Developing Countries in the World Economy

World Scientific Studies in International Economics

(ISSN: 1793-3641)

Vol. 34 Applied Trade Policy Modeling in 16 Countries: Insights and Impacts from World Bank CGE Based Projects
by David G Tarr (Consultant and Former Lead Economist, The World Bank, USA)

Vol. 35 The Floating World: Issues in International Trade Theory
by Wilfred J Ethier (University of Pennsylvania, USA)

Vol. 36 Trade Policy in Asia: Higher Education and Media Services
edited by Christopher Findlay (University of Adelaide, Australia), Hildegunn Kyvik Nordas (Organisation for Economic Co-operation and Development, France) & Gloria Pasadilla (APEC Secretariat, Singapore)

Vol. 37 The Path of World Trade Law in the 21st Century
by Steve Charnovitz (The George Washington University, USA)

Vol. 38 International Trade, Distribution and Development: Empirical Studies of Trade Policies
by Paul Brenton (The World Bank, USA)

Vol. 39 Evolving Patterns in Global Trade and Finance
by Sven W Arndt (Claremont McKenna College, USA)

Vol. 40 Shadow Banking Within and Across National Borders
edited by Stijn Claessens (International Monetary Fund, USA), Douglas Evanoff (Federal Reserve Bank of Chicago, USA), George Kaufman (Loyola University Chicago, USA) & Luc Laeven (International Monetary Fund, USA)

Vol. 41 Modeling Developing Countries' Policies in General Equilibrium
by Jaime de Melo (FERDI, France & University of Geneva, Switzerland)

Vol. 42 Developing Countries in the World Economy
by Jaime de Melo (FERDI, France & University of Geneva, Switzerland)

The complete list of the published volumes in the series can be found at
http://www.worldscientific.com/series/wssie

42 World Scientific Studies in International Economics

DEVELOPING COUNTRIES IN THE WORLD ECONOMY

Jaime de Melo

FERDI, France & University of Geneva, Switzerland

World Scientific

NEW JERSEY • LONDON • SINGAPORE • BEIJING • SHANGHAI • HONG KONG • TAIPEI • CHENNAI

Published by

World Scientific Publishing Co. Pte. Ltd.

5 Toh Tuck Link, Singapore 596224

USA office: 27 Warren Street, Suite 401-402, Hackensack, NJ 07601

UK office: 57 Shelton Street, Covent Garden, London WC2H 9HE

Library of Congress Cataloging-in-Publication Data

Developing countries in the world economy / Jaime de Melo.
pages cm. -- (World scientific studies in international economics ; 42)
ISBN 978-9814494892 (alk. paper)
1. Developing countries--Foreign economic relations. 2. Developing countries--Commerce.
3. Developing countries--Economic conditions. 4. Developing countries--Economic policy.
5. Economic development--Developing countries. I. De Melo, Jaime
HF1413.D286 2015
337.091724--dc23

2014040801

British Library Cataloguing-in-Publication Data

A catalogue record for this book is available from the British Library.

In-house Editor: Qi Xiao

Typeset by Stallion Press
Email: enquiries@stallionpress.com

Credits

The author would like to thank the following publishers for granting permission to reprint respective chapters.

Reprinted with kind permission from University of Chicago Press:

Chapter 1

Corbo, Vittorio, Jaime de Melo and James Tybout. 1986. "What Went Wrong with the Recent Reforms in the Southern Cone", *Economic Development and Cultural Change*, 34(3), 607–640.

Chapter 2

Melo, Jaime de and James Tybout. 1986. "The Effects of Financial Liberalization on Savings and Investment in Uruguay", *Economic Development and Cultural Change*, 34(3), 561–587.

Reprinted with kind permission from Oxford University Press:

Chapter 3

Devarajan, Shantayanan and Jaime de Melo. 1987. "Adjustment with a Fixed Exchange Rate: Cameroon, Côte d'Ivoire and Senegal", *The World Bank Economic Review*, 1(3), 447–487.

Chapter 11

Carrère, Céline and Jaime de Melo, "Are Different Rules of Origin Equally Costly? Estimates from NAFTA", in Olivier Cadot, Antoni Estevadeordal, Akiko Suwa-Eisenmann and Thierry Verdier, eds., *The Origin of Goods: Rules of Origin in Regional Trade Agreements*. New York: Oxford University Press, 191–212.

Chapter 12

Brun, Jean-François, Céline Carrère, Patrick Guillaumont and Jaime de Melo. 2005. "Has Distance Died? Evidence from a Panel Gravity Model", *The World Bank Economic Review*, 19(1), 99–120.

Chapter 15

Cadot, Olivier and Jaime de Melo. 2008. "Why OECD Countries Should Reform Rules of Origin", *World Bank Research Observer*, 23(1), 77–105.

Reprinted with kind permission from John Wiley & Sons:

Chapter 5

Riccardo Faini and Jaime de Melo. 1989. "Adjustment, Investment and the Real Exchange Rate in Developing Countries", *Economic Policy*, 5(11), 491–519.

Chapter 7

Melo, Jaime de, Marcelo Olarreaga and Wendy Takacs. 2000. "Pricing Policy Under Double Market Power: Madagascar and the International Vanilla Market", *Review of Development Economics*, 4(1), 1–20.

Chapter 17

Bilal, Sanoussi, Jean-Marie Grether and Jaime de Melo. 2003. "Attitudes Towards Immigration: A Trade Theoretic Approach", *Review of International Economics*, 11(2), 253–267.

Reprinted with kind permission from Elsevier:

Chapter 4

Faini, Riccardo, Jaime de Melo, Abdelhak Senhadji and Julie Stanton. 1991. "Growth-Oriented Adjustment Programs: A Statistical Analysis", *World Development*, 19(8), 957–967. Chapter 6

Carrère, Céline and Jaime de Melo. 2012. "Fiscal Spending and Economic Growth: Some Stylized Facts", *World Development*, 40(9), 1750–1761.

Chapter 8

Melo, Jaime de and Shujiro Urata. 1986. "The Influence of Increased Foreign Competition on Industrial Concentration and Profitability", *International Journal of Industrial Organization*, 4(3), 287–304.

Chapter 9

Tybout, James, Jaime de Melo and Vittorio Corbo. 1991. "The Effects of Trade Reforms on Scale and Technical Efficiency: New Evidence from Chile", *Journal of International Economics*, 31, 231–250.

Chapter 10

Melo, Jaime de and Alan Winters. 1993. "Do Exporters Gain from VERs?", *European Economic Review*, 37, 1331–1349.

Chapter 14

Cadot, Olivier, Jaime de Melo and Marcelo Olarreaga. 2003. "The Protectionist Bias of Duty Drawbacks: Evidence from Mercosur", *Journal of International Economics*, 59(1), 162–182.

Reprinted with kind permission from Taylor & Francis Group:

Chapter 16

Grether, Jean-Marie, Jaime de Melo and Tobias Müller. 2001. "The Political Economy of International Migration in a Ricardo–Viner Model", in Slobodan Djajic, ed., *International Migration: Trends, Policy and Economic Impact*. London: Routledge, 42–68.

Chapter 19

Gourdon, Julien, Nicolas Maystre and Jaime de Melo. 2010. "Openness, Inequality and Poverty: Endowments Matter", *Journal of International Trade and Economic Development*, 17(3), 343–378.

Chapter 22

Grether, Jean-Marie, Nicole Mathys and Jaime de Melo. 2012. "Unravelling the Worldwide Pollution Haven Effect", *Journal of International Trade and Economic Development*, 21(1), 131–162.

Reprinted with kind permission from MIT Press:

Chapter 18

Melo, Jaime de, Florence Miguet and Tobias Müller. 2004. "The Political Economy of Migration and EU Enlargement: Lessons from Switzerland", in Helge Berger and Thomas Moutos, eds., *Managing European Enlargement.* Cambridge, MA; London, UK: MIT Press, 129–167.

Reprinted with kind permission from INSEE/GENES:

Chapter 20

Ivlevs, Artjoms and Jaime de Melo. 2010. "FDI, the Brain Drain and Trade: Channels and Evidence", *Annals of Economics and Statistics*, 97/98, 103–121.

Reprinted with kind permission from Cambridge University Press:

Chapter 13

Melo, Jaime de, Arvind Panagariya and Dani Rodrik. 1993. "The New Regionalism: A Country Perspective", in Jaime de Melo and Arvind Panagariya, eds., *New Dimensions in Regional Integration.* UK: Cambridge University Press, 159–192.

Reprinted with kind permission from DE Boeck Université:

Chapter 21

Melo, Jaime de. 2013. "Trade in a 'Green Growth' Development Strategy", *Revue d'Economie du Développement*, 2013/4, 25–58.

About the Author

Jaime de Melo is Directeur Scientifique at the Fondation pour les Etudes et Recherches sur le Développement International (FERDI). He is also Emeritus Professor from the University of Geneva, where he taught from 1992 to 2012, a non-resident fellow at Brookings Institute, a CEPR fellow and a member of EU–GDN. He is an adjunct professor at the Bologna Center of the Johns Hopkins University and, since 2008 he also teaches at the Formation Universitaire à distance, Suisse. He is a founding member of the World Trade Institute. From 1972 to 1976 he worked at USAID and from 1976 to 1980 he taught at Georgetown University. From 1980 to 1993, he held several positions in the research department at the World Bank. He has consulted for the IMF, OECD, SECO, IGC, the EC Commission, and several governments. From 1986 to 1992, he was Professor Associé at Centre d'études et de Recherches sur le Développement International (CERDI) at the Université d'Auvergne. Since 2011, he is affiliated with FERDI. He has held several editorial positions and was Editor-in-Chief of *The World Bank Economic Review* (2005–2010). He holds degrees in Political Science (B.A. from Syracuse University, 1968), International Relations (M.A. from Johns Hopkins SAIS, 1970), and Economics (PhD from John Hopkins University, 1975). His publications are available at http://ideas.repec.org/e/pde173.html. His research interests focus on developing countries, particularly issues related to trade policy, migration, and the environment.

Preface and Acknowledgments

Modeling Developing Countries' Policies in General Equilibrium and *Developing Countries in the World Economy* are a collection of mostly co-authored work at Universities and at the World Bank.

My years at the Research Department at the World Bank brought me a lot. The research department was instrumental in the development of general equilibrium modeling and the papers in *Modeling Developing Countries' Policies in General Equilibrium* owe a great deal to the atmosphere there. For anyone interested in developing countries, the World Bank was, and still largely remains, a place to be.

For the twenty years at the University of Geneva, I am thankful for the opportunity to enter into new collaborations and to start working on the political economy of trade and migration policies. Several papers in *Developing Countries in the World Economy* are the result of these collaborations.

But my longest and closest affiliation — almost thirty years — has been with CERDI, the premier department in France for studying development, especially problems on Africa, and now with FERDI, its closely affiliated think-Tank that has just celebrated its tenth anniversary. Lectures and seminars at CERDI were the source of collaborations and served as springboard for work in progress. And now, at FERDI we are involved in the debate and design of sustainable development strategies and on how to finance them in an inclusive way. Some of the challenges ahead are raised in the papers in *Developing Countries in the World Economy*.

All of the papers have previously been published in academic journals or in books. I thank the publishers for the permission to reprint them. I thank Bob Stern for inviting (and prodding) me to reflect and put these volumes together and the staff at World Scientific Publishing for seeing through the production process. I also owe a great debt to my family, Isabelle, Lea, Elissa and Ines for their patience and support.

Looking back, I have had the good fortune of engaging in these collaborations. Reflecting on them, I have mostly been on the receiving side in the exchange of ideas. I owe my co-authors a great debt and feel fortunate that many a collaboration has turned into a lasting friendship. I dedicate these volumes to them.

Geneva, January 2015

Contents

Credits v

About the Author ix

Preface and Acknowledgments xi

Introduction 1

Part I: Reforms, Adjustment and Growth **19**

Chapter 1 (with Vittorio Corbo and James Tybout) What Went Wrong with the Recent Reforms in the Southern Cone 21

Introduction
The Reforms and Their Intent
Stylized Outcomes
What Went Wrong
Conclusions

Chapter 2 (with James Tybout) The Effects of Financial Liberalization on Savings and Investment in Uruguay 55

Introduction
Financial Reforms, Financial Deepening and Financial Crisis
Stylized Outcomes: Savings, Investment and Growth
Financial Liberalization, Savings and Investment
Financial Resource Allocation at the Micro Level
Conclusions

Chapter 3 (with Shantayanan Devarajan) Adjustment with a Fixed Exchange Rate: Cameroon, Côte d'Ivoire, and Senegal 83

Case Studies of Adjustment: Cameroon, Cote d'Ivoire, and Senegal
A Model of Medium-Term Adjustment
Determinants of the Current Account and Real Exchange Rates
Conclusions
Appendix A: Symbols Used in the Text
Appendix B: Solution of the Model
Appendix C: Parameters for Model Simulation

Chapter 4 (with Riccardo Faini, Abdelhak Senhadji and Julie Stanton) Growth-Oriented Adjustment Programs: A Statistical Analysis 125

Introduction
External Environment and Adjustment Lending
A Model to Measure Effectiveness of IMF–WB Programs
Statistical Results
Sustainability of Adjustment: Output Loss Estimates from Investment Cuts for a Group of Intensive Adjustment Lending Recipients
Conclusions

Chapter 5 (with Riccardo Faini) Adjustment, Investment and the Real Exchange Rate in Developing Countries 137

Introduction
The Controversy
External Adjustment and the Real Exchange Rate
Investment, the Real Exchange Rate and the Debt Overhang
Looking Ahead
Appendix A: Forward-Looking Model of Investment

Chapter 6 (with Céline Carrère) Fiscal Spending and Economic Growth: Some Stylized Facts 167

Introduction
Defining Events
Patterns of Fiscal and Growth Events
Understanding Fiscal Events
Conclusions
Appendix A: Growth Acceleration
Appendix B: Fiscal Events
Appendix C: Sensitivity Analysis

Part II: Trade Policies, Market Structure and Market Access **197**

Chapter 7 (with Marcelo Olarreaga and Wendy Takacs) Pricing Policy Under Double Market Power: Madagascar and the International Vanilla Market 199

Introduction
Trends in the Natural Vanilla Market
Alternative Pricing Policies in a Price-Leadership Model
Estimation of the Price-Leadership Model
Evaluating Madagascar's Pricing Strategy
Conclusions

Chapter 8 (with Shujiro Urata) The Influence of Increased Foreign Competition on Industrial Concentration and Profitability 219

Introduction
A Comparison of Concentration and Profitability in 1967 and 1979
Industry Structure and Performance: Cross-Section Regression Analysis
Conclusion

Chapter 9 (with Vittorio Corbo and James Tybout) The Effects of Trade Reforms on Scale and Technical Efficiency: New Evidence from Chile 237

Overview
A Glance at the Data
Better Measures of Efficiency Changes
Concluding Remarks
Appendix: Production Technology Estimates

Chapter 10 (with Alan Winters) Do Exporters Gain from VERs? 257

Introduction
A Simple Model of a Competitive Industry Subject to a VER
Estimation
Welfare and Distributional Effects of VERs: Some Illustrative Simulations
Conclusions
Appendix A: Data Sources for Econometric Estimates

Chapter 11 (with Céline Carrère) Are Different Rules of Origin Equally Costly? Estimates from NAFTA 277

Introduction
NAFTA RoO Map, and Non-Parametric Cost Estimates
A Simple Model
Cost Estimates by Type of RoO and Category of Activities
Evaluating Estevadeordal's Synthetic Index
Value Content Restrictions
Conclusions
Appendix: the Model

Chapter 12 (with Jean-François Brun, Céline Carrère and Patrick Guillaumont) Has Distance Died? Evidence from a Panel Gravity Model 299

Is There a Puzzle?
Explaining the Puzzle

Robustness
Conclusion
Appendix A: Data Sources and Data Preparation
Appendix B: Estimation Method
Appendix C: Evolution of $|\beta|$ by Subperiod
Appendix D: Additive Transport Cost Function

Part III: Political Economy **321**

Chapter 13 (with Arvind Panagariya and Dani Rodrik) The New Regionalism: A Country Perspective 323
Introduction
Welfare Economics of FTAs
Institutional Dimensions of RI
Growth Effects of RI Schemes
Conclusions

Chapter 14 (with Olivier Cadot and Marcelo Olarreaga) The Protectionist Bias of Duty Drawbacks: Evidence from Mercosur 359
Introduction
Tariff Drawbacks and Lobbying
Customs Union and Duty Drawbacks
Application to Mercosur
Concluding remarks

Chapter 15 (with Olivier Cadot) Why OECD Countries Should Reform Rules of Origin 381
Rules of Origin: Definition and Measurement
Quantifying the Effects of Rules of Origin
Direct Evidence
An Exception and a Quasi-Natural Experiment
Indirect Evidence
Implications for Reform
Appendix: Glossary of terms

Chapter 16 (with Jean-Marie Grether and Tobias Müller)
The Political Economy of International Migration in a Ricardo–Viner Model 411

Introduction
Is There an Immigration Surplus?
Determinants of Individual Preferences over Immigration Policy
Why Illegal Migrants?
Dual Labor Markets and 'Guest-Worker' Migration
Conclusions

Chapter 17 (with Sanoussi Bilal and Jean-Marie Grether)
Attitudes Towards Immigration: A Trade Theoretic Approach 439

Introduction
The Model
Attitudes Towards Immigration
Comparative Statics
Discussion
Conclusions

Chapter 18 (with Florence Miguet and Tobias Müller)
The Political Economy of Migration and EU Enlargement: Lessons from Switzerland 455

Introduction
The Political Economy of Immigration Policy
The Shaping of Switzerland's Immigration Policy
Determinants of Attitudes and Voting Behavior
Conclusions

Part IV: Challenges Ahead — An Inclusive Globalization and Environmental Policies 495

Chapter 19 (with Julien Gourdon and Nicolas Maystre)
Openness, Inequality and Poverty: Endowments Matter 497

Introduction
Framework and Data

Trade Liberalization and Inequality: Endowments Matter
Openness, Inequality and Poverty: Further Results
Conclusions
Appendix 1: Data and Data Sources
Appendix 2: Data Construction

Chapter 20 (with Artjoms Ivlevs) FDI, the Brain Drain and Trade: Channels and Evidence 533

Introduction
Migration, Trade and FDI: A Skeleton Model
Empirical Specification and Data
Results
Conclusion

Chapter 21 Trade in a 'Green Growth' Development Strategy: Issues and Challenges 553

Preliminaries
Natural Resources, the Environment, and Trade: Channels of Interaction
Direct Trade-Environment Linkages
Pollution Havens, Trade Leakages and Border Tax Adjustments
Implementation Difficulties: Political Economy Considerations
Concluding Remarks: Trade Policies for a Green Growth Strategy

Chapter 22 (with Jean-Marie Grether and Nicole Mathys) Unravelling the Worldwide Pollution Haven Effect 581

Introduction
The Pollution Content of Trade: A Framework
Measuring the PCI
Unravelling the Pollution Haven Effect
Robustness Checks
Conclusions

Introduction

The papers in this volume deal with developing countries' policies and how they faced the challenges they had to confront in the global economy where they are becoming increasingly important players. During the 1980s, attention focused on how countries would adjust to an adverse external environment while reforming inefficient and, often inequitable, policies of the past. Quantifying the gains from successful adjustment and reduction in distortions was the order of the day. In the 1990s, as the Cold War ended and trade and communication costs were falling rapidly, a new regionalism with increasing migratory pressures took hold. Understanding the political economy of policy decisions drew increasing attention. More recently, preoccupations have turned towards inclusive growth and the potential conflicts between trade policies conducive towards a more integrated world economy and environmental policies to conserve natural resources and mitigate climate change. Chapters in this volume cover selected aspects of these shifting concerns.

Part I: Reforms, Adjustment and Growth

Except for chapter 6, all chapters in Part I collect papers evaluating the challenges posed by carrying out deep reforms or by adjusting to the rapidly shifting external environment of the 1970s and 1980s. Chapters 1 to 3 use a case-study approach and chapters 4 to 6 cross-country comparisons. All focus on medium term outcomes rather on the long-term determinants of growth.

The first challenge, widely debated at the time, is the causes of the failures in the policy packages of the 'Southern Cone' countries of Latin America — Argentina, Chile and Uruguay. All three were in a situation of economic and political crisis in the mid-1970s when, under military control, they embarked on what would, a decade later, have been called 'structural adjustment programs'. The packages were a mix of policies to stabilize the economy and of micro reforms to generate growth. What policies were adapted, what happened, and did these reforms fail? Chapters 1 and 2 analyze these reforms.

The second relates to countries in the Franc zone. While these countries faced the same shocks as the rest of the developing world, they shared a common currency, the CFA Franc backed by the Banque de France under conditions that induced a sense of monetary and fiscal discipline while also presumably favorable to foreign investment. In contrast with the Southern Cone countries that started from a closed capital account, CFA-zone members already had a convertible currency but they had to adjust to the shocks under a fixed exchange rate. Chapter 3 analyzes the adjustment experience of Cameroon, Côte d'Ivoire and Senegal over the 1970s up until the mid-1980s.

The third deals with the adjustment challenge developing countries faced during the 1980s when, in the wake of expansionary policies, they faced declining terms-of-trade, rising real interest rates on their external debt, and, for middle-income countries, the drying up of commercial lending. These events required them to effect a financial transfer towards industrialized countries. The IMF and the World Bank disbursed loans conditional on carrying out stabilization and structural reforms. These quick-disbursing loans were to generate 'adjustment with growth'. Here too, outcomes fell short of expectations. Chapters 4 and 5 relate aspects of that episode.

Chapter 6 explores fiscal spending episodes and subsequent growth for 107 (84 developing) countries over the 1972–2006 period to examine the 'fiscal space' contention that extending public investment in capital expenditure — while simultaneously controlling the government budget deficit — can raise growth.

Chapter 1 dissects one of the most comprehensive set of rapidly adopted (two to three years) reforms in the 20th Century. The three Southern Cone countries started from a situation of extreme macro disequilibrium (high inflation and large fiscal deficits) combined with heavily controlled financial systems, extensive government intervention and large anti-export biases. Within their first two years, the new economic teams inspired by the 'Chicago school' carried out orthodox anti-inflationary policies while differing on the order of liberalization of financial, goods and labor markets. Then, in what we called phase II, as inflation was still between 50% and 150%, all three adopted an active crawling peg with pre-announcement of the path of the exchange rate according to the so-called *tablita* (the ledger on which each central bank would announce the rate of exchange rate devaluation for the coming month). The idea was to break long-standing inflationary expectations. Phase II ended in a major financial crisis in 1981–1982 in all three countries with large increases in external debt (much coming from private-sector capital flight as controls on capital flows had been removed).

Drawing on work carried for that project (see Corbo and Melo, 1985), the paper argues that some efficiency gains were realized in Chile and Uruguay (see chapters 2, 8 and 9) but that these initial gains were overshadowed by policy inconsistencies, implementation difficulties, and overlooked market frictions (interest rates and traded goods prices took longer to converge to world levels than anticipated). Key factors in the outcome were the use of the exchange rate to bring down inflation under an open capital account and, at the micro level, a lack of prudential regulation allowing firms to exploit negative real financial costs from borrowing in dollars.

Particularly influential in the design of the phase II episode was the 1979 *tablita* blueprint based on Dornbusch's over-shooting model where interest parity holds continuously for financial markets and the law of one price holds for tradables (see Rodriguez, 1982). Initial developments followed the blueprint with large capital inflows, a real exchange rate appreciation and negative real interest rates (as inflation was only falling gradually). However, the policies also went beyond the blueprint. In Argentina, the fiscal deficit was never tackled, and in Chile, wage indexation was inconsistent with the policy of pre-announcement of the exchange rate. As documented in figures 1 to 3 in the paper and, as confidence waned, the spread between peso and dollar denominated interest rates widened. Capital flight ensued, and the *tablita* was abandoned. The end-result was that reforms under an open capital account exacerbated capital flight with rising income inequality (see also Melo, 2015, chapter 10).

Chapter 2 analyzes Uruguay's unusual opening sequence where the capital account was liberalized prior to the current account. By 1974, the financial system was deregulated with domestic residents allowed to hold dollar-denominated accounts in the Uruguayan banking system. The paper examined whether, crisis notwithstanding, the dramatic switch in the regulatory regime led to the benefits expected from the literature on financial deregulation popularized by Ronald McKinnon and Edward Shaw. After detecting some evidence of higher growth during the post-reform period, the paper studied the response of private savings and private investment to the reforms, identifying in each case a structural break around the time of the reforms, especially so for private savings. For private savings, over the pre-reform 1962–1973 period, interest rates had the expected sign and explanatory power while in the 1974–1981 'open economy' period it was the real exchange rate that picked up explanatory power. In the open economy period, a real exchange rate appreciation discouraged savings by making traded goods less expensive and encouraging expenditures on imported consumer durables. An upward shift in the investment function was also detected during the reform period but the standard variables (real interest rate variations and the accelerator mechanism) were not significant. In conclusion the quasi-laboratory experiment offered by the sharp and rapid financial reforms led to many outcomes predicted by proponents of financial reform but little evidence of improved efficiency in the allocation of credit across firms.

Chapter 3 contrasts the adjustment to external shocks in Cameroon, Côte d'Ivoire and Senegal during 1973–1984 when adjustment called for a depreciation of the real exchange rate and/or a sharp reduction in spending. The paper starts with a description of the evolution of a common set of indicators (terms-of-trade, two indicators of external competitiveness, a decomposition of the evolution of the current-account deficit). The interpretation of the different paths of the real exchange rate paths shows that they could be accounted for by different patterns of external borrowing, public expenditure levels and taxation of windfall gains from the commodity boom. These differences were then incorporated in a two-sector medium-term macro model, in which exports are not consumed domestically, the current account deficit is equated with the government deficit and a semi-tradable sector competes with imports. This skeleton model tracks well the different adjustment responses to similar shocks across the three countries. Regressions of the correlates of the current account and the real exchange supported the model.

Chapters 4 and 5 were written while the IMF and World Bank structural programs of the 1980s were still in progress. Since the programs were aimed at restoring growth, emphasis was on the investment response to the reforms to see if the required reduction in the expenditure–income gap came mostly from a reduction in expenditure or from an increase in output. Chapter 4 focuses on growth and investment in a sample of 93 countries. Because of the short time period (only three to five years after receiving loans), it was not possible to control for self-selection into adjustment lending programs. However, after controlling for initial conditions and the size of the external shock, no differences in growth rates and investment rates were found for recipients of adjustment programs relative to the control group. A closer look at output and investment rates was also carried out for a smaller group of 14 countries that received a large amount of adjustment lending. A growth model where investment is the only constraint on growth was used to detect any increases in the marginal efficiency of investment during the adjustment period. No increases in marginal efficiency were detected but the estimates showed large output losses coming from lower aggregate (private and public) investment.

Chapter 5 focuses on the core policy lever in these adjustment programs: a large depreciation of the real exchange rate (for the 83 countries examined, on average the real exchange rate depreciated by 40% over 1978–1988). To be sure, a sharp deterioration of the real exchange rate was called for because of overly expansionary policies prior to 1982 (partly spurred by the large volumes of recycled petrodollars), but the sharp depreciation was also supposed to elicit a strong tradable-sector response and to remove pervasive distortions in the factor markets that had previously favored capital-intensive investments.

By 1988, recovery was only in sight for East Asian countries. Econometric evidence from a forward-looking investment model showed that the fall in investment in middle-income countries outside of East Asia was not caused by a rise in the cost of capital. Rather, investment was negatively related to debt and to foreign exchange availability indicators (suggesting that debt relief would raise investment as well as consumption) and to real exchange variability, a proxy for macroeconomic instability.

Two conclusions were drawn. The East Asian countries were resilient with a successful adjustment as they carried out adjustment from a situation reflecting 20 years of productivity-led growth under their outward-looking strategy — a rapid recovery that was repeated a decade later following the East Asian financial crisis. So for middle-income manufacturing exporters, the conclusion was that sustainable growth would be within reach if the micro reforms could be sustained long enough. By contrast, for low-income primary exporters, the lack of export supply and investment response attributable to uncertainty led us to conclude that there would be a high payoff to achieving macroeconomic stability first with partial debt relief and a postponement of microeconomic reforms as successful implementation could be jeopardized by uncertainty (25 years later one would put greater emphasis on institutional quality as a prerequisite for success!).

Chapter 6 uses 'event-analysis' (i.e., reorganizing data around events) to explore the relation between a significant change in fiscal spending — approximated by primary spending to purge non-discretionary expenditures — and subsequent growth (definition of fiscal and growth events and robustness tests to the selection criteria are discussed in the paper). Subject to precautions in interpreting results, among developing countries, the probability that a fiscal event is followed by a growth event is higher for the middle-income countries in Latin America. The probability of a fiscal event not followed by a growth event is significantly higher in Sub-Saharan Africa, suggesting that the success of a growth-oriented fiscal expenditure package might hinge on the quality of the institutional environment. Other patterns were also detected. First, fiscal events followed by growth events devote fewer resources to general public services and/or are accompanied by a growing share of transport and communication expenditures while fiscal events not followed by a growth event are followed by a falling share of expenditure of transport and communication expenditures. Second, controlling for other growth-related events, the probability that a growth event occurs in the five years following a fiscal event is increased as the associated fiscal deficit is limited.

Part II: Trade Policies, Market Structure and Market Access

That high-growth countries have integrated the world economy by trading more than laggards is accepted and the bulk of the evidence increasingly points towards trade being an engine of growth. Beyond geography-related factors (landlocked, small and/or distant from all markets), differences in trade performance can be assigned to three categories: countries' own trade policies (protection and/or direct discrimination against exports and non-tariff barriers (NTBs)); partners' policies impeding access (protection other than tariffs for industrialized countries); and behind-the-border measures that raise trade costs (deficient hard and soft infrastructure, etc.). Papers in part II cover each aspect of these three categories of trade performance.

Chapters 7 to 9 deal with developing countries' own trade policies. Chapter 7 is a case study of the market for natural vanilla in which Madagascar had a dominant position (and was at one time the leader of a cartel). The production and export of Malagasy vanilla was controlled by a marketing board (the Vanilla Marketing Board (VMB)) which was supposed to protect small producers from fluctuations in the world market. By setting up and estimating a model of the vanilla market in which Madagascar had double market power, on the export side as the major supplier of vanilla on the world market and on the supply side via the VMB, the paper showed that the VMB policies did not protect producers. Actual policies were compared with the optimal policies suggested by the model with double market power. Simulations suggested that producers would have had over 10 times their actual revenues under a policy of laissez-faire. Not surprisingly, the VMB collapsed as unsold stocks that had accumulated over the years under Madagascar's high export taxes were eventually burned. In a follow-up paper (Cadot *et al.*, 2009), we estimated that the elimination of the VMB might have contributed to lifting up to 20,000 individuals above the poverty line. In reality, as noted in the introductory quote to the chapter, as was the case with many marketing boards elsewhere, the VMB ended up reflecting the disparity in political effectiveness between the urban political elites and the unorganized rural population, resulting in what Mancur Olson has described as 'the exploitation of the many by the few'.

Analyzing Chile's trade liberalization, chapters 8 and 9 report early micro evidence in support of the argument that protection reduces industrial sector efficiency as barriers to entry and the absence of foreign competition would result in inefficient industrial structures with firms leading an 'easy life'. In some industries, monopolies or collusive oligopolies would earn excessive profits. Firms could also fail to reach scale efficiency and technical efficiency. And in markets characterized by Chamberlinian competition, trade protection would attract inefficient small producers. Detecting these effects, however, requires access to firm-level data and preferably access to a laboratory-like environment where one can contrast an industrial structure under a protected trade regime with one in the same country under a liberalized trade regime.

At the time, Chile had embarked on a deep trade liberalization. Moreover, Chile had two manufacturing censuses for 1967 and 1979 and the change in trade regime took place between the two censuses. Thus, we were fortunate to have both an interesting experiment since there was a dramatic change in the trade regime between the two manufacturing censuses (1967 and 1979) and to have access to the two censuses (in fact when Vittorio Corbo expressed his regret at not being granted access to the 1979 census he said he already had the 1967 census — which the Census Bureau had apparently lost — so a gainful exchange was rapidly concluded!). So even though other reforms and adjustments were ongoing (deregulation of the labor and financial markets), the changes in the trade regime were sufficiently large that one could detect trade-policy-related changes in industrial performance in spite of measurement problems.

Chapter 8 focuses on aggregate industry performance, looking for evidence in support of the 'import-discipline' hypothesis that had been verified for some developed countries. To give orders of magnitude of the changes between the two census years, in 1967, tariffs averaged around 50% with many NTBs. By 1975, when reforms started, half of tariff rates were over 80% and NTBs were pervasive. By 1977 all NTBs had been removed and replaced with a 10% uniform tariff — no exceptions except for cars over 850cc! This reduction in protection was certainly among the most drastic ever observed in such a short period of time in recent history. By 1977, Chile had one of the lowest and most uniform protection in the developing world. The chapter shows that the reduction in protection led to inter-industry specialization, an increase in concentration and a decrease in profitability. Cross-section estimation of a simultaneous equation model of concentration and price-cost margins for 1967 and 1979 showed that profits were highest in the most concentrated sectors. As to the 'import-discipline hypothesis', evidence in its support was found for 1979: after controlling for other factors, the penetration of imports reduced most the profitability of the highly concentrated sectors.

Chapter 9 also draws on the two censuses to study changes in the distribution of plants at the 3-digit ISIC level between the two census years to detect changes in scale and technical efficiency. Were returns to scale above unity getting closer to unity in the 1979 relative to 1967 and was technical efficiency increasing (i.e., plant dispersion from the frontier falling)? Comparison of the two census years revealed that the greatest improvement in productivity occurred in the industries undergoing the most reduction in protection. Detailed examination of the distribution of plants in both census years revealed that small plants in the increasing returns region either expanded or exited the market. Expansion in plant size thus partly accounted for the estimated reduction in unexploited economies of scale between the two census years even though reductions in protection probably also forced firms to price more competitively, which would have also shown up as reduction in unexploited returns to scale.

Chapters 10 and 11 address barriers to access by developing countries to developed country markets. Chapter 10 examines a neglected aspect of the Voluntary Export Restraints (VERs) that were negotiated between importing and exporting countries outside the GATT. The administration of VERs by exporting countries gave them rents — the price that importing countries had to pay to negotiate outside the GATT. It was accepted (at least implicitly) that exporting countries gained because they received the rents. Chapter 10 shows that, notwithstanding a rent transfer, exporting countries might lose as VERs forced firms out of industries in which they were most productive. A general model is set up in which competitive firms supply to a restricted and an unrestricted market. Drawing on quarterly data of Taiwanese leather footwear exports over 1974–1986, demand and supply elasticities are then estimated to study the welfare effects of the US VER on Taiwanese exports of leather footwear to the US during 1977–1981. Simulations show that with an upward sloping supply curve (which is likely as industries under

VERs were growing rapidly), the VER would result in a misallocation of resources as the VER breaks the equality of marginal revenue of factors from sales to the restricted and unrestricted markets. In addition to the possibility of a welfare loss in spite of receiving rents from the restriction, a VER would also raise industry profits while industry wages would be reduced, increasing income inequality.

Chapter 11 is first of two dealing with Rules of Origin (RoO). These are necessary to prevent trade deflection — importing in the low-tariff partner, then re-exporting to the high-tariff partners in the zone — in the Free Trade Areas (FTAs) that have been spreading around the world. Suspicions about this legitimate objective of preventing screwdriver assembly were first raised by Anne Krueger (1999) in the context of Mexican exports to the US under NAFTA. Detailed scrutiny at the HS6 level on NAFTA reported in chapter 11 (also see complementary evidence in Melo, 2015, chapter 19) confirms these suspicions. The paper shows that utilization rates by Mexican exporters to the US barely increased with preference margins (in textiles and apparel the preference margin was 10.4% but the utilization rate for 618 products was only 79%). A model relating utilization rates to the preference margin and to an index of the restrictiveness of the product specific RoO was then estimated. The results suggest that compliance costs — as captured by rates of utilization of preferences — are the highest for technical requirements followed by a regional value content, with the least cost associated with a change of tariff classification. Interestingly in NAFTA, technical requirements and regional value content requirements at the tariff-line level happen to be the selected RoO criterion for those tariff lines with the highest preferential margins.

Chapter 12 addresses the 'distance puzzle' which went against the widespread perception that the current wave of globalization should have led to a 'death of distance', as captured by a fall in the absolute value of the coefficient of distance in the gravity trade model when it is estimated repeatedly over time. After correcting for shortcomings in previous studies, repeated estimation over the period 1962–1996 produced the robust result that trade costs have indeed been falling (i.e., the absolute value of the distance coefficient is falling over time). However, this is only the case for bilateral trade between rich countries. The paper suggests that low-income countries might have become marginalized (this result still holds in an update to data covering the period 1962–2006 published in the *Journal of Economic Surveys* in 2013). Since the estimates control for geographic factors (landlockedness, multilateral resistance and other country characteristics including factors specific to bilateral trade), if one accepts the gravity model as the standard for estimating bilateral trade, and that shortcomings in the quality of the data for low-income countries have not systematically biased results, it could well be that behind-the-border impediments to trade are falling less rapidly in low-income countries.

Part III: Political Economy

Regional trade agreements (FTAs) for the vast majority and an increasing mobility of people are important developments in the current globalization (another is the relation of trade and the environment covered in part IV). Until recently regionalism was discussed in relation to multilateralism, usually neglecting the political economy of trade liberalization (it is politically easier to liberalize trade bilaterally or in a small group of countries than multilaterally). Chapters 13 to 15 discuss three aspects of the political economy of FTAs. Likewise, early discussions on the mobility of labor neglected political economy motives as people were only considered a factor of production like capital. Then, following Robert Mundell's reasoning in a world where trade in goods-only leads to factor price equalization, the arbitrage gains from trade would be achieved equally by a movement of factors in the absence of trade in goods, or vice-versa, and countries should then be indifferent between the two forms of market integration. But in the case of the movement of labor, the political economy of policies towards migration become important. Chapters 16 to 19 discuss this political economy of migration. The papers take inspiration from the Swiss case where voting on immigration policy has taken place regularly and where the share of foreign population has risen from 6% in 1950 to 23% in 2012.

Chapter 13 was written in 1991 for a co-edited book on the 'new' regionalism, which argued that developing countries, then engaging in FTAs with Northern partners, were experiencing a new regionalism quite different from the first wave of South–South regionalism of the 1960s. The chapter starts with a review of the standard Vinerian analysis of the efficiency of preferential trade liberalization, noting that nothing more can be obtained on a preferential basis than on a non-discriminatory basis. However, the significance of the chapter is that it went on to suggest that a successful regional integration should be what we would call today 'deep' integration, i.e., going beyond an FTA in goods-markets only and also beyond the multilateral agenda by setting up regional institutions. A model is introduced in which the government is confronted with pressures from the private sector lobbying for policies that depart from those desired by the government, thereby imposing welfare costs on the government. In this set-up, when two countries integrate, there are three channels through which delegation in decision-making would alter economic outcomes: (i) a preference-dilution effect as factional interests have a smaller role in a larger political community (on the assumption that sector lobbies do not join forces across countries); (ii) a preference-asymmetry effect as the patterns of compromise at the regional level among members with different structures and preferences lead to a more efficient outcome for some, and to a less efficient one for others; (iii) an institutional-design effect as setting-up an institution from scratch may enhance efficiency for all members.

Chapter 14 is an example of the institutional-design effect accompanying regional integration in the case of Mercosur. Prior to integration, as in many developing countries, Mercosur members granted duty drawbacks to exporters by reimbursing them for duties paid on their imported inputs. In a political economy setting where tariffs and rebate systems are endogenously determined by lobbying in an influence-driven framework à la Grossman-Helpman (1994), the existence of duty drawbacks reduces the incentives for exporters to counter-lobby against high tariffs on their inputs (with a full duty-drawback, tariffs on intermediates for exporters are irrelevant). With the creation of a regional bloc, duties on intra-regional exports are eliminated. In the case of a Customs Union like Mercosur, exporters are now beneficiaries of the area's Common External Tariff (CET), and at the margin their incentives to lobby against intermediate-goods protection rises on goods that are used heavily in sectors where intra-regional exports are large. The paper gives evidence that this is indeed what happened in the case of Mercosur where all members had duty drawbacks that they eliminated rapidly when integrating. The estimates suggest that in the absence of counter-lobbying, the CET would have been on average 3.5 percentage points higher with the top tariff reductions being in intermediates (see Table 3 in the chapter).

The Mercosur study is an example of how 'deep' integration can give rise to a positive institutional-design effect. It is also consistent with the positive appraisal of the new regionalism given in chapter 13 and by others who have also argued that this new regionalism was accompanied by a simultaneous reduction in MFN (most favored nation) tariffs. A second conclusion is that with a 'deep' integration like a Customs Union — if it is accompanied by a formula for revenue sharing as in the case of the South Africa Customs Union (SACU) — then the costly-to-satisfy RoO requirements can be eliminated. Unfortunately, almost all regional trade agreements among developing countries have difficulties going beyond FTA status because the heterogeneity of interests among members (coastal and landlocked, resource-rich and resource-poor, large and small) produces a sharp trade-off between the benefits of internalizing the spillovers and the costs of moving away from the preferred national policy (loss of sovereignty).

Chapter 15 reviews what we know about the complex RoO used by OECD countries (the EU has over 500 product-specific RoO) in their Generalized Systems of Preferences and how they impact on the Least Developed Countries (LDCs). Both direct and indirect evidence drawing on the use of preferences by LDCs leads to the conclusion that RoO adopted by OECD countries impose substantial compliance cost by design. The paper shows that the US and the EU, the two main protagonists in preferential trade agreements with LDCs, impose complex RoO for products in which preferential margins are anything but negligible, complementing the results reported for Mexican exports to the US under NAFTA in chapter 11 (also see Melo, 2015, chapter 19). In sum, preferential agreements are two-handed: with one hand preferences are granted and with the other they are taken away with RoO that are in effect 'business-owned' rather than 'business-friendly'. Suggestions are given on how OECD might simplify their RoO and hopefully harmonize them at the WTO.

Chapters 16 to 18 deal with immigration policies in receiving countries. Chapter 16 develops a trade-theoretic model of the decision on immigration under direct democracy. It takes a pure trade-theory view to the determination of attitudes towards immigration in a price-taking economy with three factors (capital, skilled labor and unskilled labor) and two households (low and high skill) where attitudes towards immigration are entirely determined by economic self-interest. Decisions on letting in migrants are the result of voting as in the Swiss case. Among the propositions derived in this setting, it is shown that when capital ownership is evenly distributed within each group of households, low and high-skill households always have opposite attitudes towards immigration. More interestingly, the model shows that an increase in inequality (which has occurred) would result in a stiffening of attitudes towards capital-poor immigrants.

Chapter 17 goes beyond the direct-democracy case and surveys the literature on the determinants of attitudes towards immigration in industrialized countries in a medium-term Ricardo–Viner economy. The paper distinguishes between infinitesimal and sustained migration and includes the case of an unequal distribution of capital. The discussion is then extended to the case of segregation against immigrants. In this case, confining illegal migrants to the non-traded sector is likely to engender support for immigration. So is segregation via a 'guest-worker' program in an efficiency-wage setting where working conditions are not the same between the primary and secondary sectors. The upshot of the survey is that natives are more likely to vote in favor of immigration if the government applies a 'guest-worker' system rather than a 'melting-pot' system.

Written when the EU was about to take in 10 new members, chapter 18 suggested lessons from the Swiss experience with a large absorption of immigrants (I am among them, having taken the Swiss nationality 15 years after joining the University of Geneva). The paper recounts the characteristics and the evolution of immigration in Switzerland and how the government navigated between economic interests seeking to avoid a tightening of immigration quotas and popular pressure seeking to tighten them (the popular vote of February 2014 was the first time that popular pressure carried the day). Results from estimating a direct-democracy model for the year 2000 vote to restrict foreigners to less than 18% of the population show that opposition was highest among low-skill and among right-wing voters. People from the extremes of the political spectrum were also more likely to vote as well as those with higher education. Comparing results from attitude surveys with those from actual voting also suggest that results from opinion polls are subject to a 'hypothetical bias' and hence probably over-pessimistic.

Part IV: Challenges Ahead — An Inclusive Globalization and Environmental Policies

Globalization has expected benefits but presents many challenges. On the positive side, absent a more positive attitude towards immigrants, an inclusive globalization would be one of general convergence through increased trade and increased FDI on the expectations that this would reduce migratory pressures through convergence in incomes and wages while increased openness should lead to less inequality and greater poverty reduction in developing countries. On the challenges side, our increasingly integrated world economy may be harmful for the environment. To state it in journalistic terms, globalization resulting in more trade would be good for growth, itself good for poverty reduction while more trade would accelerate the deterioration of the environment including accelerated climate change. The papers in part IV address some of these challenges.

Chapter 19 revisits inconclusive results on the link between openness (understood as the ease with which goods and services and factors move across countries), inequality and poverty, with a larger sample of developing countries than in previous studies. The paper draws on a panel data set so that the effects of trade policy changes are more directly linked to changes in a country's variables. Results show that differences in factor endowments matter: trade liberalization is consistently associated with decreases in inequality in countries relatively well endowed with primary-educated (unskilled) labor but with increases in inequality in countries relatively well endowed with workers lacking basic education. The results carry over, though more tentatively, when the decile data is used rather than aggregate measures of inequality. Suggestive simulations of the effects of trade liberalization on aggregate measures of income inequality are reported.

Taking data on emigration by skill categories for 1990 and 2000, chapter 20 tests whether trade and migration are substitutes and whether FDI and migration are also substitutes. A skeleton Ricardo–Viner model with skilled and unskilled labor in which migration is exogenous but FDI flows respond to differences in rates of return to capital suggests that high-skill migration should be positively correlated with FDI as the price of the non-traded goods would be raised while higher tariffs would be associated with lower FDI. Over the period 1990–2000, for a sample of 102 countries, controlling for several factors, an increase in the emigration rate of high-skill workers is positively correlated with an increase in FDI while linguistic fractionalization is negatively correlated with FDI inflows. Further work on the trade–FDI–migration nexus is needed to confirm if the skill composition of emigrants matters.

Chapter 21 reflects on the role of trade in a green-growth development strategy. It starts from the observation that the current trade and finance framework built around the Bretton Woods institutions is not designed to handle the increasing physical linkages between countries. Trade specialists are concerned that climate change negotiators will seek to impose limits on trade outside the WTO process while environmentalists and climate change specialists fear that international trade interests will thwart attempts to arrest the depletion of natural resources and undercut policies to reduce CO_2 emissions. Because natural resources are concentrated in low-income countries with weak institutions and the poor are concentrated on fragile land, there is a legitimate concern that the current open trading system could exacerbate the natural resource curse and prevent an inclusive green-growth path.

The chapter then identifies channels of interaction between natural resources, the environment and trade. The survey identifies four roles for trade in a green-growth development strategy: (i) an open World Trading System to help diffuse the technologies needed for a low-carbon economy: (ii) a carbon-credit trading system to separate where abatement takes place from who pays the costs; (iii) border tax adjustments to correct for carbon leakage; (iv) an enforcement mechanism to deter free-riding. The chapter closes with a discussion of principles to guide trade policies needed for the trading system to be supportive in our quest to control global warming.

Chapter 22 addresses the pollution haven argument that, due to more stringent environmental policies in the North, dirty industries will migrate to the South. It does so by estimating a model of bilateral trade in which the Pollution Content of Imports (PCI) is broken down into fundamental determinants of trade and into environment-related determinants (differences in factor endowments and differences in an index of environmental policies). While previous studies focused on a single country and a few pollutants, the estimates reported here are for 10 pollutants covering 79 four-digit manufacturing sectors in a sample of 48 countries. Decomposition results reported in the paper show consistently a pollution-haven effect (countries with lax environmental policies have a comparative advantage in polluting industries) and a factor endowment effect in the opposite direction across all pollutants. When the sample is split in two by per capita income, the results show that when taking into account the volume of intra-regional trade, the total effects are small because in this period (1986–1988) much trade was among high-income but low-polluting partners. Thus for the sample year, differences in factor endowments in and in environmental policies only marginally affected the worldwide pollution content of world trade suggesting that the pollution-haven effect was not quantitatively important.

References

Cadot, Olivier, Laure Dutoit and Jaime de Melo (2009) "The Elimination of Vanilla's Marketing Board, 10 Years on", *Journal of African Economies*, 18(3), 388–430.

Corbo, Vittorio and Jaime de Melo (1985) "Overview and Summary", *World Development*, 13(8), 863–866.

Grossman, Gene and Elhanan Helpman (1994) "Protection for Sale", *American Economic Review*, 84(4), 833–850

Krueger, Anne O. (1997) "Free Trade Agreements versus Customs Unions", *Journal of Development Economics*, 54(1), 169–187.

Melo, Jaime de (2015) *Modeling Developing Countries' Policies in General Equilibrium*, Singapore: World Scientific.

Rodriguez, Carlos (1982) "The Argentine Stabilization Plan of December 20th", World *Development*, 10(9), 801–811.

Part I

Reforms, Adjustment and Growth

What Went Wrong with the Recent Reforms in the Southern Cone

Vittorio Corbo
World Bank and Pontificia Universidad Catolica de Chile

Jaime de Melo
World Bank

James Tybout
Georgetown University and World Bank

I. Introduction

For decades, Argentina, Chile, and Uruguay pursued inward-looking development strategies that relied heavily on extensive government intervention. Accordingly, these economies were characterized by antiexport biases, high spreads in protection across sectors, and heavily controlled financial systems. Likewise, each economy suffered from recurrent balance-of-payments crises and low growth. During the 1970s, these countries attempted to switch from import-substitution-led industrialization to a more neutral strategy. Furthermore, to improve resource allocation, the three countries moved (in varying degrees) toward liberalization of markets. Commodity price controls were practically eliminated, government deficits were reduced and/or eliminated, trade barriers were reduced, interest rates were decontrolled, constraints on capital flows were reduced, and constraints on labor markets were relaxed. However, except for Chile, many forms of intervention still remained.

The reforms started around 1974 in Uruguay and Chile and 1976 in Argentina. At that time, all three countries were in severe macroeconomic disequilibrium with acute foreign exchange shortages and severe fiscal-deficit-induced inflation. Hence, the reform packages entailed short-term rescue operations and stabilization policies as well as long-term policies to progressively remove government intervention across product and factor markets.

0013-0079/86/3403-0009$01.00

The outcome of these reform packages is well known. All three economies experienced initial success with the early stages of their stabilization and liberalization programs. But each eventually encountered a boom-bust cycle, large increases in external indebtedness, and major internal financial crises. What did the reform packages accomplish, and why did they ultimately fail?

The thesis of this paper is that initially some efficiency gains were made but that these were ultimately overshadowed by problems with policy inconsistencies, implementation difficulties, and overlooked market frictions. These factors generated a sustained appreciation of the real exchange rate and a large spread between the costs of dollar-denominated and peso-denominated loans. In turn, the appreciation and interest-rate spreads created protracted opportunities for arbitrage that distracted firms from the business of production. Eventually, firms became sufficiently in debt, so that as expectations of a major devaluation developed, they were forced into crisis borrowing to cover soaring interest costs.

To lay the basis for our argument, we review briefly in Section II the initial conditions facing each country on the eve of the reforms and the sequencing of reforms in each country. A distinction is made between stabilization policies (to reduce inflation and balance-of-payments crises) and liberalization policies (to promote better resource allocation). Section III reviews the stylized outcomes of the three reform packages. Section IV traces problems experienced in each country to particular ways in which policy was implemented. Lessons to be drawn from the experience of the reforms follow in Section V.

II. The Reforms and Their Intent[1]

When the military seized power, both Argentina and Chile were experiencing high fiscal deficits, severe inflation, and balance-of-payments crises.[2] Annual inflation rates were approaching 1,000% in Chile (September 1973) and 2,300% in Argentina (March 1976). In the prereform crisis the government deficit as a share of GDP was 12.0% in Argentina and 16.1% in Chile (table 1). Moreover, net Central Bank exchange reserves were negative in Argentina and close to zero in Chile. To compound these problems, both countries suffered from numerous microeconomic distortions such as tariffs, interest ceilings, and price controls.

In Uruguay, macroeconomic imbalances were not as pronounced when the military came to power: inflation was only 97% in 1973; the government deficit had averaged a relatively modest 3.2% of GDP over the previous several years (table 1); and partly because of severe restrictions on trade and international capital flows, there was no immediate crisis of Central Bank reserves. Nonetheless, the economy was suffering from widespread microeconomic distortions and had registered almost zero growth for 20 years.

The first task facing the economic teams in each country was to restore macroeconomic stability. But these teams also diagnosed excessive government intervention as the fundamental cause of inefficient resource allocation and low growth. In their view, the cure called for a deregulation of commodity and factor markets, including the removal of barriers to free trade and capital flows. Such measures would improve resource allocation, eliminate recurrent bottlenecks, and lead to higher growth.

A. Liberalization Policies

With different timing and intensity, all three countries removed price controls, liberalized interest rates, decentralized intermediation, and partly deregulated labor markets. All three countries also relaxed restrictions on international trade and liberalized capital inflows. But with the exception of domestic financial market deregulation, which proceeded rapidly in all cases, the sequencing of reforms was different in each country. Early on, Uruguay removed all controls on capital flows and many commodity price controls, but it progressed more slowly toward liberalizing foreign trade. Chile, on the other hand, went the furthest in eliminating domestic price controls, the endemic fiscal budget deficit, and trade barriers, but it kept controls on short-term capital flows for a long time and maintained important labor market regulations. Argentina also eliminated price controls and removed most restrictions on short-term capital flows before implementing a tariff reform. Below, we review the major features of each country's policies.

1. *Commodity market deregulation.* Two kinds of reforms were implemented in commodity markets: deregulating domestic prices and reducing tariff and nontariff barriers to trade. Chile went furthest on both counts. In the early stages of implementation, prices in the domestic commodity market were deregulated, and subsidies were practically eliminated. Most nontariff restrictions to trade were eliminated, and the commodity market was indirectly deregulated by privatizing over 500 enterprises that had been seized or nationalized during the Allende years. The multiple exchange rate system was unified with an initial large devaluation. All nontariff restrictions were lifted, and the tariff structure was also reformed. Over 5 years, starting in 1974, the average tariff was brought down from 90% to a uniform 10% (except for automobiles over 850 cubic centimeters).

In Argentina, after a substantial price deregulation, price controls were reinstated as part of the stabilization effort in 1977 but abandoned thereafter. Initially, the liberalization also included the unification of the exchange rate with a sharp real devaluation (close to 25%), some reduction in tariffs, and a substantial reduction of taxes on traditional exports. Furthermore, most nontariff barriers were eliminated except for basic metals. Redundant protection nonetheless remained until late

TABLE 1

MACROECONOMIC PERFORMANCE IN THE SOUTHERN CONE

	Import Substitution Period	Prereform Crisis	Reforms: Phase 1		Reforms: Phase 2	Postreform Recession
			Chile			
	1965–70	1971–73	1974–76	1977–78	1979–81	1982–83
Average annual growth rate (%):						
GDP	4.3	.5	3.1	9.0	7.3	−7.8
Expenditure	5.1	1.3	−8.2	11.9	10.2	−14.4
Gross fixed investment	5.3	−9.8	−7.8	16.7	17.8	−26.6
CPI	23.3	149.7	358.0	79.0	30.2	11.7
Average (%):						
Fiscal deficit/GDP	2.1	16.1	5.1	1.3	−2.1	3.1
Unemployment rate	6.0	4.6	14.2	13.6	12.2	22.2
Real wage (1969 = 100)	98	98	69	82	100	82
			Uruguay			
	1965–70	1971–73	1974–76	1977–78	1979–81	1982–83
Average annual growth rate (%):						
GDP	1.9	−.4	4.3	3.2	4.7	−7.2
Expenditure	2.9	−.2	1.9	3.6	5.6	−11.2
Gross fixed investment	7.3	−10.8	25.0	10.5	6.9	−24.8
CPI	49.8	62.7	69.2	51.3	54.0	33.3

Average (%):						
Fiscal deficit/GDP	1.9	3.2	3.8	1.9	0.0	6.4
Unemployment rate	8.2	8.1	9.7	12.4	8.4	13.7
Real wage (1968 = 100)*	104	102	86	70	64	54

	Argentina				
	1965–73	1973–75	1976–78	1978–80	1981–83
Average annual growth rate (%):					
GDP	4.2	2.9	.8	3.7	−3.0
Expenditure	4.2	3.3	−1.6	8.6	−6.1
Gross fixed investment	6.6	.1	4.9	4.0	−15.1
CPI	23.5	77.6	245.6	128.3	188.5
Average (%):					
Fiscal deficit/GDP	3.0	12.0	7.7	7.9	17.8
Unemployment rate	5.7	2.4	3.4	2.2	4.7
Real wage (1976 = 100)	125	154	100	118	111

SOURCES.—National accounts and papers mentioned in n. 1.

NOTE.—Averages for the period 1965–70 were estimated by fitting $\ln x = a + bT$; T = time trend; for the other periods a compounded average is used.

* Until October 1980, the index reflects only legislated increases in wages.

in 1979, and the peso appreciation of 1979 and 1980 provided a de facto trade liberalization.

In Uruguay, price controls were nearly eliminated by the end of 1979. But from 1974 to 1980, commercial policy reforms were much less pronounced than in the other two countries. However, import quotas that were widespread in the early seventies were eliminated in 1975, and taxes on traditional exports were removed. Unlike Chile and Argentina, until early 1979, Uruguay encouraged nontraditional exports with direct subsidies and credit subsidies. Tariffs were somewhat reduced, with maximum tariff rates lowered from 300% in 1975 to 150% by 1977. But tariffs were levied on reference prices, usually much higher than landed prices. Thus, the realized protection was often a multiple of the nominal formal tariffs, and there was redundant protection throughout 1979. A formal program of tariff reductions was initiated in January 1980, with a uniform 35% tariff rate to be achieved by December 1985. As in Argentina, an appreciating real exchange rate in 1980 and 1981 was the main source of increasing external competition.

2. *Financial market deregulation.* The rapid deregulation of domestic financial markets, also a common feature of reforms in the three countries, was important because of many years of nonprice allocations of credit and highly negative real interest rates. In all three countries, domestic capital markets were substantially deregulated in two ways. First, interest rate ceilings were progressively eliminated.[3] Second, restrictions on financial intermediaries were reduced. Argentina went from 100% reserve requirements and directed credit programs to a decentralized fractional reserve system. The Chilean government first loosened its control of the financial system by allowing nonbank intermediaries to operate without interest rate controls. Then in the next several years, interest ceilings on commercial banks were removed, and publicly held intermediaries were returned to the private sector. In Uruguay, dollar deposits were legalized early on, and directed credit programs were dismantled. Later, in 1977, controls on entry into the banking system were removed.

Each country also tried to open its economy to international capital flows, but the speed and extent of this action varied. In Uruguay, unrestricted movements of private capital were legalized as early as 1974, and full convertibility was reached by early 1977.[4] In Argentina, most controls on capital movements were eliminated with the reforms of 1979. In Chile, medium-term capital flows were progressively deregulated, with global limits on borrowing eliminated in 1979 and restrictions on the monthly inflow eliminated in April 1980. Restrictions on short-term capital inflows remained until late 1981.[5]

3. *Labor market deregulation.* In all three countries, labor market liberalization was relatively minor. These markets continued to be controlled through penalties or prohibitions on labor dismissals, legis-

lated wages, and/or wage indexation. But the weakening of trade union power was a de facto deregulation in the early stages of the reforms. In Chile, mobility was increased by the new labor laws of late 1979 and the social security reform of May 1981.[6] But until June 1982, Chilean wages were fully indexed to the consumer price index (CPI) for the private and public sectors. In Uruguay, labor mobility was increased with the social security reform of 1979, which created a unified social security fund financed mainly by government revenue from general taxes. Argentina's labor market was deregulated even less than those of Chile and Uruguay. This reflected the military's ongoing concern with political stability and the potential threat posed by the Peronist labor movement.

B. Stabilization Policies

In each country, the new economic teams had to immediately contend with two forms of macro imbalance: internally, extremely high inflation rates and, externally, major balance-of-payments crises. Programs to redress these imbalances were implemented in two identifiable phases.

In the first phase, anti-inflationary policy was based on major reductions in monetary growth and fiscal deficits. These "orthodox" measures were recognized to be contractionary, but it was thought that the potential benefits would easily outweigh the temporary costs of recession.[7] Absorption reductions were much more important in Chile than in Argentina and Uruguay; hence, not surprisingly, the Chilean recession was the most extreme (table 1).

Anti-inflationary policy measures were, in themselves, viewed as insufficient to eliminate balance-of-payments crises. Hence, phase-1 policies in each country also included major expenditure-switching attempts. In Chile and Argentina, switching was achieved through large real devaluations, and in Uruguay, switching included a combination of real devaluation and promotion of nontraditional exports. To avoid repetition of external crises, these initial adjustments were followed with a passive crawling peg exchange rate regime aimed at maintaining purchasing-power parity.

These initial policies successfully eliminated balance-of-payments crises. But, several years after the contractionary policies had been implemented, although the rate of inflation came down considerably in each country, it remained disturbingly high (Chilean inflation was still around 50% in late 1977, Argentinian inflation 166% in late 1978, and Uruguayan inflation roughly 50% in late 1978—see table 2). This persistence of inflation motivated a major shift of stabilization tactics toward what we will call "phase-2" policies.

Because the economies were seen as being more open to trade and capital flows, the new approach consisted of using the exchange rate as an anti-inflationary tool. Expectations about inflation and devaluation

TABLE 2

Exchange Rates, Prices, and Interest Rates during the *Tablita* Period (Phase 2) (Annual Growth Rates)

Year and Quarters	Argentina				Chile				Uruguay			
	Inflation	Real Exchange Rate Index (1978:4 = 100)	Real Interest Rate (P)	Ex Post P/$ Spread	Inflation	Real Exchange Rate Index (1978:4 = 100)	Real Interest Rate (P)	Ex Post P/$ Spread	Inflation	Real Exchange Rate Index (1978:4 = 100)	Real Interest Rate (P)	Ex Post P/$ Spread
1977:												
1	191.0	175.4	−26.2	−42.0	90.4	118.6	...	...	64.5	106.0	−1.5	...
2	122.0	163.1	3.7	−16.3	74.7	99.9	58.0	44.8	58.6	102.7	2.1	...
3	161.9	135.4	−15.9	18.5	53.5	92.6	...	...	68.4	97.3	−3.8	...
4	215.2	138.5	37.9	137.5	49.9	101.5	...	...	45.5	94.7	21.4	23.0
1978:												
1	196.3	126.2	28.8	112.8	33.0	104.6	...	...	23.7	93.9	43.1	54.8
2	185.1	115.4	−1.1	94.8	34.7	101.4	43.8	32.3	52.5	96.4	13.4	4.8
3	126.3	104.6	17.6	78.0	33.4	98.7	...	...	47.6	99.9	17.9	1.8
4	166.8	100.0	−9.7	38.0	27.2	100.0	...	...	49.4	100.0	15.6	12.5
1979:												
1	204.3	96.9	−23.0	33.3	25.4	100.8	22.6	8.2	68.9	86.5	.4	14.8
2	138.4	95.4	−11.5	42.3	34.6	105.6	19.4	−13.0	73.2	87.6	−5.3	14.8

3	169.5	86.2	−4.8	73.9	51.8	119.5	6.1	70.1	90.0	79.4	−14.6	20.5
4	96.7	76.9	53.3	63.7	41.1	110.0	20.0	23.3	86.9	68.7	−11.1	28.6
1980:												
1	97.1	70.8	19.5	44.3	29.5	108.2	22.8	36.6	66.7	61.9	.4	30.0
2	98.2	60.0	9.2	48.3	33.4	106.0	10.4	25.6	41.8	60.7	18.6	22.1
3	73.2	56.9	42.6	74.5	28.1	102.0	10.9	26.4	57.4	57.6	5.4	14.5
4	87.6	49.2	13.9	60.8	34.4	94.5	8.6	23.8	34.6	55.8	22.6	13.3
1981:												
1	71.6	50.8	52.8	20.0	18.3	89.2	36.5	28.0	25.1	54.7	30.9	17.1
2	129.8	81.5	−19.6	−1280.6	11.7	82.4	37.2	27.6	29.7	49.8	23.1	19.6
3	177.2	80.0	28.9	51.0	9.3	76.7	37.5	27.0	40.4	46.6	13.0	11.4
4	125.0	81.5	1.0	−1041.7	6.7	74.1	48.4	31.7	25.2	45.2	27.4	16.2
1982												
1	161.8	...	...	...	2.9	68.5	54.6	7.1	7.7	45.3	38.5	9.4
2	71.3	...	...	...	−.8	69.7	47.7	4.8	11.4	46.6	36.1	8.2
3	324.5	...	...	...	26.1	93.6	...	...	22.7	45.9	32.3	7.3
4	342.6	...	...	...	55.8	116.6	...	...	18.8	115.8	44.0	−96.5

SOURCES.—IMF, *International Financial Statistics*, various issues; papers mentioned in n. 1; and Petrei and Tybout (n. 34).

NOTE.—Annual growth rates are computed as follows: (1) inflation = CPI = $(CPI_t/CPI_{t-1})^4 - 1$ where CPI_t = CPI in quarter t; (2) real exchange rate index (RER) (1978:4 = 100) = $0.5\{PX^{\$}(1 + \text{subsidy}) + 0.5[PM^{\$}(1 + \text{tariff})]\}/CPI$ where $PX^{\$}$ = export prices in dollars, $PM^{\$}$ = import prices in dollars, and both $PX^{\$}$ and $PM^{\$}$ are trade-weighted divisia indices (of manufacturing wholesale prices of trading partners ($PM^{\$}$) and of dollar prices of major exports ($PX^{\$}$); (3) real interest rate (P) = $[(1 + r)/(1 + \hat{CPI})] - 1$ where r = average annual interest rate during quarter; (4) P/$ spread = $\{(1 + r)/[(1 + \hat{FXR})(1 + r^{\$})]\} - 1$ where $\hat{FXR}$ = devaluation rate, $r^{\$}$ = lending rate in $.

were recognized as important in determining the dynamics of stabilization, and it was assumed that preannounced exchange rate targets (up to 6 months in advance) would break inflationary expectations. The rate of devaluation was set by a preannounced schedule (the *tablita*) at less than the existing difference between domestic and world inflation. This policy corresponds to an "active" crawling peg.

Proponents of the new approach thought that purchasing-power parity and interest parity—both resulting from the forces of competition in freely operating commodity and capital markets—would obtain fairly rapidly. In Argentina and Uruguay, anti-inflationary policy took precedence over other economic objectives with the adoption of the *tablita* in December 1978. Similarly, although Chile was also implementing other liberalization reforms, bringing inflation down also became a major concern when the *tablita* was adopted in February 1978.

Since conditions differed in the three countries, there is no one model to describe how policymakers envisaged the path toward a stable economy. The Rodriguez model probably comes closest to describing how the preannouncements were supposed to work—at least in Argentina and Uruguay.[8] In this model, interest rate parity obtains continuously because of the absence of controls on capital flows and the assumption of perfect asset substitutability. The law of one price holds for tradables, and the rate of change in the prices of nontradable goods is a function of inflationary expectations—which are assumed to form adaptively—and of excess demand for nontradable goods. The model predicts that the implementation of a *tablita* should immediately reduce nominal interest rates and, to a lesser extent, inflation. The decline in real interest rates should first stimulate demand, creating an excess demand for nontradable goods and thereby inducing a temporary appreciation (that is, a fall) of the real exchange rate.[9] As inflation falls, both the real interest rate and the real exchange rate should increase, approaching their long-run equilibrium from below. The economy should stabilize without undergoing the recession associated with traditional contractionary measures. The avoidance of a recession associated with this new approach was quite attractive politically, especially in Argentina, where the military stated that increases in unemployment should be avoided at all costs.

In Chile, the vision of phase-2 stabilization was less closely linked to an integrated macro model. Policymakers there believed that the rate of domestic inflation would converge rapidly to world inflation simply because of competitive pressure. These policymakers were relatively concerned about the inflationary pressures that capital inflows might create; hence the *tablita* policy was initially pursued with substantial restrictions on the volume and rate of foreign credit use. Undoubtedly this contributed to an unemployment rate somewhat higher than the one that could have resulted with free capital inflows.

III. Stylized Outcomes

There is no easy bench-mark for judging the reforms. When they were initiated, each country was in a state of chaos. And as the reforms came to an end, each country was plunging into a deep recession. To give as balanced a picture as possible, we report average values of macroeconomic indicators for five periods (table 1). The first period corresponds to years representative of the import-substitution-led development strategy, the second to the period of instability directly preceding the reforms. The next two periods correspond to the reforms. Phase 1 is broken into two subperiods to isolate better the conditions that prevailed immediately before the *tablita* (phase 2) period (during which all three countries used the exchange rate as a stabilization instrument). The fifth period covers 2 years of deep recession after the abandonment of the *tablita*.

A. Phase 1

Phase 1, which combined liberalization with orthodox stabilization packages, was successful because the contractionary effects of the reduction in expenditures reduced macroeconomic imbalances. In Argentina, the central government budget deficit was reduced from an average of 12% of GDP in the prereform crisis period to 8%, and inflation was nearly cut in half. But growth never returned to the rates achieved during Argentina's period of import-substitution-led industrialization. In Chile, despite the 1975 recession when GDP fell 13% mainly because of a sharp external shock, the initial stabilization program was more successful. The government budget deficit was brought down from 16% of GDP during the prereform crisis to 1% by the end of phase 1, and inflation fell from 150% to 79%. In Uruguay, the turnaround was the most dramatic. Years of stagnation during the import-substitution phase gave way to 8 years of rapid growth, and the budget deficit (3% of GDP during the crisis) was progressively reduced. Inflation, meanwhile, was down from a historic peak of 97% in 1973 to 51% by the end of phase 1.

There were, nevertheless, differences in adjustment in the three countries during phase 1. Although real wages fell in all three countries, the trajectories of real wages and employment varied (see table 1). In Argentina, where unemployment remained low until 1981, the adjustment involved a drastic reduction in real wages and little change in unemployment. In Chile and Uruguay, by contrast, a reduction in employment accompanied the fall in real wages. Both countries also had to cope with severe external shocks caused by the rise in oil prices and the fall in the dollar prices of their main exports (copper in Chile and wool and beef in Uruguay). Balassa has estimated that the output effect of the external shock during 1974–78 (expressed as a percentage of average GDP for the period) was only 1% for Argentina but 4% for

Chile and 7% for Uruguay.[10] Argentina differed from Chile and Uruguay in another important dimension. Chile and Uruguay were both ultimately successful at eliminating their fiscal deficits and even at achieving a surplus, but although Argentina managed to reduce the deficit of its public enterprises, the fiscal deficit was never eliminated. (The lowest values of the Argentine public-sector deficit were 4.8% of GDP in 1977 and 6.9% of GDP in 1978.)

The countries also differed in terms of their liberalization policies during phase 1. Although all three countries reduced or removed taxes on traditional exports, only Uruguay gave strong fiscal and financial incentives to exporters of nontraditional products. Unlike the other countries, Uruguay managed to combine expansionary government (and later private) investment growth with a reduction in consumption.[11] Most of the increase in investment came from foreign savings, reflecting a reversal in a long-established trend of capital flight before the reforms. By contrast, Chile kept close control of capital flows and more rapidly liberalized domestic interest rates, which became positive early in the reforms. Furthermore, a sharp cut in the size of the public sector was introduced from the beginning. As a result, Chile's initial adjustment phase was more contractionary.

B. Phase 2

The outcomes of phase 2, when all three countries pursued the same general exchange-rate-based stabilization policy, are strikingly similar (table 2). In terms of inflation alone, the stabilization policies ultimately achieved their goal. In Chile, inflation fell from an annual rate of 35% in 1978:2 to −1% in 1982:2. In Uruguay, it fell from an annual rate of 49% in 1978:4 to 23% in 1982:3, and in Argentina, it fell from 167% in 1978:4 to 72% in 1981:1.

However, because these stabilization programs created other major imbalances, they proved unsustainable. Table 2 shows that the immediate impact of the *tablita* was to induce a decline in the marginal cost of dollar borrowing and to thereby create major opportunities for financial arbitrage. Hence, given the simultaneous increase in excess world liquidity and the lifting of capital controls, large capital inflows were induced. (In Argentina, public-sector borrowing significantly augmented private demand for foreign credit.)

The *tablita*-induced inflows financed a large excess of absorption over income, which drove up the relative prices of nontraded goods sharply. When it became apparent that this rapid real exchange rate appreciation was unsustainable, all three countries began to experience highly positive real interest rates. And the spreads between domestic and foreign borrowing costs increased. (Reasons for this outcome are further discussed in Section IV.) As confidence in the *tablita* policies waned, rates of capital inflows dropped dramatically, and the economic

TABLE 3

SOURCES OF INCREASES IN GROSS EXTERNAL DEBT (Billion US$)

Country and Period*	Increase in Gross External Debt (1)	Current Account (Surplus = +) (2)	Direct and Portfolio Capital Inflow (3)	Reserve Change (Gain = +) (4)	Residual (Capital Flight)† (5)
Argentina:					
1976–78	4.2	3.6	.5	3.5	4.8
1979–83‡	30.9	−12.9	8.0	−3.8	29.8
Chile:					
1975–78	2.0	−2.0	.2	1.0	−.8
1979–83	11.2	−12.4	1.5	1.5	−1.2
Uruguay:					
1973–78	0.5	−.6	.4	.7	−.4
1979–83	3.3	−1.9	.5§	−.3	2.2

SOURCES.—Col. 1—*Morgan International Data* (New York: Morgan Guarantee Trust Co., 1984); col. 2—IMF, *International Financial Statistics* (1984); col. 3—IMF, *Balance of Payments Statistics*; col. 4—IMF, *International Financial Statistics* (1984), line 1 l.d and 1 an d.

* For each country, the first period corresponds to phase 1, the second to phase 2 and its aftermath.

† Computed as col. (1) + col. (2) + col. (3) − col. (4).

‡ Banco Central de la Republica Argentina estimates for 1983.

§ Assumes zero values for 1983.

booms became busts. In Uruguay and in Argentina, where there were no controls on capital movements, major outflows occurred (table 3). In Chile, where individuals were prohibited from making large dollar purchases, speculation against the exchange regime took the form of purchases of imported consumer durables.[12]

C. Productivity and Growth

The reform packages were to bring down inflation and lead to a better resource allocation and a fuller use of labor and capacity. Was this the case? The evidence is sketchy and sensitive to how comparisons are made. We nevertheless argue that in terms of investment, employment, and growth, the reforms improved resource use in Chile and Uruguay but not in Argentina.

The evidence for Uruguay is clearest. During 1955–73, GDP grew 1.0% a year; during 1974–83, the years of the reforms, it grew 2.4% a year. Even though the rising investment-to-GDP ratio mostly reflected foreign savings, the marginal efficiency of investment (defined by the incremental capital output ratio [ICOR]) was higher during the reforms than during 1967–73. Furthermore, evidence from financial statements clearly indicates that capital formation was concentrated in exportable products during phase 1.[13]

In Chile, GDP growth was sustained in spite of relatively low investment rates and low rates of employment growth. This suggests that productivity and capacity utilization increases contributed significantly to growth. Calculations from a simulation model for 1977–81—in which account was taken of capacity utilization increases during 1977–79—suggest that reform-induced productivity gains increased the GDP in 1981 by 19% over what would have been achieved with historical total factor productivity (TFP) growth rates for the period 1950–74.[14] Further analysis based on comparisons of the 1967 and 1979 manufacturing censuses shows that although concentration increased in 1979 relative to the prereform period (1967), average price-cost margins fell. The increase in concentration was due to the greater opportunities that the trade liberalization and other reforms favoring mergers opened up for exploiting economies of scale. Furthermore, the fall in profitability was attributed to two factors: the reduction in oligopolistic conduct because of exposure to foreign competition and the increase in the elasticity of demand facing domestic firms caused by the entry of imports.[15]

Case study interviews with entrepreneurs in each country provide additional evidence of increased productivity. In each country, several entrepreneurs said that they achieved productivity gains beyond expectations. In addition to labor dismissals, the most frequently cited source of productivity gains was consolidation of production lines and the use of existing distribution channels to market imported goods. Entrepreneurs also often noted that foreign competition forced them to improve product quality. An additional factor in the case of Argentina was the purchase of foreign technological know-how, which enabled firms to compete with imports by upgrading the quality of their products and by producing them more efficiently.[16]

IV. What Went Wrong

We saw in Section II that the use of the exchange rate as an anti-inflationary instrument was expected to result in temporary capital inflows and temporary appreciation of the real exchange rate. Authorities hoped that these characteristics of the transition to price stability would be short-lived and mild. However, the combination of the *tablita* with inappropriate financial policies generated dramatic boom-bust cycles that culminated in the abandonment of each liberalization effort. Why were these effects so large, protracted, and damaging? We argue that three problems undermined the experiments: policy inconsistencies, the overlooking of market frictions, and the creation of adverse incentives to exploit the new environment.

In a nutshell, uncontrolled fiscal deficits (initially in Argentina and later also in Uruguay) and wage indexation (in Chile) clashed with the *tablita* program, making the tendency for currency appreciation worse.

Various unanticipated frictions did the same (see below). In turn, this caused a large volume of credit to flow into the countries. Despite this capital inflow, confusing signals regarding the administration of the *tablita* (especially in Argentina) increased exchange risk and tended to maintain a large spread between ex post borrowing costs in pesos versus dollars. With each economy failing to converge toward a steady-state equilibrium for so long, economic agents shifted their attention from the traditional objective of maximizing operating earnings to exploiting the various arbitrage possibilities that arose. In particular, the absence of basic regulatory constraints on financial activities facilitated this process. Even though we cannot isolate the effect of each factor on the outcome of the reforms, we take up each factor separately for expositional purposes, starting with policy inconsistencies, moving to frictions and adjustment lags, and then examining evasions of the intended objectives.

A. Policy Inconsistencies

To begin, several policies worked at cross-purposes. At the macro level, the economies were pulled in opposite directions by the clash of strong incentives to borrow abroad, lack of fiscal restraint (Argentina and Uruguay), wage policies (Chile), and the confusing management of the exchange rate (Argentina). These macro policies generated real exchange rates that discriminated against exports and induced risky corporate financial structures. In addition, contrary to announced intentions, micro reforms of both commercial and financial sector policies failed to eliminate important distortions.

1. *Exchange rate preannouncement, fiscal deficits, and wage indexation.* To be successful, the preannouncement model had to meet certain conditions. One of them was that the initial real exchange rate appreciation had to be moderate and short-lived in order to minimize foreign debt accumulation and adverse effects on the earnings of tradable-producing sectors. Otherwise, the *tablita* would be judged unsustainable, and expectations of a devaluation—reflected in growing dollar-peso spreads—would set in. But a growing externally financed fiscal deficit—starting in Argentina in 1980 and in Uruguay in 1981—increased capital inflows. This led to an increase in absorption over and above the one supposed to arise under the dynamic adjustment called for by the *tablita*. The deterioration in the real exchange rate was thus compounded to levels that jeopardized confidence in the sustainability of the *tablita* and ultimately inspired the capital flight documented in table 3.[17]

Cumby and van Wijnbergen have developed a formal model that links the probability of collapse in the exchange rate regime to fiscal policies. The credibility of the policy is analyzed in a world of uncertainty and in a setting of rational expectations by focusing on the con-

FIG. 1.—One-period-ahead probabilities of the collapse of the *tablita* in Argentina, 1979:1–1980:2. See Robert Cumby and Sweder van Wijnbergen, "Fiscal Policy and Speculative Runs on the Central Bank under a Crawling Peg Regime: Argentina, 1974–81" (Washington, D.C.: World Bank, 1983), fig. 1.

sistency between fiscal and domestic credit policies and the preannounced rate of crawl. The model for Argentina is estimated with monthly data. Cumby and van Wijnbergen's estimates, reproduced in figure 1, show that the probability of collapse of the exchange rate regime was very high from the beginning. In early 1980, the high estimated probability values for the collapse reflect the domestic credit expansion (63% in April and 46% in May) caused by the rescue of financial institutions. As a result of this episode, the stock of credit more than doubled in 2 months, and the probability of collapse shot up to 99%. Later, the probability of collapse was high because of growing fiscal deficits. Simulations of the effect of a 2% temporary increase in the growth of domestic credit (not reported here) suggest that the probability of collapse returns to a slightly higher equilibrium value after about 9 months (the probability is permanently raised by a temporary increase in domestic credit because this permanently increases the stock of credit).[18]

Fiscal deficits were not a problem in Chile. Indeed, the government budget had a surplus during the *tablita* period. But capital inflows in Chile were concentrated during the *tablita* years as capital controls were being relaxed at a time when the *tablita* and inflation inertia were making foreign borrowing highly profitable. Furthermore, as discussed below, the existence of 100% backward wage indexation made the recovery of the real exchange rate a lengthy process. This in turn undermined the credibility of the *tablita* policy.

2. *Announcement inconsistencies and exchange risk.* Another source of inconsistency relates to the preannouncement of the exchange rate and to the lack of explicit guarantees that the government would honor the *tablita*. This problem was particularly important in Argentina, where no exchange insurance was provided and many ambiguities shrouded the announcements. The declarations were often vague about the future, and the resulting premium for exchange risk increased the spread between the domestic interest rate and the international interest rate (plus the announced rate of devaluation). At the beginning, Central Bank Resolution 807 produced a substantial downward trend in the spread, which reached a minimum in February 1979 (fig. 2). After reaching this minimum, the spread increased as the re-

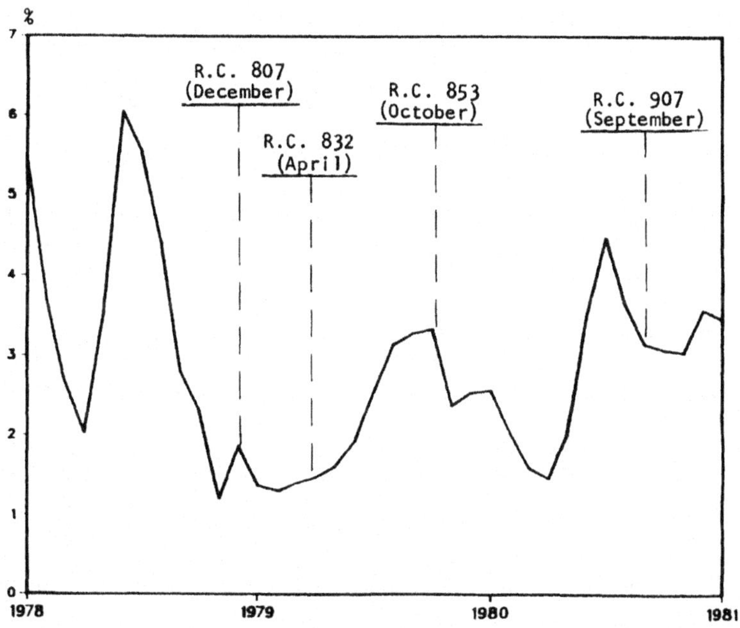

FIG. 2.—The "news" and peso/dollar spreads in Argentina (monthly observations). The spread is computed subtracting the U.S. prime rate plus the rate of devaluation from the average domestic lending rate. See Roque Fernandez, "The Expectations Management Approach to Stabilization in Argentina during 1976–82," *World Development* 13, no. 8 (1985): 871–92.

maining period of the devaluation schedule became shorter and shorter. Despite its ambiguity, Resolution 853, in October 1979, produced another downward trend because most agents initially interpreted that the schedule had been extended until March 1981. Indeed, Martinez de Hoz made it clear that he did not want a perfectly determined schedule because that would imply "free exchange insurance." But after the failure of the Banco Intercambio Regional, in March 1980, credibility waned so much that further resolutions would no longer reduce the spread.

In Uruguay, no ambiguities surrounded the announcements, yet the spreads remained fairly wide. Moreover, commercial banks seldom took open positions, despite the profitability (and encouragement from authorities) of transforming dollar liabilities into peso assets. There was a brief period in 1981 when the Central Bank sold guarantees (March–September 1981), but even then, although the spread declined, it remained fairly high (see fig. 3). Hanson and de Melo tested a simple model of interest-rate determination using monthly data for the period November 1978–December 1981 and showed that—except for the period of exchange guarantees—the spread obtained between peso and dollar interest rates was constant. The evidence suggests that the exchange risk remained high and that loans denominated in dollars were imperfect substitutes for loans denominated in pesos.[19]

3. *Conflicts between commercial and exchange rate policies.* Even if the unexpectedly large real appreciation had not generated speculative outflows (and the associated collapse of the *tablita*), it would still have imposed major costs on the economy in terms of resource allocation. Activities in the tradable sector that were profitable on the eve of the *tablita* were squeezed dramatically by the time phase 2 was nearing its collapse. The effect on exporters and import-competing producers was not symmetric, reflecting a further conflict between commercial and exchange rate policies. Despite announced intentions to promote exports while subjecting import-substituting firms to greater competition, the real appreciation tended to reduce export profitability relatively more.

The authorities' signals about trade liberalization policies turned out to be somewhat at odds with the de facto system of incentives that emerged. In all three countries, and especially in Chile and Uruguay, the authorities stated early on that exports would become the engine of growth. But the incentives provided by the elimination of taxes on traditional exports and by the initial sharp real devaluations were soon eroded in phase 2. The appreciating real exchange rates that accompanied *tablita* policies worked against exportables more than importables because exportables lacked the buffer of redundant initial protection. Besides reducing earnings mostly in the very sector that authorities set out to promote, the conflicting signals bred uncertainty

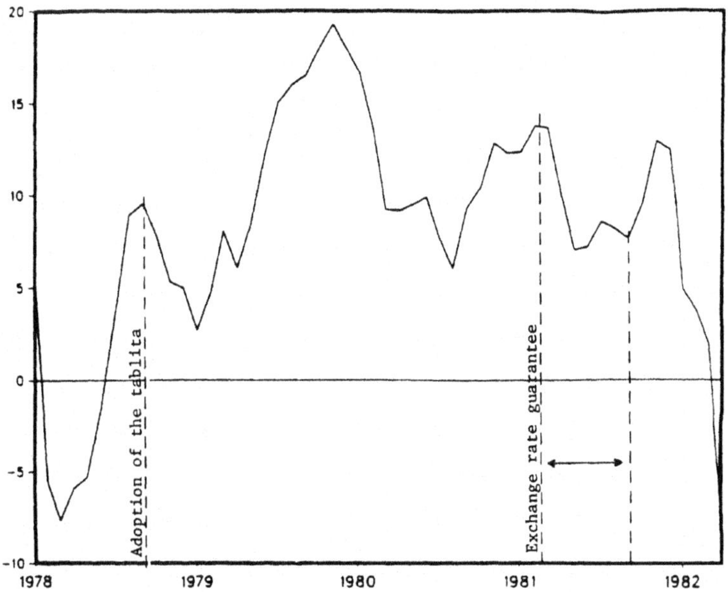

FIG. 3.—Exchange insurance and ex post spread between peso and dollar interest rates in Uruguay (monthly spreads).

$$\text{Spread} = \frac{(1 + RPD_t/100)}{(1 + RDD_t/100)\,(1 + \hat{E})} - 1$$

where RPD_t and RDD_t are annualized interest rates on 1–6 month peso and dollar deposits.

$$\hat{E} = \left(\frac{ER_{t+6}}{ER_t}\right)^2 - 1$$

is the annualized ex post rate of devaluation. Adapted from James Hanson and Jaime de Melo, "External Shocks, Financial Reforms and Stabilization Attempts in Uruguay during 1974–83," *World Development* 13, no. 8 (1985): 917–39, fig. 3.

among producers. An example is provided by the formal tariff reduction schedules of the government. The schedules were broken on one or several occasions when it was felt that inflation was not falling fast enough. Producers reacted by delaying making major resource commitments. Such wait-and-see attitudes were confirmed by interviews with 40 businessmen. The interviewees reported that they delayed taking action on government policies for periods ranging up to 6 months because they were uncertain whether the policy would be adhered to.[20]

The conflict between commercial and exchange rate policies is apparent in a comparison of gross margins trajectories for exportable

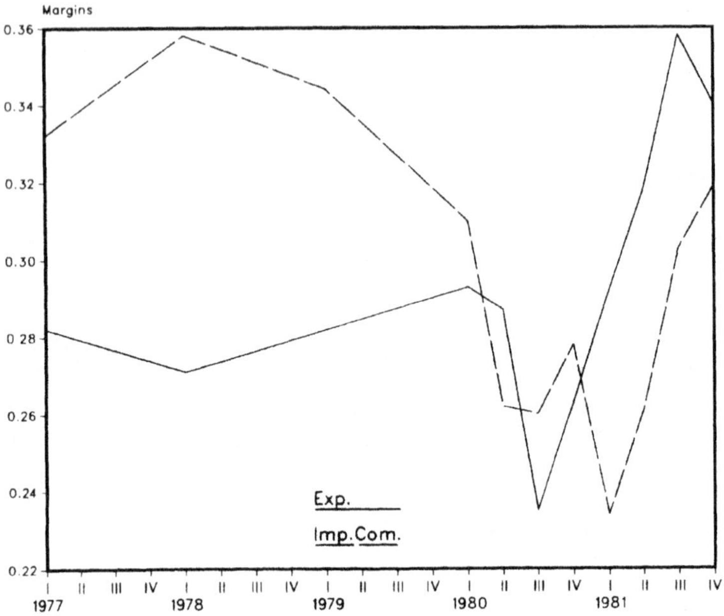

FIG. 4.—Gross margins in Argentina exportable versus import-competing goods (1977–81). Adapted from Humberto Petrei and James Tybout, "Microeconomic Adjustments in Argentina during 1976–81: The Importance of Changing Levels of Financial Subsidies," *World Development* 13, no. 8 (1985): 949–68.

manufacturing firms and those of import-competing manufacturing firms (figs. 4, 5, and 6). Whereas the reforms were supposed to raise profitability of exportable activities vis-à-vis importable activities, the reverse occurred, particularly during phase 2, when real exchange rate appreciation lowered the profitability of exportable firms more sharply than that of import-competing firms.

The inconsistency between trade liberalization and exchange rate policies was particularly apparent in Argentina. Although export taxes were reduced dramatically at an early stage in the reforms, the price-level-deflated effective exchange rate for exports followed the path of the real exchange rate closely after 1977.[21] Moreover, considerable tariff and nontariff barriers remained in place for some time. The maximum tariff rates on consumer goods were reduced from values over 200% to 100% in 1976, but import penetration in these commodities remained low. In December 1978, a general scheme for tariff reductions was announced, but the schedule put the major burden of adjustment well into the future. So the trade reforms, combined with the real exchange rate appreciation, did little to translate officially announced

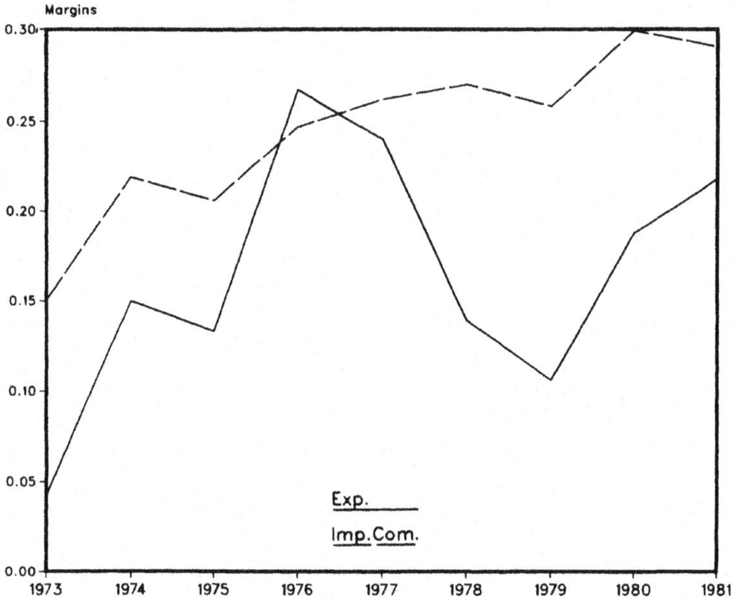

FIG. 5.—Gross margins in Uruguay exportables versus import-competing goods (1973–81). Adapted from Jaime de Melo, Ricardo Pascale, and James Tybout, "Microeconomic Adjustments in Uruguay during 1973–81: The Interplay of Real and Financial Shocks," *World Development* 13, no. 8 (1985): 995–1015.

intentions into the appropriate price signals. Instead, exporters were hurt more than import-competing producers, who were still protected by redundant protection. Figure 4 shows this perverse impact on average gross margins for firms in Argentina.[22] (The problem disappears in 1981 because of the maxi-devaluation that ended phase 2.) This outcome may have been traceable in part to the competing objectives of the Ministry of Commerce—accustomed to using protection to fight current account problems—and the Central Bank, which was using the exchange rate as a stabilization tool.[23]

In Uruguay, there was a similar discrepancy between pronouncements and policies. Exports were encouraged effectively during phase 1 with new financial incentives, increased fiscal incentives, and a real exchange rate stabilized by a passive crawling peg (fig. 5). But in 1979, the incentives that reduced the bias against export activities vis-à-vis import-competing activities were eliminated. Because there was much redundant protection in manufacturing when the tariff reform started to be implemented in January 1980, exporters were hurt, whereas import-substituting producers in manufacturing were still enjoying redundant

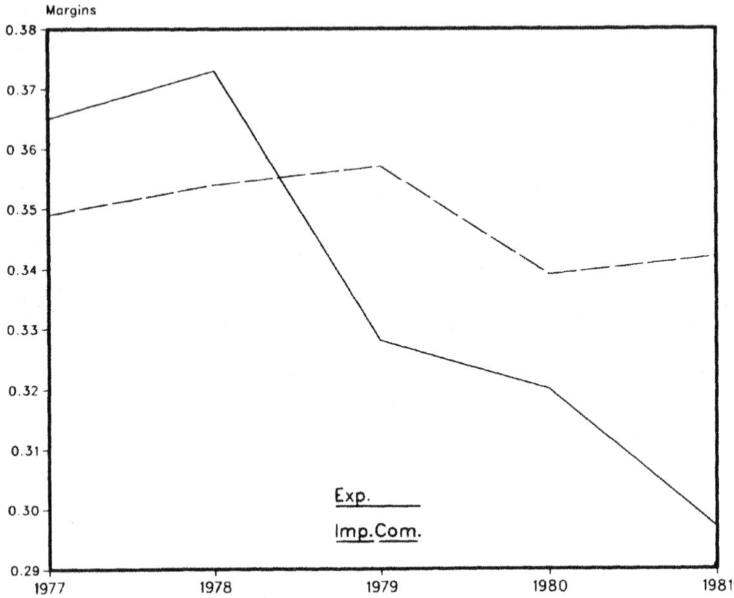

FIG. 6.—Gross margins in Chile exportable versus import-competing goods. Adapted from Julio Galvez and James Tybout, "Microeconomic Adjustments in Chile during 1977–81: The Importance of Being a Grupo," *World Development* 13, no. 8 (1985): 969–94.

protection. The rate of growth of nontraditional exports fell sharply during 1979–81.

The same pattern developed in Chile. During 1975–79, exportable-goods producers attracted resources, and nontraditional exports grew 32% a year. But the peso appreciation reversed this trend in 1979. During 1979–81, the leading growth sectors were nontradables (construction, trade, and financial services), even though the completion of the tariff reforms in June 1979 had reduced the policy-induced bias against exportables to 10% (see fig. 6).[24]

4. *Treatment of financial intermediaries*. Another inconsistency in policies was between the proclaimed reliance on free-market mechanisms and the de facto treatment of financial intermediaries. There are two ways of promoting efficient intermediaries in a deregulated financial sector. The first is flatly to refuse to provide deposit insurance and never to bail out failed banks.[25] The second is to sell insurance to banks at actuarially fair rates, determined bank by bank after careful examination of loan portfolios. Neither policy was pursued. The governments implicitly or explicitly provided deposit insurance at *no* cost and with no systematic procedures for monitoring loan portfolios, li-

quidity levels, or solvency positions. In Uruguay, banks were not even required to publish their income statements (perhaps because authorities felt that this information would spread rapidly in a deregulated economy). Moreover, in at least one case, important problems of monopoly control and conflict of interest were allowed to continue unarrested.

In Chile, authorities initially chose the "no insurance" option for financial sector deregulation. Recognizing that the provision of free deposit insurance to banks induces risk-taking, they repeatedly advised depositors that they would not be bailed out if a bank failed. Even so, when a medium-sized bank failed in 1977, the Central Bank rescued all of its depositors.[26] Thereafter, popular opinion had it that depositors no longer needed to concern themselves with their banks' portfolios. This paved the way for high-risk lending operations and the channeling of funds to affiliated enterprises in financial distress.[27] Accordingly, when adverse earnings and the dissolution of the *tablita* weakened the industrial sector, financial intermediaries were too fragile to absorb the shock. (Banks had already lost much of their capital during the Allende years.) Further bailouts and a near socialization of the banking sector were the results.

The chain of events was similar in Uruguay. No formal explicit insurance was provided, but experience generated expectations of a bailout. During the banking crisis of 1965, and again in 1979, depositors were rescued by the government from bearing the costs of failures. These precedents satisfied depositors that they need not worry about their banks' portfolios. By the end of the reform period, when firms could no longer pay the high real interest rates, 21 out of 23 banks had been bailed out by the government and sold to foreign banks.

Unlike Chile and Uruguay, in Argentina deposit insurance was explicitly provided but at no cost to the banks. This created even more incentives for loan officers to pursue risky ventures. Furthermore, rather than calling in overdue loans and registering losses, Argentine banks rolled them over and financed their new resource commitments by attracting additional deposits. As Fernandez notes, this practice may have contributed to the extremely high and rising real interest rates during phase 2 and during the aftermath of Argentine reforms.[28]

In short, the financial sector booms in the Southern Cone may have reflected something other than the flourishing of a newly liberated sector. An alternative view is that the booms were largely a consequence of rentseekers scrambling to extract the major subsidies provided by free deposit insurance, explicit or implicit. And the high real interest rates observed toward the end of the reforms in all three countries partly reflected banks' raising of deposit interest rates to attract new depositors to compensate for a growing number of nonperforming loans. A minimum set of basic banking regulations on bank portfolios would have gone a long way toward preventing the internal financial crisis.

B. Frictions and Adjustment Lags

Prominent among the assumptions of the stabilization model used in phase 2 was that tradable goods and assets were perfect (or near perfect) substitutes for their external counterparts.[29] The evidence strongly suggests that this was not the case.

1. *Price formation.* During the *tablita* period, it was thought that domestic inflation would rapidly converge to international inflation plus the preannounced rate of devaluation. However, as seen above, this was never the case, and the domestic currency invariably appreciated sharply.

In Uruguay, domestic inflation, $\dot{P}$, exceeded the rate of devaluation adjusted for international inflation ($\dot{P}W + \dot{E}$) for the first 2 years of the *tablita,* although the gap between the two narrowed as time went by. Figure 7 shows that convergence in rates of change of the wholesale price index (WPI) to the exchange-rate-adjusted WPI of trading partners only occurred 24 months after the start of the program. It deserves mention that as long as $\dot{P} > \dot{P}W + \dot{E}$ for tradables, the loss of competitiveness was increasing, and restoring competitiveness would have required a sustained period of domestic inflation *less* than world inflation. This phenomenon of limited transmission from foreign to domestic tradable prices is further supported statistically.[30]

Also in Chile there appears to have been considerable stickiness in the downward adjustment of inflation. As already stressed, part of this was due to wage indexation: being linked to a weighted average of tradable and nontradable goods prices (namely the CPI), wage inflation did not fall one-for-one with reductions in domestic tradables inflation. And statistical evidence suggests that a change in the rate of devaluation—keeping excess demand levels at their observed trajectories—would take over nine quarters to work its full impact on the inflation rate.[31]

Isolating the effect of aggregate demand from the effect of the *tablita* policy—by assuming that expenditure growth had remained the same as in the reference path—Corbo simulated the real exchange rate trajectory that would have resulted if, starting in the first quarter of 1980, devaluation rates had been passive—that is, if they had matched the difference between foreign and domestic inflation. The results, depicted in figure 8, show that real appreciation would still have been substantial. This appreciation is driven by a key assumption incorporated in the simulation, namely that the trajectory of expenditure growth is independent of the rate of crawl.

The implication of these results is that a stabilization policy based on a preannounced rate of devaluation with a decreasing rate of crawl

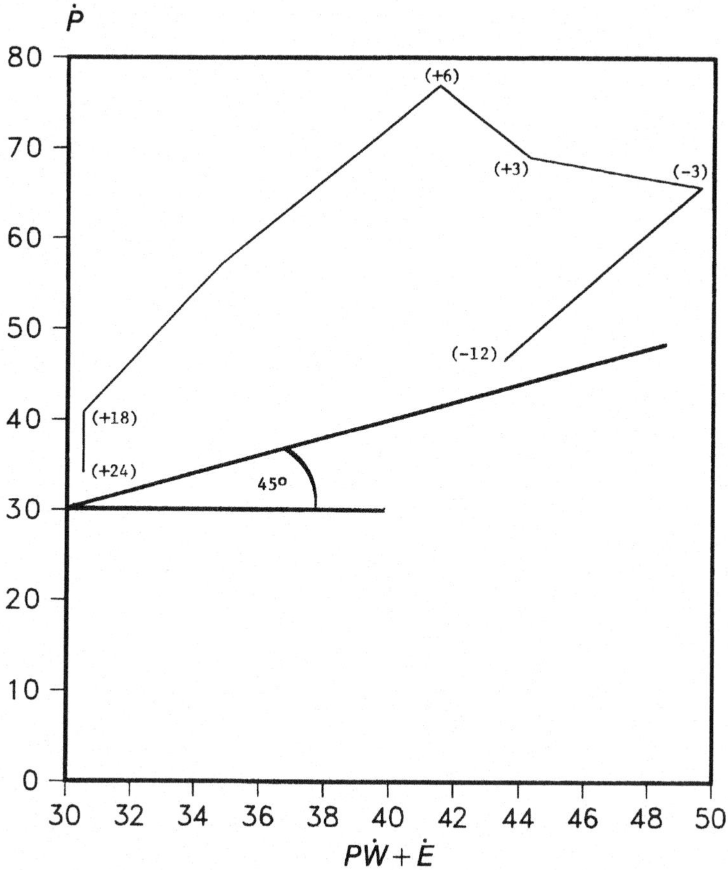

FIG. 7.—Price convergence during the *tablita* (annualized logarithmic growth rates). $\dot{P}$ = wholesale price. $P\dot{W}$ = weighted wholesale prices of 10 major trading partners. $\dot{E}$ = devaluation rate. Figures in parentheses indicate months before (−) and after (+) the start of the preannouncement of the exchange rate.

is bound to generate a lengthy period of domestic currency real appreciation. During this period, domestic tradables are losing competitiveness. To restore competitiveness to levels prevailing before the *tablita* requires domestic inflation for tradables to be less than the trading partners' inflation. This implies that the rate of crawl must be accelerated and demand policies must be restrictive to put downward pressure on aggregate demand.

Micro-level studies show that even at the commodity level, substitution between domestically produced and imported tradables was

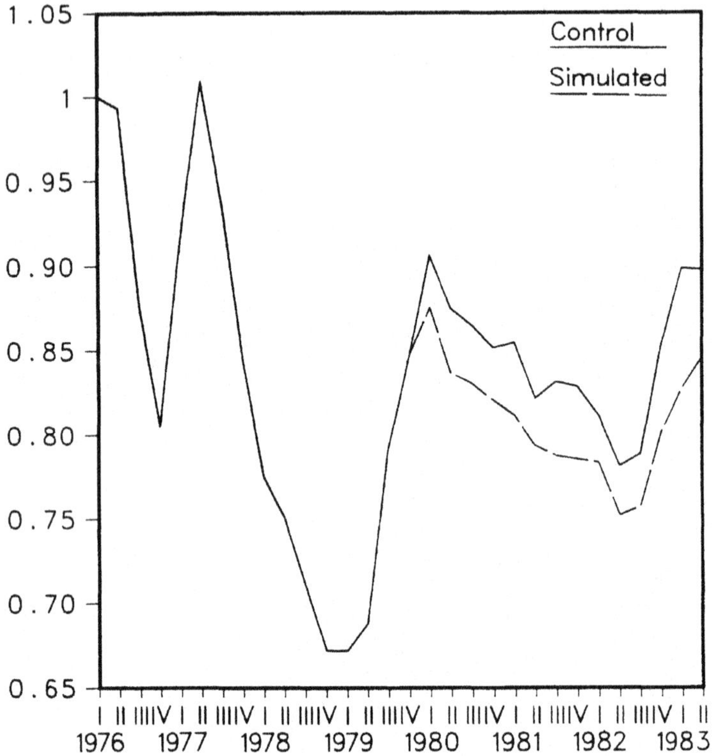

FIG. 8.—Effects of a PPP devaluation rule on the real exchange rate (P_{ext}/P_m) (1976:1 = 1.00). Real exchange rate = P_{ext}/P_m. P_{ext} = domestic currency price of similar imports (tariff inclusive); $P_{ext} = P_w^*(1 + t)ER$ where t = average tariff rate and ER = nominal exchange rate. P_m = price of differentiated domestically produced import-competing goods. Derived from a model in V. Corbo, "International Prices, Wages and Inflation in an Open Economy: A Chilean Model," *Review of Economics and Statistics* 67, no. 4 (1985): 564–73.

low. Part of the reason for this limited short-run substitutability was delayed adjustments. One factor overlooked by authorities is that it takes time to develop distribution channels for imports (especially when, as in Argentina, it takes considerable time to obtain an importer's license). The more unpredictable the environment, the longer the delay. Micro-level evidence indicates that reductions in trade restrictions took a while to affect producer pricing, even when imports and domestic goods were very similar.[32]

2. *Financial asset substitutability and monetary policy.* In the three countries the monetary authorities assumed that domestic

financial assets were perfect substitutes for foreign assets. Furthermore, they thought that instantaneous portfolio adjustment was being impeded only by capital controls. This view led monetary authorities to conclude that if controls on capital inflows were lifted, domestic interest rates would drop to equal foreign interest rates adjusted for the expected rate of devaluation. Thus, they accelerated the opening-up of the capital account to bring into equality the domestic and international interest rates. However, spreads between domestic and international interest rates not only resulted from imperfections in domestic financial markets but also from imperfect substitution between domestic and foreign assets. These frictions were overlooked by the authorities.

Corbo and Matte provide evidence of imperfect asset substitution for Chile in a model with three financial assets: money, domestic interest-bearing assets, and foreign assets.[33] In this model, if domestic interest-bearing assets are perfect substitutes for foreign assets and portfolio adjustments are instantaneous (i.e., if there is perfect capital mobility) and there is no sterilization attempt by the Central Bank, a deficit in the current account and a decrease in net domestic credit by the Central Bank are matched by an equal foreign capital inflow without reserve loss and with a constant money base. This means that under perfect (no) capital mobility, one peso's worth of domestic credit reduction would be matched by one (zero) peso's worth of capital inflow. For Chile, the estimated coefficient linking capital inflows and the change in net domestic credit creation was only -0.34 and the one linking capital inflows and the current account deficit was -0.32, suggesting that Chile's financial system during the period is best described as relatively closed rather than as open with perfect capital mobility. Furthermore, as predicted by the model, the coefficients of the change in net domestic credit and of the current account deficit in the capital flow equation were not statistically different.

These results suggest that the Central Bank was wrong in assuming that a perfect capital mobility model was a good characterization of Chile's financial market. (Indeed, a causality test reported in that paper shows that changes in reserves did not affect changes in domestic credit, suggesting that the monetary authorities did not attempt to control the money supply.) In particular, the Central Bank could have sterilized part of the high money growth during the period (M1 grew 60% in 1979, 58% in 1980, and 33% in 1981) and thus mitigated the overheating of the economy.

C. Evasions of the Intended Incentive Structure[34]

With relative prices moving rapidly in all three countries and with elements of financial disequilibria apparent, firms avoided making long-term or irreversible production adjustments.[35] Instead, the focus of their activities was largely on financial and other endeavors that held the promise of immediate returns.[36] Such activities helped firms to remain profitable, but they also allowed many firms to behave at odds with the incentive structures that governments were trying to create.

1. *Privatization of the tariff.* The quick-return activities that subverted the reform programs took several forms. One of the most interesting has become known as "tariff privatization." This term refers to instances when firms that produce importable goods before trade liberalization become retailers for the now-cheaper foreign products, selling initially at prices not much below those previously charged on domestically produced substitutes. In so doing, they delay and sometimes avoid the desired convergence of domestic relative (and absolute) prices toward international levels.

Many instances of changes in activity from producing to retailing are reported in Arriagada et al.[37] This activity developed in part because of the advantage of already having a well-established distribution framework and in part because of the uncertainties that raised the costs of entry into retailing. Tariff privatization may also help explain the slower fall in price-cost margins for importables than for exportables observed in figures 4, 5, and 6.[38]

2. *Exploiting the financial environment.* The spread between peso and dollar borrowing costs described earlier created further opportunities for quick profits. A clear shift of the profit base from real to financial activities is observable among many Argentine and Chilean firms. Earlier in the reforms, when access to dollars was relatively limited (mainly in Chile), the spread tended to generate financial rents to larger firms, especially those whose line of production put them in regular contact with foreign lenders. Later, when access to dollar loans was more general, cheap foreign credit became a popular means to offset operating losses. Since foreign borrowing was also prevalent among nontradable firms, which could not offset capital losses from a large devaluation, the stage was set for major financial crises when the *tablita* programs became unsustainable and big devaluations took place.

In Argentina, the real cost of dollar borrowing became very negative in 1977 and, except for a short period in late 1979 and early 1980, remained so until the big devaluation of 1981. Moreover, peso rates were often negative in real terms during the later 1970s. This financial environment meant that any firm with access to credit, especially dollars, could create a substantial cash flow for itself simply by expanding its nominal borrowing at a rate sufficient to keep its real debt constant. When both dollar and peso rates became positive in the last quarter of 1979, the returns from this activity evaporated. But they materialized again in 1981, when the government protected firms from the big devaluations with various exchange insurance programs. These programs gave further incentives to firms, now more indebted in dollars than ever, to shift their attention from real production to financial activities. The riskiness of the corporate sector's financial structure steadily increased as a consequence, especially among large firms, which were the most able or willing to expose themselves in dollars.[39]

The Chilean experience was somewhat different, largely because quantitative constraints substantially limited dollar credit inflows until 1980. These constraints combined with the extremely high peso cost of debts to make borrowing a very expensive endeavor for the average firm. Nonetheless, some Chilean producers, by virtue of their size or sector of activity, had direct access to cheap foreign funds. Moreover, some firms directly or indirectly held shares in major commercial banks, which in turn had access to credit from abroad. Both sets of favored firms were owned in large measure by a handful of powerful industrialists and made up the country's major "economic groups."[40] The average financial cost to group-affiliated firms was accordingly considerably below that for independent producers. Furthermore, these group-affiliated firms exploited their preferential credit access to finance large acquisitions of long-term securities, thereby generating nonoperating earnings and consolidating power. In so doing, they became heavily indebted and, having done poorly in real operations, were in an unenviable position when the opportunities for financially based profit making evaporated in 1981.

Like Argentina, Uruguay opened its capital account to capital inflows almost completely at an early stage in its reforms. Firms moved decisively to exploit negative real financial costs as a source of revenue. Especially among exportable-goods producers, who enjoyed various subsidies until 1979, the returns from holding net dollar liabilities were high. In addition, in the early stage of phase 2 (when the exchange risk was low), firms exploited large financial returns by borrowing in dollars. Net dollar liabilities of the typical firm went from a negligible share in 1973 to roughly 35% of assets for exportable producers and 13% of assets for import-competing producers in 1981. In Uruguay, as in Argentina, firm size was strongly positively correlated with dollar exposure.[41] The general pattern of the largest firms becoming very vulnerable to devaluation-induced financial crises thus characterized all three countries of the Southern Cone.

V. Conclusions

Rarely do countries carry out reform packages as profound as those in the Southern Cone. Not only did the reform packages span all markets, but they were implemented in a short time, starting from a crisis situation and heavily distorted markets. This paper has attempted to provide explanation for the most flagrant reasons for failure, despite notable growth and productivity gains in the early phases.

What then are the lessons? Obvious though it is, the fact that the three countries started with conditions much further from the reform targets than did other economies that liberalized successfully (notably, the East Asian countries) is worth remembering. Import-substitution policies had been in place since the depression of the 1930s. Interest rates had been controlled for decades. Price controls had been in place since the early 1950s, and labor markets had been subject to innumerable regulations. These initial conditions, and previously unsuccessful mild attempts at liberalization, implied that the authorities probably faced deeply entrenched political interest groups and recalcitrant expectations. The trade regime had historically discriminated against exporting activities and resulted in much redundant protection for import-competing producers. Furthermore, macro policies were frequently constrained by balance-of-payments crises.

Despite these adversities, we showed that many positive signs emerged from the phase-1 stabilization plans, especially in Uruguay and Chile. Exports and productivity growth picked up while the economies recovered rapidly from a crisis situation. Besides the relatively low real wages and high unemployment rates in Chile (not surprising under the circumstances), the most disquieting sign during phase 1 was the emergence of extremely high real interest rates as soon as deregulation took place.

We have argued that troubles started to develop in phase 2, when the approach to stabilization policy changed and the economies became increasingly open to foreign capital flows. The *tablita* policy, in combination with the removal of restrictions on capital flows, led to boom-bust cycles. The setting of the preannounced devaluation schedules at much less than the internal-external inflation differential under deregulated domestic interest rates led to large short-term capital inflows, increased dollar indebtedness, and booms. In turn, the booms caused strong peso real appreciation, which resulted in a loss of competitiveness for tradables and generated doubts about the sustainability of the *tablita*. Capital flight followed, and the economies went bust, with each country having accumulated staggering volumes of external debt.

The most obvious lesson is that use of the exchange rate as an anti-inflationary tool leads to a major macroeconomic disturbance, and this disturbance ultimately undermines the stabilization effort. A related lesson is that a properly designed reform package should coordinate the opening of the current and capital accounts. We have given examples and estimates of the adverse effects on exportable producers. We have also shown some of the costs in credibility and incentives of not coordinating fiscal and wage policies with the *tablita*.

Another lesson is to be drawn from the comparison of adjustment paths between exportable- and importable-producing firms. This juxtaposition reveals that price-cost margins fell more rapidly for the former than for the latter during real exchange rate appreciation. Redundant protection, product differentiation, delays in the establishment of importing channels, and other adjustment delays are thus likely to affect exportables more adversely than importables during a period of real exchange rate appreciation. Hence it appears that exporters are particularly vulnerable to movements in the real exchange rate.

Finally, the phenomenal opportunities for nonoperating earnings in Chile and Argentina led firms to assume risky financial structures, thereby setting the stage for widespread banking crises when the *tablita* ended. These patterns of financial behavior were abetted by access to foreign credit and by the implicit or explicit provision of commercial bank deposit insurance. We conclude that closer supervision of financial activity is advisable when financial systems that have been highly regulated for a long time are liberalized. In the Southern Cone, such supervision would have helped avert the crises encountered when operating earnings fell and the reforms were abandoned.

Notes

* Prepared for presentation at the Allied Social Science Associations' meetings, Dallas, on December 26–28, 1984. This article is a summary of research in progress at the World Bank under RPO 672-85, "Liberalization and Stabilization in the Southern Cone." We would like to thank Maria Ameal, José Miguel Sanchez, and Kalayarat Suriyasat for their unfailing support during this research and Sebastian Edwards, Arnold Harberger, Anne Krueger, and Simón Teitel for comments on an earlier draft. The World Bank does not accept responsibility for the views expressed herein, which are ours and should not be attributed to the World Bank or to its affiliated organizations. Our findings, interpretations, and conclusions are the results of research supported by the Bank; they do not necessarily represent official policy of the Bank. The designations employed, the presentation of material, and any maps used in this article are solely for the convenience of the reader and do not imply the expression of any opinion whatsoever on the part of the World Bank or its affiliates concerning the legal status of any country, territory, city, or area or the legal status of any country's authorities or the delimitation of its boundaries or national affiliation.

1. This section draws on Roque Fernandez, "The Expectations Management Approach to Stabilization in Argentina during 1976–82," *World Development* 13, no. 8 (1985): 871–92; Vittorio Corbo, "Reforms and Macroeconomic Adjustments in Chile during 1974–83," *World Development* 13, no. 8 (1985): 893–916; James Hanson and Jaime de Melo, "External Shocks, Financial Reforms and Stabilization Attempts in Uruguay during 1974–83," *World Development* 13, no. 8 (1985): 917–39.

2. The fiscal deficit was 25% of GDP in Chile, 16% in Argentina, and 7% in Uruguay.

3. In Argentina, interest rates were freed by June 1977; in Chile, by June 1975; and in Uruguay, by October 1977. Pablo Spiller and Edgardo Favaro, "The Effects of Entry Regulations on Oligopolistic Interaction: The Uruguayan Banking Sector," *Rand Journal of Economics* 15, no. 2 (1984): 244–54, show that oligopolistic interaction among incumbent Uruguayan banks was much reduced when the reforms allowed entry into the banking system.

4. Full convertibility was only introduced de jure in October 1978, but currencies other than the peso were recognized as legal tender from the start, and the spread between the floating financial and crawling commercial exchange rates was eliminated by early 1977.

5. In Argentina, capital inflows with maturity of less than 12 months were prohibited until June 1980, although in practice all controls on capital flows were lifted in early 1979. In Chile, until late 1981, short-term capital inflows (less than 24 months) were available only to finance foreign trade operations, while medium-term capital inflows were subject to a reserve requirement.

6. Even though labor dismissal was relaxed after September 1973, dismissal of more than 10 workers required special permission from the ministers of labor and the economy up until 1981.

7. For a recent presentation of the traditional orthodox approach to stabilization policy, see Rudiger Dornbusch, "Stabilization Policy in Developing Countries: What Have We Learned," *World Development* 10, no. 9 (October 1982): 701–30.

8. See Carlos Rodriguez, "The Argentine Stabilization Plan of December 20th," *World Development* 10 (1982): 226–38. The first version of the paper is dated June 1979.

9. Sweder van Wijnbergen, "The Crawling Peg, Capital Flows and the Real Exchange Rate in LDC's," photocopied (Washington, D.C.: World Bank, 1983), also obtained a temporary real exchange rate appreciation. In his model this arises because the slowing down in the rate of crawl generates an increase in wealth to holders of dollar liabilities, which in turn raises expenditure. Under certain conditions, inflation may even rise temporarily, an outcome consistent with phase 2 in Uruguay. Also see Mario Blejer and Donald Mathieson, "The Preannouncement of Exchange Rate Changes as a Stabilization Instrument," *IMF Staff Papers* 28 (December 1981): 760–92; and Sebastian Edwards, "The Order of Liberalization of the External Sector in Developing Countries," *Essays in International Finance*, no. 156 (Princeton, N.J.: Princeton University Press, 1984).

10. See Bela Balassa, "Adjusting to External Shocks: The Newly Industrializing Developing Economies in 1974–76 and 1979–81," *Review of World Economics* 121, no. 1 (1985): 116–35.

11. The average investment GDP ratio in Uruguay rose from 10% for 1967–74 to 16% for 1975–81.

12. Hanson and de Melo (n. 1 above), table 8, show that purchases of imported consumer durables shot up in Uruguay in 1980 and 1981 during the period of real exchange rate appreciation. For evidence on Chile, see Rudiger Dornbusch, "External Debt, Budget Deficits and Disequilibrium Exchange Rates," in *International Debt and the Developing Countries*, ed. Gordon Smith and John Cuddington (Washington, D.C.: World Bank, 1985).

13. See James Hanson and Jaime de Melo, "The Uruguayan Experience with Liberalization and Stabilization, 1976–81," *Journal of Inter-American and World Affairs* (November 1983), pp. 477–502. The effects of the financial reforms on private savings and private investment are analyzed in Jaime de Melo and James Tybout, "The Effects of Financial Liberalization on Savings and Investment in Uruguay," *Economic Development and Cultural Change*, this issue. The evidence from financial statements is discussed here in Section IV.

14. The simulations are reported in Timothy Condon, Vittorio Corbo, and Jaime de Melo, "Productivity Growth, External Shocks and Capital Inflows in Chile during 1977–81: A General Equilibrium Analysis," *Journal of Policy Modelling* (in press). Sebastian Edwards, "Stabilization with Liberalization: An Evaluation of Ten Years of Chile's Experiment with Free Market Policies,

1973–83," *Economic Development and Cultural Change* 33, no. 2 (January 1985): 223–54, also computes high values for reform-induced productivity gains (13% of 1979 GDP).

15. See Jaime de Melo and Shujiro Urata, "The Influence of Increased Foreign Competition on Industrial Concentration and Profitability," photocopied (Washington, D.C.: World Bank, December 1984).

16. See Vittorio Corbo and Jaime de Melo, eds. "Scrambling for Survival: How Firms Adjusted to the Recent Reforms in Chile, Uruguay, and Argentina," World Bank Staff Working Paper no. 764 (Washington, D.C.: World Bank, 1985).

17. See Domingo Cavallo and Angel Peña, "Deficit fiscal, endeudamiento del gobierno y tasa de inflacion en Argentina: 1940–82," *Estudios IEERAL,* no. 26 (April–June 1983); and Roberto Frenkel, "La apertura financiera externa: El caso Argentino," in *Relaciones financieras externas y su efecto en la economia Latinoamericana,* ed. Ricardo Ffrench-Davis (Mexico: Fondo de Cultura, 1984).

18. See Robert Cumby and Sweder van Wijnbergen, "Fiscal Policy and Speculative Runs on the Central Bank under a Crawling Peg Regime: Argentina, 1974–81," photocopied (Washington, D.C.: World Bank, 1983). Estimates in figure 1 are high, but the pattern is reasonable.

19. Fernandez (n. 1 above) discusses the ambiguities surrounding preannouncements in Argentina, and Hanson and de Melo, "External Shocks, Financial Reforms, and Stabilization Attempts in Uruguay during 1974–83" (n. 1 above), examine interest rate spreads in Uruguay. Sebastian Edwards, "Monetarism in Chile 1973–83: Some Economic Puzzles," *Economic Development and Cultural Change,* this issue, also examines why real interest rates were high in Chile during the period. Evidence of imperfect substitution between peso- and dollar-denominated loans in Chile is discussed in Section IV.

20. See Corbo and de Melo (n. 6 above).

21. See Julio J. Nogues, "Critical Overview of Stabilization and Trade Liberalization Policies: Argentina during 1976–81," photocopied (Washington, D.C.: World Bank, 1983).

22. For further documentation of this effect, see Peter Wogart and José Marques, "Trade Liberalization, Tariff Redundancy and Inflation: A Methodological Exploration Applied to Argentina," *Review of World Economics* 120 (1984): 18–39.

23. See Nogues (n. 21 above). But also see Guillermo Calvo, "Fractured Liberalism: Argentina under Martinez de Hoz," *Economic Development and Cultural Change,* this issue, for the argument that the real exchange rate appreciation started before the adoption of the *tablita.*

24. The actual bias against exportables was probably higher than figures based on tariffs and subsidies would show because most exports are homogeneous and consequently are invoiced in the country of destination, whereas the reverse would be the case for imports. Given that transport costs from trading partners to the Southern Cone countries are relatively high, this effect was probably not negligible.

25. This option is risky because (1) only the government is likely to have the resources to insure banks, and (2) in the absence of any deposit insurance, information problems may be so severe that many wealth holders are unwilling to make deposits at all.

26. For reference, the first major bank failures in each country occurred on the following dates: Argentina (Banco Intercambio Regional) March 1980; Chile (Banco Osorno), 1977; Uruguay (Banco Panamericano), 1979.

27. See Carlos Díaz Alejandro, "Goodbye Financial Repression, Hello Financial Crash," *Journal of Development Economics* 19, no. 1/2 (1985): 1–24;

José Pablo Arellano, "De la liberalización a la intervención: El mercado de capitales en Chile: 1974–83," *Estudios CIEPLAN*, no. 11 (1984): 5–50; Arnold Harberger, "Lessons for Debtor-Country Managers and Policymakers," in Smith and Cuddington, eds. (n. 12 above); James Tybout, "A Firm Level Chronicle of Financial Crises in the Southern Cone," photocopied (Washington, D.C.: World Bank, 1985).

28. Fernandez (n. 1 above).

29. We are aware that there is an identification problem: price and interest rate convergence was undoubtedly affected by expectations, which in turn were influenced by the policy inconsistencies discussed above.

30. Strong demand from Argentine tourists (and expenditures related to capital inflows) in the presence of redundant protection contributed to this outcome. See Hanson and de Melo, "External Shocks, Financial Reforms and Stabilization Attempts in Uruguay during 1974–83" (n. 1 above).

31. See Vittorio Corbo, "International Prices, Wages and Inflation in an Open Economy: A Chilean Model," *Review of Economics and Statistics* 67, no. 4 (1985): 564–73. The model is an extension of the Scandinavian model of inflation with three types of goods: homogeneous importables, differentiated importables, and nontradables.

32. See Felipe Morande, "Factores determinantes de los precios internos de bienes transables en Chile," *Estudios CIEPLAN*, no. 11 (1984).

33. See Vittorio Corbo and Ricardo Matte, "Capital Flows and the Role of Monetary Policy: The Case of Chile," Documento de trabajo no. 92 (Santiago: Instituto de Economia, Pontificia Universidad Catolica de Chile, 1984). The model is an extension of a model popularized by Penti Kouri and Richard Porter, "International Capital Flows and Portfolio Equilibrium," *Journal of Political Economy* 82, no. 3 (1984): 443–68.

34. This section draws on Tybout (n. 27 above); Humberto Petrei and James Tybout, "Microeconomic Adjustments in Argentina during 1976–81: The Importance of Changing Levels of Financial Subsidies," *World Development* 13, no. 8 (1985): 949–68; Julio Galvez and James Tybout, "Microeconomic Adjustments in Chile during 1977–81: The Importance of Being a Grupo," *World Development* 13, no. 8 (1985): 969–94; Jaime de Melo, Ricardo Pascale, and James Tybout, "Microeconomic Adjustments in Uruguay during 1973–81: The Interplay of Real and Financial Shocks," *World Development* 13, no. 8 (1985): 995–1015.

35. For evidence that increased inflation was accompanied by greater relative price variability in Argentina, see Mario Blejer, "The Dispersion of Relative Commodity Prices under Very Rapid Inflation," *Journal of Development Economics* 9 (1981): 347–56.

36. Individuals who hoarded imported consumer durables prior to the maxi-devaluations also benefited from capital gains and frustrated government policy intentions.

37. See Corbo and de Melo (n. 16 above).

38. For Chile, Galvez and Tybout show that slow convergence was only among firms that began the reform period from low levels of protection.

39. The argument and the evidence is further elaborated in Tybout (n. 27 above).

40. For evidence on the size of group-affiliated firms, see Fernando Dahse, *Mapa de la extrema riqueza* (Santiago: Editorial Aconcagua, 1979); and Galvez and Tybout (n. 34 above). For evidence on their intermediaries and on their foreign borrowing, see Danse.

41. But dollar borrowing in Uruguay, unlike that in Argentina, seems to have been limited to tradable-sector producers.

The Effects of Financial Liberalization on Savings and Investment in Uruguay*

Jaime de Melo
World Bank

James Tybout
Georgetown University and World Bank

I. Introduction

In 1973, after a military takeover, Uruguayan authorities rapidly began liberalizing their economy's tightly regulated financial system.[1] By late 1974, domestic residents could hold unrestricted dollar-denominated accounts in the Uruguayan Banking System (UBS), and the Central Bank (CBU) had started to pay interest on required bank reserves. By the end of 1976, directed credit programs had been largely dismantled and interest rate ceilings had been phased out.[2] By 1979, reserve requirements and numerous other regulations had been eliminated, leaving the UBS virtually free of government controls.

The Uruguayan financial reforms were accompanied by major macro stabilization programs, and, as detailed elsewhere, these policies ultimately combined to generate serious problems.[3] When a civilian government resumed control in March 1985, fiscal deficits, high inflation, and unemployment had returned. Unlike when the military took over, the country was also ridden with a large volume of external debt, an internal debt crisis, and an insolvent banking system.

Recent analyses of the Uruguayan reforms have focused on the crisis that emerged and its causes. But less attention has been given to the issue of whether, crisis notwithstanding, the dramatic switch in regulatory regime generated any of the efficiency and growth benefits predicted by the literature on "financial liberalization." This paper examines the Uruguayan experience for evidence of such linkages.

By the literature on "financial liberalization" we mean the perspective popularized by McKinnon and Shaw, according to which substantial improvements in growth are possible with financial market

0013-0079/86/3403-0007$01.00

deregulation.[4] This perspective encompasses both micro and macro arguments. At the micro level, it is noted that interest rate ceilings in countries with high inflation may make the real cost of credit highly negative. Thus excess demand for credit emerges, and savings are rationed according to criteria such as firm size, rather than expected returns. At the macro level, it is argued that, because the interest elasticity of private savings is positive, the removal of ceilings will raise private savings rates. This greater volume of financial resources will relax the liquidity constraint on investment, accelerating capital formation and raising growth. We look for evidence of each of these effects.

The paper contains five major sections. Section II briefly reviews the impact of the reforms and other developments on financial asset holdings and on the availability of liquidity to the private sector. Section III asks whether there is any evidence of higher growth during the reform period and, if so, whether it was accompanied by higher savings and investment. Section IV builds simple econometric models of aggregate savings and investment, which are then tested over the period 1962–83. The models are structured to indicate whether private savings responded to interest rates and whether low private investment levels in the prereform period were directly attributable to excessive financial market regulation. Section V investigates whether the reforms improved the efficiency of financial intermediation and cross-firm credit allocation. Conclusions follow in Section VI.

II. Financial Reforms, Financial Deepening, and Financial Crisis

Before formally modeling the impact of Uruguay's financial regime on real savings and investment, it is useful to establish how closely the evolution of financial variables followed the pattern prescribed by McKinnon and Shaw. In this section, we briefly review the shifts in portfolio composition that took place during the 1973–82 reform period. We note that the real magnitude of the financial sector expanded rapidly, increasing the availability of funds to the private sector. In this sense the benefits of financial liberalization should have been present. But we also note that, after 1978, much of the financial sector expansion was induced by exchange-rate-based stabilization policies rather than deregulation per se. We raise some questions whether such expansion, being largely speculative in nature, can be expected to facilitate economic growth.

Table 1 presents the evidence on financial "deepening," or increases in the real size of the financial sector. Notice that a tremendous increase in the ratio of financial assets (M2) to GDP occurred (col. 1), mainly because of a rise in assets denominated in foreign currency (col. 2). The growth in peso-denominated assets was much slower, reflecting the gradual lifting of the ceilings on peso interest rates and the con-

TABLE 1

FINANCIAL PORTFOLIO SHIFTS IN PRIVATE BANKS (UBS)

	M2/ GDP (1)	Dollar Deposits/ Total Deposits (2)	Nonresidents' Deposits/ Total Dollar Deposits (3)	Residents' Dollar Deposits/ Pesos Deposits (4)	Residents' Deposits in U.S. Banks (US$ Millions) (5)	Residents' Deposits in U.S. Banks/ Dollar Deposits in UBS (6)	Average Ex Post Real Interest Rate on Peso Deposits (% per Year) (7)
1973	14.4	.24	.0	.30	147	2.81	−32.9
1974	14.4	.27	.0	.36	164	3.53	−26.4
1975	14.5	.37	.0	.58	172	1.81	−23.3
1976	19.0	.48	1.0	.90	245	1.60	−7.0
1977	22.2	.57	1.0	1.31	243	.81	−10.6
1978	26.2	.54	4.1	1.10	231	.58	1.8
1979	28.2	.49	6.4	.90	202	.27	−17.2
1980	31.0	.45	6.0	.76	254	.24	−12.4
1981	36.6	.49	7.9	.88	367	.26	6.6
1982	49.2	.75	8.5	2.77	759	.43	20.7
1983	48.9	.67	9.3	2.75	222	.85	5.7

NOTE.—All figures are end-of-year values. Dollar deposits expressed in pesos using the end-of-year financial exchange rate (buyer).

tinued high inflation.[5] As is clear from table 1, column 7, ex post average real returns to deposits in pesos remained negative during the early stages of financial liberalization. Indeed, as the further breakdown in table 3 below indicates, it is only after interest rates were completely deregulated that returns to deposits became positive. Even after real deposit rates had turned positive, they plummeted again in 1979–80, following the announcement of the new exchange-rate-based stabilization regime.

Precisely because of this stabilization regime, it is useful to view this growth of the financial sector as occurring in two phases. During the first phase (1974–78), financial deepening was mostly due to portfolio shifts by domestic residents. Just as predicted by McKinnon and Shaw, this remarkable financial deepening included a portfolio shift from inflation hedges toward financial assets and an end to capital flight. The nominal value of the stock of dollar deposits by Uruguayan residents in U.S. banks (table 1, col. 5) rose from US$164 million in 1974 to US$245 million in 1976, then declined to US$202 million in 1979. In addition, the net errors and omissions item of the balance of payments—reflecting over- and underinvoicing and other forms of capital flight—changed drastically. Prior to the reforms, it was always negative. (The yearly average was US$40 million, or 10% of export earnings, over 1970–74.) During 1975–78, the average yearly value of net errors and omissions turned to a positive US$38 million.

During the second phase (1979–83) the financial reforms were overshadowed by a stabilization policy based on the *tablita*. This was a preannounced schedule of devaluation rates less than the differential between domestic and trading partners' inflation. It was meant to put downward pressure on inflation, both directly through international competition and indirectly through its influence on expectations. What it did, in fact, was to generate large capital inflows, which in turn caused a strong real appreciation. Hence, during the *tablita* period, financial deepening was no longer reform induced.

Argentine deposits accounted for much of the capital inflow in the second phase (table 1, cols. 2 and 3).[6] During the first 2 years of the *tablita* period, it was the extremely high peso interest rate yields to foreigners that attracted these deposits. Later, when the political and economic situation became more uncertain in Argentina in 1981–82, the UBS appeared to be a relatively safe deposit for Argentines, especially during the South Atlantic conflict. Finally, after reaching their peak in the middle of 1982, foreign deposits fell back to half their value in the next 6 months, when fears that the Mexican treatment of dollar deposits might be repeated in Uruguay.

In addition to the increase in nonresident deposits, a shift in the currency composition of portfolios took place during the *tablita* period.[7] As confidence in the *tablita* waned, portfolios were rapidly adjusted: the share of dollar deposits in the UBS (which had been falling between 1977 and 1980) started to rise again, even when expressed in pesos (see table 1, col. 2). Banks refused to arbitrage across currencies; hence many of the private sector's peso-denominated loans were renewed in dollars as they matured (table 2, cols. 5 and 6). Private capital outflows in 1982 totaled US$1.4 billion, the UBS lost US$800 million, and the Central Bank's reserves fell by US$800 million (table 1, col. 6). Flotation of the peso came in November 1982. By revaluing dollar liabilities, flotation left the UBS with a largely insolvent dollar-denominated portfolio. The reforms and stabilization attempt thus ended with the CBU attempting to forestall financial collapse by purchasing private debt and financing these purchases by printing money and borrowing heavily abroad.

In sum, the pattern of financial asset accumulation was particularly turbulent during the *tablita* period and should probably be attributed more to macro disequilibrium than to the removal of financial sector controls per se. This turbulence, and the associated increase in uncertainty, may have inhibited the mechanisms described in the financial liberalization literature from taking hold.

Even in the absence of heightened uncertainty, the benefits from deregulation are not automatic. One reason is that financial deepening does not necessarily imply greater credit availability for the private sector. Private banks could invest abroad the funds captured in Uruguay, or the government might absorb credit to fund its fiscal deficits, thereby limiting the funds available for the private sector. Did these phenomena take place in Uruguay? Table 2 shows that, although there was considerable fluctuation in the M2/credit ratio, after 1975 credit to the private sector grew rapidly.[8] This is consistent with the fact that fiscal deficits were reduced during the early years of the reform period, and investment abroad by banks took place mainly in the early years of liberalization. We conclude that, except to the extent that dollarization and macro disequilibria complicated matters, the benefits of financial decontrol should have been present.

III. Stylized Outcomes: Savings, Investment, and Growth

As a final prelude to our modeling effort, we next review what happened to saving and investment. Referring to figure 1, note first that growth rates during 1955–73 were considerably lower than those during 1974–78, despite adverse terms of trade movements during the latter period.[9] Moreover, fueled mainly by external events, further acceleration occurred during 1979–81 before recession set in. Even if one takes into account the recession years 1982–83, trend growth was statistically higher during the reform period (2.4% per annum) than during the prereform years (1.0% per annum).

The ex post incremental capital output ratio (ICOR) also fell by

TABLE 2

MONEY AND CREDIT AS PERCENTAGE OF GDP

					Credit to Private Sector (% GDP)		
	M1/GDP	M2/GDP	M2/Credit	Credit/GDP	Total	Dollars	Pesos
1973	9.5	14.4	90.4	16.0	13.4	10.3	3.1
1974	9.0	14.4	91.1	15.9	13.2	11.0	2.2
1975	7.9	14.5	81.5	17.8	13.2	11.3	2.9
1976	8.2	19.0	96.8	19.6	16.4	11.3	5.1
1977	7.6	22.2	105.6	21.0	18.4	11.1	7.3
1978	7.4	26.2	113.6	23.1	20.2	11.6	9.6
1979	7.0	28.2	127.1	22.2	23.0	12.5	10.5
1980	7.2	31.0	118.5	26.2	28.1	15.4	12.7
1981	7.1	36.6	111.1	32.9	33.2	18.0	15.2
1982	7.2	49.2	92.7	53.1	46.5	19.3	27.2
1983	5.7	48.9	67.4	72.6	53.2	14.8	38.4

NOTE.—Yearly averages. M2 includes M1 and all savings and term deposits with the banking system (defined to include BCU, BROU, and private banks). Credit includes all credit granted by the banking system.

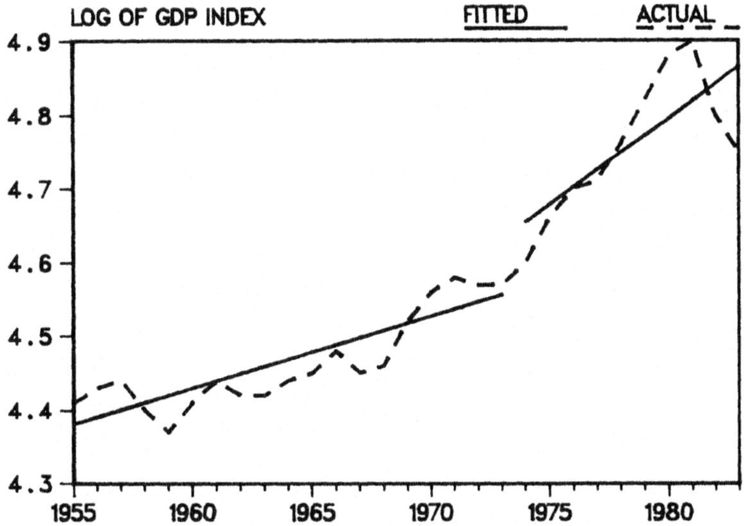

FIG. 1.—Trend growth. Annual data from 1955 to 1983:

$$\ln \text{GDP}_t = \underset{(197.1)}{4.37} - \underset{(-1.44)}{.185}\, D_t + \underset{(5.02)}{.010}\, T_t + \underset{(2.50)}{.014}\, (D \times T), \qquad \bar{R}^2 = .915,$$

where D is a dummy variable (one from 1974 to 1983, zero otherwise), T is a trend variable, and (D × T) is an interaction term. A second regression using neither the dummy variable nor the interaction term yielded the following:

$$\ln \text{GDP}_t = \underset{(185.6)}{4.31} + \underset{(12.83)}{.017}\, T_t, \qquad \bar{R}^2 = .854.$$

nearly 40% during the 1975–81 period relative to the 1967–74 period. This correlation of reforms with ICOR changes might be viewed as support for McKinnon and Shaw's hypothesis that expanded financial intermediation raises the average efficiency of investment. But there is other evidence that suggests that capacity utilization in the manufacturing sector also rose fairly steadily over the 1973–81 period.[10]

Referring to table 3, note also that simple correlation analysis would not support the view that the domestic savings rate rises in response to interest rate deregulation. To the contrary, domestic savings are slightly lower during the reform period than before, although deposit rates went from −20% (1964–73) to −17% (1974–78) to 1% (1979–83). When we separate government from private savings, we still find that private savings fell during the reform period. Indeed, private savings fell toward the end of the reforms, especially during 1979–81, when real-exchange-rate appreciation became pronounced.[11]

A final stylized pattern emerges from table 3: average private-sector investment, which had been very low during the prereform pe-

TABLE 3

COST OF CREDIT, INTEREST RATES, SAVINGS, AND INVESTMENT

	1955–63	1964–73	1974–78	1979–83
Average real borrowing rate*	−3.8	−13.4	−15.1†	2.2
Inflation (CPI)	20.1	62.2	66.9	46.2
Government deficit/GDP	...	−2.0	2.9	−2.5
Ex post real interest rate on time deposits‡	−9.8	−20.1	−16.8†	.9
Domestic savings/GDP§	11.9	12.5	11.0	11.7
Private savings/GDP‖	...	11.3	9.6	9.6
Foreign savings/GDP#	2.9	−1.7	2.5	2.9
Private investment/GDP‖	...	9.6	12.1	12.6
Real exchange rate index**	197	162	147	125

SOURCES.—IMF, *International Financial Statistics*, various issues; Banco Central de Uruguay (unpublished interest rate series); and World Bank Report no. 3652-UR (1981).

NOTE.—All annual interest and inflation rates calculated as averages from corresponding monthly rates. A consistent series for government capital expenditures could not be constructed beyond 1961.

* Weighted average of interest rates charged on different types of peso loans.

† Averages computed over 1974–77 and 1978–83.

‡ Computed as $(i - \dot{p})/(1 + \dot{p}) \times 100$, where $\dot{p}$ is the percentage of CPI inflation.

§ Computed residually from national accounts.

‖ Computed by subtracting government capital expenditures (obtained from fiscal accounts) from total investment.

\# Minus the trade balance ($TB = EX - IM$).

** Computed as: $RER = ER \times$ CPI (U.S.) ÷ CPI (URU), where ER is the commercial exchange rate (pesos per dollar).

riod, rose markedly during 1974–83. Why was private investment so low before the reforms? One obvious possibility is that financial repression made the economy to be savings constrained, but other factors might also have been important. For example, the prereform return on capital may simply have been low. Harberger and Wisecarver show that the return to private-sector investment in Uruguay was only between 6% and 7% during 1968–71.[12] They also give evidence that capital income was heavily taxed and that there was a bias in the tax structure against agriculture. This situation changed in 1974, when the taxation of capital income was reduced and made more uniform.

The removal of quotas on imports of capital goods in 1974 may also have induced investment. Indeed, between 1959 and 1974, quantitative, administrative, and other restrictions on imports had become increasingly stringent as the Uruguayan currency was becoming increasingly overvalued; by 1971, imports of capital goods were effectively prohibited.

To summarize, GDP growth picked up during the reforms even if one averages in the recession years that followed the Argentine-led boom. Private-sector investment rose, and it appears that the marginal efficiency of investment also rose. However, this rise in investment was funded by foreign savings—private domestic savings actually declined. To go beyond these stylized outcomes, it is necessary to model more explicitly savings and investment behavior. We take up this task in the following section.

IV. Financial Liberalization, Savings, and Investment

The literature on financial repression stresses that because savings levels are sensitive to real interest rates, nominal interest controls cum inflation reduce the amount of national income allocated to capital formation. In the first part of this section, we test whether the liberalization of Uruguay's financial sector and the associated improvements in real yields on bank deposits significantly influenced the level of savings, as the "financial liberalization" literature would predict.

The advocates of financial liberalization do not seek to induce savings per se but to promote an increase in the volume and efficiency of capital formation. They argue that, under financial repression, the limited supply of credit is likely to be rationed across projects according to criteria that do not correlate closely with social returns. But when interest rates are decontrolled, two types of improvements may be induced. First, a larger volume of investment can be financed because savings have increased. (If international capital movements have also been liberalized, additional funding becomes available from abroad.) Second, projects with expected returns below the new market clearing rate drop out, while previously rationed high-return projects are afforded the chance to compete for funds. Tests for the presence of the first effect will be reported in the second part of this section. Indirect tests for the second effect are deferred until Section V.

A. The Reforms and the Savings Rate

To investigate the influence of financial liberalization on savings rates, Fry, Giovannini, and others have regressed the ratio of domestic savings to GDP on real income growth, lagged savings, foreign savings, and some measure of the real interest rate.[13] Income growth is included in this specification because it proxies for deviations from "permanent" income, which, standard theory suggests, should induce savings-rate fluctuation. Lagged savings is included because the adjustment process may be spread over multiple periods, and foreign savings is included because it may "crowd out" domestic savings by allowing residents to consume more at any given rate of capital accumulation. Of course, the interest rate is included because savings behavior may be sensitive to real returns.

As a point of departure, we estimate this "traditional" model for Uruguay in 1962–83. The results appear in table 4. Because the real

TABLE 4

STANDARD SAVINGS RATE FUNCTION, 1962–83

	$s_t = \beta_0 + \beta_1 y'_t + \beta_2 r_t + \beta_3 f_t + \beta_4 s_{t-1}$			
	(1)	(2)	(3)	(4)
$\hat{\beta}_0$	9.29 (4.69)	9.21 (4.57)	10.42 (4.65)	10.2 (4.54)
$\hat{\beta}_1$	.083 (.827)	.126 (1.11)	.239 (1.46)	.290 (1.56)
$\hat{\beta}_2$	.037 (1.41)	.055 (1.50)	.048 (1.63)	.070 (1.65)
$\hat{\beta}_3$	−.538 (−3.97)	−.612 (−3.76)	−.584 (−3.87)	−.671 (−3.58)
$\hat{\beta}_4$	.283 (1.78)	.308 (1.87)	.186 (1.02)	.190 (.990)
$\bar{R}^2$	.47	.45	.38	.30
Durbin's *H*-statistic	2.53	2.80	3.85	4.64
$F(4,17)$	5.69	5.34	4.18	3.28
Endogenous variables	None	r	y'	r, y'

SOURCES.—See table 3.

NOTE.—Figures in parentheses are *t*-ratios. The variables are: s = total savings/GDP × 100; y' = real GDP growth (%); r = real ex post deposit rate (%); f = foreign savings/GDP × 100.

interest rate and/or the level of real income may be endogenous with respect to the savings rate, we reported estimates with instrumental variables applied to the different possible combinations of these variables in columns 2–4.[14] The most notable finding here is that the real interest rate exhibits a positive, albeit weak, correlation with savings rates. Hence, whereas simple correlation analysis shows no response of savings to interest rates, these results provide mild support for the claim that financial liberalization induced savings, controlling for other factors. Notice also that foreign savings appear to significantly influence the savings rate. In fact, column 1 implies crowding out on the order of 54 cents for every dollar of foreign capital inflow. Finally, the Durbin's *H*-statistics suggest that there may be problems with serial correlation or misspecification, and tests based on recursive residuals indicate that a structural break takes place around 1974 (see App.).[15]

There are a number of factors that might account for specification problems in the table-4 model. First, the financial repression literature posits a positive response of *private* savings to interest rates. But table 4 is based on *total* savings, and such responsiveness may be obscured. Second, the foreign savings rate may not be an exogenous determinant of domestic savings, particularly after the opening of the economy in 1974 to capital flows. In a world of integrated capital markets, eco-

TABLE 5

DOMESTIC PRIVATE SAVINGS RATE FUNCTION, 1962–83

	$s_t^p = \beta_0 + \beta_1 y_t' + \beta_2 r_t + \beta_3 e + \beta_4 D + \beta_5 s_{t-1}^p$				
	(1)	(2)	(3)	(4)	(5)
$\hat{\beta}_0$	−1.28 (−.384)	−.640 (−.182)	−1.23 (−.365)	−.933 (−.273)	−.154 (−.036)
$\hat{\beta}_1$	−.011 (−.092)	−.040 (−.308)	.078 (.394)	.036 (.171)	−.024 (−.195)
$\hat{\beta}_2$	−.011 (−.331)	−.030 (−.696)	−.004 (−.101)	−.020 (−0.419)	−.004 (−.108)
$\hat{\beta}_3$	.050 (2.67)	.045 (2.19)	.052 (2.66)	.048 (2.20)	.036 (1.52)
$\hat{\beta}_4$	1.76 (1.51)	1.85 (1.59)	1.61 (1.31)	1.75 (1.43)	1.43 (1.16)
$\hat{\beta}_5$	.286 (1.44)	.277 (1.37)	.249 (1.11)	.264 (1.18)	.407 (2.08)
$\bar{R}^2$	.32	.30	.29	.30	.28
Durbin's *H*-statistic	.90	.43	. . .*	. . .*	−.12
$F(5,16)$	2.97	2.82	2.74	2.84	2.67
Endogenous variables	None	r	y'	r, y'	e

SOURCES.—See table 3.

NOTE.—Figures in parentheses are *t*-statistics. The variables are: s^p = (private savings/GDP) × 100; y' = real GDP growth (%); r = real ex post deposit rate (%); D = regime dummy, equals zero through 1974 and one thereafter; e = real exchange rate (1980 = 100). For other definitions, see table 3.

* The Durbin's *H*-statistic cannot be calculated for this set of estimates.

nomic agents optimize over their present and future consumption of both domestic and foreign goods, taking interest rates, exchange rates, income, and expectations into consideration.[16] Hence, given that the level of foreign savings is simply the current account deficit, a better specification of the savings function for an open economy might exclude foreign savings and include the real exchange rate. Finally, as discussed above, many institutional changes took place in Uruguay at the same time that interest rates were being decontrolled.

To remedy each of these possible shortcomings, we reestimate the savings equation using the *private* savings rate, replacing the foreign savings rate with the real exchange rate, and including a dummy variable for the post-1974 period. The results from this "open economy" model are reported in table 5. The alternative specification performs much better in terms of Durbin's *H*-statistic, but worse in terms of overall significance levels. With respect to particular parameters, notice first that interest rates now play no role whatsoever in explaining savings rates, whereas real exchange rates exhibit a significant negative coefficient. The exchange rate coefficient is what one would expect, given that low real exchange rates encourage absorption by making traded goods less expensive and perhaps by creating the perception of an increase in real wealth. Now the mild positive interest elasticity of savings disappears completely. Finally, the dummy for the postliberalization period indicates that, after controlling for other factors, there is a mild upward shift in the savings function after decontrol. This suggests that some factors other than interest rate movements and exchange rate movements induced a general improvement in the average propensity to save.

Does this model exhibit structural stability? According to the statistical tests reported in the Appendix, it fits well for the post-1966 period but shifts significantly when this year and earlier ones are included in the sample. Interestingly, therefore, our "open economy" savings function does better in the later subperiod, when trade and capital flows were uninhibited; our "traditional" savings function does better in the 1962–73 subperiod, when trade and capital flows were relatively controlled.

These results suggest fitting the traditional model to the 1962–73 period, and the open economy model to the 1967–83 period. The results of this exercise are reported in table 6. For the traditional model, notice that the interest elasticity of savings has increased considerably in significance with the omission of 1974–83. Closer inspection reveals that this is because the years 1970–73 now receive much greater weight, and during this period both real interest rates and savings rates were very low. During these years, the real fiscal deficit grew rapidly and was financed by two mechanisms associated with financial repression. First, money creation cum interest ceilings was extracting a large tax from financial wealthholders. Second, as mentioned above, government taxes captured corporate earnings before they could be saved. Thus there appears to be some link between financial repression and Uruguayan savings problems in the prereform period, although it is not clear whether this link is due to a high interest elasticity of savings or a combination of factors.

Turning next to the "open economy" specification, notice that the interest elasticity of savings is nil. Other regressions (available on request) indicate that this result does not change significantly when we limit the sample to 1974–83—the period one would have chosen in the absence of results from structural stability tests. (Nor does it change when we fit our "traditional" model to 1973–83; these data also available on requests.) One plausible explanation for this interest insensitivity is that movements in ex post real interest rates during the *tablita* period largely reflected movements in the expected rate of devaluation, rather than fluctuations in ex ante expected returns. (The application of instruments to real interest rates does not remedy this problem.) Hence, although the responsiveness of savings rates to observed interest rates is low, our tests may be flawed by measurement problems.

TABLE 6

SAVINGS MODELS IN SUBPERIODS

	TRADITIONAL MODEL, 1962–73: $s_t = \beta_0 + \beta_1 y'_t + \beta_2 r_t + \beta_3 s_{t-1} + \beta_4 f_t$	OPEN ECONOMY MODEL, 1967–83: $s^p_t = \beta_0 + \beta_1 y'_t + \beta_2 r_t + \beta_3 s^p_{t-1} + \beta_5 e_t + \beta_6 D_t$		
	(1)	(2)	(3)	(4)
$\hat{\beta}_0$	7.89 (6.11)	−2.23 (−.836)	−1.90 (.677)	−1.70 (−.602)
$\hat{\beta}_1$	−.319 (−3.04)	−.009 (−.102)	−.009 (−.110)	−.017 (−.195)
$\hat{\beta}_2$	.083 (3.44)	.004 (.134)	.011 (.463)	.000 (.014)
$\hat{\beta}_3$	.403 (3.93)	.399 (2.49)	.428 (2.65)	.423 (2.63)
$\hat{\beta}_4$	−1.02 (−8.17)	...	...	...
$\hat{\beta}_5$	...	.045 (3.06)	.042 (2.77)	.040 (2.55)
$\hat{\beta}_6$	...	2.40 (2.80)	2.24 (2.60)	2.32 (2.67)
$\bar{R}^2$	.90	.52	.51	.51
Durbin's *H*-statistic	−1.46	−2.20	−2.10	−2.48
$F(4,7)$ or $F(5,11)$	24.69	4.52	4.42	4.44
Endogenous variables	*r*	*r*	*e*	*r*, *e*

SOURCES.—See table 3.

Two variables do emerge as significant in our "open economy" savings model for 1967–83. First, real exchange rates exhibit considerable explanatory power. This is what one would expect, given that absorption should be more sensitive to real exchange rates when the economy is open. (Regressions for 1962–73 show a much lower significance level for this variable than during 1974–83). Second, the reform dummy in the open economy model shows a significant upward shift in private savings rates after 1974. This probably is due to the removal of various forms of intervention and taxation, and it may also pick up some increase in ex ante expected interest rates that, for reasons just discussed, the real interest rate series probably fails to capture.

In sum, Uruguayan savings behavior exhibited a clear shift between the 1960s and the 1970s. During the former period, savings rates were sensitive to foreign capital inflows and appeared to have been influenced by various policies associated with financial repression. During the second period, the real exchange rate played a dominant role, and, in particular, real appreciation seems to have discouraged saving. Nonetheless, controlling for the effects of exchange rate variation, savings rates appear to have shifted upward with the implementation of financial liberalization and reforms.

B. The Reforms and Investment Rates

By liberalizing the financial sector, Uruguayan authorities hoped to quicken the pace of capital formation. We now turn our attention to the issue of whether factors associated with financial liberalization indeed accounted for the jump in investment documented in Section III.

When an economy is not savings constrained, investment should behave according to standard empirical functions that hold for industrialized countries, with the real price of capital and expected output demand (proxied by the history of demand growth) playing central roles. But when an economy is financially repressed, it does not operate on this "notional" investment demand function. Fluctuations in output induce capital formation only to the degree that they cause increases in savings, and, with intermediation repressed, firms may have to condition closely their investment spending on their own liquidity positions. Hence we should be able to detect structural shifts in the investment function from "repressed" to "unconstrained" if the McKinnon and Shaw mechanisms were empirically important in Uruguay.

For this exercise we express private investment over GDP as a function of current and lagged real income growth, current and lagged real money growth, the real interest rate, the real exchange rate, a dummy for the postreform period, and lagged investment. We then attempt to identify what periods, if any, reflect significant structural shifts.

Before discussing structural shifts in the investment function, it is useful to review the full sample (1962–83) findings. Table 7 presents these under the assumptions that current income growth is endogenous (col. 1), real exchange rates are endogenous (col. 2), real interest rates are endogenous (col. 3), and all three variables are endogenous (col. 4). The instruments used for endogenous variables are the same as those for the savings rate equations in tables 4–6.

There are several results worth noting. First, in view of the significant coefficients on lagged income and lagged investment, the standard accelerator mechanism appears to have been operative for at least part of the sample period. This implies that the economy was not savings rationed throughout the 1962–83 period, particularly given the negligible role that income growth played in inducing savings rate fluctuations (tables 4–6). Second, fluctuations in the real money stock do not appear to have been important, at least not in the sense predicted by the standard model of financial repression. Instead of allowing firms to accumulate internal funds for investment, increases in the money

TABLE 7

PRIVATE INVESTMENT RATE FUNCTION, 1962–83

	$i_t = \beta_0 + \beta_1 y'_t + \beta_2 y'_{t-1} + \beta_3 m'_t + \beta_4 m'_{t-1} + \beta_5 e_t + \beta_6 r_t + \beta_7 D_t + \beta_8 i_{t-1}$			
	(1)	(2)	(3)	(4)
$\hat{\beta}_0$	−.688	−.485	−.024	−.483
	(−.276)	(−.177)	(−.011)	(−.163)
$\hat{\beta}_1$	−.029	.035	.057	.020
	(−.261)	(.580)	(.890)	(.172)
$\hat{\beta}_2$	.293	.269	.265	.285
	(3.12)	(3.21)	(3.52)	(2.80)
$\hat{\beta}_3$	.020	.016	.009	.014
	(1.32)	(1.11)	(.657)	(1.04)
$\hat{\beta}_4$	−.020	−.021	−.024	−.021
	(−1.41)	(−1.49)	(−1.63)	(−1.47)
$\hat{\beta}_5$	.022	.022	.020	.024
	(2.12)	(1.64)	(2.04)	(1.67)
$\hat{\beta}_6$	−.028	−.015	−.009	−.011
	(−1.44)	(−.90)	(−.467)	(−.471)
$\hat{\beta}_7$	2.34	2.17	1.98	2.20
	(3.89)	(3.73)	(3.59)	(3.64)
$\hat{\beta}_8$	.584	.575	.570	.555
	(5.03)	(5.24)	(5.12)	(4.83)
$\bar{R}^2$	.81	.82	.82	.82
Durbin's *H*-statistic	.22	.33	.27	.61
$F(8,13)$	12.09	13.34	12.94	12.68
Endogenous variables	y'	e	r	y', e, r

SOURCES.—See table 3.

NOTE.—Figures in parentheses are *t*-ratios. The variables are: i = private investment/GDP × 100; y' = real GDP growth (%); m' = real money growth (%); e = real peso/dollar exchange rate (1980 = 100); r = real ex post interest rate (%); D = regime dummy; equals zero through 1974 and one thereafter. For other definitions see table 3.

stock had either a negligible or a transitory effect on the rate of capital formation. Third, the effect of the interest rate on investment is negative but weak, as is often found in industrialized countries. Fourth, the real exchange rate is positively related to investment, but this correlation is also weak. Finally, the function clearly shifts upward in the reform period, suggesting that the surge in investment documented in Section III was *not* induced by movements in the explanatory variables of this model.

The issue remains whether the investment function in table 7 describes the entire 1962–83 period or is really some aggregation over different structures. As reported in the Appendix, CUSUM and CUSUMSQ tests indicate that a clear structural break appears when

TABLE 8

RECURSIVE PARAMETER ESTIMATES FOR INVESTMENT FUNCTION

DATA BASE BEGINS IN:	$i_t = \beta_0 + \beta_1 y'_t + \beta_2 y'_{t-1} + \beta_3 m'_t + \beta_4 m'_{t-1} + \beta_5 e_t + \beta_6 r_t + \beta_7 D_t + \beta_8 i_{t-1}$					
	$\hat{\beta}_1$	$\hat{\beta}_2$	$\hat{\beta}_3$	$\hat{\beta}_4$	$\hat{\beta}_5$	$\hat{\beta}_6$
1974	−.024 (−.47)	.086 (2.87)	.012 (2.84)	−.028 (−2.67)	−.011 (−1.77)	−.121 (−3.73)
1973	.154 (1.60)	.135 (1.50)	.016 (1.21)	.010 (.508)	.003 (.158)	.004 (.072)
1972	.154 (2.18)	.135 (2.08)	.016 (1.49)	.010 (.635)	.003 (.198)	.004 (.094)
1971	.158 (3.21)	.138 (2.97)	.017 (1.76)	.011 (1.01)	.003 (.383)	.007 (.320)
1970	.121 (2.98)	.116 (2.59)	.021 (2.36)	.005 (.487)	−.003 (−.447)	−.016 (−1.41)
1969	.123 (3.57)	.116 (2.83)	.021 (2.58)	.004 (.567)	−.003 (−.495)	−.016 (−1.54)
1968	.125 (3.98)	.115 (3.00)	.020 (2.91)	.003 (.493)	−.002 (−.406)	−.017 (−1.75)
1967	.008 (.103)	.264 (2.81)	.021 (1.11)	−.011 (−.626)	.012 (.932)	−.033 (−1.26)
1966	.008 (.111)	.263 (3.03)	.022 (1.18)	−.011 (−.684)	.012 (1.02)	−.033 (−1.34)
1965	.023 (.337)	.273 (3.26)	.015 (.995)	−.015 (−.942)	.014 (1.25)	−.027 (−1.20)
1964	.023 (.349)	.274 (3.55)	.015 (1.04)	−.015 (.995)	.014 (1.39)	−.027 (−1.25)
1963	.059 (.881)	.249 (3.02)	.012 (.796)	−.021 (−1.33)	.019 (1.77)	−.011 (−.512)
1962	.057 (.859)	.265 (3.40)	.009 (.633)	−.024 (−1.57)	.020 (1.97)	−.009 (−.450)

NOTE.—Figures in parentheses are t-ratios. Real interest rates are treated as endogenous.

we begin with the 1974–83 period and add data points backward in time, but this break is not significant.

This structural shift, though mild, might constitute evidence of movement from a "notional" investment demand function in the liberalized period toward savings-rationed investment behavior in the prereform years. However, results reported in table 8 suggest that it does not. Looking at the coefficient estimates associated with the 1973–81 period, the 1972–81 period, and so on backward in time, one discovers that (1) the coefficients on income growth have explanatory power in *all* subsamples beginning earlier than 1971, although the relative importance of current and lagged income varies somewhat, and (2) coefficients on money growth were most significant during the *post*-1972 period, although even here the positive initial effect of real monetary expansion tended to be offset in the following period.[17] In short, the disappointing rates of growth that Uruguay experienced during the 1960s and early 1970s do not appear to be attributable to savings constraints per se. Rather, lack of demand for capital goods—perhaps traceable to low income growth and the excessive tax burden mentioned above—is a more plausible explanation.

What, then, accounts for the significant shift in the function indicated by our stability tests? There are two causes. First, the 1967–69 period appears to have been characterized by major outliers. This is not surprising, given the 1965 banking panic and its aftermath, as well as the major 1968 devaluation followed by a freezing of wages and prices. Second, a number of coefficients are unstable. For example, referring to table 8, one sees that in the post-1972 period there is a negative association between investment and the real exchange rate. This is what one might expect with no constraints on capital goods imports and no limits on foreign borrowing: foreign capital goods are cheap when the real exchange rate is low, and the lower this rate, the more likely that devaluation will eliminate bargains in the near future. But in the prereform period, low real exchange rates were typically associated with relatively tight import controls, as discussed in Section III above. Hence, the negative correlation disappears when prereform years are added to the sample. The increases in the interest rate sensitivity of investment from the pre- to the post-1972 period may simply reflect a nonlinearity in this relationship, given that real interest rates reached much higher levels during the later period.

V. Financial Resource Allocation at the Micro Level

For a number of reasons, one would expect that more efficient allocation of financial resources at the micro level would have resulted from the reforms. First, relaxing entry barriers into banking should narrow borrowing-lending interest rate spreads. Second, as mentioned above, removing interest rate ceilings should increase the efficiency of investment, as some firms may no longer be rationed or at least may be less dependent on self-finance. We shall examine the efficiency of financial intermediation from both the supply and demand sides. From the supply side we examine borrowing-lending spreads and review the evidence on oligopolistic banking behavior. From the demand side, we attempt to identify reform-induced changes in the allocation (and terms) of credit across firms with different characteristics.

A. Financial Intermediation

We begin by noting that spreads between borrowing and lending rates declined for each of the three most important types of loans issued by the UBS: dollar-denominated loans, preferential peso-denominated loans, and nonpreferential peso-denominated loans. This means that savers received a greater fraction of the return generated by their wealth and paid less implicit tax to the government. This reduction in spreads was one hoped-for consequence of financial liberalization and no doubt was linked to the phasing out of reserve requirements. In addition, after 1979, when deposits surged, economies of scale probably contributed to the decline in spreads.

According to McKinnon and Shaw, the relaxation of financial sector entry prohibitions in 1977 should also have helped reduce spreads by fostering competition. Indeed, the number of banking houses increased from one in 1976 to over 20 in 1980. However, in spite of evidence (reviewed below) suggesting that entry reduced the extent of oligopolistic behavior among dominant banks, it is not clear that the increased participation of banking houses contributed much toward the reduction in spreads. Banking houses were restricted to offshore banking operations and mainly intermediated foreign currency funds obtained from nonresidents. Thus, even though their share of foreign currency loans rose from 4.3% in December 1977 to 11.5% in December 1979, it remained small and probably did not affect much competition among dominant banks in the peso loan market.

Further evidence on the extent of noncompetitive pricing behavior in UBS is provided by Spiller and Favaro, who studied commercial banks' loan-pricing behavior before and after banking houses were allowed to expand.[18] After the regulatory change, average price-cost margins and the variance of interest rates across banks fell, suggesting a change in behavior. This was confirmed by empirical models of the banking sector that exhibited less oligopolistic interaction among the dominant banks after the regulatory change.

Such increases in competition may have squeezed monopoly rents in the financial sector, but the deregulation that made them possible also appears to have facilitated a more than optimal degree of risk taking. Coupled with Uruguay's macro disturbances, the results were disastrous. At the time that this article was written, UBS was in the midst of a major financial crisis, with nonperforming loans estimated at several multiples of net worth. Hence, in retrospect, to the extent that excessive deregulation may have facilitated the current crisis, the associated costs must be weighed against the reform-induced benefits we have mentioned.

B. The Allocation of Credit by Firm Size

We finally turn to evidence of improved credit allocation from the demand side. We proceed by testing whether the differences between large and small manufacturing firms' financial profiles changed appreciably after interest rates were deregulated in late 1976.[19] Because small firms are characterized by relatively uncertain earnings rates, and because they present banks with relatively high transactions costs per peso borrowed, these firms are likely to pay higher interest rates in the *absence* of ceilings. But when interest controls are imposed, banks may force small borrowers to compensate for these unattractive characteristics by reducing their leverage and/or lessening their default probability through some other mechanism, such as changes in their asset structure.

If prevalent, such phenomena would have occurred prior to 1977, that is, when interest rates were still regulated and liquidity to the private sector had not yet begun its rapid expansion (table 2). Hence, we examine a panel data set of financial statements for 69 Uruguayan manufacturing firms for changes between the 1973–77 and 1978–81 periods. Our objective is to determine (1) whether the correlation of firms' size with their leverage, liquidity, and financial costs suggested repression in the 1973–77 period and (2) whether this pattern of correlation weakened or disappeared thereafter.

Because the financial characteristics of any given firm are likely to exhibit intertemporal correlation, we adopt an error component framework for making our comparisons. In this framework, each index of financial performance—be it leverage, liquidity, or financial cost—is expressed as a function of time dummies and a firm size index:

$$y_{it} = \sum_{s=1973}^{1981} \gamma^s D_{it}^s + \beta_1 \sum_{s=1973}^{1977} D_{it}^s X_{it} + \beta_2 \sum_{s=1978}^{1981} D_{it}^s X_{it} + v_i + \epsilon_{it}. \tag{1}$$

The dummy D_{it}^s takes a value of one when $t = s$, and zero otherwise; $i = 1, 69$; $t = 1973 \ldots 1981$. The size index X_{it} is the logarithm of the ith firm's total assets in year t, measured as a deviation from the average over all firms' log assets in the same year. The error component v_i is firm specific and ϵ_{it} is pure noise.

Estimation of equation (1) allows us to test for regime-related changes in the influence of firm size on the financial characteristic y, controlling for general shifts in mean y values. The estimates of β_1 and β_2 are reported below in table 9. Several results emerge. First, as expected, in the 1973–77 period small firms are less leveraged and are more liquid. This suggests that banks indeed required small firms to be safer in terms of balance-sheet structure when institutional constraints prevented them from charging higher interest rates. It is also apparent that large firms and small firms paid similar real financial costs, although this result should be treated cautiously because the data on financial costs are fairly crude. Hence it appears there is evidence of some allocative effects of financial repression in the early years.

Second, there is mild evidence of expected shifts in the size coefficients, although these shifts are not statistically significant. With financial liberalization, small firms increased their leverage and reduced their liquidity somewhat, relative to large firms, and they paid a

TABLE 9

CORRELATION OF FINANCIAL INDICATORS AND FIRM SIZE UNDER DIFFERENT REGIMES

	$\hat{\beta}_1$ (1973–77)	$\hat{\beta}_2$ (1978–81)	$\hat{\beta}_2 - \hat{\beta}_1$
Leverage (gearing)	.045	.041	−.004
	(3.61)	(2.75)	(−.54)
Liquidity (quick)	−.0706	−.0611	.0095
	(−3.18)	(−2.14)	(.535)
Real financial costs	−.026	−.040	−.014
	(−1.08)	(−1.20)	(−.65)

NOTE.—Gearing = debt/assets; quick = (short-term assets less inventories)/(short-term debt); real financial costs = (total financial costs + monetary correction)/(net financial liabilities). The inclusion of a monetary correction essentially means deducting from nominal financial costs that amount of new borrowing necessary each period to keep *real* net financial liabilities constant.

larger premium to do so. These results lead us to conclude that there may have been some improvement in the credit allocation mechanism, but it certainly was not a dominant characteristic of the reform effort. Perhaps the major macro imbalances that rocked the Uruguayan economy soon after its liberalization prevented these effects from emerging more clearly.

VI. Conclusions

The literature on financial market liberalization in developing countries has identified a number of mechanisms through which financial market deregulation should affect resource allocation and growth: increases in the real interest rate should induce more savings; a relaxation of the liquidity constraint with financial deepening should facilitate private investment; and this relaxation, coupled with the decentralization of banking, should improve the allocation of financial resources at the micro level. The empirical relevance of these effects to Uruguay's recent financial reforms has been investigated in this paper. Our main findings are summarized below.

Beyond any doubt, the financial reforms led to many outcomes predicted by the proponents of financial market deregulation. Among them, there was financial deepening early on, as Uruguayans shifted their wealth toward financial assets and repatriated a fraction of their dollar financial assets held abroad to Uruguayan banks. In turn, this increase in dollar (and later peso) deposits increased real credit to the private sector. Also, the banking system progressively replaced the government as the channel through which savings were transferred to investors. However, much of the financial deepening during the period 1979–82 was not reform induced; rather, it was attributable to macro stabilization policies and exogenous events (instability in Argentina). These reforms were accompanied by an increase in GDP growth rates over historical trend growth, higher private investment, and lower private savings, especially toward the later years of the reforms.

Econometric estimation of private savings and private investment demand functions over the period allowed us to identify some of their underlying determinants. We found that savings behavior exhibited a clear shift with financial liberalization. During the 1960s, savings were sensitive to (mostly exogenous) foreign capital inflows and appeared to have been influenced by various policies associated with "financial repression." During the 1970s, when there were no restrictions on foreign borrowing, savings were strongly negatively correlated with the real exchange rate as one would expect where there are no restrictions on private foreign borrowing. Nonetheless, controlling for the effects of real exchange rate variations, private savings rates shifted upward with the implementation of financial reforms. Finally, we found a positive response of savings rates to real interest rates in the prereform period but no such responses after financial liberalization. However, neither of these findings seems free of measurement problems.

On the investment side, we found that standard accelerator effects were significant throughout the sample period. This suggests that the Uruguayan economy was not savings constrained, despite the presence of "financial repression" in the prereform years. Nonetheless, several shifts in the structure of the private investment function took place. First, controlling for other factors, the intercept term shifted up significantly during the reform period. Second, the responsiveness of investment to interest rates and real exchange rates appears to increase in later years. These changes are consistent with what one might expect following the changes in the regulatory environment. We conclude from this macro modeling effort that the financial reforms induced structural shifts in Uruguayan savings and investment behavior, although these shifts were not entirely as envisioned by proponents of financial deregulation.

At the micro level, we reported evidence that the efficiency of financial intermediation improved as banks' lending-borrowing spreads diminished, partly in response to less oligopolistic interaction among leading banks following relaxation of barriers to entry. We also looked for evidence of improved credit allocation from the demand side after the freeing of interest rates in late 1976. Our results provide mild evidence that, with financial liberalization, small firms increased their leverage and average financial costs relative to large firms, suggesting that there may have been some improvement in the credit-allocation mechanisms.

Appendix

To test for structural stability, we construct recursive residuals for each model. These are defined as $u_t = (y_t - \mathbf{x}_t'\boldsymbol{\beta}_{t-1})/\alpha_t$, where $(\mathbf{x}_t, y_t)$ are the period t-values for the explanatory and dependent variables, $\boldsymbol{\beta}_{t-1}$ is the k-dimensional vector of coefficient estimates based on the first $t-1$ observations, and α_t is a scaling factor—based on the explanatory variables—which ensures that the variance of u_t is constant across observations for properly specified models. When no structural shift occurs, the sum $C_j = \Sigma_{t=1}^{j} u_t$ follows a random walk, and the series $CSQ_j = \Sigma_{t=1}^{r} \tilde{u}_t^2$ increases in proportion to j. But if the tth observation behaves according to a model different from the model governing the previous $t-1$ observations, both series are likely to jump.

Brown, Durbin, and Evans derive the distributions of $1/\hat{\sigma}\, C_j$ and $1/S\ CSQ_j$ for correctly specified models, where σ is the standard error from the full regression and S is the associated sum of squared residuals.[20] We use the methodology they suggest to construct the critical bounds for these series (hereafter CUSUMs and CUSUMSQs) and then construct each series two ways. The first is done by beginning with the first K years of the sample period and adding additional years consecutively. The second is done by beginning with the last K years of the sample period and adding years moving backward in time. Results for savings models are presented in table A1, and results for the investment model are presented in table A2. In all tests, r alone is treated as endogenous.

Refer to the first six columns of table A1, which describe the "traditional" savings model. Here, when observations are added forward in time, a clear jump occurs after 1974. In fact, the CUSUMSQ series is so small as to be statistically significant at the .1 level before this jump occurs, which is to say that the model fits well until 1975. Adding data backward in time, the structural shift at 1974 appears, although here it is not as significant.

The pattern for our table 5 model is somewhat different. Going backward, no major break occurs until 1966. But going forward, CUSUM statistics rise rapidly, reaching statistical significance at the .1 level by the early 1970s. This suggests that the early period either contained an outlier or reflected a structure distinct from what emerged after 1966.

Finally, referring to table A2 for stability tests of our investment model, note that a structural break occurs in 1967, adding data backward in time. This shift is not large enough to be statistically significant at the .1 level, however.

TABLE A1

Structural Stability Tests for Savings Models

Table 4 Model						Table 5 Model						Critical Values	
Forward			Backward			Forward			Backward				
Sample Ends:	CUSUM	CUSUMSQ	Sample Starts:	CUSUM	CUSUMSQ	Sample Ends:	CUSUM	CUSUMSQ	Sample Starts:	CUSUM	CUSUMSQ	CUSUM	CUSUMSQ
1967	.414	.010	1978	−.192	.002	1967	−1.99	.233	1978	−.052	.000	± 3.50	(−.266, .384)
1968	.436	.010	1977	.437	.025	1968	−1.95	.233	1977	.449	.015	± 3.94	(−.207, .443)
1969	−.371	.048	1976	−.239	.052	1969	−2.04	.234	1976	−.766	.102	± 4.38	(−.149, .501)
1970	−.377	.048	1975	−2.03	.240	1970	−2.89	.276	1975	−1.31	.119	±4.81	(−.090, .560)
1971	−.276	.049	1974	−2.52	2.55	1971	−5.38*	.642*	1974	−.260	.184	± 5.25	(−.031, .619)
1972	−1.02	.082	1973	−1.30	.341	1972	−6.11*	.673	1973	.174	.195	± 5.69	(.028, .678)
1973	−.751	.086*	1972	−2.47	.421	1973	−7.16*	.738*	1972	.466	.200	± 6.13	(.087, .737)
1974	1.44	.369	1971	−4.67	.705	1974	−7.88*	.768	1971	−.358	.240	± 6.57	(.146, .796)
1975	3.72	.674	1970	−5.19	.721	1975	−6.53	.875*	1970	−.010	247	± 7.00	(.204, .854)
1976	4.73	.734	1969	−4.97	.723	1976	−7.04	.890	1969	.283	.252*	± 7.44	(.263, .913)
1977	6.22	.866	1968	−4.24	.755	1977	−6.40	.914	1968	1.35	.319*	± 7.88	(.322, .972)
1978	7.32	.936	1967	−3.85	.764	1978	−6.25	.915	1967	1.91	.337*	± 8.32	(.381, 1.03)
1979	8.13	.975	1966	−2.24	.917	1979	−5.96	.920	1966	5.08	.929	± 8.76	(.440, 1.09)
1980	8.59	.987	1965	−3.30	.984	1980	−5.18	.955	1965	5.23	.930	± 9.19	(.499, 1.15)
1981	8.63	.988	1964	−2.88	.994	1981	−5.79	.977	1964	6.03	.968	± 9.63	(.557, 1.21)
1982	8.98	.995	1963	−3.08	.997	1982	−6.19	.987	1963	5.33	.997	± 10.07	(.616, 1.27)
1983	...	1.00	1962	...	1.00	1983	...	1.00	1962	...	1.00	...	...

* Significant at the .1 level.

TABLE A2

STRUCTURAL STABILITY TESTS FOR INVESTMENT MODEL

	Forward			Backward		Critical Values	
Sample Ends:	CUSUM	CUSUMSQ	Sample Starts:	CUSUM	CUSUMSQ	CUSUM	CUSUMSQ
1970	−.101	.001	1975	.639	.029	± 3.18	(−.284, .426)
1971	−.871	.043	1974	−.611	.141	± 3.67	(−.212, .498)
1972	−.922	.043	1973	−1.06	.155	± 4.16	(−.141, .569)
1973	.738	.240	1972	−1.09	.155	± 4.65	(−.069, .641)
1974	1.06	.248	1971	−1.95	.208	± 5.14	(.002, .712)
1975	.101	.314	1970	−2.66	.244	± 5.63	(.074, .784)
1976	.002	.314	1969	−3.68	.318	± 6.11	(.145, .855)
1977	.909	.373	1968	−1.16	.773	± 6.60	(.216, .926)
1978	2.70	.603	1967	−1.45	.780	± 7.09	(.288, .998)
1979	3.33	.631	1966	−1.96	.798	± 7.58	(.359, 1.07)
1980	1.87	.783	1965	−1.95	.798	± 8.07	(.431, 1.14)
1981	.735	.876	1964	−.435	.962	± 8.56	(.502, 1.21)
1982	1.59	.928	1963	.268	.997	± 9.05	(.574, 1.28)
1983	...	1.00	1962	...	1.00	...	...

Notes

* This paper is part of research in progress at the World Bank under RPO 672-85, "Liberalization and Stabilization in the Southern Cone." The authors are grateful to John Cuddington, Sebastian Edwards, Alan Gelb, Nathaniel Leff, and Simón Teitel for comments. Jorge Miranda and Kalayarat Suriyasat provided able research assistance. The World Bank does not accept responsibility for the views expressed herein, which are those of the authors and should not be attributed to the World Bank or to its affiliated organizations. The findings, interpretations, and conclusions are the results of research supported by the Bank; they do not necessarily represent official policy of the Bank. The designations employed and the presentation of material used in this document are solely for the convenience of the reader and do not imply the expression of any opinion whatsoever on the part of the World Bank or its affiliates concerning the legal status of any country, territory, city, or area, or of its authorities, or concerning the delimitation of its boundaries or national affiliation.

1. The tightly regulated condition of the banking system was a response to the banking crisis of 1965, when several banks failed. These failures culminated a period of rapid branch expansion, during which financial intermediaries' offices multiplied to capture time deposits at 5% and checking deposits at 0%. (This was the only way they could compete, since interest rates were controlled.) Following the 1965 bankruptcies, a bill on banking regulations was passed in 1965 that prohibited entry into the banking system and limited the expansion of remaining branches. A remarkable contraction in the size of the financial market ensued, and regulation of the banking system was to remain until the military takeover in 1973. For further descriptions, see H. E. Daly, "A Note on the Pathological Growth of the Uruguayan Banking Sector," *Economic Development and Cultural Change* 16 (1969): 91–96.

2. In 1977, commercial banks were allowed to pay interest on checking accounts, and the BCU relaxed legislation governing banking houses by allowing de facto entry and expansion. In 1979 both the profit and deposit banking tax (amounting to 8.4% of the value of deposits) and the obligatory reserve requirements were abolished. Insofar as banking houses could not offer checking account services (they were chiefly engaged in intermediating foreign currency funds held mostly by nonresidents), some regulation still persisted. For a further description of the financial reforms, see Mario Blejer and José Gil Díaz, "Domestic and External Factors in the Determination of the Real Interest Rate: The Case of Uruguay," *Economic Development and Cultural Change*, this issue, and the app. to James Hanson and Jaime de Melo, "External Shocks, Financial Reforms and Stabilization Attempts in Uruguay: 1974–83," *World Development* 13, no. 8 (1985): 917–39.

3. Hanson and de Melo.

4. See Ronald McKinnon, *Money and Capital in Economic Development* (Washington, D.C.: Brookings Institution, 1973); and Edward Shaw, *Financial Deepening in Economic Development* (Oxford: Oxford University Press, 1973).

5. Ceiling rates on passbook savings accounts were increased from 8% to 18% in 1974. After interest rate ceilings were eliminated, passbook rates averaged 20%–25% a year. Thus, part of the increased financial deepening is the result of the shift out of checking accounts (see table 2, col. 1).

6. Official statistics may not be a good measure of the importance of nonresident deposits because they had been subject to different treatment during the period. They initially were subject to higher reserve requirements, which encouraged banks to request that nonresidents declare a Uruguayan address.

7. As long as the *tablita* appeared relatively credible, i.e., as long as Argentina was strongly appreciated vis-à-vis Uruguay, dollarization declined because the risk-adjusted return on pesos was higher. This pattern was reversed in 1981, when Argentina abandoned the *tablita* and the economy started heading toward a recession. (Demand from Argentine tourists disappeared in 1981, and Uruguayans shifted their expenditures to Argentina, especially in 1982, when Argentina underwent further massive devaluations.) Credibility of the *tablita* eroded in 1982, as the government deficit reached 8% of GDP and was financed by foreign borrowing. Hanson and de Melo discuss peso-to-dollar portfolio shifts in terms of relative yields and suggest that the pattern of peso-dollar interest rate spreads reflected a growing probability of devaluation. For an alternative view of the determination of peso interest rates, see Blejer and Gil Díaz.

8. A considerable part of this expansion was consumer credit, which went from 4% to 12% of total credit between 1979 and 1981. Hanson and de Melo also stress that the increase in liquidity went to finance and made possible two asset price bubbles: one in agricultural land, followed by one in real estate.

9. These movements are estimated to have cost the Uruguayans an average of 7% of their GDP. See Bela Balassa, "Adjusting to External Shocks: The Newly Industrializing Developing Economies in 1974–76 and 1979–81," *Review of World Economics* 121, no. 1 (1985): 116–35.

10. See James Hanson and Jaime de Melo, "The Uruguayan Experience with Liberalization and Stabilization: 1974–81," *Journal of Inter-American and World Affairs* 25 (1983): 477–507, esp. 488–89, for a discussion of investment efficiency; and Jaime de Melo, Ricardo Pascale, and James Tybout, "Microeconomic Adjustments in Uruguay during 1973–81: The Interplay of Real and Financial Shocks," *World Development* 13, no. 8 (1985): 995–1015, for evidence of increases in capacity utilization.

11. With redundant protection eliminated and the expectations of a devaluation rising, consumers stockpiled imported consumer durables by lowering savings and increasing their share in the allocation of credit. See Hanson and de Melo, particularly table 6.

12. Even when the social returns to private investment in the form of tax revenue generation are included, the social returns to private-sector investment remained low—between 8% and 9%. See Arnold C. Harberger and Daniel L. Wisecarver, "Private and Social Rates of Return to Capital in Uruguay," *Economic Development and Cultural Change* 25 (1977): 411–45, esp. table 20.

13. See Maxwell Fry, "Money and Capital or Financial Deepening in Economic Development," *Journal of Money, Credit and Banking* 10 (1978): 464–75; and Alberto Giovannini, "The Interest Elasticity of Savings in Developing Countries: The Existing Evidence," *World Development* 11 (1983): 601–7.

14. Our set of instruments includes lagged income growth, lagged real money growth, lagged inflation, the logarithm of real fiscal spending, the lagged real Uruguayan exchange rate, the current real Argentine exchange rate vis-à-vis the dollar, and a dummy for the reform period. As Giovannini notes, the application of instruments to real interest rates can be interpreted as a technique for dealing with rational expectations.

15. Durbin's H-statistic is asymptotically normal, with zero mean and unit variance if the model satisfies the classical assumptions.

16. See Lars E. O. Svenson and Assaf Razin, "The Terms of Trade and the Current Account: The Harberger-Laursen-Metzler Effect," *Journal of*

Political Economy 91 (1983): 97–125; and Rudiger Dornbusch, "External Debt, Budget Deficits and Disequilibrium Exchange Rates," in *International Debt and the Developing Countries,* ed. Gordon Smith and John Cuddington (Washington, D.C.: World Bank, 1985). We are not the first to argue that foreign savings do not belong in the domestic savings function. On this, see Giovannini and the app. to Nathaniel Leff and Kazuo Sato, "Specifying the Demand for Capital Imports in Developing Countries: Testing an Hypothesis with Latin American Data," mimeographed (New York: Columbia University, 1985).

17. This means that liquidity shocks influenced the timing more than the long-run volume of investments. Such a result is consistent with many other studies of investment behavior in the United States and developing countries.

18. See Pablo Spiller and Edgardo Favaro, "The Effects of Entry Regulation on Oligopolistic Interaction: The Uruguayan Banking Sector," *Rand Journal of Economics* 15 (1984): 244–54. They also give evidence supporting a Stackelberg-type of oligopoly model, in which conjectural variations are different between the dominant firms and others.

19. The data set is drawn from an earlier study of how manufacturing firms in various sectors (exportables, importables, etc.) adjusted to the reforms. For further discussion of the data set and adjustments made to it see de Melo et al. The logic of the tests is developed formally in James Tybout, "Interest Controls and Credit Allocation in Developing Countries," *Journal of Money, Credit and Banking* 16 (1984): 474–87.

20. See R. L. Brown, J. Durbin, and J. M. Evans, "Techniques for Testing the Constancy of Regression Relationships over Time," *Journal of the Royal Statistical Society,* Series B, 37 (1975): 149–92.

THE WORLD BANK ECONOMIC REVIEW, VOL. 1, NO. 3: 447-487

Adjustment with a Fixed Exchange Rate: Cameroon, Côte d'Ivoire, and Senegal

Shantayanan Devarajan and Jaime de Melo

As members of the Communauté Financière Africaine, Cameroon, Côte d'Ivoire, and Senegal cannot use the nominal exchange rate as a tool of macroeconomic adjustment. This article considers these countries' responses to the commodity and oil price shocks of the 1970s in light of this and other institutional constraints. Using a two-sector model, it shows that there exist instruments that, in principle, permit the real exchange rate depreciation necessary for adjusting to macroeconomic imbalances. The authors interpret the very different adjustment experiences of the three countries (despite their common economic structure and institutional setting) in terms of different uses of these instruments. Alternative assumptions about the labor market leave the qualitative nature of the results unaltered. Statistical analysis of data from the three countries confirms the model's linking of the current account and real exchange rate with the instruments of adjustment.

Like most developing countries, Cameroon, Côte d'Ivoire, and Senegal were subjected to the external shocks of commodity booms and oil price hikes in the 1970s. As members of the Communauté Financière Africaine (CFA) (a monetary union with France), however, these countries could not devalue their nominal exchange rate to adjust to the macroeconomic imbalances that followed. The purpose of this article is to interpret the adjustment experiences of these three countries in light of this and other institutional constraints.

The cases of Cameroon, Côte d'Ivoire, and Senegal are particularly interesting for another reason. In addition to sharing a common institutional framework for external adjustment, they have a similar economic structure: all three are largely primary product producers, with a small industrial base and service sector fueled by public expenditures. Yet the outcomes of their adjustment experiences were quite different. By the early 1980s, Cameroon was enjoying low foreign debt and steady, 4 percent growth in gross domestic product (GDP), while Côte

Shantayanan Devarajan is at Harvard University. Jaime de Melo is at the World Bank. The authors thank Dani Rodrik, Alan Gelb, Richard Westebbe, seminar participants at Georgetown University and at a Centre d'Etudes et de Recherches sur le Développement Internationale conference in Clermont-Ferrand for comments on an earlier draft. Gabriel Castillo, Chris Danek, Julie Stanton Gwynn, and Jackson Magargee provided much appreciated support.

d'Ivoire and Senegal were experiencing high debt-service payments and declining GDP.

Our major conclusion is that membership in the CFA zone does not, in principle, impede adjustment to macroeconomic imbalances. There exist enough instruments to achieve, for example, the real exchange rate depreciation that is necessary to redress a current account deficit. However, in practice, these instruments are not always used, or are used in the wrong direction, and this is why the outcomes were different in the three countries.

To make these points, we first describe in the remainder of this introduction the rules of CFA zone membership. Next, we look closely at the adjustment to shocks by Cameroon, Côte d'Ivoire, and Senegal, using a set of common "adjustment indicators" for 1973–84 (section I). These serve as the backdrop to a model of adjustment with a fixed exchange rate, presented in section II. The model captures the distinctive features of CFA zone economies as well as the instruments of adjustment to which they have access. While these countries cannot effect a nominal devaluation, the model shows how a real devaluation can be achieved by a reduction in government expenditure or a change in commercial policy. The roles of wage rigidity and unemployment are highlighted in the analysis. In section III, the model is tested using data from Cameroon, Côte d'Ivoire, and Senegal. Conclusions follow in section IV.

The CFA zone consists of a West and a Central African monetary union, the Union Monetaire Ouest-Africaine (UMOA) and the members of the Banque des Etats de l'Afrique Centrale (BEAC). Participation in the zone sets its members apart from most other developing countries in at least three ways: they have monetary integration, currency convertibility, and a fixed exchange rate.[1]

Monetary integration. Member countries pool 65 percent of their foreign exchange reserves with the French treasury. Each union's central bank sets monetary policy based on its overall asset position, and all bank members face the same interest rate.[2] The central bank influences an individual country's monetary position by imposing country-specific credit constraints and limiting each country's central government's borrowing to 20 percent of its previous year's fiscal receipts.[3] By pooling reserves, the countries avoid some of the seigniorage costs of holding reserves.

Currency convertibility. The CFA franc is convertible since it is guaranteed by the French franc (FF), itself a convertible currency. Each country has an operations account with the French treasury which it can overdraw at a graduated interest rate that rises to the Bank of France's rediscount rate. There

1. The institutional characteristics of the CFA zone and their implications for macroeconomic adjustment are described in Bhatia (1985) and Guillaumont and Guillaumont (1984). The implications of real exchange rate volatility are analyzed in Macedo (1984). Mundell (1972) provides a historical analysis of monetary integration in Africa. Devarajan and de Melo (forthcoming) evaluate and analyze the growth implications of participation in the CFA zone.

2. This is not strictly true for BEAC members.

3. This does not include borrowing by public enterprises, an important qualification for certain countries.

are no foreign exchange implications for transactions among zone members. Convertibility does, however, have implications for asset choice by residents and, in the longer run, for foreign direct investment.

Fixed exchange rate. The CFA franc (CFAF) is pegged to the French franc at an exchange rate (50 CFAF = 1 FF) that has remained unchanged since 1948. Parity adjustment requires unanimous agreement among zone members. Effectively, CFA countries cannot use nominal devaluation of the exchange rate as an instrument of macroeconomic adjustment.

Although a type of CFA franc had been in use during the colonial era, the two central banks were created when the majority of the members received their independence from France. In its early stages, the CFA zone was designed as a means of providing balance of payments credit to these emerging nations. In addition, it was felt that a common and stable exchange rate would attract foreign investment into these countries. Over the long run, membership in the zone has induced a sense of monetary and fiscal discipline, damping the "stop-go" cycles observed in many developing countries. Nevertheless, despite the general consensus that the monetary union has been working fairly well and that its members have probably fared better than they would have in its absence, concern has recently been raised that adjustments to macroeconomic imbalances have not been as prompt and complete as desirable, as sustained periods of real exchange rate appreciation have been observed among many zone members.

As a result of the turbulent 1970s, many CFA countries were experiencing macroeconomic "crises" in the early 1980s. Senegal and Côte d'Ivoire—the two largest UMOA members—had huge current account and public sector deficits that could in turn lead to debilitating debt-service payments in the future. Cameroon had become an oil exporter and was running sizable current account surpluses. Some observers began questioning whether the particular nature of the CFA zone prevented its members from adjusting their economies to these dramatic changes. To assess this question, we turn now to a detailed analysis of the adjustment process in Cameroon, Côte d'Ivoire, and Senegal.

I. Case Studies of Adjustment: Cameroon, Côte d'Ivoire, and Senegal[4]

All three countries experienced windfall gains from the commodity price increases of the mid-1970s.[5] Cameroon and especially Côte d'Ivoire benefited from the coffee and cocoa boom of 1975–77;[6] Senegal enjoyed a phosphates

4. For a more detailed description of these case studies, see Castillo and others (1986).

5. Davies (1983) provides a comparative study of how major commodities exporters reacted to the 1975–77 commodity boom. He shows that Cameroon and Côte d'Ivoire made extensive use of their commodity stabilization funds to tax the windfall gains to producers.

6. Following Brazil's frost in July 1975, which reduced world production by one-third, coffee prices doubled in 1976 and rose another 60 percent in 1977. The price of cocoa futures showed increases of 64 and 85 percent in 1976 and 1977.

boom in 1973.[7] In addition, Cameroon became a net oil exporter in 1980. Nevertheless, the adjustment experience of the three countries differed substantially. External borrowing patterns varied, as did the relative contributions of the private and public sectors to the trade deficits or surpluses. As suggested by the model to be presented in section II, the compositional differences in expenditures differentially affected the external sector's competitiveness in each country.

To study the adjustment experience, we use a matched set of adjustment indicators suggestive of the model to be presented below. These indicators measure the magnitude of the external shocks and help show how adjustment took place.

A first set of indicators is constructed from price indexes. The commodity terms-of-trade index is supplemented by an index measuring the ratio of the domestic producer price to the world price for the two most important export commodities (coffee and cocoa for Cameroon and Côte d'Ivoire; phosphates and groundnuts for Senegal). The impact of the shock on the structure of production is measured by two real exchange rate indexes. An index corresponding to the concept of the real exchange rate developed in the model of section II (the ratio of prices of tradables to prices of nontradables) is constructed from national accounts data (tradables include agriculture and industry, and nontradables account for the rest). A rise in the index signals an increase in the relative price of tradables. Second, a purchasing power parity index (PPPRER) is used to measure the external competitiveness of manufacturing. This index is the ratio of an import-trade-weighted manufacturing wholesale price index (WPI) of trading partners to the domestic manufacturing WPI, so that a fall in the value of the index indicates a loss of manufacturing competitiveness.[8]

The second set of adjustment indicators measures the sources of current account deficits and the composition of government expenditure. Observing that the current account (CA) is equal to net domestic savings, we decompose it into its private and public sector components:

$$CA = S_p - I_p + S_g - I_g, \tag{1}$$

where S_p and S_g are private and public savings, and I_p and I_g are private and public investment.[9] The usefulness of this decomposition derives not only from the fact

7. In 1974 phosphate prices increased by almost 400 percent.

8. In presenting the real exchange rates, we are not distinguishing between changes in the price ratio caused by external circumstances and those attributed to domestic price changes (that is, policy influenced). This is because our analysis will be based on relative prices. Regardless of what determines it, the real exchange rate remains the most important signal for domestic agents making decisions about engaging in tradable activity. Institutional monetary reforms in 1973 gave greater autonomy from France to the two central banks (BEAC, BCEAO) in setting money supply targets. As a result, money supply growth, which had averaged 10 percent annually since independence, rose to 45 percent in 1974. Obviously this change accounted for the observed drop in the PPPRER index in the three countries in 1974. For further discussion, see Castillo and others (1986).

9. The equality between the change in net foreign financial assets and CA is strictly valid only if there are no changes in the French franc–U.S. dollar exchange rate vis-à-vis the currencies in which debts are denominated.

that public sector deficits are, at least in principle, instruments of adjustment, but also from the observation that public sector spending is usually more intensive in nontradables than private sector spending, an observation that will play a crucial role in the model of section II. Finally public sector expenditure and investment patterns are tracked to see whether foreign borrowing is guided towards investment which, if it has a higher rate of return than the borrowing costs, would justify the increase in external debt.

Cameroon

Cameroon was subject to two major positive shocks in the late 1970s. First, the coffee and cocoa boom of 1975–77 led to windfall gains for the commodity stabilization fund (ONCPB), as producer prices were repressed during the boom. Second, the discovery of offshore oil, which went into production in 1978, created a one-time opportunity for the government to accelerate its development program.

How did Cameroonian policymakers respond to these favorable shocks? Figure 1 summarizes the story. At the time of the 1976–77 coffee boom, production was at its lowest point since the 1960s. The "spending effect" of the boom was therefore not substantial. The real exchange rate did not appreciate (although its rate of depreciation slowed). Nevertheless, manufacturing competitiveness continued its downward slide, reflecting the country's inward-looking industrial policy, rather than the effects of the shock. After the boom, the government raised producer prices of both cash crops while simultaneously restraining government spending (between 1976 and 1980, both government expenditure and investment declined).

The post-1978 oil boom was of much greater significance but elicited a similar response. While estimates vary, there is reason to believe that up to three-fourths of the oil revenues were saved abroad.[10] This is confirmed by the sizable current account surpluses recorded since 1978. In fact, the government has used the oil revenues to retire a small part of its foreign debt. Consequently, and in contrast to other oil exporters' experiences, Cameroon's real exchange rate continued to depreciate (even when mining is excluded from tradables) in the first few years of the oil era (see figure 1). To the extent that this windfall was spent domestically, it was channeled into investment rather than consumption; while the share of public expenditure in GDP fell slightly between 1978 and 1982, that of public investment almost doubled.

It is often observed that a period of real exchange rate appreciation is followed by a consumption boom because the private sector perceives a permanent increase in wealth. This was avoided in Cameroon. That it was private rather than public net savings which rose simply reflects the system of budget accounting in Cameroon. The bulk of oil revenues and expenditures financed by them are

10. Data about oil exports are systematically underreported in the official statistics, but oil revenue estimates are included as government receipts in our data.

Figure 1. *Adjustment Indicators for Cameroon*

Terms of trade (1973 = 100)

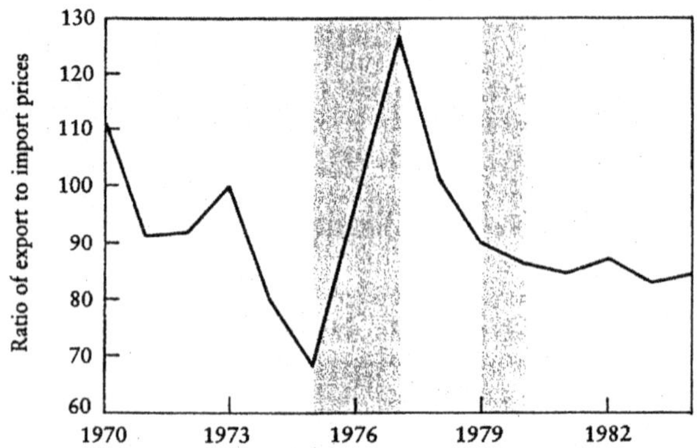

Note: Weighted index of prices of exported commodities to imported commodities.

Ratio of producer to world price (percent)

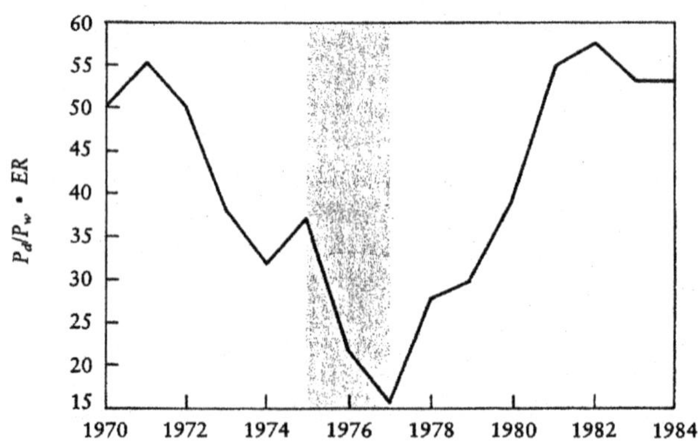

Note: For coffee and cocoa. P_d = domestic producer price; P_w = world price; *ER* = nominal exchange rate.

Figure 1 *(continued)*

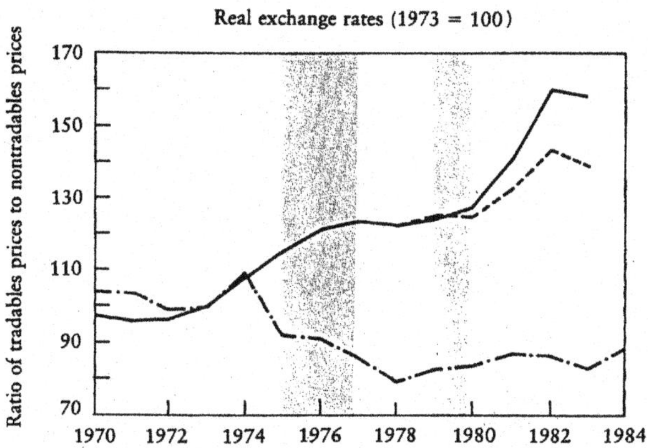

——— Price of tradables / price of nontradables
----- Price of tradables (excluding mining) / price of nontradables
—·— Manufacturing competitiveness index: import-weighted manufacturing wholesale price index of trading partners / domestic manufacturing WPI (a decline indicates a loss of competitiveness)

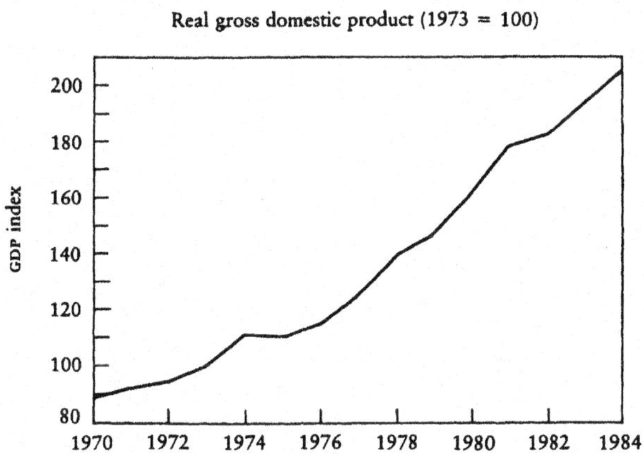

Note: Change in GDP from 1973 base value.

Figure 1 *(continued)*

Decomposition of net domestic savings (by public and private sources)

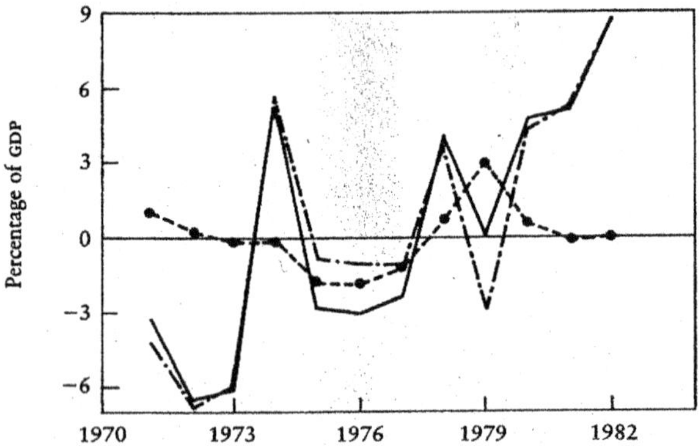

Note: All are measured as percentage of GDP.
----- Federal government budget surplus
–·–·– Private sector surplus of savings over investment
——— Trade account balance

Public expenditure and investment (shares in GDP)

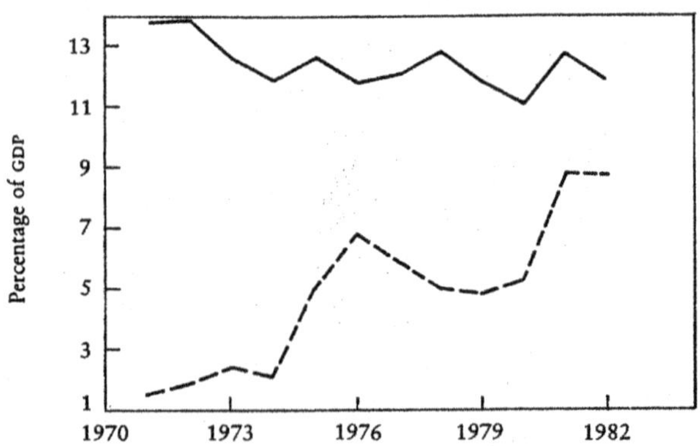

——— Public expenditure / GDP
---- Public investment / GDP

entered in the *compte hors budget,* which is outside the official public financial accounts. The government has used its liquid position to raise the producer prices of cash crops, keeping the real exchange rate from appreciating and preventing the traditional export sector from contracting Dutch disease. The bias of the public expenditure mix toward investment rather than consumption has also been beneficial for future growth. Because money and real wages have risen, however (the inevitable consequence of incomplete sterilization), manufacturing's international competitiveness has fallen, as shown by the PPPRER index.

Côte d'Ivoire

Given that coffee and cocoa account for 50 percent of Côte d'Ivoire's export earnings, the 1975–77 boom in these commodities led to a sharp but short-lived improvement in the overall terms of trade, which then deteriorated by a cumulative 37 percent between 1977 and 1980 (partly reflecting the 1979 oil price shock). As in Cameroon, the stabilization fund was the main recipient of the windfall gains between 1976 and 1978. The fund's income reached 16 percent of GDP at the peak of the coffee and cocoa boom in 1977.

Faced with these rapid changes in its external environment, Côte d'Ivoire chose a different adjustment path from Cameroon. The government accelerated the investment program it had started around 1974 (see figure 2). The increase in public investment was mainly allocated to large projects with high unit costs, long gestation lags, and low foreign exchange earning potential. Furthermore, and unlike the other two countries, the government increased the share of public expenditure in GDP immediately following the coffee boom. As suggested by the model in section II, this expenditure pattern is consistent with the observed loss of manufacturing sector competitiveness.

When the commodity boom came to an end, the government continued its investment program, initially increasing the share of public investment in GDP. Public expenditure also continued to rise rapidly; its share in GDP rose from 15 percent in 1977 to a peak of 26 percent in 1982.[11] By contrast, the private sector adjusted rapidly on both sides of the boom, as shown in the decomposition of the net domestic savings. Private expenditure surged immediately following the boom, but it fell just as quickly when the terms of trade deteriorated.

Part of the increase in public sector borrowing was financed internally (the money supply grew by 33 percent a year between 1975 and 1980), but much of it was external; the debt-service ratio (debt-service payments as a percentage of merchandise exports), which had averaged 8 percent during the 1965–75 period, quadrupled during 1980–85. When the time came to adjust in 1980, it was the private sector that generated the large surplus to service the increased external debt. Expenditure switching could have been achieved by reductions in the relative size of nontradable-intensive public expenditure; but little of this

11. The increased shares of government investment and expenditure in GDP are largely due to adjustment by the private sector.

Figure 2. *Adjustment Indicators for Côte d'Ivoire*

Terms of trade (1973 = 100)

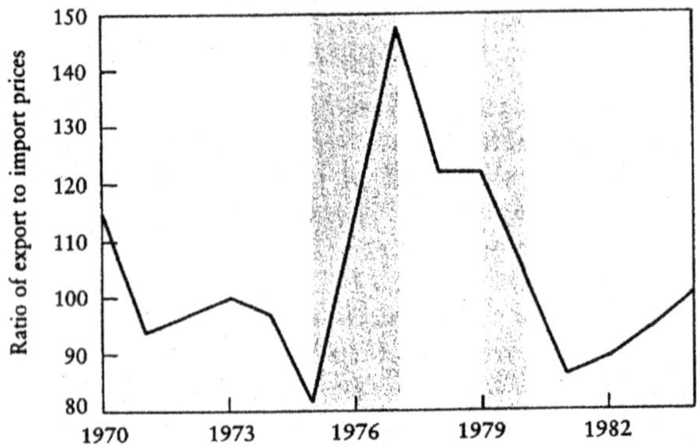

Note: Weighted index of prices of exported commodities to imported commodities.

Ratio of producer to world price (percent)

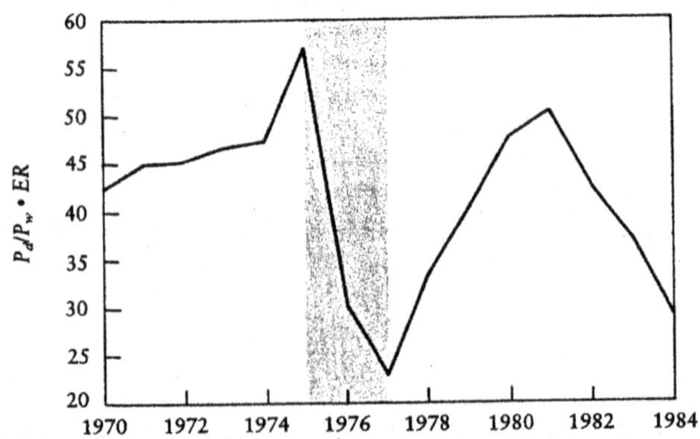

Note: For coffee and cocoa. P_d = domestic producer price; P_w = world price; *ER* = nominal exchange rate.

Figure 2 *(continued)*

Real exchange rates (1973 = 100)

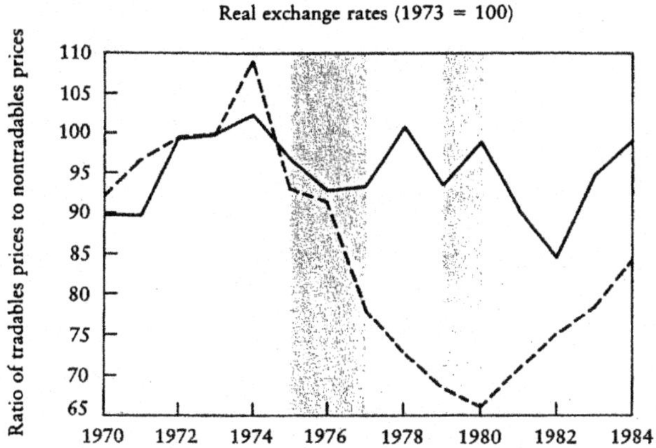

——— Price of tradables / price of nontradables
- - - - Manufacturing competitiveness index: import-weighted manufacturing wholesale price index of trading partners / domestic manufacturing WPI (a decline indicates a loss of competitiveness)

Real gross domestic product (1973 = 100)

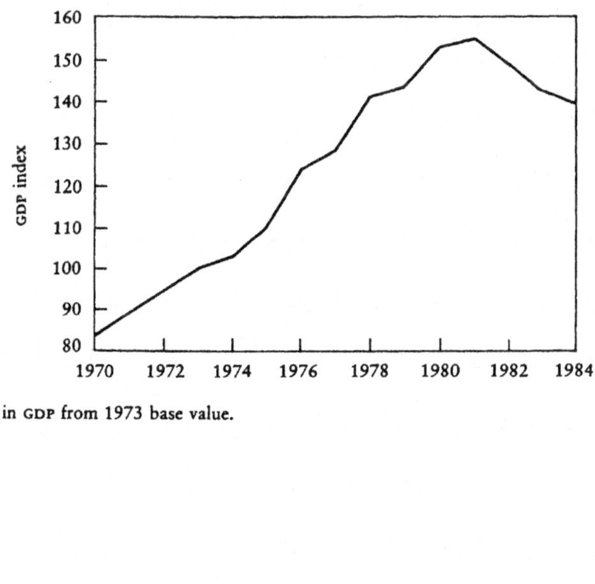

Note: Change in GDP from 1973 base value.

Figure 2 *(continued)*

Decomposition of net domestic savings (by public and private sources)

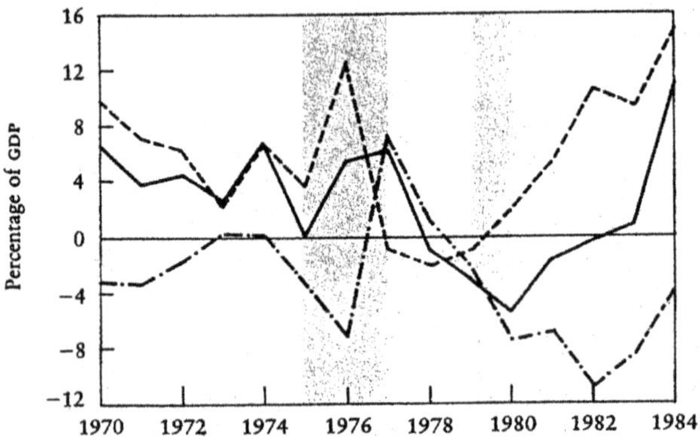

Note: All are measured as percentage of GDP.
–·–·– Federal government budget surplus
----- Private sector surplus of savings over investment
—— Trade account balance

Public expenditure and investment (shares in GDP)

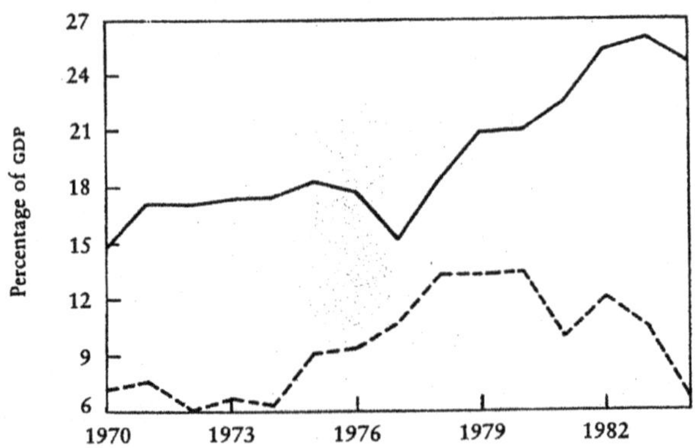

—— Public expenditure / GDP
---- Public investment / GDP

occurred. Instead the post-1980 adjustment was mostly achieved by private expenditure reduction and a consequent fall in GDP. This slow adjustment by the public sector contrasts sharply with Cameroon's experience.

The implications of Côte d'Ivoire's public sector "boom" for the real exchange rate closely follow the predictions of the model of section II: an initial real exchange rate appreciation between 1975 and 1977, accompanied by a sharper and sustained loss of competitiveness for the manufacturing sector (see figure 2). The developments following the commodity boom did not seriously reduce the prices of tradables relative to nontradables, which would have helped achieve expenditure switching toward nontradables and hence restore external balance. Two factors contributed. First, when the boom ended, taxation of coffee and cocoa was reduced, raising the relative price of a component of the tradable sector. Second, public investment had a sizable import component. Nevertheless, manufacturing lost competitiveness rapidly as the public sector deficit was financed by money creation. With a fixed exchange rate, expenditure switching would have been better achieved had the public sector curtailed its import-intensive expenditures. Unfortunately, this path was not followed.

Senegal

The 1970s were a particularly volatile period for the Senegalese economy. A phosphates boom in 1973–75[12] was followed by two droughts, in 1977–78 and 1979–80. Most observers agree, however, that the policies following these shocks, as much as the disturbances themselves, brought on the economic crisis that gripped the country in the 1980s.

The indicators in figure 3 lend credence to this view. Soon after the phosphates boom, the real exchange rate appreciated because there was little taxation of windfall gains as in Cameroon and Côte d'Ivoire. Windfall revenues were spent domestically on consumption rather than investment, as figure 3 shows. Net dissaving by the private sector dominated total net dissavings, and the share of public investment in GDP stayed almost constant.

Moreover, when the terms of trade deteriorated after 1977, Senegal continued an expansionary policy of maintaining private consumption and expanding public consumption. The latter grew in real terms at an average rate of 6.7 percent a year during 1975–80, although per capita output fell by 0.6 percent a year during the period. This contributed to the continued real exchange rate appreciation. The government responded to the shocks of the 1977–78 and 1979–80 droughts by increasing consumer subsidies, public sector employment, and transfers to the parapublic sector. Meanwhile, incentives to produce exports showed little increase, since the domestic prices of the main cash crops remained well below their world levels. The successive droughts and declining terms of trade called for an alternative adjustment path, namely, for a real exchange rate depreciation. As the model below shows, this could have been

12. Phosphates account for 10 percent of the country's exports, and groundnuts for about 50 percent.

Figure 3. *Adjustment Indicators for Senegal*

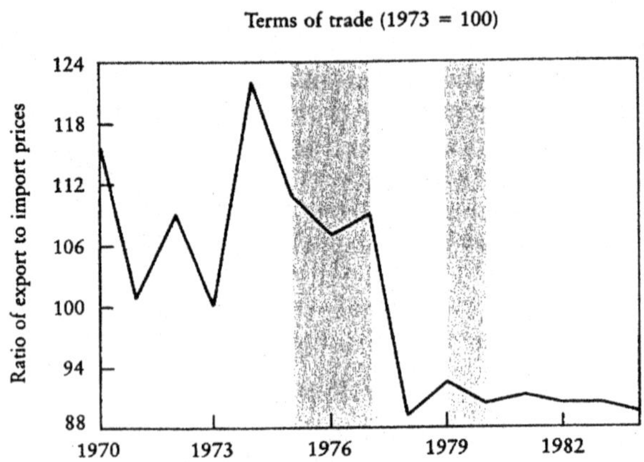

Note: Weighted index of prices of exported commodities to imported commodities.

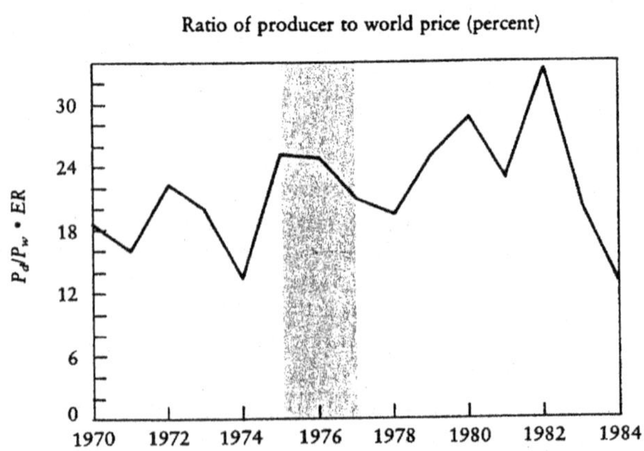

Note: For phosphates and groundnuts. P_d = domestic producer price; P_w = world price; ER = nominal exchange rate.

Figure 3 *(continued)*

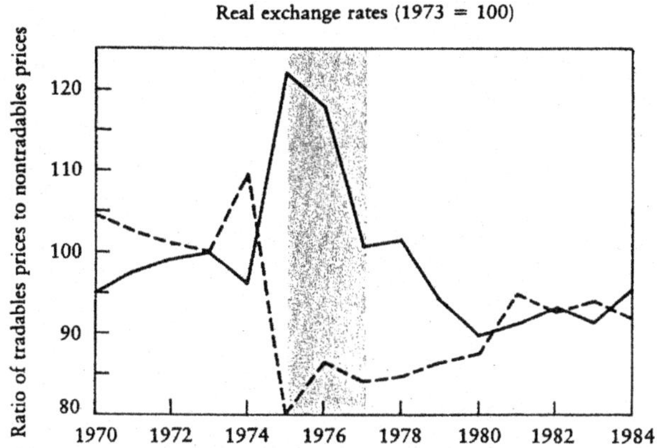

—— Price of tradables / price of nontradables

---- Manufacturing competitiveness index: import-weighted manufacturing wholesale price index of trading partners / domestic manufacturing WPI (a decline indicates a loss of competitiveness)

Note: Change in GDP from 1973 base value.

Figure 3 *(continued)*

Decomposition of net domestic savings (by public and private sources)

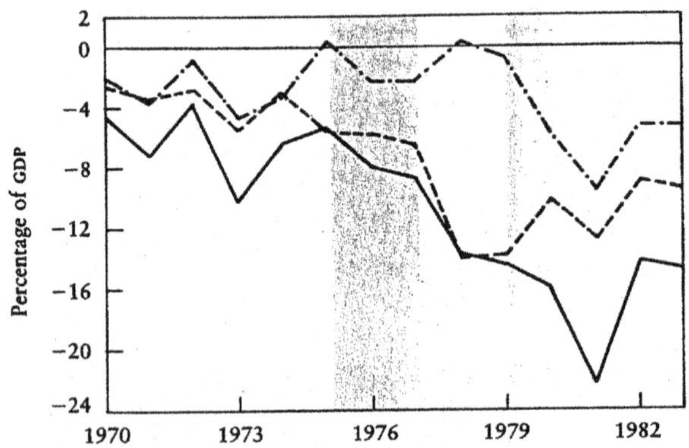

Note: All are measured as percentage of GDP.
–·–·– Federal government budget surplus
– – – – Private sector surplus of savings over investment
——— Trade account balance

Public expenditure and investment (shares in GDP).

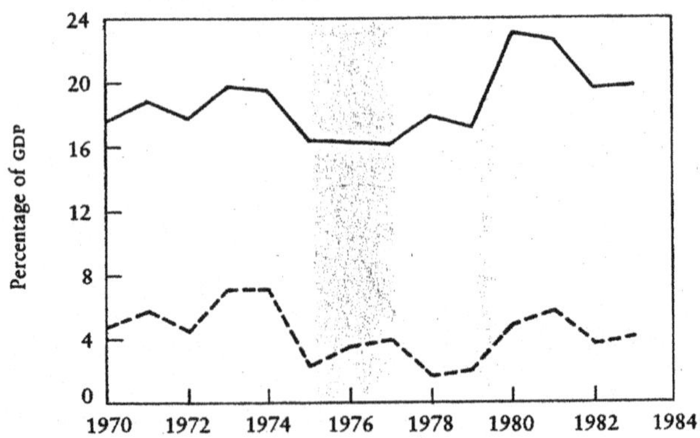

——— Public expenditure / GDP
– – – – Public investment / GDP

achieved by cutting government expenditure, even if there had been relative price rigidities.

The outcome of all this is shown in the stubbornly negative trade balance and oscillating GDP figures of the last fifteen years. In addition, Senegal faces a debt crisis, or more appropriately a "creditworthiness crisis," in the mid-1980s. The government had to undertake draconian structural adjustment measures in 1984. The results of this program have yet to be seen. There is little doubt, however, that a different set of responses to the favorable and unfavorable shocks of the 1970s would have led to less drastic cutbacks in the 1980s.

In sum, despite similar characteristics and institutional frameworks, the three countries adjusted quite differently to a common sequence of terms-of-trade shocks. None avoided loss of external competitiveness in manufacturing, and only Cameroon avoided real exchange rate appreciation. Côte d'Ivoire's manufacturing sector experienced a sustained loss of external competitiveness, and Senegal's real exchange rate appreciated. Given the magnitude of these swings one must ask whether they could have been dampened so as to avoid costly resource shifts into, and then later out of, nontradables.

In our discussion above, we attributed these different patterns of real exchange rate behavior and loss of external competitiveness to different patterns of external borrowing, public expenditure levels, and taxation of windfall gains. Below we show that this interpretation is consistent with predictions from a two-sector model. The model is also useful to determine the relative impact of alternative instruments to maintain real exchange rate stability and reduce external deficits.

II. A Model of Medium-Term Adjustment

The popular model to analyze medium-term macroeconomic equilibrium (when nominal aggregate demand pressures are zero and the focus is on real variables) is the "dependent economy" model due to Salter (1959) and Swan (1960). In that model, the equilibrium real exchange rate or relative price between tradables and nontradables depends on fundamentals (tastes and technology in the relevant sectors), the level of capital inflows, and the extent of price rigidity in the labor market or the nontradable sector.[13] When a current account deficit (that is, absorption of goods and services exceeding current income[14]) must be eliminated, a policy that allows the real exchange rate to depreciate is required. The real exchange rate is defined as RER = $(PT/PN)e$, where e is the nominal exchange rate and PT and PN are price indexes of tradable and nontradable sectors. In the case of the CFA zone, where e is fixed, depreciation of the real

13. Recent presentations are Bruno (1976), Dornbusch (1980), Corden (1977). Jones and Corden (1976) present the analytics of the case with fixed nominal wages and sector-specific capital. Prachowny (1980) provides a detailed analysis of the standard model with sector-specific capital.

14. All one can say from a current account deficit is that the net financial asset position of the country is deteriorating. Private capital inflow could be so great that reserves are increasing. The country may be increasing its real assets (foreign direct investment) if expenditures are mostly for investment.

exchange rate requires a policy that lowers *PN* or the wage rate (in terms of foreign prices) or a fiscal policy that raises the relative price of tradables, *PT*. Thus a policy which *switches* expenditures toward nontradables is required in addition to an initial reduction in the *level* of expenditures so as to achieve external balance without experiencing a rise in unemployment.

The above analysis leaves out the role of monetary policy in dealing with external imbalance. A current account deficit means the net financial asset position for the nation as a whole is deteriorating (for example, private capital inflow may be so great that central bank reserves are increasing). As indicated by equation 1 above, the deficit may reflect a public or private sector deficit. With the exchange rate fixed, if there is a budget deficit that exceeds net private saving and autonomous capital inflow, foreign exchange reserves will be run down and, unless there is sterilization, the domestic assets of the banking system will decline. The automatic monetary mechanism will then tend to eliminate the deficit as the price of nontradables falls relative to tradables. In practice, of course, there is at least partial sterilization of these monetary effects so that the flow equilibrium deficit is partly maintained.

The implication of monetary union membership for CFA zone countries is that there is a limit to the extent to which any individual country can sterilize the monetary implications of its external deficit.[15] Effective monetary policy will thus speed up the *monetary* adjustments that are called for by a current account deficit if there is some relative price rigidity in the economy. But the implications for the real economy of a current account deficit remain, regardless of the effectiveness of monetary policy. In the remainder of the paper, we are concerned with these adjustments in the real economy.

We return therefore to the standard analysis of expenditure policy mixes to restore external balance that are analyzed in the Salter-Swan "dependent economy" model.[16] Here we propose to highlight more precisely what adjustment in real variables is required to correct an external deficit; this is done by extending the standard dependent-economy model to consider features typical of CFA zone countries.[17] First, a current account deficit is a national deficit. As such

15. In the CFA zone, the monetary mechanism to eliminate an external deficit implies ending sterilization so as to let the money supply fall. Even though the monetary reforms of 1974 included some decentralization of power, with credit policy becoming less controlled by the Bank of France and more by each union member, monetary policy remains by and large in the hands of each union's central bank, which sets targets for total central bank financing in each member state and has other means to control domestic credit (for example, setting reserve requirements for individual commercial banks and varying interest rates). In turn, the central bank of each monetary union must maintain a certain level of total external reserves for its union with the Bank of France (for example, the statutes of BCEAO require it to act whenever its level of external reserves falls below 20 percent of its sight liabilities).

16. For recent case studies of macroadjustment using this approach see Ahamed (1985).

17. So many applications of the dependent economy are available that most options we introduce have been treated in one form or another in the literature. For example, the distinction between private and public deficit, which is usually not made, has been exploited, though in a simpler model, by Soderstrom (1985). Perhaps our model is closest in spirit to Jones's (1974) two-sector model, in which the export good is not consumed domestically.

it is the sum of the private and public sector financial deficits, the private deficit being the excess of private investment over private savings and the public deficit being the budget deficit. The model recognizes this distinction and assumes—to approximate the case studies under review—that the private sector deficit is always zero (that is, the private sector does not borrow or lend to the government *or* from or to foreigners). Therefore the current account deficit *is* the budget deficit. Second, access to the French treasury implies that external borrowing is a possibility open to these countries whenever it is necessary to adjust to macroeconomic disequilibrium. Third, because the exchange rate cannot be used for expenditure switching, trade taxes or subsidies are an important means of adjustment to a current account imbalance. Hence, they are included in our analysis. Fourth, we consider structural characteristics in our selection of functional forms, thus departing from the standard dependent-economy analysis: the export sector is the traditional, price-taking sector but the rest of the economy produces a good which is imperfectly substitutable with the imported commodity. We refer to this sector as the "semi-tradable" sector, and the elasticity of substitution in use between this sector's output and imports reflects the extent of "dependence" of the economy.

The Model

A typical CFA zone member's economy is characterized by a primary sector producing a cash crop (coffee, cocoa, or groundnuts) that is almost entirely sold in world markets at an exogenously given dollar price, together with a small industrial sector and a sizable nontradable sector. The industrial sector produces goods and services that are imperfect substitutes for goods sold in international markets; by contrast, the cash crop is a homogenous, undifferentiated product. Hence the distinction between the two sectors. Without much loss of generality, we can aggregate the industrial and nontradable sectors into a semitradable sector. Since it includes manufacturing, the semitradable sector competes for demand with foreign goods, albeit partially.

For simplicity, we assume that output in each sector is produced by a Cobb-Douglas production function. To reflect the medium-term focus of the analysis, we assume sector-specific capital. This gives us the following production functions, with the terms for capital suppressed:

$$X = \bar{A}L_1^{\alpha} \tag{2}$$

where

X = output (equal to exports) of the primary sector

L_1 = labor employed in the primary sector

and

$$Q = \bar{B}L_2^{\beta} \tag{3}$$

where

Q = output of semitradables

L_2 = labor employed in the semitradables sector.

A bar over a variable indicates that the variable is exogenous.

The output of the semitradables sector is an imperfect substitute for imports, in private consumption. Assume that private sector preferences are described by a constant elasticity of substitution (CES) utility function. Then the demand for semitradables, C, and imports, M, is a function of the relative final prices of imports to semitradables:

$$\frac{C}{M} = \overline{K}\left[\frac{P_M^*(1+t)\overline{e}}{P}\right]^{\sigma} \tag{4}$$

where

P_M^* = exogenous world price of imports (chosen as numeraire)
P = domestic price of semitradables
$\overline{e}$ = exchange rate (fixed by assumption and set equal to unity by choice of units)
t = ad valorem tariff rate
σ = elasticity of substitution of semitradables for imports (equal to minus the own price-elasticity of demand for imports)
$\overline{K}$ = a constant
C = private demand for semitradables
M = private demand for imports.

Labor is the only mobile factor. If it is available in fixed supply ($\overline{L}$), then we have the constraint:

$$L_1 + L_2 = \overline{L}. \tag{5}$$

Alternatively, we consider the implications of a wage that is rigid in terms of consumption goods. We consider two variants suggested by the two consumption goods in the model. In the first one, we assume wage rigidity in terms of the (tariff-inclusive) import price so that any supply response will arise exclusively in the semitradable sector, unless the tariff rate changes. In the second variant, we assume rigidity in terms of the semitradable sector price, and thus supply response will come from the cash crop sector exclusively. In both instances, we relax the full employment assumption to incorporate Keynesian multiplier effects. In the first alternative, equation 5 is replaced by

$$W/[P_M^*(1+t)e] = \overline{W} \tag{6}$$

and in the second by

$$W/P = \overline{W}. \tag{7}$$

Finally, profit maximization and perfect competition require equality of the value of marginal product across the two domestic sectors:

$$\alpha P_X^*(1-s)\overline{e}\overline{A}L_1^{\alpha-1} = \beta P\overline{B}L_2^{\beta-1} \tag{8}$$

where P_X^* is the world price of the export sector and s is the ad valorem export tax rate.

We assume that the government exogenously purchases only semitradables, amounting to $\overline{G}$.[18] Material balance for semitradables requires that

$$Q = C + \overline{G}. \tag{9}$$

The government's budget constraint sets foreign borrowing plus import and export duty revenues equal to government expenditures:

$$\bar{e}(F + tP_M^*M + sP_X^*X) = P\overline{G} \tag{10}$$

where F is foreign borrowing (for example, borrowing from the operations account) by the government. Net private domestic savings are assumed to be zero.

By Walras's Law (the equality between income, including foreign borrowing by the government, and expenditure), the difference between the value of imports and exports equals the current account deficit, F, that is:

$$P_M^*M = P_X^*X + F. \tag{11}$$

Since we have assumed for simplicity that the fiscal deficit is the current account deficit, this abstracts from any real effects arising out of the government's borrowing from the central bank, and from the fact that some foreign borrowing may be done by the private sector. This roughly fits the countries studied in which private borrowing was transitory whereas public borrowing was often sustained.

Note further that (excluding the effects of taxes and subsidies) there are two relative prices in our model: P_X^* and P. A rise in P_X^* is an improvement in terms of trade. A rise in P is a rise in the price of semitradables relative to imports. A rise in P_X^*/P represents a change in the relative price of exportables to semitradables. Excluding again the effects of taxes and subsidies, P_X^*/P is the real exchange rate facing producers. In the remainder of the paper, when we speak of the real exchange rate we shall mean the value of P_X^*/P (inclusive of export taxes) since its value signals the relative profitability of engaging in exportables versus domestic production (see figure 4).

The model represented by equations 2–5 and 8–11 is sufficiently simple for qualitative analysis. Its solution in log-differential form is given in the appendix, and comparative static solutions for typical parameter values are given below. The model can also be illustrated graphically. We do so below and show the effects of the shocks experienced by Cameroon, Côte d'Ivoire, and Senegal, as well as of the policy responses (import tariffs, export taxes, and changes in government expenditure). We restrict ourselves in the graphical analysis to the full-employment case, leaving the implications of wage rigidity for the multiplier analysis reported subsequently.

18. This assumption is subjected to sensitivity analysis. Appendix A formulates the model for the case where an exogenous fraction, m, of $\overline{G}$ is spent on imports.

Figure 4. *Equilibrium in the Dependent-Economy Model*

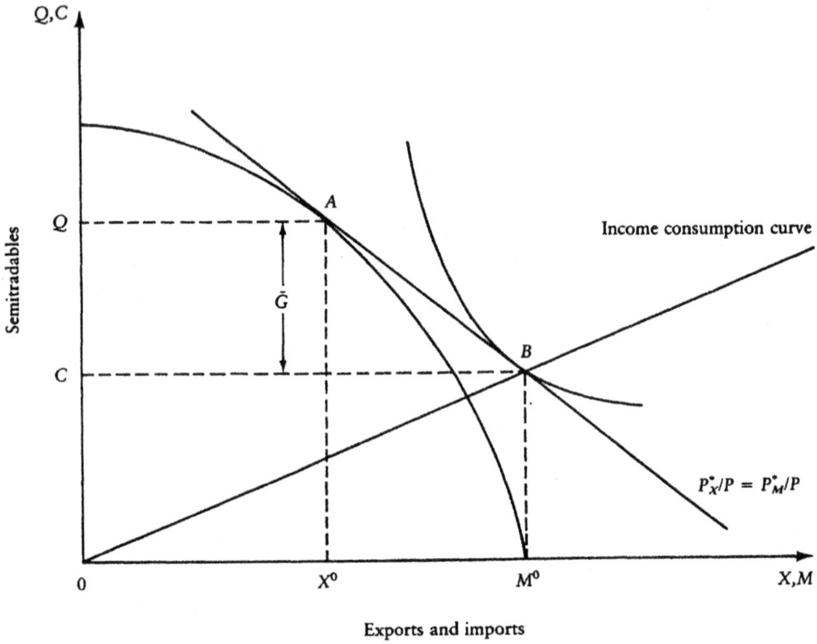

Graphical Analysis

Figure 4 portrays an equilibrium in the model for the full-employment case. Assume that export taxes and import tariffs are zero. Assume further that there are constant terms of trade, defined to equal 1 so that the price of imports equals that of exports: $P_M^* = P_X^*$. The production functions together with the full-employment condition imply that there is a well-behaved transformation frontier between X and Q, as shown. For a given price ratio P_X^*/P, production is determined at the point A, at which the slope of the tangent to the transformation frontier equals P_X^*/P. The private consumer's budget line is given by the line from the production point with slope P_M^*/P, which by assumption equals P_X^*/P, since $s = t = 0$. Private consumption is determined at the point B, where the indifference curve is tangent to this budget line. Equilibrium is defined as the price level, P, at which the production of the semitradable, Q, is exactly $\overline{G}$ units above private demand for the semitradable, C. The government budget deficit, which is here assumed to equal its consumption of semitradables, $\overline{G}$, is equal in value to the current account deficit, $OM_1 - OX$.

Now suppose an import tariff is imposed: $t > 0$. Holding P fixed, the consumer's budget line rotates clockwise (not drawn in figure 4) and is no longer equal to the producer budget line, as $P_M^*(1 + t)/P > P_X^*/P$. If the substitution effect dominates the income effect of the tariff, the demand for the semitradable, C, will rise and the relative price of the semitradable will have to rise to eliminate excess demand. In the new equilibrium, the income consumption curve (ICC) will rotate counterclockwise but by less than if P were to have remained unchanged.

In order to perform comparative statics exercises with this apparatus, it is useful first to describe the supply and demand curves for semitradables. This is done in figure 5, in which parts A–C are used to motivate the shape of the private demand curve, C, which is presented in parts D–F. For deriving total demand, we consider only cases of a budget deficit ($\overline{G} > 0$) so that the equilibrium production point on the transformation frontier is above the intersection point of the relevant income consumption curve with the budget line. As P rises, the slope of P_X^*/P flattens and Q rises. Hence, the supply curve of Q is upward-sloping. The slope of the demand curve depends on σ, the elasticity of substitution between imports and semitradables. Notice that for higher levels of P, not only does the slope of the consumer's budget line shift, but so does the point on the transformation frontier whence it is drawn. The latter represents the general equilibrium income effect while the slope rotation reflects the substitution effect. In equilibrium, the income effect of price changes for this nontraded good is not zero because the government buys a fixed amount of it, $\overline{G}$.

Now consider extreme elasticity values in parts A–C of figure 5. For $\sigma = 0$, the income-consumption paths for all prices are a unique ray through the origin. In this case, as P falls (the slope of the tangent gets steeper), private demand for Q declines. That is, the private demand curve for semitradables (C in figure 5D) is upward-sloping.[19] With $\sigma = 0$, there is no substitution effect; hence the general equilibrium income effect dominates. For values of $\sigma < 1$, the private demand curve will be upward-sloping. The intersection of C and Q in figure 5D is not an equilibrium, since exogenous government demand, $\overline{G}$, is not taken into account. Equilibrium is at the intersection of the demand curve for semitradables, $C + \overline{G}$, with the corresponding supply curve. By contrast, for very high values of σ (figure 5, parts C and F) small changes in prices bring about substantial changes in the income-consumption paths (recall that our indifference curves, being based on CES utility functions, are homothetic, so all income-consumption paths are rays through the origin). In this case, the substitution effect dominates, so that demand for Q rises as P declines and the demand curve is downward-sloping (figure 5F). When $\sigma = 1$, the income and substitution effects cancel each other and the demand curve is vertical (figure 5,

19. In the case of a budget surplus $\overline{G} < 0$, the demand curve for Q would be downward-sloping.

Figure 5. *Comparative Statics in the Dependent-Economy Model*

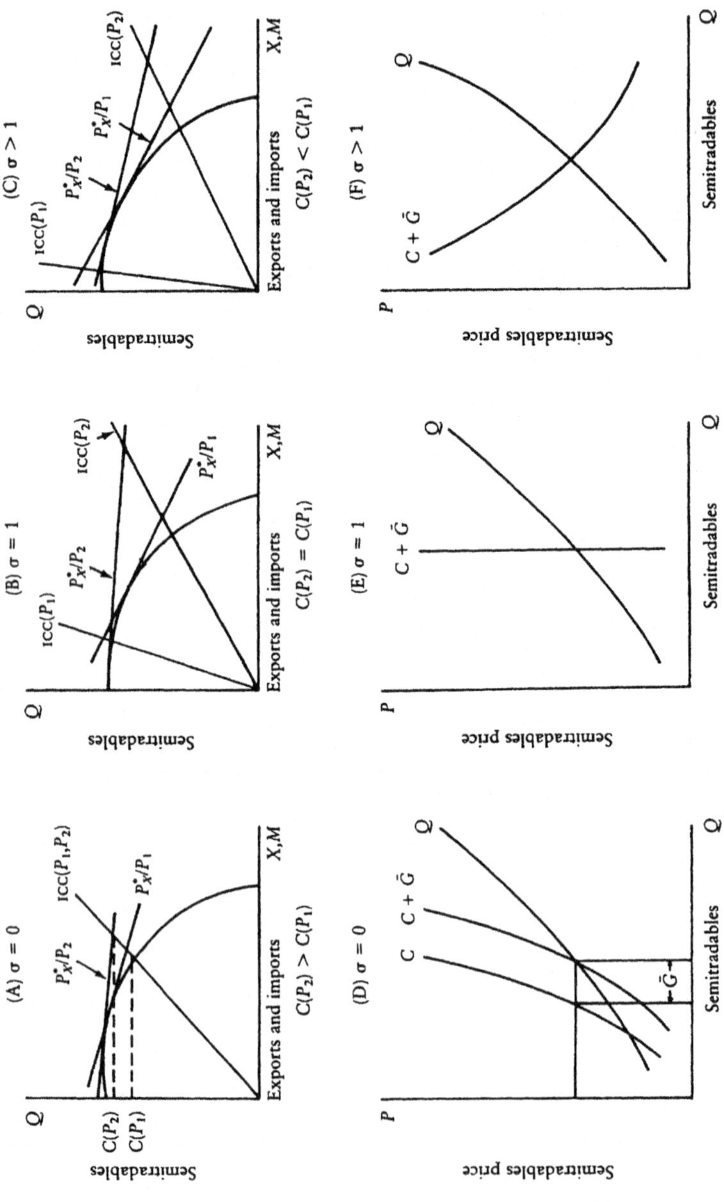

Note: $P_2 > P_1$

parts B and E).[20] Hence the demand curve is upward- or downward-sloping depending on the elasticity of substitution between imports and semitradables.

With this apparatus, we are able to anticipate much of the comparative statics multiplier results for different values of σ reported below. First, an increase in G always leads to an increase in P (and hence a real exchange rate appreciation). Whether or not the demand curve is downward-sloping, a rightward shift will raise P.

Second, the impact of a tariff increase is asymmetric depending on the elasticity of substitution. The effect of an increase in t is to make the slope of the consumer's budget line steeper in figure 4. As explained earlier, if the income effect dominates, this leads to lower demand for semitradables and imports (a decline in C and M), that is, when $\sigma < 1$. In turn, this implies that the demand curve in figure 5D shifts to the *left* so that P falls. In the extreme case where $\sigma = 0$, imports are noncompetitive so that a tariff is equivalent to a consumption tax. By contrast, if $\sigma > 1$, the tariff lowers M but raises C, causing the demand curve in figure 5F to shift to the right, raising P. Whether or not P declines, an increase in the tariff rate lowers the current account deficit. This is because we assumed no private borrowing. If the private sector always balances its budget, the increased tariff revenues contribute one-for-one toward reversing the government's deficit, and therefore the trade deficit.

Third, the same mechanism is at work for a favorable terms-of-trade shock (an increase in P_X^*). It will improve or worsen the current account deficit depending on the value of σ. This can be explained by observing that the effect of an increase in P_X^* is to shift the supply curve for Q to the left as producers move into production of exports, X. In addition, the demand curve for Q shifts to the right (the general equilibrium income effect). For low σ, this can lead to an increase in P and Q. If Q rises, X must fall, given the shape of the transformation frontier. Moreover, as P is higher, demand for M is greater. The higher M and lower X lead to an unambiguous increase in the current account deficit. For high σ, the substitution effect dominates and consumers demand less Q, thus releasing resources to the exportable sector and yielding an improvement in the current account deficit.

Finally, the effect of an increase in the export tax, s, is to shift the supply curves of semitradables in figure 5 to the *right*. Since exporting is less profitable, resources shift to semitradables. This always implies a decline in P. For $\sigma < 1$ (as in figure 5D) this shift also causes Q to decline, implying an increase in X. When $\sigma > 1$, the impact on X is in the opposite direction. In both cases, P declines. Moreover, the current account deficit improves because of the increased public revenues from the tax rise.

Adjustment with Rigidity: Parametric Analysis

We now supplement the graphical analysis with multiplier calculations derived from solving the model under different demand and supply elasticities and the

20. Note that, as drawn, figure 5B–F shows that for P private demand exceeds supply of the semitradable. Hence P will not be an equilibrium.

three different assumptions about labor market behavior embodied in equations 5, 6, and 7. Since the elasticity of substitution in demand between imports and the semitradable is an important parameter, we start with a systematic variation of σ under the three model variants. This allows us to examine simultaneously the influence of relative price rigidity and inflexibility in demand and supply.

For all calculations, we take as a starting point a small government sector in total expenditures (that is, a small budget deficit) and a small external deficit. Government expenditures are 5 percent of total expenditures, foreign exchange revenues are 95 percent of foreign exchange expenditures, and initial tariff and export taxes are 25 percent and 10 percent, respectively. These parameter values are roughly representative of the initial situation in the three countries.

Figure 6 displays the multipliers for the current account, F, and the real exchange rate, RER, where the plotted values are percentage changes in F and RER for a 1 percent change in the selected instrument (for example, the import tariff) or exogenous variable (for example, the terms of trade) under different values of σ.[21]

Starting with the current account multipliers, for a given government expenditure increase, the more elastic is domestic demand (that is, the higher the value of σ) the less is the real exchange rate appreciation and hence the smaller is the corresponding increase in the current account deficit (figure 6). The flexible wage, full-employment case lies between the two fixed wage cases. When the wage is fixed with respect to the world price of imports, the semitradable sector can expand without limit, offsetting the decline in the current account. Fixing the real wage in semitradables curtails its supply response, which raises the value of the current account multiplier. Sensitivity analysis with the assumption that all government spending is on semitradables reveals that this conclusion is qualitatively robust. If 20 percent of government spending is on imports, the full-employment deficit multiplier ranges from 3.7 to 3.4 as σ ranges from 0.2 to 100.

Besides a first-round positive impact on the current account, an improvement in the terms of trade raises real income, which contributes to an increase in the current account deficit. Recall from the earlier comparative statics discussion of a terms-of-trade shift, however, that for low values of σ an improvement in the terms of trade is likely to lead to a rise in P and an increase in Q. As shown in figure 5D, for low values of σ, the income effect dominates the substitution effect. P rises, attracting labor out of the cash crop sector (except when the wage is fixed in terms of semitradables). Regardless of supply response there will be a shift in consumption toward imports. Both effects work to raise the current account deficit. Thus when the price elasticity of demand for imports is low, the current account will deteriorate when the terms of trade improve (figure 6). For the initial conditions chosen here, the multiplier changes sign for values of σ around 2 except for the case when the wage is tied to the numeraire (P^*_M), which increases

21. Multipliers for the other endogenous variables are omitted since these variables were not discussed in the case studies.

Figure 6. *Current Account Multipliers*

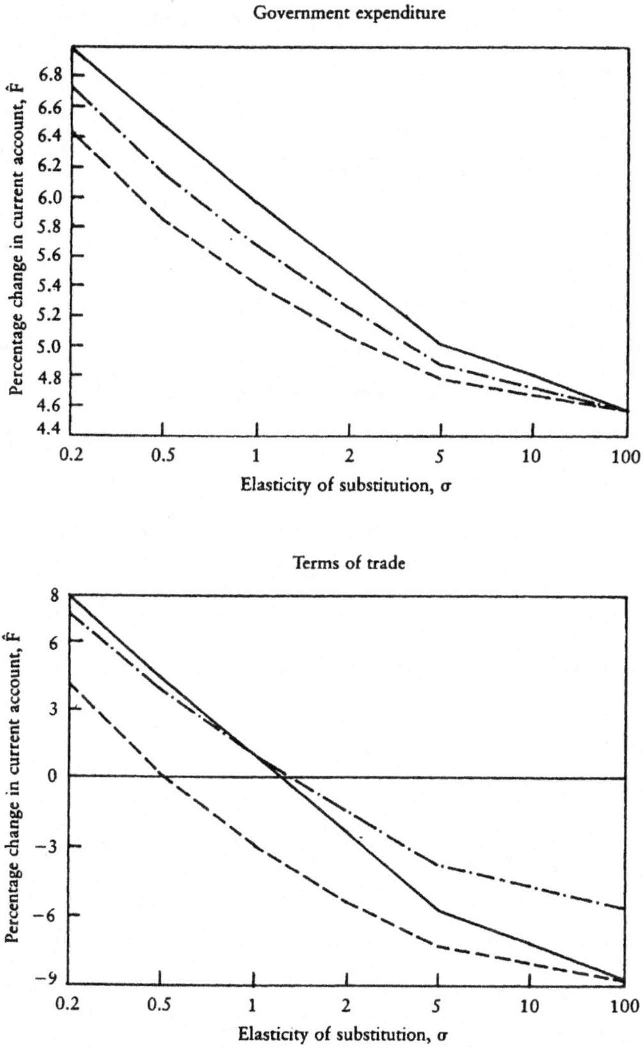

Figure 6 *(continued)*

Import tariff

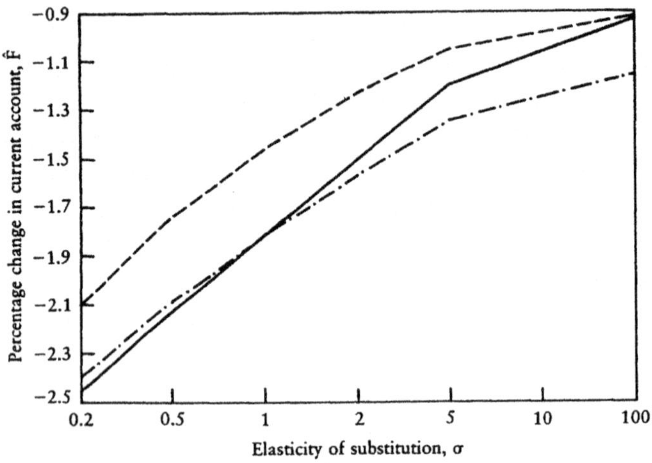

Export tax rate

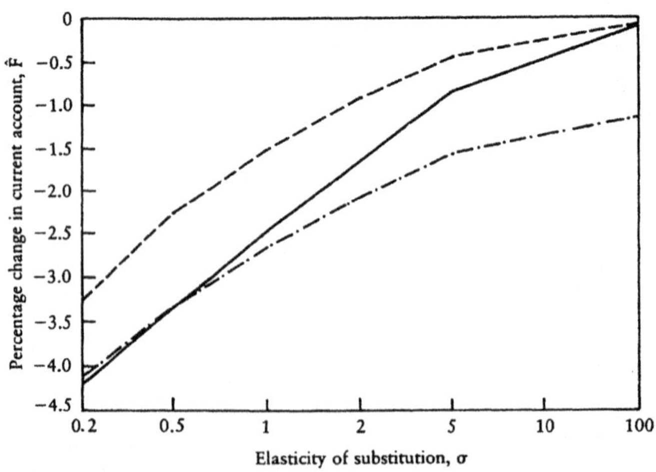

Key: —·— flexible wage, full employment; – – – fixed wage, $P_M^*(1 + t)$; —— fixed wage, P.

Note: Multipliers are defined as the percentage change in $F = \hat{F} = P_M^* M - P_X^* X$ for a 1 percent change in the corresponding exogenous variable (for example, the import tariff).

supply response. This in turn contributes to a smaller current account deficit and hence to switching at a lower value of σ.

Multiplier values with respect to export taxes and import tariffs (figure 6) should be viewed together since they are alternative instruments for achieving expenditure switching toward semitradables.[22] Raising a tariff reduces the current account deficit both because it increases government revenues and because it lowers imports. The reduction in imports is much lower than the tariff increase, so that tariff revenues always rise. However, this positive effect is mitigated by the resource shift out of cash crops into semitradables as demand shifts out of imports. In addition, with the quantity of government purchases fixed, the higher semitradable price increases total government expenditures and thus the current account deficit.

An increase in export taxes also raises government revenues and hence reduces the budget deficit. Although exports decline, the net effect is an increase in revenues from this source. It appears from the multipliers in figure 6 that an export tax is a more potent instrument than an import tariff in reducing a current account deficit, even though we assume an infinite foreign elasticity of demand for cash crop exports. This is because the current account is endogenous in our model. If the current account were fixed, then Lerner symmetry would prevail and an import tariff would be equivalent to an export tax. The two multipliers do converge to the same value as $\sigma \rightarrow \infty$ because, in this case, $\hat{F} \rightarrow 0$ and we approximate balanced trade at the margin. However, for finite values of σ, especially in the plausible range $0.5 < \sigma < 2$, the export tax dominates the import tariff because of its impact on P. An export tax increase releases resources to the semitradable sector, increasing the latter's competitiveness and thereby lowering the deficit. By contrast, an import tariff, by increasing demand for semitradables, bids up P, which counters the favorable impact of the increased tariff revenues on the deficit. In sum, raising the export tax lowers the level of exports, but the revenue effects—in reducing the government deficit—are sufficiently strong to result in an improvement in the current account deficit.

The above analysis can be used to shed light on another issue of current interest to CFA zone members. Since they cannot devalue the nominal exchange rate, some zone members (Côte d'Ivoire and Senegal in particular) have introduced an import tariff combined with an export subsidy to "simulate" a real depreciation. In our framework, this amounts to combining the effects of the import tariff and a negative export tax. Our results show that, if the current account deficit were due to a fiscal deficit, such a tariff-cum-subsidy scheme may not have the desired effect. First, to the extent that the scheme is not revenue-neutral, it will affect the current account deficit, possibly in a perverse manner. Second, even if the scheme were revenue-neutral, it would not be "deficit neutral," given the effect on the semitradable price. Unless government spending is also reduced, the tariff-cum-

22. The export tax rate is defined as a positive number. Hence an increase in the export tax is defined as a positive number. See appendix B.

subsidy scheme can worsen the current account deficit and appreciate the real exchange rate.

In comparing the impact of various tax and subsidy schemes, we are not addressing the question of allocative efficiency or its analog, consumer welfare. An export tax or import tariff may improve the deficit, but what does it do to welfare? To answer this, an explicit welfare function must be introduced, which is somewhat problematic in our model which has separate government expenditure and a non-zero trade deficit. The only result we can claim is that, if the welfare function were that implied by the demand system in equation 4, then the welfare maximizing tax to raise a given level of revenue would be an export tax rate of zero, combined with an import tariff and domestic tax on semitradables at equal positive rates. This is a special case of the result of Diamond and Mirrlees (1971) and is one of the recommendations in Shalizi and Squire (1986) for tax policy in Sub-Saharan Africa.

Real exchange rate multipliers appear in figure 7. Their interpretation is straightforward. As $\sigma \rightarrow \infty$, the domestic relative price of semitradables becomes determined by the fixed world price. Multiplier values approach zero, regardless of labor market assumptions. Also labor market assumptions do not affect multiplier values significantly in the range $0.5 < \sigma < 2$. Finally, several of the tariff and terms-of-trade multipliers change sign at $\sigma = 1$ for reasons associated with the slope of the demand curve in figure 5.

We conclude with estimates of the likely range of real exchange rate and current account multipliers. The range is derived by assigning share parameters in the production functions that bracket the range of cash crop and manufacturing sector supply elasticities in the literature which we summarize in appendix C. This is done for the flexible wage model, which is also likely to be more representative of labor market behavior in CFA countries. The multipliers are displayed in table 1 for two sets of values for m, the import share of government expenditure.

How do these figures relate to the adjustment experience of Cameroon, Côte d'Ivoire, and Senegal? Consider first the multipliers displayed in table 1 resulting from a terms-of-trade improvement with and without increases in government spending and export taxation. The figures suggest that terms-of-trade improvements will result in real exchange rate appreciation if one considers the more realistic low-elasticity case. This appreciation will be dampened by windfall taxation but is nonetheless likely to prevail. Contrast the experience of Cameroon and Côte d'Ivoire. Even though export taxes were raised in Côte d'Ivoire, government spending was increased sharply and real exchange rate appreciation occurred. By contrast Cameroon avoided real exchange rate appreciation by avoiding increases in government spending and by taxing the windfall gain.

Now consider the adjustment phase that corresponds to the need to reduce external financing. This was the situation facing Côte d'Ivoire in the early 1980s. In the absence of devaluation, expenditure switching can be achieved in principle by a combination of decreases in export taxes and government spending and

Figure 7. ***Real Exchange Rate Multipliers***

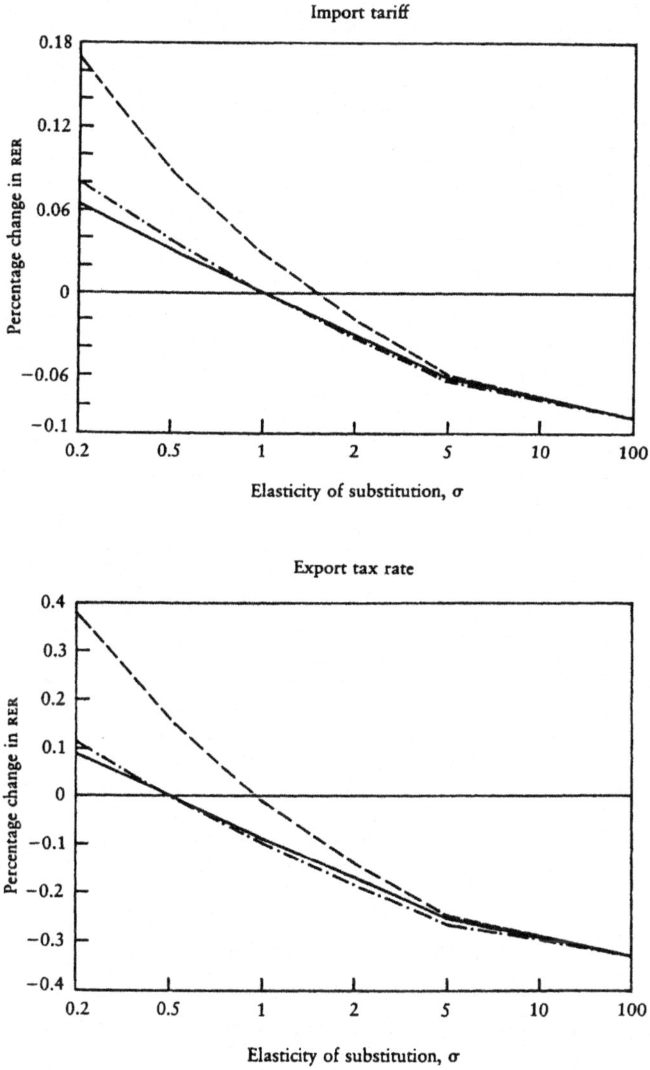

Figure 7 *(continued)*

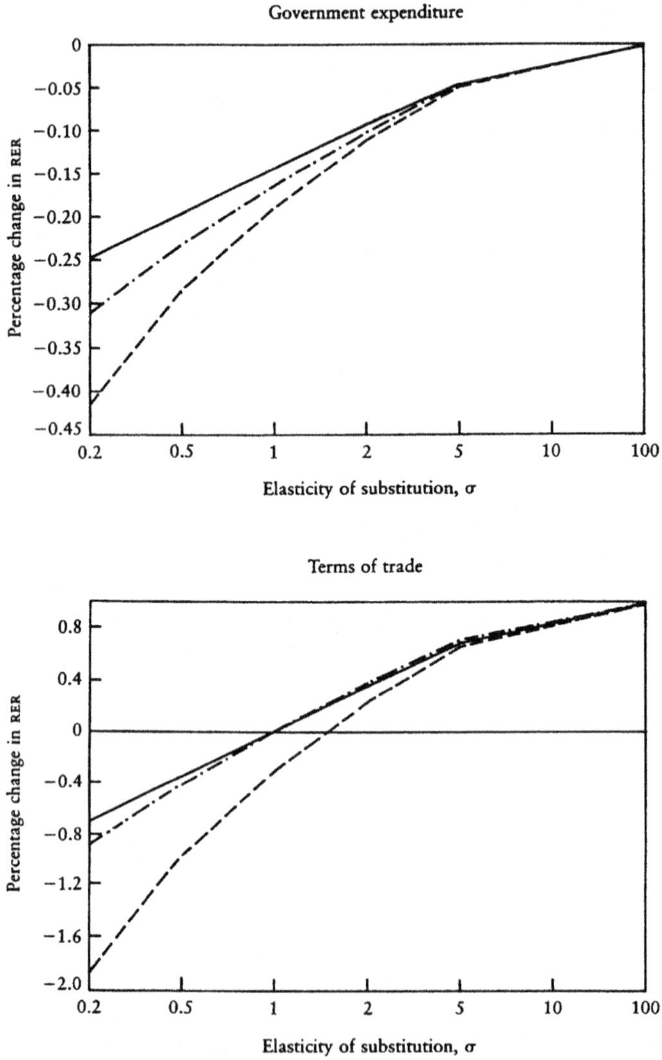

Key: —·— flexible wage, full employment; – – – –fixed wage, $P_M^*(1 + t)$; —— fixed wage, *P*.

Note: Multipliers are defined as the percentage change in the real exchange rate RER = $(P_X^*(1 - s)/P)$ for a 1 percent change in the corresponding exogenous variable (for example, the import tariff).

Table 1. *Multipliers under Different Elasticities of Supply and Demand*

	Low elasticities[a]				*High elasticities*[b]			
	Real exchange rate		*Current account deficit*		*Real exchange rate*		*Current account deficit*	
	$m = 0$	$m = 0.2$	$m = 0$	$m = 0.2$	$m = 0$	$m = 0.2$	$m = 0$	$m = 0.2$
Terms of trade	−1.7	−0.6	4.9	2.9	0.3	0.3	−1.7	−2.4
Government expenditure	−0.4	−0.1	6.7	5.5	−0.1	0.0	5.3	5.1
Export tax	0.0	0.0	−3.3	−3.0	−0.1	−0.1	−2.0	−1.8
Import tariff	0.1	0.1	−2.2	−2.1	0.0	0.0	−1.6	−1.6

Note: See appendix C for definition and derivation of parameters ϕ and Ω, which stand for supply elasticities in agriculture and semitradable sectors, respectively; m is the share of government expenditure that is imported.

a. $\sigma = 0.5$; $\phi = 0.14$; $\Omega = 0.2$.

b. $\sigma = 2.0$; $\phi = 1.7$; $\Omega = 0.85$.

increases in tariffs. However, in the low-elasticity case, changes in export taxes have no effect on the real exchange rate, whereas when the elasticity is high, import tariffs become an ineffective instrument. Nevertheless, increases in export taxes are a more effective way of reducing the external deficit than increases in tariffs even when the supply elasticity in the cash crop sector is low. Reduction in the government deficit has the highest multiplier value on the current account and is not very sensitive to the range of elasticities considered. Note finally that the results are robust to variations in the import content of government expenditure, signifying that it is the size of the budget, rather than its composition, that is crucial.

III. Determinants of the Current Account and Real Exchange Rates

The case studies as well as the model results suggest some fundamental determinants of the current account and the real exchange rate for CFA zone countries. Therefore, we conclude with a statistical analysis of the current account and real exchange rate in the three countries. Ideally, econometric analysis would proceed from full-information estimation of a structural simultaneous equation model of the current account and the real exchange rate. Unfortunately, not enough restrictions can be imposed on the model in section II for it to be identified. Availability of time series data for the three countries imposes further limitations. These considerations lead us to concentrate on reduced form estimation for the current account and the real exchange rate. Since our model suggests that these two variables are jointly and endogenously determined, neither variable is included in the estimation equation of the other.

The results from estimating the current account and real exchange rate equations appear in tables 2 and 3. For the current account equation, the dependent variable is the current account surplus over GDP, $(X - M)$/GDP, and the regressors with expected signs are the public sector surplus, [PUBDR = $(GR - GE)$/GDP](+); real national income growth, DLNY(−); the manufacturing

Table 2. *Determinants of the Current Account (CAR)*

Country and years		PUBDR (+)	DLNY (−)	WR (−)	DV (−)	$\bar{R}^2$	DW	χ^2 (prob)	ρ(−1)
	1a	0.8	−26.0		−1.6	0.99	1.6	13.7	−0.4
Côte d'Ivoire,		(2.4)**	(2.5)**		(0.7)			(0.13)	(1.5)
1965–84	1b	0.9	−19.1	0.0		0.99	1.7	10.5	−0.4
		(2.8)**	(2.5)**	(0.0)				(0.40)	(1.6)
	2a	1.1	20.6		−3.3	0.99	2.2	9.5	−0.3
Senegal,		(4.2)***	(2.5)**		(4.9)***			(0.22)	(1.6)
1965–83	2b	1.2	18.9	0.1	−5.8	0.99	2.1	5.9	(−0.3)
		(5.2)***	(2.2)**	(2.1)**	(4.2)***			(0.54)	(1.4)
	3a	0.7	20.9		−0.3	0.92	1.9	7.5	−0.4
Cameroon,		(4.6)***	(5.2)***		(0.3)			(0.58)	(1.8)
1965–83	3b	0.7	20.7	0.0		0.93	2.0	9.9	−0.3
		(4.5)***	(5.4)***	(1.2)				(0.45)	(1.5)

***Significance at 1 percent level.
**Significance at 5 percent level.
*Significance at 10 percent level.

Note: Expected signs of the variables are given under each column heading in parentheses. Definition of variables (also see text): CAR = $(X - M)$/GDP; PUBDR = $(GR - GE)$/GDP; DLNY = first difference of natural logarithm of real national income; WR = real manufacturing wage; DV = dummy variable (set to 1 for 1974–85). Estimation: Ordinary least squares with first-order correction for autocorrelation after data deflation to remove heteroskedasticity. χ^2 is White's (1980) statistic for H_0: $E(u_t^2) = \sigma^2$; value in parentheses is prob > χ^2. The expression ρ(−1) is the estimated value for the first-order autoregressive process. Intercepts omitted.

sector real wage, $WR(-)$; and a dummy variable, DV, taking a value of 1 for 1974 and beyond, zero otherwise. Since we do not report values for the intercept, a negative (positive) sign for DV implies a smaller (larger) current account surplus for the post-1973 period. The χ^2 statistic is White's (1980) joint test for misspecification and heteroskedasticity. Hence, the relatively low values of the statistic in table 2 are reassuring as they suggest both low heteroskedasticity and no serious misspecification.[23]

The results indicate that public sector deficits consistently exerted pressure on the current account in the three countries, supporting the model of section II. Real income growth also contributed to the worsening external position in Côte d'Ivoire but not in Senegal, where to the contrary the current account improved with income growth. This is not surprising since Senegal suffered from droughts which in turn hampered export earnings. The positive influence of income growth on the current account of Cameroon is also to be expected from the impact of the oil discovery. The regressions also show a marked deterioration of the average current account deficit after 1974 for Côte d'Ivoire and Senegal in comparison with the earlier period. Finally, the real wage variable does not enter significantly.

23. χ^2 values are final values after correction for heteroskedasticity. We corrected for heteroskedasticity by assuming a mixed form, that is, $E(u_t^2) = \alpha_1 + \alpha_2 Z_t$ where we chose the logarithm of real income as instrument to regress on the residuals. Estimated values of this regression were then used as deflators.

Table 3. *Determinants of the Real Exchange Rate Multiplier (RER)*

Country and years		*PUBDR* (+)	*TOT* (−)	*CONCR* (−)	*DV* (−)	$\bar{R}^2$	*DW*	χ^2 *(prob)*	$\rho(-1)$
Côte d'Ivoire, 1965–84	1a	0.7	−0.5		2.0	1.0	1.8	16.7	−0.2
		(2.6)**	(9.7)***		(2.0)*			(0.05)	(0.8)
	1b	−0.9		−7.5		0.99	1.6	11.3	−0.5
		(1.5)		(1.8)*				(0.08)	(2.7)
Senegal, 1961–83	2a	2.7	−0.0		−1.8	0.99	1.9	11.6	−0.3
		(3.2)***	(0.4)		(0.6)			(0.23)	(1.4)
	2b	2.8		2.0	−2.4	0.99	1.9	10.9	−0.3
		(3.4)***		(1.0)	(0.9)			(0.28)	(1.5)
Cameroon, 1965–83	3a	0.0	0.1		3.1	0.99	1.2	16.0	−0.7
		(0.1)	(2.7)**		(0.7)			(0.06)	(4.0)
	3b	0.2		1.2	−2.4	0.99	1.1	16.3	−0.7
		(0.6)		(0.5)	(0.4)			(0.06)	(3.9)

***Significance at 1 percent level.
**Significance at 5 percent level.
*Significance at 10 percent level.

Note: Expected signs of the variables are given under each column heading in parentheses. Definition of variables (also see table 2 and text): RER = ratio of agriculture and manufacturing price indexes to construction and services price indexes; PUBDR = see table 2; TOT = ratio of indexes of exports to imports; CONCR = official development assistance/GDP; DV = same as table 2. Estimation: Ordinary least squares with first-order correction for autocorrelation after data deflation to remove heteroskedasticity. χ^2 is White's (1980) statistic for H_0: $E(u_t^2) = \sigma^2$; value in parentheses is prob > χ^2. The expression $\rho(-1)$ is the estimated value for the first-order autoregressive process. Intercepts omitted.

This is not surprising since the wage series only pertains to manufacturing and had to be constructed from incomplete data.

Turning to the results from the real exchange rate equation estimations in table 3, the results are more mixed as misspecification and/or heteroskedasticity is present in most equations. Two new variables are introduced, concessionary lending/GDP, CONCR(−), and the terms of trade, TOT(−). For example, for Côte d'Ivoire, much of the variation is captured by the intercept. Though to a lesser degree, this also occurs for other equation estimates, probably suggesting that our measure of the real exchange rate index which corresponds closely to our model (namely the relative price of agriculture and manufacturing)[24] is inaccurately measured. However, the significantly negative value for the dummy variable in the equations for Senegal confirms a sharp real exchange rate appreciation after 1974, as government policy and droughts combined to sustain a deteriorating external balance.

IV. Conclusions

This article has addressed the theme of medium-term macroeconomic adjustment with a fixed exchange rate in three countries in the CFA zone: Cameroon,

24. Similar results were obtained when tradables were confined to agriculture. We do not include estimated equations with the real manufacturing wage, *WR*, as that variable was usually not significant.

Côte d'Ivoire, and Senegal. We showed how different adjustment responses to similar shocks took place in the three countries. In Cameroon, despite improved terms of trade and windfall gains from the oil price hike of the late 1970s, the government avoided real exchange rate appreciation by restraining public expenditure and sterilizing most of the foreign exchange gains. The real exchange rate was also stabilized by taxing the proceeds of coffee and cocoa exports during the boom and then raising producer prices when the boom was over. By contrast, Côte d'Ivoire expanded public sector investment, financing it partly by external borrowing. The real exchange rate appreciated and manufacturing sector competitiveness fell sharply for some time until adjustment to the growing external deficit took place. In Senegal, public sector subsidies continued to be financed by taxation of exports so the real exchange rate depreciation needed after successive droughts did not occur. The government remained in deficit and adjustment was postponed. Unlike Cameroon, therefore, neither Senegal nor the Côte d'Ivoire achieved the real exchange rate depreciation called for by adverse terms of trade and output trends.

We developed a stylized dependent-economy model to show the relationship between the instruments of adjustment (tariffs, taxes, and government expenditure) and the associated targets (the real exchange rate and the current account deficit). This model was then used to illustrate the combination of current account deficits and real exchange rate changes resulting from a terms-of-trade shock and different government expenditure patterns. The model also highlighted the implications for the real exchange rate of changes in taxation of cash crops and in restrictions on imports.

Finally, we used reduced-form estimation to analyze the determinants of the real exchange rate and current account in the three countries. The results indicate that a small number of variables explain a great part of the real exchange rate and current account variations in the three countries over the period 1963–85. Although a structural model corresponding to the stylized model would need to be estimated to explore further its usefulness, the reduced-form results are consistent with the model in the text, reinforcing the significance of the public sector deficit as a determinant of current account deficits and the real exchange rate in the countries analyzed.

APPENDIX A. SYMBOLS USED IN THE TEXT

C = private demand for semitradables
CA = current account, expressed as percent of GDP
e = exchange rate, assumed fixed; units chosen to set e = unity
F = foreign borrowing (conducted by government only); also equal to the fiscal deficit and the current account deficit
g = government; public sector
$\overline{G}$ = total government expenditures (semitradables only in initial presentation)
I_i = investment; $i = \{g,p\}$
L_j = labor employed in sector j; $j = \{1, 2\}$
m = share of government expenditure composed of imports
M = private demand for imports
p = private sector
P^*_X = world price of the export sector product
P = domestic semitradables price
P^*_M = world import price (exogenous; the numeraire)
Q = output of semitradables
s = ad valorem export tax rate
S_i = savings; $i = \{g,p\}$
t = ad valorem tariff rate
W = wage rate
X = output of export sector (cash crops only)
α = share of payments to labor in export sector production
β = share of payments to labor in semitradables production
Ω = supply elasticity of semitradable sector
σ = elasticity of substitution in demand between semitradables and imports
ϕ = supply elasticity of agriculture
1 = primary sector
2 = semitradables sector

APPENDIX B. SOLUTION OF THE MODEL

The model considered in the main text is repeated here for convenience in level form. Exogenous variables are indicated with a bar and parameters with Greek letters (except P^*_X, which is a parameter labeled thus for clarity). The equations describing the full employment version are

(A-1) $$X = \overline{A}L_1^{\alpha}$$

(A-2) $$Q = \overline{B}L_2^{\beta}$$

(A-3) $$\frac{C}{M} = K\left(\frac{P^*_M(1 + t)\overline{e}}{P}\right)^{\sigma}$$

(A-4) $$L_1 + L_2 = \overline{L}$$

(A-5) $$\alpha P_X^*(1 - s)\bar{e}\overline{A}L_1^{\alpha-1} = \beta P\overline{B}L_2^{\beta-1}$$

(A-6) $$Q = C + \overline{G}(1 - m)$$

(A-7) $$\bar{e}[F + tP_M^*M + sP_X^*]X = (1 - m)\,P\overline{G} + mP_M^*\overline{G}$$

(A-8) $$P_M^*(M + m\overline{G}) = P_X^*\,X + F.$$

This is a system of eight equations with the following eight endogenous variables: Q, M, X, C, L_1, L_2, P, and F. Exogenous policy variables are $\overline{G}$, t, s, and m, the fraction of government expenditures spent on imports. The terms of trade represented by P_X^* are also considered exogenous. The model is homogeneous of degree zero in all prices and the exchange rate, so we select $P_M^* = 1$ as numeraire and by choice of units we choose $\bar{e} = 1$. Thus, a terms-of-trade change will come from changes in the exogenous export price, P_X^*. When the wage is fixed in terms of the domestic price of the import good, equation A-4 is replaced by $W/[P_M^*(1 + t)\bar{e}] = \overline{W}$ and when it is fixed in terms of the price of the semitradable, P, equation A-4 is replaced by $W/P = \overline{W}$.

Log-differentiation of the above system of equations yields the following (where $\hat{Z} \equiv dZ/Z$):

(B-1) $$\hat{X} = \alpha\hat{L}_1$$

(B-2) $$\hat{Q} = \beta\hat{L}_2$$

(B-3) $$\hat{C} - \hat{M} = \sigma(\hat{\tau} - \hat{P})$$

(B-4) $$\lambda\hat{L}_1 + (1 - \lambda)\hat{L}_2 = 0$$

(B-5) $$\hat{P}_X^* + \hat{\zeta} + (\alpha - 1)\,\hat{L}_1 = \hat{P} + (\beta - 1)\hat{L}_2$$

(B-6) $$\gamma\hat{G} + (1 - \gamma)\hat{C} = \hat{Q}$$

(B-7) $$\mu_3\hat{F} + \mu_1(\hat{t} + \hat{M}) + \mu_2\,(\hat{s} + \hat{P}_X^* + \hat{X}) = (1 - \theta)\hat{P} + \hat{G}$$

(B-8) $$\hat{M} + \rho\hat{G} = \delta(\hat{P}_X^* + \hat{X}) + (1 - \delta)\hat{F}$$

where

$$\hat{\tau} = \frac{t}{1 + t}\hat{t}$$

$$\lambda = \frac{L_1}{L_1 + L_2}$$

$$\hat{\zeta} = \frac{-s}{1 - s}\hat{s}$$

$$\gamma = \frac{\overline{G}}{\overline{G} + C}$$

$$\mu_1 = \frac{tM}{mP_M^*\overline{G}},\ \mu_2 = \frac{sP_X^*X}{mP_M^*\overline{G}},\ \text{and}\ \mu_3 = 1 - \mu_1 - \mu_2$$

$$\delta = \frac{P_X^*X}{P_M^*(M + m\overline{G})}$$

$$\theta = \frac{mP_M^*\overline{G}}{(1-m)P\overline{G} + mP_M^*\overline{G}}$$

$$\rho = \frac{m\overline{G}}{M + m\overline{G}}.$$

When $W/(P_M^*[1 + t]) = \overline{W}$, B-4 becomes $\hat{W} = \hat{\tau}$, and when $W/P = \overline{W}$, B-4 becomes $\hat{W} = \hat{P}$.

Note from the definition of the parameters that an increase in the tariff rate implies an increase in $\hat{\tau}$ but that an increase in the export tax implies a *decrease* in $\hat{\zeta}$.

Combining B-1, B-2, B-4, and B-5 gives us the following output supply elasticities for the export and semitradables sectors:

(B-9) $$\hat{X} = \phi\,(\hat{P}_X^* - \hat{P} + \hat{\zeta})$$

(B-9′) $$\hat{X} = \phi^*\,(\hat{P}_X^* + \hat{\zeta})$$

(B-10) $$\hat{Q} = \Omega\,(\hat{P} - \hat{P}_X^* - \hat{\zeta})$$

(B-10′) $$Q = \Omega^*\,\hat{P}$$

where

$$\phi = \frac{\alpha\,(1-\lambda)}{\lambda(1 - \beta) + (1 - \lambda)(1 - \alpha)};\ \phi^* = \frac{\alpha}{1 - \alpha}$$

and

$$\Omega = \frac{\lambda\beta}{\alpha(1 - \lambda)}\,\phi \geq 0;\ \Omega^* = \frac{\beta}{1 - \beta}.$$

In the above expressions, an asterisk denotes the value of the parameter for the case when the wage is fixed in terms of $P_M^*\,(1 + t)$. Similar expressions can be derived for the case when the wage is fixed in terms of P. Expressions B-9 and B-10 show that an increase in the relative price of the semitradable ($\hat{P} > 0$) elicits a positive supply response for the semitradable sector and that an increase in the export tax ($\hat{\zeta} < 0$) decreases the supply of the cash crop sector.

The model is solved by matrix inversion. Letting $\hat{Y}$ and $\hat{Z}$ denote the vectors of endogenous and exogenous variables respectively and A and B the corresponding coefficient matrixes, the multipliers are obtained as

$$\hat{Y} = A^{-1}\,B\,\hat{Z}.$$

Appendix C. Parameters for Model Simulation

The parameter values used to calculate the multipliers in table 1 are

Low case	*High case*
$\sigma = 0.50$	2.0
$\alpha = 0.40$	0.8
$\beta = 0.30$	0.6
$\lambda = 0.40$	0.4
$\gamma = 0.05$	0.05
$\mu_1 = 0.40$	0.4
$\mu_2 = 0.40$	0.4
$\mu_3 = 0.20$	0.2
$\delta = 0.95$	0.95
$t = 0.10$	0.10
$s = 0.25$	0.25

The parameter values for the multipliers reported in figures 6 and 7 are the same except that $\alpha = 0.6$, $\beta = 0.4$, and $\lambda = 0.5$.

The parameter values for α, β, and λ are chosen to calibrate supply elasticities. In agriculture, the range is $0.4 < \phi < 1.7$ and in manufacturing $0.2 < \Omega < 0.85$. Berthelemy and Morrison (1985) report the following supply elasticities for agriculture from estimation of a Nerlovian production function (t-values in parentheses): Cameroon: 0.8 (3.2); Côte d'Ivoire: 0.4 (3.3); Senegal: 0.2 (1.4). Their results are statistically more significant than those reported in Bond (1983) and for the most part fall within the range of elasticities implied by our parameter choice. The crops included in their analysis are export crops: Cameroon (cocoa, coffee, cotton); Côte d'Ivoire (cocoa, cotton); Senegal (groundnuts, cotton). Berthelemy and Morrisson also find a statistically significant elasticity of agricultural supply to manufacturing output (elasticities around 0.4) which is consistent with our full employment formulation in which ϕ depends on β.

In other calculations reported in Castillo, Devarajan, Jakobeit, and de Melo (1986), we also varied the share of labor in semitradables. The resulting supply elasticities have a wider range of values, but the qualitative implications of the multiplier analysis remain unchanged.

References

Ahamed, L. 1985. "Stabilization Policies in Developing Countries." *World Bank Research Observer* 1, no. 1: 79–110.

Berthelemy, T. C., and C. Morrisson. 1985. "Offre de Biens Manufactures et Production Agricole." Paris: OECD. Processed.

Bhatia, R. 1985. *The West African Monetary Union: An Analytical Survey.* Washington, D.C.: International Monetary Fund Occasional Paper 35.

Bond, M. 1983. "Agricultural Responses to Prices in Sub-Saharan African Countries." *IMF Staff Papers* 30, no. 4: 703–26.

Bruno, M. 1976. "The Two-Sector Model and the Real Exchange Rate." *American Economic Review* 66, no. 4: 566–77.

Castillo, G., S. Devarajan, C. Jakobeit, and J. de Melo. 1986. "Growth and Adjustment in an African Monetary Union: The CFA Franc Zone." Washington, D.C.: Development Research Department, World Bank. Processed.

Corden, W. 1977. *Inflation, Exchange Rates, and the World Economy*. Chicago: University of Chicago Press.

Davies, J. M. 1983. "The Economic Effects of Windfall Gains in Export Earnings, 1975–78." *World Development* 11, no. 1: 119–39.

Devarajan, S., and J. de Melo. Forthcoming. "Evaluating Participation in African Monetary Unions: A Statistical Analysis of the CFA Zone." *World Development*.

Diamond, P., and J. Mirrlees. 1971. "Optimal Taxation and Public Production: I and II." *American Economic Review* 61: 8–27, 261–78.

Dornbusch, R. 1980. *Open Economy Macroeconomics*. New York: Basic Books.

Guillaumont, P., and S. Guillaumont. 1984. *Zone Franc et Developpement Africain*. Paris: *Economica*.

Jones, R. 1974. "Trade with Non-Traded Goods: The Anatomy of Interconnected Markets." *Economica* 41: 121–38.

Jones, R., and W. Corden. 1976. "Devaluation, Non-Flexible Prices, and the Trade Balance for a Small Country." *Canadian Journal of Economics* 9, no. 1: 150–61.

Macedo, J. de. 1984. "Collective Pegging to a Single Currency: The West African Monetary Union." Princeton, N.J.: Princeton University. Processed.

Mundell, R. 1972. "African Trade, Politics, and Money." In R. Tremblay, ed., *Africa and Monetary Integration*. Montreal: Editions HRW.

Prachowny, M. 1980. *The Two-Sector Small Open Economy Model*. New York: Oxford University Press.

Salter, W. 1959. "Internal and External Balance: The Role of Price and Expenditure Effects." *Economic Record* 35: 226–38.

Shalizi, Z., and L. Squire. 1986. "Tax Policy for Sub-Saharan Africa." Washington, D.C.: Country Policy Department, World Bank. Processed.

Soderstrom, Hans. 1985. "Exchange Rate Strategies and Real Adjustment after 1970: The Experience of the Smaller European Economies." In T. Peters, P. Praet, and P. Reding, *International Trade and Exchange Rate in the Late Eighties*. Amsterdam: North-Holland.

Swan, T. 1960. "Economic Control in a Dependent Economy." *Economic Record* 36: 51–66.

White, H. 1980. "A Heteroskedasticity-Consistent Covariance Matrix Estimator and a Direct Test for Heteroskedasticity." *Econometrica* 48, no. 4: 817–38.

World Development, Vol. 19, No. 8, pp. 957–967, 1991.
Printed in Great Britain.
0305–750X/91 $3.00 + 0.00
Pergamon Press plc

Growth-Oriented Adjustment Programs: A Statistical Analysis

RICCARDO FAINI
University of Brescia and CEPR
JAIME DE MELO
The World Bank, Washington, DC and CEPR
ABDELHAK SENHADJI
University of Pennsylvania, Philadelphia
and
JULIE STANTON*
University of Maryland, College Park

Summary. — This paper gives a statistical analysis of economic performance under International Monetary Fund (IMF) — World Bank (WB) growth-oriented adjustment programs. The evaluation is based on a sample of 93 countries and makes a comparison of the average values of economic indicators during 1982–86 with the corresponding values during 1978–81. The methodology controls for the external environment and for initial conditions. The paper finds no evidence of a statistically better (or worse) growth performance for loan recipient countries.

The paper then examines the investment-output relationship for a group of 14 countries that received a large number of growth-oriented adjustment loans. An estimate is provided of the foregone growth because of lower aggregate investment during the period of adjustment. The paper concludes that the desired signs of a sustainable recovery through higher investment were not evident, at least through 1986.

1. INTRODUCTION

The decade of the 1980s will be remembered as one of unfulfilled expectations for developing countries. Average per capita GDP growth fell from 3.1% in the 1970s to 0.6% in the 1980s, and for many countries, private per capita consumption growth was negative. Adjustment lending programs supported by the International Monetary Fund (IMF) and the World Bank (WB) were launched in response to the deteriorating external environment. Restoring growth has remained the focal concern of adjustment lending. Indeed, it is this greater emphasis on growth that distinguishes the adjustment programs of the 1980s from their predecessors. The purpose of this paper is to assess statistically the extent to which adjustment programs supported by the IMF and the World Bank restored growth.[1]

The paper offers a systematic evaluation of IMF-WB supported adjustment programs. The evaluation relies on a large sample of countries (93) and controls for some of the statistical difficulties associated with measuring the effectiveness of adjustment programs. In Section 2, we review briefly the environment under which IMF-WB lending took place, the rationale for adjustment lending, and the distribution of adjustment loans through time. The methodology is described in Section 3. The results of the statistical evaluation in Section 4 suggest that, after controlling for external factors and for initial conditions, growth is not higher in coun-

*We thank Bela Balassa, Ajay Chhibber, Patrick Conway, Vittorio Corbo, Peter Montiel, John Nash, Dani Rodrik, and three referees for helpful comments. This paper is part of research funded at the World Bank under RPO 675–32. The appendix to the paper is available from the authors upon request and is included in the discussion paper version listed in the references (Faini, *et al.*, 1990). The views contained herein are those of the authors and do not necessarily reflect those of the World Bank.

tries recipient of IMF-WB funds, but that investment was significantly lower than for nonrecipient countries. This result leads us to examine further long-term growth prospects in Section 5. There, for a group of 15 countries that received IMF-WB adjustment loans, we estimate a simple growth model where capital is the only binding factor on output. This model allows us to measure the approximate output loss incurred during adjustment programs due to the combined reduction of private and public investment. Conclusions follow in Section 6.

2. EXTERNAL ENVIRONMENT AND ADJUSTMENT LENDING

The proximate causes of the worsening performance of developing countries during the 1980s are well known. For oil-importing countries, the foreclosing of commercial credit and higher real interest rates on commercial borrowing came on top of the second oil price shock. Within this group of countries, exporters of primary commodities were further adversely affected by declining prices for primary commodities as the dollar appreciated. For oil exporters, deterioration in the terms of trade came later, but they were also adversely affected by the foreclosing of commercial funds. This adverse evolution of the external environment for developing countries is summarized in Table 1. Using these measures, in Table 2 we provide a measure of the loss in purchasing power during 1982–86 due to the unfavorable environment of the 1980s. The loss is estimated at between 3.8 and 4.5 percentage points of average GDP during 1982–86.

As can be seen from the macroeconomic indicators in Table 2, as a result of the deteriorating external environment, developing countries had difficulty improving their current account position during the 1980s and they increased substantially their external indebtedness. Table 2 also indicates that the cut in expenditures that accompanied the adjustment to the more unfavorable external environment involved a reduction in the share of investment expenditures in GDP.

It is in response to these balance-of-payments difficulties that adjustment lending was initiated by the World Bank (structural adjustment loans and sectoral adjustment loans) and that adjustment programs by the IMF (extended fund facilities and standby arrangements) were intensified.[2] Participation by these international agencies was intended to assist recipient countries in designing packages that would help achieve two objectives. First, the packages would help stabilize the economy by adopting measures to restore a sustainable balance between aggregate demand and aggregate supply. Second, the packages would help production in the shortrun, especially in tradables because of the need to generate increased net foreign exchange earnings to meet larger debt service payments. In our companion paper (Faini, *et al.*, 1991), we show that this objective was met by a significantly larger real exchange rate devaluation for countries that participated in adjustment programs

Table 1. *Terms-of-trade, real interest rates and borrowing sources*

	1980	1981	1982	1983	1984	1985	1986
Change in terms of trade (%):							
Nonfuel exporters	−5.8	−4.0	−2.0	0.6	2.6	−2.3	−2.9
Fuel exports	44.1	11.1	0.3	−8.5	0.7	−2.8	−47.9
Real interest rate*	4.4	6.5	6.7	5.8	7.0	5.0	5.0
Borrowing sources							
Net private borrowing†	73.3	72.5	48.9	25.4	14.8	13.7	2.3
Official borrowing (IMF and WB)							
Number of WB adjustment loans	8	8	5	22	10	18	28
(amount†)	(0.8)	(0.9)	(0.8)	(3.4)	(1.1)	(2.0)	(3.9)
Number of IMF loans	26	32	30	41	30	31	32
(net IMF credit†)	(2.3)	(4.7)	(3.6)	(9.4)	(4.4)	(0.9)	(−1.4)

Sources: World Bank (1989), Table 2.1, and Khan (1988), appendix.
*Percent.
†Billion current dollars.

Table 2. *Macroeconomic indicators during the 1980s**

Indicators†	1978–81 Low Income	1978–81 Middle Income		1982–86 Low Income	1982–86 Middle Income	
GDP (Growth)	2.77	4.83		2.48	1.99	
CA/GDP	−7.97	−5.52		−7.81	−5.12	
INV/GDP	20.6	27.1		18.5	22.7	
RER	1.029	1.014		1.247	1.040	
SH/GDP‡			−4.50 (LY)			−3.82 (MY)
DOD/GDP	33.8	29.3		54.2	46.6	

*Own calculations. All values are average values during the relevant period. Sample of 93 developing countries. LY = low income; MY = middle income (income per capita above $450 in 1986).
†Definitions:
GDP = Real gross domestic product.
CA = Current account surplus.
INV = Real public + private investment.
RER = Real exchange rate index (1980 = 1.0). An increase in the value of RER means a real depreciation.
SH = Measure of external shock (see equation 4).
DOD = Public or publicly guaranteed debt from *World Bank Debt Tables*.
‡Source: Faini *et al.* (1991). Estimate of the welfare loss due to lower terms of trade and higher interest rates during 1982–86 compared with 1978–81, as expressed as a share of the average GDP. Formula for the computation of the welfare loss is given in equation (4).

supported by the IMF and the World Bank. As emphasized by Corbo, Goldstein and Khan (1987), the novel emphasis of adjustment programs in the 1980s was on the restoration of long-run growth, hence the label "growth-oriented" adjustment programs.

The distribution of adjustment loans (and amounts) by the IMF and by the World Bank are given in Table 1. The table shows the sharp drop in the availability of commercial funds starting in 1982. The table also indicates a sharp increase in lending volume and in the number of loans by both institutions starting in 1983. The amount of lending by both institutions, however, far from compensated for the decline in commercial fund borrowing. While both institutions provided quick-disbursing loans, the shorter maturity of IMF loans implied sharply diminishing net credit after 1985.

In previous work, we found no correlation between the amount of IMF-WB adjustment credit during 1982–86 and the size of the external shock during that period, suggesting that adjustment lending was not targeted to countries facing the greatest deterioration in the external environment. We found, however, a significantly negative correlation between IMF-WB credit and net private credit, suggesting that IMF-WB credit served as a substitute for private credit.

3. A MODEL TO MEASURE EFFECTIVENESS OF IMF-WB PROGRAMS

(a) *Alternative approaches to evaluating adjustment programs*

The relatively short period since the beginning of adjustment lending is a reason why so little formal statistical evidence is available on performance under these adjustment programs. Apart from a recent paper by Khan (1988), most of the available evidence (Donovan, 1982; Goldstein, 1986; Cornia *et al.*, 1987; Balassa, 1988) relies on nonparametric statistics (e.g., the number of countries which show an improvement in growth in the year following implementation of an adjustment program) to assess performance. Furthermore, the samples are often small, making the interpretation of results more difficult.

Statistical evaluation of adjustment programs is fraught with difficulties. First, any evaluation must recognize that performance will be influenced by the external environment. Countries under adjustment programs which faced a more unfavorable environment would be expected to show less improvement in performance. Second, any assessement should, to the extent possible, take into account what policies would have been in the absence of IMF-WB adjustment programs.

Thus any "before and after" analysis should be complemented by a control group approach to reduce the bias in the estimated values of the selected indicators. These considerations are taken into account in the simple model presented below.[3]

Denote the set of performance indicators j for country i by y_{ij}. We postulate that changes in the value of each performance indicator depend on a vector of autonomous policy changes, Δx_i, on changes in the external environment, SH_i, and possibly on participation in IMF-WB adjustment programs:

$$\Delta y_{ij} = \alpha_{0j} + \Delta x_i' \times \alpha_i + SH_i \times \alpha_{2j} + CON \times \alpha_{3j} + \varepsilon_{ij} \qquad (1)$$

where CON is a dummy variable which takes the value of one for countries that received an IMF or World Bank adjustment loan. Because autonomous policy changes are unobservable for countries participating in IMF-WB programs, we specify the following reaction function:

$$\Delta x_i = \gamma_{0i} - \gamma_{1i}\, y_{i-1} + \zeta_{ij} \qquad (2)$$

which assumes an adjustment process of the performance indicators towards an exogenous target value, γ_{0i}. Substituting $\Delta x_i'$, the transpose of equation (2), into equation (1) gives the final equation for estimation:

$$\Delta y_{ij} = \beta_{0j} + (y_{i-1}') \times \beta_{ij} + SH_i \times \beta_{2j} + CON \times \beta_{3j} + \theta_{ij}\,. \qquad (3)$$

In this model, Δ refers to a difference between the "post" and "pre" adjustment periods, and in the statistical results reported in Section 4, each observation is an average over the pre- and postadjustment periods.

The assumption that IMF-WB lending has a fixed effect on performance may appear too restrictive. Alternatively, we introduce in equation (3) the amount of net IMF-WB lending during 1982–86 instead of the dummy variable CON. In that case, the maintained hypothesis is that, after controlling for external factors and autonomous policy changes, the change in performance is linearly related to the amount of IMF-WB disbursements.

(b) *Implementation*

Since IMF-WB programs are not often initiated in the same year, it is difficult to choose the correct point for beginning the assessment of these programs. The choice of 1982 as the cut-off point was made since 1982 corresponds most closely to the year when the external environment deteriorated sharply for developing countries (see Table 1).[4]

As detailed in the appendix (available from the authors), the sample consists of data for 93 developing countries. Among these countries, 32 did not receive any IMF-WB adjustment loans during 1982-86. Another nine received their first adjustment loan only in 1985 or 1986 which makes it difficult to assess the impact of the loan given our data. Thus, these countries are added to those that did not receive adjustment loans so that the control group includes 41 countries. The remaining 52 countries received IMF-WB adjustment lending. In this group, only two countries received their first adjustment loan in 1984. Hence one should really interpret the statistical results as pertaining to the performance of 50 countries which received adjustment credits in 1982 or 1983 and were carrying out policy reforms whose performance-enhancing effects were supposed to last throughout the period of analysis (i.e., until 1986). The performance of these countries is compared with the performance of 43 countries (of which 11 countries had been implementing adjustment lending policy reforms since 1984).

Next, we construct a proxy for the external environment, SH_i, by measuring terms of trade and interest rate shocks. To measure how significant the deterioration in the external environment was, we quantify the impact of the external disturbances associated with declining terms of trade and rising real interest rates. External disturbances are measured over 1982–86, taking average values over 1976–81 as the base period. The formula (country subscripts omitted) is:[5]

$$SH = -(\bar{R}_2 - \bar{R}_1) \times (\bar{D}/Y)_1 + (\overline{PX}_2/\overline{PX}_{1-1})(\bar{X}/Y)_1 - \bar{P}M_2/\bar{P}M_1 - 1)(\bar{M}/Y)_1 \qquad (4)$$

where subscripts 2 and 1 refer to 1982–86 and 1976–81 respectively, a bar over a variable means an average value over the relevant period and the variables are:

$\bar{R}$	=	average real interest rate (deflator is the US GDP deflator) and the nominal interest rate is the weighted interest on concessional and commercial debt.
Y	=	real GDP
PX, PM	=	export and import price indices deflated by the US GDP deflator
X, M	=	real exports and real imports
D	=	gross outstanding debt, net of reserves

In equation (4), the first term measures the contribution of higher than expected interest payments and the remaining terms measure the effect of changes in the terms of trade. The choice of periods implies that the proxy for the external environment, SH_i, is expressed as a percentage of the average value of GDP during 1976–81.

4. STATISTICAL RESULTS

Our main interest is in the effects of adjustment programs on growth. We use two indicators of growth: GDP growth and the share of investment in GDP. It could be argued that the investment share in GDP is an intermediate target. While this would be true in the long run, our limited time frame for the postloan period removes this concern. An improvement in growth alone could indicate an increase in capacity utilization. Hence the investment share is used as an additional indicator of sustainable long-run growth. We also use two indicators whose developments are followed closely by the IMF: inflation and the current account. (Another closely watched indicator, the government deficit, is not included here because it is unreliable on a comparative basis.)

The results after one round of exclusion of influential observations, and correcting for heteroskedasticity, appear in Table 3.[6] The effects of participation in IMF-WB programs are measured by the coefficient on the dummy *CON*.[7] The first remarkable result is that participation in IMF-WB programs does not appear to affect output growth in a significant manner, after having controlled for the negative influence of external shocks. We also find that adjustment lending is positively correlated with the current account performance. These results echo those in Khan (1988) where countries that participated in IMF programs had significantly lower output growth in the first year after the inception of the program. This negative effect, however, appeared to diminish when Khan allowed the effects of IMF programs to last two years. Khan also found that countries participating in IMF programs had a significant improvement in their current account. The fact that we measure performance over a three to five year period (depending on when the country received its first adjustment loan) may, therefore, account for our finding an insignificant effect of IMF-WB participation on growth.

The investment equation suggests that external shocks and the control group dummy are insignificant although all other variables in the equation have statistically significant coefficients with the expected signs. Finally, the inflation equation performed poorly. None of the explanatory variables had a significant impact on inflation. This is probably because we have not included credit in our instrument set. In that equation, however, the variable for external shocks has the right sign, i.e., external shocks push up inflation.

Table 3. *Performance under adjustment lending**

Dependent variable	Y_{-1}	I/Y_{-1}	CA_{-1}	$\hat{P}_{-1}$	SH	CON	F	$NOBS$
ΔY	−0.577	0.006	−0.134	0.010	−0.069	−0.001	28.15	79
	(−6.32)	(0.17)	(−2.68)	(0.46)	(−2.06)	(−0.19)		
$\Delta I/Y$	0.246	−0.295	0.279	−0.047	−0.049	−0.006	10.81	80
	(1.57)	(−4.51)	(2.61)	(−2.65)	(−0.56)	(−0.68)		
$\Delta\hat{P}$	−0.146	−0.072	−0.151	0.077	0.140	+0.008	1.42	79
	(−0.60)	(−0.70)	(−0.95)	(0.58)	(0.98)	(+0.43)		
ΔCA	0.395	0.133	−0.490	0.026	−0.056	+0.034	13.60	80
	(3.00)	(3.07)	(−6.55)	(1.87)	(−0.84)	(+4.83)		

*The constant term is omitted from the results, and the *t*-statistics are in parentheses.

Definition of variables: all variables are average values over 1982–86 (e.g., *Y* is average GDP growth during 1982–86). All lagged values are average values over 1978–81.

Y = GDP growth; *I/Y* = INV/GDP; *CA* = CA/GDP; *P* is the inflation rate; *SH* is the external shock estimate from equation (4); *CON* = dummy variable with value 1 if participating in IMF and/or World Bank adjustment programs; *F* = statistic; *NOBS* = number of observations used in regression.

Results are corrected for heteroskedasticity by weighing each observation by the inverse of its estimated standard error. Extreme influential observations are excluded using Belsley, Kuh, and Welsch (1980) criteria outlined in the appendix (available from the authors). The list of excluded countries is given in Table A2 of this appendix.

Our results also indicate that initial conditions play a crucial role in affecting the macroeconomic performance of the economy. For instance, it is found that a higher current account surplus and a lower inflation rate are associated with better investment performance in the following period. It is, however, more difficult to understand why lagged inflation should have a positive effect on growth, though insignificant, and on the current account.

These results should, however, be interpreted with caution. First, the effects of IMF-WB programs may not have had the time to appear as our data are only up until 1986. Second, the estimate of the dummy variable *CON* in equation (3) does not recognize the fact that the choice of a country to participate in a program is itself endogenous so that our method of direct estimation of β_{2j} suffers from self-selection bias. Recent work that extends the sample period to 1988 and that controls for nonprogram factors and self-selection bias suggests that a group of 25 countries that received two or more structural adjustment loans or three or more World Bank adjustment loans outperformed the control group when comparisons are over the period 1985–88 compared with 1981–84 (see World Bank, 1990, Chapter 2). It is interesting to note, however, that results similar to ours are found when comparisons are made for averages defined over 1981–84 and 1970–80. Taken together, these results suggest both a sensitivity of results to the methodology used and the periods over which comparisons are made and a need to include a long enough time period to allow for program effects to appear in the data.

To summarize, against the background of overall worsening indicators for developing countries as a whole, after controlling for external factors, IMF-WB supported adjustment programs appear not to have significantly affected output growth, nor to have affected the level or efficiency of investment. We conclude that the evidence on whether the growth-oriented adjustment programs of the 1980s helped recipient countries achieve higher growth and improved efficiency is still inconclusive. Given that the structural reforms advocated by these programs often require a relatively long time before their benefits materialize, the above results are not surprising. A major motivation of the adjustment programs, however, was to mobilize resources, that is to increase the volume of investment as well as to increase its efficiency in use. Therefore, in the next section we analyze further aggregate investment behaviour over a long period for a group of 15 countries which received a relatively large number of World Bank loans (usually three or more). In particular, we look for instability in the investment/output relationship after the inception of adjustment lending with a view to detect joint changes in capacity utilization due to stabilization and changes in the productivity of capital due to reforms.[8] We also estimate output loss from investment cuts during adjustment.

5. SUSTAINABILITY OF ADJUSTMENT: OUTPUT LOSS ESTIMATES FROM INVESTMENT CUTS FOR A GROUP OF INTENSIVE ADJUSTMENT LENDING RECIPIENTS

The previous results suggest that the foundations for sustained recovery were not achieved primarily due to the fall in investment during the adjustment lending period. We now investigate further the issue of long-term sustainability by studying aggregate investment and aggregate output during adjustment for a group of countries which were intensive recipients of IMF-WB adjustment loans.[9] We use a simple aggregate growth model in which the only binding factor on ouput is capital, a simplification which allows us to extend the analysis to a larger number of countries because data requirements are few, and to a period of 25 years. Labor is assumed to be in abundant supply. Foreign exchange may be scarce, but lack of its availability is, as in Taylor (1979), fully reflected in (lower) investment. As derived in the appendix (available from the authors), the estimated equation is:

$$Q_t = (1-\lambda)\ Q_{t-1} + a\ I_t + v_t \qquad (5)$$

where

Q_t = output produced during period t
λ = depreciation rate
a = output-capital ratio
I_t = investment during period t
v_t = error term

This formulation eliminates the need to depend on unreliable and incomplete data on employment. It also implicitly assumes that during the estimation period, capital stock resources were fully utilized except for a stochastic term. Since this assumption is less tenable for the adjustment years, initial estimation is carried out for the preadjustment period. Stability testing (see Table A3 in Faini *et al.*, 1990) is then used to assess whether the sample period can be extended up until 1986. In addition we test whether Q_{t-1} is correlated with the error term and for possible endogeneity of I_t. Details of the estimation procedure are described in the appendix (available from the authors).

Estimation results and estimation periods

appear in Table 4. Column (2) gives the estimate of one minus the depreciation rate, and column (3) the inverse of the incremental capital-output ratio (ICOR) ($\hat{a}$). With the exception of Zambia, the range of estimated values is in accordance with *a priori* expectations, although the average estimate for the depreciation rate (10%) is somewhat on the high side. Our interest, however, is primarily with the estimate of the ICOR, which is around three (excluding outlier Zambia). For the 13 reported countries, the values of the ICOR lend themselves to be separated into two groups: countries with ICORs above three (Kenya, Ghana, Malawi, Morocco, Côte d'Ivoire) and countries with ICORs below three (Thailand, the Philippines, Colombia, Chile, South Korea, Jamaica, Mexico, Pakistan). In general, the composition of each group fits with *a priori* expectations.

Stability tests (reported in Faini *et al.*, 1990, and available from the authors) indicate that nine out of 14 equations are stable. In interpreting this result, it should be remembered that two factors are likely to affect the ICOR during the adjust-

Table 4. *The production function*

Countries*	$(1-\lambda)$†	$\hat{a}$†	*D75*‡	$\bar{R}^2$	Stability (1)§	Period of estimation	Break year
Chile (2)	0.83 [7.89]	0.54 [2.34]	0.35 [2.6]	0.94	U	62–81	81
Colombia (2)	0.89 [6.79]	0.53 [.92]		1.0	S	61–85	84
Ghana (4)	0.82 [7.68]	0.25 [.76]		0.71	S	61–85	81
Jamaica (6)	0.84 [16.94]	0.36 [3.13]		0.94	S	61–86	80
Côte d'Ivoire (3) (fixed)‖	0.89 [20.31]	0.32 [2.27]		0.98	U	66–79	79
Kenya (3) [29.6]	0.96 [1.66]	0.24		0.99	S	66–86	81
Korea (3)	0.84 [8.50]	0.60 [2.48]		1.0	S	61–86	80
Malawi (4)	0.94 [32.55]	0.26 [2.91]		0.99	U	61–80	80
Mexico (2)	0.79 [8.22]	0.83 [2.93]		1.0	U	62–81	81
Morocco (3)	0.95 [17.53]	0.29 [1.47]		0.99	S	61–86	82
Pakistan (4)	0.97 [26.13]	0.64 [2.68]		1.0	S	61–86	79
Philippines (3)	0.90 [5.90]	0.45 [1.14]		1.0	U	61–79	79
Thailand (2)	0.96 [54.7]	0.37 [4.85]		1.0	S	61–86	81
Zambia (3)	0.90 [16.94]	0.06 [1.09]		0.92	S	61–86	83

*Number of SALs and SECALs in parentheses.
†*t*-statistics in brackets.
‡Dummy variable equal to one for the year 1975 and zero otherwise.
§*S*: stable equation (the break year is prior to the first WB adjustment loan). *U*: unstable equation.
‖For all countries, gross domestic investment was used for I_t (see equation 5), except for Côte d'Ivoire where fixed investment was used.

ment period: (1) changes in capacity utilization due to stabilization; and (2) changes in the productivity of capital due to reforms or to a change in the public and private sector shares in investment. Because these two effects on the ICOR are indistinguishable in our model and because they are likely to move in opposite directions during adjustment, it is not surprising that stability could not be rejected in the majority of cases. Furthermore, even when the equation was found to be unstable, the fitted value of output based on the preadjustment estimates did not deviate much from actual output during adjustment. This suggests that the net effect on output of changes in capacity utilization and capital productivity was not significant. Therefore, instead, we shall concentrate on measuring the extent of output loss due to lower investment during the adjustment period. This implies that we cannot evaluate, as intended, whether adjustment lending raised the marginal efficiency of investments through reforms in the system of production and investment incentives for the private sector and, for the public sector, through rationalization of public investments.

To estimate the output loss during adjustment, we estimated what output would have been, had the average investment-output ratio (I/Q) between 1970 and the initiation of WB adjustment lending prevailed afterwards. Formally, yearly output loss, L_t, is calculated as:

$$L_t = \hat{a}\ [I_t - \bar{I}_t] \qquad (6)$$

where $\bar{I}_t = (\overline{I/Q}) \times Q_t$, and $\hat{a}$ is the estimated value of the output-capital ratio from equation (5) (column 2 of Table 4). Notice that if one believes that adjustment lending led to higher efficiency in resource use and thus to a lower incremental capital-output ratio (i.e., a higher value of $\hat{a}$), then equation (6) will significantly underestimate the output loss due to the fall in investment.

Table 5 gives the estimates of the contractionary loss on output due the the lower investment levels during the period of adjustment lending. For example, Chile lost 17% of output during 1982–86 because of lower investment levels. Mexico, Chile and Malawi experienced the worst losses. Of course, one cannot ascribe the entire output loss to the adjustment to a relatively more unfavorable external environment in the early 1980s. Chile and Mexico, for example, had to also adjust to the disequilibria resulting from overly expansionary domestic policies in the late 1970s. Only South Korea raised its investment ratio during adjustment, thereby showing a positive output gain.

Excluding South Korea and Zambia, the countries fall into three groups: low, medium, and high output loss as a percentage of GDP. Colombia, Ghana, Côte d'Ivoire and Pakistan lost, on average, less than 1% of GDP per year. At the other extreme, Mexico, Malawi, Chile, and Kenya, on average, lost close to 4% of GDP per year. In interpreting this result, one must remember that for unstable countries (Côte d'Ivoire, Mexico, Malawi and Chile), the estimate of the output loss may be biased in an unpredictable direction because of a change in the value of $\hat{a}$ during the adjustment period.

In spite of these caveats, our results suggest a sizable output loss because of lower aggregate investment levels during the period of adjustment under IMF-WB lending. Since an objective of these growth oriented programs was to restore growth by, among others, raising investment, one must ask what causes this sharp decline in investment and resulting output loss. While our analysis does not allow us to measure by how much private investment actually fell, the estimated fall in aggregate investment output ratios was large enough in most countries to leave little doubt that private investment fell substantially during the adjustment. At least two factors must have contributed to the fall in private investment.

The first factor is that the expenditure-switching policies that accompanied the adjustment programs resulted in an increase in the relative price of imported capital goods. This cost increase was caused by the real exchange rate devaluation required to achieve a trade balance surplus to service the external debt. Furthermore, the interpretation of the statistical analysis of performance indicators in Section 4 suggests that scarce foreign exchange was probably tied up in purchasing intermediate goods with little left for capital goods imports.

But this interpretation does not recognize that, given capital investment partially irreversible because of sunken costs of entry and exit, the decision to invest in the activities supposedly made more profitable by the ongoing reforms depends on the probability of a policy reversal during the lifetime of the new investment. With costly resource reallocation, uncertainty is likely to have led many private investors to either keep their capital abroad or in existing activities until the subjective probability that the reforms and adjustment programs would not be reversed was high enough for them to commit to new investments.[10] Thus, the second factor would ascribe much of the fall in private investment to the lack of credibility in the adjustment programs, perhaps mostly because of the size of the required adjustment, or perhaps also because of

Table 5. *Output loss due to lower investment*

Country	Adjustment period*	Cumulative† effect	Average one-year effect	IMF-WB adjustment lending as percentage of GDP‡
Chile	82–86	−0.170	−0.034	0.010
Colombia	85–85	−0.004	−0.004	0.002
Ghana	82–85	−0.034	−0.009	0.025
Jamaica	81–86	−0.118	−0.020	0.031
Côte d'Ivorie	80–86	−0.049	−0.007	0.019
Kenya	82–86	−0.141	−0.028	0.011
Korea	81–86	0.120	0.020	0.003
Malawi	81–86	−0.260	−0.043	0.033
Mexico	82–86	−0.230	−0.046	0.004
Morocco	83–86	−0.076	−0.019	0.013
Pakistan	80–86	−0.053	−0.008	0.004
Philippines	80–86	−0.097	−0.014	0.004
Thailand	82–86	−0.083	−0.017	0.004
Zambia	84–86	−0.037	−0.012	0.005

*The adjustment period is defined as the years after receipt of the WB SAL.

†The formula used is $\sum_{t=s}^{e} \hat{a}\,(I_t - \bar{I}_t)/QF_t;\ \bar{I}_t = \left[\frac{I}{Q}\right] Q_t$

where:

$\left[\frac{I}{Q}\right]$ is the average of the investment/output ratio from 1970 until the starting dates of the adjustment program.

I_t = the level of investments.

QF_t = the fitted value of output (e.g., 5 where I_t was replaced by $\bar{I}_t$).

s = the starting date of the adjustment program.

e = the last year available during the adjustment program.

‡Average IMF-WB lending on average GDP over period 1979–86.

overambitious reforms in an unsettled macroeconomic environment.

6. CONCLUSIONS

This paper has provided a statistical analysis of performance under IMF-WB growth-oriented adjustment programs. The evaluation was based on a comparison of the average values of economic indicators during 1982–86 with the corresponding average values during 1978–81. The methodology controlled for the state of the external environment during the period when growth-oriented adjustment programs were in effect as well as for the initial conditions of the loan recipient countries. Account was also taken of the policies that would have been adopted had they not participated in IMF-WB adjustment programs.

Admittedly the methodology is crude, even though it controls for most of the pitfalls commonly made in such comparative exercises. We found that initial conditions played a significant role in affecting macroeconomic performance. For example, we found that a higher current account surplus and a lower inflation rate during 1978–81 were associated with better investment performance during 1982–86. We also found that a deterioration in the external environment during 1982–86 was associated with lower growth during that period.

The main result from our comparisons between IMF-WB recipients and countries that did not receive adjustment loans (or received them toward the end of the period so that not enough time had elapsed to include them among loan recipients) relates to growth and investment. After controlling for initial conditions and external factors, we found no evidence of a statistically better (or worse) performance for loan recipient countries. These results suggest that the positive effects on growth and resource mobilization expected from adjustment-with-growth packages had not yet occurred. Given that the structural reforms advocated by these programs often require a relatively long time before their benefits materialize, these results may not be surprising.

In the last section of the paper we analyzed in greater detail the investment output relationship for a group of 14 countries that received a large amount of growth-oriented adjustment lending. For each country, we fit a simple production function (in which capital is the only constraint on growth) over a 25-year period. We then provided an estimate of the output loss from the shortfall in investment during the period when each country was receiving adjustment lending. The results show much foregone growth because of lower aggregate (public and private) investment levels during the period of adjustment. Thus, the desired signs of a sustainable recovery through higher investment, evaluated here through 1986, were not evident.

NOTES

1. In previous work (Faini *et al.*, 1991), we evaluated performance under adjustment lending for a group of nine indicators using a before-and-after approach so that we did not control for initial conditions nor for the size of external shocks.

2. The World Bank initiated SALS (structural adjustment loans) and SECALs (sectoral adjustment loans) in 1979 and 1981 respectively. Like the EFF (Extended Fund Facility) and stand-by arrangements, World Bank adjustment loans are quick-disbursing loans. For a description of adjustment lending investments by the IMF and World Bank see World Bank (1989). All IMF upper credit tranche programs are of short duration and some Fund-supported adjustment programs were initiated before 1979. Of 288 programs during 1973–86, however, only 44 took place during 1973-78.

3. The following model draws on Goldstein and Montiel (1986).

4. Because the choice of cut-off is arbitrary, we also carried out our estimation using 1981 as an alternative cut-off point. The results were similar to those reported in Table 3.

5. The formula derives from a two-period maximization by firms and households under assumptions of perfect competition and wage-price flexibility. See Dornbusch (1985), pp. 354–356.

6. One round of exclusion tests results in about 5% loss of observations. Excluded countries are reported in the appendix (available from the authors). The exclusion criteria were determined by the value of Cook's *D*-statistic. See Belsley, Kuh and Welsch (1980), and section A3 of Faini *et al.* (1990).

7. Similar results, not reported here, were obtained in an alternative estimation based on a model in which *CON* is replaced by the intensity of IMF-WB adjustment lending.

8. Because we fit the growth model to a relatively large number of countries, we kept it as simple as possible so that we were not able to distinguish between capacity and productivity effects nor between private and public investment.

9. The 14 countries (see Table 4) were selected on the basis of the number of SALs. Turkey, included in that sample, had to be dropped from our analysis because regime changes did not allow us to get stable estimates.

10. This interpretation is emphasized in a broader context in the literature on credibility (Calvo, 1986; Dornbusch, 1988; Rodrik, 1988).

REFERENCES

Balassa, B., "Quantitative appraisal of adjustment lending," PPR Working Paper Series No. 79 (Washington, DC: The World Bank, 1988).

Belsley, D., E. Kuh and R. E. Welsch, *Regression Diagnostics Analysis* (New York: John Wiley & Sons, 1980).

Blejer, M. and M. Khan, "Government policy and private investment in developing countries," *IMF Staff Papers*, Vol. 31, No. 2 (1984), pp. 379–403.

Buffie, E., "Devaluation investment and growth in LDCs," *Journal of Development Economics*, Vol. 20 (1986), pp. 361–379.

Bufie, E., "The macroeconomics of trade liberalization," *Journal of International Economics*, Vol. 17 (1984), pp. 121–137.

Calvo, G., "Incredible reforms," mimeo (Philadelphia: University of Pennsylvania, 1986).

Cline, W. R., "International debt: From crisis to recovery?" *American Economic Review*, Vol. 75 (1985), pp. 185–190.

Corbo, V., M. Goldstein, and M. Khan (Eds.), *Adjustment with Growth* (Washington, DC: IMF, 1987).

Corden, M., "Macroeconomic adjustment in developing countries," Mimeo (Washington, DC: IMF, 1988).

Cornia, G., R. Jolly, and F. Stewart, *Adjustment with a Human Face,* Vol. 1 (Oxford: Oxford University Press, 1987).

Dadkhah, K. M., and F. Zahedi "Simultaneous estimation of production functions and capital stocks for developing countries," *The Review of Economics and Statistics*, Vol. LXVIII, No. 3 (1986), pp. 443–451.

Dell, S., "Stabilization: The political economy of overkill," in J. Williamson (Ed.), *IMF Conditionality* (Washington, DC: Institute for International Economics, 1983), pp. 7–46.

Diaz-Alejandro, C., "Southern cone stabilization problems," in W. Cline and S. Weintraub (Eds.), *Economic Stabilization in Developing Countries* (Washington, DC: Brookings Institution, 1981).

Donovan, D. J., "Real responses associated with exchange rate action in selected upper credit tranche stabilization programs," *IMF Staff Papers* (1981), pp. 698–727.

Dornbusch, R., "Notes on credibility and stabilization," Mimeo (Cambridge, MA: MIT, 1988).

Dornbusch, R., "The effects of OECD macroeconomic policies on non-oil developing countries," World Bank Staff Working Papers, No. 793 (Washington, DC: World Bank, 1986).

Dornbusch, R., "Policy and performance links between LDC debtors and industrial nations," *Brookings Papers on Economic Activity,* No. 2 (1985), pp. 303–368.

Faini, R., J. de Melo, A. Senhadji, and J. Stanton, "Performance under adjustment lending," in V. Thomas, A. Chhiber, M. Dailami, and J. de Melo (Eds.), *Restructuring Economies in Distress: Policy Reform and the World Bank* (Oxford: Oxford University Press, 1991).

Faini, R., J. de Melo, A. Senhadji, and J. Stanton, "Growth-oriented adjustment programs: A statistical analysis," PPR Working Paper No. 426 (Washington, DC: The World Bank, 1990).

Genberg, A., and A. K. Swoboda, "The medium-term relationship between performance indicators and policy: A cross section approach," EPD Discussion Paper No. EPD-01 (Washington, DC: The World Bank, 1987).

Goldstein, M., and P. Montiel, "Evaluating fund stabilization programs with multicountry data: Some methodological pitfalls," *IMF Staff Papers*, Vol. 33, No. 2 (1986), pp. 314–344.

Hausman, J. A. "Specification tests in econometrics," *Econometrica,* Vol. 46 (1978), pp. 1257–1270.

Khan, M., "The macroeconomic effects of fund-supported adjustment programs: An empirical assessment," Mimeo (Washington, DC: IMF, 1988).

Khan, M., and M. Knight, "Stabilization programs in developing countries: A formal framework," *IMF Staff Papers*, Vol. 28, No. 1 (1981), pp. 1–53.

Kiviet, J. F., "On the rigour of some misspecification tests for modelling dynamic relationships," Vol. 53, *Review of Economic Studies,* Vol. 53 (1986), pp. 241–261.

Kiviet, J. F., "Model selection test procedures in a single linear equation of a dynamic simultaneous system and their effects in small samples," *Journal of Econometrics,* Vol. 28 (1985), pp. 327–362.

Mitra, P. K., "Adjustment to external shocks in selected semi-industrial countries, 1974–1981," Mimeo (Washington, DC: The World Bank Public Economics Division, 1984).

Rodrik, D., "Liberalization, sustainability, and the design of structural adjustment programs," Mimeo (Washington, DC: The World Bank, 1988).

Sachs, J., and H. Huizinga, "U.S. commercial banks and the developing country debt crisis," *Brookings Papers on Economic Activity* (Washington, DC: Brookings Institution, 1987).

Sargan, J. D., "The estimation of economic relationships using instrumental variables," *Econometrica,* Vol. 26 (1958), pp. 393–415.

Taylor, L. *Macro Models for Developing Countries* (New York: McGraw Hill, 1979).

van Wijnbergen, S., "Exchange rate management and stabilization policies in developing countries," *Journal of Development Economics,* Vol. 23 (1986), pp. 227–247.

van Wijnbergen, S., "Stagflation effects of monetary stabilization policies: A quantitative analysis of South Korea," *Journal of Development Economics,* Vol. 10 (1982), pp. 133–269.

World Bank, "Adjustment lending policies for sustainable growth," PRS Series No. 14 (Washington, DC: The World Bank, 1990).

World Bank, "Adjustment lending: An evaluation of ten years of experience," PRS Series No. 1 (Washington, DC: The World Bank, 1989).

Economic Policy October 1990 Printed in Great Britain

LDC adjustment packages

Riccardo Faini and Jaime de Melo

Summary

Developing countries have been hit by a fall in their terms of trade, high real interest rates on their external debt, and a drought in commercial lending from abroad. Their subsequent adjustment packages, often supported by loans from the IMF and World Bank, focused on a sharp real exchange rate depreciation to restore external balance and a host of microeconomic reforms to secure a simultaneous supply-side improvement. This paper examines the success of these 'adjustment with growth' packages in a large sample of developing countries.

We find these packages have been much more successful in LDCs which export manufactures than they have in those concentrating on primary exports (primarily low-income African countries); the latter have not resumed sustainable growth, and most of their external adjustment has arisen from expenditure reduction, not an increase in supply. The longer-term prospects for manufacturing exporters are also brighter: there we detect signs of increased efficiency and a smaller decline in investment than in primary exporters. But we also find that a high external debt burden and an unstable macroeconomic environment impede investment in all LDCs. In the longer term, adjustment with growth packages will succeed only if they are accompanied by a more stable macroeconomic environment and appropriate debt relief.

Adjustment, investment and the real exchange rate in developing countries

Riccardo Faini and Jaime de Melo
Johns Hopkins University, Bologna; and World Bank, University of Geneva and CEPR

1. Introduction

The developing countries have been in crisis since 1982. The combination of deteriorating terms of trade, rising real interest rates on their external debt and the drying up of commercial lending have forced them to pursue drastic economic adjustment policies. Faced with a sharp withdrawal of commercial bank funds that was only partly compensated by official lending, and unwilling to default, developing countries had to effect a positive transfer to developed countries. The crisis required a sharp adjustment: developing countries had to earn foreign exchange by exporting more or save it by importing less. It is now recognized that the brunt of adjustment fell on absorption, in particular on investment. In most developing countries, with the significant exception of East Asian countries, adjustment was achieved by cutting investment rather than by increasing saving. Both public and private investment fell. Admittedly, prior to 1982 many countries had embarked on overly ambitious investment programmes, partly because recycled petrodollars were all too readily available. Yet the fall in investment, particularly private investment, could have adverse implications for a sustained recovery.

In response to the debt crisis, the IMF increased its lending, and the World Bank responded by introducing quick-disbursing adjustment loans to help countries achieve both macroeconomic equilibrium and efficient structural adjustment. In many quarters, the crisis was viewed as an opportunity to carry out much-needed microeconomic reforms

We acknowledge partial funding from RPO 675-32 at the World Bank. We thank Carlo Maggi, Ceyla Pazarbasioglu and Alex Pfaff for extremely valuable research assistance, Maria D. Ameal for unfailing logistic support and Richard Baldwin, Charles Bean, David Begg, Mansoor Dailami, Giancarlo Perasso, Lant Pritchett and members of the Economic Policy Panel for helpful comments. An appendix describing data sources and country classifications is available from the authors on request. The views expressed are those of the authors not those of their affiliations.

that would raise efficiency and allow adjustment to take place without a loss in growth despite the reduction in investment.

Whatever the differences in the depth of the crises affecting them, most developing countries have now been undergoing structural adjustment for almost a decade. What can be said overall about its success? In this paper, we evaluate adjustment packages by focusing on two key issues: did the sharp devaluation of the real exchange rate (advocated by international organizations) generate a supply response, and did microeconomic rationalization sufficiently raise the marginal efficiency of investment to compensate for the adverse effects of adjustment on the volume of investment? In other words, are there signs that the structural reforms are bearing fruit, and, if there is recovery, is it sustainable?

We term real output growth sustainable if it exceeds population growth. Sustainability has assumed particular importance because the sharp drop in living standards that has accompanied adjustment programmes in many countries has created tensions that affect investment decisions. Is this uncertainty preventing investment in countries that would otherwise attract investment precisely because of the lower real wages? If investors are waiting to see whether economic conditions will deteriorate, then their expectations could become self-fulfilling, and could lead to the abandonment of otherwise well-conceived adjustment packages.

To set the tone for our analysis, we need first to get a general sense of how adjusting countries are doing. Just as the severity of the crises differed widely across countries, so too has the burden of adjustment and its timing. No classification system for grouping countries can fully capture this diversity. Table 1 summarizes the latest available figures. Here we choose a country grouping based on economic structure: fuel exporters, manufacturing exporters, and, as a residual category, primary exporters. Period averages are taken for four macro-indicators: GDP growth, the share of investment in GDP, the ratio of debt service to exports and the real exchange rate.

Three facts stand out. One is that only manufacturing exporters (mostly the East Asian countries) have resumed growth at pre-crisis levels. Although the debt-service burden of this group is high (partly because of a few Latin American countries in the grouping), it has stabilized. Growth among the fuel exporters has deteriorated throughout the three periods. Primary exporters have recuperated most of their loss in growth, but they have not arrested a worsening trend in their external debt service.

The second significant fact is the universal, and pronounced, decline in the investment share in GDP. For the non-fuel groups, the share has

Table 1. Macroeconomic indicators (annual averages, %)

		Primary exporters	Manufacturing exporters	Fuel exporters
GDP growth	1978–81	2.8	4.8	6.6
	1982–86	1.4	2.4	2.0
	1986–88	2.4	4.9	0.9
Investment/GDP	1978–81	21	26	28
	1982–86	18	23	25
	1986–88	17	22	19
Debt service/exports	1978–81	15	25	18
	1982–86	20	28	25
	1986–88	29	29	39
Real exchange rate (1980 = 100)	1978–81	103	103	100
	1982–86	113	112	95
	1986–88	139	139	135

Notes: Unweighted averages of sample of 83 countries with population exceeding 1 mn. in 1980. Throughout the paper, an increase in the real exchange rate denotes a real exchange rate depreciation.

fallen by about 20%, while for fuel exporters the decline was even sharper, reaching 30%. To be sure, it can be argued that the overly ambitious investment programmes following the oil boom needed to be scaled down. But the declines for the primary and manufacturing exporters are very high and may cause concern about the prospects for sustained recovery.

The declining investment share in GDP and slower rate of growth, in spite of a sharp deterioration in the real exchange rate, is even more pronounced if we divide our sample of 83 countries into currently (i.e. in 1988) severely indebted countries and others. The 36 severely indebted countries had a decline in average growth from 3.1% per annum in 1978–81 to 2.5% in 1986–88 while the average share of investment in GDP fell from 22.3% in 1978–81 to 15.7% in 1986–88. For this severely indebted group of countries, the real exchange rate depreciation was 46%.

The third significant finding from Table 1 is the sharp real exchange rate depreciation. Six years into the cirisis, the real exchange rate had depreciated by close to 40% for all three country classifications. Some real exchange rate depreciation would have been required by any adjustment programme involving an increase in the net transfer from debtors to creditors, otherwise the required shift towards tradeable activities would not have materialized.

But there is more behind this sharp and universal depreciation in the real exchange rate. When the IMF and World Bank stepped in to fill at least some of the financing gap left by the withdrawal of commercial lending, they offered 'adjustment-with-growth' packages that relied heavily on a sharp depreciation of the real exchange rate as a condition for obtaining funds. The real exchange rate is an endogenous variable that can never be fully under a country's policy control, but it is no exaggeration to say that achieving a sharp real exchange rate depreciation was the centrepiece of these adjustment packages.[1]

The failure of such a large number of countries to resume sustainable growth has given ammunition to the advocates of debt relief and to the critics of the adjustment-with-growth packages advocated by the IMF and the World Bank. The heavy emphasis on real exchange rate depreciation as a way to restore external balance and elicit a significant supply response has been at the centre of this controversy about the effectiveness of these packages. In the first part of the paper, we take a fresh look at the role of the exchange rate in the context of adjustment by distinguishing between the short-run supply effect of a real exchange rate depreciation and its long-run effect on growth of output through its impact on investment.

In addition to the emphasis on a sharp depreciation of the real exchange rate, most adjustment packages introduced a host of productivity-enhancing microeconomic reforms. Typically the reforms included a rationalization of public sector recurrent and investment expenditures; a restructuring of public enterprises; and trade, fiscal and credit policy reforms to provide more nearly neutral and transparent incentives. While it is too early to see the full effects of microeconomic reforms, one could hope to detect some effects in the form of a greater efficiency of investment. In the second part of the paper, we analyse the behaviour of investment during adjustment, looking first into the efficiency and cost of investment. Can one attribute most of the decline in private investment to the rising cost of capital goods? Did the efficiency of investment improve during adjustment? Because investment decisions are at least partially irreversible, we look into the influence of the macroeconomic environment, particularly the debt overhang, on investment decisions.

In what follows, we address the evidence for a large sample of developing countries. In Section 2 we state succinctly the controversy surrounding the role of the real exchange rate in achieving external balance and restoring growth. Section 3 gives evidence on adjustment in the external balance and the supply-side effects of a real depreciation.

[1] See Edwards (1989b) and World Bank (1988) for a description of IMF-/World Bank-supported adjustment packages.

Section 4 looks at the effects on investment of real depreciation and other factors. Conclusions and implications for a sustained recovery are discussed in Section 5.

2. The controversy

A standard framework for analysing the effects of adjustment programmes is the two-sector dependent-economy model with exogenous terms of trade. Consider the situation prevailing before the crisis. Before 1981, many countries could run a trade deficit financed by external borrowing. When foreign borrowing was foreclosed or, at the least, greatly reduced, the absorption-income gap had to be reduced to reduce the current account deficit. (Many countries had to produce a trade surplus to service the increased payments on their external debt caused by higher real interest rates.)

When resources are initially fully and efficiently employed, closing the absorption-income gap by reducing absorption is often referred to as the *primary cost*, or inevitable cost, of reducing a current account deficit. If closing the gap also entails a reduction in resource use because of relative price (or other) rigidities, there is also a *secondary cost* of adjustment. Over the medium term, adjustment policies to reduce the external deficit would include both expenditure-reducing and expenditure-switching policies (e.g. a real exchange rate depreciation). In addition, if the adjustment package is introduced at a time of inflation, a cutback in demand is desirable to reduce inflationary pressures. When resources are not fully or not efficiently employed one can also expect a supply response to a depreciation of the real exchange rate.

The relative effectiveness of expenditure-reducing and expenditure-switching policies depends on the marginal propensity to consume tradeables and on supply responsiveness. The lower the marginal propensity to consume tradeables, the less external adjustment will be obtained from a given demand reduction. And the more difficult it is to shift existing resources from non-tradeable to tradeable activities, the greater the required relative price shift (real exchange rate depreciation).

To give some idea of the scope for substitution in demand, note that many countries, especially primary exporters, do not consume exports domestically. Also, close substitutes for imports are typically not available in the short to medium run. Data for a group of 40 developing countries indicates that the share of consumer good imports fell from 30% in 1980 to 25% in 1987. Such a shift toward the inelastic component of total imports is likely to reduce the effectiveness of expenditure-switching policies.

The traditional structuralist argument against devaluation is that it has a small impact on the trade balance because of low elasticities. This traditional argument has been buttressed by the contention that the redistributive mechanisms brought into play by devaluation (i.e., the shift from low savers to high savers) are contractionary from the demand side (Krugman and Taylor, 1977). Traditional stabilization packages reach the point of 'overkill' (Diaz-Alejandro, 1980; Dell, 1982) when it is further recognized that restrictive monetary policy may have a contractionary effect on supply through higher interest costs (Cavallo, 1977; Bruno, 1979).

These shortcomings did not go unnoticed within the international agencies. But it was not until the advent of adjustment lending in the early 1980s ($26 bn. from the IMF and $16 bn. from the World Bank during 1980–87) that these agencies made an explicit attempt to combine short-run stabilization goals with growth-oriented policies. In this new framework (see Corbo *et al.*, 1987, and Thomas *et al.*, 1990), devaluation of the real exchange rate still played an essential role, not only to restore external balance but also to achieve a more efficient resource allocation: the positive supply response to a real devaluation would dominate its contractionary demand effects.

This new emphasis on growth did not diminish the criticism, however. A 'new' structuralist critique pointed out that devaluation could be contractionary, this time from the supply side. The effect would come through the higher cost of imported inputs (Buffie, 1984); a lower volume of real credit (because of higher input prices with constant nominal credit) and consequently higher interest costs for firms (Van Wijnbergen, 1986); and, in the presence of widespread wage indexation, through higher labour costs. Finally, in the longer run, the negative effect on supply could be compounded if a real depreciation depressed investment because of a higher cost of imported capital equipment (Buffie, 1986).

Consider the following back-of-the-envelope calculation of the contractionary effects of a devaluation that increases the costs of intermediate inputs. For the countries in Table 1, the real exchange rate depreciated by approximately 25% between 1980 and 1987. Assuming an economy-wide value-added ratio of 0.5, imported intermediates at 30% of total intermediates, and long-run demand and supply elasticities of 1 and 2 respectively, the contractionary effect would be 5% of GDP. (In addition, the contractionary effects from the demand side could conceivably lead to excess supply among non-traded sectors.[2])

[2] Lizondo and Montiel (1989) give an exhaustive discussion of the various factors contributing to the contractionary effects of devaluation. Also see Edwards (1989a, chapter 8).

This 'new' critique assumes that a nominal devaluation results in a real devaluation on impact – as has been the case in the 1980s. The amount of the real devaluation will probably be less than the nominal devaluation, but it will be substantial, as the figures in Table 1 show. Over the longer term, as various studies have pointed out (e.g. Edwards, 1989a), there is a tendency for the real devaluation to erode because of wage indexation and other factors. The critique remains worthy of closer investigation, however, in view of the pronounced depreciation in the real exchange rate apparent from Table 1 and the difficulties many countries have had in resuming growth.

Finally, a related critique from the advocates of debt relief is that the resulting overkill from the extreme severity of adjustment programmes combined with a deteriorating external debt position has inhibited private investment. According to these critics, the debt overhang has acted as a tax on the proceeds of investment (Sachs, 1989) and uncertainty has created negative incentives for private investment (Rodrik, 1989; Dornbusch, 1988). As pointed out earlier, the criticism rests upon the consequences of uncertainty on the decision to invest in a world where the investment decision is at least partially irreversible. The argument here is that uncertainty about the future course of an adjustment package will lead potential investors to adopt a wait-and-see attitude. In the typical Latin American case, flight capital will not be repatriated for investment because uncertainty about the outcome of the ongoing adjustment package is high.

3. External adjustment and the real exchange rate

Developing countries responded to the shocks of the 1980s by depreciating their real exchange rate.[3] How effective has real exchange rate depreciation been? First, we analyse the evolution of the trade balance to see how much of the improvement in the trade balance was accounted for by real exchange rate depreciation after controlling for time trends and country-specific effects. Second, we look for evidence of supply response to the real exchange rate.

For each of the three country groupings in Table 1, we pool countries and correlate the trade balance-GDP ratio with absorption, the real exchange rate, country dummies and a time trend. Unfortunately,

[3] Real exchange rate depreciation was even stronger for recipients of World Bank/IMF adjustment loans. Thirty countries that did not receive adjustment loans with a major trade-reform component depreciated in real terms by less than 2% between 1980–82 and 1985–87 whereas 40 countries that received structural adjustment loans depreciated by 22% in real terms (see World Bank, 1988).

Table 2. Determinants of the trade balance
(Dependent variable: the ratio of trade balance to GDP)

Effect of 1% increase in	Manufacturing exporters	Fuel exporters	Primary exporters
Real absorption	−0.16 (0.07)	−0.78 (0.76)	−0.49 (0.12)
Real exchange rate	0.18 (0.08)	0.10 (0.11)	0.20 (0.84)
Real exchange rate in previous year	0.07 (0.07)	0.15 (0.12)	0.08 (0.09)

Notes: Estimated over 1965–85, excluding countries for which less than four observations. There are 20 manufacturing exporters, 11 fuel exporters and 18 primary exporters for which data is available. Standard errors of estimates shown in parenthesis. Equations estimated by instrumental variables using real money, and lagged values of absorption and the real exchange rate as instruments. Time trend and country-specific intercepts not reported.

because of lack of data, we are unable to separate out directly the effects of demand switching and supply response. Results are reported in Table 2. All coefficients for the real exchange rate are significant with the exception of that for fuel exporters, which is not surprising since natural-resource-based economies usually have price-insensitive supply structures. (Generally the lagged value of the real exchange rate is insignificant.) The coefficient on absorption is even more significant. For our sample, then, we conclude that the real exchange rate depreciation contributed to improving the trade balance.

We also re-estimated the same equation adding dummy variables for the post-1981 period on the coefficients of absorption and the real exchange rate. For the primary-exporter group a significantly negative value showed up for the real exchange rate dummy variable, suggesting no contribution of real exchange rate depreciation to trade balance improvements. This is consistent with other studies that have attempted to link the trade balance with the real exchange rate.

It is interesting to measure the relative contribution of changes in absorption and of the real exchange rate to the trade balance. The index $R = a_2/a_1$ (elasticity of the trade balance with respect to price/elasticity of the trade balance with respect to absorption) measures the relative impact on the trade balance of a reduction in absorption and of a real depreciation. For our three country groupings, this index is 1.13 for manufacturing exports, 0.13 for fuel exporters, and 0.41 for primary exporters. The exchange rate contributes to trade balance improvements most for manufacturing exporters. This is exactly what the 'old' structuralists would argue. For the rest of the developing world, the relative effectiveness of expenditure-switching policies is very low indeed. Falling in this category are small low-income countries, which are at a relatively early stage of industrialization with a small and undiversified industrial sector. These countries have few opportunities for expanding exports, which are concentrated in a few primary commodities. The scope for export expansion is typically even more limited for natural-resource-based economies such as fuel exporters, although there may be room for adjustment on the import side if they have a larger share of consumer imports. These are the prototypical 'structuralist' economies (see Chenery, 1975; Taylor, 1982).

One can also use the estimates in Table 2 to see how much of the improvement in trade balance was accounted for by real exchange rate depreciation after controlling for country-specific effects and the time trend. For manufacturing exporters (primary exporters) the average trade balance-GDP ratio was 4.9 (2.3) percentage points higher in 1983–85 than in 1979–81. For manufacturing exporters real exchange depreciation accounted for a 2.1 percentage point improvement in the trade balance, while for primary exporters real exchange rate depreciation only accounted for a 0.8 percentage point improvement.

The limited scope for import substitution is also apparent from the evolution of the composition of non-fuel imports during the 1980s. The data (not shown here) indicates some import substitution in consumer goods with a rising share of intermediate goods in imports. But since the share of consumer goods in total imports was already low at the onset of adjustment (about 20%), it is likely that little supply response could be expected from the replacement of imports with domestically produced substitutes for the majority of developing countries.

Turn now to supply response. We assume that output supply at each point of time is a function of the capital stock, the cost of variable inputs, and, because adjustment takes time, of lagged supply. Because of lack of data for our large sample, we approximate the cost of variable inputs by the real exchange rate. This variable is also intended to proxy the costs of labour and, more importantly, the presumed supply-augmenting effects of adjustment programmes based on real exchange rate depreciation. As before, dummy variables capture country-specific effects. The country-classification is unchanged. After taking a quasi first difference of the supply equation, one obtains the reduced form of Table 3.

Interestingly, when it comes to the coefficient on the real exchange rate, one finds consistently a negative and significant contribution to supply (the lagged effects appear insignificant): a real depreciation (which increases our measure of the real exchange rate) reduces current output supply, other things equal. It must, of course, be recognized

Table 3. The real exchange rate and output supply (Dependent variable: logarithm of real output)

Effect of 1% increase in	Fuel exporters	Primary exporters	Manufacturing exporters
Output last year	0.44	0.31	0.21
	(0.15)	(0.07)	(0.11)
Output two years ago	−0.04	0.07	0.13
	(0.07)	(0.03)	(0.05)
Real exchange rate	−0.10	−0.17	−0.08
	(0.04)	(0.06)	(0.03)
Real exchange rate last year	0.07	0.15	−0.01
	(0.08)	(0.06)	(0.05)
Real gross fixed investment	0.12	0.11	0.16
	(0.03)	(0.01)	(0.02)
Diagnostic statistics:			
Wald test	477	853	82
Sargan test	5.4	4.6	0.9

Notes: Maximum sample 1965–85, countries with less than four years data excluded. Standard errors in parenthesis. Estimated by instrumental variables, using as instruments: world demand, real money, real GDP, real investment. The Wald test measures joint significance, the Sargan test the accuracy of the instrument set (see Arellano and Bond, 1988a). Both test statistics have five degrees of freedom.

that our simple reduced form is certainly a short-cut way of trying to capture the supply-enhancing effects of a real depreciation. In terms of the framework developed earlier, the results in Table 3 suggest that the presumed resource-switching towards tradeables elicited by the massive real exchange rate depreciation involved at least a temporary output loss. In a world where factor specificity plays an important role, switching policies would be expected to lead to some resource idleness. It may well be that non-tradeable activities used factors not easily transferable to tradeable activities. Probably the real exchange rate variable also captures other adjustment effects associated with terms-of-trade loss like lack of foreign exchange. Nonetheless, taken together, the results in Tables 2 and 3 give support, though perhaps only suggestive, to the concerns raised by the structuralist critique.

4. Investment, the real exchange rate and the debt overhang

The sharp fall in the share of investment in GDP in developing countries (Table 1) does not bode well for a consolidation of adjustment achievements to date in the absence of a significant increase in the efficiency of investment. Lower investment not only reduces future productive capacity, it also engenders lowered expectations for future growth. These expectations may be socially destabilizing. In addition, lower investment limits the scope for resource reallocation in response to reforms throughout the economy. Yet it is resource reallocation to the new set of incentives created by the reforms that is expected to play a crucial role in most adjustment-with-growth programmes.

The disappointing investment rate in developing countries may be attributable to the extreme economic and financial distress of the most recent period, or it may be attributable to the design of adjustment policies. Two components of the adjustment-with-growth programmes may have been responsible for the investment slump. The first has to do with the effects of a real depreciation; the second with the microeconomic reforms that were part of the conditionality provisions of the adjustment packages supported by the World Bank. Consider again the impact of a real depreciation. It has been argued (e.g. Blejer and Khan, 1984), that the availability of foreign exchange exerts a powerful influence on investment both because it is needed to purchase mostly foreign-produced capital goods and because it may permit a less restrictive monetary policy. A real exchange rate depreciation is expected to promote investment by increasing the availability of foreign exchange. This may not happen, however, since a real exchange rate devaluation may substantially raise the real cost of capital goods (Buffie, 1984).

The second way in which adjustment programmes may have contributed to the slump in investment comes from the cut in public expenditures required by IMF stabilization programmes and by the strong public-sector management-reform component in World Bank structural adjustment programmes. Structural adjustment programmes aimed at restoring growth not only by rationalizing fiscal and financial incentives through economy-wide market and financial-sector reforms, but also by strengthening public-sector management. Many structural adjustment packages required a combination of divestiture of some public enterprises and a freeze on the creation of new ones and on employment levels in existing ones – in other words, a reduction in public-sector expenditure. It was hoped that private-sector investment would move in to replace public-sector investment and that, as a result of the policies aimed at rationalizing price incentives and reforming public-sector management, the overall marginal efficiency of investment would rise.

To evaluate the proximate causes of the fall in the investment share in GDP, we collected time-series data on public-sector investment for a sample of 32 countries. The data can be used to provide a rough breakdown of total investment by public- and private-sector components. The remainder of the paper is based on analysis of these data.

Table 4. Investment efficiency and the cost of capital (Annual averages, unweighted averages in country groups)

	Manufacturing exporters			Primary exporters			Developed countries		
	70–74	75–82	83–86	70–74	75–82	83–86	70–74	75–82	83–86
Investment/GDP									
private (%)	13	15	12	15	14	11	21	19	18
public (%)	6	8	7	6	7	6	4	4	3
total (%)	19	23	19	21	22	17	25	23	21
ICOR									
private	1.1	2.1	1.9	1.3	1.5	1.5	2.1	2.2	1.9
total	1.6	3.4	2.7	1.8	2.3	2.3	2.5	2.6	2.2
Cost of capital (1975–82 = 100)	54	100	233	38	100	158	76	100	152

Notes: Developed country data for the G-7: US, UK, France, Germany, Japan, Italy and Canada. The incremental capital-output ratio is the ratio of real investment to real output growth. Real GDP growth is the denominator in both the private and total ICOR. Thus a higher total ICOR implies a lower efficiency of investment. The real cost of capital is measured by (nominal interest rate + depreciation rate − rate of price increase of investment goods) multiplied by the price of investment goods relative to the GDP deflator.

4.1. Efficiency of investment and the cost of investment

The longer-term trends (1970–86) of public and private investment rates are displayed by sub-period for the manufacturing and primary exporter groups in Table 4. Comparable trends for the G-7 countries are also provided as a reference. Broadly similar trends apply to developed and to developing countries. For all country groupings, private and public investment falls in the post-1982 period, and the cost-of-capital index rises. Fluctuations, however, are more pronounced for developing than for developed countries.

For developing countries, four stylized facts emerge. First is an increase in the share of public investment during the period of 'easy' credit, when there was ample liquidity in the world capital markets following the first oil price rise. Second is a sharp downward shift in the share of private investment in GDP after the crisis, especially for primary exporters. Third is a steady increase in the real cost of capital. Fourth is a sharp swing in the incremental capital output ratio (ICOR) for manufacturing exporters, with an improvement during 1983–86, when the ICOR fell and the efficiency of investment increased, whereas the ICOR for primary exporters remained stable.

On the basis of these broad trends, one would be tempted to conclude that adjustment programmes were largely successful, at least for manufacturing exporters. For this group, the fall in public- and private-sector investment was accompanied by an increase in the efficiency of total investment. It could also be argued that the reduction in the size of the public sector's capital expenditures weeded out the most inefficient investments and that the rationalization of public-sector investments raised the marginal efficiency of public investment.

Also, by emphasizing the need for a real exchange rate depreciation, adjustment programmes compounded the increase in the cost of capital. It was hoped that the higher cost of capital would increase the efficient use of capital. And, helped by financial-sector reforms, distortions in factor prices favouring capital-intensive production techniques would be eliminated. In the final analysis, this means that the same growth rates can now be achieved with a smaller investment effort if the efficiency-augmenting effects are sufficiently strong.

These findings and interpretations are at best suggestive, but certainly not conclusive. The fall in the ICOR may reflect a higher rate of capacity utilization of a slowly increasing (or perhaps even shrinking) volume of capacity. It may also reflect a cutback of projects with long gestation lags (particularly public investment projects), or in investment in maintenance. In both cases the decline in the ICOR may not be sustainable and is likely to be reversed. Better information (like a breakdown of GDP into public- and private-sector components) would be needed for a sounder verdict.[4] We can, however, go a bit further and verify whether the real exchange rate depreciation was a cause of the increase in the real cost of investment. We can also verify whether the major cause of the decline in private investment was the increase in the cost of investment or other factors such as depressed demand.

We start with the cost of capital goods. Table 5 displays estimates of the elasticity of the relative price of capital goods in terms of the real exchange rate. The results show that a real exchange rate devaluation significantly increases the relative price of investment. The effect is stronger for manufacturing exporters than for primary exporters. At first sight this appears paradoxical. However, the result is less surprising when we consider that the share of construction in total investment is usually higher in lower-income countries (see Chenery, Syrquin and Robinson, 1986). In sum, the results in Tables 4 and 5 suggest that our data are at least consistent with the 'new' structuralist critique, namely, that depreciation of the real exchange rate will have some contractionary

[4] Because of the impossibility of distinguishing between the public- and private-sector components of GDP in our sample, the ICOR calculations in Table 4 are at best suggestive of trends in the efficiency of investment. Also, these rough calculations do not account for changes in capacity utilization. For alternative calculations that indicate an increase in the efficiency of investment during the 1980s see Easterly and Wetzel (1989).

Table 5. The real exchange rate and the relative price of investment goods (Dependent variable: logarithm of price of investment goods relative to the GDP deflator)

	Manufacturing exporters	Primary exporters
Effect of 1% devaluation	0.46 (0.07)	0.26 (0.07)

Notes: Data and country classification as in Table 4. Estimated by instrumental variables, using lagged real exchange rate, real money, public investment and country intercepts as instruments. Standard errors in parenthesis. Country intercepts not reported.

effects on supply in the medium to long term. Of course, the undesirable effects of these contractionary pressures must be balanced against any efficiency-enhancing effects resulting from less distortion in the cost of capital.

We turn next to the causes of the decline in private investment. A contributing factor must have been the income loss that resulted from the combination of worsening terms of trade and higher debt-service payments. For the same group of countries as those in Table 1, Faini *et al.* (1990) estimate a loss in income of 2.5% of the average GDP between 1978–81 and 1982–86 (period averages). To sort out further the effects on private investment of demand-side shocks and of the cost of capital, we estimate a standard accelerator model in which the growth of absorption and the expected cost of capital are the main determinants of investment demand. The simplicity of the accelerator model makes it attractive for separating the effects on investment due to the combined effects of changes in the level of aggregate demand and changes in the expected cost of capital. We also examine whether the different components of the cost of capital (the real interest rate and the real price of investment goods) affect investment differently.[5] Finally, we look for any significant impact on private investment of foreign exchange availability (measured as the sum of export receipts and non-monetary capital flows) and of public investment.

As expected, private investment is positively related to real GDP growth and negatively related to the cost of capital (Table 6). The long-run elasticity of the investment rate with respect to the cost of capital is 0.16 for manufacturing exporters and 0.12 for primary exporters. Foreign exchange availability exerts a positive, but statistically weak, impact for primary exporters and no effect at all for manufacturing exporters. Public-sector investment never proved to be statistically

[5] We also tested for a separate and/or different effect of the real exchange rate but found none.

Table 6. Investment determinants: output and substitution effects (Dependent variable: ratio of private investment to GDP)

Effect of unit increase in	Manufacturing exporters	Primary exporters
Private investment/GDP, last year	0.61	0.39
	(0.11)	(0.11)
Output growth	0.12	0.17
	(0.06)	(0.06)
Output growth last year		0.15
		(0.08)
Capital cost last year	−0.06	−0.07
	(0.03)	(0.03)
Depreciation	−1.43	−1.03
	(0.46)	(0.46)
Depreciation last year		−1.11
		(0.53)
Foreign exchange/GDP		0.01
		(0.007)
Diagnostic statistics		
Wald test	84 (4)	84 (7)
Sargan test	56 (43)	34 (59)

Notes: Standard errors in parenthesis. Country intercepts not reported. Estimated by instrumental variables. Capital cost defined as (real interest rate + depreciation rate) multiplied by price of investment goods relative to GDP deflator. (Depreciation rate taken as 7% p.a.) Depreciation defined as depreciation rate times relative price of investment goods. Degrees of freedom in parenthesis.

significant in any of the equations. Our data were unable to detect any significant complementarity (or substitutability) between public and private investment once we control for the real interest rate and the cost of capital. This may be because our data did not distinguish between investment in infrastructure and investment by public enterprises.

It is instructive to apply the estimates in Table 6 to the investment and cost-of-capital figures of Table 4 to calculate the portion of the decline in investment between 1975–82 and 1983–85 accounted for by variations in the cost of capital. This estimate is obtained by multiplying the long-run elasticity of investment with respect to the various components of the cost of capital by the change in the average value of these components between the two periods. The calculation indicates that only a relatively small fraction of the fall in private investment is attributable to increases in the cost of capital, even for manufacturing exporters, where investment is more sensitive to changes in the cost of capital. We find that 34.6% of the decline in private investment is attributable to increases in the cost of capital. Comparable figures for primary exporters are 24.2% of private investment. We, therefore, conclude that the output (and other) effects were a more important contributing factor to the decline in investment than the substitution effect.

4.2. Investment and the debt overhang

While the accelerator model is useful for sorting out the contribution of demand shocks and of changes in the cost of capital, the calculations presented above suggest that other factors must have played an important role in explaining the recent dramatic decline in investment among developing countries. To explore these other factors, we now turn to a forward-looking approach to the investment decision. Clearly, entrepreneurs consider the future before committing long-term resources to production, basing their decision on their expectations about the future path of the main determinants of the investment's return.

In a context where investment is at least partially irreversible once capital is installed, the decision to invest is intrinsically tied to the level of uncertainty about the future evolution of the economy. A high level of uncertainty will reduce the propensity to invest: it increases the possibility that highly productive capacity installed today will be of no use tomorrow if economic conditions deteriorate sharply. Under these circumstances, entrepreneurs would prefer to wait for the uncertainty to dissipate rather than make the decision to invest today. In turn, low investment today increases the probability of economic deterioration tomorrow, making the initial prophecy self-fulfilling (Rodrik, 1989). The economy becomes trapped in an inefficient, low-investment equilibrium.

This outcome is not simply a theoretical quibble. The scenario we have just sketched matches the situation in many developing countries, where the debt overhang and widespread symptoms of adjustment fatigue provide a gloomy outlook for the recovery of private investment. A recent World Bank report (1988) concludes that the long-run sustainability of the adjustment effort is threatened by low investment rates, persistent debt overhang, worsening income distribution and burgeoning fiscal deficits. Under these circumstances, it is no wonder that forward-looking entrepreneurs are quite reluctant to sink resources into nearly-irreversible activities.

To model the forward-looking nature of the investment decision, we assume that the representative firm is constrained by a putty–clay technology and operates in an imperfectly competitive output market. (The model is derived in the appendix.) Production techniques are

Table 7. Investment and the macroeconomic environment (Dependent variable: the adjusted ICOR)

Effect of unit increase in	Investment	
	Private	Total
Debt/exports	1.01	1.34
	(0.21)	(0.62)
(Debt/exports) × (value ICOR)	−0.74	−0.40
	(0.15)	(0.28)
Value ICOR	2.74	2.17
	(0.35)	(0.60)
Real exchange rate, last year	−2.56	−2.66
	(1.07)	(1.91)
(Real exchange rate, last year) × (value ICOR)	3.00	2.60
	(0.90)	(0.87)
Foreign exchange/GDP	−1.11	−2.76
	(0.69)	(0.84)
(Foreign exchange/GDP) × (value ICOR)	−0.10	0.11
	(0.38)	(0.34)

Notes: Sample pools manufacturing and primary exporters. Standard errors in parenthesis, country intercepts not reported. The adjusted ICOR at time t is defined as

$$(q\,IC/p)_t - (1-d)/(1+r)_t(q\,IC/p)_{t+1}$$

where q is the price of investment goods, p the GDP deflator, IC the ICOR, d the depreciation rate and r the real interest rate. The value ICOR is simply $(q\,IC/p)$.

flexible *ex ante* but, once chosen, they cannot be changed in response to subsequent variations in factor prices. Capital-market imperfections are summarized by an agency cost function in which a high leverage is associated with higher costs for the firm. Only debt and retained earnings are available as sources of investment finance. Finally, we dispense with the assumption that the interest rate and the entrepreneur's discount rate are identical. Market imperfections prevent such equalization. The risk premium (i.e., the difference between the discount rate and the interest rate) is assumed to be a function of the macroeconomic environment. The resulting first-order condition (see the appendix) relates the quasi-forward difference in the marginal capital-output ratio (multiplied by the ratio of the investment to the output deflators) to the determinants of the risk premium.

This framework is convenient for investigating whether variables such as the debt ratio, foreign exchange availability, the real exchange rate and public investment have a significant bearing on the investment decision through their impact on the macroeconomic environment.

Table 8. Investment and macroeconomic stability
(Dependent variable: country-specific fixed effects of investment in Table 7)

	Total investment	Private investment
Constant	1.69	1.45
	(0.29)	(0.21)
Standard deviation of real exchange rate	−0.30	−0.15
	(0.12)	(0.09)

Notes: OLS cross section on 20 countries, standard errors in parenthesis.

Estimation of the optimality condition helps isolate the effect of the macroeconomic environment on investment by controlling for the more direct impact that these variables have on investment through other channels such as the cost of capital.

We estimate this model for a smaller sample that combines manufacturing and primary exporters. Table 7 indicates several important results. First, an increase in the debt–export ratio is associated with a lower propensity to invest, possibly because of a higher risk premium. Second, a depreciated real exchange rate and a greater availability of foreign exchange both promote investment.

We also investigated whether the debt–export ratio became more significant during the crisis period. Tests for in-sample stability show that the debt–export ratio has a significantly higher coefficient after 1982.

The picture that emerges from these estimates is that the macroeconomic environment is likely to have had a significant impact on investment. The sample of 20 countries is smaller than one would wish ideally, and the assumption of continuous optimization by agents is a strong one. Yet the results support the often-heard contention that a credible macroeconomic environment is a prerequisite for a sustainable recovery.

Further support for this hypothesis is given in Table 8, which reports the results of regressing the fixed country effects of Table 7 on the standard deviation of the real exchange rate, σ. If fluctuations in the real exchange are a good proxy for macroeconomic instability, then the results in Table 8 confirm the view that investment responds positively to a stable macroeconomic environment.[6] Taken together,

[6] The sample is the same as that in Tables 4–6 except that countries with negative ICORs have been eliminated.

the results in Tables 7 and 8 suggest that the state of the macroeconomic environment explains much of the cross-country variation in investment.[7]

5. Looking ahead

Six years into the crisis that hit developing countries, three facts stand out. First, only manufacturing exporters have resumed growth to pre-crisis levels and stabilized their debt-service burden. Second, the investment share in GDP has declined substantially. Third, the real exchange rate has depreciated sharply, by about 40% compared with its level around 1980. Arguably, a sharp real exchange rate depreciation was called for by the need to service higher interest payments. However, a substantial depreciation was also clearly at the heart of the adjustment-with-growth packages supported by the IMF and World Bank.

Complemented by microeconomic reforms for rationalizing incentives and by other measures aimed at mobilizing resources, depreciation of the real exchange rate was expected to help remove long-standing distortions in factor markets that favoured capital-intensive projects and distortions in goods markets that penalized the production of tradeables, notably exports. The evidence shows that for most countries, adjustment occurred mainly through a reduction in expenditures. To say the least, the econometric evidence is certainly consistent with structuralist arguments that real depreciation elicits little supply response in the short run.

A sustainable recovery requires that income growth exceed population growth. For low-income countries, population growth is around 2% a year. Per capita income growth was still negative during 1986–88 for fuel exporters and positive but less than 0.5% for primary exporters. These countries have not yet achieved sustainable recovery in the strong sense of a growth in per capita income of 1% or more a year. Since adjustment also worsened income distribution in many countries because of the combination of capital flight and plummeting real wages, a sustainable recovery has not yet been achieved.

Yet there is evidence that sustainable growth may be within reach if productivity-raising microeconomic reforms can be sustained long enough. This has been clearly demonstrated by the successful adjustment experience of the East Asian countries during the recent crisis and the spectacular increases in total factor productivity growth they

[7] Alesina and Tabellini (1989) analyse the effects of macroeconomic instability in terms of political decisions.

achieved during a 20-year period of outward orientation. The calculations presented in this paper show signs, in the form of a higher efficiency of investment, that productivity is rising. However, up to now, this effect has been quantitatively small. We also show that only a small part of the decline in investment can be accounted for by the substitution effect arising from the higher cost of investment associated with the sharp real exchange rate depreciation. We therefore conclude that in spite of some investment efficiency improvements, especially among manufacturing exporters, much of the decline in private investment must be accounted for by factors other than the cost of capital. The impact of lower investment on growth was significant. Indeed, if one applies end-of-period ICORs to the estimated elasticities of investment with respect to the real cost of capital, one finds a yearly loss in growth of 1.8% for primary exporters and 1.1% for manufacturing exporters from the lower investment levels that is not caused by a higher cost of capital.

The decline in real income caused by the unfavourable external environment also contributed to the decline in private investment. However, the evidence also supports the contention that, in a world where capital is at least partially sunk once installed, uncertainty about the future course of the economy will lead investors to wait. Econometric evidence from a forward-looking model of investment behaviour shows that investment was negatively related to debt and foreign exchange availability indicators. Therefore, contrary to what has often been asserted, debt relief would raise investment as well as consumption. Evidence was also found that investment was negatively affected by real exchange variability, a proxy for macroeconomic instability.

Two lessons emerge for the design of adjustment programmes. First, in low-income, primary-exporting countries the large real exchange rate devaluation that is central to the adjustment-with-growth strategy may not be effective for a number of reasons. These include the attendant rise in the cost of (mostly) imported capital inputs and the general lack of supply-responsiveness to the real exchange rate depreciation. Second, the microeconomic reforms that have been at the heart of many recent adjustment packages may not bear fruit if there is uncertainty about the sustainability of the stabilization effort. Investors will wait for the uncertainty surrounding a stabilization programme to be resolved, and low investment, in turn, will increase the probability of future economic deterioration. Under these circumstances, there is a high pay-off for achieving macroeconomic stability by taking appropriate measures for partial debt relief and postponing microeconomic reforms if successful implementation is jeopardized by the uncertainty investors feel about the economy. At the same time, the use of funds available from debt relief should be monitored so as to improve the position of both the creditors and the debtors. As argued by Sachs (1989) and by Claessens and Diwan (1990), debt relief should come with enhanced conditionality to provide the country with the incentive to adjust and, perhaps more crucially, to avoid the resumption of unsustainable macroeconomic policies.

Discussion

Richard Baldwin
Columbia Business School, NBER and CEPR

This paper examines the adjustment of developing countries (LDCs) to the external shocks of the 1980s. The size and scope of the sample are impressive. The authors use a variety of empirical techniques to shed light on the effects on aggregate supply and investment of two typical components of adjustment packages: significant real exchange rate depreciation and microeconomic reforms.

Table 1 studies the determinants of the trade balance. Although the authors are careful to draw only weak conclusions from the evidence, it is worthwhile pointing out some problems with these findings. Consider briefly the theory behind this regression. An accounting identity together with a semi-log approximation imply that:

$$\left(\frac{TB}{GDP}\right)_t = \alpha + (-1)\ln A_t + \ln GDP_t + \gamma_t$$

where γ is the approximation error. Assuming that GDP is a function of the real exchange rate gives us the Table 1 equation. Theory tells us that the coefficient on $\ln A$ should be exactly minus one; the fact that the estimates are consistently greater suggests that the instrumental variables have not fully dealt with the simultaneity problem. For instance, a Keynesian relationship between demand and output could account for the estimated coefficients. If lower demand lowered output as well as improving the trade balance, the coefficient on $\ln A$ would be upward biased. The fact that the estimate is consistently too high casts doubt on the estimation procedure; all the estimates are likely to reflect the impact of the RER. Since the coefficients are all undoubtedly biased it is probably best to think of them as multiple-correlation coefficients. We can therefore say no more than that depreciations are positively correlated with trade-balance improvement in this sample. Table 2 does not shed any light on whether this comes from the contractionary effects of devaluation on demand or its impact on aggregate supply.

The easiest way to avoid confounding supply and demand considerations is directly to estimate the impact of RER on output as is done in Table 3. Here we see that in fact devaluations are correlated with *lower* output; they appear to have a negative supply effect. Of course, as the authors mention, it is difficult to interpret even the signs of coefficients in such a simple estimation of the GDP function.

The evidence in Table 4 suggests that adjustment programmes have improved the aggregate efficiency of LDCs' investment. But since the private ICOR of developed countries (DCs) improved as much as that of the LDCs it is not at all evident that the improvement can be attributed to the adjustment programmes. And although the LDCs' public ICOR improved more than the DCs', this may again be for a large number of reasons. In particular, since the improvement is for only four years, 1983–86, it is very possible that this represents a reduction of public investment which does not directly contribute to GDP, rather than a weeding out of inefficient projects. For example, postponing maintenance on roads and bridges, reduced education expenditures and elimination of long-term public health projects would tend to boost the public ICOR yet may not represent efficiency gains.

The most convincing evidence in the paper is presented in Table 7. The regression results are for a well-specified model of the investment decision. The table presents evidence that devaluation promotes investment, yet a greater debt-to-export ratio discourages investment. Although this is not directly related to the effects of depreciation and microeconomic reforms on supply, it does address an important issue. It suggests that a sustainable macroeconomic environment is important for growth and that acquiring debt to stabilize the economy may be a self-defeating policy.

Charles Bean
London School of Economics

This stimulating and provocative paper seeks to marshall econometric evidence from a panel of developing countries on the wisdom or otherwise of the 'adjustment with growth' packages forced on many of them over the last decade. While I have sympathy with many of the arguments the authors advance, the econometric results are sometimes not as convincing as one would like, and their case might usefully have been buttressed by case studies of individual countries.

My first comment is perhaps more appropriately directed at the IMF and the World Bank than at the authors of this paper. A key feature in these adjustment packages has been real exchange rate depreciation, and Faini and de Melo follow this line of thinking by treating the real exchange rate as a largely exogenous variable under the control of the authorities. But how are such real depreciations achieved? In the short run a monetary relaxation i.e. a nominal devaluation/depreciation, will do the trick, but in the medium term one would expect the consequent improvement in competitiveness to be whittled away as domestic wages and prices adjust. In the long run a real exchange rate depreciation can be sustained only if it is accompanied by other real changes such as a fiscal contraction or a successful incomes policy. The effect on the economy will differ depending on the nature of the supporting policies (the latter is supply enhancing; the former is generally not), and the authors fail to control for this.

Turning next to the results of Tables 2 and 3 in Section 3, I must confess to some unease at the rather cavalier treatment of the question of identification, with the real money supply, surely an endogenous variable, playing a major instrumental role. Faini and de Melo admit that they cannot sort out whether their trade balance equation reflects demand switching or a supply response. But I do not see why their supply equation should be any more successfully identified, especially since for lack of data it omits important supply-side variables such as the capital stock and own-product wages (for which the real exchange rate seems likely to be a poor proxy). This may not matter too much if the equations are used for reduced form 'historical accounting' exercises such as those to which the trade balance equation is put, but should make one wary of making policy recommendations based on an assumed channel of response.

The discussion of the adverse effect of a real exchange depreciation on the cost of capital and thence investment provides an interesting counterpart to the literature on European unemployment which has identified the terms of trade deterioration following OPEC I and II as a potential source of wage pressure and adverse supply-side developments in the 1970s and early 1980s. However, the results suggest that increases in the cost of capital account for only a third (quarter) of the decline in private investment in manufacturing (primary) exporters. Since virtually all of the action comes from variations in the real interest rate rather than the price of capital goods (see Table 4), it would appear that the impact on investment of the real depreciations via the cost of capital is essentially negligible.

The authors then go on to consider a more structural model of investment in which the impact of the macroeconomic environment can be more directly assessed. Although the main text makes much of the effect of uncertainty and irreversibility in leading to a 'wait-and-see' attitude on the part of entrepreneurs, the model of the appendix does not explicitly incorporate this feature (it is in fact valid only under point expectations). Instead there is an *ad hoc* risk premium which depends on macroeconomic variables such as the debt–export ratio and the availability of foreign exchange. The results in Table 7 suggest that these variables are statistically important. Unfortunately, because the estimated equation is an intertemporal optimality condition it is not easy to gauge their quantitative significance, which requires solving the full optimization problem facing the entrepreneur. It would have been useful if the authors had given the reader some guidance here.

Finally, the discussion sometimes confuses the issue of macroeconomic uncertainty with the question of the credibility of economic policies (when the reader is told, for example, that the results 'support the often-heard contention that a credible macroeconomic environment is a prerequisite for a sustainable recovery'). A set of announced policies can be completely 'incredible' i.e. unsustainable, and consequently the path of future policy instruments entirely predictable. By contrast a set of announced policies can be 'credible' i.e. sustainable, but there can be considerable uncertainty about whether the government will actually stick to them. Identifying an adjustment programme that is both credible and successful is child's play *ex post*; identifying it *ex ante* is another matter entirely!

General discussion

Many panelists focused on the difficulty of interpreting regression equations at this degree of aggregation. In particular, it was hard to know how best to capture the effect of uncertainty: Jean-Paul Lambert thought that some measure of the variability of export prices might be more appropriate for many primary commodity exporters. Horst Siebert pointed out that microeconomic determinants of uncertainty (such as the probability of expropriation) had been changing significantly in many countries during the period under consideration. He also thought it important to control explicitly for unanticipated changes in fiscal and monetary policy. Daniel Cohen was unhappy with the interpretation given to the debt–export ratio, which could represent many different influences on investment.

There was some discussion also of policy implications. David Newbery pointed out that primary commodity exporters faced a serious difficulty: if the elasticity of demand for their products was less than unity, an expansion of exports along the lines demanded in structural adjustment programmes might lead to their becoming worse off overall. Paul Seabright suggested that devaluation meant very different things for primary commodity and for manufactured exporters: for the former, a devaluation would have little effect on the foreign currency price of their exports but would change mainly the relative domestic price of tradeables and non-tradeables; it was unsurprising that dramatic effects were hard to find in the short term. For manufactured exporters, however, devaluations changed the prices of their goods relative to competing products and could be expected to yield appreciably greater results in the short term.

Appendix. A forward-looking model of investment

The representative firm is assumed to be constrained by a putty–clay technology and to operate in an imperfectly competitive output market. Imperfections in capital markets constrain the financing choice of the firm. There is no well-functioning stock market. There are, as a result, only two sources of finance: (short-term) debt and retained earnings. Entrepreneurs discount future returns at a rate, i, which is assumed to be larger than the risk-free interest rate, r (otherwise firms would accumulate financial assets). Therefore, debt is the privileged source of finance (perhaps also because of its favoured tax status). However, an internal solution to the optimal debt decision is obtained by assuming that higher outstanding debt relative to the firm's capital is associated with increasing agency costs.

The firm's problem can be written as:

$$\max \sum \left(\frac{1}{1+i}\right)^t [p_t(Q_t)Q_t - w_t N_t - q_t I_t + B_t - B_{t-1} - r_t B_{t-1} - A[(B_t, p_t(\cdot)Q_t)] \quad \text{(A1)}$$

s.t.

$$Q_t = \sum_{v=t-L}^{t} (1-\delta)^{v-t} I_v f(k_v)/k_v \quad \text{(A2)}$$

$$N_t = \sum_{v=t-L}^{t} (1-\delta)^{v-t} I_v / k_v \quad \text{(A3)}$$

where Q_t, N_t, and I_t represent output, employment and investment, respectively, $p_t(Q_t)$ is the inverse demand function, and w_t and q_t are labour and investment costs, respectively. On the financial side, r_t is the risk-free interest rate and $A(B_t, p_t(\cdot)Q_t)$ with $A_1 > 0$, $A_2 < 0$ and $A_{11} > 0$ is the agency cost function. Equations (A2) and (A3) define the production and the labour demand function for a putty–clay technology, where L is the average life of capital goods, δ denotes their depreciation rate, and $f(k_v)$ and k_v represent the *ex ante* production function (in intensive form) and the capital-labour ratio.

The first-order conditions for output and debt are:

$$g(q_t, \bar{w}_t) - \frac{1-\delta}{1+i} g(q_{t+1}, \bar{w}_{t+1}) = MR_t - MR_t A_2 \tag{A4}$$

$$(1+i)(1-A_1)-(1+r)=0 \tag{A5}$$

where MR_t denotes marginal revenue and $g(\ )$ is an increasing function of factor prices (Nickell, 1979). The function g represents the present discounted value over a lifetime of marginal costs of installed capacity for a machine after allowing for depreciation. At an optimum, the cost of an extra unit of capacity today is equated to marginal revenue plus the discounted saving of not having to install more capacity tomorrow. The variable $\bar{w}$ represents the present discounted value of labour costs over the lifetime of a machine. Even after parameterizing the agency cost function and the *ex ante* production function, one cannot estimate (A4) since $\bar{w}$ is not observable. We can, however, substitute out for $\bar{w}$ by using the first-order condition for k_v (not reported in the text), which relates the marginal rate of substitution between labour and capital in the *ex ante* production function to $q_t/\bar{w}_t$. We find that $g(\ ) = q_t/f'(k_t)$.

For the purpose of estimation, we assume that $f(k_t)$ is Cobb–Douglas and $A(\ )$ is quadratic, i.e.:

$$A(B_t, p_t(\ )Q_t) = a/2\left[\frac{B_t^2}{(p_tQ_t)^2} - C\right]p_tQ_t \tag{A6}$$

Substitution and manipulations yield:

$$\frac{q_tIC_t}{p_t} - \frac{1-\delta}{1+i^r}\frac{q_{t+1}IC_{t+1}}{p_{t+1}}$$

$$= \frac{(\varepsilon-1)\alpha}{\varepsilon}[1/2a(i-r)^2/(1+i)^2 + 1 + ac/2] \tag{A7}$$

where IC_t denotes the incremental capital-output ratio, i^r is the real interest rate, $[1+i^r = (1+i)p_t/p_{t+1}]$ and ε and α represent the price elasticity of demand and the capital elasticity of output, respectively. The right-hand side of (A7) is equal to $MR_t(1-A_2)$ after substituting from (A5) and (A6) and multiplying by α/p_t. To interpret the left-hand side of (A7) notice that a large value of IC indicates a relatively more capital-intensive technique on the latest vintage which in turn must be attributed, for a given q, to a relatively high level of $\bar{w}$, i.e. of the present discounted value of labour costs over the lifetime of machine. As a result the present value of marginal costs associated with a machine (the function $g(\ )$) will be also large and lead, as indicated by (A4), to a lower capacity output. For a given value of δ, (A7) could have been estimated had we assumed that $i = r$. Suppose though that $1 + i = (1 + r)(1 + \rho)$, where ρ is a multiplicative risk premium that depends on the macroeconomic environment. Multiply (A7) by $1 + \rho$ and bring the unobservable terms from the left-hand to the right-hand side. We then assume that ρ can be expressed as a function of the state of the macroeconomic environment.

Equation (A7) provides the basis for estimation. We experiment over different values of δ. Notice that if ρ is not equal to zero, then the lagged value of $q(IC/p)$ should belong on the right-hand side of the equation. Fixed-effect estimation under these circumstances would be problematic: the speed of convergence is a function of the number of observations per country. To circumvent this problem, we rely on a modified Anderson–Hsiao (1982) procedure. To eliminate the fixed effect, we take first differences of the original equation. By doing so, however, the error term, if it was white noise to begin with, is transformed into a first-order unit-root moving average process which is correlated with the first difference of $q(IC/p)$. Therefore, we use an (efficient) instrumental variable procedure by exploiting all the orthogonality restrictions between the error term and $q(IC/p)_{t-i}$ where $i > 1$. This generalized method of moments estimator was implemented in the DPD programme developed by Arellano and Bond (1988b).

References

Alesina, A. and G. Tabellini (1989). 'External Debt, Capital Flight and Political Risk', *Journal of International Economics.*

Anderson, T. and C. Hsiao (1982). 'Formulation and Estimation of Dynamic Models Using Panel Data', *Journal of Econometrics.*

Arellano, M. and S. Bond (1988a). 'Some Tests of Specification for Panel Data: Montecarlo Evidence and an Application to an Employment Equation', IFS Discussion paper 88/4.

—— (1988b). 'Dynamic Panel Data Estimation Using DPD', IFS Discussion paper 88/10.

Blejer, M. and M. Khan (1984). 'Government Policy and Private Investment in Developing Countries', *IMF Staff Papers.*

Bruno, M. (1979). 'Stabilization and Stagflation in a Semi-Industrialized Economy', in R. Dornbusch and J. Frenkel (eds.) *International Economic Policy: Theory and Evidence.* Johns Hopkins University Press: Baltimore.

Buffie, E. (1984). 'The Macroeconomics of Trade Liberalization', *Journal of International Economics.*

—— (1986). 'Devaluation, Investment and Growth', *Journal of Development Economics.*

Cavallo, D. (1977). 'Stagflationary Effects of Monetarist Stabilization Policies', Ph.D Thesis, Harvard University.

Chenery, H. (1975). 'The Structuralist Approach to Development Policy', *American Economic Review.*

Chenery, H., S. Robinson and M. Syrquin (1986). *Industrialization and Growth,* Oxford University Press: Oxford.

Claessens, S. and I. Diwan (1990). 'Liquidity, Debt Relief, and Conditionality', in I. Husain and I. Diwan (eds.) *Dealing with the Debt Crisis.* The World Bank: Washington, D.C.

Corbo, V., M. Goldstein and M. Khan (eds.) (1987). *Growth-Oriented Adjustment Programs.* World Bank: Washington, D.C.

Dell, S. (1982). 'Stabilization: The Political Economy of Overkill', *World Development.*

Diaz-Alejandro, C. (1980). 'Southern Cone Stabilization Plans', in W. Cline and S. Weintraub (eds.) *Stabilization in Developing Countries.* Brookings Institution: Washington, D.C.

Dornbusch, R. (1988). 'Notes on Credibility and Stabilization', (mimeo), MIT: Cambridge, MA.
Easterly, W. and D. Wetzel (1989). 'Policy Determinants of Growth: Survey of Theory and Evidence', PPR Discussion Paper No. 313, World Bank: Washington, D.C.
Edwards, S. (1989a). *Real Exchange Rates, Devaluation and Adjustment: Exchange Rate Policy in Developing Countries*, MIT Press: Cambridge MA.
—— (1989b). 'The International Monetary Fund and the Developing Countries: a Critical Evaluation', *Carnegie Rochester Conference Series on Public Policy*.
Faini, R., J. de Melo, A. Senhadji-Semlali and J. Stanton, (1990). 'Growth-Oriented Adjustment Programs: A Statistical Analysis', PRE Discussion Paper No. 426, World Bank, Washington, D.C., Forthcoming in *World Development*.
Krugman, P. and L. Taylor. (1977). 'Contractionary Effects of Devaluation', *Journal of International Economics*.
Lizondo, S. and P. Montiel (1989). 'Contractionary Devaluation: An Analytical Overview', *IMF Staff Papers*.
Nickell, S. (1979). *The Investment Decision of the Firm*. Cambridge University Press: Cambridge.
Rodrik, D. (1989). 'Policy Uncertainty and Private Investment in Developing Countries', NBER Working Paper No. 2999, National Bureau of Economic Research, Cambridge, MA.
Sachs, J. (1989). 'The Debt Overhang of Developing Countries', in G. Calvo, R. Findlay, P. Kouri and J. de Macedo (eds.) *Debt, Stabilization and Development: Essays in Memory of Carlos Diaz-Alejandro*, Basil Blackwell: Oxford.
Taylor, L. (1982). *Structuralist Macroeconomics*. Basic Books.
Thomas, V., A. Chibber, M. Dailami and J. de Melo (eds.) (1990). *Structural Adjustment and the World Bank*. Oxford University Press: Oxford (forthcoming).
Van Wijnbergen, S. (1986). 'Exchange Rate Management and Stabilization Policies in Developing Countries', *Journal of Development Economics*.
World Bank (1988). 'Adjustment Lending: An Evaluation of Ten Years of Experience', Policy and Research Series No. 1, World Bank, Washington, D.C.

Chapter 6

Fiscal Spending and Economic Growth: Some Stylized Facts

Céline Carrère and Jaime de Melo*
University of Geneva, Switzerland
Fondation pour les Etudes et Recherches sur le Développement International, Clermont-Ferrand, France
Centre for Economic Policy Research, London, UK

Summary — Using an "event analysis", this paper complements the cross-country approach to the study of fiscal correlates of growth. Data on fiscal expenditures and growth for a database of 140 countries (118 developing countries) over 1972–2005 are reorganized around turning points providing a summary but encompassing description of "what is in the data". For this sample, the probability of occurrence of a fiscal event is about 10%, and, the probability of a growth event once a fiscal event had occurred is around 26%. For developing countries, fiscal events followed by growth events occur under situations of (i) significantly lesser deficit, (ii) fewer resources devoted to non-interest general public services and (iii) shift in primary expenditures toward transport & communication. After controlling for the growth-inducing effects of positive terms-of-trade shocks and of trade liberalization reform, probit estimates indicate that a growth event is more likely to occur in a developing country when surrounded by a fiscal event. Moreover, the probability

*We thank Christopher Adam, Jean-François Brun, Antonio Estache, Robert Flood, Peter Heller, participants at the CERDI seminar, and three referees for comments on an earlier draft. An annex describing the data base and construction of variables is available in Carrère and de Melo (2007). Final revision accepted: January 9, 2012.

of occurrence of a growth event in the years following a fiscal event is greater the lower is the associated fiscal deficit, confirming that success of a growth-oriented fiscal expenditure reform is associate with a stabilized macroeconomic environment (through limited primary fiscal deficit).

Keywords — fiscal space, primary spending, growth acceleration, event analysis, developing countries

1. INTRODUCTION

A renewed focus on fiscal policy and growth has spawned a lively debate over demands for what has been dubbed greater "fiscal space" to support growth. Besides a few case studies (see World Bank, 2007), so far the exploration of fiscal space and performance in developing countries has proceeded along two paths: (i) studies of the efficiency of specific public sector expenditures — e.g., several studies on infrastructure (Calderón & Servén, 2004) or on other components of social infrastructure (Estache, Gonzalez, & Trujillo, 2007), and (ii) cross-country growth regressions in which government expenditures are included among the regressors (Adam & Bevan, 2005 or Devarajan, Swaroop, & Zou, 1996). Perotti (2007) reviews critically the contributions of the production function and growth regression approaches. Among the more interesting lessons from these exercises (Adam & Bevan, 2005; Bose, Haque, & Osborn, 2007; Kneller, Bleaney, & Gemmell, 1999), using dynamic panels have persuasively shown that capital expenditure, as well as spending on education, health, and transport and communication can be favorable to growth when the government budget constraint is *simultaneously* taken into account in the equation.

As pointed out in several studies (e.g., Easterly, Kremer, Pritchett, & Summers, 1993; Jones & Olken, 2008), growth tends to be highly unstable in low-income countries. This makes it difficult to unveil the relation between growth and its fundamentals leading Hausmann, Pritchett, and Rodrik (2005) to pay attention to turning points by relying on an event analysis. This paper applies this approach over a large data base of 140 countries over the period 1972–2005 providing a description of the correlates between significant public spending "shocks" and growth accelerations, reorganizing the data around turning points, or "events" (calendar time is transformed into "event time"). This descriptive analysis should be viewed as complementary to the approaches described above.

More specifically, we construct growth "events" along the lines of Hausmann *et al.* (2005). Lacking information on mile-stone events in fiscal reforms similar to those available for trade reforms as in Wacziarg and Welch (2008), we define an "event" on the fiscal side using an approach similar to the definition of an event on the growth side, i.e., based on conditional changes in primary fiscal expenditures but taking into account the government budget constraint. This descriptive approach should be informative as it provides an easy-to-understand exploration of the correlates between fiscal policy (here fiscal expenditures) and performance (here per capita GDP growth). It avoids imposing a single common linear model for all countries as done in cross-countries regressions. When applied to a large database, as done here, it gives a more encompassing description of "what is in the data" and is thus complementary to the three other approaches mentioned above.

To highlight the main findings, in this sample, the probability of occurrence of a fiscal event is about 10%, and the probability of a growth event once a fiscal event has occurred is in the 22–28% range. The probability of occurrence of a fiscal event is higher for the bottom half of the income distribution of countries. For the developing country group which is the focus of this study, fiscal events followed by growth events occur under situations of a significantly lesser deficit, and a shift in discretionary expenditures toward transport & communication is only observed for fiscal events followed by growth events. After controlling for the growth-inducing effects of positive terms-of-trade shocks and of trade liberalization reform, the statistical analysis in which the probability of a growth event is conditioned on the occurrence of a fiscal event in surrounding years confirms that growth events are, on average, more likely when a fiscal event has occurred. Moreover, the probability of occurrence of a growth event in the five years following a fiscal event is greater the lower is the associated fiscal deficit, confirming that success of a growth-oriented fiscal-expenditure package is associated with a stabilized macroeconomic environment (through limited fiscal deficit).

The paper unfolds as follows. Section 2 presents the identification conditions of both growth and fiscal events (with details and sensitivity analysis left to the Carrère & de Melo, 2007, Annex A.3). Section 3 studies the characteristics of growth and fiscal events, and the relation between the two. The descriptive analysis computes fiscal event (unconditional) probabilities and probabilities that fiscal events are followed (or not) by growth events. Section 4 investigates the characteristics of fiscal events, in particular the ones followed by a growth event, in terms of geography, underlying changes in expenditure composition, and in the level of associated primary deficit. Then the statistical analysis turns on the growth side, the objective being to see if, based on probit estimates, growth events are more likely to occur in a developing country when surrounded by a fiscal event. Section 5 concludes.

2. DEFINING EVENTS

We are interested in the relation between a "significant" change in fiscal spending and a "significant" change in GDP growth — what Hausmann, Pritchett and Rodrick (henceforth HPR, 2005), call "growth acceleration". Per capita GDP *growth* and primary fiscal expenditures (in GDP %) *growth* are then our two indicator values. Call these growth indicators, z. Average annual *changes*, $z_{t,n}$, are computed for each year over successive windows of length n. Here, because of the limited sample size for the fiscal data (1972–2005) we choose a succession of windows of 5 years ($n = 4$). So we compute $\Delta z_{t,n}$:

$$\Delta z_{t,n} = z_{t,t+n} - z_{t-n-1,t-1}$$

If the change $\Delta z_{t,n}$ in the average indicator value satisfies certain conditions (see below), we will say that an "event" has taken place for z in t. The appendix details how we selected the parameter values defining an event and how sensitive our sample of events is to changes in the conditioning values so here we only describe the conditions for our "benchmark" set of parameters starting with GDP per capita growth, and then turning to primary fiscal expenditures. In this benchmark case, the sample produces 58 growth events and 95 fiscal events. Sensitivity of the number of events to the choice of parameter values is reported in appendix.

(a) *Growth events*

As in HPR, a growth event will have taken place in t if the following conditions are met:

(i) an increase in the average per-capita growth of 2 ppa or more (percentage points per annum, ppa),
(ii) growth acceleration sustained for at least 5 years $[t; t+4]$,
(iii) an average annual growth rate of at least 3.5 ppa during the acceleration period $[t; t+4]$,
(iv) a post-acceleration output exceeding the pre-episode peak level of GDP.

With this selection process, several events could follow one another over consecutive years capturing in fact the same event. To select the more "relevant" year, we fit a spline regression and choose the year for which the change in indicator value is statistically the most significant. Finally, we impose the restriction that two events must be separated by at least 5 years. This method is used for both growth and fiscal events. See details in Appendices A and B.

(b) *Fiscal events*

The core of this study is the definition of a fiscal event. Defining an event was easier for Wacziarg and Welch (2008) where the objective was to identify when significant reductions in trade distortions took place. Here a fiscal event could be a fiscal policy aimed at stabilizing the economy or a fiscal policy aimed at improving the efficiency of the economy (e.g., expenditures to enhance the productivity of private investment or to devote resources to improve property rights enforcement). While both types of fiscal policy, if successful, would raise the growth rate, in the case of stabilization, the economy would be returning to trend growth while in the second case, the growth rate would go up. Like WW, we have in mind a fiscal policy that has more permanent effects on growth.

Barro's (1990) endogenous growth model provides the framework to identify the growth effects of public expenditures. In this model, productive government capital expenditures increase the marginal productivity of private expenditure. Unless government revenue can be raised in a non-distortionary way — which is highly unlikely in practice — increases in government spending can raise or lower steady-state growth. In this model, government expenditures that only provide consumption services are negatively correlated with growth since the government has to raise taxes in a distortionary way.

This framework which puts the emphasis of fiscal policy on growth — the focus of this paper — underlines the importance of the composition of expenditures and of tax structure. While we can deal with the composition of government expenditures, in our large sample (140 countries over 1972–2005), unfortunately we cannot deal with the growth effects resulting from the choice of tax structure.

While Barro's model provides a useful framework, implementing the event-analysis in the spirit of WW is much more difficult as there is much more fungibility in fiscal policy than in trade policy. This makes it difficult to identify the fiscal space levers, so it is much more difficult to identify the expected effects of changes in these levers. Here, we restrict fiscal reform to a change in total primary fiscal expenditures and, in a second step, we study the underlying evolution of many components of potential interest (e.g., education, health, or transport and communication).

Faced with limitations and constraints on data availability, we rely on changes in consolidated central government total fiscal expenditures, TFE (taken from the GFS, see details in Carrère & de Melo, 2007, Annex Al) as "event" changes in government expenditures. Since we are looking for autonomous fiscal expenditures, events are defined on expenditures purged of non-discretionary components such as wages and interest payments, *IP*.[1] Lacking information on the wage component for each functional expenditure category, we consider as discretionary TFE purged of interest payments. So, we define discretionary fiscal expenditure, DFE, as $DFE = T - FE - IP$ which is equivalent to focusing on primary spending. We also compute the primary fiscal deficit, *def*, as the difference between the total revenues and *grants* and the discretionary fiscal expenditure, DFE (so a deficit is negative).

For the developing countries in the sample used here, average *DFE* is 24% of GDP and average central government primary fiscal deficit, *def*, is −2% of GDP. An increase in *DFE* will be declared as fiscal event in t when the following conditions are met over the following five year window:

(i) An increase in DFE average growth of 1 ppa (percentage point per annum),
(ii) If in deficit (i.e., $def < -2\%$ of GDP), deficit does not increase,
(iii) If in surplus (or in $def > -2\%$ of GDP), the increase in DFE does not lead to a deficit exceeding 2% of GDP.

The 5-year (rather than a longer period) window was dictated by the length of the time-series and our desire to have enough fiscal and growth events for statistical analysis. Sensitivity of events to parameters in the above conditions is discussed in the Appendix.[2]

This first cut at defining a "fiscal event" could be improved upon in several ways. First, the objective is to capture the availability of budgetary room that allows a government to provide resources for a desired purpose "without any prejudice to the susceptibility of a government's financial position" (Heller, 2005). Hence, ideally one would define conditions (ii) and (iii) based on formal tests of debt sustainability such as those used by Chalk and Hemming (2001). However, lack of data on indebtedness leads us to use the value of the deficit level.

Second, unfortunately, the "event" cannot be interpreted as entirely discretionary (or unanticipated). The large set of expenditures included in DFE implies that the fiscal event captures non-discretionary elements in the definition and more restrictive definitions of discretionary fiscal expenditures could certainly be built around one of the functional components of fiscal expenditures, although any greater volatility in narrower series may be difficult to interpret.[3] Thus, the most plausible interpretation of the constructed "events" is as significant changes in fiscal policy and refrains from attributing any government objective to the event — even if in case of developing countries, the pro-cyclicality of fiscal policy (see the discussion on the evidence below) suggests that the discretionary element dominates.

Third, in view of the links we are seeking to establish between fiscal spending events and growth events, one might consider whether the selection of the fiscal event (in particular through conditions (ii) and (iii)) is biased toward selecting as fiscal events those that are followed by growth.

Actually, due to the automatic response of government spending and taxes to output growth, a period of growth acceleration soon after the fiscal event will lead, other things equal, to a lower deficit. Hence, by construction, if there is an overlap in the fiscal and growth events definition' periods, we are more likely to select as fiscal events those that are followed by growth since a condition is imposed on the evolution of the fiscal deficit. However, as noted by Ilzetski and Végh (2008) or Perotti (2007) among the papers that have studied the cyclical behavior of fiscal policy in developing countries (see also Frankel, Végh, & Vuletin, 2011; Kaminsky, Reinhart, & Végh, 2004 and Gavin & Perotti, 1997), it is widely accepted that fiscal policy in these countries is typically pro-cyclical, i.e., the budget deficit is positively correlated with economic growth.

Several explanations have been advanced to explain the pro-cyclicality of fiscal policy in developing countries. Gavin and Perotti (1997) have argued that developing countries face credit constraints that prevent them from borrowing with slow growth. Tornell and Lane (1999) show that competition for a common pool of funds among different units (ministries, provinces) leads to the so-called "voracity effect" whereby expenditure could actually exceed a given windfall. Alesina, Campante, and Tabellini (2008) show that procyclicality is an optimal behavior in the presence of voters with imperfect information and corrupt politicians. (Végh & Vuletin, 2012) give evidence that the other pillar of fiscal policy, taxation, is also pro-cyclical in developing countries. This evidence comes in addition to earlier evidence by Talvi and Végh (2005) that the inflation tax falls during expansion.

Hence, according to this pro-cyclical effect, if a growth event occurs in the year following a fiscal event, this should increase the deficit, and hence weaken the probability of observing fiscal events followed by a growth event (recall that an increase in discretionary fiscal expenditure associated with an increase in the fiscal deficit does not qualify as a fiscal event). One might even suspect our definition of fiscal event to underestimate, for the developing countries, the correlation with subsequent growth.

Fourth, we would not want to exclude countries that sought fiscal space through highly concessional borrowing even if this led to an increase in their deficit (since, despite high grant percentage as a share of the loan, such loans are not treated as grants). This suggests that one might wish to take an estimate of the grant component of such loans and include that portion in government revenue thereby relaxing the budgetary constraint. However, there is no data on the grant component of these loans. As an alternative, we redefined our fiscal event with a fourth condition allowing Low-income countries to increase their fiscal deficit during the fiscal spending growth period up to 4% of GDP (considering that for low income countries, external borrowing is likely to be on highly concessional terms). Results are reported in next section.

Finally, with better indicators of performance of government expenditures than GDP per capita growth, this "event-type" analysis could be extended directly to the indicators of fiscal expenditure that concern the debate on fiscal space, e.g., health and/or education expenditures and expenditures on transport & communication capturing, for instance, event in budget reallocation between government functions for a given amount of total outlays. Unfortunately, as already mentioned, given the low quality of fiscal data, volatility in narrower series may be more difficult to interpret.

3. PATTERNS OF FISCAL AND GROWTH EVENTS

Keeping in mind the shortcomings of this methodology, we take an exhaustive approach by constructing fiscal events for as many countries as possible. Since we are interested in the various components of fiscal expenditures, the best database is the IMF Government Financial Statistics (GFS). GFS statistics are available for a large number of countries since 1972 and up to 2005.[4] Following most previous studies on fiscal expenditures we use data on fiscal expenditures by function (instead of expenditures by economic classification — i.e., by current *vs.* capital expenditures).[5] As described in Carrère and de Melo (2007, Annex Al), after reconciling the fiscal data, our "fiscal sample" includes 140 countries, of which 118 are developing (i.e., non High Income OECD countries).

For the growth database, we use the Penn World Table PWT 6.2 (see Heston, Summers, & Aten, 2006) as our baseline data source.[6] Hence, the "growth" database covers 187 countries over the same period as the fiscal data base, i.e., 1972–2004. Taking into account missing data, the sample includes 5380 observations hence 87% of the potential number of observations ($= 6171 = 187$ countries $*$ 33 years).

Turn now to the construction of growth and fiscal events as defined in Section 2 and in the appendix. As mentioned above, due to the limitations imposed by the availability of fiscal data, we choose 5-year periods for both fiscal and growth events, i.e., $n = 4$. This means that the exercise covers the period 1977–2000. Because there are missing data, we have also imposed that data be available for four out of the 5 years entering each "window". If this condition is not satisfied, a missing value is entered for that "window". Having computed the fiscal and growth events on their respective databases, we merge the two into a final dataset (see Carrère & de Melo, 2007, Annex A.2 for details). The resulting database includes 107 countries (84 developing countries, i.e., all non-High Income OECD countries), over 1977–2000. This leads to 1452 observations hence 57% of the potential number ($= 2568 = 107$ countries $\times$ 24 years).

For this sample and for the parameter values selected here, we get 58 growth events and 95 fiscal events. This is our benchmark data set over which exploration takes place. As discussed in Table 6, the number of events is relatively insensitive to a range of plausible parameter values. Nor are changes in the pattern of events surprising when we change parameter values. Figure 1 plots a subset of events in this benchmark case: 25 fiscal events are simultaneous or followed by a growth event, 23 fiscal events are preceded by a growth event. The residual (47) events that are neither followed nor preceded by a growth event are not shown in the figure (also see the details in Table 6).

Table 1 reports unconditional probabilities of these fiscal events.[7] For the whole sample and given our construction of a fiscal event, the probability of occurrence of a fiscal event is 9.7% and the probability of a growth event once a fiscal event has occurred is 26.3%. Table 1 also reports probabilities across countries ranked according to their income per capita and by region. Column 5 shows that, although the probability of occurrence of a fiscal event is fairly evenly spread across the income quartiles, the probability is higher for the lower quar-tiles (first and second). It is difficult to interpret this pattern since, as explained above, this definition of a fiscal event does not distinguish between fiscal policy shocks and systematic fiscal policy. If one can assume that fiscal policy shocks are not more prevalent among low and middle income countries, then the pattern would seem to indicate that fiscal policy is more volatile among low-income countries.[8] The probability that a

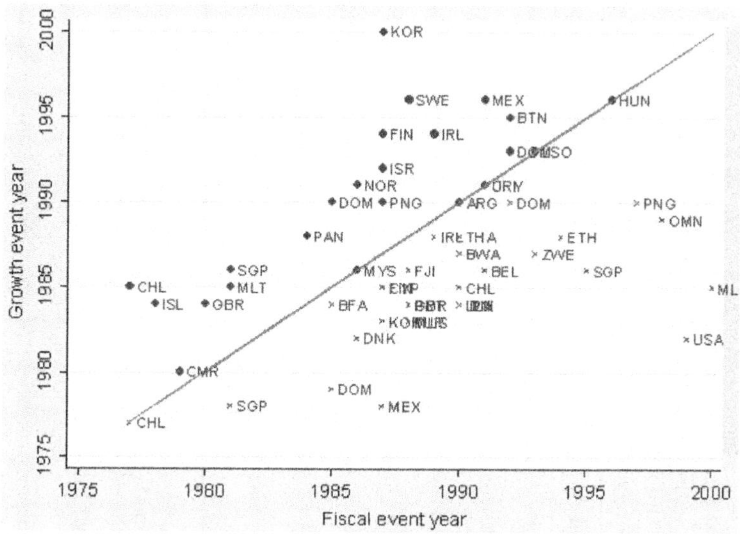

Figure 1. *Growth events vs. fiscal events. Notes:* (a) *19 points strictly above the red line (growth event strictly preceded by fiscal event);* (b) *23 points strictly below the red line (growth event strictly followed by fiscal event);* (c) *six points on the red line (growth event simultaneous to fiscal event, of which four in Latin America). 95 − 48 = 47 fiscal events with no associated growth events not shown in the figure. ARG, Argentina; BTN, Bhutan; CHL, Chile; CMR, Cameroon; CRI, Costa Rica; DOM, Dominican Republic; FIN, Finland; GBR, United Kingdom; HUN, Hungary; IRL, Ireland; ISL, Iceland; ISR, Israel; KOR, Korea, Rep.; LSO, Lesotho; MEX, Mexico; MLT, Malta; MYS, Malaysia; NOR, Norway; PAN, Panama; PNG, Papua New Guinea; SGP, Singapore; SWE, Sweden; URY, Uruguay.*

Source: *Authors' computation from GFS and PWT 6.2 data. (For interpretation of the references to colour in this figure legend, the reader is referred to the web version of this article.)*

fiscal event is followed by a growth event is much higher for the third quartile (i.e., for middle-income countries which are largely in Latin America). Note however, that the patterns suggest that fiscal policy may be pro-cyclical (but not destabilizing given our definition of fiscal event) in Latin America since, out of the nine fiscal events associated with growth in Latin America, four are simultaneous (see Figure 1), which seems to confirm earlier results (see e.g., Gavin & Perotti, 1997; Kaminsky *et al.*, 2004 and Perotti, 2007). At the same time, it is clear that low-income countries have both a higher probability of having a fiscal event, but a lower probability of having a fiscal event followed by a growth event. This pattern is largely

Table 1. *Fiscal event probabilities*[a]

	Number of fiscal events				Probability of occurrence			Probability that a fiscal event is followed by a growth event
	Total fiscal events	Followed by a growth event	NOT followed by a growth event	Obs.[b]	Total fiscal events	Fiscal events followed by a growth event	Fiscal events NOT followed by a growth event	
	(1)	(2)	(3)	(4)	(5) = 1/4	(6) = 2/4	(7) = 3/4	(8) = 6/5
Total	95	25	70	977	9.7%	2.6%	7.2%	26.3%
First GDP pc quartile[c/]	26	4	22	233	11.2%	1.7%	9.4%	15.4%
Second GDP pc quartile	27	8	19	228	11.8%	3.5%	8.3%	29.6%
Third GDP pc quartile	19	9	10	268	7.1%	3.4%	3.7%	47.4%
Fourth GDP pc quartile	23	4	19	248	9.3%	1.6%	7.7%	17.4%
High income OECD countries	21	6	15	297	7.6%	2.2%	5.4%	28.6%
Developing countries	74	19	55	680	12.2%	3.1%	9.1%	25.7%
Asia	17	5	12	171	11.0%	3.3%	7.8%	29.4%
Middle East & Africa	28	3	25	198	14.1%	1.5%	12.6%	10.7%
Latin America & Carib.	20	9	11	235	8.5%	3.8%	4.7%	45.0%
Europe & Central Asia	9	2	7	76	11.8%	2.6%	9.2%	22.2%

Source: Authors' computation from GFS and PWT 6.2 data.

Notes: High income country, i.e., with a 2006 GNI per capita (calculated using the World Bank Atlas method) greater than $11,116, Classification of July 2007.

[a] Computations based on benchmark set of parameters from Table 6, row 1 (58 growth events and 95 fiscal events).

[b] Obs. in which a fiscal event could have occurred.

[c]"First GDP pc Quartile" corresponds to "low income" and some "lower middle income" countries. "Second GDP pc Quartile": "lower middle income" and some "upper middle income" countries. "Third GDG pc Quartile": "high income" countries. "Fourth GDP pc Quartile": "upper middle income" countries.

reflecting the distribution of fiscal and growth events in the Middle East and Sub-Saharan Africa. Suppose then that the success of a fiscal event can indeed be measured by whether or not it is followed by a growth event. One is then tempted to add that these patterns could reflect the quality of underlying institutions. Indeed, according to many indicators, Sub-Saharan Africa and the Middle East have bad scores on several indicators of institutional quality.

Note that when we use the alternative definition of fiscal event allowing Low-income countries to increase their average fiscal deficit during the fiscal spending growth period up to 4% of GDP, three additional fiscal events followed by a growth event are identified: Mali, Mauritius, and Burkina Faso. Then, under this scenario, the probability that a fiscal event is followed by a growth event in Middle East and Africa increases from 11% to 21%.

4. UNDERSTANDING FISCAL EVENTS

(a) *The anatomy of fiscal events*

The benchmark set of parameters selected 95 fiscal events. Table 2 describes the changes in the composition of fiscal expenditures around these events. The table shows average values and changes for the 5-year period preceding the event and the 5-year period following the event, comparing between events that preceded a growth event and events that did not precede a growth event, focusing on "Low and Middle Income" countries.

First note that the level of the deficit in GDP is lower during fiscal events followed by a growth event, a result that is corroborated by the regression analysis below.[9]

Three other significant differences appear when one compares the evolution of fiscal expenditure for the two groups of events. First, fiscal events followed by growth events devote fewer resources to general public services. Second, fiscal events followed by a growth event are characterized by a growing share of transport and communication expenditure whereas the pattern is the opposite when the fiscal event is not followed by a growth event. Third, though the difference in means is not statistically significant, there is a higher growth in education expenditures when the fiscal event is followed by a growth event than when it is not (and the opposite pattern holds for health expenditures). These results support findings in a growth regression framework. Easterly and Rebelo (1993),

Table 2. *Characteristics of fiscal events in developing countries according to their timing with growth events*[a]

	Fiscal event followed by a growth event			Fiscal event NOT followed by a growth event		
	14/63			49/63		
	Average level			Average level		
	Pre-event (1)	Post-event (2)	Change pp (3) = (2) − (1)	Pre-event (4)	Post-event (5)	Change pp (6) = (5) − (4)
% Of public expenditure in GDP	25.4*	24.0*	−1.4	23.0*	21.7*	−1.3
% Of public deficit in GDP	−3.4	−0.3*	3.2*	−3.4	−1.2*	2.3*
Expenditures by function (in % of total public exp.)			Change % = (2 − 1)/(1)			Change % = (5 − 4)/(4)
Education	12.8	14.4	13%	14.1	15.3	9%
Health	8.4*	8.8*	5%	5.7*	6.2*	8%
Transport and communication	6.4	6.6*	3%*	6.3	5.8*	−7%*
General (non-interest) public services	16.5*	15.4*	−7%*	21.3*	19.3*	−10%*
Defense	6.0*	5.5*	−8%*	11.7*	10.0*	−14%*
Housing and community amenities	4.5*	4.2	−7%*	2.7*	3.9	43%*
Recreation, culture, and religion	1.5	1.0	−30%	1.7	1.4	−13%
Others (residual)	43.9	44.1	0%	36.5	38.0	4%

Source: Authors' computation from GFS and PWT 6.2 data.

Notes: Developing countries are defined as low and middle income countries, with a 2006 GNI per capita (calculated using the World Bank Atlas method) lower than $11,116, Classification of July 2007.

[a]Based on the benchmark set of parameters, see Table 6, row 1.

*Test of difference in mean between fiscal event NOT followed by a growth event compared to fiscal event followed by a growth event (i.e., cols. 4, 5, 6 compared to cols. 1, 2 and 3, respectively). An asterisk indicates significance at 5% level.

Kneller *et al.* (1999) or Gupta, Clements, Baldacci, and Mulas-Granados (2005) found that "balanced budget and investment in transport and communication are consistently correlated with growth in a sample of low income countries" (Gupta *et al.*, 2005). The latter also provide evidence that countries where spending is concentrated on wages tend to have a lower growth.

(b) *Correlates of growth events*

As a final exercise, as in HPR, we check if fiscal events enter the set of growth event correlates. The dependent variable is then a dummy that takes the value of 1 in the 3-year window around the date of growth acceleration (and 0 otherwise), the 3-year window (as in HPR) reflecting the uncertainty attached to the identification of the first year of a specific growth event.[10] The comparison group for a growth event consists of the countries that have not had a growth episode in the same 3 years. We estimate the following probit[11] where the binary dependant variable (the 3-year window around the date of the year of the growth event, GE_{it})is regressed on several determinants:

$$\Pr(GE_{it} = 1) = \phi\left(\alpha_0 + \alpha_1 FE_{it} + \alpha_2 WW_{it} + \alpha_3 TOT_{it} + \alpha_4 HI_{it} + \sum_{t-1} \beta_t D_t\right) \quad \text{for } i = 1, \ldots, 104; \; t = 1, \ldots, 24 \qquad (1)$$

where ϕ is the cumulative normal distribution; FE_{it} is a dummy variable that takes the value of 1 at the date of the fiscal event as defined in the benchmark above and during the four years following this date; WW_{it} is a proxy for trade (and other) reforms, i.e., a dummy taking the value of 1 during the first five years of a transition toward openness as defined by Wacziarg and Welch (2008); TOT_{it} is a proxy for any external shock, i.e., a dummy taking the value of 1 if the change in the terms of trade for country i and year t is in the upper 90% of the entire sample. Following HPR, this variable is introduced to capture exceptionally favorable external circumstances[12]; HI_{it} is a dummy equals to one for High Income countries; $\sum_{t-1} D_t$ is a full set of year effects.

In Eq. (1), the year dummies capture the effects of omitted time-related variables like common shocks across countries that could account for a growth event. As to the fiscal dummy event variable, FE_{it}, it is a way to test whether, on average, growth events are preceded by fiscal events. The inclusion of the WW_{it} dummy for trade reform is both to capture the potential growth effects of a trade reform, and also the effects of other ongoing reforms since, very often, trade reforms are part of a broader package of reforms. Finally, as pointed out by Easterly *et al.* (1993), it is also plausible that many growth accelerations are triggered by favorable external conditions, especially in our context where, due to the short length of time series, we defined growth events over a 5-year window.[13] To control for this, we introduce the TOT_{it} dummy.

Before commenting on the results, one should caution about the endogeneity problems, especially of the fiscal event dummy. It could be that in country-events when growth is anticipated to be unusually high, one might think that policy-makers would increase discretionary public spending (simultaneous bias if this increase occurs with a decreasing associated deficit). Unfortunately, we lack appropriate instruments, so the results should be interpreted accordingly.

Columns (1) and (2) in Table 3 report the marginal coefficients corresponding to the estimation of (1) on the whole and on the "non high income" samples respectively. Hence, the reported coefficients give directly the change in the probability that a growth event occurs for a discrete change of the corresponding dummy variable from 0 to 1.

Column (1) which reports estimates for *all* countries, shows that the coefficient associated with FE_{it} is significantly positive (at the 10% level) implying that, on average, a fiscal event increases the probability of experiencing a growth event in the five consecutive years by 5.5% points.

Turning to the variable that captures the five years following economic reform (other than fiscal) through trade liberalization, WW_{it}, surprisingly, the coefficient is negative in col. (1) and (2), only significant in col. (2). This coefficient was also negative and not significant in HPR. However, this surprisingly negative coefficient does not necessarily contradict Wacziarg and Welch (2008) results since when they study the timing of the growth response to trade liberalization they find that, in the 3 pre-liberalization

Table 3. *Probit estimates of growth events*

	Probit	Probit	Probit	**Probit**	Logit	Logit
Col.	(1)	(2)	(3)	**(4)**	(5)	(6)
Dependent variable: Dummy for the timing of growth events						
FE_{it} (fiscal event dummy)	.055*	0.065*	0.075**	0.094**	0.072**	0.088**
	0.033	0.04	0.035	0.044	0.034	0.04
$FE_{it} * \overline{def}_{t-4,t-1}$	—	—	0.026**	0.039**	0.025**	0.043**
			0.010	0.017	0.01	0.018
$\overline{def}_{t-4,t-1}$			0.001	0.0002	0.0008	0.004
			0.003	0.004	0.003	0.037
WW_{it} (Trade liberal dummy)	−0.050	−0.082*	−0.038	−0.051	−0.031	−0.042
	0.050	0.037	0.053	0.052	0.054	0.722
TOT_{it} (Terms of trade dummy)	0.162*	0.154*	0.153*	0.139*	0.145*	0.938
	0.105	0.108	0.101	0.100	0.11	0.707
DC_t (developed-country dummy)	0.008	—	0.009	—	0.01	—
	0.035		0.033		0.031	
Year effects	Yes	Yes	Yes	Yes	Yes	Yes
Sample	All	Non-I	All	Non-HI	All	Non-HI
Obs.	977	518	977	518	977	518
Pseudo R^2	0.07	0.08	0.09	0.10	0.09	0.10
Observed proportion of $GE_{it} = 1$	13.2%	13.5%	13.2%	13.5%	13.2%	13.5%

Source: Authors' computation.
Estimation by probit. Coefficients are marginal probabilities evaluated at the sample means. See text for definition of variables.
HI stands for "High Income" countries as defined by the World Bank, July 2007.
We allow for a five-year lag between a change in the underlying determinant and a growth event. The timing of the growth event is the three year window centered on the initiation dates.
Standard errors below coefficients: heteroscedasticity consistent and adjusted for country-level clustering.
$^{*}p = 0.1$.
$^{**}p = 0.05$.

years, growth is slightly depressed and that, in the 3 years following liberalization, the effect is not significantly different from zero. However, an increase in growth becomes noticeable (of around 1.5% point) after 4 years.[14]

As expected, we observe a strong conditional correlation between external shocks and the probability of a growth event: a large positive terms-of-trade shock increases the probability of experiencing a growth event by 16.2% points (significant at a 10% level). This confirms that the incidence of external shocks and, in particular, fluctuations in the terms of trade play an important role. Finally, the high income dummy is not significantly different from zero so that when we limit our sample to "non high income" countries (see col. 2), coefficients remains very similar.

Recent literature assessing the effects of public expenditures on growth (e.g., Bose *et al.*, 2007; Kneller *et al.*, 1999, and Adam & Bevan, 2005) has emphasized the importance of incorporating the budget constraint. Here we then introduce the average deficit in the years preceding the potential growth event, i.e., the deficit/surplus level $\overline{def}_{t-4,t-1}$ (we do not include year t in the average to limit the reverse causation bias). The introduction of this variable provides insights on the correlation of the stabilization *vs.* growth objective of fiscal policy and acceleration in growth which cannot be done by the introduction of the fiscal event dummy alone (as our definition of fiscal event is based on a mix of these two objectives).

We also check whether the impact of a fiscal event on the probability of a growth event is directly correlated with the level of the current deficit by introducing the fiscal event dummy FE_{it} interactively with its associated deficit/surplus level.[15]

Results reported in cols. (3) and (4) show that, if the deficit by itself is not significant, the interaction coefficient is significantly positive (at 5% level) indicating that the marginal impact of a fiscal event depends on both coefficients (associated to FE_{it} and $FE_{it} * \overline{def}_{t-4,t-1}$). This means that the probability of occurrence of a growth event in the 5 years following a fiscal event is greater the lower the associated fiscal deficit, confirming the prima facie appropriateness of fiscal policy as a stabilizing device.

This also suggests that acceleration in the growth rate is not associated with stabilization alone: it needs to be accompanied by an increase in fiscal expenditure, and more so if the increase in expenditure is geared toward

Table 4. *Interpretation of probit model results*'[a]

	No fiscal event	Fiscal event associated with an average deficit of				
		−3%	−2%	−1%	0%	1%
Probability of occurrence of a growth event in the 5 following years[b]	9.70%	7.39%	10.75%	15.08%	20.44%	26.80%
Change in growth event probability from a no fiscal event situation		2.26 pp	1.10 pp	5.43 pp	10.79 pp	17.15 pp

Source: Authors' computation.
Notes: *pp* stands for percentage points.
[a]Evaluation based on coefficients of the equation reported in column 4, Table 3.
[b]Evaluation of $\phi(\alpha_0 + \alpha_1 FE_{it} + \alpha_1 FE_{it} * def_{t-5,t-1} + \alpha_2 \overline{WW}_{it} + \alpha_3 \overline{DC}_{it} + \sum_{t-1} \beta_t \bar{D}_t)$ for different values of FE_{it} and $def_{t-5,t-1}$, all other variables evaluated at their sample mean, ϕ representing the standard cumulative normal distribution.

expenditures on infrastructure as we have shown in Table 2. Coefficient values associated with WW_{it} and TOT_{it} remain unchanged.

To ease interpretation, Table 4 reports for a typical Low and Middle Income country, the relationship between a fiscal event and the occurrence of a growth event for different values of the associated deficit/surplus. As indicated in the table, for a typical Low or Middle Income country and in the absence of a fiscal event in the five preceding years, the probability of a growth event is around 9.7%.[16] This probability is quite higher than in case of a fiscal event with an associated fiscal deficit equal to 3% of GDP (−2.26% point of difference).[17] The probability of a growth event increases to 10.8% in case of a fiscal event in a deficit situation of 2% of GDP, and reaches 26.8% in a surplus situation of 1%, implying an increase in growth event probability of 17.2% points compared to the no-fiscal-event alternative. Remember that to be qualifying as fiscal event this deficit can not increase with public expenditure.

Finally, Table 5 reports statistics of the predictive ability of this Probit model. It is customary to take a prediction rule with a threshold value of $p^* = 0.5$, on the basis that we would predict 1 if the model says 1 is more

Table 5. *Prediction accuracy of the probit model*[a] *share of actual* GE_{it} *predicted by the model*

		Actual		
		GE = 1	GE = 0	Total
Predicted	GE = 1	10.0%	35.1%	45.2%
	GE = 0	3.5%	51.4%	54.8%
Total		13.5%	86.5%	100%

Source: Authors' computation.
Correctly classified = 61.45%.
[a]Computation based on coefficients reported in column 4 in Table 3, cut off = 13.4% (value for determining whether an observation has a predicted positive outcome).

likely than zero:

$$\widehat{GE}_{it} = 1 \quad \text{if the predicted probability } \hat{\phi} > p^*$$

However, because of the unbalanced sample with many more 0s than 1s, we set p^* equal to the proportion of l's in the sample (which corresponds to the average predicted probability in the sample).

Taking this criterion, Table 5 suggests that the basic model as defined in Table 3, col. (4), successfully predicts 74% of the growth events (i.e., $GE_{it} = 1$) and 56.4% of total cases of no growth events (i.e., $GE_{it} = 0$). Hence, 61.4% of total growth event observations are correctly predicted. Since this measure of goodness of fit depends on the cutoff selected to classify the predicted $\widehat{GE}_{it}$, one should only interpret the results in Table 5 as indicative orders of magnitude.

We carry out four robustness checks. First, as discussed above, we estimate a logit function (which has fatter tails and may be more appropriate for our sample with many zero values for the dependent variable). Results in cols. (5) and (6) of Table 3 show that the logit specification does not change the qualitative conclusions based on results in cols. (3) and (4). Second, we change the definition of FE_{it} with (i) the dummy that takes the value of 1 at the date of the fiscal event and during the 9 years following this date (instead of 4), giving more time for the effects of a fiscal event to have an impact on growth and (ii) different parameters in the "fiscal event" definition (corresponding to the sensitivity analysis in Table 6). Third, we

Table 6. *Benchmark events and sensitivity analysis*

	Total number of events in		Growth events preceded by a fiscal event		Fiscal event: Followed by a growth event		Including the ones simultaneous to growth events		Also preceded by a growth event		Only preceded by a growth event		W/o any growth event		Total
	Growth	Fiscal													
	(1)	(2)	(3)	(3)/(1)	(3)	(3)/(2)	(4)	(4)/(2)	(5)	(5)/(2)	(6)	(6)/(2)	(7)	(7)/(2)	(3) + (6) + (7)/(2)
Benchmark growth event — unchanged ($\alpha = 0.035$; $\beta = 0.02$; $y_{t+n} \geq \max\{y_i\}$)															
Fiscal event conditions															
1. $\phi = 0.01$; $\lambda = 0$; $\gamma = -0.02$; $\delta = 0$	58	95	25	43.1%	25	26.3%	6	6.3%	7	7.4%	23	24.2%	47	49.5%	100%
2. $\phi = 0.005$; $\lambda = 0$; $\gamma = -0.02$; $\delta = 0$	58	123	28	48.3%	28	22.8%	6	4.9%	6	4.9%	29	23.6%	66	53.7%	100%
3. $\phi = 0.02$; $\lambda = 0$; $\gamma = -0.02$; $\delta = 0$	58	49	14	24.1%	14	28.6%	4	8.2%	1	2.0%	11	22.4%	24	49.0%	100%
4. $\phi = 0.02$; $\lambda = 0$; $\gamma = -0.02$; $\delta = -0.02$	58	95	25	43.1%	25	26.3%	6	6.3%	6	6.3%	24	25.3%	46	48.4%	100%
5. $\phi = 0.01$; $\lambda = -0.02$; $\gamma = -0.02$; $\delta = 0$	58	107	27	46.6%	27	25.2%	7	6.5%	6	5.6%	26	24.3%	54	50.5%	100%
6. $\phi = 0.01$; $\lambda = 0.01$; $\gamma = -0.02$; $\delta = 0$	58	81	23	39.7%	23	28.4%	5	6.2%	4	4.9%	19	23.5%	39	48.1%	100%
7. $\phi = 0.01$; $\lambda = 0$; $\gamma = -0.02$; $\delta = 0$; $ge_{t,t+n} > 0$	58	87	21	36.2%	21	24.1%	3	3.4%	8	9.2%	22	25.3%	44	50.6%	100%
8. $\phi = 0.01$; $\overline{def}_{t,t+n} \geq 0$	58	37	15	25.9%	15	40.5%	3	8.1%	4	10.8%	10	27.0%	12	32.4%	100%
Fiscal event condition unchanged ($\phi = 0.01$; $\lambda = 0$; $\gamma = -0.02$; $\delta = 0$)															
Growth event conditions															
9. $\alpha = 0.035$; $\beta = 0.02$; $y_{t+n} \geq \max\{y_i\}$	58	95	25	43.1%	25	26.3%	6	6.3%	7	7.4%	23	24.2%	47	49.5%	100%
10. $\alpha = 0.02$; $\beta = 0.02$; $y_{t+n} \geq \max\{y_i\}$	74	95	31	41.9%	31	32.6%	5	5.3%	9	9.5%	27	28.4%	37	38.9%	100%
11. $\alpha = 0.035$; $\beta = 0.01$; $y_{t+n} \geq \max\{y_i\}$	70	95	28	40.0%	28	29.5%	6	6.3%	9	9.5%	25	26.3%	42	44.2%	100%
12. $\alpha = 0.02$; $\beta = 0.01$; $y_{t+n} \geq \max\{y_i\}$	95	95	33	34.7%	33	34.7%	6	6.3%	14	14.7%	30	31.6%	32	33.7%	100%
13. $\alpha = 0.035$; $\beta = 0.02$;	72	95	29	40.3%	29	30.5%	6	6.3%	6	6.3%	25	26.3%	41	43.2%	100%

Source: Authors' computation from GFS and PWT 6.2 data.

reran the benchmark regression without the trade liberalization dummy. Fourth, as fiscal data became more reliable over time, we checked the robustness of our results by restraining the sample to the 1990–2000 period. Fourth, we considered the dependent variable as censored at zero and used a Tobit estimator. Reflecting poor-quality fiscal data, estimates from the Tobit regression using actual values for growth and primary spending yielded large standard errors. In all four robustness checks, the results were largely unchanged, so we do not report them here.

5. CONCLUSIONS

This paper constructed growth and primary spending expenditures (i.e., net of interest payments) "events" over the period of 1972–2005 for 118 developing and 22 High Income OECD countries. Fiscal expenditures were compiled by Government function, and "events" were sought over 5-year rolling windows. Significant "events" were approximately constructed as follows. For GDP per capita, acceleration in the average annual growth rate of 2% point per annum (ppa) between any rolling 5-year window would qualify for a growth "event". For fiscal expenditures (expressed in GDP%), an increase in the average growth rate of approximately 1 ppa that would not be accompanied by an aggravation of the (consolidated central government) fiscal deficit beyond 2% of GDP would likewise qualify for a fiscal "event". The resulting benchmark constructed data set (merging both fiscal and growth databases) had 58 growth events and 95 fiscal events over a sample that included 107 countries (84 developing countries) over 1977–2000 (1452 observations).

For this sample, the (unconditional) probability of occurrence of a fiscal event is about 10%, and, for a large range of parameter values for the selection of a "significant" event, the probability of a growth event once a fiscal event had occurred is in the 22–28% range. The probability of occurrence of a fiscal event is higher for the bottom half of the income distribution of countries, but the probability that this fiscal event is followed by a growth event is higher for the third quartiles, corresponding to middle income countries (which are largely in Latin America). The probability of a fiscal event *not* followed by a growth event is significantly higher for the Africa region, prompting us to note that this result is coherent with the view that the success of a growth-oriented fiscal expenditure package hinges on the quality of the institutional environment.

Concentrating on the Low and Middle Income sample of 84 countries, the paper investigates the differences in the pattern of functional expenditures for fiscal events followed by growth events compared to those not followed by a growth event. In addition to a significantly lower fiscal deficit for fiscal events followed by a growth event (which is partly an outcome of the way events were constructed), three other significant differences appear. First, fiscal events followed by growth events devote fewer resources to general public services. Second, fiscal events followed by a growth event are characterized by a growing share of transport and communication expenditure whereas the pattern is the opposite when the fiscal event is not followed by a growth event. Third, though the difference in means is not statistically significant, there is a higher growth in education expenditures when the fiscal event is followed by a growth event than when it is not.

This description of the anatomy of fiscal events and their relation to growth events is completed by statistical analysis where a few controlling factors are included in a probit estimate of growth events on fiscal events. On average, we find that a growth event is more likely to occur when surrounded by a fiscal event. Second, controlling for the growth-related effects of other reforms and for favorable external conditions shocks, we estimate that for a typical developing country, the probability of occurrence of a growth event in the five years following a fiscal event is increased as the associated fiscal deficit is limited.

NOTES

1. Heller (2005) considers wages and interest payments as the two non-discretionary expenditures in developing countries. In our fiscal data set which is decomposed by "function" rather than "economic" use we do not have a wage component for each function so we cannot include wages as non-discretionary. See Carrère and de Melo (2007, Annex Al) for the definitions of these components.
2. Our desire to have a transparent and economically sensible homogeneous framework across countries led us not to use procedures that treat break dates as unknown variables to be estimated (see e.g., Bai &

Perron, 1998; Bai & Perron, 2003). However, all turning points in GDP per capita growth or in primary expenditure growth that are qualified as "event" are significant at a 10% level. Hence, only smaller but statistically significant breaks may be identified by endogenous procedures. Moreover, as shown in the appendix, changes in "event" parameters do not affect results.

3. As discussed by Perotti (2007), it is very difficult even in developed countries like United States where quarterly data and external information on GDP elasticities of revenues and transfers are both available to apply time-series methodologies to detect a fiscal discretionary policy shock (i.e., an unanticipated shock) in the data. Data requirements are too demanding to apply these (controversial) time-series methodologies to developing countries.
4. There was a major change in the GFS in 1989 causing concern about the comparability of data before and after that date (see details on the data reconciliation in Carrère & de Melo (2007, Annex A.1.2). Using box-plots, we explored the possibility of lack of comparability for the series of interest. Fortunately, as discussed in the Carrère & de Melo (2007, Annex A.1.2, Figure Al), this is not the case.
5. Eight six percent of the observations rely on data consolidated at the central government sector level and the remainder 14% at the budget central government level (see Carrère & de Melo, 2007, Annex A.1.3 for further discussion).
6. Using WDI database is an alternative. As shown by HPR, this does not affect the results.
7. These probabilities are computed by dividing the numbers of events by the number of country-year observations in which an event could have occurred. The latter is calculated by summing all the observations in the sample and eliminating: (i) a 4-year window after the occurrence of each event since our qualifying conditions take this period as belonging to the same episode; (ii) the potential competing dates before the event that have been eliminated by the spline regression.
8. This in accordance with Végh and Vuletin (2012) who found that tax policy is more volatile in developing countries than in industrial countries in the sense that developing countries change their tax rates by larger amounts than industrial economies.

9. As discussed in Section 2, insofar as the growth event occurs during the 5-year period when the fiscal deficit is computed, there could be a mechanical effect whereby the fiscal deficit will be lower during spells of high growth. On the other hand, the evidence for developing countries shows that fiscal expenditures and fiscal deficits are higher during periods of high growth (more capital inflows and "voracity" effects in the political cycle).
10. Growth events are computed according to the same benchmark with 58 growth events. Because we are interested in predicting the timing of growth events, we drop all data corresponding to years $t + 2 \ldots t + 4$ of a growth event. The sample then consists of all countries for which the relevant data are available, including countries that have not experienced growth episodes.
11. We also fit a *logit*. Both *probit* and *logit* fit maximum likelihood models with dichotomous dependent variables coded as 0/1. With a *logit* model, Eq. (1) would be identical except for ϕ which is the cumulative logistic distribution rather than the cumulative normal distribution. It is difficult to theoretically justify the choice between these two models. Note that the logistic distribution being very similar to the normal one, results are usually identical. However, some differences in results could appear in very unbalanced sample, i.e. in a sample in which there are many more 0s than 1s, which is our case. This is why, as a robustness check, we also present logit estimation results.
12. The change in the terms of trade is computed as the first difference of the log of the terms-of-trade index, the latter defined as the ratio of export prices to import prices using the current and constant price values of exports and imports from WDI. We use this index instead of the more traditional net-barter index because of its broader coverage. However, this measure has the disadvantage that it includes the service export sector (see the discussion in Loayza and Raddatz (2007)).
13. Easterly *et al.* (1993) showed that about 10 percent of the variation in GDP growth and a quarter of the variation in growth volatility can be explained by the observed differences in the volatility of terms-of-trade changes.
14. Remember that one of the conditions for a growth event in this paper is an increase in the annual growth rate of per capita GDP of at least 2 pp.

Hence, if we redefine the dummy WW_{it} in order to capture the years $[t+5$ and more$]$ after the trade liberalization instead of $[t;\, t+4]$ as previously, we obtain a positive coefficient but not statistically significant.

15. Of course, the fiscal deficit/surplus situation is implicitly already taken into account as one of the conditions defining what we call a "Fiscal event" is that a deficit situation must improve.
16. Based on results in Table 3, col. (4) with $FE_{it} = 0$, all other variables set at their sample mean.
17. Based on results in Table 3, col. (4) with $FE_{it} = 1$, all other variables set at their sample mean.

REFERENCES

Adam, C. S., & Bevan, D. L. (2005). Fiscal deficits and growth in developing countries. *Journal of Public Economics*, *89*, 571–597.

Alesina, A., Campante, F., & Tabellini, G. (2008). Why is fiscal policy often procyclical?. *Journal of the European Economic Association*, *6*(5), 1006–1036.

Bai, J., & Perron, P. (1998). Estimating and testing linear models with multiple structural changes. *Econometrica*, *66*(1), 47–78.

Bai, J., & Perron, P. (2003). Computation and analysis of multiple structural change models. *Journal of Applied Econometrics*, *18*, 1–22.

Barro, J. R. (1990). Government spending in a simple model of endogenous growth. *Journal of Political Economy*, *98*, 103–125.

Bose, N., Haque, M. E., & Osborn, D. R. (2007). Public expenditure and economic growth: A disaggregated analysis for developing countries. *The Manchester School*, *75*(5), 533–556.

Calderón, C. A., & Serven, L. (2004). The effects of infrastructure development on growth and income distribution. World Bank Policy Research Working Paper No. 3400.

Carrère, C., & de Melo, J. (2007). Fiscal spending and economic growth: Some stylized facts. World Bank Policy Research Working Paper No. 4452.

Chalk, N., & Hemming, R. (2001). Assessing fiscal sustainability in theory and practice. IMF Working Paper No. 00/81.

Devarajan, S., Swaroop, V., & Zou, H.-F. (1996). The composition of public expenditure and economic growth. *Journal of Monetary Economics*, *37*, 313–344.

Easterly, W., & Rebelo, S. (1993). Fiscal policy and economic growth: An empirical investigation. NBER Working Paper No. 4499.

Easterly, W., Kremer, M., Pritchett, L., & Summers, L. (1993). Good policy or good luck? Country growth performance and temporary shocks. *Journal of Monetary Economics*, *32*(3), 459–483.

Estache, A., Gonzalez, M., & Trujillo, L. (2007). Government expenditures on education, health, and infrastructure: A naïve look at levels, outcomes, and efficiency. World Bank Policy Research Working Paper No. 4219.

Frankel, J. A., Végh, C. A., & Vuletin, G. (2011). On graduation from fiscal procyclicality. NBER Working Paper No. 17619.

Gavin, M., & Perotti, R. (1997). Fiscal policy in Latin America. NBER Macroeconomics Annual 1997 (Vol. 12, pp. 11–72). MIT Press.

Gupta, S., Clements, B., Baldacci, E., & Mulas-Granados, C. (2005). Fiscal policy, expenditure composition, and growth in low-income countries. *Journal of International Money and Finance*, *24*(3), 441–463.

Hausmann, R., Pritchett, L., & Rodrik, D. (2005). Growth accelerations. *Journal of Economic Growth*, *10*, 303–329.

Heller, P. S. (2005). Understanding fiscal space. IMF Policy Discussion Paper, PDP/05/4.

Heston, A., Summers, R., & Aten, B. (2006). Penn world table version 6.2. Center for international comparisons of production, income and prices at the University of Pensylvania, September 2006.

Ilzetski, E., & Végh, C. (2008). Procyclical fiscal policy in developing countries: Truth or fiction? NBER Working Paper No. 14191.

Jones, B., & Olken, B. (2008). The anatomy of start-stop growth. *The Review of Economics and Statistics*, *90*(3), 582–585.

Kaminsky, G., Reinhart, C, & Végh, C. (2004). When it rains, it pours: Procyclical capital flows and macroeconomic policy. NBER Macroeconomics Annual 1994 (Vol. 19, pp. 11–84). MIT press.

Kneller, R., Bleaney, M., & Gemmell, N. (1999). Fiscal policy and growth: Evidence from OECD countries. *Journal of Public Economics*, *74*, 171–190.

Loayza, N., & Raddatz, C. (2007). The structural determinants of external vulnerability. *World Bank Economic Review*, *21*(3), 359–387.

Perotti, R. (2007). Fiscal policy in developing countries: A framework and some questions. World Bank Policy Research Working Paper No. 4365.

Talvi, E., & Végh, C. (2005). Tax base variability and procyclicality of fiscal policy. *Journal of Development Economics*, 78(1), 156–190.

Tornell, A., & Lane, P. (1999). The voracity effect. *American Economic Review*, *89*, 22–46.

Végh, C., & Vuletin, G. (2012). How is tax policy conducted over the business cycle? NBER Working Paper No. 17753.

Wacziarg, R., & Welch, K. H. (2008). Trade liberalization and growth: New evidence. *World Bank Economic Review*, *22*(2), 187–231.

World Bank (2007). Fiscal policy for growth and development: Further analysis and lessons from country case studies. Background Report No. 4, Joint World Bank and IMF Development Committee (Washington).

APPENDIX A. GROWTH ACCELERATION

The criterion is GDP per capita growth at time t over horizon t to $t + n$, i.e., $g_{t,t+n}$ defined by the following:

$$\ln(y_{t+i}) = a + g_{t,t+n} * i, \quad i = 0, \ldots, n \tag{2}$$

y_t being the GDP per capita (from the PWT 6.2, see Heston *et al.*, 2006). The change in the criterion function is given by the change in the OLS estimated growth rate over horizon n across that horizon:

$$\Delta g_{t,n} = \hat{g}_{t,t+n} - \hat{g}_{t-n-1,t-1} \tag{3}$$

Growth acceleration will be identified when, during rapid growth episodes, the following conditions are all satisfied:

$$\begin{aligned} &\hat{g}_{t,t+n} \geq \alpha \text{ ppa growth is rapid} \\ &\Delta g_{t,n} \geq \beta \text{ ppa growth accelerates} \\ &y_{t+n} \geq \max\{y_i\},\ i \leq t \text{ post-growthoutput exceeds pre-episode peak} \end{aligned} \tag{4}$$

where *ppa* is percentage points per annum, α is minimum per capita growth that must be satisfied during the period (3.5 ppa for HPR and for us in our base case), and β is the minimum acceleration that must be satisfied (2.0 ppa in the benchmark case). Since several years of events could be following one another, the timing of the initiation of the growth acceleration episode is chosen by fitting for each candidate year the following spline regression:

$$\ln(y_{t+i}) = a_0 + g_{t-n-1,t+n} * i + a_1 DE + v g_{t+i,t+n} * i * DE, \quad i = -n-1, \ldots, n \tag{5}$$

where *DE* is a dummy variable that takes a value of 1 for the candidate event year. Eq. (5) is estimated by OLS over each candidate year, and the selected event year is the one for the regression with the highest F-test (i.e., highest R^2).

APPENDIX B. FISCAL EVENTS

From the GFS data, we define primary expenditures (*dfe*) as total fiscal expenditures less interest payments (*ip*). The government budget constraint (small case variables represent variables expressed as a share of GDP) is:

$$trg \equiv dfe + ip + def \tag{6}$$

with *trg* the total revenue and grants in % of GDP, and *def* the fiscal deficit/surplus in % of GDP ($def < 0$ is defined as a deficit and $def > 0$ a surplus). Using the same notation as above to define the length over which changes in the ratio of primary spending takes place:

$$(dfe_{t+i}) = a + g^{dfe}_{t,t+n} * i, \quad i = 0, \ldots, n \tag{7}$$

An acceleration in primary spending will be identified when there is an increase in the estimated growth of ratio of primary expenditures as a percentage of GDP, $\Delta \widehat{g^{dfe}}$. Define now $\overline{def}_{t,t+n}$ as the average deficit (as a % of GDP) over the period so that the change in deficit between two adjacent periods is

$$\Delta def_{t,n} \equiv \overline{def}_{t,t+n} - \overline{def}_{t-n-1,t-1} \tag{8}$$

We impose two criteria for an increase in ratio of primary expenditures growth, Δdfe, to qualify as a fiscal "event". The first criterion deals with situations when the increase in expenditures takes place from a situation of fiscal deficit. Take then the case of a fiscal deficit in the period preceding the candidate fiscal event and let δ be the selected threshold value for the central government deficit. In our sample, for developing countries, the average (central government) fiscal deficit was 2%. So, if increasing primary expenditures take place from a situation of deficit, i.e., when ($\overline{def}_{t-n-1,t-1} < \delta$), we require an improvement in the fiscal deficit of λ (with $\lambda = 0$ corresponding to a situation of no deterioration). This gives rise to the condition on the second line of (9).

$$\begin{aligned} &\Delta g^{dfe}_{t,t+n} \geq \phi, \quad \phi > 0 \quad \text{discretionary expenditure growth is rapid} \\ &\begin{cases} \Delta def_{t,n} \geq \lambda & \text{if } \overline{def}_{t-n-1,t-1} < \delta \quad \text{a deficit situation must improve} \\ \overline{def}_{t,t+n} \geq \gamma & \text{if } def_{t-n-1,t-1} < \delta \quad \text{a limit on a growing deficit} \end{cases} \end{aligned} \tag{9}$$

In the case of a more favorable initial situation (i.e., ($\overline{def}_{t-n-1,t-1} > \delta$)), we wish to exclude events where the shift to a deficit results in an average deficit in excess of γ during the period $(t, t+n)$. This is the criterion in the third line of (9).

APPENDIX C. SENSITIVITY ANALYSIS

Table 6 reports the results of a sensitivity analysis. In the benchmark case, we choose $\alpha = 0.035$; $\beta = 0.02$; $y_{t+n} \geq \max\{y_i\}$ in Eq. (4). This case reported in row 1 yields 58 growth events. For the corresponding benchmark fiscal events, we settled for the following fiscal parameter set $\phi = 0.01$; $\lambda = 0$; $\gamma = -0.02$; $\delta = 0$ which yields 95 fiscal events. As shown in Table 6, tighter conditions always lead to less qualifying events. However, the ratio of fiscal events followed by a growth event remains in the 22–28% range, except when we require that the fiscal event be accompanied throughout by a fiscal *surplus* in which case 41% of fiscal events are followed by a growth event (row 8). Likewise, rows 9–13 carry out similar sensitivity analysis for the growth event parameters. Finally, note that if we define periods of 8 years instead of 5 ($n = 7$), the benchmark set of parameters leads to 52 fiscal events and 18 growth events over the reduced period of 1980–1997.

Part II

Trade Policies, Market Structure and Market Access

Review of Development Economics, 4(1), 1–20, 2000

Pricing Policy Under Double Market Power: Madagascar and the International Vanilla Market

*Jaime de Melo, Marcelo Olarreaga, and Wendy Takacs**

Abstract

This paper uses a price-leadership model of the international vanilla market to study the welfare consequences of alternative pricing policies for Madagascar, the leader, that also controls domestic production through a single-channel marketing system. Econometric estimates of the model are used for simulations of welfare and revenue changes and internal redistribution of income. Results indicate that Madagascar could have gained between 0.9% and 2.6% of GDP per year on average over the period 1981–91 by following optimal pricing policies, and that producers were overtaxed suggesting that political economy considerations played a role in the pricing decisions.

1. Introduction

> The policies of the marketing-boards is a conspicuous instance of the disparity in political effectiveness between the urban political elites and the unorganized and inarticulate rural population. Bauer (1987, p. 235).

Despite success at export diversification, in many developing countries traditional commodity exports remain an extremely important source of export and tax revenue. For some commodities, certain exporting countries have sufficient market share to influence, or even control, the world market prices of their principal export commodity. In these cases the exporting country is in a position to improve its terms of trade and national welfare through appropriate pricing policies. Many countries that believe they are in this position tightly control internal production, distribution, and pricing of the export commodity and give monopoly export rights to state-owned marketing-boards.

Marketing-board control of distribution and prices has crucial implications for the government budget. When marketing-boards control production and distribution of important staples for internal distribution, political pressures often result in high producer and low consumer prices and a significant deficit that contributes to macroeconomic imbalance. When the products in question are exported and there is a significant spread between producer and export prices that exceeds processing, transport and storage costs, the marketing-board raises revenue for the state through implicit taxation of producers. This implicit taxation has also important implications for income distribution within the exporting country. Where the agricultural sector consists of a large number of small producers, heavy implicit taxation of export crops can increase inequality in income distribution.[1]

*de Melo: University of Geneva, 102 bl Carl Vogt, 1211 Geneva 4, Switzerland; and CEPR, London, UK. Tel: 22-705-8273; Fax: 705-8293; E-mail: demelo@ibm.unige.ch. Olarreaga: World Bank, DECRG, 1818 H street, Washington, DC 20037, USA; and CEPR, London, UK. Tel: 202-458-8021; Fax: 522-1159; E-mail: molarreaga@worldbank.org. Takacs: University of Maryland, Baltimore County, Baltimore, MD 21228, USA. Tel: 410-455-2174; E-mail: wtakacs@umbc2.umbc.edu. Without implicating them, we thank Olivier Cadot, Jaya Krishnakumar, Maurice Schiff, James Tybout, Alan Winters, and a referee for suggestions on an earlier draft. An earlier version was presented at the conference "Recent Developments in International Economics", Aix-en-Provence (July 1995), and appeared as CEPR DP #1447.

The pricing policies of marketing-boards for export crops have received heavy criticism for overtaxation of agriculture, for overestimating the actual degree of market power in international markets, and for lack of pricing flexibility in the face of changing world market conditions.[2]

A prime example would be OPEC's underestimation of consumer and producer response and its loss of market share and market power over time.

Another example is the international vanilla market, which historically has been dominated by a cartel led by Madagascar. In recent years the cartel has continued to restrict exports and maintain high prices despite drastic loss of market share to its principal competitor, Indonesia. These developments have led observers to question whether the vanilla marketing authorities in Madagascar have overestimated their market power and followed a pricing policy that has reduced their country's welfare.

Outside observers' arguments for dismantling marketing-boards and a "hands-off" policy are based on the principle that taxation of producers is both inefficient and detrimental on distributional grounds. But governments with weak fiscal systems need to raise revenue and trade taxes may be the only instrument at hand. A marketing-board (or other parastatal agency) is a way of raising revenue through implicit taxation, which may be politically more acceptable than transparent high tax rates.[3] In the case of export crops these organizations redistribute income from (usually) small farmers to an urban political elite. Not surprisingly, the political economy of pricing policy in such an environment is likely to lead to excessive rent extraction on the part of the parastatal at the expense of the poor.[4]

The economics of marketing-boards in the context of international trade have been studied in several settings. Among the more significant recent contributions, Markusen (1984) compares welfare-maximizing and revenue-maximizing export taxes with profit-maximizing marketing-boards in a two-good general equilibrium model. Krishna and Thursby (1992) introduce strategic interaction and concentrate on the nature of competition between two duopolist marketing-boards in the international market. These contributions are concerned with policy design in different environments, a concern we share as well. However, by not confronting the model's predictions with actual pricing decisions, these authors cannot address, even indirectly, whether political economy factors may have been important in explaining actual pricing.[5]

Our model of double market power differs from theirs and others in the literature, and allows us to contribute an empirical case study of pricing policy in this environment. By comparing several alternative strategies to the actual strategy followed by Madagascar, we obtain some idea of the extent to which the operation of marketing-boards reflects political economy motives of internal redistribution as suggested by the above quote. More generally, this is a case study of overlapping marketing-board objectives as revenue-raising, welfare-maximizing and internal income redistribution instruments.

We develop and estimate a price-leadership model of the international vanilla market which allows us to focus on the welfare and internal distributional implications of alternative pricing policies on the part of the vanilla marketing authorities in Madagascar. Has Madagascar overestimated its market power, as is usually claimed by the opponents of taxation of primary commodities? Or does the double market power of the marketing authorities as a monopsony buyer in their own country and a price leader internationally give them an incentive to raise prices above the optimal level from the point of view of the country as a whole? Has the operating of the marketing-board gone even further and served primarily as a means to redistribute income internally?

2. Trends in the Natural Vanilla Market

Natural vanilla[6] is a tree crop that is exported after a relatively elaborate preparation that involves drying and curing.[7] In 1990, Madagascar was the largest producer (tons in square brackets) [1800] followed by Indonesia [600]. Other suppliers were on the fringe: Comoros [140], Reunion [16], Tonga [40], Tahiti [50]. Madagascar, Comoros, and Reunion produce bourbon vanilla which is considered high quality both because of high vanillin content and of fragrance which distinguishes it from the vanilla offered by other suppliers.

In 1960, the international market for natural vanilla was dominated by Madagascar, the world's lowest-cost producer of the high-quality bourbon vanilla. From its dominant position of 60% of world volume of natural vanilla exports, Madagascar organized the bourbon vanilla cartel with Comoros and Reunion, setting high prices and restricting supply. The cartel's share exceeded 80% of the world market in 1974 but dropped to 30% starting in the mid 1980s as Indonesia's market share climbed rapidly to over 30% of world exports.

These developments in the natural vanilla market are summarized in Figures 1, 2 (volume and value trends) and Figure 3 (price and taxation trends). The market has grown, with Indonesia increasing significantly its output since the mid-1980s (Figure

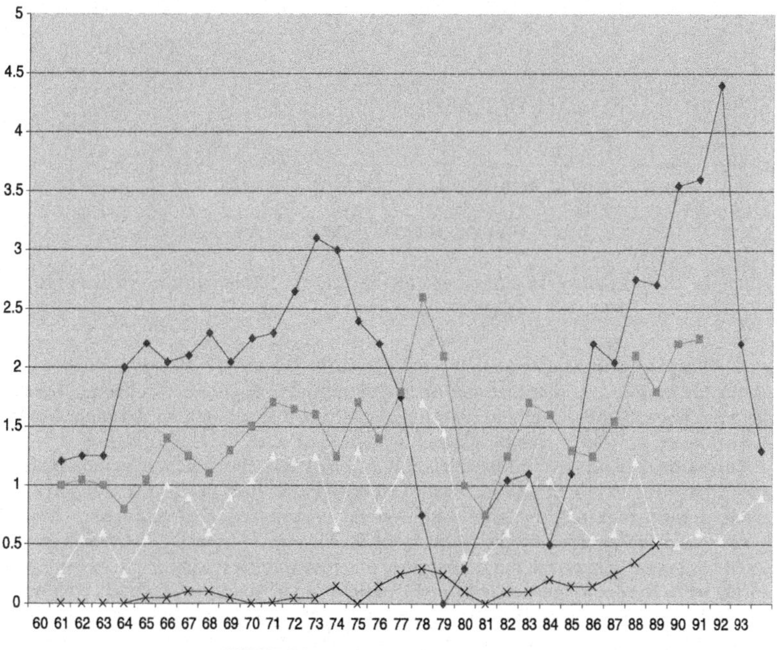

Figure 1. Madagascar/Indonesia/World Export Volumes and Madagascar's Stocks

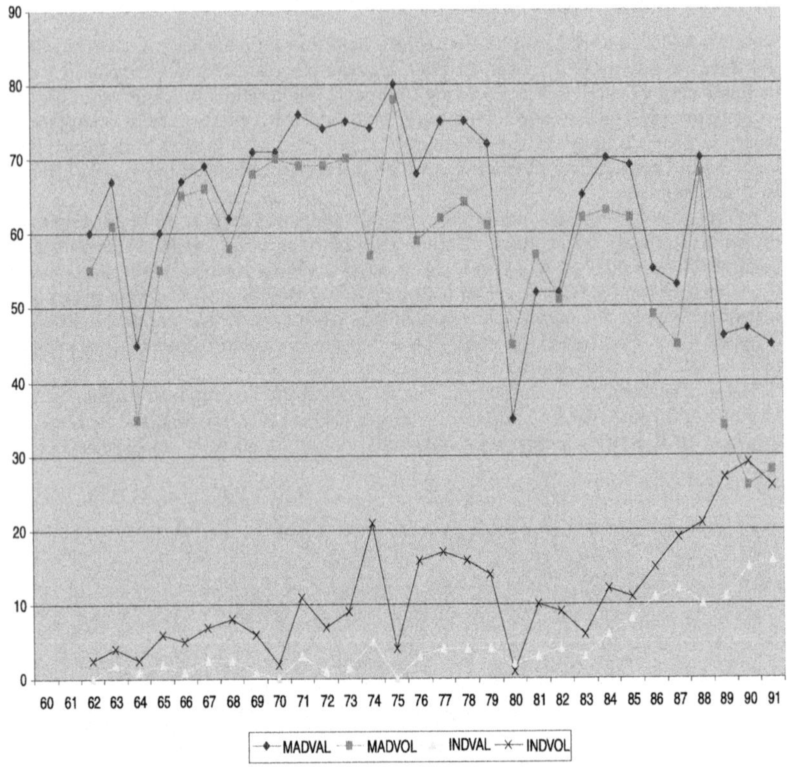

Figure 2. Export Values (in US$) and Volume Shares of Madagascar and Indonesia

1), catching up with Madagascar by the late 1980s (Figure 2). However, higher unit values for bourbon vanilla (see the price differential in Figure 3)—reflecting quality differentials and the cartel's pricing policies—have contributed to maintain a high market share in value terms for Madagascar, at least until 1987 (also Figure 2).

During the period covered by this study (up to 1991), the domestic vanilla market was highly regulated in Madagascar. Licenses (valid for three-year periods) for growing were required for producers. Vanilla preparation also required a license (yearly renewable) given by the Ministry of Trade to growers and "processors–stockers", the two participants in the preparation of cured vanilla. Purchase prices from producers were fixed and guaranteed for the entire crop. A stabilization fund (CAVAGI) stabilized the price received by producers and financed stocking costs with contributions taken from export proceeds, after payment of the export tax. Finally, the Ministry of Commerce selected each year certain processors—stockers allowed to export (38 in 1989, 13 in 1990), as well as quantities exported by each exporter at the price fixed by the cartel.

Figure 1 also shows the evolution of Madagascar's vanilla stocks that resulted from the marketing-board behavior which guaranteed the purchase of the entire crop at the fixed price. Stocks grew rapidly to an all-time high of over five years' of exports in 1992. By then the stocked vanilla was deteriorating and it was clear that it could not be sold on world markets. Besides, by 1990, stocking costs accounted for over 60% of the CAVAGI budget and amounted to 0.003% of GDP. Not surprisingly, in 1993, three-quarters of the stock was burned.[8]

Figure 3 shows the evolution of the average price for the two major suppliers and the rising tax (including payments for the stabilization fund) by Madagascar. It is striking that the cartel's price remained insensitive to its loss of market share to Indonesia. The average price for Madagascar's high-quality bourbon vanilla has remained well above Indonesia's. Part of the price differential is due to the generally higher quality of the bourbon vanilla exported by Madagascar. (Towards the end of the period the vanillin content of Madagascar's vanilla was about twice that of Indonesia.) Part of the price difference would also be attributable to Madagascar's rising taxation, which reached 80% of the unit export price.

In Indonesia, by contrast, the government does not regulate the production process. Indonesian vanilla is supplied by a large number of small producers. There is no stock-

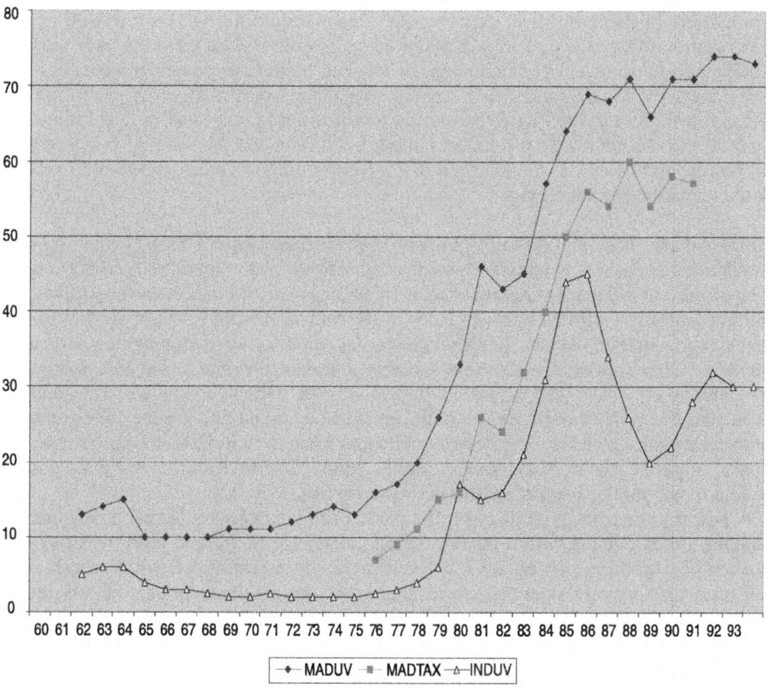

Figure 3. Export Unit Values (in US$) of Madagascar and Indonesia, and Madagascar's Tax

piling on the part of the government, and no government intervention in the export market through either export taxes or quantity controls. Two commonly cited factors contributing to the rapid growth of the industry in Indonesia are the high-price policy of the bourbon cartel whose alleged goal is to supply the high-quality end of the market,[9] and Madagascar's internal pricing policies, which have discouraged high-quality production, even though production and opportunity costs (of land especially) are low.[10] Other factors that have also contributed to the rise of Indonesia in the market include a vanilla shortage in the late 1970s[11] that encouraged vanilla purchasers to secure other sources of supply, most notably in Indonesia, and great improvements in the quality of Indonesian vanilla, which contributed especially to increased sales in the United States.[12]

3. Alternative Pricing Policies in a Price-Leadership Model

This structure of the international vanilla market and Madagascar's tight regulation of the internal market raise issues about pricing policy under double market power.

Madagascar's share of the world market and the control that the authorities exercise over both export and domestic farm-gate prices implies that the authorities have both market power in the export market and monopsony power relative to the growers. The absence of regulation of the market in Indonesia and the large number of independent suppliers imply that export supply from Indonesia can be modeled as the supply curve of a perfectly competitive industry.[13] We therefore treat the international vanilla market using a price-leadership model, with Madagascar as the price leader and Indonesian producers (and other smaller producing countries) acting as followers. Given differences in the quality of vanilla produced in Madagascar and in Indonesia, we treat the two countries' products as imperfect substitutes. We develop first a graphical representation of the model, then the corresponding structural model that is used in the simulations in section 5.

Graphical analysis Figure 4 uses a linear representation (the model, estimations and simulations are based on constant-elasticity specification) to illustrate the market position of the vanilla marketing authorities in Madagascar: We use it to investigate the welfare and distributional consequences of alternative pricing policies. Market power in the export market implies that Madagascar faces a downward-sloping demand curve for its vanilla exports, D, with the associated marginal revenue curve MR. Note that the demand curve shows the quantity that Madagascar would sell in the world market at various prices for Madagascar vanilla, given the demand and supply conditions for Indonesian vanilla and the resulting equilibrium price in that market. S is the upward-sloping supply curve of Madagascar's vanilla producers; the resulting marginal cost of vanilla to the marketing authorities is shown by MC.

A *laissez-faire* pricing strategy on the part of Madagascar would result in a market equilibrium at point *a*, with a free-trade equilibrium price P_M^F and quantity of vanilla exports Q_M^F. Ignoring processing and transport costs, the producers would receive the full price paid by buyers in the world market, so the producer price PP_M^F would not diverge from the export price. This *laissez-faire* pricing strategy represents the optimal policy *for the world* (i.e., free trade) where price to consumers equals the marginal cost of production.

A pricing strategy by the vanilla marketing authorities to exploit Madagascar's market power in the world market and maximize the country's profits from vanilla production and export would imply an export quantity of Q_M^* (the quantity at which

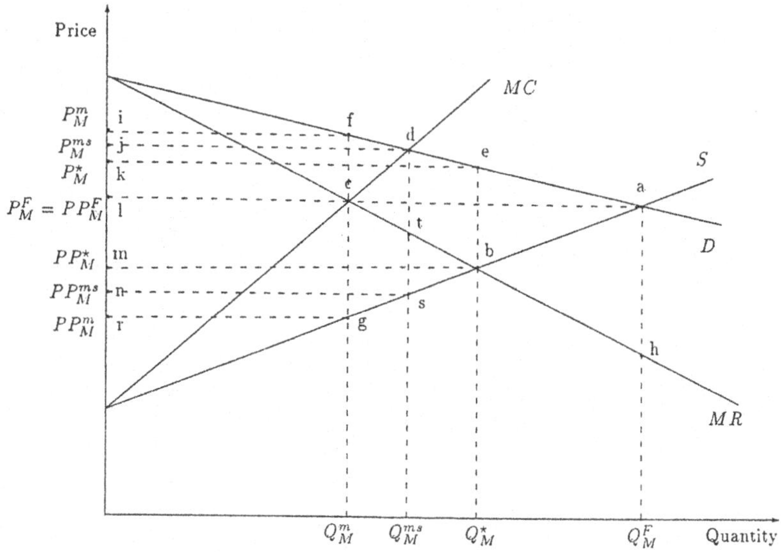

Figure 4. Madagascar Pricing Strategies

marginal revenue from exporting equals the true marginal production cost for vanilla), an export price of P_M^*, and a producer price at PP_M^*.[14] This pricing strategy represents an optimal policy *for the country*; i.e., exploitation of the country's monopoly power in the world market to improve its terms of trade.

A third marketing-board pricing strategy would exploit simultaneously market power in the world market and monopsony power relative to the growers to maximize marketing-board profits, which is equivalent to maximizing vanilla tax revenue. The equilibrium quantity under this pricing strategy would be Q_M^m, where the marginal cost of vanilla to the marketing-board equals its marginal revenue from export sales at point *c*.

Equilibrium export price under this pricing strategy would be P_M^m and producer price would be PP_M^m. This monopoly/monopsony pricing strategy would be optimal *for the marketing-board*; i.e., the exploitation of both monopoly and monopsony power which maximizes marketing-board profits. Maximizing marketing-board profits is not optimal from the point of view of the country as a whole because the exploitation of the board's monopsony position *vis-à-vis* the growers involves a loss to domestic producers from lower producer prices and reduced output.

One other pricing strategy, which is not likely to be chosen, but is included in the discussion here for the sake of completeness, would be exploitation of monopsony power over the growers, but without simultaneously taking advantage of market power in the world market. This monopsony-only equilibrium would be at point *d*, where MC to the marketing authorities equals price. Export price would be set at P_M^{ms}, and producer price at PP_M^{ms}. Note that the geometry of Figure 4 indicates that if the S and D curves are symmetric around *a*, then the same solution would be obtained by either the exploitation of monopsony power or by the exploitation of monopoly power.

Given the divergence of interests of the marketing-board, the growers, and consumers abroad, it is useful to identify gains and losses to the world, to Madagascar as a whole, and to the vanilla producers, of the alternative pricing strategies. From the point of view of Madagascar as a whole, Q_M^* is the optimal export quantity. This pricing strategy results in marketing-board profits of $\widehat{kebm}$ and a loss to producers of $\widehat{labm}$ compared with free trade. The world suffers deadweight losses equal to triangle $\widehat{eab}$ in Figure 4 because price exceeds the true marginal production costs represented by the height of the supply curve S. But from the point of view of Madagascar, any divergence of export levels below or above Q_M^* involves losses. Compared with free trade, the monopoly pricing strategy nets Madagascar gains of $\widehat{bah}$.

When the marketing-board maximizes profits at Q_M^m, tax revenue is $\widehat{ifgr}$, producer losses (compared with free trade) are $\widehat{lagr}$, and triangle $\widehat{cbg}$ represents the loss of welfare *to the country as a whole* (compared with the optimal at Q_M^*). For export levels below Q_M^*, $MR >$ supply price implies the extra revenue the country could earn by increasing exports exceeds actual incremental production costs. But the deadweight losses *from the point of view of the world as a whole* of triangle $\widehat{fag}$ are even larger. Because both free-trade and the tax-revenue-maximizing solutions are second-best from the country's point of view, one cannot tell *a priori* which would lead to greater welfare.

The monopsony-only pricing strategy is not the optimal policy from any particular group's point of view. Marketing-board profits of $\widehat{sdjn}$ would be lower than at Q_M^m, Madagascar's profits from producing and exporting would be lower than at Q_M^* by an amount $\widehat{tbs}$, and world losses (compared with free trade) would be $\widehat{das}$.

Algebraic formulation The graphical model used above has a straightforward algebraic equivalent. We give its representation in the following equations with the constant-elasticity functional forms used in the simulations in section 5.[15]

Note however, that this model does not correspond exactly to the reduced-form model used in section 4 to obtain the demand and supply elasticities needed for the simulation analysis. Hence the other variables influencing demand and supply relationships (e.g., the price of substitutes, income, etc.) are subsumed in the constant term in the equations that follow (and in the simulations in section 5).

Assume then that both countries export their entire vanilla crop and face constant-elasticity demand curves of the form:

$$D_M = A\frac{P_I^{\alpha}}{P_M^{\beta}}, \tag{1}$$

$$D_I = B\frac{P_M^{\delta}}{P_I^{\gamma}}, \tag{2}$$

where $P_j, j = I,M$ is the export price, $A,B > 0$ are constants, and $\alpha,\beta,\gamma,\delta > 0$ represent own and cross-price elasticities of demand. Other factors influencing demand (e.g., income per capita and the price of substitutes) are subsumed in the constant term.[16] The supply functions are:

$$S_M = C(PP_M)^{\varepsilon}, \tag{3}$$

$$S_I = D(PP_I)^{\phi}, \tag{4}$$

where PP_j is the producer price, $C,D > 0$ are constants, and $\varepsilon,\phi > 0$ are supply elasticities with other intervening factors again subsumed in the constant term.

First, assume there is no intervention by Madagascar and that free trade prevails on the vanilla market. Madagascar's export price is obtained as follows:

$$P_M^F = \underset{P_M}{\text{argsol}}(D_M = S_M \quad \text{and} \quad D_I = S_I) = \left[\frac{A}{C}\left(\frac{B}{D}\right)^{\alpha/(\gamma+\phi)}\right]^{1/(\varepsilon-\lambda)}, \tag{5}$$

where

$$\lambda = \alpha\delta/(\gamma+\phi) - \beta < 0 \tag{6}$$

is Madagascar's elasticity of demand under the assumption of price leadership.

Under the price-leadership assumption, if Madagascar pursues a national welfare-maximizing pricing strategy, its optimal export price is given by:

$$P_M^* = \underset{P_M}{\text{argmax}}\left(P_M D_M - P_M \frac{1+\lambda}{\lambda} S_M\right) = \left(\frac{\lambda}{1+\lambda}\right)^{\varepsilon/(\varepsilon-\lambda)} P_M^F, \tag{7}$$

where

$$PP_M^*/P_M^* = (1+\lambda)/\lambda \tag{8}$$

is the ratio of producer to selling price in the leader–follower model that tends to 1 as $\lambda \to -\infty$.[17]

Correspondingly, if Madagascar behaves as a monopsonist on the domestic market but does not intervene in the export market, the export price is given by:

$$P_M^{ms} = \underset{P_M}{\text{argmax}}\left(P_M D_M - P_M \frac{\varepsilon}{\varepsilon+1} S_M\right) = \left(\frac{\varepsilon+1}{\varepsilon}\right)^{\varepsilon/(\varepsilon-\lambda)} P_M^F, \tag{9}$$

where

$$PP_M^{ms}/P_M^{ms} = \varepsilon/(1+\varepsilon) \tag{10}$$

is the ratio of producer to selling price in the monopsonist model that tends to 1 as $\varepsilon \to \infty$.

Finally, if Madagascar behaves as a monopsonist on the domestic market and as a price leader on the export market, we proceed in the same way but the price wedge is now given by:

$$\frac{PP_M^m}{P_M^m} = \Omega = \frac{1+\lambda}{\lambda}\frac{\varepsilon}{\varepsilon+1}. \tag{11}$$

Note that monopsony power in the domestic market vanishes as $\varepsilon \to \infty$. Likewise the optimal export tax is a decreasing function of the value of the elasticity of demand. The optimal price under the price-leader–monopsonist assumptions is:

$$P_M^m = \underset{P_M}{\text{argmax}}(P_M D_M - P_M \Omega S_M) = \Omega^{\varepsilon/(\varepsilon-\lambda)} P_M^F. \tag{12}$$

It can easily be verified that $P_M^* \to P_M^F$ as $\lambda \to -\infty$; that $P_M^{ms} \to P_M^F$ as $\varepsilon \to \infty$; and that $P_M^m \to P_M^F$ as λ and $|\varepsilon| \to \infty$.

This is a first model of the international vanilla market.[18] To compare Madagascar's actual observed pricing policy with the alternative pricing scenarios described here, we need estimates of the crucial supply and demand parameters. We now discuss the econometric model used to obtain the elasticities needed for the simulation analysis.

4. Estimation of the Price-Leadership Model

This section reports the results of our estimation of the model described above. On the supply side, econometric tests confirmed that supply decisions depend on lagged prices. Demand parameters were estimated from panel data, so that demand and supply error terms are not correlated, thereby allowing us to estimate separately demand and supply sides of the model. As will be seen from the discussion, results from the demand estimates are remarkably robust, those for supply estimates less so.

Demand

We estimated import demand equations for each of the four major importing countries of the form $D_J^H = f(P_H^H, P_I^H; PV^H; GDP^H)$ where (H = Japan, USA, France, Germany) and ($J = M$ for Madagascar and I for Indonesia), D_J^H is quantity imported per capita, PV^H is the deflated price of the synthetic substitute vanillin, ($P_M^H; P_I^H$) are the CIF export prices of Madagascar and Indonesia vanilla, and GDP^H is real GDP per capita for importing country H. We estimated these import demand equations under partial equilibrium assumptions. This means that we did not impose cross-equation restrictions taking, as it were, refuge behind the observation that expenditures on vanilla are a sufficiently small share of total expenditures to be considered in isolation. Estimation is carried out separately for Madagascar and Indonesia using panel data for the period 1964–91. Results for the within estimators are reported in Table 1.

Our estimation strategy was as follows. First, we tested for the inclusion of dummies for each importing country through Leamer critical F value for large samples, and had to reject the null hypothesis of no country dummies ($F(12,84) = 4.9$ for Madagascar and $F(12,84) = 5.0$ for Indonesia). Second, we estimated the model with a random and fixed effects estimators. Even though our sample is not random (the four largest vanilla importers), since fixed-effects models are conditional on the effect prevailing in the observed sample, it is preferable to treat individual effects as random (Mundlak, 1978). The Hausman test (random effects vs within estimator) rejected the hypothesis of no correlation of the individual effects with other regressor for Indonesia but could not reject it for Madagascar. Therefore we settled for a fixed-effects estimator for Indonesia and a random-effect estimator for Madagascar. Demand for Indonesia is estimated with heteroskedastic-robust standard errors. Madagascar demand is estimated with a 2SLS procedure (using the estimated value of Indonesia's price in Madagascar's demand equation) to account for the simultaneity bias due to Madagascar's price-leader and Indonesia's price-follower behavior.

The results appear in Table 1. All price coefficients have the expected signs and are significant at the 1% (5%) level for Madagascar (Indonesia). Three-quarters of the variance is accounted for by the price and income variables. Even though no restrictions were imposed on the cross-price elasticities, they turned out to have practically the same values. Under the price-leadership assumption (see definition of λ above), the own-price demand elasticity is (–1.39) which is lower than the estimate for Indonesian vanilla (–1.98). This result is intuitively plausible if, indeed, bourbon vanilla is in a "category of its own."

For both countries, the price of synthetic substitutes is significant even though the estimated value is much higher for Indonesia than for Madagascar. This is probably credible in relative terms since Indonesia produces lower-quality vanilla which might be considered a closer substitute for artificial products. In sum, even though the stan-

Table 1. Panel Demand Estimates (1966–91)

	Dependent variable[a]: ln *D*	
	Madagascar	*Indonesia*
Constant	–40.29	
	(–7.54)**	
$\ln P_M$	–2.53	1.66
	(–3.54)**	(2.23)*
$\ln P_I$	1.73	–1.99
	(2.70)**	(–3.73)**
$\ln PV$	1.01	1.85
	(4.24)**	(4.37)**
$\ln GDP$	3.31	4.79
	(5.80)**	(4.38)**
Adjusted R^2	0.79	0.77
SER	0.59	1.36
F-test H0:no-dummies	4.1**	3.6**
Leamer *F* H0:no-dummies	4.9**	5.3**
D–W	1.9[b]	1.2[c]
Hausman H0:random eff.[d]	5.0	4.7[+]

[a]Data sources are: CAVAGI, COMTRADE, and FAO. Madagascar's demand is estimated with a random effect technique and Indonesia's demand is estimated with a White robust within-estimator. In both cases random and within-estimators yielded very close estimates. Figures in parenthesis are *t*-statistics: * is for significance at the 5% level and ** at the 1% level.

[b]Significant at 5% following Bhargava et al. (1981) tables.

[c]Following Bhargava et al. (1981) we cannot reject the hypothesis of autocorrelation (1.2 is below the lower bound).

[d]We choose a 20% significance level (noted +) since the Hausman test drops all variables for which the fixed-effect estimator is more efficient than the random-effect estimator and therefore biases the test towards accepting the null hypothesis (H0). For Madagascar the test follows a chi-squared of order 4 and for Indonesia a chi-squared of order 3.

dard error of the regression is on the high side,[19] in overall terms these results are remarkably good.

Supply

The estimated supply functions are inspired by the literature on the determinants of tree crops where lags in production are important. The supply functions are estimated in double log form and take the form: $S_J = f(P_J;\ PS_J;\ R_J;\ H_J;\ T;\ DUM)$. As before, ($J$ = Madagascar, Indonesia), P_J are one-period lag unit values for Madagascar and Indonesia, PS_J is the price of other factors affecting supply (e.g., wages or the price of rice), R_J is rainfall deviations from optimal rainfall quantity to produce vanilla, H_J is harvested area, T is a time trend to capture exogenous factors affecting supply, and DUM is a dummy variable that captures the effects of cyclonic conditions in Madagascar. Time subscripts and lags have been omitted. A separate supply function is estimated for each country over the period 1964–91 according to the following strategy. In the presence of autocorrelation in OLS estimates, a Wald test was used for selecting between maximum-likelihood iterative AR1 estimates and lagged endogenous variables leading to the selection of the AR1 method to correct for autocorrelation. The results appear in Table 2.

In spite of relatively high significance for the main coefficients (usually around 95% for all coefficients in both equations, and no evidence of heteroskedasticity in the estimates as shown by the Breusch–Pagan test), the supply estimates posed problems owing to a lack of data (e.g., the lack of data on rainfall for Madagascar), and the consequent need to search for the best specification on a trial-and-error basis.[20] For instance, in the case of Madagascar, a dummy variable (*DUM*) was used to account for the 1976 cyclone and for unfavorable climatic factors during 1966–70. Also, the search for best-fitting lag structures yielded generally insignificant results so we opted for a single lag on prices for both countries.[21]

The results in Table 2 yield similar long-run supply elasticity estimates (0.48 for Madagascar and 0.52 for Indonesia). Perhaps because of measurement problems, real wages in the vanilla growing regions were insignificant in both supply equations. For Madagascar though, the price of rice (PR_i) was significant and was included as an alternative variable measuring opportunity costs (being insignificant in the case of Indonesia, it was not included). The absolute deviation of rainfall from the recommended amounts, R_I, does not enter significantly into Indonesia's supply function. The time trend coefficient was positive and significant for Madagascar, but the harvested area

Table 2. Supply Estimates (1964–91)

	Dependent variable[a]*:* ln S	
	Madagascar	*Indonesia*
Constant	4.80	–5.50
	(2.98)**	(–3.40)**
$\ln PP_{t-1}$	0.49	0.52
	(2.00)*	(4.92)**
$\ln PR_{t-1}$	–1.44	
	(–3.79)**	
$\ln R_{t-1}$		–0.04
		(–1.23)
Dummy	–0.87	
	(–5.63)**	
$\ln H$		1.08
		(5.38)**
Time	0.10	
	(5.33)**	
Adjusted R^2	0.84	0.85
SER	0.31	0.31
Wald H0:AR1	6.9	1.6
Breusch/Pagan[b]	9.3	6.7
D–W	1.8**	1.9**

[a] Data sources are: CAVAGI, COMTRADE, and FAO. Estimation by a maximum-likelihood iterative first-order serial correlation (AR1) technique. Figures in parenthesis are t-statistics: * is for significance at the 95% level and ** at the 99% level.
[b] H0:homoskedacity.

was insignificant (probably owing to the significant correlation between the time trend and the harvested area), in contrast to Indonesia where the harvested area was significant (but the time trend insignificant).

In view of the above, it is not surprising that in contrast with the demand estimates, the supply estimates were sensitive to the selection of explanatory variables, especially for Madagascar (for example, in equations including harvested area or wage instead of time produced supply estimates around 0.8). However, in all instances, positive and significant supply estimates were obtained. Hence, the use of a range of estimates in the simulations reported in Tables 4 and 5.

5. Evaluating Madagascar's Pricing Strategy

The demand and supply estimates were used to compute Madagascar's optimal prices and quantities under each of the alternative pricing strategies pictured in Figure 4 and expressed in equations (3)–(12). These "optimal" prices (and quantities) were then compared with actual observed prices and quantities. Comparisons were for the years 1981–91, the period when Indonesia came into the market and, more importantly, the period when Madagascar began to accumulate large stocks and to tax producers heavily. The calculations were carried out using standard calibration techniques.[22] Welfare and revenue comparisons are discussed, followed by comparisons of the resulting internal redistribution between producers and the marketing-board.

Welfare and Revenue

Table 3 compares actual average prices and quantities with the calculated average optimal prices and quantities under the alternative scenarios. Actual producer prices are quite close to optimal producer prices under the government revenue-maximization assumption. However, because optimal selling prices are much lower than actual ones, optimal quantities are correspondingly higher than actual ones. Thus there would appear to be overtaxation.

For welfare calculations, we express the triangular welfare losses (areas *tbs*, *cbg*, and *bah* in Figure 4) generated by deviations from the welfare-maximizing strategy. Welfare and marketing-board revenue changes appear in Table 4 and producer surplus changes in Table 5. Neglecting internal vanilla consumption, welfare change equals the change in the marketing-board revenue plus the change in producers' surplus:[23]

Table 3. Calculated Optimal Prices and Quantities

	Export price[a]	*Producer price*	*Implicit tax*[b]	*Quantities*[c]
Actual (average 1981–91)	66	5	61	877[d] (1,569)[e]
Price-leader	36	11	25	2,447
Monopsony	35	12	23	2,578
Price-leader/Monopsony	49	5	44	1,634
Free trade	26	26	0	3,860

[a] All prices are in $/kilo.
[b] The implicit tax is given by the difference between export and producer prices.
[c] In metric tonnes.
[d] Actual exports.
[e] Actual production.

Table 4. Welfare and Marketing-Board Revenue Gains (1981–91 average)

	Percentage of export revenue (ER) and GDP[a]			
	Price-leader	*Monopsony*	*Price-leader/ monopsony*	*Free trade*
Walfare (% ER)	(44)[b] **48**[c] [127][d]	(42) **48** [118]	(43) **41** [100]	(22) **26** [114]
Gains (% GDP)	(0.90) **0.99** [2.63]	(0.86) **0.98** [2.44]	(0.87) **0.85** [2.08]	(0.46) **0.53** [2.36]
M-B revenue (% ER)	(47) **28** [19]	(30) **22** [63]	(51) **42** [72]	(–83) **–83** [83]
Gains (% GDP)	(0.98) **0.57** [0.39]	(0.63) **0.46** [1.29]	(1.06) **0.87** [1.49]	(–1.72) **–1.72** [–1.72]

[a] Actual export revenue represents 2.1% of GDP during this period and 715% of producers' revenue. Valued at export [producer] price vanilla production was 15.2% [1.5%] of GDP.
[b] Figures in parenthesis are higher-bound estimates obtained by decreasing Madagascar's elasticity of supply by one standard deviation and its demand elasticity by 1/2 (to avoid an inelastic demand estimate). $\varepsilon = 0.24$, $\beta = 1.7$, $\lambda = -1.06$. Other elasticities take the values in note *c*.
[c] Figures are for estimated elasticities. $\alpha = 1.70$, $\beta = 2.53$, $\delta = 1.66$, $\gamma = 1.99$, $\lambda = -1.39$, $\varepsilon = 0.49$, $\phi = 0.52$.
[d] Figures in square brackets are for lower-bound estimates obtained by taking one standard deviation above the mean estimate; i.e. $\alpha = 1.05$, $\beta = 3.25$, $\delta = 0.92$, $\gamma = 2.51$, $\lambda = -2.94$, $\varepsilon = 0.73$, $\phi = 0.62$.

$$\Delta W^j = \Delta\Pi^j + \int_{PP^{ac}}^{PP^j} \hat{S}(PP)\cdot dPP, \qquad (13)$$

where ΔW^j is the change in welfare had the marketing-board followed policy j; $\Delta\Pi^j$ is the change in marketing-board revenue; PP^{ac} is the actual producer price; PP^j is producer price under policy j, and $\hat{S}$ is the estimated supply function for Madagascar. Under the assumption that internal general equilibrium repercussions of alternative vanilla pricing policy can be neglected, ΔW^j, is an approximation of welfare change.

Consider first the bold figures (figures in parenthesis and brackets are corresponding estimates under high and low elasticities) which compare actual outcomes with either set of optimal policies, welfare-maximizing (price-leader) or revenue-maximizing (price-leader/monopsony). The estimates show very large welfare losses, almost 50% of the annual value of exports, or 1% of realized annual GDP. Given that the cumulated stocks were destroyed, *ex post* these estimates reflect the interpretation of a misguided policy. If, instead, tax revenue maximization was indeed Madagascar's intended objective, the profile of quantities exported would have been about equal to actual production which is about twice actual exports, or 70% of exports under national welfare maximization. Then welfare gains would have been 0.8% of actual GDP.

Comparing the alternative policies, in terms of the tradeoff between welfare and revenue maximization, the elasticity estimates here suggest that, in terms of welfare, the departure from welfare maximization to revenue maximization would be justified. A Pigouvian-type calculation indicates that going for revenue maximization only lowers average GDP by 0.16% per year while yielding an average yearly revenue gain of 0.3% (i.e., a tradeoff between a 14% higher welfare gain under welfare maximization and a government revenue 52% as large under tax revenue maximization).

Table 5. Producers' gains/losses (1981–91 average)

	Percentage of producers' total revenue (TR) and GDP[a]			
	Price-leader	*Monopsony*	*Price-leader/ monopsony*	*Free trade*
Surplus (% TR)	(–25)[b] **143**[c] [855][d]	(83) **179** [397]	(–65) –6.8 [203]	(754) **778** [1411]
Gains (% GDP)	(–0.07) **0.42** [2.37]	(0.24) **0.52** [1.14]	(–0.19) **–0.02** [0.59]	(2.18) **2.26** [4.08]
Revenue (% TR)	(–40) **215** [1315]	(94) **270** [661]	(–89) **–7.40** [327]	(926) **1,162** [2417]
Gains (% GDP)	(–0.12) **0.62** [3.81]	(0.27) **0.78** [1.91]	(–0.26) **–0.02** [0.95]	(2.68) **3.37** [7.00]

[a] Actual producers' revenue represents 0.29% of GDP during this period and 13.98% of export revenue.
[b] See note *b* in Table 4.
[c] See note *c* in Table 4.
[d] See note *c* in Table 4.

What about a hands-off policy, the choice usually advocated in the policy circles in international organizations? A noninterventionist policy would have resulted in a total revenue loss for the marketing-board of 1.7% of GDP on an annual basis, a loss that, arguably, might be politically hard to sustain in a country with a weak fiscal system. However, in terms of welfare, a non-interventionist policy would have yielded a gain which amounts to 0.5% of GDP, which supports the hands-off policy, especially since in addition it would have been more equitable (see below).

How sensitive are these calculations to variations in elasticities? In a first scenario (values in parenthesis in Tables 4 and 5) we increase Madagascar's monopoly power in the export market and monopsony power in the domestic market; and in a second scenario we do the opposite (values in square brackets in Tables 4 and 5). First, note that the pattern of demand and supply elasticities is such that there is little difference between the monopoly and monopsony solutions, this regardless of the pattern of elasticities. If the set of elasticities brackets the extent of potential double market power over the period, actual pricing resulted in a welfare loss of between about 0.9% and 2.6% of GDP in comparison with either welfare-maximizing or revenue-maximizing policies. On the other hand, *laissez-faire* would have increased welfare above the actual outcome by 0.5% to 2.4% of GDP. If fiscal revenue was the primary objective, revenue-maximizing pricing policy would have yielded between 0.9% and 1.5% (in terms of GDP) more annual revenue than obtained under the observed outcome.

Internal Redistribution

The above results suggest that pricing policy had objectives other than welfare or revenue maximization, probably reflecting political-economy considerations. Table 5 reports the revenue and surplus producers would have had under each of the scenarios in relation to their average total revenue over the period and as a percentage of GDP. That *laissez-faire* would have been more equitable is already clear from the above, as vanilla growers would not have been taxed so heavily. For example, producers' gain (in comparison with the actual pricing policy) is estimated at 2.2% = 0.5 + 1.7) of GDP (or over 11 times their actual revenue) under *laissez-faire*. Under a more realistic welfare-maximizing strategy producers would have gained on average 0.4% (= 1.0 – 0.6) of GDP (or over twice their actual average revenue).

As already suggested by the price and quantity comparisons in Table 3, the producer surplus calculations reported in Table 5 indicate that producers obtained approximately what they would have if the marketing-board had followed a profit-maximizing strategy. Yet selling price was held about 20% above the profit-maximizing level, despite falling international market share and accumulating vanilla stocks. Not surprisingly this high price wedge resulted in cases of under-invoicing and rumours of smuggling.

One explanation of this pricing policy is simply an overestimation on the part of the vanilla market authorities of Madagascar's degree of market power, or an underestimation of the degree of substitutability between Madagascar and Indonesian vanilla. But then the puzzle is why producer prices were not set accordingly.

Another possible explanation, along political-economy lines, is that a high-price policy served the interest of what Findlay (1989) refers to as the "bureaucratic capitalist" alliance. The high-price policy would then be viewed as reflecting the clearing price in the power struggle in the urban sector. It is also consistent with the widely held view that marketing-boards have developed into rent extraction entreprises (see e.g., Helleiner (1964) and Gilbert (1993)).

Our main objective in this paper is an evaluation of Madagascar's pricing policies for vanilla, but a similar analysis could be applied to other export-oriented marketing-boards or any other arrangements or regulations that give monopsony power to a single marketing entity. In each case careful attention must be paid to institutional arrangements that influence the distribution of the gains and losses. For example, Trouillot (1988) and Slocum (1996) describe export marketing arrangements for bananas in St Lucia and Dominica in which banana growers' associations hold legal monopsony power, but long-term contractual arrangements provide that all bananas exported from Dominica and St Lucia are sold in the United Kingdom by a single multinational banana trading company that effectively sets the price paid to banana growers and also accounts for a large percentage of total UK banana sales. This marketing arrangement may well give the simultaneous price-leader/monopsony power to the multinational. The likely result is a pricing structure that maximizes profit for the multinational, rather than revenue for the Caribbean banana growers' associations.

6. Conclusions

For the last decade, Madagascar has followed a high-price strategy in the natural vanilla market. This paper has attempted to evaluate the welfare and internal distribution consequences of Madagascar's vanilla pricing policy. We developed and estimated a simple price-leadership model of the international vanilla market that takes into account both the marketing authority's buying power relative to growers and the selling power in the international market. On the assumption that there was no economic rationale for stocking (since stocks were burnt), the simulations indicated a large welfare loss from the pricing policies followed by Madagascar during the period 1981–91. Even though *laissez-faire* would have been far from optimal and probably not an option in an economy with a weak fiscal system and no mechanisms for lump-sum transfers, it would have been preferable to the policies actually followed on both efficiency and distributional grounds.

This said, the model and methods used here are only a starting point in the evaluation of alternative pricing policies for countries with weak fiscal systems and double market power. In particular, it leaves out several important factors (e.g., stockholding motivated by supply uncertainty, incentive effects for the development of synthetic substitutes, and quality mix choice) that would have affected optimal pricing strategy. The link between pricing policies and the erosion of market power due to entry of new suppliers and possible entry-deterrence strategies on the part of Madagascar, and the possibility of cooperation between the two major exporting countries, were not considered.

Nonetheless, this case study suggests that though prices paid to producers might have been compatible with revenue maximization, overly high official selling prices constituted implicit overtaxation of producers. In political-economy terms, this case study suggests that the pricing policy followed by Madagascar was closer to that predicted by a predatory view of the state than by a revenue-maximizing bureaucratic state.

References

Bauer, Peter T., "Marketing-Boards," in John Eatwell et al. (eds.) *The New Palgrave: A Dictionary of Economics*, New York: Macmillan (1987).

Bhargava, Alok, Luigi Franzini, and Wiji Narendranathan, "Serial Correlation and the Fixed Effects Model," *Review of Economic Studies* 49 (1981):533–49.

Cardenas, Mauricio, "Stabilization and Redistribution of Coffee Revenues: A Political Economy Model of Commodity Marketing-Boards," *Journal of Development Economics* 44 (1994): 351–80.

Denis, Jean-Emile, "Export Performance of the Marketing-Boards in LDCs—the Case of Cocoa and Coffee in West Africa," in Michel M. Kostecki (ed.) *State Trading in International Markets*, New York: St Martin's Press (1982).

Findlay, Ronald, "Is the New Political Economy Relevant to Developing Countries?" Country Economics Dept., World Bank (1989).

Gilbert, Christopher L., "Domestic Price Stabilisation Schemes for Developing Countries," in Stijn Classens and Ronald Duncan (eds.) *Managing Commodity Price Risk in Developing Countries*, Baltimore: Johns Hopkins University Press (1993).

Guillaumont, Patrick and Sylviane Guillaumont, "Dévaluation et Prix Réels Payés aux Producteurs agricoles dans les Pays en Developpement: Explication d'un Paradoxe," in Patrick Guillaumont (ed.) *Economie des Politiques Agricoles dans les Pays en Developpement*, Paris: Revue Francaise d'Economie (1994).

Helleiner, Gerald, "The Fiscal Role of the Marketing-Boards in Nigerian Economic Development, 1947–61," *Economic Journal* 74 (1964):582–610.

Idachaba, Francis S., "Marketing Boards as Potential Stabilizers of Government Revenue in Developing Countries: The Nigerian Experience," *Economic Bulletin of Ghana: Second Series* 3 (1973):23–30.

Just, Richard E., Andrew Schmitz, and David Zilberman, "Price Controls and Optimal Export Policies under Alternative Market Structures," *American Economic Review* 69 (1979):706–14.

Kolawole, M. I., "The Reform of Commodity Boards in Nigeria: An Analysis of New Producer Policy," *Economic Bulletin of Ghana: Second Series* 3 (1973):14–19.

Kostecki, Michel M., "State Trading by the Advanced and Developing Countries: the Background," in Kostecki, Michel M. (ed.) *State Trading in International Markets*, New York: St Martin's Press (1982).

Krishna, Kala and Marie Thursby, "Optimal Policies and Marketing-Board Objectives," *Journal of Development Economics* 38 (1992):1–15.

Krueger, Anne, Maurice Sehiff, and Alberto Valdes, *The Political Economy of Agriculture Price Interventions in Latin America*, San Francisco: ICS Press (1992).

Lloyd, Peter J., "State Trading and the Theory of International Trade," in Michel M. Kostecki (ed.) *State Trading in International Markets*, New York: St Martin's Press (1982).

Markusen, James R., "The Welfare and Allocative Effects of Export Taxes vs Marketing-Boards," *Journal of Development Economics* 14 (1984):19–36.

Mundlak, Yair, "On the Pooling of Time Series and Cross Sectional Data," *Econometrica* 46 (1978):69–80.
Nielsen, *The Story of Vanilla*, Nielsen Massey Vanilla, Illinois (1992).
Slocum, Kelly, *Producing under a Globalizing Economy: The Intersection of Flexible Production and Local Autonomy in the Work, Lives and Actions of St Lucian Banana Growers*, PhD dissertation, University of Florida (1996).
Trouillot, Michel, *Peasants and Capital: Dominica in the World Economy*, Baltimore: Johns Hopkins University Press, 1988.
Van Kooten, G. C. and John Spriggs, "A Comparative Statics Analysis of the Welfare Impact of Supply Restricting Marketing-Boards," *Canadian Journal of Agricultural Economics* 55 (1984):221–30.
Wickens, M.R. and James Greenfield, "The Econometrics of Agricultural Supply: An Application to the World Coffee Market," *Review of Economics and Statistics* 55 (1973):443–40.

Notes

1. Cardenas (1994) argues that the redistribution implications of marketing-boards depend on the type of institutional agreement. He shows that in the case of coffee marketing-boards, countries which have a more proactive behavior by stabilizing producer prices and heavily taxing exporting have generally followed an industrialization policy at the expense of agriculture.
2. For an early assessment of distortions that marketing-boards may introduce between food and export crops, see Idachaba (1973). Kolawole (1973) examined the potential role of marketing-boards to stabilize government revenue and concluded that, in the case of Nigeria, the strong and positive correlation between government revenue exclusive of marketing-boards' contributions and marketing-boards' revenue suggested a tendency towards destabilization. For evidence on lack of flexibility in pricing policy on the part of cocoa and coffee marketing-boards in West Africa, see Denis (1982).
3. Kostecki (1982) and Lloyd (1982) suggest that governments opt for marketing-boards rather than taxes and subsidies because the taxation is more covert and less likely to prompt political opposition.
4. This view is forcibly expressed in the above quote from Bauer. For a political economy model of the predatory state, see Findlay (1989). For a review of the differing roles of parastatals in agriculture see Krueger (1992, ch. 5), and for indirect evidence at the macroeconomic level of rent-extraction from agricultural producers via exchange rate devaluations in African countries, see Guillaumont and Guillaumont (1994).
5. An exception is Van Kooten and Spriggs (1984). However, they focus on the Canadian marketing-boards and assume perfectly competitive markets where free trade is the first-best policy.
6. Natural vanilla beans account for only a small fraction of the vanilla flavouring market. The market share for natural vanilla bean production is generally considered to be protected from the far lower-cost artificial synthetic substitutes on two grounds: first a shift in tastes towards natural and organic foods; and second labeling regulations which allow a "vanilla" label to be used only on products made from natural vanilla (new bioengineered products which derive vanillin from vanilla plant tissues pose little threat because of high costs and low probability that new labeling definitions will be created for the biotechnical food industry in the next ten years).
7. Harvesting begins four years after planting, with peak yields after seven years and an average tree life of 15 years. Preparation costs are about the same among the major suppliers. Thus Madagascar's comparative advantage (production costs less than half of its competitors, Comoros and Indonesia) derives from climatic conditions and from the lower opportunity cost of land and labor.
8. It could be argued that the accumulation of stocks was partly aimed towards building a credible strategy of limit pricing, as for instance in the case of Brazilian coffee stock policy. However, levels were beyond those required for such a strategy.

9. The Alliance de la Vanille negotiates, each year, prices and quantities exported with a small group of buyers in the three major purchasers of natural vanilla (percentage shares of world demand in parenthesis): US (60%), France (15%), Germany (15%). The cartel also distributes quota shares among the three exporting members. In recent years, Madagascar has filled between 60% and 70% of its allocated quota share. Until 1993 when it was lowered to $60 per kg, the price was set at around $73 per kg.

10. Madagascar's production costs (including preparation to the exporting stage) are estimated at less than half those of its competitors (Indonesia and Comoros). Because of bulging stocks (until they were burnt in 1993), purchase prices received by producers have fallen drastically in recent years. The barter terms of trade with rice has fallen from 10 to 4.

11. Stocks were depleted in 1978 following a world crisis in the vanilla market resulting from cyclonic conditions among Indian Ocean producers. It could therefore be argued that precautionary stocking to face uncertainty was a rational policy, though not to the levels observed in the 1980s.

12. Significant improvements in harvesting, drying, and curing techniques improved the quality of Indonesian vanilla during the last half of the 1980s, which made bourbon and Indonesian vanilla more readily substitutable.

13. The noninterventionist policy followed by Indonesia implies that the international vanilla market differs from the duopoly marketing-board model developed by Krishna and Thursby (1992). Our model also differs from theirs and Just (1979) in that we treat the parastatal marketing-board as part of the government, rather than assuming an independent marketing-board with its own objectives that the government must influence with tax and/or subsidy policies. These models and Markusen (1984) also assume the existence of domestic demand, so the existence or lack of domestic price regulation and market segmentation becomes important.

14. Here we have assumed that the producer price is set to equate quantity produced with quantity exported, which assumes no domestic demand and no accumulation of stocks. Given the variability of production due to climactic conditions, some positive level of stockholding would be optimal, an issue not addressed here.

15. Since our interest is in checking the plausibility of alternative pricing rules followed by CAVAGI rather than in predicting trends in the international vanilla market, we did not test for alternative functional forms (e.g., linear demand and supply functions). Constant-elasticity demand and supply curves around a trend are also easier to calibrate and interpret.

16. One can consider them as constants in the optimization problem as these are clearly not strategic variables.

17. If $\lambda \geq -1$, then there is no interior solution to Madagascar's optimization problem.

18. In particular, the model abstracts from the potential effects of Madagascar's pricing policy on the supply of substitutes by Indonesia which in turn would affect the extent of Madagascar's market power. This is inherently a dynamic problem which must address the substitutability issue and the precautionary motive for holding stocks in the face of uncertainty.

19. This is mostly because of the large fluctuations in small markets (e.g., Japan). Also because the calculated D–W statistic for panel data (see Bhargava et al., 1981) could cast doubts on robustness—not so much because autocorrelation affects efficiency, but because of the possibility of spurious regressions—we tested for cointegration by applying the Dickey–Fuller test to the residuals. The significant coefficient suggests that variables are integrated. But, though estimation in first differences led to lower t-statistics, signs and values on price elasticities remained correct and close to those reported in Table 1 (except for the cross-price elasticity of Madagascar vanilla with respect to Indonesia which became insignificant). Similar results were obtained with AR1 estimates.

20. According to Nielsen (1992), no pesticides or fertilizers are used in growing vanilla beans. We could not obtain information on planting, the number of trees and their average age. Because it takes around nine months for the bean to mature from pollination time, current prices are not included (this was also confirmed econometrically).

21. The search for lag length was on the basis of the best fits after having tried out geometric and Almon lags. For Madagascar, we obtained plausible results with a two-period Shiller lag,

20 *Jaime de Melo, Marcelo Olarreaga, and Wendy Takacs*

which is not unreasonable given that it takes about three years for a tree to yield harvestable beans. However this lag structure yielded virtually identical values for the lag coefficients and gave the same long-run elasticity estimate as with a one-period lag. Given that for Indonesia, best results were obtained with a one-period lag, we opted for a one-period lag for both countries, thereby treating them symmetrically. As we are interested in long-run estimates rather than adjustment paths, this seemed reasonable. Better data over a longer period would have allowed modeling tree stock response based on forward-looking expectations of future prices as in, for example, Wickens and Greenfield (1973).

22. Each constant in equations (1) and (2) was calculated from the corresponding prices and quantities in each year using the selected estimated elasticity. The constants entering in (1)–(4) are the average values for the period 1981–91 taken by the other factors influencing demand and supply decisions. Thus the estimates are intended to represent long-run estimates.

23. This measure accounts for nonlinearity of demand and supply functions.

International Journal of Industrial Organization 4 (1986) 287–304. North-Holland

THE INFLUENCE OF INCREASED FOREIGN COMPETITION ON INDUSTRIAL CONCENTRATION AND PROFITABILITY*

Jaime de MELO and Shujiro URATA

The World Bank, Washington, DC 20433, USA

Final version received December 1985

This paper uses the Chilean manufacturing censuses of 1967 and 1979 to examine the effects of the Chilean reforms in the mid-1970s on market structure and performance. The reforms substantially increased the concentration in industry and substantially reduced profitability. These outcomes are interpreted in the light of hypotheses about the effect of potential entrants on market structure and on the pricing behavior of incumbents. Next, a cross-sectoral simultaneous equations model of structure and performance is estimated to isolate the contribution of import and export shares to cross-sectoral variations in concentration and profitability and to test for structural change between the two censuses. The analysis confirms that the liberalization of trade changed the way import and export shares determined profitability and supports the import discipline hypothesis.

1. Introduction

Because of increasing international linkages in national product markets, the fields of international trade and industrial organization have moved closer together. Recent developments in the theory of international trade have introduced the effects of imperfect competition and product differentiation [Krugman (1979), Lancaster (1980)]. And recent developments in the theory of industrial organization have recognized the effects of foreign trade

*This paper is part of the World Bank Research Project on Liberalization with Stabilization in the Southern Cone (RPO 672-85). An earlier version of the paper was presented at the annual EARIE meetings, Cambridge, September 11–13, 1985. We thank participants and Alexis Jacquemin for helpful comments. This is a shortened and revised version of an earlier paper [de Melo and Urata (1984)]. We also thank a referee, Vittorio Corbo, John Kwoka, James Tybout and especially Eric Swanson for helpful discussions, Gabriel Castillo, Narayana Poduval and Kalayarat Suriyasat for extremely efficient research assistance, and Bruce Ross-Larson for editorial help. An appendix is available from the authors. The World Bank does not accept responsibility for the views expressed herein which are those of the authors and should not be attributed to the World Bank or to its affiliated organizations. The findings, interpretations, and conclusions are the result of research supported by the Bank; they do not necessarily represent official policy of the Bank. The designations employed and the presentation of material in this document are solely for the convenience of the reader and do not imply the expression of any opinion whatsoever on the part of the World Bank or its affiliates concerning the legal status of any country, territory, city, area, or of its authorities, or concerning the delimitation of its boundaries, or national affiliation.

in determining market structure, conduct, and performance [Jacquemin (1982), Huveneers (1981), Geroski and Jacquemin (1981)]. Most of this theoretical work has been motivated by the quest for better theories of the pattern of international trade among developed countries and by the desire to provide better underpinnings for the empirical research on the structure–conduct–performance paradigm initiated by Bain. The recent literature has emphasized the effects of potential entrants – such as importers [Geroski and Jacquemin (1981)] or multinational companies [Sleuwagen (1983)] – on market structure and the pricing behavior of incumbent firms. This literature has given rise to the import-discipline hypothesis: the threat of entry by foreign competitors will constraint domestic firms to adopt entry-forestalling prices that more closely approximate competitive prices. This hypothesis will hold even if exposure to foreign trade reduces the number of domestic producers.

Paralleling these developments, cross-sectoral empirical studies have generally shown, almost exclusively for developed countries, that sectoral price–cost margins are inversely correlated with sectoral import shares.[1] Though valuable, these results cannot be interpreted as conclusive support of the import-discipline hypothesis. They usually do not consider conduct. Nor do they take into account the joint determination of market structure and performance.[2]

For developing countries pursuing a policy to relax severe foreign trade restrictions, one would expect that the import-discipline hypothesis would have even more force. Yet, most empirical studies of the effects of the trade regime in developing countries have not examined the effects of trade reforms on market structure and performance. Instead, they have sought to measure the restrictiveness of the trade regime and its relation to growth. This paper takes advantage of the remarkable experiment offered by the Chilean trade liberalization of the mid-1970s to examine the role of foreign competition on the structure and performance of the Chilean manufacturing sector. The analysis is based on a comparison of the 1967 and 1979 manufacturing censuses, the former for a highly protected economy, the latter for an economy whose high level of protection had just been reduced to roughly 10% across the board tariff.

The paper has two distinctive features. First, it offers evidence on the relationship between market structure and performance under different foreign trade regimes for a developing country. Second, it tests for differences in the structure–performance relationship under different trade regimes. The organization of the paper is as follows. Section 2 summarizes the main

[1]An exception is Jones, Laudadio and Percy (1973) who report a positive correlation for Canada. See Katrak (1980) and Siddharthan and Dasgupta (1983) for India.

[2]Exceptions are Jacquemin, de Ghellinck and Huveneers (1980) and Pugel (1980) which present simultaneous equation models of structure and performance.

characteristics of the trade regime in both census years, and compares concentration and profitability in the two years. Section 3 presents a simultaneous equation model of the structure–performance relationship to examine whether the Chilean trade reforms altered the determinants of concentration and profitability. Conclusions follow in section 4.

2. A comparison of concentration and profitability in 1967 and 1979

Since the Chilean economy of 1979 had undergone significant reforms spanning commodity and factor markets, we begin by briefly describing the reforms, emphasizing those for foreign trade. We then compare average concentration and profitability in both census years, interpreting the changes in the light of foreign competition.

2.1. The Chilean reforms

Until the fall of the coalition government in 1973, the general tendency was to increase government intervention in commodity and factor markets. The domestic credit market was highly controlled as in most other developing countries. Many firms had no access to credit, while those with official access enjoyed negative real interest rates. Labor legislation made labor dismissal difficult (because of high severance payments) and discouraged potential entrants by raising sunk costs. As a result there were high de facto barriers to entering industry.

In foreign trade, there had been some short-lived liberalizations of foreign trade restrictions, but the general tendency was toward greater restrictiveness, and quantitative restrictions (QRs) were widespread. There are several estimates of the restrictiveness of the foreign trade regime around 1967, the year of one of the Chilean manufacturing censuses used in this study. Corbo and Meller (1981, tables 3.7 and 3.8) show that there was general discrimination against export activities and for import-substituting ones – as well as against agriculture and mining and for manufacturing.[3] Another study of price comparisons for 92 manufacturing products found a nominal protection rate of 48% and an effective protection rate of 133% [de la Cuadra (1974), in Behrman (1976, table 5.3)]. Further estimates of nominal protection reconstructed for this study from the specific and ad valorem tariffs at the product level show even higher average rates of protection and a greater dispersion across sectors (see table 3 below). There were some incentives to exports at the time, such as a system of drawbacks for up to 30% of the

[3]For 1966–68 the average effective exchange rate (*EER*) on imports excluding premiums on import licenses was estimated at 10.6 while that for exports was 9.8 and the bias (i.e., the ratio of *EER* in industry to *EER* in agriculture) against agriculture and for manufacturing was estimated at 42%.

value of exports. But the estimates leave little doubt that Chile's foreign trade regime in 1967 was very restrictive and that products of domestic firms faced little competition on the local market from imports.

By 1979 the situation was reversed. A rapid and pervasive liberalization of foreign trade restrictions took place between September 1973 and June 1979. The pace and extent of the liberalization can be appreciated from the following summary figures taken from Corbo (1985). In September 1973 ad valorem tariff rates ranged from 0 to 750%, with half the tariffs above 80%. In addition, import prohibitions applied to 187 tariff positions as defined by the Brussels Tariff Nomenclature, and for 2,872 tariff positions there was a deposit requirement of 10,000% of the c.i.f. import value, due 90 days before importing. By August 1975 the maximum tariff rate had been reduced to 105%, the average to 65%. Most redundant protection has been eliminated, and within the next four years a uniform tariff of 10% was achieved (except for motor vehicles above 850 cc) and all other restrictions on imports and incentives to exports were eliminated. The resulting pattern of protection (see table 3 below) was one of the lowest and most uniform in the world.

There were also other reforms – including the deregulation of domestic labor and financial markets and the removal of price controls on sales in the domestic market – that affected the profitability of domestic firms and their number and size. Controls on interest rates were removed, and new labor legislation made it easier for firms to dismiss workers. Another important reform was a massive sale of public enterprises to the private sector. In sum, very different patterns of concentration and profitability would be expected in the Chilean manufacturing sector in 1979 and in 1967.

2.2. Concentration and profitability: 1967 vs. 1979

Before examining the factors associated with interindustry differences in concentration and profitability in section 3, we look at manufacturingwide changes in concentration and profitability between the two census years. The data come from the two manufacturing censuses and refer to establishments (that is, to plants not firms).

We start with a comparison of concentration in both census years. Table 1 gives the frequency distribution of the number-equivalent (*NEQ*) Herfindahl indices of sales for the 41 Chilean manufacturing sectors in both years.[4] A comparison of the two frequency distributions for the *NEQ* index (simply the number of equal-sized firms that would give the same value of the Herfindahl

[4]A description of the data and the aggregation schemes is provided in the appendix which also describes our sample selection. We purged firms whose data appeared to have been recorded incorrectly or that would be inconsistent with the implicit production framework adopted in our analysis and deleted twelve industries which appeared very heterogenous. As a result we lost 28% of observations for 1967 and 49% for 1979.

Table 1

Frequency distribution of number-equivalent Herfindahl indices for 41 Chilean manufacturing sectors.[a]

Equivalent number of firms	Number of sectors 1979	1967	Percentage 1979	1967
0–5	6	1	14.6	2.4
5–10	11	5	26.8	12.2
10–20	13	16	31.7	39.0
>20	11	19	26.8	46.3
	41	41	100.0	100.0

[a]*Source*: appendix tables A.4 and A.5.

index) shows a dramatic increase in the concentration of plants in 1967 and 1979.[5] Only six sectors had *NEQ* firm indices between 0 and 10 in 1967, compared with 17 in 1979. Only five sectors showed a decline in the Herfindahl index between 1967 and 1979.

Further confirmation of this dramatic increase in concentration is provided by a comparison with trends in the U.S. and U.K. (table 2). Although concentration also increased in the U.S. and U.K., the increase was far greater in Chile. Moreover, the firgures for Chile are a lower bound, for they refer to plants rather than firms whereas those for the U.S. and U.K. refer to multiplant firms. In Chile, mergers started in 1975, concentrating the assets of the industrial sector in the hands of a few conglomerates, even though there was a drastic decline in profitability. Regardless of whether these mergers changed the extent of multiplant operations between the two years, the concentration of firms in Chile would be greater than that of establishments.

The concentration of plants would be expected to increase over the 12 years for two main reasons. The first is that there were several barriers to

[5]The Herfindahl index (*HD*) is defined as $HD=\sum_i (S_i/\sum_i S_i)^2 \equiv n\sigma^2 + 1/n$, where n is the number of establishments in the industry, S_i is sales of establishment i, σ^2 is the variance in market shares in sales. The number equivalent (*NEQ*) is defined as the inverse of *HD* because *NEQ* assumes that $\sigma^2=0$. We are aware that *HD* defined on total sales is likely to be a biased measure since export sales should be excluded from the numerator and imports added to the denominator [Utton and Morgan (1983)]. Lacking export data at the firm level, we could not correct for the first source of bias. As to the inclusion of imports in the definition of market size, their effect on market power is likely to be ambiguous. On the one hand, taking account of the rise in import share would lower the estimates of the increase in concentration between the two census years reported in table 2. On the other hand, recognizing that imports were often made by the leading domestic producers of similar products [see Corbo and de Melo (1985)] would raise the estimates of concentration. In sum, we think that the bias resulting from these data deficiencies is likely to be small.

Table 2

Trends in industrial market concentration (annual percentage growth rate in parentheses).[a]

	U.S.		U.K.		Chile	
	1947	1970	1968	1975	1967	1979
Unweighted	40.9	42.7	63.4	65.1	38.9	50.1
	(0.2)		(0.4)		(2.1)	
Weighted[b]	38.7	42.6	64.4	65.9	49.0	61.6
	(0.4)		(0.3)		(2.5)	

[a]*Source*: U.S.: Mueller and Hamm (1974, table 1); U.K.: Hart and Clarke (1980, table 3.5); Chile: appendix table A.4. The 4-firm concentration ratio is used for the U.S. and for Chile; the 5-firm concentration ratio for the U.K. Data for U.S. and U.K. are firm based and data for Chile are plant based.

[b]Weighted by value of shipment.

entry in 1967. Imports were highly restricted, capital was immobile because of the direct allocation of investment funds to existing firms, and labor mobility was impaired because of restrictive labor legislation. So, both domestic and foreign entry and exit are likely to have been low in 1967, indicating that both efficient and inefficient firms simultaneously existed. By contrast, the capital and labor markets had been deregulated in 1979, and there were no restrictions on imports other than the 10% ad valorem tariff. The liberalization forced inefficient firms out of markets, which resulted in a smaller number of firms. The second reason is related to the formation of conglomerates during the reforms, which is likely to have speeded up concentration by increasing mergers and plant consolidation, and indirectly speeded up exit for firms which did not have access to conglomerate financial resources. These conglomerates included financial firms as well as medium-sized and large non-financial firms. Dahse (1979) argues that the conglomerates used their banks to keep their firms afloat while small firms that did not belong to a conglomerate had to adjust or disappear. This new environment facilitated the entry, but especially the exit, of firms. With most of the exits by small firms, concentration increased. The interindustry changes in concentration, though showing some variation, were mostly across the board: the rank correlation of Herfindahl indexes for 1967 and 1979 is 0.80, showing that the interindustry pattern of concentration did not change much.

Between the two census years there was a significant decline in average protection (and its dispersion) and an increase in export (*ES*) and import penetration (*MS*) shares. The index of intraindustry specialization (*B*) increased, showing that greater participation in manufacturing trade led to

Table 3

Protection, exposure to trade, concentration, and profitability.[a]

	Year	Mean	Standard deviation	Difference of means (1979–67)[b,c]
Tariff protection (TAR)	1967 1979	73.6 12.6	56.4 2.3	−61.0 (a)*
Export share (ES)	1967 1979	0.04 0.13	0.07 0.22	0.09 (b)*
Import share (MS)	1967 1979	0.20 0.29	0.22 0.27	0.09 (c)
Intraindustry trade index (B)	1967 1979	0.14 0.28	0.20 0.31	0.09 (b)*
Price–cost margin (PCM)	1967 1979	0.48 0.32	0.10 0.10	−0.16 (a)
Herfindahl index (HD)	1967 1979	0.07 0.12	0.07 0.11	0.05 (b)*

[a]*Source*: appendix tables A.4 and A.5. Definition of variables: TAR = tariff, ES = exports (EX)/sales (S), MS = imports $(M)/(S-EX+M)$, $B=1.0-|EX-M|$ $(EX+M)$, $PCM=(S-\text{cost of inputs}-\text{wages})/S$, HD = Herfindahl index of sales.

[b]Significantly different from zero at: (a) 1% level, (b) 5% level, (c) 10% level.

[c]For entries marked with *, equality of variances rejected at 1% level. Satterthwaite's (1946) approximation to degrees of freedom is used to construct the t-statistic when the equality of variances is rejected.

intraindustry not interindustry specialization. And the increase in concentration was accompanied by a sharp and statistically significant decrease in the weighted average price–cost margin.

At first glance it might seem counterintuitive that a marked increase in concentration would be accompanied by a decline in profitability. The reason is that in a closed economy concentration and profitability would be expected to move in the same direction but, for an economy changing from discriminating against exports and imports towards approximating a free-trade situation, it would be expected that firms would exploit the substantial economies of scale resulting from the opportunities to export and from the disappearances of small inefficient firms. The opening to foreign trade thus led to an increase in concentration. In turn, the decline in profitability was caused by the opening towards free trade which reduced the difference between home prices and international prices.

Another reason for profitability and concentration to move in opposite directions is the effect of the reforms on the elasticity of demand facing domestic firms. Import penetration, by introducing close substitutes, must have raised the elasticity of demand facing domestic firms. Conjectural variation models predict that the price–cost margin in equilibrium is jointly determined by concentration and by the elasticity of demand, with the price–cost margin proportionately related to concentration and inversely related to the elasticity of demand [Cowling and Waterson (1976), Urata (1984)]. The depressing effect of an increase in the elasticity of demand on profitability may well have more than compensated for the increased concentration.

Alternatively, a change in conduct, prompted by the liberalization of trade, may have caused the decline in profitability (despite the increase in concentration). The increase in actual and potential competition from abroad probably curtailed the collusive behavior by domestic firms.

3. Industry structure and performance: Cross-section regression analysis

The theoretical analyses just referred to and the empirical evidence, suggest that cross-sectoral variations in exposure to foreign trade should influence variations in concentration and profits across sectors.[6] To go beyond the aggregate analysis for manufacturing, we specify and estimate a simultaneous equation model to study the effects of international trade on concentration and profits.

3.1. The two-equation model

In the two-equation model presented below, concentration and profitability are endogenously determined and foreign variables are assumed to be exogenous. The model is the outcome of a specification search that considered a three-equation simultaneous model that also determined the import share endogenously to reflect the possibility that imports were attracted to sectors where profits were highest. The results show that the endogeneity of imports can be rejected, so we describe only the two-equation model.[7] The model is recursive, and the expected signs are entered below the variables.

Concentration equation:

$$HD = f\left(VA, CDR, \underset{?}{MS}, \underset{?}{ES} \right). \tag{1}$$

[6]The role of foreign trade variables in industrial organization studies is reviewed in The Symposia in the *Journal of Industrial Economics* (1980), in *Recherches Economiques de Louvain* (1981), and in Jacquemin (1982).

[7]We thank Jacquemin for suggesting this possibility and for suggesting using the interaction term in the profitability equation. Complete results from 2SLS estimation of the three-equation system – where the coefficient of *PCM* in the *MS* equation is not statistically different from zero, even at the 30% level for 1967 and 1979 – are reported in an appendix available from the authors on request.

Profitability equation:

$$PCM = g\Big(\underset{+}{KO}, \underset{+}{HD}, \underset{?}{MS}, \underset{?}{ES}, \underset{-}{MS \cdot HD}\Big), \qquad (2)$$

where

HD: Herfindahl index computed on total sales,
VA: Value added (net of taxes) expressed in 1979 prices,
CDR: cost–disadvantage ratio, which is value added per worker in the smaller establishments accounting for half of sales in the industry divided by the corresponding values in the larger plants accounting for the balance,
MS: import share (imports/[sales − exports + imports]),
ES: export share (exports/sales),
PCM: price–cost margin: ([sales − input costs − wages]/sales),
KO: capital–output ratio, which is the book value (net of depreciation), of buildings, machinery, and vehicles divided by the gross value of production, all in current prices.[8]

In the concentration equation, the Herfindahl index (*HD*), is used to measure concentration, because it is the measure associated with the oligopoly models discussed in section 2.[9] Two measures of scale economies in relation to market size (*VA* and *CDR*) and two measures of foreign influence (*MS* and *ES*) are in the equation determining the concentration ratio. Although industry sales are often used to measure market size [see Jacquemin, de Ghellinck and Huveneers (1980), Pagoulatos and Sorensen (1981)] we side with Caves, Porter and Spence (1980) in using value added, *VA*, as a more appropriate proxy for market size. It is more appropriate because plant size depends not on the value of shipments (which includes purchased inputs) but on value added. The effect of market size on concentration is expected to be negative because a larger market can support a larger number of efficient plants. The cost-disadvantage ratio (*CDR*) is a rough indicator of diseconomies of scale and is also expected to exert a negative influence on concentration.[10]

[8]Data sources, data preparation, and construction of variables are described in the appendix. All the data, except imports and exports, are directly aggregated from establishment data. We also performed the outlier and influentiality tests suggested by Belsley, Kuh and Welsch (1980). The deletion of two sectors with studentized residuals above 2.5 did not affect our results because these observations do not have leverage. Hence all observations are included in the estimations.

[9]The correlation coefficient between the Herfindahl index and the four-firm concentration ratios which is also an appropriate measure for a dominant firm cartel model [see Dickson (1979)] is 0.872 in 1967 and 0.870 in 1979.

[10]We have not used the standard index of minimum efficient scale (*MES*) used in many empirical studies because it is by construction extremely highly correlated with the Herfindahl index. Inclusion of the standard proxy for *MES* [Comanor and Wilson (1967)] raised the $\bar{R}^2$ for the concentration equations to 0.93 (1967) and 0.71 (1979) with significant coefficients for *MES*

The impact of foreign trade on concentration is ambiguous because it is difficult to predict the reaction of domestic producers to imports. The import share (*MS*) would increase concentration if threats from imports induce mergers of domestic firms. But it would reduce concentration if producers were induced to improve efficiency and thereby raise the number of efficient producers. This second outcome would be expected for 1979 because interviews with business managers and preliminary calculations suggest that sectors most exposed to foreign competition increased their productivity the most. The expected impact of the export share (*ES*) on concentration is also ambiguous. If an expansion in export opportunities reduces average costs because of scale economies from increased market size, producers engaged in exporting activities should be able to increase their market share, showing a positive relation. This relationship is more likely if the fixed cost of entering exporting activities is high. But a negative relationship may be observed if the fixed cost of exporting activities is low. A negative relationship may also be observed if economies of scale in production or distribution are not important because a larger market size resulting from export opportunities can support more producers.

Turning to the price–cost margin equation, the variation in the gross price–cost margin across industries is attributed to four variables. The capital–output ratio (*KO*) is included in order to control for the normal rate of return since the gross price–cost margin includes both normal and excess rates of return. The sign on the *KO* ratio is thus expected to be positive. The Herfindahl index (*HD*) should affect the price–cost margin positively because the possibility of collusion (which enables producers to exploit excess profits) tends to increase in a more concentrated industry environment. Finally, the foreign trade variables from the concentration equation – the import share (*MS*) and the export share (*ES*) – are also included in the price–cost margin equation.

The expected sign of the two foreign trade coefficients in the price–cost margin equation is ambiguous. Normally the profit rate is expected to be negatively related to the import share because greater competition from foreign producers should restrain the market power of domestic firms in the domestic market. But simple non-cooperative models by Geroski and Jacquemin (1981), Urata (1984), and de Melo and Urata (1984) have recently shown the possibility of a positive relationship by explicitly incorporating the conduct of firms. The first two studies showed that the price–cost margin

(*t*-statistics of 21 and 8). We experimented with the measure proposed by Lyons (1980), aggregating the results in his table 1 to our 41 sectors. Unfortunately, the resulting coefficients, though of the right sign, were not statistically significant so we did not report them in the text. Jacquemin, de Ghellinck and Huveneers (1980) and Caves, Porter and Spence (1980) further discuss the expected influence of market size and economies of scale, but their use of standard proxies suffers from the drawbacks pointed out by Lyons.

may be positively associated with the import share if domestic and foreign producers collude. The third derived a positive relationship by assuming that domestic producers simultaneously produce and import. However, the general expectation is that a high rate of import will affect negatively the price–cost margin for two reasons. First, because a high rate of imports may reveal a comparative disadvantage and hence may be associated with lower profits. Second, because, as mentioned above, imports increase the degree of actual competition faced by domestic firms.

Furthermore, the simple non-cooperative oligopoly models referred to above suggest that, in equilibrium, the price–cost margin is determined by the interaction of concentration with imports. Furthermore, as argued by Jacquemin, de Ghellinck and Huveneers (1980), import competition and the uncertainty it brings about are likely to modify the expected reactions of rivals to oligopolistic decisions with the constraining effect of import competition on market conduct and performance of domestic producers being stronger the higher is industrial concentration. Hence we also experiment with the multiplicative term $MS \cdot HD$ in the profitability equation.

The expected sign of the export coefficient is also ambiguous. A negative relationship will obtain if one assumes that export activities constrain non-competitive oligopolists to behave competitively as long as the oligopolists cannot discriminate between domestic and foreign markets. The manufacturing exports of most developing countries consist of undifferentiated products for which the scope for discrimination across markets is likely to be small. So, exports can be expected to depress profitability. But exporting firms must be rewarded by a risk premium if there is greater uncertainty in dealing with foreign markets. In that case, industries with higher export sales may have higher rates of return. However, the general presumption is that export activities have a constraining influence on pricing behavior especially if exports are not differentiated as is likely to be the case for a semi-industrial country like Chile.

3.2. *Statistical results*[11]

The two-equation simultaneous model in the previous section is recursive. The correlations between the disturbances of the concentration and profit equations are small and insignificant for both 1967 and 1979. So, the ordinary least squares method, which leads to consistent and asymptotically efficient estimates under such conditions, is applied to both equations.[12] The

[11] We also tried a double log specification, but we do not report the results because they are virtually the same. The only significant difference is a lower significance level for the coefficient of *ES* in the *PCM* equation for 1967.

[12] The correlation coefficients between the disturbance terms of the two equations for 1967 and 1979 are −0.049 and −0.166. Neither is significant, even at the 25% level. Application of 3SLS squares to gain asymptotic efficiency yielded extremely close results.

results compare favorably with many other cross-section estimates of structure and performance though the predictive power of the concentration equation for 1967 is weak.

In the concentration equations reported in table 4, the negative coefficients for the *CDR* showing that economies of scale are positively associated with concentration in Chile's manufacturing sector, are expected. But the positive and statistically significant sign for *VA* is puzzling, since a larger market would be expected to allow a greater number of efficient size establishments. However, one should bear in mind that the domestic market Chilean producers face is relatively small over the relevant production range. Hence it may well be that producers are still operating in the range of the declining long-run average costs, in which case the sign on *VA* would be positive. The results may also indicate overemployment of factors of production in concentrated industries. Finally, foreign trade factors have no significant effect on concentration, either in 1967 or in 1979.

Turning to the profit equations in table 5, as expected, the capital–output ratios for both years show a positive and statistically significant relationship with the price–cost margin. The Herfindahl index also has the expected positive sign but its value is significant only for 1979. This result is somewhat unexpected in view of the arguments presented in section 2.2 which suggest a reduction in collusive behavior in 1979. First the positive impact of mergers on profitability via increased productivity may have dominated the dampening effect of a reduction in collusive behavior. It is also probable that in 1967 when protection was 'made to measure', concentration had little effect on profitability as there was room for coexistence for a wide variety of firms with different sizes and efficiency levels. By contrast, in 1979, in the face of increased competition, only large firms could operate profitably. (Recall that the discussion in section 2 reports that the reforms induced many mergers and plant consolidations, in part as a defensive response to the new environment provided by the trade reforms.) Second, in 1979, Chile was still adjusting to trade liberalization. In the long run, however, after adjustments

Table 4

Regression estimates: Concentration equation.[a]

Independent variable	Sample	Equation	Constant	VA^b	CDR	ES	MS	R^{2c}
HD	1967	(1a)	0.08 (a)	6.56 (b)	−0.06	−0.05	0.01	0.182
			(2.79)	(2.11)	(−1.30)	(0.19)	(0.12)	
	1979	(1b)	0.18 (a)	12.15 (a)	−0.20 (c)	−0.11	−0.05	0.308 (a)
			(3.93)	(3.64)	(−2.02)	(−1.41)	(−0.70)	

[a] *t*-values in parentheses. (a): significant at 1% level; (b): significant at 5% level; (c): significant at 10% level.

[b] *VA* expressed in 1979 × 10^6 pesos.

[c] Tests on R^2 are equivalent to an *F*-test that all coefficients (other than the intercept are jointly zero.

Table 5

Regression estimates relating price–cost margins to domestic and international variables.[a]

Independent variable	Equation	Sample	Constant	*HD*	*KO*	*ES*	*MS*	*MS·HD*	R^2 [b]
PCM	(2a)	1967	0.38 (a) (9.97)	0.32 (1.49)	0.18 (b) (2.16)	−0.78 (a) (−2.73)	0.17 (b) (2.53)	—	0.276 (b)
	(2b)	1967	0.38 (a) (8.31)	0.28 (0.58)	0.18 (b) (2.13)	−0.78 (a) (−2.69)	0.16 (1.15)	0.18 (0.09)	0.276 (b)
	(2c)	1967	0.41 (a) (11.43)	−0.14 (−0.46)	0.17 (b) (2.10)	−0.74 (b) (2.58)	—	2.11 (b) (2.20)	0.249 (b)
PCM	(2d)	1979	0.21 (a) (5.82)	0.26 (b) (2.06)	0.16 (a) (3.27)	−0.14 (b) (−1.93)	0.02 (0.27)	—	0.326 (a)
	(2e)	1979	0.17 (a) (3.58)	0.47 (b) (2.40)	0.19 (a) (3.59)	−0.14 (c) (−1.91)	0.15 (1.34)	−1.15 (−1.40)	0.362 (a)
	(2f)	1979	0.21 (a) (5.87)	0.29 (c) (2.00)	0.17 (a) (3.32)	−0.12 (c) (−1.68)	—	−0.21 (0.48)	0.329 (a)

[a] *t*-values in parentheses. (a): significant at 1% level; (b): significant at 5% level; (c): significant at 10% level.
[b] Tests on R^2 are equivalent to an *F*-test that all coefficients (other than the intercept) are jointly zero.

to the almost free-trade situation would have taken place, one would expect that concentration would have a significantly reduced impact on profitability as domestic prices for a small open economy would tend to be determined in foreign markets. In sum, market structure is an important element in determining market performance in the Chilean manufacturing sector, a result found often for developed countries.

As expected, the significance of the foreign trade variables is more pronounced on profitability than on concentration. In the absence of the interaction term [eqs. (2a) and (2d)], a significant positive relation holds in 1967 between the import share and profitability. If one considers that the Chilean manufacturing sector of 1967 was severely foreign-exchange-constrained, the non-observance of the import-discipline hypothesis does not appear so surprising. Only 13% of imports in that year were consumer goods, and few imports were competitive with similar domestically produced goods. The positive relation may well reflect the concentration of QRs in sectors which would have had a natural comparative disadvantage under free trade. Those were probably the sectors with the highest import share. With QRs more binding in those sectors, one would expect a positive relation between the import share and the price–cost margin. In 1979, the correlation between the import share and profitability is insignificant.

The hypothesis that the constraining effect of import competition on market conduct and performance may be more pronounced the higher the degree of industrial concentration, finds moderate support for 1979 in eq. (2e). However, the statistical significance is, at best, marginal. Dropping the import share from the equation lowers the negative significance of the interaction term in 1979 [eq. (2f)] but produces a significantly positive coefficient for 1967. This result would suggest that in the foreign-exchange-constrained economy of 1967, import penetration was greatest in the more concentrated sectors with the highest protection – perhaps because of the more successful lobbying activities of large firms. Imports were thus concentrated in the more highly concentrated sectors which were also the more profitable.[13]

Finally in table 6, we report tests for structural shifts in the coefficients in the concentration and profitability equations between the two years. The null hypothesis of no structural change is strongly rejected for the profitability equation but not for the concentration equation.[14] Moreover, there is a

[13]We do not report results of equations in which the export share is dropped since they only result in a loss of goodness of fit and did not affect the sign or statistical significance of the import share (or other) coefficient in either year.

[14]The Chow test is applied to test the presence of structural change. The null hypothesis is $H_0{:}\alpha_i^{67}(\beta_i^{67}) = \alpha_i^{79}(\beta_i^{79})$, where α_i^j and β_i^j indicate coefficients in concentration and profit equations in year j, respectively. The relevant test static is

$$F(k+1, n_1+n_2-2k-2) = \frac{(RRSS-URSS)/(K+1)}{URSS/(n_1+n_2-2k-2)},$$

Table 6

Structural change test (pooled 1967 and 1979).[a]

Independent variable	Equation[b]	$D \cdot$Constant	$D \cdot VA$	$D \cdot CDR$	$D \cdot HD$	$D \cdot KO$	$D \cdot ES$	$D \cdot MS$	$D \cdot (MS \cdot HD)$	R^2[c]
HD	(1a)+(1b)	0.10 (b) (1.97)	5.60 (1.16)	−0.14 (−1.37)			−0.07 (−0.22)	−0.01 (−0.62)		0.32 (a)
PCM	(2a)+(2d)	−0.17 (a) (−3.28)			−0.06 (−0.26)	−0.01 (−0.13)	0.64 (b) (2.22)	−0.15 (c) (−1.76)	—	0.57 (a)
PCM	(2b)+(2e)	−0.22 (a) (3.29)			0.19 (0.37)	0.02 (0.16)	0.64 (b) (2.23)	−0.01 (−0.08)	−1.34 (−0.65)	0.58 (a)
PCM	(2c)+(2f)	−0.21 (a) (−4.09)			0.44 (1.31)	−0.0004 (−0.004)	0.62 (b) (2.18)	—	−2.32 (b) (−2.27)	0.56 (a)

[a](a): significant at 1% level; (b): significant at 5% level; (c): significant at 10% level.

[b]Only differences in the values of the coefficients are reported but the test on R^2 is on the whole equation; D=dummy variable (1967=0, 1979=1). Equation numbers refer to equations in tables 4 and 5.

[c]Tests on R^2 are equivalent to an F-test that all coefficients other than the intercept are jointly zero.

marked decline in the absolute values of the export and import share coefficients in the profit equation.[15]

The decline in the value of the export share coefficient suggests that the negative influence of exports on profitability was moderated after trade liberalization. Contributing factors to this decline would be the reduction in discrimination of the incentive system against exporting activities and possibly an increase in market power brought about by increased product differentiation indicated by the rising value of the intraindustry specialization index, B (see table 3) in 1979. The decline in the value of the import share coefficient in the equation excluding the interaction term tends to support the import-discipline hypothesis. The statistically significant decline in the value of the interaction term when the import share is excluded also supports the import-discipline hypothesis. It suggests that the rising import share hit hardest the highly concentrated sectors which showed the greatest decline in profitability because of increasing import competition. In sum, the tests for structural change suggest that the pattern of profitability across sectors was affected by the reforms, and that changes in exposure to foreign trade contributed toward explaining that change.

4. Conclusion

This paper has drawn on Chile's far-reaching reforms in the mid-1970s to examine how the reforms affected the structure–performance relation in manufacturing. A comparison of manufacturingwide concentration and profitability before (1967) and after (1979) the reforms reveals a big increase in concentration and a big reduction in the profit rate. The increase in concentration was attributed to the greater opportunities that the trade liberalization and other reforms favoring mergers opened for exploiting economies of scale and forcing the exit of inefficient firms. However, as trade

---

where $RRSS$ and $URSS$ are restricted and unrestricted residual sum of squares, $K+1$ is the number of linear restrictions, and n_1 and n_2 are the number of observations in each year. F statistics for the HD and PCM equations are 1.79 and 15.24 while the 5% and 10% significance points for F (5, 72) are 1.94. Further testing of homogeneity of coefficients on trade variables [H_0: $\beta_3^{67}=\beta_3^{79}$ and $\beta_4^{67}=\beta_4^{79}$, where β_3 and β_4 are coefficients for ES and MS in the PCM eqs. (2a) and (2d)] yielded F (2, 72) = 3.35 which is significant at 5%, indicating structural change in the coefficients for the trade variables. We also tested the hypothesis that all the trade variable coefficients are zero [H_0: $\beta_3=\beta_4=\beta_5=0$ in the PCM eqs. (2b) and (2e)]. The results yielded: F (3.35) = 3.78 for 1967 and F (3.35) = 2.04 for 1979 which indicate that the null hypothesis can only be rejected for 1967 at 5%. The absence of significance of the trade variables in 1979 may be due to the cancelling effects of increased openness: a decrease in costs due to increased productivity on the one hand and a decrease in price due to a reduction in protection, on the other.

[15]Hitris (1978) also examined structural change in profits in a single equation framework for the U.K. Except for the constant term, he could not reject the equality of coefficients in 1962 and in 1967.

liberalization reforms were just completed by June 1979, the manufacturing sector had not yet reached its new long-run equilibrium in 1979. The seemingly inconsistent fall in profitability (while concentration rose) was attributed to two factors: the reduction in oligopolistic conduct because of exposure to foreign competition and the increase in the elasticity of demand facing domestic firms caused by the entry of imports.

A cross-sectoral simultaneous equation model estimated for 1967 and 1979 confirmed these significant changes in concentration and profitability. The model also confirmed some results found for developed countries: the excess profit rate was highest in the most concentrated sectors, and a proxy measure for economies of scale is positively correlated with concentration. When we examined how imports and exports determined variations in concentration and profitability, unlike most previous studies, we found that the import share was positively correlated with the excess profit rate before the liberalization of trade. We explained that this finding is consistent with the highly restrictive foreign trade regime of Chile's manufacturing sector in 1967. This result raises questions about the applicability of the import-discipline hypothesis in developing countries where quantitative import restrictions are prevalent. However, the comparison between 1979 and 1967 gives support to arguments put forth by proponents of the import-discipline hypothesis: the penetration of imports reduced most the profitability of the highly concentrated sectors.

Finally, statistical tests showed that the structural relationship between profitability and foreign trade variables changed significantly between the two years. Specifically trade liberalization was accompanied by improved profitability in exporting activities and reduced profitability in import competing activities. The rise in profitability for exporting activities was attributed to increased product differentiation and the decline in profitability of import competing activities was attributed to increased competition, the latter interpretation supporting predictions of the dynamic import-discipline hypothesis.

References

Behrman, J., 1976, Foreign trade regimes and economic development: Chile (Columbia University Press, New York).

Belsley, D., E. Kuh and R. Welsch, 1980, Regression diagnostics (Wiley, New York).

Caves, R., M. Porter and M. Spence, 1980, Competition in the open economy: A model applied to Canada (Harvard University Press, Cambridge, MA).

Clarke, R. and S.W. Davies, 1980, Market structure and price-cost margins, Economica 49, 277–287.

Comanor, W. and T. Wilson, 1967, Advertising, market structure and performance, Review of Economics and Statistics 49, 423–440.

Corbo, V., 1985, Reforms and macroeconomic adjustments in Chile: 1974–83, World Development, 893–916.

Corbo, V. and J. de Melo, eds., 1985, Scrambling for survival: How firms adjusted to the recent reforms in Chile, Uruguay, and Argentina, World Bank Staff Working Paper no. 764 (Washington, DC).
Corbo, V. and P. Meller, 1981, Alternative trade strategies and employment implications: Chile, in: A. Krueger et al., eds., Trade and employment in developing countries (University of Chicago Press, Chicago, IL).
Cowling, K. and M. Waterson, 1976, Price-cost margins and market structure, Economica 43, 267–274.
Cuadra, Sergio de la, 1974, La proteccion efectiva en Chile, Documento de trabajo no. 22 (Instituto de Economia, Universidad Catolica, Santiago).
Dahse, F., 1979, Mapa de la extrema riqueza (Editorial Aconcagua, Santiago).
Dickson, V.A., 1979, The Lerner index and measures of concentration, Economics Letters 3, 275–279.
Geroski, P. and A. Jacquemin, 1981, Imports as competitive discipline, in: P. Geroski and A. Jacquemin, eds., Symposium on industrial organization and international trade, Recherches Economiques de Louvain 47, 197–208.
Hart, P.E. and R. Clarke, 1980, Concentration in British Industry, 1935–75 (Cambridge University Press, Cambridge).
Hitris, T., 1978, Effective protection and economic performance in U.K. manufacturing industry 1963 and 1968, Economic Journal 88, 107–120.
Huveneers, C., 1981, Price formation and the scope for oligopolistic conduct in a small open economy, Recherches Economiques de Louvain 41, 209–242.
Jacquemin, A., 1982, Imperfect market structures and international trade – Some recent research, Kyklos 35, 75–93.
Jacquemin, A., E. de Ghellinck and C. Huveneers, 1980, Concentration and profitability in a small open economy, Journal of Industrial Economics 28, 131–144.
Jones, J., L. Laudadio and M. Percy, 1973, Market structure and profitability in Canadian manufacturing industry: Some cross section results, Canadian Journal of Economics 6, 356–368.
Katrak, H., 1980, Industry structure, foreign trade and price-cost margins in Indian manufacturing industries, Journal of Development Studies 17, 63–79.
Krugman, P., 1979, Increasing returns, monopolistic competition, and international trade, Journal of International Economics 9, 469–479.
Lancaster, K., 1980, Intraindustry trade under perfect monopolistic competition, Journal of International Economics 10, 151–176.
Lyons, B., 1980, A new measure of minimum efficient plant size in manufacturing industry, Economica 47, 19–34.
Melo, J. de and S. Urata, 1984, Market structure and performance: The role of international factors in a trade liberalization, DRD Discussion Paper no. 71 (World Bank, Washington, DC).
Mueller, W.F. and L.G. Hamm, 1974, Trends in industrial market concentration, Review of Economics and Statistics 56, 511–520.
Pagoulatos, E. and R. Sorensen, 1981, A simultaneous equation analysis of advertising, concentration and profitability, Southern Economic Journal 47, 728–741.
Pugel, T.A., 1980, Foreign trade and U.S. market performance, Journal of Industrial Economics 29, 119–129.
Satterthwaite, E.W., 1946, Am approximation distribution of estimates of variance components, Biometrics Bulletin no. 2, 110–114.
Siddhartan, N. and A.K. Dasgupta, 1983, Entry barriers, exports and inter-industry differences in profitability, The Developing Economies 21, 14–23.
Sleuwagen, L., 1983, Multinational enterprises, industrial concentration and the degree of monopoly, Presented at 10th EARIE Conference, Aug.
Urata, S., 1984, Price-cost margins and imports in an oligopolistic market, Economics Letters 15, 139–144.
Utton, M. and A. Morgan, 1983, Concentration and foreign trade (Cambridge University Press, Cambridge).

Journal of International Economics 31 (1991) 231–250. North-Holland

The effects of trade reforms on scale and technical efficiency

New evidence from Chile

James Tybout

Georgetown University, Washington, DC 20057, USA, and the World Bank (CECTP)

Jamie de Melo and Vittorio Corbo*

The World Bank (CECTP and CECMG), Washington, USA

Received June 1989, revised version received November 1990

This paper analyzes the changes in industrial sector performance that accompanied Chile's dramatic trade liberalization of the 1970s. Comparisons of pre- and post-liberalization manufacturing census data reveal little productivity improvement overall. However, adverse macro conditions may have masked the positive effects of trade reforms: industries undergoing relatively large reductions in protection experienced relatively large improvements in average efficiency levels, and relatively large reductions in cross-plant efficiency dispersion. These conclusions are based on maximum likelihood technology estimators that deal with measurement error and incomplete observations.

1. Overview

For several reasons, development economists routinely argue that trade protection reduces industrial sector efficiency. First, in markets characterized by entry barriers, the absence of foreign competition allows domestic producers to enjoy monopoly power and excess profits. Consequently, these firms may fail to produce at minimum efficient scale (achieve 'scale efficiency') and/or to get the maximum possible output from their input bundles (achieve 'technical efficiency' or 'X-efficiency'). Second, in markets characterized by Chamberlinean competition, trade protection may attract inefficiently small producers, causing similar increases in average production

*This paper was prepared for the World Bank research project 'The Effects of Trade Regimes on Industrial Competition and Efficiency' (RPO 764-46). We thank Raul Galleguillos and Jose Miguel Sanchez for their painstaking work in preparing the data used in this study, and Julie Stanton for very able research assistance. Helpful comments from Bela Balassa, Zvi Griliches, Gene Grossman, Ramon Lopez, Cristian Moran, Dani Rodrik and three anonymous referees were received on an earlier draft. The views are those of the authors, not those of the World Bank.

costs.[1] It is sometimes claimed that these two *intra*-industry effects of protectionism are more important sources of welfare loss than the traditional comparative advantage effects.

Disturbingly, the body of empirical evidence supporting these claims is ambiguous. For example, Rodrik (1988a) notes that 'there is practically no direct evidence on the importance of scale economies in specific industrial sectors of the developing countries'. Similarly, Pack (1988) observes that 'to date there is no clear confirmation of the hypothesis that countries with an external orientation benefit from greater growth in technical efficiency in the component sectors of manufacturing'. Finally, Bhagwati (1988) concludes 'although the arguments for the success of the export promotion strategy based on economies of scale and X-efficiency are plausible, empirical support for them is not available'. One is left wondering whether the received wisdom is more a matter of faith than fact.

The lack of clear evidence is not accidental. To examine the intra-industry effects of trade reforms directly, one must make 'before and after' comparisons of a large sample of plants. Sufficient data are rarely available for the appropriate countries at the appropriate times. Fortuitously, however, the Chilean trade liberalization of 1974–79 was preceded and followed by industrial censuses, providing a natural experiment. This paper is an effort to document the evidence that emerged.

The paper is divided into three remaining sections. After some background on Chilean reforms, section 2 presents descriptive measures of the size distribution and productivity of each industry in each census year. Changes in these measures across census years are then correlated with industry-specific changes in effective protection rates. The results are suggestive, but suffer from conceptual problems, measurement error and missing data problems. Hence section 3 corrects for these shortcomings and re-examines patterns of association. The results reinforce and extend the findings in section 2: although *overall* industrial efficiency did not improve between the two census years, the three-digit industries that underwent relatively large reductions in protection improved relative to others.

2. A glance at the data

2.1. Changes in the Chilean economy between the census years

In this section we take a first look at the data to familiarize the reader with general magnitudes and sources of variation. But before discussing

[1]For more detail on arguments involving scale effects, entry and exit, see Roberts and Tybout (1990). For a compact review of the literature linking trade and technical efficiency in LDCs see Rodrik (1988b).

descriptive statistics, it is worth reviewing the major changes that took place in Chile between the two census years.[2]

Like most developing countries, Chile pursued an import-substituting industrialization strategy in the 1950s and 1960s. By 1967 – the first year for which we have plant-level data – quantitative restrictions (QRs) were widespread. The cross-sectoral dispersion in tariff rates was extremely high, and the average effective protection rate for manufacturing was over 100 percent [Behrman (1976)]. In addition, market entry and exit were limited by extensive controls on the domestic credit market and by labor laws that made worker dismissal difficult. Finally, price controls on domestic commodity markets were pervasive.

By 1979 – the other year for which we observe plants – the situation had changed dramatically. All QRs had been removed in 1974, and between 1975 and 1979, the average effective protection rate had been brought down below 15 percent, while cross-sectoral dispersion in tariff rates had been virtually eliminated. Thus by 1979, Chile had achieved one of the lowest and most uniform protection structures in the world. The domestic labor and financial markets had also been deregulated and price controls on sales in the domestic market had been removed.

2.2. Industry-wide changes in structure

Table 1 summarizes the ways in which industrial structure, productivity and exposure to foreign competition changed between the two census years. Referring to the top panel, notice that the dramatic drop in protection was accompanied by clear increases in import shares, export shares, and intra-industry trade. So trade liberalization apparently did place domestic manufacturers in more direct competition with their foreign rivals. Also, however, it combined with macro stabilization policies to create unemployment problems that still lingered in 1979.

The middle panel of table 1 describes the plant size distribution. Here notice that output per plant remained surprisingly stable between 1967 and 1979, while the number of plants fell slightly. This lack of expansion presumably reflected the same forces that created recession and unemployment during the second half of the 1970s. Notice also that, while the largest plants expanded, most others contracted. So if small plants were below minimum efficient scale in 1967, they were probably more so after the liberalization.

Measures of value-added per unit input give a crude sense for productivity

[2]See Corbo (1985) for further details.

Table 1

Aggregate industrial structure, 1967 and 1979.

	1967 (1)	1979 (2)	Ratio (2)/(1)
Market conditions[a]			
Effective protection	120%	15%	0.13
Export share	4%	13%	3.25
Import penetration rate	20%	29%	1.45
Intra-industry trade index	0.14	0.28	2.00
Manufacturing unemp. rate	5%	13%	2.60
Plant size distribution[b]			
Average gross output per plant	37,241	37,425	1.01
Number of plants	7,060	6,771	0.96
10th output percentile	1,430	1,051	0.74
25th output percentile	3,006	2,358	0.78
Median output	7,203	5,723	0.79
75th output percentile	20,972	16,126	0.77
90th output percentile	75,536	60,442	0.80
99th output percentile	507,189	595,724	1.17
Factor use and productivity[a]			
Value-added per plant	21,403	15,978	0.75
Workers per plant	39	34	0.88
Efficiency labor per plant[c]	188	185	0.98
Capital per plant[d]	30,760	59,853	1.95

[a]All figures refer to manufacturing. Trade flow data are taken from de Melo and Urata (1986). Let X, M and Q represent exports, imports and domestic production, respectively. Then the export share is X/Q; the industry penetration rate is $M/(Q+M-X)$, and the index of intra-industry trade is $1.0-|X-M|/(X+M)$. Effective protection figures are taken from Behrman (1976) and Aedo and Lagos (1984). We omit the glass industry in calculating mean effective protection rates because its 1967 value of 3,500% was an extreme outlier. Unemployment figures come from Banco Central de Chile (1986).

[b]These figures refer to the census data after cleaning. Variables values in 1967 prices were converted to 1979 prices.

[c]Wage bill divided by the minimum wage, which is held constant in real terms across census years.

[d]Figures are based on plants reporting complete capital stock data. Such plants constituted 38 percent of the sample in 1967 and 35 percent in 1979.

levels; these can be inferred from the bottom panel of table 1. Referring to the last column, note that value-added per plant fell more rapidly than workers per plant (however measured) between 1967 and 1979, so labor productivity dropped. Similarly, for those plants reporting complete capital stock data, value-added per unit capital fell. Taken together, these results suggest an unequivocal fall in total factor productivity for the manufacturing sector as a whole between 1967 and 1979. Like the low output growth, this productivity drop probably reflected the relatively slack demand for manufactured products in 1979, coupled with a gradual change in the mix of products and the nature of technology.[3] Measurement error is also likely, especially in capital stocks and the price deflators.[4]

2.3. Sector-specific structural change

For several reasons, we caution against viewing the patterns of adjustment in table 1 as driven exclusively, or even mainly, by trade policy. First, as already noted, the available price indices may exhibit general biases over time, and some of the variables are measured with error. Second, and more importantly, Chile underwent many major macro shocks between 1967 and 1979, including hyperinflation during 1973, a major recession during 1974–76, exchange rate appreciation thereafter, and large increases in the real interest rate. In terms of influence on manufacturing sector aggregates, these forces could easily have masked the effects of commercial policy.

Comparisons of adjustment patterns among the different three-digit industries are more likely to reveal something about the effects of trade liberalization. This is because all industries were subject to roughly the same measurement errors and changes in macro conditions, but different industries underwent very different amounts of change in protection. Therefore, deviations of particular industries from the typical pattern of adjustment probably partly reflected the amount of new foreign competition that these industries faced.

To see whether changes in trade exposure correlate with changes in structure and performance, we construct a set of industry-specific variables. First, we measure the change in protection between 1967 and 1979 with

$$PROTEC_j = (1 + R_j^{79})/(1 + R_j^{67}),$$

where R_j^t is the effective protection rate for the jth industry in year t.[5] Similarly, we construct a set of industry-specific measures of change in size, factor use and productivity. But for these variables, we provide extra detail by looking at the shape of the entire cross-plant distribution in each year –

[3] Reductions in the ratio of industrial value added to industrial output are typically observed as the process of economic development unfolds. See, for example, Chenery, Syrquin and Robinson (1986).

[4] Capital stocks are reported by only a fraction of the plants and are expressed in historic cost deflated by a general capital stock price index. We used official price series at the three-digit industrial classification level from Chile's Instituto Nacional de Estadastica to deflate outputs, and combined these prices with the 1977 Chilean input–output table to impute sector-specific intermediate input price deflators. Experimentation with other price indices did not significantly change our findings. Further details of the data preparation procedures are available from the authors.

[5] Estimates of the effective rates of protection by industry and year are taken from Behrman (1976) and Aedos and Lagos (1984).

just as in the middle panel of table 1. For example, we measure changes in the size distribution of plants with the following six variables:

$$RQn_j=(1+Qn_j^{79})/(1+Qn_j^{67}), \quad n=10, 25, 50, 75, 90, 99$$

Here Qn_j^t represents the output of the plant at the *n*th percentile during year *t*, given that plants in this industry and year have been sorted in order of increasing output. So if median plant size falls between the census years for industry *j*, $RQ50_j$ will be less than one. Also, if the *shape* of the size distribution changes, this will be reflected by different values for the different percentiles. We construct analogous variables to measure changes in value-added, *RVn*, employment, *RLn*, value-added per efficiency unit, *RVEn*, value-added per unit capital, *RVKn*, gross output per efficiency unit, *RQEn*, and gross output per unit capital, *RQKn*.[6]

We choose these variables for several reasons. First, use of the ratio form makes it possible to ignore any macro shock or data bias that affects all industries equally.[7] It also allows us to ignore industry-specific effects that do not vary over time. Second, by including both gross output and value-added in our set of variables, we can see whether the findings hinge critically on measurement problems with the latter.

Different three-digit industries presumably react differently to changes in protection. So, to avoid forcing all industries into the same mold, we use Spearman rank correlations to look for dominant patterns of association between *PROTEC* and the various measures of structure and performance. These correlations are reported in table 2 for each variable and percentile, along with associated *t*-ratios.

Several conclusions can be drawn. First, sectors with relatively large declines in protection have shown a somewhat greater tendency toward employment reductions. For example, the correlation between changes in protection and changes in the 50th employment percentile is 0.260, indicating that reductions in protection are associated with reductions in employment among plants with no more than the median number of workers. This reduction is most striking among plants in the third largest quartile, and is strongest when employment is measured in terms of number of workers. Second, however, reductions in protection are associated with *higher* value-added and output among the smallest plants. This effect is strongest in the lowest decile, and is nonexistent among plants above the median. So there is

[6]Ratios involving capital are constructed using only the subset of plants reporting complete capital stock data.

[7]By 'equally' we mean that the shock or bias scales the ratio of interest by an amount that is independent of *j*.

Table 2

Cross-industry rank correlations – changes in protection with changes in industrial characteristics.

	Percentiles (*n*)					
PROTEC **correlated with:**	10th	25th	50th	75th	90th	99th
Gross output (*RQn*)	−0.327 (1.50)	−0.193 (0.86)	−0.062 (0.26)	−0.157 (0.69)	−0.133 (0.59)	−0.108 (0.47)
Value-added (*RVAn*)	−0.481 (2.39)	−0.338 (1.56)	−0.251 (1.13)	−0.168 (0.74)	0.003 (0.01)	0.054 (0.23)
Employment (*RLn*)	0.251 (1.13)	−0.055 (0.25)	0.260 (1.17)	0.520 (2.67)	0.397 (1.89)	0.251 (1.13)
Efficiency labor (*REn*)	0.075 (0.33)	−0.018 (0.08)	0.318 (1.61)	0.395 (1.87)	0.222 (0.99)	0.181 (0.80)
Value-added per efficiency labor (*RVAEn*)	−0.577 (3.08)	−0.434 (2.10)	−0.410 (1.96)	−0.304 (1.39)	−0.414 (1.98)	−0.071 (0.31)
Value-added per unit capital (*RVAKn*)	−0.392 (1.85)	−0.246 (1.11)	−0.199 (0.88)	−0.323 (1.48)	−0.236 (1.06)	−0.221 (0.98)
Gross output per unit efficiency labor (*RQEn*)	−0.451 (2.20)	−0.418 (2.01)	−0.462 (2.27)	−0.319 (1.47)	−0.516 (2.63)	−0.022 (0.09)
Gross output per unit capital (*RQKn*)	−0.218 (0.96)	−0.143 (0.62)	−0.158 (0.70)	−0.414 (1.98)	−0.419 (2.01)	−0.358 (1.67)

Note: Absolute values of *t*-ratios are in parentheses.

some evidence that as protection falls, small plants increase production levels toward minimum efficient scale, shedding labor at the same time.[8]

Given that labor use falls and output rises as protection is reduced, it is unsurprising that value-added per efficiency worker and output per efficiency worker both rise. As with the output effects, these responses are concentrated among the smaller plants.[9] This finding supports X-efficiency arguments linking trade exposure and productivity.

Finally, and less strikingly, output per unit capital and value-added per unit capital tend to rise most in those industries where the reductions in protection were most dramatic. Hence, given that reductions in protection are associated with increases in both output per employee and output per unit capital, any standard index of total factor productivity growth con-

[8]Comparing plants' employment levels in Chile (1979–86) and Colombia (1977–87), Roberts and Tybout (1990) found that high rates of protection were associated with relatively *large* plants – both in terms of output and in terms of employment – once industry and country effects were controlled for. This finding is consistent with the present paper's findings regarding correlations of protection with workers per plant, but not with its findings regarding output per plant.

[9]Efficiency effects aside, a reduction in effective protection can cause an increase in value-added to the extent that technology allows plants to substitute away from intermediate goods usage as their relative price rises. We are grategul to Ramon Lopez for this point.

structed from these data would probably correlate negatively across industries with changes in protection.

3. Better measures of efficiency changes

All of the above is very suggestive, but it glosses over two types of measurement problems. The first is that table 2 is limited to single factor productivities. Accordingly, it does not allow us to measure overall productivity of the input bundle, or to distinguish between scale effects and X-efficiency effects. The second problem concerns data quality. Value-added and capital stock figures are likely to be biased because of inflation-distorted bookkeeping. Moreover, even without inflation, book values of capital stocks reflect historic cost rather than economic worth, and the discrepancy in values should increase as the capital ages. Finally, for many enterprises capital stock figures are missing entirely. This section presents an attempt to come to grips with all of these shortcomings.

3.1. Indices of scale and technical efficiency

First, by going to a parametric representation of production technologies, we can easily construct better measures of efficiency. Assume that intermediate inputs are used in fixed proportion to gross output, and let the maximum value-added attainable with given amounts of capital, K^*, and labor, E, be represented by the production function $f(K^*, E)$. Then returns to scale are simply the sum of the elasticities of $f(\cdot)$ with respect to its arguments. If this sum exceeds one for a given vector of inputs, the associated plant is said to suffer from *scale inefficiency*. Also, if the ith plant is using inputs, (K_i^*, E_i), and producing value-added, V_i, then $e_i = f(K_i^*, E_i) - V_i$ is an index of the plant's level of *technical inefficiency*.[10]

Our objective is to infer something about the changes in these efficiency measures that accompany trade liberalization. Ignoring econometric and data problems for the moment, imagine we are able to obtain consistent estimates of the following Cobb–Douglas production function for each industry and year:

$$V_i = \beta_0 + \alpha K_i^* + \beta_1 E_i + \beta_2 D_{1i} + \beta_3 D_{2i} + \beta_4 D_3 + u_{1i}. \tag{1}$$

Here D_1 through D_3 are dummies that control for things like type of firm ownership, u_1 is a disturbance term, and all other variables are assumed to be measured in logarithms. (More detailed variable definitions are provided in the appendix.) Then inferences regarding scale and technical efficiency can be based on estimates of α, β_0, β_1, and $\mathrm{var}(u_1)$.

[10]This definition, which began with the work of Farrell (1957), is fairly standard for empirical work. For literature surveys, see Forsund, Lovell and Schmidt (1980) and Schmidt (1985–86).

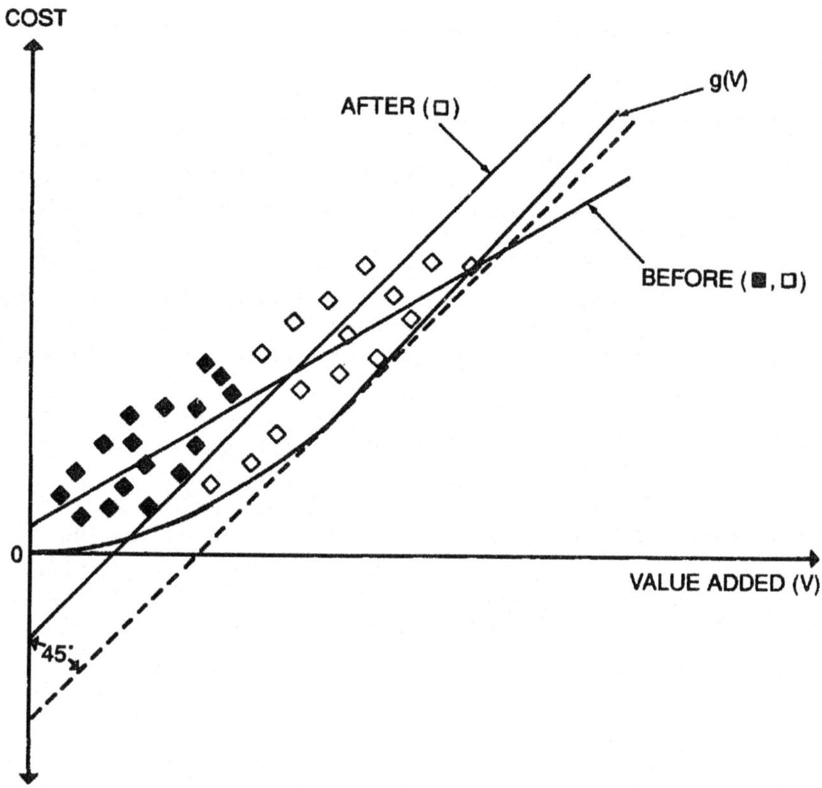

Fig. 1. Fitted cost function before and after trade liberalization.

To see how, refer to fig. 1. Here we represent $f(K^*, E)$ indirectly with its dual, the technically efficient cost function, $g(V)$. This allows us to work in two dimensions. All variables are in logarithms, so $1/g'(V)$ reflects returns to scale, and $g(\cdot)$ follows the usual pattern of increasing returns in low output ranges, then constant or diminishing returns. Open squares and solid squares are hypothetical data points; they represent cross-sectional observations on plants in a given industry. All data points lie above $g(V)$ to indicate that the associated plants are not operating at maximum technical efficiency.[11] Assuming that deviations from the efficient technology are Hicks-neutral, the

[11]With measurement error in value-added, some observed data points might fall below the cost function. Measurement error does not alter the analysis unless its variance changes across census years in a way that is correlated with changes in protection rates. We assume this does not occur.

horizontal distance from the cost function for the ith plant is a monotonic positive function of its technical inefficiency level, e_i.

Suppose that trade liberalization forces some plants in the increasing returns region to expand or exit the market, eliminating the data points represented by solid squares in fig. 1. Then Cobb–Douglas estimates of the returns to scale, $(\alpha+\beta_1)$, are likely to fall, as the 'before' and 'after' regression lines make clear.[12] The cost function intercept is also likely to fall, or equivalently, the production function intercept, β_0, is likely to rise. Finally, given that the Cobb–Douglas technology implies a log-linear relationship between costs and output, it should fit the data better after plants in the increasing returns range have been eliminated. So the variance in $u_1(\sigma_1^2)$ is likely to drop with trade liberalization unless offseting changes in measurement error occur.

There is another reason why σ_1^2 may fall and β_0 may rise as efficiency improves. Imagine that heightened exposure to foreign competition forces all plants to move toward the efficient technology, so that the data points in fig. 1 drift to the right, and cluster more closely above the efficient cost function. Then the residual variation and the intercept of the estimated cost function would fall.[13] These effects can occur without any change in the estimated returns to scale, so by examining the changes in β_0, σ_1^2, and $\alpha+\beta_2$ together, we may be able to learn something about the relative importance of scale effects versus technical efficiency effects.

3.2. Dealing with imperfect data

Problems of missing data and measurement error complicate the analysis. As mentioned above, capital stock figures do not accurately reflect true stocks, and for many plants they are missing entirely. We deal with these problems by employing an estimator that combines errors-in-variables techniques developed by Goldberger (1972) with missing data treatments exposited in Gourieroux and Monfort (1981). The estimator provides maximum likelihood estimates for eq. (1), given the following relationships [Tybout (1990)]:

$$K_i^* = \gamma Z_i + \delta_0 + \delta_1 E_i + \delta_2 D_{1i} + \delta_3 D_{2i} + \delta_4 D_{3i} + i_{2i}, \tag{2}$$

$$K_i = K_i^* + u_3. \tag{3}$$

[12]Returns-to-scale estimates should fall for the estimated production function as well as the estimated cost function, since cost is simply an index of factor usage. Interpreted this way, fig. 1 may be viewed as representing the inverse production function.

[13]Much of the microeconometric literature on efficiency measurement is devoted to capturing these two effects [e.g. Schmidt (1985)]. We depart from this literature somewhat because of the data problems discussed in the following subsection.

Here K is the book value of capital stock, which differs from the true stock by the measurement error u_3, and is missing entirely for a fraction of the sample. Also Z is an instrument for the true capital stock (see the appendix for details). When estimating the system (1) through (3), we assume that all disturbances are independent of one another, and labor and capital are exogenous.[14] Also, we assume that the missing data pattern is 'ignorable' [e.g. Little (1982)], and hence does not create selectivity bias.[15]

3.3. *The estimated effect of trade reforms on productive efficiency*

Estimates of the system (1) through (3) for each industry and year are presented and discussed in the appendix. We use the results to construct industry-specific indices of the changes in returns to scale, average efficiency level (i.e. production function intercept), and dispersion in efficiency levels between 1967 and 1979. For the jth industry ($j=1,21$), these measures are:

$$SCALE_j=(\hat{\alpha}_j+\hat{\beta}_{1j})_{79}/(\hat{\alpha}_j+\hat{\beta}_{1j})_{67},$$

$$EFFIC_j=(\hat{\beta}_{0j})_{79}/(\hat{\beta}_{0j})_{67},$$

$$DISPER_j=(\hat{\sigma}^2_{1j})_{79}/(\hat{\sigma}^2_{1j})_{67},$$

Here, a circumflex indicates an estimated value, and subscripts outside parentheses refer to the year of the census from which the estimates were obtained. As with our descriptive statistics of subsection 2.3, these indices are relatively robust with respect to industry-specific distortions in estimators. Such distortions will not matter if they bias estimators by the same factor in each year, or (when comparing across industries) if the factor of bias is common to all industries.

The top panel of table 3 presents estimated values for each parameter ratio of interest, industry by industry, along with associated *PROTEC* values. As in table 1, there is still no evidence of *overall* improvements in productive efficiency for the manufacturing sector. Of the 21 manufacturing industries analyzed, only 10 showed reductions in estimated returns to scale, only 9

[14]This exogeneity assumption is justifiable if firms choose input levels before observing current period shocks to technology and to real input prices [e.g. Zellner, Kmenta and Drèze (1966)]. This condition seems to suit 1967 particularly well, given that labor laws were very strict, and labor dismissal was difficult. Nonetheless, we experimented with an alternative version of the model in which it was assumed that firms observe current period wages without error and freely adjust employment levels to maximize short-run profits. This extension yielded implausible results, suggesting the approach taken here is a closer approximation to behavior.

[15]This assumption can be relaxed [Tybout (1990)]. However, experiments in which we did so suggested that selectivity bias was minimal, so we opted for the simpler estimator.

Table 3

Values and rank correlations of *PROTEC*, *SCALE*, *EFFIC* and *DISPER*.

Industry	Estimated parameter ratios *PROTEC*	*SCALE*	*EFFIC*	*DISPER*
Food	0.24	0.97	0.97	1.89
Beverages	1.47	1.02	1.06	1.38
Textiles	0.19	1.01	1.14	2.44
Apparel	0.98	0.95	1.02	2.21
Leather products	0.96	0.99	0.54	3.06
Footwear	1.01	1.00	0.83	4.07
Wood and cork	1.13	1.26	0.53	2.85
Wood furniture	1.11	1.18	0.76	2.10
Pulp and paper	0.60	1.18	0.25	1.03
Printing	1.31	1.00	0.91	3.17
Indus. chemicals	0.69	0.98	0.94	1.47
Other chemicals	0.95	1.17	0.81	2.32
Rubber products	0.28	1.04	3.36	1.03
Plastic products	0.50	0.88	1.41	2.18
Glass[a]	0.03	0.72	1.49	1.09
Nonmetal materials	1.13	1.13	0.65	3.42
Iron and steel	0.87	0.79	1.15	1.90
Metal products	0.60	1.09	0.85	2.72
Nonelectrical machinery	0.64	0.92	1.42	0.91
Electrical machinery	0.20	0.90	1.72	0.91
Transport equipment	0.39	1.06	0.77	0.98

	Spearman rank correlations[b] *SCALE*	*EFFIC*	*DISPER*
PROTEC	0.387 (1.83)	−0.523 (−2.68)	0.548 (2.86)
SCALE	–	−0.731 (−4.67)	0.271 (1.23)
EFFIC	–	–	−0.505 (−2.55)

[a]This industry exhibited such an extreme reduction in measured protection that we redid the analysis without it. None of the results (available on request) were significantly affected.
[b]*t*-ratios are in parentheses.

showed evidence of Hicks-neutral productivity improvements, and only 5 registered reductions in our index of efficiency dispersion.

Recall, however, that many macro shocks hit the Chilean manufacturing sector between the census years, masking the effects of commercial policy in sector-wide analyses. Therefore, to isolate the influence of trade reforms from shocks that are common to all industries, we once again turn to cross-industry comparisons. Spearman rank correlations and *t*-ratios for *PROTEC*, *SCALE*, *EFFIC*, and *DISPER* are reported in the bottom panel of table 3. Notice that relatively large reductions in protection are associated with relatively marked declines in the estimated returns to scale. Although this association is statistically weak, it builds on our findings in table 2. There we saw that small plants tend to drop out or grow as protection is removed; here we find evidence that this process generates some efficiency gains.

More strikingly, the intercept of the production function appears strongly negatively associated with the level of protection, as does the dispersion in output levels conditioned on inputs. These correlations are partly due to a flattening of the regression line, as the correlation between *SCALE* and *EFFIC* makes clear.[16] However, *SCALE* does not correlate as strongly with reductions in protection as does *EFFIC*, so we are tempted to conclude that such reductions are associated with movements toward the efficient technology across a wide range of plant sizes. That is, the apparent changes in overall efficiency were probably not exclusively attributable to small inefficient plants expanding or dropping out.

Taken together, the rank correlations in table 3 are wholly consistent with the finding in table 2 that industries undergoing the most reduction in protection showed the most productivity improvement. They also appear to confirm the adjustment processes discussed in connection with fig. 1. Nonetheless, there are alternative plausible explanations for our findings. Consider the scale result first. Changes in returns to scale are negatively associated with changes in average plant size across the two censuses, as one would expect.[17] So it appears that expansions in plant size do partly account for reductions in estimated returns to scale. But other factors may also be at work. Specifically, our data deflation procedure is strictly justified only if products are homogeneous at the three-digit level. This is obviously unlikely, and could lead to misinterpretations. That is to say, when value-added is deflated by an industry price deflator, we are not really isolating a physical quantity, even if intermediate inputs are always used in fixed proportions to output. This means that if big firms achieve larger mark-ups because of market power, they will appear to have more output per unit input – that is, they will appear more scale efficient. Moreover, if reductions in protection force these firms to price competitively, it will appear that returns to scale in the industry have decreased.[18] This is surely a result in favor of trade liberalization, but not the one we have stressed.

Several alternative explanations also come to mind for the technical efficiency findings. For example, the positive correlation between *PROTEC* and *DISPER* might have been generated by a reduction in product diversity within certain three-digit industries, making intra-industry technology more

[16]Even when the underlying population remains unchanged, sampling error is likely to induce a negative correlation between the intercept and the sum of the slope coefficients, so we caution against reading too much into the high t-ratio for the rank correlation of *SCALE* and *EFFIC*.

[17]The rank correlation between average plant size changes and scale changes is about −0.30.

[18]Using the same data, de Melo and Urata (1986) found that price–cost margins decreased slightly between the two census years. They attribute this to increased competitive pressures from liberalization.

uniform across plants. This, too, would reduce observed deviations from the estimated technology. As for the association between *PROTEC* and *EFFIC*, it might partly reflect a downward shift of the efficient cost function, $g(V)$, for industries exposed to world competition.

Finally, despite our very encouraging findings, it should be stressed that they reflect a number of somewhat arbitrary decisions regarding data preparation and model specification. First, there was some specification search involved in choosing the capital stock instrument. Initially electricity consumed was used, and when it became clear that this led to very inaccurate estimates, we switched to machinery and equipment.[19] Second, our protection estimates for 1967 are crude. Third, with respect to specification, it must also be recognized that our crude measure of labor input is probably not strictly exogenous. So if labor usage depends on output demand and some omitted variables – e.g. the wage–price ratio – changes in the omitted variable can change the estimated relationship between labor and output. (Changes in the structure of protection alter the cross-sectoral pattern of wage–price ratios, and hence in principle could change the apparent pattern of scale economies.)

Little could be done about these shortcomings. However, we did test for robustness by trying alternative variable definitions and model specifications. With respect to data, we experimented with two alternative industry-specific deflators for gross output and found that our results were robust to the gross output deflator (results available upon request). We also developed an extension of the model treating labor as endogenous (see footnote 14). Unfortunately, this yielded implausibly low estimates for returns to scale, probably reflecting problems with our wage variable and the imposition of too much structure on the data.[20]

4. Concluding remarks

This paper provides new micro evidence on the relationship between choice of development strategy and industrial sector performance. Our contribution departs from the existing literature in several respects. First, unlike virtually all other evidence, ours is at the establishment level. Thus, we are able to address theories of intra-industry adjustment much more directly than has been possible in the past. Second, there is dramatic variation in the trade regime between our sample years. This gives our analysis a laboratory-

[19]However, tests for the association between protection and efficiency were not performed until we had settled on our instrument, nor did we even compare results from the two census years industry by industry. Hence our search in itself did not bias the results in favor of our priors.

[20]Our data do not specify location of establishments, so we are unable to control for the possibility that firms in different localities may face difference wage–price ratios.

like flavor, and creates sufficiently large changes in industrial performance to be detectible, despite measurement problems. Finally, unlike much of the literature, our study tracks a single country through time, eliminating the complicating influence of country-specific effects.

Although the findings are suggestive, much more plant-level work must be done before we can be confident of the 'stylized facts' regarding intra-industry adjustments to trade reforms. We are currently attempting to generate further evidence by analyzing additional liberalization episodes and by exploiting panel data that follow individual plants through time.

Appendix: Production technology estimates

This appendix presents more detail on our estimates of eqs. (1) through (3) of the text.

A.1. Variable definitions

The variables we used to estimate these equations are presented in table A.1. We draw the reader's attention to several details. First, following Maddala (1977) we use a size dummy, D_3, as an instrument for the capital stock. This dummy also appears in the production function (1), because imposing an exclusion restriction would have vastly complicated estimation [Tybout (1990)]. Empirically, coefficients on D_3 in eq. (1) are all very close to

Table A.1

Variable definitions for section 3 estimates.

V	= logarithm of value added corrected for inflation distortions and expressed in 1979 prices
E	= logarithm of labor, expressed in efficiency units[a]
D_1	= 1 if the firm is a proprietorship, 0 otherwise
D_2	= 1 if the firm is a partnership, 0 otherwise[b]
D_3	= −1 if the firm is among the smallest third of the industry sample; 0 if the firm is among the middle third of the industry sample; and 1 if the firm is among the largest third of the industry sample
K	= logarithm of the reported value of the capital stock, i.e. machinery and equipment plus vehicles, plus land and buildings (this variable is considered 'missing' if at least one component takes a zero or missing value)
Z	= logarithm of machinery and equipment

[a]This variable is constructed as the wage bill divided by the minimum wage. The wage bill includes an imputation for owners and family help. See Griliches and Ringstad (1971) for a similar definition. In earlier work [Corbo and de Melo (1985)], we tested several specifications of the labor variable to deal with heterogeneity in the labor force and found that labor input measured by the total number of unskilled equivalent workers was the best.

[b]Partnership could not be distinguished in the 1967 data, so all firms with between 1 and 10 owners were considered partnerships in that year.

Table A.2

Industry-wide production technologies, 1967 vs. 1979.

Industry/description	Year	n/n_c	Intercept β_0	Capital α	Labor β_1	σ_1^2	σ_2^2	σ_3^2	σ_v^2	Returns to scale $\alpha+\beta_1$
312 Food products	67	1,543/	2.802	0.345	0.645	0.425	0.199	0.058	2.26	0.990
		801	(15.54)	(11.94)	(16.43)	(23.37)	(5.11)	(1.57)		(−0.35)
	79	1,880/	2.720	0.329	0.632	0.803	0.124	0.101	2.90	0.961
		696	(15.18)	(11.81)	(15.08)	(28.97)	(2.43)	(1.98)		(−1.27)
313 Beverages	67	429/	2.383	0.389	0.682	0.786	0.241	−0.061	2.57	1.071
		122	(4.05)	(5.19)	(9.81)	(12.60)	(2.48)	(−0.67)		(1.00)
	79	138/	2.521	0.315	0.783	1.087	0.046	0.133	4.18	1.098
		74	(2.78)	(2.78)	(4.56)	(8.17)	(0.28)	(0.80)		(0.69)
321 Textiles	67	666/	3.191	0.332	0.611	0.312	−0.025	0.188	2.23	0.943
		271	(11.52)	(7.83)	(12.77)	(17.92)	(−0.60)	(4.31)		(−1.69)
	79	657/	3.635	0.133	0.819	0.762	0.324	−0.219	3.17	0.953
		216	(12.50)	(3.26)	(12.32)	(17.74)	(2.21)	−(1.51)		(−0.91)
322 Wearing apparel	67	582/	2.569	0.504	0.613	0.406	−0.074	0.257	1.94	1.118
		104	(4.25)	(5.29)	(7.51)	(15.82)	(−1.57)	(4.49)		(1.77)
	79	621/	2.610	0.268	0.791	0.896	0.445	−0.252	2.74	1.059
		149	(6.43)	(4.08)	(9.40)	(15.50)	(3.27)	(−1.96)		(0.93)
323 Leather products	67	128/	4.693	0.163	0.698	0.224	−0.091	0.260	2.06	0.861
		56	(6.89)	(1.50)	(6.77)	(8.03)	(−0.58)	(1.60)		(−1.71)
	79	109/	2.531	0.483	0.364	0.686	−0.063	0.155	2.86	0.847
		49	(3.69)	(4.46)	(2.02)	(7.53)	(−0.81)	(1.85)		(−1.08)
324 Footwear	67	323/	3.385	0.260	0.738	0.287	0.142	0.071	2.14	0.998
		81	(9.49)	(3.83)	(9.85)	(11.10)	(1.24)	(0.64)		(−0.05)
	79	2,661/	2.826	0.200	0.794	1.169	0.211	−0.086	3.34	0.994
		57	(4.19)	(1.83)	(5.56)	(11.26)	(0.82)	(−0.34)		(−0.06)

331 Sawmills, wood and cork	67	732/	5.143	0.206	0.636	0.383	0.158	0.135	1.71	0.842
		266	(18.62)	(4.67)	(12.31)	(17.89)	(1.52)	(1.31)		(−4.11)
	79	502/	2.737	0.210	0.847	1.091	0.272	0.065	3.34	1.058
		196	(6.12)	(2.93)	(8.28)	(15.26)	(1.29)	(0.31)		(0.79)
332 Wood furniture	67	416/	4.041	0.194	0.714	0.365	0.525	−0.189	1.64	0.908
		108	(13.05)	(3.31)	(9.68)	(11.51)	(2.68)	(−1.05)		(−1.78)
	79	368/	3.063	0.162	0.908	0.765	0.632	−0.259	2.45	1.070
		93	(7.12)	(2.26)	(8.93)	(12.44)	(1.77)	(−0.75)		(0.90)
341 Pulp and paper	67	39/	3.997	0.303	0.579	0.227	0.111	0.005	3.77	0.882
		24	(5.26)	(2.79)	(3.99)	(3.93)	(0.91)	(0.04)		(−1.04)
	79	68/	0.978	0.623	0.417	0.234	0.314	−0.070	4.95	1.040
		29	(1.60)	(6.00)	(2.77)	(1.36)	(1.07)	(−0.84)		(0.39)
342 Printing	67	302/	3.928	0.413	0.530	0.199	0.106	0.063	1.97	0.943
		76	(12.44)	(7.98)	(7.61)	(8.75)	(1.68)	(1.08)		(−1.12)
	79	388/	3.555	0.183	0.755	0.631	0.233	−0.135	2.43	0.938
		106	(12.03)	(4.00)	(10.50)	(13.48)	(1.73)	(−1.02)		(−1.13)
351 Chemicals (industrial)	67	81/	4.578	0.227	0.642	0.441	−0.302	0.406	2.55	0.869
		45	(5.87)	(2.38)	(4.78)	(6.67)	(−2.34)	(2.89)		(−1.12)
	79	51/	4.303	0.309	0.542	0.650	0.196	−0.143	3.00	0.851
		24	(4.61)	(2.88)	(2.61)	(4.73)	(1.49)	(−1.15)		(−0.81)
352 Other chemicals	67	206/	3.841	0.478	0.335	0.333	0.070	0.153	2.35	0.813
		109	(6.16)	(5.16)	(3.51)	(8.48)	(1.14)	(2.41)		(−2.54)
	79	188/	3.120	0.343	0.606	0.772	0.303	−0.110	4.30	0.948
		112	(4.99)	(4.23)	(4.85)	(8.57)	(2.52)	(−0.99)		(−0.51)
355 Rubber products	67	61/	0.925	0.784	0.176	0.467	−0.145	0.410	3.15	0.960
		31	(0.60)	(3.26)	(0.68)	(5.93)	(−2.81)	(4.30)		(−0.22)
	79	83/	3.128	0.240	0.761	0.481	−0.293	0.409	3.32	1.001
		39	(4.34)	(1.92)	(4.45)	(6.67)	(−2.02)	(2.60)		(0.01)
356 Plastic products	67	100/	3.122	0.257	0.817	0.260	−0.204	0.385	2.16	1.074
		39	(4.79)	(3.39)	(7.48)	(7.47)	(−1.73)	(2.82)		(0.70)
	79	185/	4.398	0.025	0.914	0.566	−1.098	1.398	2.34	0.938
		64	(6.58)	(0.24)	(7.28)	(9.60)	(−0.53)	(0.67)		(−0.69)

Table A.2 (continued)

Industry/description	Year	n/n_c	Intercept β_0	Capital α	Labor β_1	σ_1^2	σ_2^2	σ_3^2	σ_v^2	Returns to scale $\alpha+\beta_1$
362 Glass	67	51/	2.726	0.357	0.703	0.389	0.068	0.047	3.67	1.060
		27	(2.47)	(2.09)	(3.81)	(4.72)	(0.56)	(0.39)		(0.38)
	79	37/	4.072	0.349	0.416	0.424	0.035	0.109	3.91	0.764
		17	(3.41)	(2.03)	(1.97)	(4.12)	(0.20)	(0.61)		(−1.26)
369 Nonmetallic mineral products	67	146/	3.105	0.305	0.708	0.242	0.263	0.069	2.17	1.013
		67	(7.68)	(4.79)	(7.20)	(6.24)	(1.80)	(0.53)		(0.18)
	79	152/	2.024	0.243	0.898	0.828	−0.045	0.222	4.41	1.142
		43	(3.73)	(2.68)	(6.13)	(8.68)	(−0.19)	(0.92)		(1.40)
371 Iron and steel	67	52/	2.624	0.449	0.619	0.241	0.024	0.042	2.82	1.068
		28	(3.22)	(5.35)	(5.30)	(4.77)	(0.43)	(0.74)		(0.52)
	79	41/	2.997	0.463	0.387	0.459	0.272	−0.160	4.26	0.850
		18	(2.98)	(3.08)	(1.92)	(3.26)	(1.72)	(−1.33)		(−0.89)
381 Metal products	67	636/	4.136	0.206	0.702	0.285	0.459	−0.212	2.33	0.908
		238	(16.13)	(5.18)	(15.01)	(13.97)	(4.67)	(−2.45)		(−2.63)
	79	625/	3.505	0.124	0.866	0.775	0.261	−0.083	3.23	0.991
		224	(10.49)	(2.52)	(12.87)	(17.41)	(−1.29)	(−0.41)		(−0.18)
382 Nonelectrical machinery	67	289/	2.705	0.063	0.905	0.869	−0.240	0.445	3.20	0.967
		99	(4.43)	(0.73)	(8.10)	(12.03)	(−0.36)	(0.66)		(−0.36)
	79	173/	3.848	0.259	0.633	0.795	−0.040	0.134	2.89	0.893
		71	(5.81)	(3.12)	(4.81)	(9.32)	(−0.32)	(1.06)		(−0.90)
383 Electrical machinery	67	95/	2.183	0.287	0.826	0.637	0.120	0.011	3.61	1.113
		45	(2.61)	(2.61)	(5.47)	(6.61)	(0.84)	(0.08)		(0.81)
	79	76/	3.746	0.066	0.934	0.579	1.356	−1.244	3.39	1.000
		48	(4.09)	(0.49)	(4.92)	(5.85)	(2.32)	(−2.19)		(−0.00)
384 Transport equipment	67	184/	4.403	0.266	0.717	0.586	−0.012	0.134	3.00	0.983
		76	(7.70)	(3.52)	(7.14)	(9.53)	(−0.10)	(1.14)		(−0.20)
	79	164/	3.376	0.115	0.927	0.576	0.240	−0.042	2.75	1.041
		65	(6.63)	(1.81)	(8.55)	(8.92)	(0.65)	(−0.11)		(0.45)

zero, so the only cost of proceeding this way is apparently a small loss of power.

Second, notice that Z, which serves as another instrument for the true capital stock, is defined to be machinery and equipment. This reflects several considerations. One is that machinery and equipment are almost always reported.[21] (When total capital is missing, it is usually because firms have rented their buildings, land, or vehicles.) The other consideration is that the instrument Z should be correlated with true capital, but not with the measurement error u_2. If measurement error in capital is essentially due to the longer term items – i.e., buildings and land – machinery and equipment satisfy this condition.[22]

A.2. Parameter estimates

Table A.2 reports estimated output elasticities with respect to capital, α, and labor, β_1, their sum, $\alpha+\beta_1$, the intercept, β_0, and estimates for σ_1^2, σ_2^2 and σ_3^2. To give some sense for the overall fit, we include total variation in V, σ_V^2, for comparison with σ_1^2. Numbers in parentheses are asymptotic 'Z' ratios for the null hypothesis that the coefficient estimated immediately above is zero *except* in the case of returns to scale, where the null is that returns to scale are unity. Finally, the number of observations used for each industry, n, and the number for which capital stocks are observable, n_c, are also reported.

Observe first that the scale estimates are generally very plausible, although the labor coefficient is sometimes larger than one would expect. We found that although the scale estimate $\alpha+\beta_1$ was insensitive to the instrument (Z) used, the choice of instrument did affect the breakdown of returns to scale between α and β_1. So, although the scale estimates seem robust, these individual magnitudes should be viewed with some caution.

Note next that the estimated variances of u_1 are always significantly positive, while those of u_2 and u_3 sometimes are not. However, for these latter two disturbances, only 3 out of 84 estimated variances are significantly negative at the 95 percent level.[23] This gives us some degree of confidence that our model is reasonably specified, and we take these variance estimates to shed some light on the importance of capital stock measurement error. In

[21]This is less true in 1979 than in 1967. Obviously, observations that do not include machinery and equipment must be excluded from the estimation altogether. Details of the data preparation are available from the authors.

[22]We also tried electricity consumption as an instrument for capital but found it had low predictive power. (It was also unattractive conceptually because electricity is subject to relatively severe endogeneity problems.) Installed horsepower was an alternative to machinery and equipment, but this variable was only available in the 1967 census.

[23]Negative variance estimates could in principle be eliminated by restricting the parameter space when we maximize the likelihood function, but this would vastly complicate the calculations [see Tybout (1990) for details]. Given that the variances of u_2 and u_3 are nuisance parameters with little bearing on our analysis, we do not grapple with this problem.

particular, we observe that all but six sectors showed reductions in the amount of measurement error from 1967 to 1979, perhaps reflecting the fact that firms were instructed to adjust their book values to market worth in the latter year.[24]

[24]This one-time revaluation was termed the 'Retacacion Tecnica', or 'technical adjustment'.

References

Aedo, F. and F. Lagos, 1984, Protección efectiva en Chile: 1974–79, Documento de Trabajo no. 94 (Pontificia Universidad Catolica de Chile, Santiago).

Banco Central de Chile, 1986, Indicadores Economicos y Sociales 1960–1985 (Departamento de Informaciones Estadistrical y Publicacions del Banco Central de Chile, Santiago).

Behrman, J., 1976, Foreign trade regimes and economic development: Chile (Columbia University Press, New York).

Bhagwati, J., 1988, Export-promoting trade strategy: Issues and evidence, The World Bank Research Observer 1, 27–58.

Chenery, H., S. Robinson and M. Syrquin, 1986, Industrialization and growth (Oxford University Press, Oxford).

Corbo, V., 1985, Reforms and macroeconomic adjustments in Chile during 1974–84, World Development 13, 893–916.

Corbo, V. and J. de Melo, 1985, Structural change in production in the Chilean manufacturing sector: 1967 vs. 1979, Mimeo., The World Bank.

Farrell, M.J., 1957, The measurement of productive efficiency, Journal of the Royal Statistical Society A120, pt. 3, 253–281.

Forsund, F., M. Lovell and P. Schmidt, 1980, A survey of frontier production functions and of their relationship to efficiency measurement, Journal of Econometrics 13, 5–25.

Goldberger, A., 1972, Maximum likelihood estimation of regressions containing unobservable independent variables, International Economic Review 13, 1–15.

Gourieroux, C. and A. Monfort, 1981, On the problem of missing data in linear models, Review of Economic Studies 68, 579–586.

Griliches, Z. and V. Ringstad, 1971, Economies of scale and the form of the production function (North-Holland, Amsterdam).

Little, R., 1982, Models for non-response in sample surveys, Journal of the American Statistical Association 77, 237–250.

Melo, J. de and S. Urata, 1986, The influence of increased foreign competition on industrial concentration and profitability, International Journal of Industrial Organization 4, 287–304.

Maddala, G.S., 1977, Econometrics (McGraw-Hill, New York).

Pack, H., 1988, Industrialization and trade, in: H. Chenery and T.N. Srinivasan, eds., Handbook of development economics (North-Holland, Amsterdam).

Roberts, M. and J. Tybout, 1990, Size rationalization and trade exposure in developing countries, in: R. Baldwin, ed., Empirical studies of commercial policy (University of Chicago Press, Chicago), forthcoming.

Rodrik, D., 1988a, Imperfect competition, scale economies and trade policy in developing countries, Mimeo., Harvard University.

Rodrik, D., 1988b, Closing the technology gap: Does trade liberalization really help, Mimeo., Harvard University.

Schmidt, P., 1985–86, Frontier production functions, Econometric Reviews 4, 289–328.

Tybout, J., 1990, Making noisy data sing: Estimating production technologies in developing countries, Journal of Econometrics, forthcoming.

Zellner, A., J. Kmenta and J. Drèze, 1966, Specification and estimation of Cobb-Douglas production models, Econometrica 34, 784–795.

European Economic Review 37 (1993) 1331–1349. North-Holland

Do exporters gain from VERs?

Jaime de Melo*

The World Bank, Washington DC, USA and Centre of Economic Policy Research, London, UK

L. Alan Winters

University of Birmingham, Birmingham, UK and Centre of Economic Policy Research, London, UK

Received October 1989, final version received October 1991

Previous literature has concentrated on the rent transfer accruing to exporting countries when a voluntary export restraint (VER) is binding. This paper studies the efficiency and distributional effects arising when VERs force factors out of industries in which they are most productive. A theoretical model of the industry under the VER is developed to establish qualitative conditions under which a VER will result in: Spillovers of exports to unrestricted markets; industry contraction; and loss in national welfare. Key parameters of demand and supply are estimated for leather footwear exports from Taiwan subject to the U.S. Orderly Marketing Agreement, and their implications explored in a calibrated simulation exercise. The results make a strong indictment of VERs. For most plausible parameter values, VERs distort exports, reduce industry size and cause overall economic losses, especially if the affected industry is large.

1. Introduction

The distinguishing feature of voluntary export restraints (VERs) is that they are administered by exporting countries. So long as the VER is binding, exports of the product under the VER earn a scarcity premium. Much work has been done to estimate the cost to importing countries – and hence the

Correspondence to: L. Alan Winters, Department of Economics, University of Birmingham, Edgbaston, Birmingham B15 2TT, U.K.

*Our thanks to two referees and to Arvind Panagariya and Jean Waelbroeck for helpful suggestions that led to substantial improvements over an earlier draft (de Melo and Winters 1990b, WPS discussion paper 326, World Bank, Washington, DC). We are very indebted to Ramon Lopez for suggesting and helping with the simplified presentation of the model in section 2. Helpful comments were also received on an early draft by Bela Balassa, Paul Brenton, Shanti Chakravarty, Nicóla Rossi, Wendy Takacs and to participants of the STEP-CEPR Conference 'Adjustment in Developing Countries' (May 1989), the European Research Workshop in International Trade (June 1989) and the George Washington University Economics Seminar. We thank Alexander Pfaff, Julie Stanton and Rebecca Sugui for logistic support. The views contained herein are those of the authors and do not necessarily reflect those of the World Bank. This research has been financed by World Bank Research Project 672-40.

gain to exporting countries – from this transfer.[1] There are, however, other effects in exporting countries arising from a binding VER. These effects stem from the contractionary pressure on the industry subjected to the VER and hence against factors employed in it. By forcing factors out of industries in which they are most productive, VERs can impose significant efficiency losses on exporters. Curiously, these losses, which must be balanced against the rent transfer from abroad, have been neglected in the literature. The purpose of this paper is to explore these effects systematically by econometric estimation and simulations in the context of the U.S. Orderly Marketing Agreement (OMA) for Taiwanese leather footwear exports during 1977–1981.

This paper is organized as follows. In section 2, we develop a simple theoretical model of a perfectly competitive industry subject to the VER. The industry sells its output to two markets, one restricted and one unrestricted. We examine the effects of a VER in the restricted market on sales in the unrestricted market (spillover effect), on industry size and national welfare. The analysis suggests that the effects of a VER depend crucially on a few product supply and factor demand elasticities. This leads us, in section 3, to estimate these key elasticities for the case of leather footwear exports from Taiwan during the U.S. OMA. Although not as precise as desirable because of data limitations, these econometric estimates suggest that the demand and supply of footwear are quite elastic. They also lend strong support to the qualitative prediction that the OMA induced some spillover to unrestricted markets and some contraction of the industry with attendant efficiency losses. Finally, in section 4, we combine the results of the previous two sections into a partial equilibrium simulation model which analyzes the likely effects of a VER on national welfare and income distribution, taking into account efficiency losses.

For plausible elasticity values we establish that a typical VER will lead to a worsening income distribution, as profits in the affected industry rise and the returns to other factors – notably labour – fall. We also establish that exporting countries are likely to incur an overall welfare loss in spite of the rent transfer gain even when the industry under the VER is of non-negligible size. The results of this paper are therefore a strong indictment of VERs. To be sure, VERs are less harmful to exporting countries than are equivalent-sized import quotas administered by the importing country, but nonetheless, they can impose notable welfare losses wherever they restrict industries accounting for significant shares of the exporters' economic activity, or when these industries make use of particular and relatively immobile skills or physical capital.

[1]See, e.g., Greenaway and Hindley (1985), Tarr and Morkre (1984), and Feenstra (1984). On the developing country side most work has concentrated on detecting rents and quality upgrading [see Aw and Roberst (1986); de Melo and Winters (1989)].

In previous work [de Melo and Winters (1990a)], we investigated the effects of the U.S. OMA for Korean leather footwear producers. We relied, however, on a restrictive technology allowing for separability between the input decisions (how much footwear to produce) and the allocation of sales to restricted and unrestricted markets. This led us to the econometric estimation of an export allocation model that concentrated on establishing that in the short run a VER reduced the marginal revenue product of factors in the Korean footwear industry and that sales were diverted from the restricted towards the unrestricted markets. This paper develops a substantially more general model of a competitive industry subject to a VER, and provides econometric estimation for the Taiwanese footwear industry that go well beyond our earlier export allocation approach. It analyzes a full supply–demand model of the footwear industry, and is to our knowledge, the first empirical attempt at the econometric estimation of the welfare (and distributional) effects of a VER on the exporting industry.

2. A simple model of a competitive industry subject to a VER

Consider the following partial equilibrium model of the effects of a VER. For convenience we call the restricted industry footwear, but the results generalize to virtually any competitive industry. Assume that many identical firms in an exporting country produce two different types of footwear for two markets, U and R (for unrestricted and restricted), using a single composite variable factor of production, Z. To simplify the welfare analysis, suppose that the entire output of the representative firm is exported. Assume, however, that the two types of footwear may differ and allow for the possibility that the marginal costs of one may depend on the output of the other. One possible justification for this is the existence of a second implicit factor of production which is fixed in supply, e.g., entrepreneurship or infrastructure. The one-input two-output technology, G, corresponding to our empirical formulation is given by

$$G(X_U, X_R, Z)=0, \tag{1}$$

where X_U and X_R are outputs and Z is a composite input. The technology is well behaved in the sense that a well-behaved profit function exists,[2] and G is also assumed to be twice differentiable.

We assume many identical price-taking representative firms in the footwear industry. Each firm maximizes profits $\tilde{\pi}$, defined as

[2]The assumptions are that G is nonempty, closed and convex, bounded from above, with free disposability of X and Z and satisfies the assumption of weak essentiality. For further discussion see, e.g., Fuss and McFadden (1978) or Chambers (1988, chapter 7).

$$\tilde{\pi} \equiv p_U X_U + p_R X_R - wZ, \tag{2}$$

subject to the technology described in (1). For the technology described in (1) and under the assumption of price-taking behavior for firms in both export markets and in the market for the composite input Z, one can write a profit function $\tilde{\pi}(p_U, p_R, w)$ which describes the maximum profits attainable by the representative firm. Profit maximization insures convexity of the profit function.

The purpose of the model is to consider the consequences of imposing a VER on exports to market R while exports to market U remain unrestricted. A VER in market R, restricting exports to level $\bar{X}_R < X_R^*$ – where X_R^* is the free trade level at price P_R^* – will introduce a wedge between the price received by the firm, p_R^s, and the price paid by footwear importers, p_R^d. Assume that the rents associated with the VER, defined as

$$R \equiv (p_R^d - p_R^s)\bar{X}_R \tag{3}$$

are redistributed such that they do not affect marginal decisions. For example, assume a lump-sum redistribution. Then firms' allocation decisions are unaffected by the presence of rents,[3] and the representative firm's restricted profit function can be written as

$$\pi = \pi(p_R^s, p_U, w), \tag{4}$$

where the firm's subscript has been omitted.

The industry faces an upward sloping inverse supply curve for its composite factor Z:

$$w = w(Z), \quad w' > 0, \tag{5}$$

and downward sloping demand curves for sales in U and R:

$$X_U = X_U(p_u), \; X_R = X_R(p_R^d), \qquad X_R', X_U' < 0. \tag{6}$$

The price-taking behavior assumption implies that firms cannot exploit monopsony in the market for Z, nor can they exploit monopoly power in their respective export markets. This price-taking behavior assumption on the part of firms may not be representative of industries with few producers of a highly differentiated product, but it certainly approximates the Taiwanese footwear industry where there is a large number of small firms producing relatively undifferentiated footwear.

Since π is differentiable in its arguments, the unique industry profit

[3]With few exceptions (e.g. Korea), rents are redistributed lump sum. If, however, rents affected firms' allocation decision as in the case of the two-tier quota allocation mechanism used by Korea [see Bark and de Melo (1989)], one would include a description of the rent allocation mechanism as an argument in the restricted profit function (4).

maximizing supply functions and derived-demand function can be obtained by application of Hotelling's lemma.[4] Therefore, under a binding VER, equilibrium in the industry will be described by the following three equations:

$$\pi_1(p_R^s, p_U, w) = \bar{X}_R, \tag{7}$$

$$\pi_2(p_R^s, p_U, w) = X_U(p_U), \tag{8}$$

$$-\pi_3(p_R^s, p_U, w) = Z, \tag{9}$$

where π_i is the partial derivative of π w.r.t. its ith argument and the demand function in the restricted market has been replaced by the VER in (7).

With a few more restrictions on technology to be given shortly, it is a straightforward comparative statics exercise to show that in this simple two-output, one-input model, a VER will lead to a contraction of the industry. To parallel the empirical work that follows, we consider two cases. The first case (corresponding to model I in section 3) is one where the industry is small in the market for its variable factor of production so that $w' = \infty$ in (5) and the industry faces a perfectly elastic supply for Z. In the second more plausible case (corresponding to model II in section 3), we allow for the upward sloping supply curve for Z in (5) to take into account the possibility that the industry is large in the market for Z.

To establish that the industry will contract when the VER is tightened ($\mathrm{d}\bar{X}_R < 0$) we need to establish the conditions under which $(\mathrm{d}Z/\mathrm{d}\bar{X}_R) > 0$, i.e., that $\mathrm{d}Z < 0$. Totally differentiate (9) with respect to $\mathrm{d}\bar{X}_R$ to obtain

$$\mathrm{d}Z/\mathrm{d}\bar{X}_R = -\pi_{31}(\mathrm{d}p_R^s/\mathrm{d}\bar{X}_R) - \pi_{32}(\mathrm{d}p_U/\mathrm{d}\bar{X}_R) - \pi_{33}[(\partial w/\partial Z)(\mathrm{d}Z/\mathrm{d}\bar{X}_R)]. \tag{10}$$

For the first case (model I), the last term on the RHS of (10) is zero. Therefore, consider the general case (model II). To sign (10) we make the further assumption of normality of Z, i.e., that an increase in w causes profit maximizing outputs to decline. Then $\pi_{3i} < 0$, $i = 1, 2$ and $\pi_{33} > 0$ by convexity of the profit function. Rewrite (10) as

$$\mathrm{d}Z/\mathrm{d}\bar{X}_R = (1 + \pi_{33}\,\partial w/\partial Z)^{-1}[\cdots], \tag{10'}$$

where the expression in brackets corresponds to the first two terms on the RHS of (10). The expression in parentheses is positive by (5) and by the

[4]Profit maximization under price-taking behavior on the part of identical firms implies that the conditions for aggregation (that industry supply be independent of output distribution across firms) are met.

assumption of convexity. To sign the expression in brackets, totally differentiate (7) and (8). This yields

$$\mathrm{d}p^{s}_{\mathrm{R}}/\mathrm{d}\bar{X}_{\mathrm{R}} = |H|^{-1}(\pi_{22} - X'_{\mathrm{U}}) > 0, \tag{11}$$

$$\mathrm{d}p_{\mathrm{U}}/\mathrm{d}\bar{X}_{\mathrm{R}} = -|H|^{-1}\pi_{12} > 0, \tag{12}$$

where

$$|H| \equiv \begin{vmatrix} \pi_{11} & \pi_{12} \\ \pi_{21} & \pi_{22} - X'_{\mathrm{U}} \end{vmatrix} < 0 \quad \text{by convexity of } \pi.$$

The positive sign of expression (11) follows from the property of the profit function that it is non-decreasing in the price of one of its outputs and from the sign of (6). The positive sign of expression (12) follows from the gross complementarity of X_{U} and X_{R} imposed by adding up for the two-output technology, G. This implies that the expression in brackets is positive so that (10′) is positive. Thus, in the two-output case, normality of Z in production of both goods insures that the industry subjected to the VER will contract. In the multiple-output case, one would also have to impose gross complementarity as it would no longer follow from adding-up as in the two-output case.[5]

The sign of expression (12) also establishes that there will be a deflection of sales towards the unrestricted market. Thus competitive firms will respond to a VER by increasing sales in unrestricted markets, the cause of what Hamilton (1989) terms the domino effect, or in the terminology here, the 'domino diversion' of exports. This is an important effect since it also explains why importing countries not participating in a VER follow suit and negotiate VERs with major exporters so as to avoid having their own markets flooded by deflected sales from restricted markets.

Finally, what are the effects of the VER on the national welfare of the exporting country? As the simulation model demonstrates, this will depend on demand elasticities in the restricted and unrestricted markets, on the elasticity of factor supply to the affected industry, and on the parameters of the production function.[6]

3. Estimation

We now describe two attempts to estimate the principal parameters of the

[5]In a multiple-output technology, gross complementarity would be satisfied provided that there are no strong economies of joint production. For exact conditions, see Lopez (1984).

[6]For expressions of the determinants of national welfare in terms of demand and supply elasticities, the interested reader is referred to our earlier (and more detailed) version of the paper [de Melo and Winters (1990b)].

above model for Taiwanese exports of leather footwear (CCCN 6402). The purpose of this estimation is to establish the plausibility of our approach and to obtain 'ball-park' estimates of the critical parameters for later policy simulations. Thus we have not experimented with large numbers of specifications, nor have we concerned ourselves much about insignificant but implausible estimates of non-critical parameters. Most Taiwanese footwear exports are sold in the U.S.A. and were subject to an OMA between July 1977 and June 1981. The OMA has been investigated several times from the U.S.A.'s point of view [e.g., Pearson (1983) and Aw and Roberts (1986)] but with the exception of Aw's (1989) analysis of quality upgrading, not for Taiwan. We estimate the model for leather footwear sales because they were all affected by the OMA, whereas the other major aggregate available to us (CCCN 6401), although accounting for a larger share of Taiwanese footwear exports, comprises rubber and plastic footwear, the former of which was not limited by the OMA. We distinguish two markets for footwear, the U.S.A. and the rest of the world and use quarterly data for 1974–1986.[7,8]

In our application, we represent the profit function by Diewert's (1974) generalized Leontief form. The corresponding profit function is

$$\pi \equiv \sum_i \sum_j \gamma_{ij}(-p_i^{1/2} p_j^{1/2}), \tag{13}$$

where $i = \mathrm{R, U, Z}$ and p_Z is just the wage (w). Concavity of the profit function requires $\gamma_{ij} = \gamma_{ji}$ and $\gamma_{ij} \geqq 0$ if $i \neq j$. Outputs ($X_\mathrm{R}, X_\mathrm{U}$) are measured with positive signs and inputs (Z) with negative signs. Differentiating (13) yields the general 'netput' equation ('netputs' are both inputs and outputs):

$$X_i = \gamma_{ii} - \sum_{j \neq i} \gamma_{ij}(p_j/p_i)^{1/2}. \tag{14}$$

Eq. (14) presumes unfettered optimization in response to prices. When X_R is considered, however, it requires modification, even for the unconstrained variables, X_U and X_Z. Neary and Roberts (1980) show that a constrained equilibrium can be expressed in terms of the parameters of the unconstrained compensated demand or supply functions by means of virtual prices. Virtual prices are the prices at which the actual quantities traded would have been traded voluntarily according to the compensated functions. For unconstrained netputs, virtual prices equal actual prices, and for constrained netputs they may be derived by inverting the compensated netput functions.

[7]We assume that all output is exported and that the exports to the rest of the world are not constrained.

[8]We estimate the various parameters of the model presented in section 2 in a simultaneous system of non-linear equations using three stage iterative instrumental variable methods from SAS's SYSNLIN procedures.

Solving (14) for $\tilde{p}_R$, the virtual price of sales to market R given a value of $\bar{X}_R$ and substituting into the two unconstrained netputs functions yields

$$\bar{X}_k = -\left[\gamma_{kk} - \frac{\gamma_{kR}^2}{(\bar{X}_R + \gamma_{RR})}\right] - \left[\gamma_{kl} - \frac{\gamma_{kR}\gamma_{Rl}}{(\bar{X}_R + \gamma_{RR})}\right]\begin{bmatrix} p_l \\ p_k \end{bmatrix}, \quad k, l = \mathrm{U}, \mathrm{Z}. \quad (14')$$

Our first attempt at estimation (model I) recognized the paucity of data on the production side of the model. We therefore estimated a system comprising only demand curves and an export allocation model to divide a given volume of exports between markets. We fix total inputs (Z) exogenously and, as suggested by an allocation model, proxy Z by total exports of footwear (X). This allows us to write $X_R = F(\tilde{p}_R, p_U)X$, which, using a generalized Leontief form, specializes to

$$X_R/X = -\gamma_{RR} - \gamma_{RU}(p_U/\tilde{p}_R)^{1/2}. \quad (15)$$

The corresponding equation for X_U is implicit in (15) given adding up.

Eq. (15) was estimated along with demand functions for leather footwear for the U.S.A. and for the rest of the world. These were normalized to express the price of Taiwanese footwear relative to a linear combination of the prices of locally produced footwear (p_i^L) and Korean exports to the market concerned (p_i^K) as the dependent variable. Normalizing the demand curve on price is necessary if the data are to have the opportunity to record infinitely elastic demands. The additional explanatory variables were a cyclical variable (the index of industrial production, Q_i) and the quantity of exports. Thus the two demand curves were of the form

$$p_i = (\beta_0^i + \beta_1^i Q_i + \beta_2^i X_i)(1 - \beta_3^i)p_i^L + \beta_3^i p_i^K), \quad i = \mathrm{U}, \mathrm{R}. \quad (16)$$

All three equations were given seasonal dummies and, in view of the evident serial correlation when estimated straightforwardly, were also adjusted for first-order serial correlation. The resulting model is labelled model I in table 1.

During the OMA the demand equations still applied, relating actual prices and quantities, but the allocation function was over-ridden by the VER and its implication, given Z, for sales X_B. Thus the quarters 1977,3–1981,2 had to be removed from the estimation of eq. (15).[9] The set of instrumental

[9]When the serial correlation adjustment was made, 1981,3 also had to be dropped because no unrestricted lagged value of X_R was available from 1981,2. For the omitted quarter, actual values of X_R and X_U were used in eq. (16) because they were exogenous. Following Neary and Roberts (1980), we set virtual prices equal to actual prices for unconstrained netputs, and for constrained netputs we obtain virtual prices by inverting the corresponding compensated demand function.

Table 1

Estimates of supply and demand functions for Taiwanese footwear.[a]

	Model I		Model II	
	Coefficient	*t*-statistic	Coefficient	*t*-statistic
γ_{RR}	4.67	(1.81)	–	
γ_{RU}	4.31	(2.14)	1.32	(0.90)
γ_{RZ}	–		0.49	(0.19)
γ_{UU}	–		–	
γ_{UZ}	–		−0.05	(0.09)
ρ	0.87	(0.12)	1.00	(–)
R				
β_1	0.0003	(0.0094)	0.0010	(0.0080)
β_2	−0.0016	(0.0018)	0.0009	(0.0012)
β_3	−0.308	(0.366)	−0.087	(0.242)
U				
β_1	0.0389	(0.0564)	−0.0031	(0.0519)
β_2	0.0108	(0.0130)	0.0073	(0.0103)
β_3	0.5941	(0.171)	0.625	(0.147)
R^2/DW	R^2	DW	R^2	DW
X_R	0.903	1.93	0.964	1.98
X_U	–	–	0.958	2.06
P_R	0.985	1.86	0.988	2.08
P_U	0.955	2.46	0.965	2.52

[a]For description of models, see text.

variables included the exogenous variables used in (15) and (16). The initial estimates of (16) were highly unstable: The serial correlation coefficients fluctuated around unity and consequently the resolution on the constant terms β_0^i was very weak. The only solution appeared to be to estimate the demand equations in first difference form, dropping the constants. Table 1 reports these results as model I.

The most striking feature of model I is its strong positive estimate of γ_{RU}: Given total exports the share allocated to market A rises strongly as their relative prices rises. This result confirms negative spillovers between markets and consequently that 'domino diversion' certainly occurs, at least in the two-market case. The elasticity of the U.S.A. share of exports with respect to its price implied by the estimate is about 3.5 in 1976/1977; that is, holding total exports constant, a 1% increase in the price available in the U.S.A. would have increased exports to the U.S.A. by 3.5%.

On the demand side, the results indicate that the U.S.A.'s demand for Taiwanese footwear is insensitive to the state of the business cycle and appears to be related only to local footwear prices rather than to those of competing suppliers from Korea. The price is, however, negatively related to the quantity of exports with an elasticity of about −14, evaluated at the mean levels of exports and prices in the year prior to the OMA (1976,3–

1977,2).[10] The demand in the rest of the world seems to be fairly strongly influenced by the state of demand (prices rise with the cycle), and to be related to the prices of both local footwear and competitive footwear from Korea. The positive term on exports is very fragile, depending on the dynamics of the equation system; it is probably best interpreted as indicating a horizontal demand curve rather than a perverse one. Thus comparing the U.S.A. market in which Taiwan is an important supplier with the world market in which it is less so, we find a lower elasticity of demand (-14 vs. $-\infty$) and less direct competition from Korea. This seems intuitively plausible. Omitting the two implausible coefficients (β_3^R and β_2^U) has little effect on the other parameter except for increasing absolutely γ_{RR} and γ_{RU} by about 0.25. Finally, the R^2 and Durbin–Watson statistics are acceptable.

The second estimation exercise (model II) attempts to incorporate the size of the industry into the system of estimating equations. As argued above, this is most easily accomplished by means of the profit function. Thus in addition to the two demand curves (16), we attempted to estimate three supply functions: Eqs. (14) for $i=R,U$ and (14) for $i=U$. Eqs. (14) rule during periods of free trade and eq. (14) during the OMA. The factor demand equation, (14) with $i=Z$, is not estimable because no data exist on factor inputs, but with the exception of γ_{ZZ}, its parameters are recoverable from the other equations by symmetry. If the stochastic behavior of the supply model is unaffected by the OMA, the error structure of (14) is derivable from that of (14).[11] However, it would be exceedingly complex to do this, as Brenton and Winters (1990) have shown using other functional forms, so it seemed most rational to treat (14) as a separate equation with its own stochastic errors.

We approached the incorporation of supply responses with great trepidation. The factor price data necessary for eqs. (14) are available only on ISIC rather than on SITC commodity classifications and refer only to wages. Data were also available to us only annually for the earlier part of our sample, and thus had to be interpolated into quarterly series. Moreover, it is possible that wages are endogenous. Hence, wages have to be instrumented in our estimation procedure. For instruments, we used employment and wages in the whole of Taiwanese manufacturing. Thus, one should not place great reliance on the results of the expanded estimation.

The results of the full estimation are reported as model II of table 1. As previously, severe serial correlation suggested that working in first differences was a necessary simplification, but this time it affected all equations. This

[10]Our estimate of the U.S. price elasticity of demand for Taiwanese footwear may appear on the high side. For example, Aw (1989) reports an average price elasticity of demand of about 3.0, a result higher than previous global estimates [Szenberg et al. (1977)].

[11]The term $(X_R+\gamma_R)$ in (14′) would become $(X_R+\gamma_{RR}-u_R)$ where u_R is an error term distributed identically throughout our sample period.

made it impossible to estimate the constants of the supply functions which, in turn, meant that (15) was inestimable. Thus our final system comprised four rather than five equations. The estimates of the demand functions are even less well defined in model II than in model I; the only notable change is that the coefficient relating prices to the quantities of exports in the U.S.A. is significantly positive. As before, we interpret this as indicating a horizontal, not an upward-sloping, demand curve.

Turning to the supply responses, we find them reduced by the inclusion of factor prices. For sales to the U.S.A. – the major market – both terms are positive: Exports to the U.S.A. depend positively on their price relative to the prices of both sales elsewhere and factor inputs. The implied elasticity of supply is around 3.1 in 1977. The coefficients on relative prices for exports to the rest of the world are positive relative to the price of U.S.A. sales but just negative relative to factor inputs. The latter sign implies implausible behavior at some set of prices, but does not disturb the signs of the elasticities at the prices experienced over our sample period. The own price elasticity of supply for exports to the rest of the world is about 1.0 in 1977, but grows to 1.5 by 1986.

The results for model II are disappointing in their lack of precision. However, they do suggest that important supply responses exist and that a more detailed study with better data would be rewarding. They also suggest that responses are around the levels suggesting that it is fruitful to study the effects of VERs on resource allocation and welfare. Thus, until firmer empirical work is undertaken, we take the estimates here as bases from which to explore the effect of different elasticity assumptions on the costs of VERs to developing country exporters.

4. Welfare and distributional effects of VERs: Some illustrative simulations

The econometric estimates in section 3 for Taiwanese leather footwear exports suggests that factor demand and output supply responsiveness are sufficient to produce 'domino diversion' towards unrestricted markets and industry contraction. However, both because we were unable to estimate precisely all the demand and supply parameters, and because our estimates may not be representative of those in other sectors subject to VERs, we complete the analysis with some counterfactual simulations inspired by our earlier results. We loosely base these calibrated simulations on Taiwanese leather footwear exports to the U.S.A. and to the ROW using volume and price data at the eve of the OMA agreement.

The partial equilibrium model consists of two constant-elasticity export demand curves (17), a constant elasticity supply curve (18) and the generalized Leontief allocation model described in section 3. Bars over a variable indicate an exogenous parameter, stars denote the initial unconstrained equilibrium, and a tilde over a variable, ˜, refers to the prices at which unconstrained producers would replicate the input and output allocation decisions imposed on them by binding constraints in the relevant market.

$$X_k = \bar{A}_k P_k^{-e_k}, \quad e_k > 0, \; k \in \{\mathrm{R}, \mathrm{U}\}, \tag{17}$$

$$X_z = Z = \bar{A}_z \tilde{P}_z^{e_z}, \quad \tilde{P}_z = \tilde{P}_3, \; e_z > 0, \tag{18}$$

$$X_i = -\gamma_{ii} - \sum_{j \neq i}^{3} \gamma_{ij} (\tilde{P}_j | \tilde{P}_i)^{1/2}, \quad i,j \in \{\mathrm{R}, \mathrm{U}, \mathrm{Z}\}, \tag{19}$$

$$\tilde{P}_{\mathrm{R}} < P_{\mathrm{R}} \quad \text{when} \quad \bar{X}_{\mathrm{R}} < X_{\mathrm{R}}^*. \tag{20}$$

Eqs. (17) and (18) describe the output demand and factor supply curves facing the all-around price-taking firms in the industry subject to the VER. Eq. (19) is obtained from applying Sheppard's lemma to the generalized Leontief restricted profit function

$$\pi(P; \alpha) = K \left(\sum_{i=1}^{3} \sum_{j=1}^{3} \gamma_{ij} [-(\tilde{P}_i \tilde{P}_j)^{1/2}] \right), \tag{21}$$

where K is a fixed factor (not modelled) which ensures a determinate firm size. Eq. (20) states that when export volumes in the restricted market are below their free trade values, the price $\tilde{P}_{\mathrm{R}}$ at which unconstrained suppliers would have voluntarily supplied the restricted quantity $\bar{X}_{\mathrm{R}}$ is less than the premium-ridden price at which sales are actually made, i.e., $P_{\mathrm{R}} > P_{\mathrm{R}}^* > \tilde{P}_{\mathrm{R}}$ where P_{R}^* is the free trade price in the restricted market.

Industry profits, π, is the difference between sales revenues and costs, both evaluated at the VER-ridden prices, whereas 'virtual' profits given by (21) are evaluated at virtual prices $\tilde{P}$. The welfare measure is

$$\Delta W = W_1 - W^* = (\Delta \pi + \Delta P_Z L) / P_Z^* Z_3 \tag{22}$$

where $W_1(W^*)$ is the value of the welfare indicator with (without) the VER, and L is a scalar indicating the size of the industry in the market for Z. ΔW is the sum of the changes in profits and factor incomes divided by their free trade values.

The elasticities in tables 2 and 3 are used to calibrate the parameters γ_{ij} appearing in the factor demand equations. Calibration is completed by treating parametrically initial price and quantity data and by choosing an initial parametric value for Z so that profits are initially equal to zero.

Table 2

Sensitivity results to elasticity specification (small industry case) (10% reduction in exports to restricted market).[a]

Elasticities	(1)	(2)	(3)	(4)	(5)	(6)	(7)	(8)	(9)
Factor demand elasticity (ε_z^d)[b]	−1	−1	−1	$-\frac{1}{4}$	$-\frac{1}{4}$	$-\frac{1}{4}$	−2	−2	−2
Output supply elasticities $(\varepsilon_R^s=\varepsilon_U^s)$[c]	2	2	2	$\frac{1}{2}$	$\frac{1}{2}$	$\frac{1}{2}$	4	4	4
Export demand elasticities $(\varepsilon_R^d=\varepsilon_U^d)$	$\frac{1}{2}$	2	4	$\frac{1}{2}$	2	4	$\frac{1}{2}$	2	4
Exports to unrestricted market (% change)	0.016	0.036	0.046	0.034	0.049	0.053	0.009	0.026	0.036
Factor use (% change)	−0.053	−0.045	−0.041	−0.041	−0.036	−0.034	−0.056	−0.050	−0.045
Change in profits[d]	7.954	1.452	0.592	6.702	0.989	0.259	8.375	1.649	0.708
Change in 'virtual' profits[e]	−3.287	−2.709	−2.428	−9.699	−7.997	−7.541	−1.778	−1.540	−1.381

[a]Initial values: $P_R=1.54$; $X_R=27.5$; $P_U=1.25$; $X_U=22.0$. Small industry case, i.e., P_Z fixed.

[b]Holding output prices constant.

[c]Holding P_Z constant.

[d]Initial profits equal to zero. Change in sales revenue minus change in value of factor inputs.

[e]Initial profits equal to zero. Restricted profits evaluated at virtual prices.

Table 3

Distributional and welfare effects of a VER.

Elasticities	Factor supply elasticity = 1			Factor supply elasticity = 5			Factor supply elasticity = 10			Factor supply elasticity = ∞		
	Low[a]	Medium[b]	High[c]	Low[a]	Medium[b]	High[c]	Low[a]	Medium[b]	High[c]	Low[a]	Medium[b]	High[c]
Exports to unrestricted markets (% change)	0.042	0.065	0.084	0.036	0.043	0.051	0.035	0.040	0.044	0.049	0.036	0.036
Factor use (% change)	−0.038	−0.033	−0.027	−0.041	−0.042	−0.040	−0.041	−0.043	−0.043	−0.036	−0.045	−0.045
Factor price (% change)	−0.038	−0.033	−0.027	−0.008	−0.009	−0.008	−0.004	−0.004	−0.004	0.0	0.0	0.0
Change in profits	8.849	3.302	2.198	7.166	1.924	1.156	6.936	1.696	0.947	0.987	1.452	0.708
Change in virtual profits	−8.451	−1.775	−0.647	−9.429	−2.472	−1.162	−9.563	−2.586	−1.265	−7.997	−2.709	−1.381
Change in welfare[d] (1)	0.088	0.014	0.005	0.094	0.019	0.008	0.095	0.020	0.009	0.0	0.0	0.0
(5)	−0.065	−0.120	−0.103	0.061	−0.015	−0.024	0.078	0.002	−0.008	0.0	0.0	0.0
(10)	−0.257	−0.287	−0.237	0.020	−0.058	−0.065	0.057	−0.020	−0.030	0.0	0.0	0.0
(20)	−0.641	−0.621	−0.506	−0.063	−0.143	−0.146	0.015	−0.064	−0.073	0.0	0.0	0.0

[a] Same elasticities as table 2, column (5).

[b] Same elasticities as table 2, column (2).

[c] Same elasticities as table 2, column (9).

[d] Numbers in parentheses refer to factor market size in relation to initial factor allocation in the industry. Change in welfare calculated from eq. (20) and expressed as a percentage of initial factor income in the industry before the VER.

The results of simulations under different assumptions about demand and supply elasticities are reported in table 2. All simulations refer to a negotiated 10% cut in exports of Taiwanese leather footwear to the U.S.A. The objective of the simulations is to establish how sensitive the results are to systematic variations in demand and supply elasticities. At this stage, we assume that the footwear industry is small in the market for its factor Z, so that P_Z, the price of the factor, is fixed.

In all the simulations, we rely on pairwise variations in the parameters of the generalized Leontief production function. For all pairwise variations, the conditions for local concavity of the profit function (i.e., $\gamma_{ij}>0$) are met, as suggested by our econometric estimates. All simulations assume identical pairwise supply and demand elasticities, since we have no a priori ground for presuming that supply elasticities to restricted and unrestricted markets should be different or for presuming that export demand elasticities should be different (although market shares in the restricted and unrestricted markets are different, however).

The simulations in columns (1–3) show that the spillover is an increasing function of export demand elasticities. The results of varying export demand elasticities also show that, other things equal, the rent transfer gain decreases as the size of the spillover increases. This is because with more spillover there is less contraction and less reduction in costs.

More interesting are the results of varying factor demand and output supply elasticities. Raising output supply responses alone increases the spillover and hence reduces profit to the industry as there is less contraction. This negative effect on industry profits is offset if the elasticity of demand for the factor of production is raised. Doubling the elasticity of factor demand approximately halves the size of the spillover effect. Holding export demand elasticities constant, doubling all production function elasticities [columns (1)–(3) to columns (7)–(9)] reduces the spillover effect by about 35% and increases marginally the amount of contraction and hence profits.

The VER breaks the equality of marginal revenues of the industry factor between sales to the restricted and unrestricted markets and creates an inefficiency [see de Melo and Winters (1990a)]. A measure of that inefficiency is provided by industry profits evaluated at 'virtual' prices. Virtual prices are the set of prices which would cause actual quantities to be supplied voluntarily i.e., the set of prices which, with maximizing behavior, would support the observed quantity outcome. Given such prices, 'virtual' profits are the maximum that exporters could earn and thus changes in them represent the efficiency losses that the VER imposes. In the absence of the VER, actual profits equal virtual profits, both being equal to zero. As can be seen from the last row of table 2, virtual profits are more negative (i.e., efficiency losses are greater) the lower demand and supply elasticities.

In practice, however, industries that enter into VERs are not small in their domestic economy. Indeed, it is precisely because these industries have been rapidly gaining market shares in developed-country markets, that VER arrangements are negotiated in the first place. In table 3, we recognize that the industry faces an upward sloping supply curve for its factor, Z, so that contraction is accompanied by a fall in the wage of the industry, P_Z. Because the share of the industry in the market for Z is likely to vary from case to case, we report welfare effects for different assumptions about the size of the industry in the factor market. Welfare calculations are reported in the bottom of table 3 as a percentage of the income of factors in the industry prior to the VER and for factor market sizes ranging from 1–20 times the initial allocation of factors in the industry. Of course, the elasticity of factor supply to the industry is not independent of its size in the market for factors, so that the welfare estimate grid should be interpreted accordingly with high values of the elasticity of factor supply corresponding to cases where the industry is small in the market for its factors. For example, elasticities of factor supply in the range between 1 and 5 and factor market sizes in the range between 1 and 5 times the initial factor allocation, could be taken as representative for analyzing a VER in textiles. On the other hand, for a smaller industry like footwear, a more likely factor supply elasticity range would be between 5 and 10 with a correspondingly higher range for the size of the factor market in relation to the footwear industry.

With wage flexibility, the distributional effects of a VER are more pronounced than earlier. Industry profits rise relatively more as they shed factors and use remaining factors at a lower wage. Taking the medium elasticity scenario as a reference, with an industry factor supply elasticity of 5, profits rise by 30% more than in the case of infinite supply elasticity, and industry wages fall by one percent. In addition to producing redeployment, a VER raises profits and lowers wages. Thus it has a strong adverse effect on the distribution of income.

The harmful effects of a VER, however, are not confirmed to the adverse distributional shifts arising from higher profits, lower wages and lower factor use. In addition, as can be seen from the grid of welfare changes displayed in the bottom of table 3, for most factor market sizes and for factor supply elasticities of below 10, the VER results in a net welfare loss. For example, with medium elasticities as a reference, a VER reducing exports to the restricted market by 10% would lead to a welfare loss of 12% of factor income (prior to the VER) for a factor supply elasticity of 1 and a factor market 5 times the size of the initial factor allocation in the industry. Of course, higher factor supply elasticities mitigate the welfare loss and so would differential export demand elasticities (with relatively lower demand elasticities in the restricted market). However, the results in the bottom of table 3 suggest that for most plausible elasticity configurations, a VER is more likely than not to reduce national welfare in the exporting country.

5. Conclusions

Most work on VERs has focused on establishing the welfare loss to the importing country arising from the conjunction of an income transfer loss and a distortionary efficiency loss in the importing country. Implicit in that work is that the exporting country is likely to receive adequate compensation for any induced inefficiency losses through the often large rent transfer. This paper has argued that this view is misconceived. A fairly general theoretical model of a competitive industry subject to a VER shows that a VER is likely to lead to both industry contraction and spillover to unrestricted export markets. We call spillover 'domino diversion' since it lends support to the pre-occupation of countries that have not negotiated VERs with seeing their markets flooded by sales diverted from the restricted markets. Our econometric estimates for Taiwanese leather footwear exports to the U.S.A. lend support to the fairly general conditions under which spillover and industry contraction will occur, namely that with rising marginal costs in the production of sales to both restricted and unrestricted markets, any increase in the output of one product does not reduce much (or increases) the marginal cost of the other product.

We also show that in addition to the expected contraction of the industry, a VER will lead to rising private profits (because of the rent transfer from abroad), and to a lower wage for the factors employed in the industry, especially those with skills with few alternative uses in other industries. Thus VERs have strongly negative distributional implications for exporting countries as profits rise and wages and employment fall. Finally, illustrative simulations show that for a plausible range of elasticities and relative sizes of the restricted industry, national welfare may well fall in spite of the rent transfer from abroad.

Appendix A: Data sources for econometric estimates

Exports and export unit values. Foreign Trade of China, Taiwan Province CCN 6402; pairs and US$ per pair;

Korean export unit values. Korean Customs data [see de Melo and Winters (1989) for details];

Domestic prices/unit values. U.S.: Bureau of Census Current Industrial Report non-rubber footwear RoW: British Footwear Manufacturers Federation, U.K. domestic production unit value and I.F.S. average exchange rate (rf);

Indices of industrial production.

Wholesale prices. I.F.S.,

RoW = OECD less U.S.A. weighted by GDP weights;

Exchange rate.

Wages and unemployment. Yearbook of Labor Statistics, Republic of China wages and employment in leather footwear and average exchange rate.

All data were quarterly except for Taiwanese wages and employment for which only annual data were available consistent form. These were interpolated into quarterly series as follows.

We assume each series grows by a constant amount throughout each year. Thus in any year

$$q_{tj}=x_t+(j-2.5)y_t, \qquad j=1\ldots4,\ t=1\ldots n,$$

where q_{tj} is the observation for quarter j year t, x_t is the annual observation, y_t is the quarterly growth in year t.

Observation x_t is centered between quarters 2 and 3 and q_{tj} at the centers of their respective quarters.

In addition, there is a requirement that the continuous function represented by x connect at the end of each year and at the beginning of the next. Thus

$$x_{t+1}+2y_t=x_{t+1}-2y_{t+1},$$

from which

$$2y_t+2y_{t+1}=x_{t+1}-x_t=\Delta x_{t+1}.$$

Writing this in matrix form yields

$$\begin{bmatrix} 2\ 0 & \ldots & 0 \\ 2\ 2\ 0 & \ldots & 0 \\ 0\ 2\ 2\ 0 & \ldots & 0 \\ . & & . \\ . & & . \\ . & & . \\ 0 & \ldots & 0\ 2\ 2 \end{bmatrix} \begin{bmatrix} \\ \\ \\ y \\ \\ \\ \\ \end{bmatrix} = \begin{bmatrix} \\ d \\ \\ \Delta x \\ \\ \\ \\ \end{bmatrix}, \tag{A.1}$$

where d is an arbitrary starting condition. (A.1) is solvable once d is known and we choose d to minimize the variance in growth rates (i.e., we choose to make the quarterly series q_{tj} as smooth as possible).

Minimizing $y'y$ w.r.t. d yields

$$d = -\left[\sum_{t=2}^{n} \Delta x_t (m_{t1} + m_{it})\right] \bigg/ 2m_{11},$$

where m_{ij} is an element of M, and $M = N'N$, where N is the matrix in (A.1).

References

Aw, B.Y., 1989, An empirical model of mark-ups in a quality differentiated export market, Mimeo. (The Pennsylvania State University, University Park, PA).

Aw, B.Y. and M. Roberts, 1986, Measuring quality change in quota-constrained import markets, Journal of International Economics 21, 45–60.

Bark, T. and J. de Melo, 1989, Efficiency and export earnings implications of two-tier quota allocation rules, International Economic Journal 3, no. 3, 31–42.

Brenton, P.A. and L.A. Winters, 1990, Non-tariff barriers and rationing: UK footwear imports, discussion paper no. 365 (CEPR, London).

Chambers, R.G., 1988, Applied production analysis: A dual approach (Cambridge University Press, Cambridge).

Diewert, E., 1974, An application of the Sheppard duality theorem: A generalized Leontief production, Journal of Political Economy 79, 481–507.

Feenstra, R., 1984, Voluntary export restraints in US autos: 1980–1981: Quality, employment and welfare effects, in: R. Baldwin and A. Krueger, eds., The structure and evolution of recent US trade policy, NBER (University of Chicago Press, Chicago, IL).

Fuss, M. and D. McFadden, 1978, Production economics: A dual approach to theory and applications (North-Holland, Amsterdam).

Greenaway, D. and B. Hindley, 1985, What Britain pays for voluntary export restraints, Thames essay no. 43 (Trade Policy Research Centre, London).

Hamilton, C., 1989, The political economy of transient 'new' protectionism, Weltwirtschaftliches Archiv, 522–546.

Lopez, R., 1984, Estimating substitution and expansion effects using a profit function framework, American Journal of Agricultural Economics 66, 358–367.

Melo, J. de and L.A. Winters, 1989, Price and quality effects of VERs revisited: A case study of Korean footwear exports, WPS discussion paper 216 (World Bank, Washington, DC).

Melo, J. de and L.A. Winters, 1990a. Voluntary export restraints and resource allocation in developing countries, World Bank Economic Review 4, no. 2, 209–233.

Melo, J. de and L.A. Winters, 1990b, Do exporters gain from voluntary export restraints?, WPS discussion paper 326 (World Bank, Washington, DC).

Neary, P. and K.W.S. Roberts, 1980, The theory of household behavior under rationing, European Economic Review 13, 25–42.

Pearson, C., 1983, Emergency protection in the footwear industry, Thames essay no. 36 (Trade Policy Research Centre, London).

Szenberg, M., J. Lombardi and E. Lee, 1977, Welfare effects of trade restrictions: A case study of the U.S. footwear industry (Academic Press, New York).

Takacs, W. and L.A. Winters, 1991, Labour adjustment costs and British footwear protection, Oxford Economic Papers.

Tarr, D. and M. Morkre, 1984, Aggregate costs to the Unites States of tariffs and quotas on imports: General tariff cuts and removal of quotas on automobiles, steel, sugar and textiles (Federal Trade Commission, Washington, DC).

7

Are different Rules of Origin equally costly? Estimates from NAFTA†

Céline Carrère and Jaime de Melo

7.1 Introduction

Rules of Origin (RoO) are a key ingredient in any preferential trading agreement (PTA) short of a customs union, as well as in any preferential market access scheme such as the Generalized System of Preferences (GSP) or the more recent 'Everything But Arms' (EBA) and Africa Growth Opportunity Act (AGOA) initiatives. Low rates of utilization have led many observers to question the extent of market access, not only because of lower Most Favored Nation (MFN) tariffs worldwide or because there may be significant learning effects that contribute to low utilization rates in the early years of implementation, but mostly because of the presumed cost-raising effects of these seemingly 'made-to-measure' RoO. Yet, there is little systematic direct evidence documenting the cost-raising effects of RoO. This chapter provides more systematic evidence for NAFTA.

Useful anecdotic evidence abounds. For example, there is ample documentation of the stringent requirements that must sometimes be satisfied to meet origin (i.e. the definition of 'vessel' under the EBA (Brenton 2005), the description of the triple-transformation rule widely applied in textiles or the detailed description of RoO in SADC (Flatters and Kirk 2005)). Several contributions have used gravity trade models with dummy variables or synthetic indices to capture the effects of RoO. These studies

† We thank conference participants, our discussant Ana Maria Mayda, and Olivier Cadot, Alberto Portugal-Pérez, Marcelo Olarreaga, Pablo Sanguinetti, and Ernesto Stein for helpful comments.

typically conclude that, after controlling for other factors, trade volumes are indirectly related either to indices of the presence of RoO or of their levels of restrictiveness (see, e.g., Augier *et al.* 2005; Estevadeordal and Suominen 2005; Cadot *et al.* 2005).[1]

Another promising approach, inspired from earlier work on EFTA (Herin 1986) has used revealed preference to estimate upper and lower bounds on the cost of RoO. The assumption here is that for sectors with utilization rates close to 100%, the utilization rate would give an upper bound on the costs of RoO, while for sectors with close to zero utilization rates, preference rates would provide a lower bound of the costs associated with RoO. Under the assumption that transitional adjustment to the administrative requirements of the RoO has taken place, this non-parametric method is a useful way to obtain bounds on the costs of RoO when one has data on utilization rates (see, e.g., Anson *et al.* 2005 and below).

While useful, these comparisons of utilization rates do not exploit the variance in the types of RoO used across sectors. Estevadeordal (2000) was the first to recognize explicitly the importance of different RoO in terms of their potential cost-raising effects by constructing a synthetic index, r_i, that explicitly accounted for differences in types of RoO.[2] The appeal of a synthetic index is potentially of great practical use since, like suitably constructed effective rates of protection that provide a summary description of a country's trade regime, a synthetic index describing the set of RoO that accompany a preferential agreement could also provide an overall idea of the restrictiveness of the system of RoO.

As explained below, the observation rule is not confronted with the data. For example broad categories of sectors (raw materials, intermediates and final goods) may not be affected in the same way by a given RoO (say a

[1] Other contributions have sought to provide more direct estimates. For example, in the context of The Europe Agreements, Brenton and Manchin (2003) have observed that several East-European partners have preferred to enter the EU market under overseas processing trading (OPT) arrangements than under the presumably more generous market access provided by the FTA. More recently, in an assessment of market access provided by the EU under the EBA and the GSP, Brenton (2005) concludes that the low take-up of preferences under the EBA must at least partly be due to costs associated with the accompanying RoO.

[2] Estevadeordal built an observation rule that relied on this assumption: a RoO requiring a change of chapter heading would be more restrictive than one requiring a change of classification at the tariff line (HS-8) level, and (other things being equal), adding a regional value-content requirement or a technical requirement would make the RoO more restrictive (and hence more costly), resulting in an ordinal integer index at the HS-8 level, r_i, in the range $[1 < r_i < 7]$, with the property that larger values of r_i would correspond to a more restrictive RoO. This synthetic index was constructed on the same data for Mexican exports to the US under NAFTA.

change of chapter). Nor is its usefulness as a measure of restrictiveness of RoO under NAFTA systematically analysed. Within the limits imposed by data availability (the effects of different types of RoO can only be captured by dummy variables and firm heterogeneity accounting for observations at the tariff line cannot be controlled for), this chapter provides a more direct estimate of the costs of the three important categories of RoO under NAFTA: change of tariff classification, existence or not of a regional value content (RVC) scheme, and the presence or not of a technical (TECH) requirement. Our estimates also allow us to check the reasonableness of the assumptions used in building the Estevadeordal's r_i index described above. Finally, for sectors subject to a RVC, we provide illustrative simulations of the cost-raising effects of these RoO.

The remainder of the chapter is organized as follows. Section 7.2 discusses the particular characteristics of the RoO map negotiated under NAFTA that are relevant for the econometric estimates that follow, and present non-parametric estimates that can be obtained by the use of a synthetic index. Section 7.3 presents a simple model leading to econometric estimates that take into account differences across broad categories of goods and across types of RoO. Results from estimating this model are presented in Section 7.4. How these cost estimates compare with Estevadeordal's index is discussed in Section 7.5. Section 7.6 then carries out illustrative cost calculations in the case where RoO take the form of a RVC. Conclusions follow in Section 7.7.

7.2 NAFTA RoO map, and non-parametric cost estimates

Section 7.2.1 describes briefly the main RoO in NAFTA, along with utilization rates in 2001, a year when NAFTA was just about in full force, since the average preferential rate of 4.1% for Mexican exports was almost equal to the average US MFN tariff (4.3%). Section 7.2.2, then turns to non-parametric cost estimates for 2000 and 2001, based on the r_i index.

7.2.1 *Preferences and utilization rates under NAFTA*

Table 7.1 describes the data used in the calculation of the compliance cost estimates for Mexican exporters of RoO under NAFTA. All data are for 2001, when NAFTA was in full force, and are defined at the HS-6 level of aggregation, only for tariff lines with positive exports to the US. This

Table 7.1 RoO map, preferences and utilization rates

Section	Obs	%	Export to US %	u_i Mean	τ_i Mean	CC %	CH %	CSI %	E %	TECH %	RVC %	r_i Mean	Interm %	Final %
1 Live Animals	80	2.3	0.71	30.7	4.1	100	0	0	15	0	0	6	6.3	23.8
2 Vegetable Prod.	150	4.2	2.17	70.3	3.6	100	0	0	0	0	0	6	12.7	8
3 Fats & Oils	27	0.8	0.02	77.9	5.1	100	0	0	0	0	0	5.9	0	100
4 Food. Bev. & tob.	123	3.5	1.75	76.6	7.6	79.7	18.7	1.6	17.1	0.8	0	5.6	11.4	86.2
5 Mineral Products	86	2.4	7.17	11.8	0.3	80.2	19.8	0	19.8	0	0	5.6	16.3	4.7
6 Chemicals	430	12.1	1.35	62.3	3.4	75.4	20	4.7	84.7	1.2	0.9	5.5	73.5	26.3
7 Plastics & Rubber	175	4.9	1.36	71.7	3.8	11.4	88	0.6	26.3	5.7	64	4.9	60.6	30.9
8 Leather Goods	52	1.5	0.18	51.3	4	61.5	38.5	0	42.3	0	0	5.5	32.7	46.2
9 Wood Products	55	1.5	0.24	37.3	2.1	7.3	92.7	0	7.3	0	0	4.2	43.6	45.5
10 Pulp & Paper	97	2.7	0.52	56.2	0.7	57.7	42.3	0	42.3	0	0	5.2	39.2	55.7
11 Textiles & Apparel	618	17.4	7.35	79.9	10.4	80.3	19.7	0	97.9	41.6	0	6.0	40.9	53.9
12 Footwear	47	1.3	0.28	67.6	6.8	19.2	80.9	0	72.3	0	48.9	4.9	0	100
13 Stone & Glass	129	3.6	1.15	60.1	3.2	54.3	43.4	2.3	43.4	0	0	5.0	10.1	89.9
14 Jewellery	35	1	0.37	45.5	2.7	60	40	0	40	0	0	5.2	34.3	40
15 Base Metals	430	12.1	3.56	67.9	2	42.6	56.1	1.4	45.4	1.2	0	4.8	50.5	48.1
16 Mach. & Elec. Eq.	631	17.7	39.52	35.5	1.5	0	81.3	18.7	31.9	4.6	1.4	3.8	0	100
17 Transp. Equip.	85	2.4	20.38	56.4	3.4	2.4	91.8	5.9	14.1	0	22.4	4.2	0	100
18 Med. Instruments	170	4.8	3.69	45.2	2.1	15.3	76.5	8.2	14.7	0	3.5	4.2	0	100
19 Arms & Ammunition	8	0.2	0.02	13.4	0.5	62.5	37.5	0	0	0	0	5.3	0	100
20 Misc. Manufact.	127	3.6	8.2	40.4	3.1	82.7	11.8	5.5	0.8	0	0	5.4	0	100
Total	**3555**	**100**	**100**	**58**	**4.1**	**50**	**45.1**	**5**	**47**	**8.6**	**4.9**	**5.1**	**29.5**	**61.2**
Raw	330	9.3	9.4	34.2	1.8	95.2	4.5	0.3	10.3	0.9	0	5.9	-	-
Interm.	1048	29.5	4.1	74.2	4.8	58.4	39.4	2.2	68.4	0.2	8.7	5.2	-	-
Final	2177	61.2	86.6	53.9	4.2	39.1	53.9	7	42.2	13.9	3.8	4.9	-	-

Notes: total Mexican exports to US under NAFTA = $131 million
All calculations are at the 6-digit level of the HS (so the table presents simple *average* by sector and category and not the *aggregate* indicator.
i.e. weighted by the imports values of each line).
u_i = utilization rate of the NAFTA regime; τ_i = tariff preference margin; r_i = the Estevadeordal (2000) index of Rules of Origin ($1 < r_i < 7$, a higher value indicating a more restrictive RoO. see text).
CC = Change in Chapter / CH = Change in Heading / CS = Change in Subheading / E = Exception to Change of Tariff Classification / RVC = Regional Value Content / TECH = Technical Requirement.

represents 3555 observations[3], 99 chapters and 20 sectors. Utilization rates, denoted u_i, are defined as the ratio of USA imports from Mexico under US-NAFTA preferential tariffs to total USA imports from Mexico (at the 6-digit HS-level). Tariff preference margins, $\tilde{\tau}_i$ are also calculated at the product line level and are defined as:

$$\tilde{\tau}_i = \frac{t_i - \tau_i}{1 + \tau_i}; \quad (t_i = t^{\text{us}}_{i,\text{mfn}}\,;\, \tau_i = t^{\text{us}}_{i,\text{mex}}), \tag{7.1}$$

where world prices are set equal to one by choice of units. Table 7.1 also reports the average value of Estevadeordal's index (which takes values in the range $1 < r_i < 7$). All data in Table 7.1 are simple (unweighted) averages at the HS-2 level, i.e. for 20 sectors (with the number of HS-6 level tariff lines in each sector for 2001).

In Table 7.1, all data on RoO refers to percentage of tariff lines subject to the corresponding RoO. Take for example sector 11 (textiles and apparel, henceforth T&A) with 618 observations at the HS-6 level, and that represents 7.35% of the total Mexican exports to US in 2001. T&A has an average utilization rate of 79.9% and an average tariff preference margin of 10.4%, with 54% and 41% of the observations falling under the final and intermediate good, respectively. Within that sector, 80% [19.7%] of observations had to satisfy a change of classification at the chapter [heading] levels, and 42% of the tariff lines had technical requirements.

Only T&A has an average tariff preference margin above 10%. Note also that some sectors with a substantial number of observations (i.e. over 100) have relatively high utilization rates in spite of low preference margins (e.g. stone and glass, sector 13).

According to stages of processing, raw materials are the least important sector, since about 30% of observations fall under the intermediate category (which represents only 4% of the total exports) and the remainder falls under the final good category (61% of the observations accounting for 87% of Mexican exports to the US). Finally, in spite of large dispersions within sectors, on average, tariff preference margins are the same for final- and intermediate-goods-producing sectors, even though average utilization rates are much higher for the intermediate-goods sectors (74% vs. 54%). If indeed, Mexico has a comparative advantage in final-goods-producing activities, it would appear that RoO that are only slightly more

[3] In view of the econometric estimates that follow, we have eliminated 5 outliers with $\tilde{\tau}_i > 100\%$, 3 belonging to Chapter 24 (Tobacco) and 2 to Chapter 12 (Vegetables). These 5 outliers are classified as 'raw materials' according to the WTO, and faced only a Change of Chapter, without exception, technical requirement or regional value content. The utilization rates for these five products are 100%.

restrictive according to the r_i synthetic index for final-goods-producing activities, have a greater impact on utilization rates than for intermediate-producing activities.

Turn next to the distribution of types of RoO, recalling that their effects can only be captured by the use of dummy variables in the statistical analysis below. About 45% of the tariff lines have to meet a Change of Heading (CH) with the remainder (50%) having to meet a Change of Chapter (CC). This means that it would be futile to attempt to capture the effects of both types of changes in tariff classification since the dummy variables would be almost quasi-perfectly collinear. Along the same lines, note that exceptions (whose effects on costs are difficult to interpret anyway), denoted E, cover about half of the tariff lines, being present for 98% of the lines in T&A (sector 11) and 85% in chemicals (sector 6). Turning to the technical requirements (TECH) that cover only 8.6% of the lines and 6 sectors, they are concentrated in sector 11. Regional value content (RVC) is prevalent in four sectors, and covers 5% of the observations.

Finally, we look at the cumulative frequency distribution of the two variables of interest, utilization rates, u_i, and preference margins, $\tilde{\tau}_i$. Utilization rates are evenly distributed around three groups of values: one-third of the total sample with u_i equal to zero, one quarter with u_i equal to 1 and the remainder in-between. As to preference rates, the sample average preference is 4.11% with the following quartile distribution: [25%:0%]; [50%:2.58%] and [75%:5.5%].

The distribution of utilization rates and preference margins are quite different between intermediate and final goods: zero utilization rates ($u_i = 0\%$) apply for 20% [34%] for intermediate [final] goods. Full utilization rates ($u_i = 100\%$) apply for 50% [16%] for intermediate [final] goods. As to the extent of preferential access, the distribution of $\tilde{\tau}_i$, the average for the intermediate goods sample is around 4.81% and the quartile repartition are: [25%: 0.6%]; [median or 50%: 3.7%] and [75%: 7.36%], whereas for the final goods the average is 4.13% and the quartile distribution: [25%: 0%]; [median or 50%: 2.5%] and [75%: 5.0%]

7.2.2 *Non-parametric estimates*

Based on data for 2000 (very close to the data reported in Table 7.1), Anson *et al.* (2005) used revealed preference arguments and Estevadeordal's (2000) synthetic index, r_i, to estimate the total compliance costs for Mexican exporters to NAFTA. As a starting point, we carry out the same exercise here with 2001 data when the average margin of preference was almost the same (4.11% in 2001 vs. 4.10% in 2000) and the average utilization rate slightly higher (58% vs. 57%). We also compare these estimates with those for 2000 to see if one can detect any learning effects through time.

As a first step, we reproduce for 2001, the non-parametric estimates of compliance costs of RoO, c_i, expressed as a percentage of unit price, of Anson *et al.* carried out for 2000. This involves comparing preference margins and utilization rates for selected values of the index of restrictiveness, r_i. By revealed preference, for headings with $u_i = 100\%$, the preference margin is an upper-bound for compliance costs (as c_i cannot be greater than the benefit conferred by $\tilde{\tau}_i$). Likewise, for headings with $u_i = 0\%$, the preference margin gives a lower-bound estimate. For the remaining sectors with $0\% < u_i < 100\%$, assumptions must be made. Anson *et al.* (2005) assumed that firms were indifferent to export to the US under the NAFTA or the MFN regimes (heterogeneity of firms notwithstanding). Then, an approximation of compliance costs would be given by the average rate of tariff preference computed for the remaining sectors, i.e. on the sample $0\% < u_i < 100\%$. Applying this reasoning, we obtain for 2000, [2001], $c = \tilde{\tau} = 6.11\%, [c = \tilde{\tau} = 6.16\%]$.

Anson *et al.* further break down total compliance costs, c_i, into an administrative component, δ_i, and a distortionary component, σ_i:

$$c_i = \delta_i + \sigma_i, \tag{7.2}$$

where all variables expressed as a percentage of unit price. To come up with an estimate of administrative costs, they assume that administrative costs would be negligible for firms on their participation constraint, $(0\% < u_i < 100\%)$, provided that they would also have low values of r_i, i.e. values corresponding to a change of tariff classification at the heading level, CH, i.e. when $r_i \leq 2$ (not much paperwork is involved in 'proving' a change of heading). Hence, calculating preference margins for utilization rates close to 100% (say $u_i = 95\%$) when $r_i \leq 2$, gives an upper bound of the distortionary component, σ_i. These average preference margins for 2000, [2001] are $\tilde{\tau} = 4.30\%$ $[\tilde{\tau} = 4.44\%]$. Recalling that the average total compliance costs for 2000, [2001] are $c = \tilde{\tau} = 6.11\%, [c = \tilde{\tau} = 6.16\%]$ we get average administrative cost estimates for δ of $\delta = 6.11\% - 4.30\% = 1.81\%$ $[\delta = 6.16\% - 4.44\% = 1.72\%]$.

Both estimates are close, though interestingly the administrative cost estimate for 2001 is less than that for 2000 both in absolute terms and in relative terms, as it falls from 45% to 42% of the total compliance costs (by assumption equal to the average preference margin). These non-parametric estimates confirm the hunch that there may be significant learning effects that could explain low utilization rates in early years of preferential access (see, e.g., Brenton 2005 in his explanation of low take-up under EBA).

7.3 A simple model

The above non-parametric cost estimates are averages across sectors, rely entirely on values taken by the r_i index, and potentially gloss over differences across types of RoO.[4] If one is ready to assume that utilization rates provide some information on the stringency of RoO and to make a few additional assumptions, one can sketch a simple model that improves along these two dimensions.

Assume first that aggregation from the firm to the tariff line level does not introduce systematic biases (which we can't check for anyway in the absence of firm-level data). Assume next that the utilization rate of NAFTA for product line *i* is a positive function of the difference between the tariff preference rate, $\tilde{\tau}_i$, and (unobserved) total compliance costs, c_i, again expressed as a percentage of unit price, associated with applying the RoO criteria, i.e.:

$$u_i = f(\tilde{\tau}_i - c_i); f'(.) > 0, \tag{7.3}$$

where $\tilde{\tau}_i$ is defined in eqn (7.1). This assumption is only defensible in the absence of firm-level information (see Appendix) that would recognize that the utilization rate is a zero–one decision for the firm. So think of eqn (7.3) as a specification for costs at the aggregated HS-6 level that circumvents the problems associated with heterogeneous behavior associated with firm heterogeneity (see Ju and Krishna 2003 and Krishna 2005).

For compliance costs associated with the RoO, c_i, assume a linear relation with each of the set of relevant RoO, i.e.:

$$c_i = \delta + \beta' RoO_i + v_i. \tag{7.4}$$

Here, RoO_i is a vector of dummies capturing the RoO described in Table 7.1 and δ captures the administrative cost of RoO. For reasons discussed below, we will include dummy variables for tariff classification change at the chapter level (CC_i), regional value content (RVC_i), and technical requirement ($TECH_i$).

[4] Spreads in utilization rates are also assumed to reflect differences in administrative costs rather than firm heterogeneity. Unfortunately, we have no data to control for firm heterogeneity, so this source of bias in the model presented here, cannot be controlled for.

Equations (7.3) and (7.4), lead to the following reduced form for estimation:[5]

$$u_i = \alpha(\tilde{\tau}_i - \delta - \beta' RoO_i) + (\mu_i - \alpha v_i). \tag{7.5}$$

Hence we estimate the following equation:

$$u_i = \lambda + \alpha\tilde{\tau}_i + \theta RoO_i + \varepsilon_i. \tag{7.6}$$

Estimation of (7.6) yields estimates of $\hat{\alpha}$ and $\hat{\theta}$ that can then be used to approximate the distorsion costs generated by RoO, $\hat{c}_i$, i.e.:[6]

$$\hat{c}_i = \frac{\hat{\theta}}{\hat{\alpha}} RoO_i. \tag{7.7}$$

Equation (7.7) states that the costs of a RoO will be proportional to the responsiveness of the utilization rate to the RoO (just like the costs of protection are an increasing function of the elasticity of import demand) and inversely proportional to the responsiveness of the utilization rate to the preference margin.

Since the dependent variable (the utilization rate) takes a value of only between zero or one, the appropriate estimation procedure for the reduced form (7.6) is a two-limit (or double-censored) Tobit (see, Appendix and e.g., Maddala 1983, Chap. 6).[7]

In this model setup, it is assumed that preferential rates and RoO are both exogenous. In reality, RoO are negotiated knowing that the preference margin will be the MFN tariff (unless it is also under negotiation multilaterally). So there is a potential multicollinearity between the RoO and $\tilde{\tau}_i$ variables in eqn (7.6). An endogeneity problem would arise if a second equation can explain RoO as a function of $\tilde{\tau}_i$ and another variable that would also influence the endogenous variable u_i. While this may be the case, in any event we do not have at our disposal a good variable to instrument the RoO variable. Moreover, instrumenting would be difficult anyway since it would take place over dummy variables.

[5] See details in Appendix.

[6] We do not estimate total compliance costs of RoO, i.e. $\hat{c}_i = (\hat{\lambda}/\hat{\alpha}) + (\hat{\theta}/\hat{\alpha}) RoO_i$ because it is difficult to give an economic interpretation for the regression constant term (notably due to the econometric procedure used and to the introduction of dummy variables for section and stage of production—see Section 7.4).

[7] The use of the maximum likelihood Tobit estimates of the linear model coefficients is preferred to the standard OLS estimates using the White correction for heteroskedacity, because the Tobit model makes expected values of the dependent variable conditional on the probability of censoring in the sample. Since there is censoring, we will usually report double-censored estimates.

Are different Rules of Origin equally costly? Estimates from NAFTA

In general (and certainly in the case of NAFTA as explained by Estevadeordal 2000) negotiations can be viewed as a 'game' played by three parties in which negotiation is over two instruments: speed of preferential tariffs *phase-in* and RoO criteria. Moreover, in our NAFTA application, we use data for 2001, a year quite late in the NAFTA process of preferential tariff liberalization (the preference margin for Mexican imports was equal to the US MFN tariff for 3215 tariff lines out of 3555 at HS-6 level). Finally, the US MFN tariff cannot be suspected of endogeneity with the NAFTA RoO. Nonetheless, a more ambitious assessment of RoO would rely on a political-economy approach as in Cadot *et al.* (2005).

7.4 Cost estimates by type of RoO and category of activities

The usefulness of costs estimates obtained from eqn (7.7) depends on the plausibility of the first-stage results for the reduced-form estimation, and should satisfy the revealed-preference criterion used in the non-parametric estimates above. Estimation is carried out for the whole sample and for broad categories of goods (intermediates and final goods[8]) adding sector dummy variables, D_k, to control for sector-specific heterogeneity:

$$u_i = \lambda + \alpha\tau_i + \theta RoO_i + \sum\nolimits_k D_k + \varepsilon_i, \qquad (7.8)$$

where $i = 1, \ldots, 3225; k = 1, \ldots, 20; RoO_i = CC_i, TECH_i, RVC_i$.[9]

Expected signs in eqn (7.8) are $\hat{\alpha} > 0, \hat{\theta}_1 < 0, \hat{\theta}_2 < 0, \hat{\theta}_3 < 0$.

Note the bounds on the estimated coefficient values in eqn (7.8). Since all variables are in the interval [0,1] (we have eliminated the five preference rates above one), when plugging values obtained from eqn (7.8) into eqn (7.7), one should obtain reasonable cost estimates provided that measurement errors and biases for the coefficients in the numerator and denominator are not systematic. One would also expect different coefficient values for the dummy variables across broad category of goods: for example a change of chapter should have a greater negative impact on utilization rates for final than for intermediate goods.

[8] Adding raw materials does not affect overall results as this category represents only 9% of the sample. Furthermore, the only RoO component for these products is a CC. However, as previously explained, we eliminated this part of the sample because all the outliers in terms of tariff preference margins belonged to this category.

[9] For multicollinearity reasons (see Section 7.2), we could not add a dummy for CH and for E in addition to CC_i. Note also that the vector RoO_i depends on the category considered, since some categories of goods do not face certain types of RoO (e.g. intermediates do not face technical requirements).

Table 7.2 Determinants of utilization rates and total costs of RoO

	Total sample		Intermediate goods		Final goods	
u_i	OLS	Tobit	OLS	Tobit	OLS	Tobit
$\tilde{\tau}_i$	2.2757**	4.3683**	3.0389**	9.0450**	2.0910**	3.9310**
	(0.41)	(0.20)	(0.47)	(0.54)	(0.45)	(0.21)
CC_i	−0.0684**	−0.1676**	−0.0604**	−0.2122**	−0.0801**	−0.1447**
	(0.02)	(0.04)	(0.03)	(0.09)	(0.02)	(0.04)
$TECH_i$	−0.2088**	−0.4975**	–	–	−0.2288**	−0.4391**
	(0.03)	(0.08)			(0.04)	(0.09)
RVC_i	−0.1065**	−0.1517**	−0.2850**	−0.4058*	−0.1147**	−0.1811*
	(0.05)	(0.04)	(0.12)	(−0.24)	(0.05)	(0.11)
Obs.	*3225*	*3225*	*1048*	*1048*	*2177*	*2177*
R^2-adj	*0.39*		*0.38*		*0.40*	
Log likelihood		*−2995.5*		*−959.8*		*−2024.8*

Notes:
Constant and dummy variables for section and stage of production are included but not reported in order to save space
OLS: coefficients estimate with Ordinary Least Squared with White correction.
TOBIT: coefficients estimate with the Two-Limit Tobit Model.
Standard deviations in parenthesis.
** and *, respectively, significant at the 5% and 10% level.

We start with the results for the two broad categories of sectors (intermediates and final goods), then comment briefly on results for the T&A sector. Table 7.2 reports the results of the OLS and two-limit Tobit estimates of eqn (7.8). For the entire sample (3225 observations) all coefficients are strongly significant with the expected sign: the tariff preference margin influences positively the utilization rate and the sign of the dummy variables relative to RoO are all negative, indicating that these requirements reduce the use of the NAFTA regime. In this linear specification, in terms of magnitude, the strongest negative impact on utilization rates comes from the TECH requirement, a plausible result if one recalls that these requirements are added when it is felt that a change of tariff heading is 'insufficient'.

Turning to the comparison of estimates for final and intermediate goods, note that TECH is only present for final goods (and applied mostly to the T&A sector), but RVC is present and significant for both categories.[10]

Turn now to the magnitudes of the coefficients on RoO dummies, recalling that only 5% of the tariff lines have an RVC, and less than 9% a TECH requirement. Model shortcomings deserve to be mentioned. First, according to eqn (7.3), the coefficient for $\tilde{\tau}_i$ in eqn (7.6) represents the

[10] When the reduced form is estimated for raw materials, the tariff preference margin is positive and strongly significant (due to some outliers). But CC, the only RoO faced by this category is not significant. This is not surprising, and conforms with *a priori* expectations.

impact of the difference between $\tilde{\tau}_i$ and c_i on the utilization rate. If so, a given increase in $(\tilde{\tau}_i - c_i)$ has an impact on u_i about three times as large for intermediates than for final goods. Secondly, differences in coefficient values on the RoO variables (which combine the impact of the RoO variables on the cost c_i and the impact of the difference $(\tilde{\tau}_i - c_i)$ on u_i discussed above), cannot be easily interpreted within the model. This said, all coefficient values have the expected signs and are significant at the 5% level, justifying turning to the compliance cost estimates obtained by plugging estimates of eqn (7.8) into eqn (7.7). The contributions to costs of the different RoO are reported in Table 7.4, columns 3 and 4, and will be discussed later.

For the estimates to be useful, they should meet the revealed preference criterion used in the non-parametric estimates reported in Section 7.2.2. This means that the estimated compliance costs should, on average, be lower [greater] than the average preference margin for products with an utilization rate of NAFTA of 100% [0%], whatever the category (total, final or intermediate). This is indeed the case for all product categories, for utilization rates of 100% [0%]. As to the products with $0\% < u_i < 100\%$, the estimated compliance costs are systematically inferior to the tariff preference margin, often by non-negligible margins. Given that the preference margins are almost at the same level for sectors with non-zero utilization rates, it could be that the absence of variation in the data prevents identifying costs, so that even with sector dummies, there is too much uncontrolled firm heterogeneity.

Unfortunately, the problem of uncontrolled firm heterogeneity cannot be alleviated by turning to sector-level estimates, because plausible results could only be obtained for one sector. Indeed, among the 2-digit sectors with more than 100 observations and average preference margins above 4% (an estimate of total compliance costs of 3% of which there are 6 sectors if one omits the misc. manuf. category), only the largest sector (the T&A sector with 618 observations) gives significant and plausible results. Since this is an important sector for Mexico in NAFTA and for developing countries engaged in preferential market access with Northern countries (e.g. under EBA and AGOA, or under other FTAs by the EU and US), estimates are reported in the last column of Table 7.3.[11]

[11] The estimation of eqn (7.8) for T&A sample (618 observations) by the two-limit Tobit model, yields the following first stage results:

$$u_i = \underset{(0.06)}{1.15} + \underset{(0.32)}{3.11}\,\tau_i - \underset{(0.06)}{0.21}\,CC_i - \underset{(0.05)}{0.37}\,TECH_i,$$

with standard errors in parenthesis and associated compliance cost estimates reported in the last column of Table 7.3.

Table 7.3 Costs and preference rates

	Total sample			Intermediate goods			Final goods			Textiles and apparel		
	Obs	$\bar{\tau}_i$	$\hat{c}_i^{TOBIT}$	Obs	$\bar{\tau}_i$	$\hat{c}_i^{TOBIT}$	Obs	$\bar{\tau}_i$	$\hat{c}_i^{TOBIT}$	Obs	$\bar{\tau}_i$	$\hat{c}_i^{TOBIT}$
$0\% < u_i < 100\%$	1410	5.92%	3.86%	322	5.28%	2.04%	1088	6.10%	4.17%	337	11.82%	13.01%
$u_i = 0\%$	954	0.38%	1.71%	211	0.76%	1.69%	743	0.27%	1.43%	34	1.87%	6.63%
$u_i = 100\%$	861	6.32%	3.01%	515	6.17%	1.61%	346	6.55%	3.69%	247	9.71%	5.65%

Notes:
Computed from coefficients estimated in eqn (7.8) applied to eqn (7.7).
$\hat{c}_i^{TOBIT}$: cost obtained from Two-Limit Tobit Model estimations.

Comparing the estimates for the T&A sector with those for larger categories of activities, it is clear that both CC and TECH criteria represent larger costs (respectively 6.7% vs. 3.01% and 11.8% vs. 9.17%) which reflects the fact that utilization rates are not much higher than average in the T&A sector in spite of high preferential margins. In interpreting these results, one should be cautious since the CC and TECH coefficients must capture some of the effects associated with 'exceptions' (98% of the lines face an exception in sector 11!). Also according to the distribution of TECH requirements, these are mostly on production processes (33% of technical requirements) with the remaining (9%) on both product and process.

To summarize, among the significant results, the revealed preference criterion is satisfied and the data classification of the RoO components in terms of estimated compliance costs is reasonable since $CC < RVC < TECH$. This is precisely the ranking assumption about restrictiveness used by Estevadeordal (2000) in setting up his observation rule to construct his synthetic index.

Perhaps more importantly, estimates conform to *a priori* expectations with respect to the costs of RoO across broad categories of goods. For instance, the costs of each component are found to be different across the stages of production with CC and RVC representing a greater cost for final-goods producing sectors than for intermediate-goods producing sectors. Since final-goods producers also faced technical requirements, it is not surprising to find total compliance costs (on average over all product lines) that are greater for final-goods-producing sectors than for intermediate-goods-producing sectors (3.2% vs. 2.0%). And given that the tariff preference margin is lower for final goods than for intermediate (4.3% vs. 4.8%), we can also expect (still in average terms over all product lines), a lower utilization rate for final-goods-producing sectors, than for intermediate-goods-producing sectors. This is indeed confirmed in Table 7.2 (utilization rates are 53.9% and 74.3%, respectively).

7.5 Evaluating Estevadeordal's synthetic index

Can synthetic indices of RoO regimes serve the same summary descriptive roles as effective rate of protection for trade regimes? We raise this question for Estevadeordal's index, constructed from the same data set, and subsequently used by Estevadeordal and Suominen (2005) to summarize RoO for several FTAs.

Consider first the following calculation. Take US sectors with tariff peaks, i.e. 3 times or more the 2001 average US tariff around 4% and compare the corresponding average value of r_i in those sectors with the corresponding values in the low-tariff sectors (less than one-third the average tariff). Values for the index (number of observations in each group in parenthesis) are in decreasing order of protection: $r_i = 6.0(257)$, and $r_i = 4.8(1432)$. Since tariff escalation according to the stage of processing is widely observed across all countries, tariff peaks are concentrated in the final-goods sectors. It follows that, at least according to this index of restrictiveness, under NAFTA, RoO would protect final-goods-producing sectors.

Are costs similar across types of RoO? Recall from eqn (7.7) that the costs of a given RoO are assumed to depend on how utilization rates react to the RoO and to the response of utilization rates to preferential rates. Computations of the costs of each type of RoO (when it applies) according to eqn (7.7) are reported in columns 3 and 4 of Table 7.4. RVC criteria have similar effects for intermediate and final goods: the imposition of an RVC on a product generates a cost estimated at 4.5% [4.6%] for intermediate [final] goods. As one would expect, a change of classification at the chapter level (CC) generates a higher cost for final (3.7%) than for intermediate goods (2.3%).[12] Finally, again according to intuition, the greatest cost for final products results from technical requirements, with an impact of 11% on total compliance costs.

To evaluate Estevadeordal's index, we make the necessary assumptions to come up with a lexicographic ordering suggested by our estimates, then compare it with his constructed from the observation rule used to construct the r_i index.[13] Both rankings are summarized in Table 7.4. On the one hand, Estevadeordal's (2000) is built around a finer distinction for the type of change of classification heading (CH, CS, CI levels), which was

[12] This result still holds when one replaces the CC_i dummy by a CH_i dummy.

[13] We have assumed that for the RoO not included in our econometric indices, they would have taken a value of 1. This is probably plausible though one may question that CH would take a value of 1 (our justification for this ranking is that cost estimates for CC are low). However, we use question marks to indicate that the rankings are assumed rather than estimated.

Table 7.4 Comparison of Estevadeordal's index and costs estimates

RoO criteria	obs.	Estevadeordal's index	Costs estimates[a/]		
			Total	Final	rank
CI	9	1	N.A.	N.A.	1(?)
CS	134	2	N.A.	N.A.	1(?)
CS + RVC[b/]	2	3	3.84%	4.61%	3
CS + TECH[b/]	30	3	11.39%	11.17%	4
CH	1400	4	N.A.	N.A.	1(?)
CH + RVC[b/]	167	5	3.84%	4.61%	3
CH + TECH[b/]	16	5	11.39%	11.17%	4
CH + RVC + TECH	4	5	15.23%	15.77%	6
CC	1209	6	3.47%	3.68%	2
CC + TECH	254	7	14.86%	14.85%	5

Notes:
a/ Estimates obtained from substituting values obtained in eqn (7.7) and in eqn (7.8).
b/ No distinction between CH and CS in econometric estimates (See text).
N.A. Not applicable (See text).

impossible to carry out in the econometric estimates due to quasi-perfect multicollinearity between the CC and CS dummy variables. On the other hand, for the more restrictive RoO (e.g. for the combination of RoO with values equal to or greater than 5), our cost estimates allow for a finer distinction (5 values instead of 3) and for a non-linear classification. Furthermore, we propose an index different according to the stage of production, allowing the data to determine if the same RoO represents a different cost for intermediate-goods-producing sectors or for final-goods-producing sectors.

Table 7.4 shows that the ranking of costs according to the estimates corresponds to Estevadeordal's selection of observation rule: costs of CC < costs of RVC < costs of TECH. However, the two indicators do not generate the same rank ordering. For instance, since the costs of an RVC is greater than the costs of a CC, a combination of CH + RVC is more costly than the cost generated by a CC.

Overall, however, for the sample of 3225 observations used in the estimations, the correlation between the two indices of costs of RoO is 0.66.

Comparisons based on RoO applied only for one preferential market access case cannot be expected to yield stylized facts, nor a robust assessment of the usefulness of a synthetic index. On the basis of the above, however, it is fair to say that the observation rule yields plausible results both in terms of relative rankings in terms of assumed costs of different types of RoO and in terms of restrictiveness when confronted with US tariff peaks (on the assumption that, for political-economy reasons, RoO should be expected to be more restrictive in sectors with tariff peaks compared with sectors with low rates of protection). However, if other comparisons point in the same direction, it might be worthwhile to distinguish changes in tariff classification in terms of the broad categories of sectors they apply to.

7.6 Value content restrictions

Import content requirements (either in the form of value or quantity) are frequently used (see Estevadeordal and Suominen 2005, Tables 1 and 3): Out of 87 PTAs, 68 require an import content for at least from products; 7 requiring some form of RVC, and another 67 use some restriction on the value of parts (VP). When applied, they usually require between 30% and 60% of the value (or quantity) under constraint to originate in the region. Among the types of RoO considered in this paper, import-content restrictions hold the greatest promise for direct quantification of their cost-raising effects. As a first step in this direction, one can check orders of magnitude suggested by some simple simulations imposing accepted functional forms and cost-minimizing behavior in a competitive environment. The simulations below compute the extent of preferential market access necessary that would leave a cost-minimizing firm indifferent under different import restrictions.

Suppose then that a Mexican firm, or some other Southern partner firm, produces under constant returns to scale and perfect competition a final good, X that it can sell either in the US (Northern) partner market, or on the ROW market. The final good is produced with value added, VA, and intermediates, Z, i.e. $X = F(VA, Z)$. Value added is produced by capital and labor, i.e. $VA = H(K, L)$ at exogenously determined prices, (w, r) while intermediates either come from the US partner, Z^A, or from the ROW, Z^C so that $Z = G(Z^A, Z^C)$, also with exogenously given prices $p^{Z,A}$ and $p^{Z,C}$. Let $F(.)$ be Leontief, and $H(.)$ and $G(.)$, be CES functions. Profit maximization will imply that the unit cost function can be written as:

$$c(.) = a_z P^z + a_v P^v, \tag{7.9}$$

where a_z, a_v are the per-unit input coefficients for intermediates and value added, respectively, with P^z, P^v their corresponding per-unit prices. Under the CES aggregation functions, the expressions for unit prices are:

$$P^z = CES(P^{z,a}, P^{v,c}; \gamma_z, \alpha_z, \sigma_z), \tag{7.10}$$

where γ_z is a calibration parameter, α_Z is the share parameter and σ_Z is the elasticity of substitution between intermediates of different origin. Likewise, the unit value-added price is given by:

$$P^v = CES(w, r; \gamma_v, \alpha_v, \sigma_v), \tag{7.11}$$

where the parameters have the same meaning as in the previous expression. Perfect competition implies that the unit price for the good, P^X equals unit cost, i.e.:

$$P^X = C(.). \tag{7.12}$$

Finally, let there be some market segmentation (or product differentiation by destination) by assuming that it is costly to reallocate X across markets. Then unit prices obtained in each market are $P^{X,A}$ in the US and $P^{X,C}$ in the ROW. Let the ease of substitution across markets be captured by the constant elasticity of transformation (CET) function, with unit sales given by:

$$P^X = CET(p^{X,A}, p^{X,C}; \gamma_X, \alpha_X, \sigma_X), \tag{7.13}$$

where the parameters have the same meaning as in the CES case.

Let, t^A be the US *ad valorem* tariff, and let the RoO be a RVC in quantity terms. If subscript zero denotes the optimal per-unit use of the intermediate originating in the US, and subscript one, the corresponding choices by the firm when it faces a RoO and preferential access, on the cost side:

$$z^R = Z_1^A/Z^C > z^* = Z_0^A/Z^C; Z_1^A > Z_0^A,$$

leading to the restricted cost function, $c^R(.)$. Since $c^R(z^R) > c^0(z^0)$, one can ask what rate of preference in the US market is necessary to leave the Mexican firm indifferent between choosing to export under NAFTA or under MFN, i.e. compute $\tau = (P_1^{X,A})/(P_0^{X,A})$ so that:

$$P_1^X = CET(p_1^{X,A}, p^{X,C}) = c^R(.). \tag{7.14}$$

Table 7.5 reports the results of illustrative simulations that calculate the margin of preference that would leave indifferent a Mexican (Southern) exporter facing an RVC for intermediate purchases.

Columns (1) to (4) could be representative of a final-producing goods industry, with a relatively low value-added ratio, while columns (5) to (8) could be representative of an intermediate-goods industry with a higher value-added ratio (less roundaboutness in the methods of production).

All simulations start from an initial equilibrium situation in which all prices are unity and in which the share of exports to the US is 50%. For simplicity, we assume that the two elasticities in the simulations are

Are different Rules of Origin equally costly? Estimates from NAFTA

Table 7.5 RVC and compensating preference margins

	(1)	(2)	(3)	(4)	(5)	(6)	(7)	(8)
Value added	30%	30%	30%	30%	60%	60%	60%	60%
Intermediates	70%	70%	70%	70%	40%	40%	40%	40%
Initial Vus/(Vus + Vrow)	20%	30%	40%	50%	20%	30%	40%	50%
Final Vus/(Vus + Vrow) [RoO]	40%	40%	60%	60%	40%	40%	60%	60%
Initial share of exports to US	50%	50%	50%	50%	50%	50%	50%	50%
Final share of exports to US	55.9%	51.5%	55.3%	51.4%	53.6%	50.9%	53.2%	50.8%
Initial Pus*	1	1	1	1	1	1	1	1
New Pus*	1.13	1.03	1.11	1.03	1.07	1.02	1.07	1.02

unity: a Cobb–Douglas for the substitution for intermediates of different origin and an elasticity of transformation across export destinations of unity. In this partial equilibrium setup, we also assume that the industry is a price-taker in input markets and in the market for export sales. Finally, to ease the interpretation of results, we also limit the amount that is exported to the initial equilibrium quantities, so that all firms do is readjust the export mix in response to the change in incentives to sell in the US market.[14]

Interpreting the results, note first that the required preferential access is higher for each RVC constraint in the final (low value-added activity). This is of course inherent in the model setup. Next we turn to orders of magnitude, given that it is not clear what the extent of restrictiveness is. For example, Estevadeordal and Suominen report that, when they are used, RVC percentages are 50% or 60%. So suppose it is 60%. According to the simulations, if the initial RVC was 40% [50%], a preference margin of 11% [3%] would be needed to leave the Mexican exporter indifferent.

7.7 Conclusions

Exporters benefitting from preferential market access have to contend with a vast array of RoO whose cost-raising effects have, so far, escaped

[14] If one were interested in computing welfare effects, one would incorporate a price responsive demand curve for total exports, so that binding RoO would then have two effects: a change in volume and a change in export destination mix. The model would be closed by specifying an upward-sloping supply curve for primary factors on production in the industry.

quantification. Using the RoO map negotiated under NAFTA, this chapter has attempted to quantify these costs. Using non-parametric methods based on a widely used synthetic index, we have estimated total compliance costs and the administrative component of total costs. Comparisons between 2000 and 2001 reveal some learning effects as utilization rates increased in spite of insignificant changes in market access. Calculations also revealed that administrative costs fell in absolute terms, but also as a percentage of total compliance costs.

Turning to the econometric estimates carried out for broad categories of goods (final and intermediates), results are in accordance with *a priori* expectations with respect to the type of RoO and to the costs of a given set of RoO across broad categories of goods. Other things being equal, compliance costs are the least for a change of tariff classification (here captured by CC), followed by a regional value content (RVC) and by a technical requirement (TECH). Regarding stages of production, an RVC is more costly for final-goods producing sectors than for intermediate-goods producing sectors. Estimates also showed that the lower rate of utilization for final-goods producing sectors under NAFTA (presumably the sectors in which Mexico had a comparative advantage) could be attributed to the battery of RoO they faced (after controlling for differences in preferential access).

Synthetic indices, such as the one proposed by Estevadeordal, which will continue to be used notably when utilization rates are not available, can give a summary measure of overall restrictiveness of a given RoO map. We have therefore compared the lexicographic ordering used by Estevadeordal in his observation rule with the ordering emerging from our cost estimates. We find that his ordinal ranking is the same as ours when it comes to individual RoO. However, they differ when several RoO enter simultaneously, and especially when it come to the distinction between final-goods-producing activities and intermediate-goods-producing activities. This suggests that it might be useful to build different synthetic indexes for broad categories of activities.

Finally, we have estimated rates of preferential market access that would be needed to counteract the cost-raising effects for regional value-content requirements when they apply. Under cost-minimization assumptions, and under acceptable functional forms, it would appear that preference margins of about 10% would be needed to compensate for a 'typical' regional value content RoO. While much still remains to be done before we better understand the cost-raising effects of RoO, the evidence presented here suggests that RoO go a long way towards negating the benefits of preferential market access for the Southern partners that are the presumed beneficiaries of these preferences.

References

Anson, J., Cadot, O., Estevadeordal, A., de Melo, J., Suwa-Eisenmann, A., Bolorma T. 2005. Rules of Origin in North-South Preferential Trading Arrangements with an application to NAFTA. *Review of International Economics*, 13(3): 501–517.

Augier, P., Gasiorek, M., C. Lai-Tong. 2005. 'The Impact of Rules of Origin on Trade Flows'. In *The Origin of Goods: Rules of Origin in Regional Trade Agreements* edited by Cadot, O., Estevadeordal, A., Suwa, A., T. Verdier. *CEPR*/ IADB / Oxford University Press, this volume Chap. 14.

Brenton, P., M. Manchin. 2003. Making EU Trade Agreements Work: The Role of Rules of Origin. *World Economy*, Vol.26 (may): 755–769.

Brenton, P. 2005. 'Rules of Origin and Utilization of Trade Preferences in non-Reciprocal Agreements'. In *The Origin of Goods: Rules of Origin in Regional Trade Agreements* edited by Cadot, O., Estevadeordal, A., Suwa, A., T. Verdier. *CEPR*/ IADB / Oxford University Press, this volume Chap. 13.

Cadot, O., Estevadeordal, A., A. Suwa-Eisenmann. 2005. 'Rules of Origin as Export Subsidies'. In *The Origin of Goods: Rules of Origin in Regional Trade Agreements* edited by Cadot, O., Estevadeordal, A., Suwa, A., T. Verdier. *CEPR*/ IADB / Oxford University Press, this volume Chap. 6.

Estevadeordal, A. 2000. Negotiating Preferential Market Access: The case of the North American Free Trade Area. *Journal of World Trade* 34(1): 141–166.

Estevadeordal, A., K. Suominen. 2005. 'Rules of Origin: A World Map and Trade Effects'. In *The Origin of Goods: Rules of Origin in Regional Trade Agreements* edited by Cadot, O., Estevadeordal, A., Suwa, A., T. Verdier. *CEPR*/ IADB / Oxford University Press, this volume Chap. 4.

Flatters, F., R. Kirk. 2005. 'Rules of Origin as Tools of Development: Lessons from SADC'. In *The Origin of Goods: Rules of Origin in Regional Trade Agreements* edited by Cadot, O., Estevadeordal, A., Suwa, A., T. Verdier. *CEPR*/ IADB / Oxford University Press, this volume Chap. 12.

Herin, J. 1986. Rules of Origin and Differences Between Tariff Levels in EFTA and in the EC. EFTA Occasional Paper no. 13.

Ju, J., K. Krishna. 2003. Firm Behavior and Market Access in a Free Trade Area with Rules of Origin. Mimeo, Penn State University.

Krishna, K. 2005. 'Understanding Rules of Origin'. In *The Origin of Goods: Rules of Origin in Regional Trade Agreements* edited by Cadot, O., Estevadeordal, A., Suwa, A., T. Verdier. *CEPR*/ IADB / Oxford University Press, this volume Chap. 2.

Maddala, G.S. 1983. *Limited-Dependent and Qualitative Variables in Econometrics*, Cambridge (GB).

Appendix: The model

This appendix develops the firm's decision to indicate the link between the variables determined at the firm level and the observed data at the HS-6 level, and justifies the econometric specification.

Firm' decision

Let index i refer to an HS-6 tariff line observation (this is the product line for which we have observations on utilization rates and preference rates). Let there be $j = 1, \ldots, n$ Mexican firms exporting to the US under product category i. Rank firms so that $j = 1, \ldots, k$ export to the US under NAFTA regime and $j = k+1, \ldots, n$ export under the MFN regime. Let $u_j = 1[0]$ represent the firm's decision to export under NAFTA [MFN], and E_j firm's j exports to the US. Finally, total unit compliance costs, c_j, associated with RoO include an administrative component, δ_j, and a distortionary cost associated with implementing the RoO requirement itself, σ_j, i.e. $c_j = \delta_j + \sigma_j$. The above relations suggest that we can write the firm's costs as:

$$c_j = f(RoO_i, \delta_j). \tag{7.15}$$

Implicitly, in eqn (7.15) we have assumed that all firms differ in their costs when they sell product i only because of costs associated with implementing RoO, an assumption that will certainly be violated in practice. With this notation, the firm's decision will boil down to:

$$\begin{array}{lll} u_j = 0 \Leftrightarrow E_j = E_j^{MFN} & \text{if} & \tilde{\tau}_i < c_j \\ u_j = 1 \Leftrightarrow E_j = E_j^{NAFTA} & \text{if} & \tilde{\tau}_i \geq c_j. \end{array} \tag{7.16}$$

Note that the rate of preference is observed at the HS-6 product level, while the utilization rate decision takes place at the firm level. However, the utilization rate in the data is also observed at the product level, and it is defined as:

$$u_i = \frac{\sum\limits_{j=1,\ldots,k} E_j^{NAFTA}}{\sum\limits_{j=1,\ldots,k} E_j^{NAFTA} + \sum\limits_{j=k+1\ldots,n} E_j^{MFN}} \quad \text{with} \quad \begin{cases} u_i = 0 & \text{if } k = 0 \\ u_i = 1 & \text{if } k = n \\ 0 < u_i < 1 & \text{if } 0 < k < n. \end{cases} \tag{7.17}$$

We assume linear specifications for the utilization rate of NAFTA at the product level:

$$u_i = \alpha(\tilde{\tau}_i - c_i) + \mu_i, \tag{7.18}$$

with c_i, the unit costs associated with RoO at the product level. c_i is a weighted average of the firms' costs c_j. Unfortunately, we have no information on the distribution of these c_j in each HS-6 level, i. However, we can reasonably assume that:

$$c_i = \delta + \beta' RoO_i + v_i, \tag{7.19}$$

where β is a $t \times 1$ vector of unknown parameters and RoO_i is a $t \times 1$ vector of explanatory variables.

Are different Rules of Origin equally costly? Estimates from NAFTA

Equations (7.18) and (7.19), lead to the reduced form for estimation:

$$u_i = \alpha(\tilde{\tau}_i - \delta - \beta' RoO_i) + (\mu_i - \alpha v_i). \tag{7.20}$$

Econometric specification

The dependent variable being truncated at both high and low values, the model becomes:

$$u_i^* = \lambda + \alpha\tilde{\tau}_i + \theta' RoO_i + \varepsilon_i, \tag{7.21}$$

where u_i^* is the latent variable, ε_i are residuals that are independently and normally distributed, with mean zero and a common variance σ^2 and:

$$\begin{cases} u_i = 0 & \text{if } u_i^* \leq 0 \\ u_i = u_i^* & \text{if } 0 < u_i^* < 1 \\ u_i = 1 & \text{if } u_i^* \geq 1. \end{cases}$$

Here, 0 and 1 are the lower and upper limits. The likelihood function for this model is given by:

$$\begin{aligned} & L(\lambda, \alpha, \beta, \sigma | u_i, \tilde{\tau}_i, RoO_i, 0, 1) \\ & = \prod_{u_i=0} \Phi\left(\frac{0 - \lambda - \alpha\tilde{\tau}_i - \theta' RoO_i}{\sigma}\right) \prod_{u_i=u_i^*} \frac{1}{\sigma}\phi\left(\frac{u_i - \lambda - \alpha\tilde{\tau}_i - \theta' RoO_i}{\sigma}\right) \\ & \times \prod_{u_i=1}\left[1 - \Phi\left(\frac{1 - \lambda - \alpha\tilde{\tau}_i - \theta' RoO_i}{\sigma}\right)\right]. \end{aligned} \tag{7.22}$$

In eqn (7.22), $\phi(.)$ and $\Phi(.)$ are, respectively, the density function and distribution function of the standard normal evaluated at $(\lambda + \alpha\tilde{\tau}_i + \theta' RoO_i)/\sigma$ (see Maddala 1983, Chap. 6 for algebraic details).

Has Distance Died? Evidence from a Panel Gravity Model

Jean-François Brun, Céline Carrère, Patrick Guillaumont, and Jaime de Melo

The estimated coefficient of distance on the volume of trade is generally found to increase rather than decrease through time using the traditional gravity model of trade. This distance puzzle proved robust to several ad hoc versions of the model using data for 1962–96 for a large sample of 130 countries. The introduction of an "augmented" barrier to trade function removes the paradox, yielding a decline in the estimate of the elasticity of trade to distance of about 11 percent over the 35-year period for the whole sample. However, the "death of distance" is shown to be largely confined to bilateral trade between rich countries, with poor countries becoming marginalized.

There is a widespread perception that the current wave of globalization, much like the first, should have led to the "death of distance." Other things equal, globalization should generate a dispersion of economic activity reflecting a decline in transaction costs, especially transport costs. But studies based on the traditional gravity model of international trade—the workhorse for studies on the pattern of trade and the influence of transport costs—do not reach that conclusion. Although some studies based on the gravity model have used direct

Jean-François Brun is associate professor of economics at the University of Auvergne; his email address is j-f.brun@u-clermont1.fr. Céline Carrère is assistant professor of economics at Ecole des Hautes Etudes Commerciales, University of Lausanne; her email address is c.carrere@u-clermont1.fr. Patrick Guillaumont is professor of economics at the University of Auvergne; his email address is p.guillaumont@u-clermont1.fr. Jaime de Melo is professor of economics, Department of Political Economy, at the University of Geneva; his email address is demelo@ecopo.unige.ch. All authors are associated with the Center for Studies and Research in International Development (CERDI). This article was submitted in May 2003, and all editorial matters were handled by Alan Winters. This is a revised version of Brun and others (2002). The authors gratefully acknowledge helpful comments from participants at seminars at CERDI and the World Trade Organization and at the Second Research and Training Network Workshop on "Trade, Industrialization, and Development," November 27–28, 2003, in London, as well as comments from three anonymous referees. Jeffrey Bergstrand, Agnès Bénassy-Quéré, Olivier Cadot, Paul Collier, Marcel Fafchamps, Caroline Freund, David Hummels, Jaya Krishnakumar, Maurice Schiff, and Alan Winters gave helpful suggestions on an earlier draft.

THE WORLD BANK ECONOMIC REVIEW, VOL. 19, NO. 1, pp. 99–120 doi:10.1093/wber/lhi004 measures of transport cost barriers to trade,[1] most rely on distance as a proxy for transport costs, obtaining an estimated elasticity of bilateral trade with respect to distance in the range [−1.3; −0.8]. However, as will be detailed, when the model is estimated separately for several years, the absolute value of the coefficient almost always increases over time. This is puzzling, because the common perception of globalization is that distance should be becoming less important in international trade, implying decreasing rather than increasing values for the estimated coefficient of distance.

This paradoxical result was initially investigated by Brun and others (1999) in a traditional gravity model framework. Earlier, Leamer and Levinsohn (1995, pp. 1387–88), reviewing the literature on international trade and distance, noted that "the effect of distance on trade patterns is not diminishing over time. Contrary to popular impression, the world is not getting dramatically smaller." They conclude that "dispersion of economic mass is the answer, not a shrinking globe" for this result. In a recent examination of the paradox Coe and others (2002) review explanations in the literature. One is the exclusion of zero observations from the model, which could bias estimation of the impact of distance over time because of the changing composition of trade. Another is that the traditional gravity model omits what is now being referred to as "multilateral trade resistance." Both explanations are tested here. The paradoxical result remains. A third, obvious explanation is examined here as well: the possibility of misspecification of the transport cost function due to omitted-variable bias.

Each of these potential explanations is examined for a large sample of 130 countries spanning bilateral trade over 35 years. The contribution of this study comes from the combination of more appropriate estimation techniques and a more thorough treatment of transport costs. The article first considers whether the puzzle still holds when estimation is carried out in a random-effects panel procedure with correction for endogeneity (Hausman and Taylor estimator) and for potential selection bias. The puzzle is found to be a robust result in a large sample. Next, a better specified gravity equation is considered. To bring it closer to accepted theoretical foundations, it includes a measure of remoteness in the estimates. Most important, it also defines an "augmented" transport cost function that includes indexes of infrastructure, price of oil, and composition of trade as arguments, all of which turn out to be statistically significant along

1. Some recent studies use direct measures of transport costs in a gravity model. Baier and Bergstrand (2001) use c.i.f.-f.o.b. price ratios over 1970–85 for 16 Organisation for Economic Co-operation and Development countries. Arguing that such comparisons provide limited information (Hummels and Lugovskyy 2003), Hummels (1999, 2001a, b) has studied determinants of freight costs based on more reliable customs data (such as German shipping data over the past 40 years or U.S. customs data at the five-digit SITC level over the period 1974–98). In the same way, Limao and Venables (2001) estimate maritime and land transport costs using 1990 transport cost data for container shipments from Baltimore to 64 destination cities, and Estevadeordal and others (2003) use British maritime transport cost data for a sample of 46 countries over the period 1870–1938.

predicted lines and contribute to the solution of the puzzle. To check for robustness, the sample is split into low-income countries and high-income countries.

To anticipate the main results: Once remoteness is included in the model, the increasing impact of distance on trade vanishes, and with the introduction of an augmented transport cost function into the log-linear specification of the gravity model, the absolute value of the elasticity of bilateral trade with respect to distance decreases significantly over time. Furthermore, when the sample is split into low- and high-income countries, the elasticity of bilateral trade with respect to distance reveals no trend for low-income countries' trade, whereas it falls for bilateral trade between high-income countries, a result in accordance with estimates obtained using more reliable customs data on transport cost (available for only a handful of countries). This result may reflect the fact that low-income countries have been marginalized in the current wave of globalization.

I. Is There a Puzzle?

The puzzle is found in the results for the traditional gravity model using cross-sectional data. This section examines whether the puzzle remains when panel data for a sample of 130 countries for 1962–96 are used. It also addresses issues raised by alternative treatments of missing observations and by potential selection bias. The bulk of the literature that reaches the conclusion that the coefficient for distance increases in absolute value over time is based on the traditional gravity model. Estimated in cross-section, this model is a variant of the following log-linear equation:

$$(1) \quad \ln(T_{ij}) = \alpha_0 + \alpha_1 \ln(Y_i Y_j) + \alpha_2 \ln(N_i N_j) + \beta \ln(D_{ij}) + \alpha_3 DUM_{ij}^k + \varepsilon_{ij},$$

where T_{ij} is the total volume of trade between country i and country j, which depends on the product of partners' income, $Y_i Y_j$, the product of partners' respective populations, $N_i N_j$, the distance between i and j, D_{ij}, and a vector of dummy variables, $DUM^k{}_{ij}$. These dummy variables usually capture a common language, a common land border, a common colonizer, the condition of being landlocked, the existence of a free trade area, and sometimes a common currency.

Typically, equation 1 is estimated in a cross-section setting for different years (with or without importer and exporter fixed effects). The puzzle is revealed in a negative impact of distance ($\beta < 0$) that increases absolutely through time. For example, in a sample of 74 countries for 1965 and 1992, Frankel (1997, table 4.2) obtains $\beta^{65} = -0.48$ and $\beta^{92} = -0.77$. Likewise, Leamer (1993) estimates distance elasticities, which did not fall between 1970 and 1985. As pointed out by Coe and others (2002), several other studies have failed to find a declining coefficient for distance over time, and most have found a significant increase in the absolute value of the estimated coefficient. For instance, estimating equation 1 over a sample of 130 countries for 1962 and 1996 yields: $\beta^{62} = -0.86$ and $\beta^{96} = -1.34$, representing an increase of the impact of distance on bilateral trade of about 36 percent over 35 years.[2]

Setting the theoretical underpinnings of the gravity equation aside until the following section, this puzzling result is put to the scrutiny of typical econometric problems. Estimated in cross-section, equation 1 has several shortcomings. First, because the dummy variables capture only part of the unobservable heterogeneity of country pairs, the remaining unobservable heterogeneity could potentially bias estimates of the coefficient for distance. Second, the typical ordinary least squares estimates may be prone to omitted-variables bias. Third, there is a potential selection bias due to missing values in bilateral trade data.

The use of panel data, with a time dimension in addition to the traditional importer and exporter dimensions, can address the issue of unobservable heterogeneity of country pairs. The usual correction introduces three specific effects: exporter, importer, and time effects (see Matyas 1997; Soloaga and Winters 2001). But the model with three specific effects is only a restricted version of the more general model adopted here, which allows for country-pair heterogeneity (see Cheng and Wall 1999; Egger and Pfaffermayr 2003). These bilateral specific effects are included to capture all unobservable time-invariant characteristics of the bilateral trade relationships that might otherwise be captured by the distance coefficient.

Moreover, because the focus is on the death of distance, panel data with a time dimension allow estimating a time-varying elasticity of trade with respect to distance. Thus, β is allowed to change over time but not across countries (differences across countries are permitted in section III, which splits the sample into groups). Finally, a quadratic term is used to allow for the existence of a turning point:

$$\begin{aligned}\ln(M_{ijt}) &= \alpha_0 + \alpha_1.\ln Y_{it} + \alpha_2.\ln Y_{jt} + \alpha_3.\ln N_{it} + \alpha_4.\ln N_{jt} + \beta_0.t + \beta_1.\ln D_{ij} \\ &\quad + \beta_2.t.\ln D_{ij} + \beta_3.t^2.\ln D_{ij} + \varepsilon_{ijt} = Z_1\psi_1 + \beta_t.\ln D_{ij} + \varepsilon_{ijt},\end{aligned} \tag{2}$$

where t is a time trend, $\varepsilon_{ijt} = \mu_{ij} + v_{ijt}$ with μ_{ij} is a specific bilateral random effect, and v_{ijt} is the idiosyncratic error term with the usual properties.

In this equation, used as a starting point for examining the puzzle, bilateral imports (of i from j) rather than total bilateral trade (M_{ij} instead of T_{ij}) are used as the dependent variable, and a random-effects estimation procedure is used to avoid eliminating the coefficient for distance in the equation (the within-transformation in a bilateral fixed-effects model removes variables that are cross-sectional

2. Appendix C reports the evolution of the distance coefficient (equation C1) when equation 1 is estimated for each year with country fixed effects as in the recent literature (Rose and Van Wincoop 2001; Anderson and van Wincoop 2003; Feenstra 2003).

time-invariant). The cost of moving to a random-effects estimation procedure is that some explanatory variables should be correlated with the bilateral random effects, a potential problem addressed later. An instrumental procedure is used to correct for this potential endogeneity (see appendix B).

The data set covers 130 countries for the years 1962–96, a period that captures most of the current wave of globalization during which transport costs have purportedly fallen. Import trade statistics are taken from the United Nations Commodity Trade Statistics (Comtrade) database.

Although the usual restriction of equal coefficients for origin and destination countries is rejected by the data (especially for the population coefficients), the difference in specification has no effect on the values of the parameters of interest β_1, β_2, and β_3 (table 1, columns 1 and 2).[3] The impact of distance on trade increases over time, because $|\beta_t|\tilde{}\ 1.321 + (0.0052.t) - (0.0001.t^2)$ (table 1, column 2). Thus estimation on panel data including bilateral specific effects does not resolve the puzzle observed in the literature based on cross-section data.

However, endogeneity tests find the gross domestic product (GDP) variables to be endogenous—correlated with the bilateral specific effects (see details in appendix B). It is therefore sensible to take the results corresponding to equation 2 estimated with the instrumental variables estimator proposed by Hausman and Taylor (1981) as typical of the results for a gravity trade model using distance as a proxy for transport costs (table 1, column 3). The overall fit is good (R-squared = 0.61), and all variables have the expected sign and plausible values. As suggested by theory, the elasticity of trade to income is significant and close to unity. The population variables have the expected negative sign, capturing the often observed phenomenon that trade tends to constitute a smaller percentage of GDP for larger countries, as discussed later. The conclusion from this preliminary inquiry is that the puzzle persists, yielding the following estimate of the evolution of the absolute value of the coefficient for distance:

$$|\beta_t|\tilde{}1.268 + (0.0062.t) - (0.0001.t^2).$$

This evolution of $|\beta_t|$ over 1962–96, as estimated in equation 2, is plotted in figure 1. These estimates indicate that a 10 percent increase in distance would reduce bilateral trade by 12.7 percent in 1962 and by 13.8 percent in 1996, or an 8.7 percent increase in the impact of distance over 35 years instead of the expected decrease.

How robust is this result? The first concern is the large number of missing values. The sample has a potential of $130 \times 129 \times 35 = 586{,}950$ observations.

3. Several recent studies use panel data without a time-series dimension but with country fixed effects (for origin countries and destination partners). This estimation procedure forces them to impose identical coefficient values on the income and population variables (Rose and Van Wincoop 2001; Coe and others 2002; Anderson and van Wincoop 2003).

TABLE 1. Distance in a Traditional Panel Gravity Model

Variable	1 GLS	2 GLS	3 HT	4 HT (with zero values)	5 HT (with variables for selection bias)
$\ln Y_{it}$		1.000 (98.76)	0.833 (39.80)	0.764 (43.13)	0.808 (40.77)
$\ln Y_{jt}$		1.159 (115.87)	1.218 (54.81)	1.571 (104.42)	1.057 (46.82)
$\ln(Y_{it}Y_{jt})$	1.080 (141.55)				
$\ln N_{it}$		−0.076 (5.95)	−0.049 (2.44)	−0.057 (4.90)	−0.022 (1.15)
$\ln N_{jt}$		−0.164 (12.90)	−0.251 (12.51)	−0.554 (40.85)	−0.175 (8.81)
$\ln(N_{it}N_{jt})$	−0.121 (13.30)				
$\ln D_{ij}$	−1.320 (51.90)	−1.321 (52.17)	−1.268 (70.93)	−1.309 (76.40)	−1.203 (69.48)
t	−0.027 (6.11)	−0.027 (6.01)	−0.030 (5.14)	−0.044 (8.32)	−0.011 (1.91)
$t.\ln D_{ij}$	−0.0052 (9.52)	−0.0052 (9.63)	−0.0062 (9.10)	−0.0043 (6.59)	−0.0064 (9.49)
$t^2.\ln D_{ij}$	0.00010 (22.04)	0.00010 (22.06)	0.00009 (14.76)	0.00009 (16.04)	0.00010 (16.95)
No. observations	171,998	171,998	171,998	216,511	171,998
R-squared	0.58	0.59	0.61	0.59	0.64
Hausman test	401.62 $\chi^2(5)$	619.85$\chi^2(7)$			
GLS vs. HT			9666.27 $\chi^2(8)$	13,727.05$\chi^2(8)$	2418.34$\chi^2(8)$

Source: Authors' computations based on data described in appendix A.

Note: Numbers in parentheses are *t*-statistics. GLS is generalized least squares estimator and HT is Hausman and Taylor (1981) estimator.

FIGURE 1. The Elasticity of Bilateral Trade to Distance $|\beta_t|$

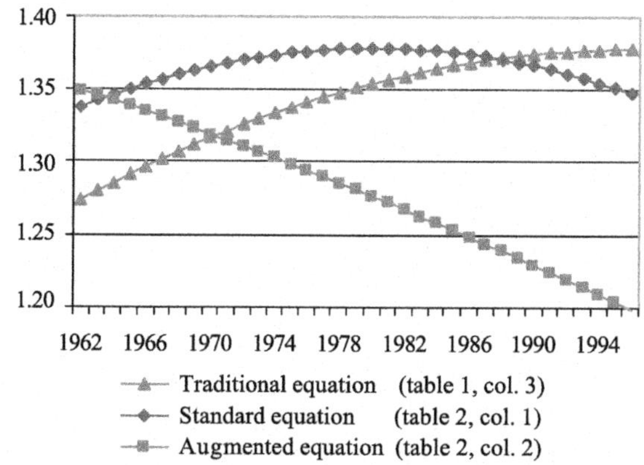

Source: Authors' computations based on data described in appendix A.

Missing values are reported for 71 percent of the potential observations, resulting in 171,998 observations. The database does not distinguish between countries that do not report their trade statistics (missing values) and country pairs with no bilateral trade (zero trade). Some country pairs report missing values at the beginning of the sample period and positive trade at the end. For them, the missing values can be suspected of being zeroes (perhaps because transport costs are too high at the beginning of the sample period). Excluding these zeroes would bias the results. The missing values are assumed to equal zero if they occur before 1975, provided that positive trade is observed thereafter. As in Frankel (1997, p. 145), zeroes are replaced by $M_{ijt} = 1$. The total number of observations rises by 26 percent. Results under this specification do not change the increasing impact of distance on trade (see table 1, column 4).

The missing values are a source of potential selection bias. Following Nijman and Verbeek (1992), three additional explanatory variables are introduced into equation 2 to correct for the selection bias (see table 1, column 5).[4] Even if two of these proxies are significant, the estimates for β_1, β_2, and β_3 remain similar.

Estimates of the evolution of β_t could also be biased because some series may contain a unit root, in which case the estimates in table 1 would be spurious if the relations were not cointegrated. So, a Levin and Lin (1993) unit root test

4. The following variables are added in the equation (coefficient; *t* Student): the number of years of presence of the couple *ij* in the sample (0.04; 31.98); a dummy variable that takes the value 1 if *ij* is observed during the entire period (0.016; 0.74); and a dummy variable that takes the value 1 if *ij* is present in $t-1$ (0.54; 35.02). Together, these variables have been shown in Monte Carlo experiments by Nijman and Verbeek (1992) to be good proxies for the Heckman correction term for selection bias.

was applied to the series for GDP, population, and bilateral imports. This test rejects, very significantly, the null hypothesis of a unit root for all series.

Finally, to check that the increasing impact of distance on trade does not capture tendencies in other coefficients, two sets of regressions were estimated: year-by-year regressions with country fixed effects and regressions over three-year subperiods with bilateral effects and the Hausman and Taylor (1981) estimator. The estimated coefficients from 1962 to 1996, plotted in appendix figure C1, show that the increasing impact of distance over time is unaffected.

From these robustness checks it can be concluded that the estimated value of $|\beta_t|$ increases over time in the traditional gravity model. The puzzle remains.

II. Explaining the Puzzle

The puzzle could be the result of a misspecification of the traditional gravity equation. A more solid theoretical foundation for the gravity equation is found in the currently popular application of the gravity model to aggregate trade between economies assumed to be specialized in differentiated products. As shown by Deardoff (1998) and Anderson and Van Wincoop (2003, 2004), utility maximization of an identical constant elasticity of substitution (CES) utility function (over countries) yields the following expression for the cost, insurance, and freight (c.i.f.) value of bilateral imports,

$$M_{ijt} = (Y_{it}Y_{jt}/Y_w)(\theta_{ijt}/\tilde{P}_{it}\tilde{P}_{jt})^{1-\sigma}, \quad (3)$$

where Y_w is world income, θ_{ijt} is bilateral transport costs, σ is the elasticity of substitution in the CES utility function, and $\tilde{P}_{it}$, $\tilde{P}_{jt}$ can be interpreted as multilateral trade resistance indexes whose values are given by:

$$\tilde{P}_{it}^{1-\sigma} = \Sigma_j(Y_{\text{it}}/Y_w)(\theta_{ijt}/\tilde{P}_{jt})^{1-\sigma}. \quad (4)$$

Estimation of the system of equations 3 and 4 raises issues related to estimation of the multilateral trade resistance index and estimation of transport costs. For the trade resistance index, suppose, as in the literature, that estimation proceeds on a cross-section basis. In that case either data for the price indexes are available (as in Baier and Bergstrand 2001), or $\tilde{P}_i$ and $\tilde{P}_j$ can be estimated directly (from the structural model with nonlinear least squares), following Anderson and Van Wincoop (2003). Alternatively, as explained by Anderson and Van Wincoop (2003) and Feenstra (2003), country-specific effects can be used to capture the variation in $\tilde{P}_i$ and $\tilde{P}_j$.[5]

Thus, a first method of estimating the gravity equation uses panel data techniques relying on a cross-section specification with a fixed-effects estimator

5. See the discussion by Anderson and Van Wincoop (2004, p. 712) on the three ways to estimate the theoretical gravity model on a cross-section basis.

that includes importer and exporter dummy variables (Rose and Van Wincoop 2001; Coe and others 2002; Anderson and Van Wincoop 2003). However, the preferred approach, used here, relies on a random-effects estimator, with the two dimensions being country-pair and time-specific effects. Of these two panel techniques the country fixed-effects estimator offers more variability on the distance coefficient because it is estimated year by year. But the risk with this method is that the distance coefficient will capture all unobserved bilateral characteristics that cannot be included in the specification (other than the usual dummy variables for common language, common border, and so on). The country-pair random effects estimator with a time dimension controls for all the unobserved bilateral specific effects, but at the cost of imposing a trend specification for the evolution of distance. After weighing the tradeoffs, the country-pair random-effects estimator is selected (but for illustrative purpose, appendix C reports the results for year-by year estimations with country fixed effects). The choice of this method requires replacing the multilateral trade resistance indexes with a remoteness measure.[6] This implies substituting values of R_{it} and R_{jt} for $\tilde{P}_{it}$ and $\tilde{P}_{jt}$ in equation 3.

Estimation of bilateral transport costs, θ_{ijt}, starts with the standard transport cost function in which distance reflects marginal transport costs. (Later, an augmented version is proposed.) In the standard implementation, used by Hummels (2001a) and Anderson and Van Wincoop (2003) among others, transport costs include distance (D_{ij}) and a vector of dummy variables for common border (B_{ij}) and being landlocked ($L_{i(j)}$). Assuming the standard multiplicative form yields:

$$(5) \qquad \theta_{ijt} = (D_{ij})^{\gamma_t} e^{\delta_1 . B_{ij} + \delta_2 L_i + \delta_3 L_j}$$

with expected signs $\delta_1 < 0$, $\delta_2 > 0$, and $\delta_3 > 0$. Once more, because bilateral specific effects capture the time-invariant characteristics of bilateral trade, equation 5 is estimated without including the dummy variables. The elasticity of transport costs to distance, γ_t, is assumed to be approximated by a quadratic time trend (t):

$$(6) \qquad \gamma_t \equiv ([\partial\theta_{ijt}/\theta_{ijt}]/[\partial D_{ij}/D_{ij}]) = \gamma_1 + \gamma_2 .t + \gamma_3 .t^2.$$

6. As explained, the literature on estimating the theoretical gravity model, notably using multilateral trade resistance indexes, is based on cross-section data. With a time dimension added in the estimation, none of the three suggestions is applicable: Price indexes are not available; the structural estimation method proposed by Anderson and Van Wincoop (2003) is not suitable for three dimensions (importer, exporter, and time); and country dummy variables no longer capture the multilateral resistance indexes, which change over time. Hence, the multilateral trade resistance indexes are replaced by a remoteness measure (as in Soloaga and Winters 2001) even if, as Anderson and Van Wincoop (2003) show, the functional form of the remoteness variable is not in conformity with the theory and can introduce a bias. However, it is comforting that the year by year estimations with country fixed effects—without bias due to the remoteness variables—reported in appendix C yield similar results.

Finally, in estimating a gravity model using panel data with a long time dimension (35 years in this case), it is essential to capture the effects of changes in relative prices, because a normalization of prices to unity can no longer be justified. For a large sample of countries for which representative price indexes are not available, real exchange rate indexes have to be used. As in Soloaga and Winters (2001) and Bayoumi and Eichengreen (1997), among others, the bilateral real exchange rate between i and j, RER_{ijt} is introduced into the equation. Also, RER_{ijt} may be interpreted as a proxy for unobservable movement of multilateral resistance indexes through time.[7]

Under these working assumptions, estimation of the standard trade barrier function in the gravity model boils down to plugging equation 5 into a modified version of equation 3 that also includes population to proxy Engel effects and, on the supply side, differences in factor endowments (Bergstrand 1989; Frankel 1997; Soloaga and Winters 2001; Coe and others 2002).[8] This yields an equation similar to equation 2, except for the inclusion of "remoteness" that takes into account relative transport costs, and the real exchange rate that takes into account the effects of the evolution in relative prices. This results in:

$$(7)\quad \begin{aligned} \ln(M_{ijt}) &= Z_1\psi_1 + \beta_t.\ln D_{ij} + \alpha_5.\ln R_{it} + \alpha_6.\ln R_{jt} + \alpha_7.\ln RER_{ijt} + \varepsilon_{ijt} \\ &= Z_1\psi_1 + Z_2\psi_2 + \beta_t.\ln D_{ij} + \varepsilon_{ijt} \end{aligned}$$

with $\alpha_5 > 0$, $\alpha_6 > 0$, $\alpha_7 < 0$, and according to equations 3 and 5, $\beta_t = (1-\sigma)\gamma_t > 0$. Estimation results for equation 7 are reported in table 2, column 1, and should be compared with those in table 1, column 3.

Broadly speaking, coefficient estimates for GDP and population have values similar to those in table 1, while the coefficient for distance continues to be estimated at around -1.3. The coefficient for the real exchange rate (RER_{ijt}) has the expected negative sign: An increase of the real effective exchange rate that reflects a depreciation of the importing country's currency against that of the exporting country reduces i's imports from j. Likewise, the remoteness variable is positive and significant: The more remote a pair of countries is from the rest of the world, the more they will tend to trade with each other. Notably, the introduction of bilateral real exchange rates and relative transport costs almost eliminates the trend for β_t, with an estimated turning point in 1981 (see figure 1). Finally, a 10 percent increase in distance would reduce bilateral

7. We thank an anonymous referee for this observation.

8. As Bergstrand (1989) points out, a negative coefficient estimate for exporter population, N_j, can be interpreted as a positive relationship between per capita income and trade (because capital-abundant countries tend to produce and export more). A negative coefficient estimate for importer population, N_i, may reflect tastes (however, this coefficient is generally not significantly different from zero, indicating an income elasticity of demand of approximately unity). Note that Coe and others (2002) introduce the population variables as a measure of geography: For larger countries, the cost of trading among themselves rather than with other countries is relatively low compared with the cost for smaller countries. This implies that large countries will tend to trade less than small countries.

TABLE 2. Distance in Standard and Augmented Panel Gravity Models

Variable	Standard 1 All	Augmented 2 All	Standard 3 P-P	Augmented 4 P-P	Standard 5 R-R	Augmented 6 R-R	Standard 7 P-R	Augmented 8 P-R
$\ln Y_{it}$	0.906 (44.74)	1.039 (71.33)	0.951 (27.27)	1.196 (43.65)	0.831 (17.76)	0.788 (22.53)	0.852 (14.60)	0.913 (21.21)
$\ln Y_{jt}$	1.164 (57.87)	1.103 (86.34)	1.352 (31.72)	1.299 (38.39)	1.005 (23.39)	0.982 (28.44)	1.303 (24.55)	1.236 (35.78)
$\ln N_{it}$	−0.015 (0.80)	−0.072 (5.63)	0.007 (0.18)	−0.288 (8.95)	−0.020 (0.54)	−0.176 (5.76)	−0.191 (3.83)	−0.272 (7.47)
$\ln N_{jt}$	−0.200 (11.04)	−0.184 (15.34)	−0.350 (8.00)	−0.249 (9.15)	−0.179 (4.38)	−0.323 (10.27)	−0.298 (5.49)	−0.292 (8.59)
$\ln D_{ij}$	−1.333 (70.46)	−1.353 (74.37)	−1.019 (39.37)	−1.059 (41.10)	−0.715 (25.62)	−0.716 (24.83)	−0.993 (38.29)	−0.978 (40.36)
$\ln R_{it}$	0.368 (10.74)	0.525 (15.45)	0.419 (6.73)	0.692 (12.21)	0.127 (1.63)	0.085 (1.05)	0.136 (1.99)	0.061 (0.86)
$\ln R_{jt}$	1.909 (59.98)	2.214 (65.72)	1.647 (29.72)	1.877 (33.39)	0.165 (2.83)	0.169 (2.74)	1.658 (34.47)	1.867 (37.30)
$\ln RER_{ijt}$	−0.0005 (6.44)	−0.0005 (6.02)	−0.0007 (5.39)	−0.0007 (5.20)	−0.0003 (2.00)	−0.0003 (2.39)	−0.0008 (4.58)	−0.0007 (7.77)
t	−0.028 (4.76)	−0.063 (10.83)	−0.009 (1.28)	−0.038 (5.28)	−0.028 (2.64)	−0.029 (2.60)	−0.028 (3.22)	−0.0666 (4.40)
$t.\ln D_{ij}$	−0.0047 (6.80)	0.0034 (4.11)	−0.0072 (8.52)	−0.0042 (4.56)	0.0009 (1.05)	0.0048 (3.33)	−0.0069 (1.05)	−0.0053 (2.06)
$t^2.\ln D_{ij}$	0.00012 (20.84)	0.00003 (2.46)	0.00008 (10.07)	0.0001 (8.90)	−0.00005 (3.79)	−0.00005 (3.26)	0.00007 (6.44)	0.00014 (6.44)
$\ln K_{it}$		0.088 (6.24)		0.194 (12.13)		0.0727 (3.78)		0.0552 (1.96)
$\ln K_{jt}$		0.184 (12.18)		0.147 (8.35)		0.115 (5.02)		0.159 (7.51)
$\ln P_{Ft}$		−0.097 (6.70)		−0.007 (0.35)		−0.408 (19.70)		−0.523 (20.77)
$\ln \pi_{jt}$		−0.216 (21.48)		−0.184 (12.60)		0.027 (1.34)		−0.153 (11.72)
No. observations	171,998	171,998	57,332	57,332	57,332	57,332	57,332	57,332
R-squared	0.64	0.64	0.56	0.58	0.62	0.64	0.56	0.59
GLS vs. HT	33,548 $\chi^2(11)$	15,410$\chi^2(15)$	900 $\chi^2(11)$	628$\chi^2(15)$	458 $\chi^2(11)$	716 $\chi^2(15)$	804$\chi^2(11)$	876$\chi^2(15)$

Source: Authors' computations based on data described in appendix A.

Note: Numbers in parentheses are t-statistics. GLS is generalized least squares estimator and HT is Hausman and Taylor (1981) estimator. P-P is bilateral trade between the poorest tercile of countries, and R-R is bilateral trade between the richest tercile.

trade by 13.4 percent in 1962 and by 13.5 percent in 1996, which is not significantly different.

However, the expected decreasing trend fails to be observed over the 35-year period. The puzzle remains. Except for explanations pertaining to the specification of the transport cost function, all possible explanations for the existence of the puzzle that have been raised in the literature have now been exhausted.[9]

Several new factors are added to the standard specification of the transportation cost function (equation 5). First, as in Limao and Venables (2001), an index is introduced for the quality of infrastructure in period t, $K_{i(j)t}$, with larger values indicating better infrastructure.[10] Also included is the cost of oil, P_{Ft}, arguably the main factor affecting the marginal cost of transport. Finally, differential freight costs between primary products and manufactures are considered by including the share of primary products in total exports, π_{ijt}, as a proxy.[11] Because of data unavailability, π_{ijt} is proxied by π_{jt}, the share of primary export products in total exports for country j regardless of destination. Thus, the augmented transport cost function becomes:[12]

$$(8) \qquad \theta_{ijt} = (K_{it})^{\rho_1}(K_{jt})^{\rho_2}(P_{Ft})^{\rho_3}(\pi_{jt})^{\rho_4}(D_{ij})^{\gamma_1+\gamma_2.t+\gamma_3.t^2}$$

with the elasticity of transport costs to distance given by equation 6, and with the following expected signs: $\rho_1 < 0$, $\rho_2 < 0$, $\rho_3 > 0$, $\rho_4 > 0$. Inserting equation 8 into equation 7 gives the augmented gravity model:

$$(9) \qquad \ln(M_{ijt}) = Z_1\psi_1 + Z_2\psi_2 + \beta_t.\ln D_{ij} + \alpha_8.\ln K_{it} + \alpha_9.\ln K_{jt} + \alpha_{10}.\ln P_{Ft} + \alpha_{11}.\ln \pi_{jt} + \varepsilon_{ijt}$$

The expected signs in equation 9 are $\alpha_8 = (1-\sigma)\rho_1 > 0$, $\alpha_9 = (1-\sigma)\rho_2 > 0$, $\alpha_{10} = (1-\sigma)\rho_3 < 0$, $\alpha_{11} = (1-\sigma)\rho_4 < 0$. In comparing results from the augmented

9. Also addressing the distance puzzle, Coe and others (2002) estimate a nonlinear cross-section gravity model in which they consider the possibility that the error term enters additively in equation 3 instead of as a multiplicative exponential, as implicitly assumed here. They find that when estimated nonlinearly, the coefficient for the distance variable shows a decline between 1975 and 2000, whereas it presents no clear trend when estimated with the standard log-linear specification (as in equation 7). Coe and others recognize, however, that theoretical models are nonstochastic and that they have not formally tested the appropriateness of an additive rather than a multiplicative error structure, which limits the inferences that can be draw from their comparison of the two estimation procedures.

10. The index constructed by Limao and Venables (2001) from data in Canning (1996) is used. The index is a simple average of four indexes (roads, paved roads, telephone lines, and railways) corrected for density. Appendix A describes how this index was constructed.

11. Including the mode of transport would also be desirable, but that information is not available for such a large sample.

12. The elements in this function capture several barriers to trade beyond transport cost. The phrases *trade barrier*, *transactions costs*, and *transportation costs* are used interchangeably to remind readers that this reduced form goes beyond capturing transport costs. For a similar interpretation of the values taken by the distance coefficients in the standard gravity model, see Rauch (1999).

specification with those from the standard specification, it should be noted that the standard specification excludes the four variables in the second line of equation 9.

The coefficient estimates for the augmented transport cost function in column 2 of table 2 are relatively close in value to those obtained in column 1, even though the estimated values for the remoteness variables are now larger. All the variables included in the augmented transport cost function carry the expected signs and are significant. The coefficient for the price of oil is negative and significant. Likewise, infrastructure improvement significantly increases the volume of trade (see Limao and Venables 2001). Finally, the share of primary products in total exports of *j* has a significant negative impact on trade, capturing the stylized fact that freight costs are greater for primary products than for manufactures (Hummels 2001a).

Thus, with the augmented trade barrier function, the puzzle disappears. The expected decreasing trend for β_t is shown in figure 1. According to the estimates in table 2, column 2, a 10 percent increase in distance would reduce bilateral trade by 13.5 percent in 1962 and by 12.0 percent in 1996—a decrease in the impact of distance of about 11.1 percent over 35 years.

Each of the transport cost function components is also introduced separately in the standard gravity equation to see how much each contributes to solving the puzzle. Oil prices solve much of the puzzle, explaining around 45 percent of the change in the elasticity of bilateral trade to distance. Infrastructure variables are also significant, explaining about 40 percent of the puzzle. Trade composition explains about 15 percent.

Next, the results are tested for sensitivity to the standard misspecification problems of endogeneity, sample selection bias, and nonvarying coefficients. To check for sensitivity to potential endogeneity for the infrastructure, remoteness, distance, and population variables, the variables (in addition of those for GDP) are instrumented according to the Hausman and Taylor (1981) method. There is no effect on the evolution of the elasticity of bilateral trade to distance. The results are unaffected when the other coefficients are allowed to change over subperiods of three years (see appendix C, equation C4). The declining trend in the distance coefficient remains unaffected when the three variables used earlier to correct for a potential selection bias are introduced.

Finally, the dummy variables for regional agreements added in equation 9 have no effect on the estimated values for β_t (even if most of regional agreements considered have a positive and significant direct impact on bilateral trade).[13]

The conclusion is thus that correction of some of the obvious misspecifications in the gravity equation that relies on distance as a proxy for transport or

13. Trade agreements taken into account are the European Union, Mercosur, Association of Southeast Asian Nations, Andean Community, West African Economic and Monetary Union, Central African Economic and Monetary Community, Economic Community of West African States, Southern African Development Community, and Common Market for Eastern and Southern Africa.

trade barriers yields plausible results for the coefficients and also yields a plausible reduction in the barrier to trade represented by distance.

III. Robustness

The gravity model is known to be sensitive to sample and product selection. Evenett and Keller (2002) find that it performs better than the Hecksher-Ohlin model in explaining trade patterns for manufactures, which are largely differentiated products. It has also been found repeatedly that the standard gravity model derived under the hypothesis of complete specialization in different products performs better for industrial countries than for developing economies (see Feenstra 2003, chap. 5). The suitability of the aggregate gravity model as a description of trade patterns and an approximation of barriers to trade in a heterogeneous sample of countries deserves to be explored further.

The sample is broken down into three groups of equal size with selection according to the income per capita of each bilateral trade partner so that P-P is bilateral trade between the poorest tercile of countries in each time period and R-R between the richest tercile.[14]

With the standard specification the overall fit is approximately the same for both groups, though coefficient values for the distance and remoteness variables are much larger for P-P bilateral trade than for R-R bilateral trade (table 2, columns 3 and 5). In the standard specification the puzzle remains for both groups, although more pronounced for the P-P group.

Results from the augmented specification for the P-P and R-R groups (columns 4 and 6 of table 2) reveal larger discrepancies across coefficients than those for the standard specification (columns 3 and 5), but larger values are again found for the coefficients for distance and remoteness for the P-P group. The coefficients for infrastructure are significant in both groups but are larger for the P-P group. The price of oil is significant only for R-R trade, whereas the share of primary commodities in trade is significant only for P-P trade.[15] Thus the results from the augmented gravity model suggest the death of distance for trade between high-income countries and marginalization for low-income countries.

14. As noted by an anonymous referee, this means that the sample is likely to change depending on relative income growth and then to be endogenous to trade. However, over the whole period the maximum changes noted in the P-P group of 45 countries are the entry of 4 countries and the exit of 2. For the R-R group of 39 countries, 2 countries entered and 1 exited. These changes represent only 4.7 percent of the P-P sample observations (2740/57,332) and 3 percent of the R-R sample observations (1730/57,332).

15. Again, the introduction of variables checking for selection bias does not affect the evolution of β_t. However, the coefficient values for these variables are larger for the P-P regressions, which would be consistent with some remaining specification problems.

The results for the R-R group accord with those obtained by Hummels (2001a) for freight rate estimates for U.S. imports at the commodity level for 1974–98. Estimating freight rate costs as a function of weight, distance, commodity fixed effects, and a time trend (and a time trend squared), Hummels finds that the distance coefficient falls over time, but only after containers are introduced (in 1980). Of course, this is only very indirect evidence that an augmented trade barrier function in a gravity equation may capture some of the determinants of transport costs isolated in a more reliable data set, but it is reassuring, nonetheless.

The apparent marginalization of low-income countries is confirmed in another breakdown reporting exports from the poorest tercile of countries to the richest tercile of countries (P-R) (see table 2, columns 7 and 8). As expected, coefficients for exporters are close to the corresponding values in the P-P group and coefficients for importers are close to the corresponding values in the R-R group. The distance trend exhibits an evolution similar to that in the P-P group. In sum, the marginalization of poor countries with respect to trading partners still holds.

That said, the results, especially those for the P-P group, must be interpreted with caution. First, the diverging evolution of β_t between the standard gravity model (see table 2, columns 3 and 5) and the augmented model (columns 4 and 6) in the two samples can be explained by the rate of improvement of the infrastructure index, which is twice as large for the high-income portion of the sample as for the low-income portion. The impact of infrastructure is, in principle, controlled for through the index $K_{i(j)t}$. But at least two variables that have a bearing on the impact of distance are correlated with $K_{i(j)t}$ but are not included in the model. One is time in transit, which is higher for P-P bilateral trade.[16] Another is mode of transport, which has changed more for the R-R group. Hence, when $K_{i(j)t}$ is included, $|\beta_t|$ decreases significantly for R-R while remaining unaffected in the P-P sample.

Second, explaining the puzzle for the P-P group probably requires a reconsideration of the specification of the augmented equation. One candidate is bilateral foreign direct investment, which has increased more rapidly for the R-R group and could be correlated with any of the factors independent of distance included in the model. Exchange rate volatility and various omitted trade costs could also be involved. Rose and Van Wincoop (2001) use a gravity model framework to argue that countries with currency unions trade more than three times as much with each other as with other countries. Likewise, Obstfeld and Rogoff (2001, p. 9) find that currency conversion costs and exchange rate uncertainty can boost trade costs. The same applies for informational costs associated with international trade, such as search costs (Rauch 1999), for corruption and imperfect contract enforcement (Anderson and Marcouiller

16. Using shipments of manufactures to the United States, Hummels (2001b) estimates the cost of an extra day in transit at 0.5 percent of the value shipped. At equal distance time in transit is higher for P-P bilateral trade, in part because ships travel routes less frequently.

2002), or for technological changes in transport during the period under analysis (such as containerization, which raises the quality of shipping and lags behind in poorer countries; see Hummels 2001a). Finally, the changing composition of trade over time should be investigated beyond the rough decomposition into primary and manufactured products used here.[17]

A final issue is the realism of the standard multiplicative form assumed for "trade frictions" in all gravity models, including this one. In equation 6 the elasticity of transport costs to distance depends only on time. Suppose instead that transport costs have two components, one that is fixed with respect to distance (such as the quality of infrastructure) and one that is variable (such as the price of oil). It can easily be shown that the elasticity of transport costs to distance could increase if the fixed cost component were falling sufficiently faster than the variable cost component (appendix D). As detailed in appendix D, efforts to estimate the resulting highly nonlinear model in the transport cost variables were unsuccessful, preventing exploration of alternatives to the standard multiplicative form for the transport cost function. However, Limao and Venables (2001) conclude that the multiplicative form of their transport cost function fit their data better than did the additive form.

IV. Conclusion

Several variants of a panel gravity model were used to address the distance puzzle for a sample of 130 countries over the period 1962–96. The puzzle proved robust to several ad hoc versions of the gravity model, but it was significantly reduced when the gravity model was correctly specified to include remoteness (or an index of multilateral trade resistance). Adding an augmented trade barrier function (real price of oil, index of infrastructure, and share of primary exports in total bilateral trade) that corrects for the misspecification inherent in the standard representation of transport costs by distance yielded plausible estimates of the expected death of distance.

Despite the many shortcomings associated with gravity-based indirect estimates of transport costs, several intuitively plausible results emerge from the model estimations: an elasticity of trade to income close to unity (as suggested by theory), a significant impact of the real exchange rate on the volume of bilateral trade, and expected significant signs for exporter and importer country characteristics and for the impact of remoteness on the volume of trade.

The model produces an estimate of the elasticity of trade with respect to distance that is very close to direct estimates obtained from transport cost data, and the results are consistent with those obtained using more reliable data on U.S. transport costs. The model with the augmented trade barrier function

17. Actually, changing the composition of trade toward more distance-sensitive goods can be expected to increase the elasticity of trade to distance. However, Berthelon and Freund (2004) find no support for this argument.

yields a plausible estimate of an 11 percent decrease in the impact of distance on bilateral trade over the 35-year period.

Splitting the sample into three equal-size groups by income per capita revealed significant differences in bilateral trade coefficient estimates for low-income bilateral trade and high-income bilateral trade. The coefficients capturing barriers to trade, including distance, have much higher values for the low-income group (P-P). The puzzle remains for low-income bilateral trade in the standard and the augmented models, while it remains for high-income bilateral trade only in the standard model. Even though problems of interpretation persist, the results from this sample-splitting procedure are consistent with recent claims that poor countries have been marginalized by the current wave of globalization while rich countries have benefited from a death of distance.

Appendix A. Data Sources and Data Preparation

- M_{ijt}: Total bilateral imports, in current U.S. dollars, by country *i* from country *j* at date *t*. UN Comtrade. The original database does not contain any zero entries.
- $Y_{i(j)t}$: GDP of country *i* (*j*) at date *t*, in constant 1995 U.S. dollars. World Bank (1999).
- $N_{i(j)t}$: Total population of country *i* (*j*) at date *t*. World Bank (1999).
- D_{ij}: Distance in kilometres between the main city in country *i* and the main city in country *j*. Database developed by CVN. Usually, the main city is the capital city, but for some countries the main economic city is considered. The distance used is orthodromic—it takes into account the sphericity of the Earth.
- B_{ij}: Dummy variable equals 1 if *i* and *j* share a common land border, and 0 otherwise.
- $L_{i(j)}$: Dummy variable equals 1 if *i* (*j*) is a landlocked country, and 0 otherwise.
- $K_{i(j)t}$: Infrastructure index, built using four variables from the database constructed by Canning (1996): number of kilometers of roads, paved roads, railways, and number of telephone sets or lines per capita. The first three variables are ratios to the surface area (World Bank 1999) to obtain a density. Each variable is normalized with a mean equal to one. An arithmetic average is then calculated over the four variables. Data for 1996 are extrapolated because 1995 is the final year for the database.
- P_{Ft}: World oil price index. International Monetary Fund (IMF) International Financial Statistics database.
- π_{jt}: Ratio of primary export products to total exports of the country *j* at date *t*. UN Comtrade.
- RER_{ijt}: Bilateral real exchange rate. IMF International Financial Statistics database. It is computed as follows:

$$RER_{ijt} = (CPI_{jt})/(CPI_{it}).(NER_{it/\$t}/NER_{jt/\$t}),$$

where $NER_{i(j)t/\$t}$ is country *i*'s (*j*'s) currency value for US\$1 at date *t* and $CPI_{i(j)t}$ is the consumption price index for country *i* (*j*) at date *t*. If the CPI is not available, the GDP deflator is used. For each pair of countries, the real exchange rate is specified such that its mean over the period is zero.

- $R_{i(j)t}$: Remoteness index defined as the weighted distance to all trading partners of country *i*:

$$R_{it} = \Sigma_j w_{jt} D_{ij} \text{ for } i \neq j \text{ and with } w_{jt} = Y_{jt}/\Sigma_j Y_{jt}.$$

Appendix B. Estimation Method

Write the model as:

$$\text{(B1)} \qquad M_{ijt} = X_{ijt}\varphi + W_{ij}\delta + \varepsilon_{ijt} \text{ with } \varepsilon_{ijt} = \mu_{ij} + \nu_{ijt},$$

where X represents k variables varying over time, and W represents g variables that are time invariant.

Some explanatory variables, such as GDP, are likely to be correlated with the bilateral specific effects, which is confirmed by the χ^2 value for the Hausman test in column 2 of table 1. This test rejects the null hypothesis of no correlation between the bilateral specific effects and the explanatory variables. Hence the generalized least squares (GLS) estimator in columns 1 and 2 of table 1 gives inconsistent estimates. The instrumental variables estimator proposed by Hausman and Taylor (1981) is used to deal with this issue.

Assume that the X_1 terms (dimension k_1) are exogenous variables, and the X_2 terms (dimension $k - k_1$) are endogenous variables (correlated with the random specific effects). Variable X_2 includes the income variables, Y_{it} and Y_{jt}. Breusch and others (1989) suggest using $[QX_1, QX_2, PX_1, W]$ as instruments, which are then taken within the model. (Here Q is a matrix that expresses deviations from country-pair means, and P is a matrix that averages the observations across time for each country pair.) The resulting estimator is consistent but not efficient because it is not corrected for heteroscedasticity and serial correlation. Following the suggestion of Hausman and Taylor (1981), first-round estimates are used to compute the variance of the specific effects, μ_{ij}, and the variance of the error term, ν_{ijt} (see, for example, Guillotin and Sevestre 1994). The instrumental variable estimator is then applied to the following transformed equation:

$$\text{(B2)} \qquad [M_{ijt} - (1-\theta)M_{ij.}] = [X_{ijt} - (1-\theta)X_{ij.}]\varphi + (\theta W_{ij})\delta + \{\theta\mu_{ij} + [\nu_{ijt} - (1-\theta)\nu_{ij.}]\},$$

where

$$\theta = (\sigma^2{}_{\nu}/[T\sigma^2_{\mu} + \sigma^2{}_{\nu})^{1/2}$$

The test proposed by Guillotin and Sevestre (1994) is used to compare the Hausman and Taylor (HT) estimator, β_{HT}, and the GLS estimator, β_{GLS}. The Hausman statistic is based on:

$$\text{(B3)} \qquad (\beta_{GLS} - \beta_{HT})[\text{var}(\beta_{HT}) - \text{var}(\beta_{GLS})]^{-1}(\beta_{GLS} - \beta_{HT})'.$$

Under the null hypothesis, this test statistic is distributed as a χ^2 with degrees of freedom equal to the dimension of the vector β_{GLS} $(k+g)$, constant excluded. If the calculated statistic is greater than the critical value, the null hypothesis is rejected and the Hausman and Taylor estimator is preferred to the GLS estimator. The values of the χ^2 statistic for that test in table 1 turn out to be always superior to the critical value, so that the null hypothesis is rejected and the Hausman and Taylor estimator in column 3 of table 1 is preferred to the GLS estimator when GDP variables are instrumented.

Appendix C. Evolution of |β| by Subperiod

$$\text{(C1)} \qquad \begin{aligned} \ln(M_{ij}) &= \alpha_1 + \lambda_i + \kappa_j + \alpha_1.\ln(Y_iY_j) + \alpha_2.\ln(N_iN_j) \\ &\quad + \beta\ln(D_{ij}) + \alpha_3.B_{ij} + \nu_{ij} \end{aligned}$$

with $B_{ij} = 1$ if i and j share a common land border. Estimated for each year with country fixed effects (corresponding to equation 1).

$$\text{(C2)} \qquad \ln(M_{ijt}) = Z_1\psi_1 + \beta.\ln(D_{ij}) + \mu_{ij} + \nu_{ijt}$$

Estimated by subperiods of three years with bilateral random effects (corresponding to equation 2).

$$\text{(C3)} \qquad \ln(M_{ijt}) = Z_1\psi_1 + Z_2\psi_2 + \beta.\ln(D_{ij}) + \mu_{ij} + \varepsilon_{ijt}$$

Estimated by subperiods of three years with bilateral random effects (corresponding to equation 7).

$$\text{(C4)} \qquad \begin{aligned} \ln(M_{ijt}) &= Z_1\psi_1 + Z_2\psi_2 + \beta.\ln(D_{ij}) + \alpha_8.\ln(K_{it}) \\ &\quad + \alpha_9.\ln(K_{jt}) + \alpha_{10}.\ln(P_{Ft}) + \alpha_{11}.\ln(\pi_{jt}) + \mu_{ij} + \nu_{ijt} \end{aligned}$$

Estimated by subperiods of three years with bilateral random effects (corresponding to equation 9).

FIGURE C1. Evolution of the Coefficient of Distance $|\beta|$ by Subperiod

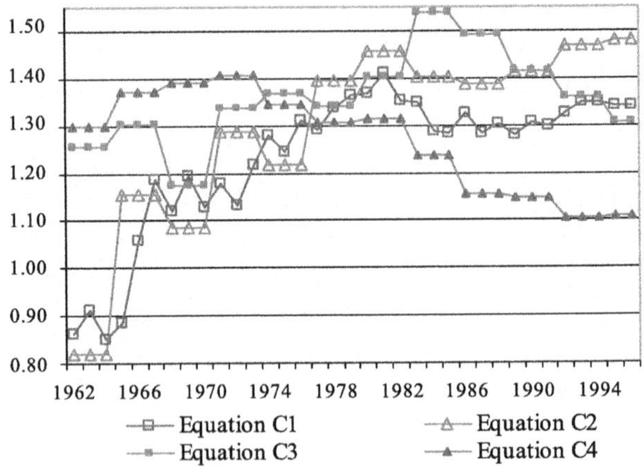

Source: Authors' computations based on data described in appendix A.

APPENDIX D. ADDITIVE TRANSPORT COST FUNCTION

Under the standard multiplicative form used in the article, the elasticity of trade costs to distance depends only on time (equation 6). Suppose now that transport costs have two components, one that is fixed with respect to distance, $\theta^F{}_{ijt}$, and one that is variable, $\theta^V{}_{ijt}$, that is, $\theta_{ijt} = \theta^F{}_{ijt} + \theta^V{}_{ijt}$.

In that case equation 8 would be rewritten as:

$$\text{(D1)} \qquad \theta_{ijt} = \underbrace{(K_{it})^{\rho_1}(K_{jt})^{\rho_2}}_{\theta^F_{ijt}} + \underbrace{(P_{Ft})^{\rho_3}(\pi_{jt})^{\rho_4}(D_{ij})^{\gamma_1+\gamma_2 \cdot t+\gamma_3 \cdot t^2}}_{\theta^V_{ijt}}$$

Under the specification in equation D1, it can be shown that equation 6 is now given by:

$$\text{(D2)} \qquad ([\partial\theta_{ijt}/\theta_{ij}]/[\partial D_{ij}/D_{ij}) = [\theta^V{}_{ijt} \times (\gamma_1 + \gamma_2.t + \gamma_3.t^2)]/(\theta^F{}_{ijt} + \theta^V{}_{ijt}).$$

From equation D2 it can be seen that the elasticity of transport costs with respect to distance could increase if the fixed cost component were falling sufficiently faster than the variable component. Substituting equation D1 into the modified version of equation 3 yields:

$$\text{(D3)} \qquad \ln(M_{ijt}) = Z_1\psi_1 + Z_2\psi_2 + \phi \ln[(K_{it})^{\rho_1}(K_{jt})^{\rho_2} + (P_{Ft})^{\rho_3}(\pi_{jt})^{\rho_4}(D_{ij})^{\gamma_1+\gamma_2.t+\gamma_3.t^2}]$$

where $\phi = (1 - \sigma)$. Expression D3 is highly nonlinear. Attempts to estimate equation D3 failed to yield convergence in the estimates even when estimated only for the R-R group (where errors in the variables measurement problems are likely to be smallest). The only consolation is that Limao and Venables (2001), who have real transport cost data for a sample similar to the one used here, claim that the multiplicative form is supported by their data.

References

Anderson, J. E., and D. Marcouiller. 2002, "Insecurity and the Pattern of Trade: An Empirical Investigation." *Review of Economics and Statistics* 84(2):342–52.

Anderson, J. E., and E. Van Wincoop. 2003. "Gravity with Gravitas: A Solution to the Border Puzzle." *American Economic Review* 93(1):170–92.

———. 2004. "Trade Costs." *Journal of Economic Literature* 42(September):691–751.

Baier, S. L., and J. H. Bergstrand. 2001. "The Growth of World Trade: Tariffs, Transport Costs, and Income Similarity." *Journal of International Economics* 53(1):1–27.

Bayoumi, T., and B. Eichengreen. 1997. "Is Regionalism Simply a Diversion? Evidence from the Evolution of the EC and EFTA." In T. Ito and A. Krueger, eds., *Regionalism versus Multilateral Trade Arrangements*. National Bureau of Economic Research East Asia Seminar on Economics, vol. 6. Chicago, Ill.: University of Chicago Press.

Bergstrand, J. H. 1989. "The Generalized Gravity Equation, Monopolistic Competition, and the Factor-Proportions Theory of International Trade." *Review of Economics and Statistics* 71(1):143–53.

Berthelon, M., and C. Freund. 2004. "On the Conservation of Distance in International Trade." World Bank Working Paper 3293. Washington, D.C.

Breusch, T., G. Mizon, and P. Schimdt. 1989. "Efficient Estimation Using Panel Data." *Econometrica* 57(3):695–700.

Brun, J. F., P. Guillaumont, and J. de Melo. 1999. "La distance abolie? Critères et mesures de la mondialisation du commerce extérieur." In A. Bouet and J. Le Cacheux, eds., *Globalisation et politiques économiques: les marges de manœuvre*. Paris: Economica.

Brun, J. F., C. Carrere, P. Guillaumont, and J. de Melo. 2002. "Has Distance Died? Evidence from a Panel Gravity Model." CEPR Discussion Paper 3500. Centre for Economic Policy Research, London.

Canning, D. 1996. "A Database of World Infrastructure Stocks, 1950–1995." *World Bank Economic Review* 12(3):529–47.

Cheng, I. H., and H. J. Wall. 1999. "Controlling for Heterogeneity in Gravity Models of Trade." Federal Reserve Bank of St. Louis Working Paper 99-010A. St. Louis, Mo.

Coe, D. T., A. Subramanian, N. T. Tamirisa, and R. Bhavnani. 2002. "The Missing Globalization Puzzle." IMF Working Paper WP/02/171. International Monetary Fund, Washington, D.C.

Deardorff, A. 1998. "Determinants of Bilateral Trade: Does Gravity Work in a Neoclassical World?" In J. A. Frankel, ed., *The Regionalization of the World Economy*. Chicago, Ill.: University of Chicago Press.

Egger, P., and M. Pfaffermayr. 2003. "The Proper Panel Econometric Specification for the Gravity Equation: A Three-way Model with Bilateral Interaction Effects." *Empirical Economics* 28(3):571–80.

Estevadeordal, A., B. Frantz, and A. M. Taylor. 2003. "The Rise and Fall of World Trade, 1870–1939." *Quarterly Journal of Economics* 118(May):359–407.

Evenett, S. J., and W. Keller. 2002. "On Theories Explaining the Success of the Gravity Equation." *Journal of Political Economy* 110 (2): 281–316.

Feenstra, R. 2003. "Increasing Returns and the Gravity Equation." *Advanced International Trade: Theory and Evidence*. Princeton, N.J.: Princeton University Press.

Frankel, J. 1997. *Regional Trading Blocs in the World Economic System*. Washington, D.C.: Institute for International Economics.

Guillotin, Y., and P. Sevestre. 1994. "Estimations de fonctions de gains sur données de panel: endogéneité du capital humain et effets de la sélection." *Economies et Prévision* 116(5):119–35.

Hausman, J. A., and E. Taylor. 1981. "Panel Data and Unobservable Individual Effects." *Econometrica* 49 (6):1377–98.

Hummels, D. 1999. "Towards a Geography of Transport Costs." University of Chicago, Graduate School of Business, Chicago, Ill.

———. 2001a. "Have International Transportation Costs Declined?" *Journal of International Economics* 54(1):75–96.

———. 2001b. "Time as Trade Barrier." Purdue University, School of Management, West Lafayette, Ind.

Hummels, D., and V. Lugovsky. 2003. "Usable Data? Matched Partner Trade Statistics as a Measure of International Transportation Costs." Purdue University, Department of Economics, West Lafayette, Ind.

IMF (International Monetary Fund). Various years. International Financial Statistics database. Washington, D.C.

Leamer, A. 1993. "The Commodity Composition of International Trade in Manufactures: An Empirical Analysis." *Oxford Economic Papers* 26(3):350–74.

Leamer, E., and J. Levinsohn. 1995. "International Trade: The Evidence." In G. M. Grossman and K. Rogoff, eds., *Handbook of International Economics*, vol. 3. New York: Elsevier, North-Holland.

Levin, A., and C. F. Lin. 1993. "Unit Root Tests in Panel Data: New Results." University of California, San Diego, Department of Economics.

Limao, N., and A. J. Venables. 2001. "Infrastructure, Geographical Disadvantage and Transport Costs." *World Bank Economic Review* 15(3):451–79.

Matyas, L. 1997. "Proper Econometric Specification of the Gravity Model." *World Economy* 20(3):363–68.

Nijman, T., and M. Verbeek. 1992. "Incomplete Panels and Selection Bias." In L. Matyas and P. Sevestre, eds., *The Econometrics of Panel Data*. Dordrecht, Netherlands: Kluwer.

Obstfeld, M., and K. Rogoff. 2001. "The Six Major Puzzles in International Macroeconomics. Is There a Common Cause?" NBER Working Paper 7777. National Bureau of Economic Research, Cambridge, Mass.

Rauch, J. E. 1999. "Networks versus Markets in International Trade." *Journal of International Economics* 48(1):7–35.

Rose, J., and E. Van Wincoop. 2001. "National Money as a Barrier to International Trade: The Real Case for Currency Union." *American Economic Review, Papers and Proceedings* 91(2):386–90.

Soloaga, I., and A. Winters. 2001. "How Has Regionalism in the 1990s Affected Trade?" *North American Journal of Economics and Finance* 12(1):1–29.

World Bank. 1999. *World Development Indicators 1999*. CD-ROM. Washington, D.C.

Part III

Political Economy

6 The new regionalism: a country perspective

JAIME DE MELO, ARVIND PANAGARIYA and DANI RODRIK

1 Introduction

Three decades ago, under the impetus of European arrangements, the developing world launched the first wave of regional integration (RI). Free-trade areas (FTAs) and customs unions (CUs) mushroomed in Latin America and Africa. Unfortunately, expectations of economic development through RI were not realised, and two decades later virtually all regional arrangements among developing countries were judged as failures.

By the early 1980s, multilateral tariff cutting by developed countries and unilateral trade liberalisation (UTL) by developing countries had substantially weakened the case for regional arrangements. Yet, paradoxically, it is then that a second round of regionalism got under way. More arrangements (eight) were signed during the 1980s than during the 1960s, and still more (half a dozen or so) are under consideration. The GATT process is running out of steam and many countries are turning back to the bilateral alternative.

From the viewpoint of developing countries, the current regionalism differs from the regionalism of the 1960s in two important respects. First, the regionalism of the 1960s represented an extension of the import-substitution–industrialisation strategy from the national to the regional level and was therefore inward-looking. The current regionalism is by contrast taking place in an environment of outward-oriented policies. Second, in the 1960s, developing countries pursued RI exclusively with other developing countries. Today these countries, especially those in Latin America, have their eyes on integration with large, developed countries.

In this chapter, we review and extend the theory of RI and evaluate empirically its contribution to growth. Our objective is to assess the benefits of RI from the viewpoint of participating countries rather than the world as a whole. In particular, we do not focus on the systemic implications of RI emphasised in Chapters 2–5. A central issue we address is whether the regional approach can accomplish objectives that cannot be accomplished via UTL. We also study the role of economic institutions in the process of regional integration. In analysing these issues, we draw a sharp distinction between the nature of RI today and that in the 1960s.

In section 2, we introduce the conventional welfare economics of RI via freer trade among partner countries. We conclude the section by alluding to the motivations behind current integration efforts which go far beyond trade integration. This theme is developed in greater detail in section 3, where it is formally recognised that integration enforces a certain degree of arbitrage among national institutions. In section 4, we provide an empirical evaluation of past integration schemes. Finally, in section 5, we turn to forward-looking lessons for the 'new' approaches to regionalism.

2 Welfare economics of FTAs

To avoid confusion, we begin by defining the terms 'preferential trading arrangement' (PTA), 'free-trade area' (FTA), 'customs union' (CU), and 'unilateral trade liberalisation' (UTL) precisely. A PTA refers to an arrangement under which partner countries impose lower tariffs on imports from each other than on imports from the outside world. An FTA involves zero tariffs on trade among partner countries but a positive tariff on imports from outside countries. Both PTAs and FTAs allow for different tariffs by partner countries on imports of similar goods from the outside world.[1] A CU is an FTA with a common external tariff (CET) by partner countries. Finally, UTL is defined as a non-discriminatory reduction in trade barriers.

The literature on RI is full of the 'anything may happen' type of results. What we present below is what we regard as helpful insights from the literature.[2] Unless otherwise noted, we assume throughout that the partner countries are small relative to the rest of the world.

In section 2.1, we present the basic Vinerian (1950) analysis and derive conditions under which an FTA is likely to be welfare-improving. In section 2.2, we consider the Kemp–Wan (1976) problem of designing a welfare-improving FTA and apply it to the analysis of FTAs in the presence of quotas. In section 2.3, we address the problem of compensation among union members. In sections 2.4–2.6, we compare FTAs successively to UTL, PTAs and CUs. In comparing FTAs to UTL, we discuss, *inter alia*, the roles of the import-substitution objective, tariff-revenue constraint and economies of scale. In comparing FTAs to PTAs, we show that when chosen correctly the latter are superior, and then proceed to explain why the GATT approach of forbidding PTAs is, nevertheless, sensible. In comparing FTAs to CUs, we pay attention to the rules of origin issue and political economy implications of the two regimes. In section 2.7, we relax the 'small union' assumption and analyse the strategic advantages of an FTA. In section 2.8, we assess explicitly the relevance of RI between developing and developed countries. Finally, in section 2.9, we summarise the main conclusions which follow from the review.

2.1 The basic economics of FTAs

Can an FTA be welfare-improving? Yes, but not always. This is the central point made by Viner in Chapter 4 of his classic work, *The Customs Unions Issue* (1950). Viner introduced the key concepts of trade creation and trade diversion, and concluded that a trade-creating CU is welfare-improving while a trade-diverting CU is welfare-worsening.[3]

In the following, we introduce the conventional analysis of an FTA formally with the help of a two-goods, three-country model. The goods are denoted 1 and 2 and countries *A*, *B* and *C*. *A* and *B* are potential partners in an FTA and *C* represents the outside world. In this setting, there are two possible trade patterns: *A* and *B* import the same good or they import different goods.

In the case when *A* and *B* import the same good, they will import it from *C* and there will be no trade between them in the initial equilibrium. Moreover, if the formation of an FTA leaves the tariff on *C* unchanged, the initial equilibrium will continue to obtain: the FTA will be vacuous. This situation may well describe the reality of some RI schemes in developing countries, particularly Africa. In many of these schemes, the partner countries had very similar patterns of trade and integration attempts had a very limited impact on trade patterns (see Foroutan, 1992, Chapter 8 in this volume).

In the more substantive case when the partner countries import different goods, assume that country *A* imports good 1 and country *B* exports it. For now, we concentrate on tariffs levied by country *A* only. Later we introduce explicitly tariffs in both *B* and *C*. In Figure 6.1, $M_1^A M_1^A$ and $E_1^B E_1^B$ are the general equilibrium import demand curve of *A* and export supply curve of *B*, respectively. The horizontal line $P^C P^C$ is the relative price at which *C* is willing to buy and sell good 1 in the world market.

Autarky prices in *A* and *B* are given by the respective heights of their curves at their points of origin. Under free trade, the gains from trade are represented by the area under the import demand curve and above the world price for *A*, and that above the export supply curve and below the

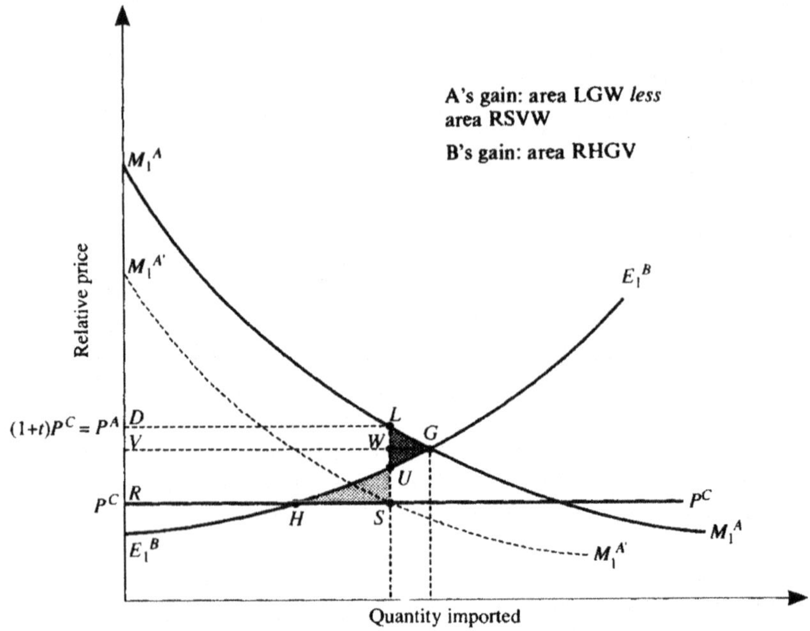

Figure 6.1 Basic analysis of an FTA

world price for *B*. Given constant costs and free trade in *C*, it neither gains nor loses from trade.

Assume that initially *A* levies a non-discriminatory tariff at rate *t* on imports from *B* and *C*. *A*'s import demand curve *as perceived by B and C* is now given by $M_1^{A'}M_1^{A'}$ where the latter lies below $M_1^A M_1^A$ by the amount of tariff per unit. The border price facing *A* is P^C and total imports are RS (= DL). Of these, *RH* comes from *B* and *HS* from *C*. Domestic price in *A* is given by P^A which is the height of the import demand curve as perceived by *A*'s residents. The gains from trade in *A* are given by area $M_1^A LD$ plus tariff revenue *DRSL* and those in *B* by area RHE_1^B.

Now introduce an FTA between *A* and *B*. Imports from *B* are no longer subject to a tariff. As drawn, there is a 'sudden death' of imports from *C* with all imports 'diverted' to *B*. The union benefits *B* both because its terms of trade improve and because its exports expand. The country's net gain equals area *RHGV*. The effect on *A* is ambiguous in general because, on the one hand, *A*'s terms of trade deteriorate (or equivalently it loses all tariff revenue) while, on the other, the distortion between the domestic and (new) border price is eliminated. The country gains or loses as area

LGW is larger or smaller than the rectangle *RSWV*. As drawn, the country loses. The effect on joint welfare of *A* and *B* is also ambiguous. They benefit jointly if area *LGU* is larger than the vertically shaded area, *HSU* but lose otherwise. As drawn, the union as a whole loses from the FTA.[4] That is to say, *B*'s gains exceed the losses of *A* and it can compensate the latter.[5]

Figure 6.1 has been drawn in such a way that an FTA between *A* and *B* eliminates the imports from *C* entirely. This is done to highlight the point that an FTA will generally generate both positive and negative effects and that the effect on the union's welfare is likely to be ambiguous.[6] If we draw *B*'s export supply curve so that it crosses *A*'s solid curve to the left of point *L*, the FTA does not eliminate imports from *C*. In this case, the internal price facing *A* is unchanged while its terms of trade with *B* deteriorate by the full amount of the tariff. *B*'s share in imports rises but total imports remain unchanged. *A*'s welfare declines because its terms of trade with *B* worsen without any improvement in efficiency; *B*'s welfare rises because its terms of trade improve and exports expand; and the union's welfare declines because over some range imports coming from *B* cost more than *C*'s price and there is no gain in efficiency in *A*.

What factors make the gains from an FTA larger or the losses smaller? If we are willing to restrict ourselves to the case depicted in Figure 6.1 where both positive and negative effects are present, a number of points can be made.[7] First, the higher the initial tariff in a given sector, the larger the favourable effect (area *LUG*) and smaller the unfavourable effect (area *USH*) of the FTA. Second, the lower the post-FTA tariff on extra-union countries the less likely that the lower-priced goods of the latter will be displaced. Third, the higher the tariffs in the outside world on the partner, the larger will be the gain or the smaller the loss. In terms of Figure 6.1, the higher the tariff in *C*, the higher will be P^C facing *A* and *B* and the smaller will be the area *HSU*. Fourth, the greater the complementarity in import demands of *A* and *B*, the larger the gains from FTA. In terms of Figure 6.1, the farther apart are the import demand and export supply curves of *A* and *B*, the larger will be the gains (area *LGW*) and the smaller the losses (area *HSU*).

On this last issue, it is worth noting that at low levels of income, complementarity is more likely to arise between countries that are different in terms of factor endowments and perhaps, therefore, countries with different *per capita* incomes. As we will discuss in section 2.3, this is precisely the condition under which the compensation issue is critical and implementation difficulties most serious. Complementarities among high-income countries are more likely to arise among countries with similar *per capita* incomes. This is because the bulk of high-income countries' trade is

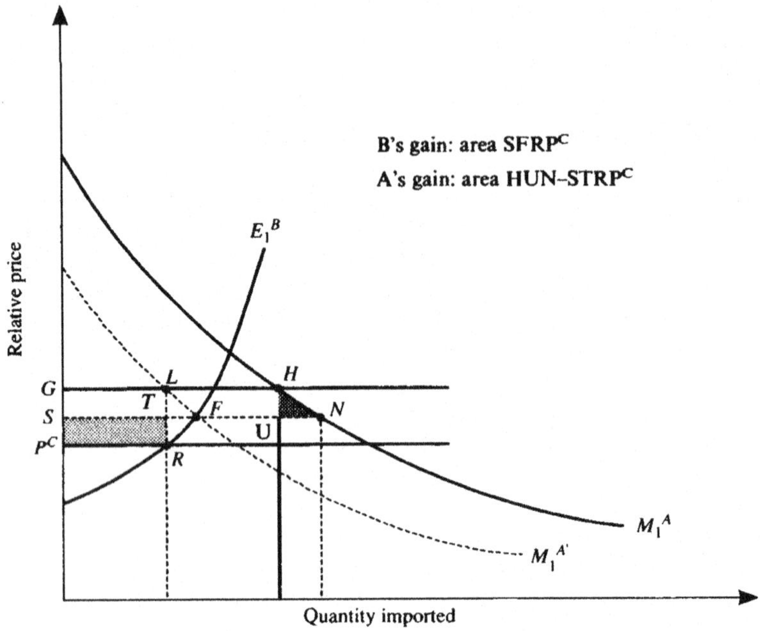

Figure 6.2 An FTA under a QR

of an intra-industry nature which correlates negatively with differences in *per capita* incomes of partner countries.

2.2 Designing a welfare-improving FTA in the presence of QRs

Can a welfare improving FTA always be designed? Yes. This is the essence of the Kemp and Wan (1976) analysis. These authors demonstrate that under very standard assumptions, *A* and *B* can adopt a set of CETs which improve their welfare without hurting the outside world. The essential idea is that the common set of tariffs may be chosen in such a way that the external terms of trade and hence the quantities traded with the outside world are unchanged while internal trade is rearranged to maximise the gains from it.

The Kemp–Wan result has important implications for the analysis of FTAs in the presence of quantitative restrictions (QRs). These implications have not been explored in the literature so far and will be considered here briefly. In Figure 6.2, we look at the two-good model. Suppose that initially *A* restricts its total imports to *GH* by a global quota.

Assuming that quota licences are auctioned competitively to domestic residents, quantity *GL* will be imported from *B* and *LH* from *C*. If we now introduce an FTA such that *C* is subject to a quota at its original level of imports (*LH*) while imports from *B* are freed of any restrictions, total imports will expand. Subtracting quantity *LH* horizontally from $M_1^A M_1^A$ everywhere, we obtain $M_1^{A'} M_1^{A'}$ as the demand curve facing *B*. This yields *SF* quantity of imports from *B* and *FN* (= *LH*) from *C*. Once again, as in Figure 6.1, we have a positive effect (*HUN*) on *A* due to a reduced gap between the domestic and border prices and a negative effect ($STRP^C$) due to a deterioration in the terms of trade with *B*. The net welfare effect on *A* is ambiguous in principle, although as drawn it loses.

Country *B* necessarily gains in this case. This gain, represented by area $SFRP^C$, is larger than the loss of country *A*. Therefore, *B* can compensate *A*, should it lose from the FTA on balance. The FTA leads to unambiguous benefits for the union as a whole. In the spirit of the Kemp–Wan result, the FTA has not reduced trade with the outside world and has expanded trade between the partners. The outside world's welfare is unaffected so that the FTA improves the world's welfare as well.

2.3 *The compensation issue*

In the preceding subsections, we have considered RI from the viewpoint of the union as a whole. We implicitly relied on lump sum redistributions between partners to ensure that neither partner loses. In practice, compensation mechanisms are difficult to implement, particularly in developing countries. Because a detailed discussion of the issue is contained in Chapter 8, we confine ourselves here to brief remarks.

Partner countries in integration schemes in developing countries often have very diverse levels of *per capita* incomes. If integration leads to a migration of industries from the poor to the relatively more advanced economies, compensation is essential. In some cases, special funds are created to help the industrial development of the poorest members. The criteria for contributions to and disbursements from these funds often become contentious, leading to very complicated formulas that generally defy economic logic.

In the case of CEAO and UDEAC in Africa (see Chapter 8 below), unions have provided for preferential duties on industrial products based on the protection needs of the poorest of the members. This has resulted in different tariff rates for the import of the same product, depending on the source: the duty is lower on imports coming from the least developed members and higher on others.

2.4 FTA versus UTL

We now consider what is perhaps the strongest criticism of the regional approach from the viewpoint of small economies: an FTA is usually dominated by UTL.

To begin with, observe that in Figure 6.1 country *A*'s welfare is maximised by liberalising its trade unilaterally. That is to say, the FTA with *B* is welfare-inferior to unilateral free trade. Moreover, the same conditions which make the FTA desirable (e.g., a high initial tariff) make UTL even more desirable. There is thus nothing which *B* can offer *A* that the latter cannot get on its own. Why, then, should *A* bother to enter a bilateral arrangement with *B*?[8]

A number of complications must be introduced to answer this question. Before we do so, however, it is useful to introduce a dramatic example. Suppose the developed and newly industrialised countries (NICs) are divided into three blocs: north America, western Europe and east Asia. Also suppose that each one of these blocs allows free internal trade but imposes high duties or voluntary export restraints (VERs) on extra-bloc imports. Under these circumstances, will developing countries in Africa, Asia and Latin America benefit more from UTL or from joining one of the blocs? Common sense dictates that the latter option is likely to be welfare-superior even though it involves adopting and maintaining the bloc's barriers to trade with extra-bloc countries. In subsections 2.4.1 and 2.4.2, we develop the argument underlying this example.

2.4.1 Partner-country tariffs A natural starting point is the introduction of tariffs in *B*.[9] Figure 6.1 assumes that *B* is a free trader even before the FTA is formed. This means that *B* has nothing to offer *A* as a part of the FTA agreement. In practice, *B* will have tariffs initially and an FTA will buy *A* a tariff-free access to *B*'s markets. In terms of Figure 6.1, the deterioration in *A*'s terms of trade which accompanied the FTA need not take place. Indeed, *B* may end up offering it better terms of trade than *C*, making the FTA a better option than UTL. It turns out, however, that this cannot happen unless *B* chooses a suboptimal option for itself.

In Figure 6.3, solid curves show *A*'s general equilibrium demand for imports of good 1 and *B*'s general equilibrium supply of exports of the same good under free trade. The horizontal line gives *C*'s supply price which *A* and *B* are too small to influence. Both *A* and *B* impose tariffs in the initial equilibrium. The tariff in *A* causes its import demand *as perceived by B and C* to shift down to the dashed curve. The tariff in *B* causes its supply of export curve as perceived by *A* and *C* to shift up as

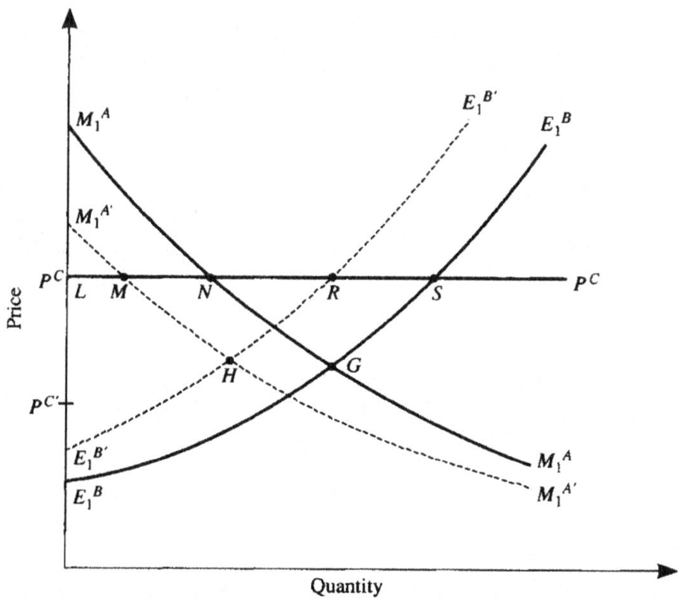

Figure 6.3 FTAs versus UTLs

shown by the upward-sloped dashed curve.[10] In the presence of non-discriminatory tariffs, *A* and *B* trade along dashed curves at the price offered by *C*. *A* imports *ML* and *B* exports *RL*. It is not necessary for *A* and *B* to trade but if they do, *B* exports up to *ML* to *A* and *MR* to *C*. Domestic prices in the two countries are given by their respective solid curves. For each country, the gains from trade are measured by the area enclosed by the world price, quantity traded, and its solid curve.

If *A* now liberalises unilaterally, its imports will rise to *LN* and its welfare will improve. The critical question is: can *A* do better by forming an FTA with *B*? Suppose *A* and *B* eliminate tariffs between themselves and impose prohibitive tariffs on *C*. This will yield *G* as the equilibrium with *A* benefiting more than from UTL.

Does this suggest that the FTA in the present case is superior to unilateral free trade? The answer is in the negative. For we have not said anything yet about *B*'s welfare. As is easy to see from Figure 6.3, compared to point *G*, country *B* can improve its welfare by liberalising unilaterally and moving to point *S*. The FTA can be superior only if *A* can compensate *B* to ensure the latter the income level at *S* and still come out ahead relative to unilateral liberalisation. This is impossible, however, since the amount by which *A*'s income at *G* exceeds its income at *N* is less than the required compensation by area *NGS*. Looked at differently, combined gains from trade of *A* and *B* under UTL are larger than those under an FTA by area *NGS*.

The conclusion from this discussion is that partner country tariffs do not negate the overall superiority of UTL over RI. Only if one of the countries – country *B* in Figure 6.3 – is willing to accept a suboptimal position for some exogenous reasons (e.g., political hegemony), can the other country benefit more from an FTA than from unilateral liberalisation.

2.4.2 Third-country tariffs Another possible explanation for a preference for an FTA over UTL is the presence of trade restrictions and/or transport costs in the outside world, country *C*. Thus, suppose that there are tariffs initially in not just *A* and *B* but also in *C*. This means that if *C* is a buyer of good 1 in the world market, it will offer a price lower than its internal price. Similarly, if *C* is a seller of good 1 in the world market, it will charge a price higher than its internal price.

In Figure 6.3, suppose now that *C*'s selling price is P^C, its buying price is $P^{C'}$, and its internal price is somewhere in the middle. This means that *B* no longer has the option of trading at *R*. Indeed, the terms offered to it by *C*, $P^{C'}$, are worse than those offered by *A*. Likewise for *A*, the terms of trade offered by *B* are better than those offered by *C*. The two countries will trade with each other at *H*. Now if *A* and *B* eliminate tariffs on each other, they can trade at *G* and both do better than if only one of them was to liberalise trade unilaterally. The FTA turns out to be superior to UTL.[11]

An important point to note is that in this example there is no difference between an FTA and complete free trade by *A* and *B*. High tariffs in *C* make that country irrelevant for optimal trade policies in *A* and *B*. In order to reach *G*, *A* and *B* do not need any external tariffs. In this sense, the only role of an FTA is to solve the Prisoners' Dilemma for the two countries and bring them to the negotiating table.

A useful application of the example provided in this subsection is that if the world gets divided into inward-looking blocs, UTL will become a less attractive option for the countries outside the bloc than it is today. The countries will then be better off either seeking access to one of the blocs and adopting its trade policy or engaging in RI so as to promote freer trade among themselves.[12] Of course, the current world being quite far from consisting of closed blocs, the example does not justify a preference for RI over UTL.

2.4.3 The import-substitution objective The most common justification for pursuing RI instead of UTL comes in the form of an implicit or explicit non-economic objective. In the early development literature, industrialisation via import substitution was considered an eminently respectable objective. This, either on grounds of infant industry, 'training ground argument' or other reasons, meant that the option of unilateral free trade was simply not available. Under such circumstances, an FTA which, in the spirit of Kemp and Wan, keeps the imports of industrial goods from country *C* fixed and exploits the gains from specialisation between partner countries is beneficial.[13]

During the 1960s, the import-substitution objective played a key role in the proliferation of RI schemes in the developing world. But the gains from specialisation expected of various schemes were not realised, for reasons we need not go into here. Suffice it to note that today the policy environment has changed dramatically and import substitution as a policy objective has fallen out of favour with policymakers, except perhaps in the early stages of development. This means that an FTA as an alternative to UTL is harder to defend on grounds of import substitution.

2.4.4 The tariff-revenue constraint Another objective which may preclude free trade as a viable option is the tariff-revenue constraint. In many developing countries, domestic tax machinery is limited and they must rely on trade taxes as the major source of revenue. In this situation, the option of UTL is simply not available, and we can ask whether RI may be a superior option than non-discriminatory tariffs.

For concreteness, assume that *A* and *B* choose their initial revenue-constrained tariffs optimally. With some qualifications, this implies relatively high tariffs on goods with low elasticities of demand. If *A* and *B* now form an FTA, they will have to restrict their tariff structure so as to impose no tariffs on each other's goods. Under standard assumptions, including fixed world prices, this restriction will lead to a lower level of welfare. The same forces which make unilateral free trade superior to an FTA under standard assumptions make non-discriminatory tariffs superior to preferential tariffs in the presence of a revenue constraint.

2.4.5 Economies of scale and product differentiation During the first wave of RI arrangements, many economists relied on the notion that an FTA could serve as a vehicle for the exploitation of economies of scale. Yet, broadly speaking, scale economies *by themselves* do not make RI superior to UTL.[14] Intuitively, if the minimum cost of production of a good along the long-run average cost curve is below the world price, both potential partners in the FTA should expand production until the marginal cost is less than or equal to the world price. They should then consume domestically as much as is demanded at the world price and export the residual. Goods for which minimum cost is above the world price should not be produced. Unilateral free trade will generally ensure this outcome.

If the case for RI over UTL already exists due to considerations cited in sections 2.4.2 or 2.4.3, scale economies generally make it much stronger. This is perhaps the reason why economies of scale are often a part of the case for an FTA. The point can be illustrated with the help of two examples, of which we develop the first one in detail and refer the reader to Corden (1972) for the second: (i) an import-substitution objective involving a target level of industrial output, as in section 2.4.2; and (ii) tariffs and transportation costs on exports to the outside world which limit access to the latter's market, as in section 2.4.3.

Suppose that both *A* and *B* have a target level of aggregate import-competing industrial output. As noted before, starting from a non-discriminatory tariff, the two countries can benefit from an FTA under such circumstances even under constant returns. If scale economies are present, however, the gains from specialisation are likely to be larger. For specialisation in the presence of scale economies yields gains in the form of larger rectangular areas rather than conventional triangular areas. Thus, the case for an FTA is stronger.

The above analysis assumes (implicitly) that products are homogeneous and the scale economies are external to the firm.[15] Suppose now that scale economies are internal to the firm and products are differentiated. These assumptions drive us automatically into the world of imperfect competition, where individual firms are able to exercise market power. In view of market power on the part of firms, potential partners in an FTA cannot be viewed as small in relation to the outside world. Therefore, their optimal tariffs are positive and UTL is non-optimal even in the absence of the import-substitution objective.

Beyond this point, the implications of imperfect competition are rather complex. Depending on the behavioural assumptions, a myriad of models can be constructed.[16] We resist temptation and restrict ourselves to the monopolistic competition model. On balance, the results which emerge from this model are intuitively more plausible than those arising from oligopoly models.[17]

Assume that potential partners consume differentiated goods for which markets are monopolistically competitive and that consumers appreciate variety. Starting from an initial protected equilibrium, formation of an FTA can yield two additional types of gains not available in the conventional models. First, after the FTA is formed, each partner will have tariff-free access to the varieties produced by the other. To the extent that consumers prefer more variety to less, welfare must rise. Second, as the market for each variety is likely to be larger in the post-FTA equilibrium, its scale of operation will expand. Given decreasing costs, this will yield further gains.

Against these gains, we must weigh the losses which are likely to accrue from increased distortion between varieties imported from the partner country and those imported from the outside world. Preferential tariff reduction will reduce imports from the outside world, which is harmful for members of the FTA. Although, in general, the net result is ambiguous, there is a strong presumption that due to decreasing costs welfare will rise. Indeed, if the members freeze their vectors of imports from country *C*, the FTA will be unambiguously welfare-improving.

Two important policy implications of this analysis may be noted. First, to the extent that intra-industry trade is predominantly among rich countries, these gains are less relevant to FTAs between poor countries. Second, contrary to the results based on models of interindustry trade, similarity among partner countries does not diminish the case for FTAs when potential trade is of the intra-industry variety.

2.5 FTAs versus PTAs

We now show that PTAs can be superior to an FTA. That is to say, partial preferences can yield a better outcome than a 100 percent preference granted under FTAs.

The point is made most easily with the help of a three-good model in which each of *A*, *B*, and *C* exports one good and imports two goods.[18] Goods imported into each country from the other two – say, those into *A* from *B* and *C* – are imperfect substitutes. *A* and *B* are small with respect to *C* so that their terms of trade are fixed. Given symmetry in the trade pattern, we need to consider the effects of a PTA on one partner only, say *A*. The effects on *B* are similar.

Denote the goods exported by *A*, *B*, and *C* by 1, 2, and 3, respectively. Assume that initially, *A* imposes the same *ad valorem* tariff on *B* and *C*. That is to say, the initial marginal distortion across *B* and *C* is the same. Suppose now that the tariff on *B* is lowered by a small amount. This will raise imports of good 2 and, given substitutability, lower imports of good 3 and raise exports of good 1. Because exports rise, there is a net expansion of imports, implying that imports of good 2 expand more than the contraction of imports of good 3 at world prices. The initial distortion in the two imports being the same, the gain from increased imports of good 2 is larger than the loss due to reduced imports of good 3. The PTA is welfare-improving.

As we lower the tariff on good 2 further, net imports will continue to expand. But the gain from the expansion of imports of good 2 will be evaluated at the lower tariff than the loss from the contraction of imports of good 3. There is therefore, no guarantee that welfare will continue to rise as we lower the tariff on good 2. Indeed, assuming monotonicity, we can find a critical, second-best optimal tariff at which the gains in good 2 from a small additional reduction in tariff are exactly offset by the losses on good 3. Any reductions beyond this tariff rate will lower welfare. By obvious extension, an FTA which pushes the tariff on good 2 down to 0 will yield a lower welfare than the PTA with the second-best optimum tariff.

This conclusion clearly brings into question the wisdom of the GATT Article XXIV, which prohibits PTAs but permits FTAs and CUs. Viner provided at least two reasons why in practice a 100 percent preference may be superior to something less than that. First, there are likely to be some economies in administrative costs. 'The burden on trade of a customs tariff', Viner reasoned, 'arises . . . also from the costs involved, for exporter and importer, in meeting the customs regulations, and the costs involved, for the tariff-levying government, in administering the customs machinery. These costs are often, in fact, more important than the duties themselves as hindrances to trade'.

A second, and perhaps more important, reason for the preference for an FTA over a PTA is that even though superior PTAs exist, there is no guarantee that those are the ones that will be picked. It is entirely possible, even plausible, that the PTAs that are actually picked are inferior to the FTA. Once again, it is worthwhile to quote Viner (1950, pp. 50–1):

> Customs Union . . . involves across-the-board removal of the duties between the members of the union; since the removal is non-selective by its very nature, the beneficial preferences are established along with the injurious ones, the trade-creating ones along with the trade-diverting ones. Preferential arrangements, on the other hand, can be, and usually are, selective, and it is possible, and in practice probable, that the preferences selected will be predominantly of the trade-diverting or injurious kind.

2.6 FTAs versus CUs

An issue of great significance in the formation of RI schemes is whether the countries should retain their own tariffs (FTA) or erect a CET (CU) on extra-union partners. Economists are divided on this issue.

There are three main arguments given in favour of FTAs. First, they do not result in an increase in tariffs in member countries. By contrast, when a common external tariff is imposed, countries with lower initial tariffs are able to raise their tariffs. This is because Article XXIV requires that the external tariff be no higher than the average of the tariffs in the partner countries prior to the formation of the union. Second, an FTA gives the member countries a greater freedom to pursue their trade-policy reforms. In a CU, more reform-oriented countries may find their hands tied by the agreement to maintain a CET. If lobbies are powerful, the CET may be set at a level high enough to protect producers in the least efficient country in the union. Finally, due to enforcement difficulties under an FTA, the union finds itself importing goods through the border of the country with the lowest tariff. This puts pressure on countries with higher tariff to bring their tariffs down to the level of the least protective country. There are thus dynamic processes at work in favour of ever-declining tariffs under an FTA.

In principle, at least some of these arguments can be turned on their heads. First, if a CU is formed, the least protective country can force the more protective countries to lower their tariffs to its level. This will make the likelihood that integration is welfare-improving higher and result in a lower cost to the rest of the world. Second, in practice, FTAs are accompanied by elaborate rules of origin and content requirement which become powerful instruments of protection. In a CU, such rules are not required. Finally, if protection lobbies are active, their effectiveness may be diluted in a CU since the latter requires union-wide lobbying, whereas under an FTA tariffs are responsive to the lobbying at the national level. In the ultimate, the issue would seem to hinge on whether we can expect institutional arbitrage across countries (in the sense of section 3) to lead to superior outcomes for all, in which case a CU would be preferable. If such arbitrage leads to worse outcomes, then it is better to leave each country with its own external tariffs. Perhaps put differently, if the 'centre' country, when one exists, has a clean trade policy, a CU can be more desirable, since we can expect that region-wide tariff policies will be determined more by this country.

2.7 Strategic advantages of an FTA

Up to this point, we assumed that the union was small in relation to the outside world. We now allow the terms of trade to change and consider the strategic advantages of an FTA for union members. Our discussion is in two parts. First, we summarise the effects resulting directly from the formation of an FTA. Second, we discuss the gains which may arise from increased bargaining power of the union *vis-à-vis* the outside world.

In the two-good model of Figure 6.1, the terms of trade effects of an FTA are straightforward. Suppose that *C*'s supply price is not constant, but increases with quantity. At a constant price of *C*, formation of an FTA reduces the demand for imports from *C*. This leads to a decline in *C*'s price. Formation of an FTA improves the union's terms of trade *vis-à-vis* the outside world.[19]

The second type of gain from an FTA can result from increased bargaining power of the union. The terms of trade of union members depend not merely on their external tariffs, but also on tariffs imposed on them by the outside world. To the extent that the level of these tariffs can be influenced through bargaining, an FTA which increases the joint bargaining power of member countries can confer further gains on the latter. Interestingly, unlike the first type of gains, these gains need not come at the expense of the outside world. The union as well as the outside world may benefit from mutual tariff reduction.[20]

Viner provides several examples from history where decisions to forge economic unions were influenced, in part, by expected gains from increased bargaining power with respect to other countries. In the United States, the Articles of Confederation had left each state with its separate tariff. The argument that this put the United States at a disadvantage *vis-à-vis* Britain and other European countries in matters of commercial policy was instrumental in mobilising public opinion in favour of a federal union with a centralised tariff policy. The recent movement for a 'United States of Europe' sprang in large part from the feeling that a European economic union was necessary to deal with a large America.

A case can be made that the existence of the European Community has been instrumental in allowing western European countries to cut out better deals with the United States in bargaining tariff reductions than would have been possible if they had dealt individually with the United States. More recently, the restraint shown by the United States towards the European Community in using 'Super 301' threats is a direct result of the Community's ability to inflict injury on the United States through retaliation. By contrast, the United States has used this instrument with relative ease against individual countries such as Japan, Brazil and India.

The bargaining power of a union is a direct function of its economic size relative to the outside countries with which it must negotiate. In this respect, formation of the European Community did prove beneficial to its member countries. By contrast, economic unions in Africa and Latin America were much too small relative to their counterparts in the developed world (see Chapters 8 by Foroutan and 9 by Nogués and Quintanilla in this volume). As a result, any expectations of these countries regarding benefits from joint negotiations with the United States and the European Community were bound to result in disappointment.

2.8 Implications for efficiency

The above discussions give some clues about the likely effects of RI arrangements. First, countries with high barriers to trade (e.g., India) are likely to benefit most from UTL. The gains from such liberalisation are likely to be much bigger than those from FTAs. Only if the world is divided into closed trading blocs is RI a superior option. Second, in the absence of closed trading blocs, the case for FTAs must be based on an exogenous objective such as import-substitution industrialisation. Third, economies of scale by themselves do not provide a reason for justifying RI over UTL. If there are other reasons for a preference for RI, however, economies of scale can reinforce them. Fourth, RI among low-income, developing countries is unlikely to yield major gains. This is because either these countries import very similar goods from developed countries or because differences in income levels among them lead to very diverse distribution of gains. In the former case, gains from specialisation between partner countries are limited while in the latter case compensation schemes which emerge are highly distortionary. Fifth, similarity in *per capita* incomes reinforces the gains from RI among developed countries. Sixth, *a priori*, it is not clear whether an FTA is superior to a CU. Much depends on how these are implemented. Finally, the larger an FTA, the greater the strategic advantages. For instance, the European Community has been generally insulated from the US 'Super 301' threats while countries such as Japan, India and Brazil have had to face them.

As a prelude to section 3, nothing has been said explicitly so far about North–South integration, which has been gaining popularity in recent years, e.g., Mexico and the United States. Countries engaged in this type of integration have relatively free trade regimes (the average Mexican tariff is 9 percent). The gains for a developing country from integration with a rich country go beyond the trade efficiency gains discussed here. First, should the world get divided into inward-looking blocs, such integration guarantees future access to a large market.[21] With this large market, the competitive pressure to ensure efficiency and availability of new technology is also guaranteed. Second, such integration involving international obligations ensures that the country's reforms will not be reversed. This is critical for the credibility of the country's policies. Finally, as a part of the integration effort, the country may be able to import pro-growth economic institutions (e.g., more liberal labour markets, stable macroeconomic policies, etc.) of the developed country.

We now proceed to develop this last point in greater detail.

3 Institutional dimensions of RI

The implications of RI go beyond trade in goods, services, and factors. Almost by definition, any regional arrangement worth its name entails the imposition of some common rules of conduct on the countries entering the arrangement and a set of reciprocal commitments and obligations. RI thereby enforces a certain degree of arbitrage among national institutions, just as it brings about arbitrage in markets for goods and services. The importance of this political dimension of RI may well exceed that of the more direct implications having to do with trade flows.

That the effects of RI can extend beyond trade has long been recognised. More than two decades ago, Hirschman (1971, p. 22) argued that surrendering autonomy to supranational authorities had both costs and benefits for governments:

> [C]ommon markets would not only provide preferential treatment for the industrialists of the participating countries; for these mutual arrangements to be durable, monetary and foreign exchange policies would have to become more uniform and stable than they have been; and such a development would be even more important than the customs preferences themselves in promoting exports from the common market countries, not only to each other, but also to third countries. It is, however, precisely the prospect of less freedom of movement in monetary and foreign exchange policies which makes national governments so skittish about entering effective common market commitments.

The issues go well beyond monetary and foreign exchange policies, and skittishness about losing autonomy is not confined to them alone. RI can also serve as a conduit for industrial policies, environmental preferences, social and welfare policies, and so on.

If the cost of integration is reduced autonomy, the benefit (as Hirschman suggests) may be superior economic outcomes. Much of the recent trend towards RI can be understood as reflecting the desire of certain countries to 'borrow' or 'import' desirable institutions from their neighbours. A central aim of the exchange rate mechanism (ERM) of the European Community was to enhance the credibility of anti-inflationary policies by effectively surrendering monetary autonomy to the Bundesbank. By entering a quasi-irrevocable arrangement in the context of the North American Free-Trade Area (NAFTA), the Mexican government is as anxious to cement its new, open trade policies as it is to obtain specific trade privileges via the arrangement.[22] In both cases, RI is used to commit to desirable policies in a context where discretion is feared to produce suboptimal results.

The literature on rules versus discretion provides the natural reference point for evaluating such institutional implications (see Fischer, 1990, for a survey). However, we should be clear that membership in an RI scheme does not purchase commitment in any direct way. The arrangements that occur in practice rarely involve the complete subordination of a member's preferences to exogenous rules or to the preferences of another member. We will highlight here three other channels through which regional institutions can alter economic outcomes.

(*a*) *The preference-dilution effect:* Irrespective of the institutional setup, a regional arrangement implies a larger political community and hence a smaller role in determining policy for politically important groups in each of the countries. This renders decisionmaking less responsive to factional interests, and may thereby enhance efficiency.

(*b*) *The preference-asymmetry effect:* Unless members have identical economic structures and preferences, policymaking at the regional level will have to compromise over the perceived needs of different countries. Somewhat paradoxically, the compromise solution may present a more efficient outcome for some members than could be obtained in the absence of integration. For others, the compromise solution may be worse.

(*c*) *The institutional-design effect:* Within established nation-states, policymakers have to live with the inherited institutional setting. But when a regional institution is set up from scratch, it may be possible to optimise in the choice of certain institutional dimensions in a way that would not normally be possible in the domestic context. This greater flexibility in institutional design may enhance efficiency in all members.

3.1 An exploratory model

To make these arguments more concrete and to draw some implications, we now turn to a simple model. As in the literature on rules versus discretion, our focus is on the interaction between governments and their private sectors, and the changes in this interaction that would follow from integration. We develop the case of a single country first, and then turn to the case where two countries become integrated.

We suppose that government behaviour can be summarised by a

quadratic-loss objective function which allows for both an economic motive and a non-economic ('political') motive:

$$G = -[(\bar{g} - g)^2 + \gamma(\theta - g)^2]. \tag{1}$$

The government's choice variable is denoted by g. It represents government intervention on some relevant policy dimension (e.g., trade protection, industrial subsidies, aggregate demand-management policies, etc.). The optimal level of g in a strictly economic sense is given by $\bar{g}$. Hence, the first term in (1) captures a purely economic motive in government decisionmaking. In addition, we suppose that the government also comes under pressure to intervene on account of political motives, represented here by the second term in (1). Politically powerful groups in the private sector have a most preferred level of intervention given by θ. The second term captures the idea that the government pays a penalty whenever g diverges from θ. γ is the relative weight placed by the government on the political motive. We attach no normative importance to this objective function; it is simply meant to characterise government behaviour in a transparent fashion.

The level of θ is endogenous, and is selected by a lobby representing politically active groups in society. These groups derive private benefits from government intervention, but they also bear a cost whenever g diverges from the economically most efficient level. This trade-off is represented by a utility function of the following sort:

$$U = ag - (\theta - \bar{g})^2. \tag{2}$$

The first term here represents the private benefits of government intervention, while the second term stands for its economy-wide costs. These costs are positive whenever the private-sector lobby expresses a preference for a g that is different from $\bar{g}$, and they are assumed to be partly internalised by the lobbying group.

The game proceeds as follows. In the first stage, the private-sector lobby announces θ, its most preferred level of government intervention, taking into account how the government will respond to this announcement. In the second stage, the government determines its optimal level of g, taking θ as given. As we shall see, in this sequence the government suffers a loss in welfare from being unable to precommit to a specified level of g in advance of the political process.

We solve the second stage of the game first. Maximising (1) with respect to g yields:

$$g = (1 + \gamma)^{-1}(\bar{g} + \gamma\theta) \equiv g(\theta). \tag{3}$$

This is the government's best-response function with respect to θ. In the first stage of the game, the lobby in turn maximises (2) subject to (3). The solution is:

$$\theta = \bar{g} + a\gamma/2(1 + \gamma), \tag{4}$$

which is larger than $\bar{g}$ as long as $a > \theta$. Substituting this back in (3), we get the equilibrium level of government intervention:

$$g = \bar{g} + (a/2)[\gamma/(1 + \gamma)^2]. \tag{5}$$

Hence g exceeds $\bar{g}$ as long as a and γ are both positive. There is therefore more intervention than is economically desirable. We can also show that:

$$(\theta - g) = (a/2)[\gamma/(1 + \gamma)^2] > 0, \tag{6}$$

which implies that the government chooses to moderate the lobby's demands. For future reference, we substitute (5)–(6) in (1) to express the value taken by the government's objective function in the non-integrated equilibrium:

$$G_N = -(a^2/4)[\gamma/(1 + \gamma)]^3. \tag{7}$$

By being responsive to political pressure, the government suffers a cost. To see that this cost originates from the specific timing of moves adopted here, suppose that we reverse the order of moves. Now the government can precommit to a specific level of g. Since the lobby moves second, it must take g as given. In view of (2), its optimal θ is then equal to $\bar{g}$. In turn, the government can maximise (1) by setting $g = \bar{g}$. Hence, when the government can precommit, its objective function attains its bliss point (of zero). We can interpret this framework also in terms of time-inconsistency: the government's optimal *ex ante* policy diverges from its optimal *ex post* policy. We note that the private-sector lobby is the beneficiary of this time-inconsistency, as it attains a higher level of utility when the government cannot precommit than when it can.

3.2 Modelling RI

We now turn to the case where two countries decide to integrate. We model this integration by requiring that the level of government intervention be the same in the two economies. We suppose that the two countries differ only with respect to the economically desirable level of intervention. Hence, the foreign government's objective function is given by:

$$G^* = -[(\bar{g}^* - g^*)^2 + \gamma(\theta^* - g^*)^2], \tag{8}$$

while the private-sector lobby in the foreign country maximises:

$$U^* = ag^* - (\theta^* - \bar{g}^*)^2. \tag{9}$$

Note that a and γ are common to the two countries.

How is decisionmaking accomplished at the regional level? It is natural to think that the regional institution will maximise an objective function that has the same structure as the ones in the two countries:

$$G_r = -[(\bar{g}_r - g)^2 + \gamma(\theta_r - g)^2], \tag{10}$$

where the subscript r refers to the regional institution. To save on notation, we do not subscript g, as this is now common to both countries – it may stand, for example, for the CET. As this expression makes clear, there are basically two issues here: first, given that $\bar{g}$ and $\bar{g}^*$ differ, what objective does the centre see itself as fulfilling (i.e., what is $\bar{g}_r$)? Second, as the respective lobbying demands θ and θ^* may in principle differ also, how does the regional institution 'aggregate' these preferences (i.e., what is the relationship between θ and θ^*, on the one hand, and θ_r, on the other)? We make what seems to be the neutral assumption by equating $\bar{g}_r$ and θ_r to the averages of the preferences in the two countries. That is,

$$\bar{g}_r = \tfrac{1}{2}(\bar{g} + \bar{g}^*) \tag{11}$$

$$\theta_r = \tfrac{1}{2}(\theta + \theta^*). \tag{12}$$

Note that having the regional institution maximise the sum of the two governments' objective functions would yield equivalent results to the approach taken here.[23]

Now we can solve for the outcome of the game under RI once again by working backwards. The regional institution's best-response function is:

$$g = (1 + \gamma)^{-1}(\bar{g}_r + \gamma\theta_r) \equiv g(\theta_r). \tag{13}$$

The national lobbies in turn maximise their objective functions, internalising this best-response function, but taking the actions of the other lobby as given. Using (12), this yields:

$$\theta = \bar{g} + a\gamma/4(1 + \gamma) \quad \text{and} \quad \theta^* = \bar{g}^* + a\gamma/4(1 + \gamma). \tag{14}$$

By comparing (14) with (4), we can see that RI moderates the national lobbies' demands for intervention. The reason is simple: each lobby now has a smaller impact on decisionmaking, as the central institution has to contend with not one but two groups clamouring for attention. Since the marginal benefits of lobbying have gone down, the groups rationally choose to do less of it.[24] This is the preference-dilution effect mentioned above.

That larger political communities may be less susceptible to harmful factionalism is in fact an old insight. This was one of the main arguments used in *The Federalist Papers* in support of a 'well-constructed Union' of American states. As James Madison argued, individual factions could well come to dominate the political agenda in small political communities, but they would be unlikely to do so in a federal setup where they would have to contend with many more pressure groups:

> The smaller the society, the fewer probably will be the distinct parties and interests composing it; the fewer the distinct parties and interests, the more frequently will a majority be found of the same party; and the smaller the number of individuals composing a majority, and the smaller the compass within which they are placed, the more easily will they concert and execute their plans of oppression. Extend the sphere, and you take in a greater variety of parties and interests; you make it less probable that a majority of the whole will have a common motive to invade the rights of other citizens; or if such a common motive exists, it will be more difficult for all who feel it to discover their own strength and to act in unison with each other (Hamilton *et al.*, 1981 [1787], p. 22)

However, note that θ and θ^* also depend on $\bar{g}$ and $\bar{g}^*$, respectively, so that the overall pressure for intervention may not be reduced for both countries simultaneously. Combining (12) and (14),

$$\theta_r = \bar{g}_r + a\gamma/4(1+\gamma) = \tfrac{1}{2}(\bar{g} + \bar{g}^*) + a\gamma/4(1+\gamma). \tag{15}$$

On account of the second term, each of the two countries experiences a reduction of lobbying (cf. (4)). But the effect of the first term works differently for the two countries. This is the preference-asymmetry effect mentioned above. If $\bar{g} > \bar{g}^*$, the home country gets an additional reduction in lobbying from regional integration, while the foreign country gets an offsetting increase. Using (14), we can now state the equilibrium level of intervention in the union:

$$g = \tfrac{1}{2}(\bar{g} + \bar{g}^*) + (a/4)[\gamma/(1+\gamma)]^2. \tag{16}$$

Comparing this with (5), we can see that the direction of change in g after integration depends on the relative magnitudes of the preference-dilution and preference-asymmetry effects. The first effect pulls g down in both countries, while the second effect reduces g in one country but increases it in the other.

Now we are ready to evaluate the consequences of integration for each of the two countries. We will do this from two different perspectives, and ask in turn: (i) does integration lead to more efficient outcomes from a strictly economic standpoint? and (ii) does integration make each of the governments better off in terms of their own objective functions, including their political motives?

3.3 Economic consequences of RI

The economic evaluation hinges on whether integration helps close the gap between the economically desirable levels of government intervention and the actual levels chosen in equilibrium. That is, we need to check whether $(\bar{g} - g)^2$ and $(\bar{g}^* - g^*)^2$ are smaller under integration. Let us denote the economic component of the government's objective function by $\bar{G}$ and use the subscripts N and I to refer to the non-integrated and integrated cases respectively. Then:

$$\bar{G}_N = \bar{G}_N^* = -(\bar{g} - g)^2|_N = -(a^2/4)[\gamma/(1+\gamma)]^4, \qquad (17)$$

$$\bar{G}_I = -(\bar{g} - g)^2|_I = -\{\tfrac{1}{2}(\bar{g} - \bar{g}^*) - (a/4)[\gamma/(1+\gamma)]^2\}^2 \qquad (18)$$

$$\bar{G}_I^* = -(\bar{g}^* - g)^2|_I = -\{\tfrac{1}{2}(\bar{g}^* - \bar{g}) - (a/4)[\gamma/(1+\gamma)]^2\}^2. \qquad (19)$$

(Asterisks denote the foreign country as before.)

Consider first the case where $(\bar{g} - \bar{g}^*) = 0$, that is when the two countries are identical. By inspection, we can see that in that case $\bar{G}_N = \bar{G}_N^* < \bar{G}_I = \bar{G}_I^*$. This is due entirely to the preference-dilution effect, and represents the beneficial economic consequence of a larger political union. This effect operates for both countries. When $(\bar{g} - \bar{g}^*) \neq 0$, on the other hand, the preference-asymmetry effect comes into play. For 'small' differences, this effect benefits the country with the larger level of economically desirable intervention. The reason is as follows. In the absence of integration, government intervention is overprovided in both countries. Under integration, the preference-asymmetry effects works to reduce g in the country with the higher level of desirable interventions, and to increase it in the other country. Given the initial distortion, this benefits the first country and hurts the second. For a 'large' divergence between $\bar{g}$ and $\bar{g}^*$, however, *both* countries are made worse off by integration.

Finally, note an important implication. As the number of countries entering an arrangement increases, the condition that each must be made better off becomes more and more stringent, as long as the countries are not identical. Hence the relatively small number of participants is one significant advantage of regionalism over multilateralism.[25]

We have assumed so far that the regional institution selects as its target for intervention the simple average of the two countries' targets (i.e., $\bar{g}_r = \tfrac{1}{2}(\bar{g} + \bar{g}^*)$). As discussed above, this creates a positive externality for the high-intervention country and a negative externality for the low-intervention country. Now suppose that the regional institution can be designed in a manner that would maximise the joint economic benefits to the two countries. In terms of the present framework, this would allow us to select the weighting of the two countries' economic targets in an optimal manner. That is, through weighted voting or other means, the regional institution's objective function could be altered to the benefit of both economies. Hence we now assume that the countries could jointly commit to an institutional setup at the regional level, even though they cannot commit to particular policies, once the institutions are in place. The fact that these institutions are being set up from scratch may enable such institutional engineering at the international level when they are ruled out domestically.

The analysis proceeds as before, except that the game is now in three stages, with the first stage of the game consisting of choosing the weighting scheme that determines the importance to be attached by the regional institutions to each country's bliss point. It can be shown (see de Melo, Panagariya and Rodrik, 1992) that the institutional design question will result in putting a larger weight on the low-intervention country's preferences.

3.4 Political consequences of RI

Our framework suggests that political considerations and the constraints placed by private-sector lobbying activities should be taken into account in evaluating the benefits of RI. For the same reasons, political considerations should also weigh heavily in the determination of when countries are likely to enter regional arrangements.

The maximised values of G and G^* in the absence of integration are:

$$G_N = G^*_N = -(a^2/4)[\gamma/(1+\gamma)]^3, \tag{20}$$

Using (14) and (16), we obtain the analogous expression under integration:

$$G_I = G^*_I = -\{[(1+\gamma)/4](\bar{g}-\bar{g}^*)^2 + (a^2/16)[\gamma/(1+\gamma)]^3\}. \tag{21}$$

Consider first the case where the two countries are identical and $\bar{g} = \bar{g}^*$. In this case, integration is unambiguously beneficial. This derives entirely from the preference-dilution effect discussed above. Integration reduces the influence of the national lobby, and allows the government to get closer to achieving its dual objectives. When $\bar{g} \neq \bar{g}^*$, on the other hand, the benefits of integration are unambiguously reduced for both partners. The reason is that any economic gains from preference asymmetry are offset by political losses arising from a wider gap between the national lobby's preferences (0 and 0^*) and the common level of intervention. This captures the political cost of giving up national autonomy: while economic performance may be improved, this comes at the cost of a reduction in the government's ability to satisfy politically important groups' demands. On balance, asymmetry hurts. A comparison of (20) and (21) makes clear that RI would not pay for either government when $\bar{g}$ and $\bar{g}^*$ are too far apart.

To summarise, RI entails a commitment to abide by supranational rules. However, since these rules are endogenous and chosen by governments themselves, there is no real sense in which integration can solve the dynamic-inconsistency problems that afflict policymaking. What integration can do, as this framework has highlighted, is to alter the parameters of the situation in certain ways to alleviate the costs of dynamic inconsistency. Hence RI can help governments achieve superior outcomes, even when integration does not involve specific commitments either to other partners' policies or to arbitrarily selected policies. Under certain conditions, the arbitraging of institutions across national borders can be mutually beneficial. But regional partners have to cross a threshold of similarity before integration can become beneficial in this institutional sense and, as argued by Winters (1992, Chapter 7 in this volume), the adoption of common policies and common rules become additional objectives in their own right.[26]

4 Growth effects of RI schemes

The institutional considerations discussed above suggest that successful RI schemes benefit from a convergence in objectives, from having few partners, and from the willingness of countries to surrender some national autonomy and to commit to supranational rules. If these institutional considerations are met, it is likely that dynamic gains, reflected in higher growth, will be reaped. We have not referred above to the 'dynamic' effects, not only because they are rarely addressed in empirical work[27], but also because, like scale efficiency effects, they are not particular to RI arrangements. However these effects, though difficult to identify, are in practice likely to be more important than the static efficiency effects alluded to above. On macroeconomic grounds 'good' policy coordination and less instability is likely to raise long-run growth. In past RI schemes, the benefits of coordination through delegation to supranational bodies was largely absent from developing country arrangements because of a combination of conflicting objectives (e.g., in Africa) and weak central institutions. On the other hand, such benefits were apparent in the European Community (see Foroutan, 1992 and Winters, 1992, Chapters 8 and 7 in this volume).

The most often cited dynamic effects are spillover effects and moving down learning curves. For example, technological diffusion is more likely to be rapid if increased competition from trade puts pressures on domestic firms to adopt these new technologies. An enlarged market also increases the stimulus for investment to take advantage of the enlarged market and to meet the expanding competition. Reduced barriers to trade would thus provide another strong impetus to the convergence predictions of neo-classical growth theory based on diminishing returns. On Gershenkronian grounds, one would argue that this catchup effect would be stronger for developing countries provided, of course, that few impediments exist on the importation of technology from developed countries. Since such barriers were erected rather than removed as they were part of the inward-looking development strategy, this dynamic effect was not exploited to its full potential for former developing country RI schemes.

Perhaps the most important potential dynamic benefit for developing RI schemes comes from economic cooperation in areas where significant externalities and public goods (education, research and development, infrastructure, environment) exist. Of course, cooperation can take many different forms ranging from the simple exchange of information through the provision of joint training facilities to the mutual recognition and adoption of rules and regulations, to the implementation of joint policies and the establishment of joint institutions with quasi-legislative powers. Given the general lack of institutional development when the early RI schemes were implemented in the early 1960s, it would appear that the potential for gains even from limited regional cooperation would be great.

Is there any evidence of positive dynamic effects from RI? In other work (de Melo, Montenegro and Panagariya, 1992) we look for the evidence by fitting a simple growth equation to a cross-section of 101 countries stratified into a group of OECD developed (23) and developing (78) countries. We test for the eventual influence of belonging to an RI scheme by the inclusion of a dummy variable. The model is estimated over the period 1960–85 and by subperiods (1960–72 and 1973–85). Besides investment, the explanatory variables include initial *per capita* income and an estimate of the stock of human capital.

We tested for the effects of RI by including dummy variables for the following arrangements (years of implementation in parenthesis): (i) among developed countries, EC (1960) and EFTA (1960); (ii) among developing countries CACM (1960), LAFTA (1960, replaced by LAIA in 1980), SACU (1969) and CEAO (1974) (see Chapters 8 and 9 below). Among the latter group, SACU (Botswana, Lesotho, South Africa and Swaziland) is an example of a North–South RI scheme and CEAO which includes former French colonies are also part of a monetary union since they are all members of the CFA zone.[28]

Three results stand out. First, with one exception,[29] none of the integration dummies was significant. Insofar as splitting the sample controls for some of the effects of omitted variables, which would capture the effects of RI, belonging to an RI had no apparent effect on long-run growth. There was apparently no effect of membership, even for developed countries when the sample was split into two subperiods: 1960–72 and 1973–85. To some extent this should not come as a surprise since trade liberalisation was being carried out multilaterally and benefits were therefore being spread fairly evenly. There is thus no apparent effect of membership in terms of higher growth even for the European Community, EFTA and CACM during the 1960s when intra-regional trade was growing rapidly.

The second result is that splitting the sample into developed and developing country groups reveals an interesting difference in the role of investment and education in explaining growth. Investment has the expected positive (and statistically significant) sign for both groups and both periods, but the human capital variable, though of the right positive sign, is significant only for the developing country group. This result has two interesting interpretations. First, as emphasised by the 'new' growth literature, human capital is a contributing factor to growth for poor countries. Second, as emphasised in the institutional analysis, and in the literature emphasising cooperation, there would appear to be benefits from institution-building and joint training. This aspect of integration, largely neglected during the first wave of RI arrangements, would appear to promise benefits.

Third, initial *per capita* income enters with a negative and statistically significant sign for all regressions except for developed countries during 1973–85. This corroborates findings in the growth literature (e.g. Barro, 1991). From the point of view of RI arrangements this result, which supports the catchup hypothesis of neoclassical growth theory, suggests that the new form of North–South RI is promising for developing country members.

The first result, however, invites a note of caution in interpreting the no-effect results on growth. It could be argued that some of the regressors are correlated with the dummy variable controlling for RI membership – for example, the investment share in GDP could be higher among RI countries because of the positive effect of membership on the macro and institutional environment. In particular, it was found that the investment rate in the European Community, and especially in EFTA, was significantly higher (about 5 percentage points) than for other developed countries until 1973. This significantly higher investment rate is consistent with the positive effects that one would expect from effective integration among institutions and also corresponded to the period when the liberalisation policies were strongest and the European Community's relative growth performance was strongest. While this result is not strong evidence of 'dynamic' effects of RI, it suggests the possibility of an association between comprehensive RI and growth. Interestingly, the same increased investment effect also accompanied the announcement of NAFTA negotiations in Mexico (see Whalley, 1992, Chapter 11 in this volume).

5 Conclusions

Where do we stand? The evidence discussed in section 4 supports earlier findings that countries involved in RI schemes did not fare any better than comparators. But, then, neither was their performance any worse. The outcome was thus quite consistent with the theoretical discussion in section 2, which demonstrated that conflicting factors determine the efficiency consequences of RI arrangements. However, history will not repeat itself as circumstances today are quite different from those prevailing during the first wave of RI arrangements: fewer trade restrictions, an agenda in most RI arrangements that extends beyond the measures considered under the GATT, and a new form of integration involving reciprocal arrangements between developed and developing partners. On the whole, our conclusion is that, under today's circumstances, the new form of arrangement is likely to result in a more favourable outcome for RI schemes if real authority is delegated to well-designed regional institutions that do more than respond to pressure groups, which is a big 'if'.

What the discussion in section 3 showed is that regional partners have to cross a threshold of similarity in their economic objectives before such partial surrender of national autonomy can be mutually beneficial. This has apparently occurred. The political benefits of RI are maximised by integrating with countries that are as similar as possible in their objectives. But from an economic perspective, as discussed in section 3, there is an optimal degree of dissimilarity: Mexico hopes to benefit from NAFTA precisely because standards of government intervention and private property are much more stringent in the United States (and Canada) than they are in Mexico. Normally, these benefits are one-sided: continuing the example, US (and Canadian) institutions may well be contaminated by the less advantageous Mexican institutions. But as we have discussed, the economic benefits of dissimilarity can be shared by all parties provided the common institutions are designed in a way that weights the objective functions of each country appropriately. Hence ability to mould regional institutions from scratch is an important determinant of the gains from integration. However, as the experience of the European Community suggests, regional institutions should resist communitarising restrictive unilateral actions by members, and the necessary pragmatic approach to negotiating changes should avoid excessive compliance with provisions catering to sectional interests.

Looking ahead, the lessons are:

(1) If the current trend of unilateral liberalisation continues, integration is less likely to have negative efficiency effects and can help cement hard-fought reductions in protection.

(2) By including on their agenda areas not covered by multilateral negotiation, such as standards and government procurement, RI arrangements can serve as a catalyst in the pursuit of removing market fragmentations.

(3) Integration can confer substantial institutional benefits, but only if real authority is delegated to central institutions. As long as multilateral institutions are weak, and regional arrangements allow for a greater surrender of national autonomy, regionalism may paradoxically remain attractive to reforming governments. However, strengthened multilateral institutions will provide greater benefits than regional ones as they will present a larger political community and a greater scope for the preference-dilution effect.

(4) To benefit from integration, some convergence in national economic objectives is necessary. This explains why the prospect of integration with rich neighbours was so unattractive to developing countries when they still believed in import substitution, and why it has become more desirable as they have opened up their economies. It also explains why multilateral institutions may be inherently more difficult to sustain than regional institutions in light of the underlying diversity of national interests.

(5) However, too much convergence may undercut the economic gains from integration. This explains why developing countries currently stand to benefit least (in economic terms, at least) by integrating with other developing countries with similarly unsettled domestic institutions.

(6) The benefits of integration are greater the higher the possibility of shaping the institutions that go along with it in an economically desirable way. Recent regional attempts perhaps offer an additional degree of freedom in this regard compared to existing multilateral institutions.

NOTES

The authors are grateful to Sumana Dhar, Claudio Montenegro, and Francis Ng for superb assistance, and to conference participants for helpful comments.

1 This means that transshipment rules are necessary to prevent imports of high-tariff countries from being channelled via low-tariff countries in the area.

2 In addition to the literature cited later, important contributions include

Corden (1968, 1970, 1972, 1976), Kemp (1969), Lipsey (1957, 1960, 1970), Riezman (1979) and Vanek (1964). Two excellent surveys of the literature are Corden (1984) and Lloyd (1983).

3 According to Viner, trade creation occurs when the formation of an FTA or a CU leads to a switching of imports from a high-cost source to a low-cost source. Analogously, trade diversion occurs when imports switch from a low-cost source to a high-cost source. Subsequent authors noted crucial limitations of Viner's conclusion and demonstrated that in general trade diversion need not be welfare-worsening and trade creation need not be welfare-improving. The concepts have remained highly influential in policy debates, however, and authors have continued to equate trade creation with welfare improvement and trade diversion with welfare deterioration.

4 In terms of Viner's terminology, the FTA just described is trade-diverting. Yet the net effect of it on welfare is ambiguous. This is the point made in the post-Viner literature alluded to in n. 2.

5 As we will argue later, this is easier said than done. In practice, compensation schemes can turn even a welfare-enhancing FTA into a disaster.

6 In section 2.5, we will see that once we recognise that the imports from *B* and *C* are *imperfect* substitutes, the positive and negative effects emerge without elimination of trade with *C*. Figure 6.1 also provides a less extreme representation of the standard Vinerian analysis in which the supply curves of both *B* and *C* are horizontal.

7 In the case described in the previous paragraph, the FTA is unambiguously welfare-worsening. It is therefore not of much interest from a policy perspective.

8 This was the issue raised Cooper and Massell (1965a) and Johnson (1965), and also discussed by Berglas (1979) and Robson (1980).

9 The following discussion draws heavily upon Wonnacott and Wonnacott (1981). Also see Berglas (1983) and Wonnacott and Wonnacott (1984) in this context.

10 By the Lerner Symmetry Theorem, the tariff on good 2 by *B* is equivalent to an export tax on good 1 at the same time. The tariff in *B* therefore implies an upward shift in its export supply curve.

11 As Wonnacott and Wonnacott (1981) show, elimination of trade with *C* is not necessary to generate this result. What is critical is that the good imported by *C* before the FTA be different than that after it.

12 Although we did not formally consider the option of accessation to a bloc, it is clear from Figure 6.3 that if the internal price of *C* is above point *G*, *B* will be better off acceding to *C* than forming an FTA with *A*.

13 This was the main thrust of the analyses in Cooper and Massell (1965b) and Johnson (1965).

14 See Bhagwati (1968, 1990) in this context.

15 Strictly speaking, the externality implies that if the equilibrium is incompletely specialised, some intervention will be desirable and complete free trade will not be locally optimal. In the discussion just presented, we have ignored this complication.

16 The literature on imperfect competition and FTAs is almost non-existent. Therefore, the best we can do is infer such implications from the models addressing national trade policies in the presence of imperfect competition. Unfortunately, even here the results depend crucially on the specific structure of the model.

17 For examples of monopolistic competition, see Helpman (1981) and Krugman (1980).
18 This model is due to Meade (1956).
19 In models with three or more goods, the terms of trade effects are more complicated and less clear cut, although the presumption is that the union's terms of trade will improve upon the formation of an FTA. Thus, in Meade's model, as each partner country reduces its tariff on imports from the other, given substitutability, the demand for imports from the outside world declines. The union's terms of trade with respect to the outside world improve.
20 This is, of course, a scenario in which FTAs serve as stepping stones to multilateral free trade.
21 The importance of gaining market access is also stressed by Winters (1992, Chapter 7 in this volume) in his discussion of successive enlargements of the European Community.
22 'NAFTA is important to Mexico in itself . . . But it is still more important as a symbolic guarantee of the nature of the changes in the Mexican economy. Since the mid-1980s, when President Miguel de la Madrid took Mexico into GATT and slashed tariffs, its technocrats have used one word to describe the changes: "irreversible"'. A free-trade agreement would, they hoped, prove the point. 'The hard decisions . . . were taken before Mr. Salinas was publicly convinced of the case for free trade with Canada and the United States. But by signalling that within ten years he wants borderless trade within North America, he is telling both Mexico's once inefficient industries and the outside world that there really is no going back' (*The Economist*, 14 December 1991, p. 20).
23 That is because the simple sum of the objective functions differs from expression (9) only by terms that are constant from the perspective of the regional institution. Consequently, the first-order conditions are identical in the two cases.
24 A couple of things could work against this in practice. First, political groups may form transnational alliances. But even if they do, larger groups will probably suffer more from free-rider problems and from diversity of interests. Second, regional institutions may somehow turn out to be more receptive to pressure than the national institutions. This problem can be alleviated by careful institutional design (see below).
25 The advantage of a relatively small number of participants in a world of trading blocs is also made by Mancur Olson in his Discussion of Irwin (1992, Chapter 4 in this volume).
26 On the difficult role and mixed outcome of supranational institutions to help establish a common market in the European Community, see section 4 of Winters (1992, Chapter 7 in this volume).
27 Oft-cited studies of the dynamic effects are Cline (1978) for the CACM and Baldwin (1991) for the effects of 'Europe 1992' on EC growth.
28 Other RI schemes that were not included either did not have a long enough existence (e.g., SADC, the Canada–US FTA, etc.) or did not achieve much by way of integration.
29 The only exception is the significant effect for the dummy variable for SACU (which is entered for Botswana, Lesotho and Swaziland) for the period 1960–72. SACU is a highly integrated RI in existence since 1910 and the members' relation to South Africa is much like that of Liechtenstein to Austria or of Monaco to France.

REFERENCES

Baldwin, R. (1991) 'EMS Credibility: Discussion', *Economic Policy: A European Forum*, pp. 89–91.

Barro, R. (1991) 'Economic Growth in a Cross-Section of Countries, *Quarterly Journal of Economics*, **106**, pp. 407–43.

Berglas, E. (1979) 'Preferential Trading Theory: The *n* Commodity Case', *Journal of Political Economy*, **87**, pp. 315–31.

(1983) 'The Case for Unilateral Tariff Reductions: Foreign Tariffs Rediscovered', *American Economic Review*, **73**, pp. 1141–2.

Bhagwati, J. (1968) 'Trade Liberalization Among LDCs, Trade Theory and GATT Rules', in J.N. Wolfe (ed.), *Value, Capital and Growth: Essays in Honour of Sir John Hicks*, Oxford: Oxford University Press.

(1990) 'Departures from Multilateralism: Regionalism and Aggressive Unilateralism', *The Economic Journal*, **100**, pp. 1304–17.

Chenery, H. and M. Syrquin (1975) *Patterns of Development: 1950–1970*, Oxford: Oxford University Press.

Cline, W.R. (1978) 'Benefits and Costs of Economic Integration in Central America', in W.R. Cline and C. Delgado (eds), *Economic Integration in Central America*, Washington, DC: Brookings Institution.

Cooper, C.A. and B.F. Massell (1965a) 'A New Look at Customs Union Theory', *The Economic Journal*, **75**, pp. 742–7.

(1965b) 'Toward a General Theory of Customs Unions for Developing Countries', *Journal of Political Economy*, **73(5)**, pp. 461–76.

Corden, W.M. (1968) 'Customs Union Theory', unpublished manuscript.

(1970) 'The Efficiency Effects of Trade and Protection', in I.A. McDougall and R.H. Snape (eds), *Studies in International Economics: Monash Conference Papers*, Amsterdam: North-Holland.

(1972) 'Economies of Scale and Customs Union Theory', *Journal of Political Economy*, **80**, pp. 465–75.

(1976) 'Customs Union Theory and Nonuniformity of Tariffs', *Journal of International Economics*, **6(1)**, pp. 99–107.

(1984) 'Normative Theory of International Trade', Chapter 2 in R.W. Jones and P.B. Kenen (eds), *Handbook of International Economics*, Amsterdam: North-Holland.

Fischer, S. (1990) 'Rules versus Discretion in Monetary Policy', in B.M. Friedman and F.H. Hahn (eds), *Handbook of Monetary Economics*, vol. II, Amsterdam: North-Holland.

Foroutan, F. (1992) 'Regional Integration in Sub-Saharan Africa: Past Experience and Future Prospects', Chapter 8 in this volume.

Greenaway, D. (1989) 'Regional Trading Arrangements and Intra-Industry Trade', in D. Greenaway *et al.* (eds), *Economic Aspects of Regional Trading Arrangements*, New York: New York University Press.

Hamilton, A., J. Madison and J. Jay (1981 [1787]), *The Federalist Papers*, **10**, ed. Roy P. Fairfield, 2nd edn, Baltimore and London: Johns Hopkins University Press.

Helpman, E. (1981) 'International Trade in the Presence of Product Differentiation, Economies of Scale and Monopolistic Competition: A Chamberlin–Heckscher–Ohlin Approach', *Journal of International Economics*, **11(3)**, pp. 305–40.

Hirschman, A. (1971) *A Bias for Hope*, New Haven and London: Yale University Press.

Irwin, D. (1992) 'Multilateral and Bilateral Trade Policies in the World Trading System: An Historical Perspective', Chapter 4 in this volume.

Johnson, H.G. (1965) 'An Economic Theory of Protection, Tariff Bargaining, and the Formation of Customs Unions', *Journal of Political Economy*, **73** (June) pp. 256–83.

Kemp, M.C. (1969) *A Contribution to the General Equilibrium Theory of Preferential Trading*, Amsterdam: North-Holland.

Kemp, M.C. and H.Y. Wan, Jr (1976) 'An Elementary Proposition Concerning the Formation of Customs Unions', *Journal of International Economics*, **6** (February) pp. 95–8.

Kowalczyk, C. (1990) 'Welfare and Customs Unions', *NBER Working Paper*, **3476**, Cambridge, Mass.: NBER.

Krugman, P. (1980) 'Scale Economies, Product Differentiation, and the Pattern of Trade', *American Economic Review*, **70**, pp. 950–9.

Lachler, U. (1989) 'Regional Integration and Economic Development', Industry and Energy Department, *Working Paper*, **14**, Washington, DC: World Bank.

Lipsey, R.G. (1957) 'The Theory of Customs Unions: Trade Diversion and Welfare', *Economica*, **24**, pp. 40–6.

(1960) 'The Theory of Customs Unions: A General Survey', *The Economic Journal*, **70**, pp. 498–513.

(1970) *The Theory of Customs Unions: A General Equilibrium Analysis*, London: Weidenfeld & Nicolson.

Lloyd, P.J. (1982) '3 × 3 Theory of Customs Unions', *Journal of International Economics*, **12**, pp. 41–63.

Meade, J.E. (1956) *The Theory of Customs Unions*, Amsterdam: North-Holland.

Melo, J. de, C. Montenegro and A. Panagariya (1992) 'Regional Integration Old and New: Issues and Evidence', Washington, DC: World Bank (mimeo).

Melo, J. de, A. Panagariya and D. Rodrik (1992) 'Regional Integration: An Analytical and Empirical Overview', Washington, DC: World Bank (mimeo).

Nogués, J. and R. Quintanilla (1992) 'Latin America's Integration and the Multilateral Trading System', Chapter 9 in this volume.

Riezman, R. (1979) 'A 3 × 3 Model of Customs Unions', *Journal of International Economics*, **72**, pp. 820–9.

Robson, P. (1980) *The Economics of International Integration*, London and Boston: George Allen & Unwin.

Summers, R. and A. Heston (1988) 'A New Set of International Comparisons of Real Product Prices and Price Levels: Estimates for 130 Countries', *Review of Income and Wealth*, **34(1)**, pp. 1–25.

Vanek, J. (1964) 'Unilateral Trade Liberalization and Global World Income', *Quarterly Journal of Economics*, **78**, pp. 139–47.

Viner, J. (1950) The Customs Union Issue, New York: Carnegie Endowment for International Peace.

Whalley, J. (1992) 'Regional Trade Arrangements in North America: CUSTA and NAFTA', Chapter 11 in this volume.

Winters, L.A. (1992) 'The European Community: A Case of Successful Integration?', Chapter 7 in this volume.

Wonnacott, P. and R. Wonnacott (1981) 'Is Unilateral Tariff Reduction Preferable to a Customs Union? The Curious Case of the Missing Foreign Tariff', *American Economic Review*, **71** (September) pp. 704–41.

(1984) 'How General is the Case for Unilateral Tariff Reduction?', *American Economic Review*, **74**, p. 491.

Journal of International Economics 59 (2003) 161–182

Journal of INTERNATIONAL ECONOMICS

www.elsevier.com/locate/econbase

The protectionist bias of duty drawbacks: evidence from Mercosur

Olivier Cadot[a], Jaime de Melo[b], Marcelo Olarreaga[c,*]

[a]HEC Lausanne, BFSH1, CH 1015 Dorigny, Switzerland, CERDI and CEPR

[b]University of Geneva, 40 Bvd du Pont d'Arve, 1211 Geneva, Switzerland, CERDI and CEPR

[c]The World Bank, 1818 H St NW, Washington, DC 20433, USA, and CEPR

Received 9 August 2000; received in revised form 9 March 2001; accepted 12 June 2002

Abstract

In a political-economy setting where tariffs and duty drawbacks are endogenously chosen through industry lobbying, it is shown that full duty-drawbacks are granted to exporters who use imported intermediates in their production. This in turn decreases their incentives to counter-lobby against high tariffs on their inputs. In equilibrium, higher tariffs will be observed on these goods. The creation of a regional block will change the political equilibrium. Duty-drawbacks will be eliminated on intra-regional exports, which in turn will lead to lower tariffs for goods used as inputs by intra-regional exporters. Evidence from Mercosur suggests that the elimination of duty-drawbacks for intra-regional exports led to increased counter-lobbying by users of intermediate products. In its absence the common external tariff would have been on average 3.5 percentage points (25 percent) higher.

Keywords: Duty-drawbacks; Political-economy *Mercosur*; New regionalism

JEL classification: F11; F13; F15

1. Introduction

A key objective of trade reforms initiated since the early 1980s was the reduction of the anti-export bias of existing trade policies in developing countries.

*Corresponding author. Tel.: +1-202-458-8021; fax: +41-21-692-3495.

E-mail address: molarreaga@worldbank.org (M. Olarreaga).

A component of the World Bank recommendations in their trade loans was the creation or improvement of duty-drawback systems and temporary admission regimes (see Krueger and Rajapatirana, 1999). The pervasiveness of duty-drawback systems is also evident in a sample of 42 developing countries having undertaken WTO Trade Policy Reviews, for which Michalopoulos (1999) finds that all but three countries (Benin, Hong Kong and Singapore) have in place some form of duty-drawback system.

Duty drawbacks (or rebate systems) reduce or eliminate the duties paid on imported intermediates or raw materials that are used in the production of exports. When a firm imports an intermediate product for use in the production of an export good, tariff payments on the imported intermediate are either waived (duty drawback system) or returned to the producer once the final product is exported (rebate system).[1] Thus, the objective of these mechanisms is to promote exports by partially or fully compensating exporters for the anti-trade bias of existing protection, since exporters have access to their imported inputs at world prices in spite of the existing levels of tariff protection.

These incentive systems are often justified on the grounds that they tend to correct the anti-trade bias imposed by high tariff levels. The problem with this line of reasoning is that it assumes that tariffs are predetermined policy variables. If such was the case, the easiest way of reducing their anti-trade bias would be simply to eliminate them. The reason why this solution is rarely achieved is that existing levels of protection correspond to a political-economy equilibrium that is difficult to modify in the presence of lobbying pressures. Thus, it is difficult to understand the rationale for such systems or to get a complete picture of their incentive effects in the absence of a political-economy approach, which is the one taken in this paper.

Moreover, many recently-formed regional blocs have partially or completely phased out duty drawbacks on intra-regional exports. Both Mercosur and Nafta members have recently eliminate duty drawbacks to goods subsequently exported to their regional partner's markets.[2] This type of policy change, which we derive endogenously as a response to shifting government incentives, is likely to trigger a re-balancing of domestic power and incentives (see Lawrence, 1999). Indeed, in the case of Mexico, in response to the elimination of duty drawbacks in intra-Nafta exports, the Industry Promotion Programs announced the reduction of external tariffs on intermediate and capital goods for producers in 20 industries (see IADB, 2000, pp. 42–43). This process of elimination of duty drawbacks in regional blocks and its effect on the structure of the external tariffs is the focus of our analysis.

[1]For a detailed description, and comparison of, the functioning of the duty drawback systems in Taiwan (China) and Costa Rica, see Wu and Chuang (1998).

[2]See IADB (2000).

Using a common agency model of endogenous protection (Grossman–Helpman, 1994) with intermediate goods, we show that duty-drawback and rebate systems decrease exporter incentives to lobby against protection on their imported intermediate goods. Indeed, under a full duty-drawback regime, tariffs on intermediates are irrelevant to exporters since they are fully rebated. This leads, *ceteris paribus*, to higher levels of protection on intermediate goods heavily used in export industries, penalizing non-exporting users of such goods.

The formation of a regional trading bloc alters these incentives. Intra-regional exporters may be, in terms of profit levels, better off than before since they are now the beneficiaries of the area's external tariffs, but *at the margin*, their incentive to lobby against intermediate-good protection rises as duty-drawback and rebate schemes are endogenously eliminated on intra-regional exports. In equilibrium, this results in a lower level of external protection for those intermediate goods that are used heavily in sectors where intra-regional exports are large. Indirect effects of that type are at the very least consistent with the reduction in MFN tariffs that has accompanied the "new regionalism". Indeed, several authors (Ethier, 1998a; Lawrence, 1999; and Cadot et al., 2001) have argued that one of the important characteristics of the new wave of regional trade agreements is that they are accompanied by simultaneous reductions in MFN tariffs.[3]

We then try to see if the model's predictions are borne out in the case of the Common Market of the Southern Cone (Mercosur). Mercosur is an interesting case-study for at least four reasons. First, Mercosur members all had duty-drawback systems for exporters in place when they negotiated their Common External Tariff (CET) in 1994. And, as stipulated in Article 12 of mercosur/cmc/dec No. 10/94, these were no longer allowed for intra-regional trade, once convergence to the CET was achieved by December 2000. Second, Ethier (1998a) has identified Mercosur as one of the recent regional blocs satisfying the "New Regionalism" 's characteristics that preferential tariff reductions are accompanied by general MFN tariff reductions (Estevadeordal et al., 1999). Third, recent work (Olarreaga et al., 1999) has shown that industry lobbying was an important determinant of Mercosur's CET. Finally, Mercosur is one of the rare functioning Custom Union (CU) in the world, which allows us to simply specify the endogenous CET as a linear function of the pre-CU tariffs, without having to worry about industry determinants of protection. This would not have been such a simple task had we chosen a Free Trade Areas, as endogenous external tariffs are

[3]Some authors, including Ethier (1998b) or Freund (2000), have argued that the causality may be reversed from unilateral (or multilateral) liberalization towards regional integration. Others, starting with Bhagwati (1992) have expressed the fear that, on the whole, the surge in RTAs is likely to diminish the incentives to engage in multilateral non-discriminatory tariff reductions. For formal models that lead to this conclusion, see Levy (1997) and Krishna (1998). For a comprehensive review of the literature see Panagariya (2000).

typically a non-linear function of the pre-FTA tariffs due to incentives to compete over tariff revenue among FTA partners (see Cadot et al., 1999).[4]

Our approach to testing the political-economy hypothesis explained above proceeds in two steps. First, we assume that the Mercosur's CET is endogenously determined through cooperative bargaining among its members, and there is evidence that this was indeed the case as discussed later. Then, using input–output tables to trace the use of imported intermediates in downstream industries, we test whether deviations from the optimal CET are correlated with the intensity of input use in downstream industries. The interest of the exercise is two-fold. First, it gives a statistical indication of the magnitude of the lobbying effects attributable to the elimination of duty-drawback schemes. Second, it provides an indirect test of the political-support model of endogenous protection, whose empirical predictions have been the object of some controversy.[5]

To anticipate our main result, we find that during the negotiations for the Mercosur's CET, counter-lobbying against protection of intermediate goods increased following the elimination of duty-drawbacks for intra-regional exports. In the absence of this mechanism, we estimate that Mercosur's CET would have been on average 3.5 percentage points higher (25 percent higher).

The remainder of the paper is organized as follows. Section 2 develops a political-economy model à la Grossman and Helpman (1994) where, in the presence of imported intermediate products and duty-drawbacks, there are incentives to lobby for exporters. The characteristics and implications of a duty-drawback scheme are studied and compared with the alternative of no such incentive scheme. Section 3 focuses on how incentives to lobby and the resulting endogenously determined tariff structure is likely to change when two countries enter in a customs union (CU). Section 4 applies the model to the case of Mercosur, where, the formation of the CU resulted in a removal of duty rebates for exports to the region. Section 5 concludes.

2. Tariff drawbacks and lobbying

We explore exporter incentives to lobby against tariffs on intermediates products in a Grossman–Helpman (1994) model,[6] to which we add an intermediate good

---

[4]Note that the analytical results in this paper also hold for FTAs. The point here is that it would be empirically more challenging to capture.

[5]Our empirical results indirectly confirm the prediction strength of both the common-agency model of Grossman and Helpman (1994) and the Nash bargaining model of Maggi and Rodriguez-Clare (1998).

[6]There are other approaches to endogenous tariff formation, but as suggested by Helpman (1995), they all tend to lead to similar predictions. for our purposes, the advantage of the Grossman and Helpman (1994) framework is that it allows us to derive estimable reduced-form equations for tariffs that are based on microanalytic foundations.

following Cadot et al. (1997).[7] Consider, then, a small (price-taking) open economy, that produces 4 traded goods. Goods 0 and 1 are exported (but nevertheless consumed at home) while 2 and 3 are import-competing. Goods 0, 1 and 2 are final goods while 3 is an intermediate that is also used in final consumption. Good 0 is the numéraire. It is produced with labor only under Constant Returns to Scale (CRTS); good 3 (the intermediate) is produced with labor and sector-specific capital; goods 1 and 2 are produced with labor and sector-specific capital, and with good 3. The focus of the model is on the interaction between sectors 1 (exported final good) and 3 (imported intermediate).

Technologies in sectors 1 and 2 are Leontief between intermediate consumption and value added, with value-added being generated with labor and sector-specific capital. Omitting sector-specific capital, value-added is an increasing and concave function of labor, $f^i(\ell_i)$, $i = 1,2$, and output is given by

$$y_i = \min\left\{ f^i(\ell_i); \frac{v_i}{\alpha_i} \right\},$$

where y_i is sector i output, v_i is its intermediate consumption, and $\alpha_i \equiv v_i / x_i$ a fixed input–output coefficient. The tariff on good i is t_i; export goods (0 and 1) are neither taxed nor subsidized.

In the three non-numéraire sectors, the presence of sector-specific capital implies diminishing returns to labor and hence rents accruing to owners of sector-specific capital, who are also the firms' residual claimants. These rents are affected by trade policy: they are the reason for lobbying and the source of political contributions. The presence of a good produced under CRTs with labor only has the effect of pinning down the wage rate, so that there is no interindustry rivalry on the labor market which simplifies considerably the model's structure.[8] Moreover, we assume that capital ownership is sufficiently concentrated for lobbies to disregard the effect of protection on consumer prices.

Together, these assumptions ensure that the only source of interindustry rivalry are input–output linkages. Given this supply-side structure, the political line-up is as follows: sector 3 lobbies for protection, sector 1 lobbies against the protection of sector 3, and sector 2 lobbies for its own protection and against the protection of sector 3. We treat the game as if lobbies 1, 2 and 3 were acting as non-cooperative

[7] The setup is similar to Cadot et al. (1997), but their focus is on explaining the determinants of protection in the presence of lobbies' rivalry in intermediate and factor markets, whereas here we explore exporters incentives in the presence of tariff drawbacks, and abstract from factor-market effects. This simplification is defensible if protection is not too high and duty-drawbacks are not a substantial part of government tariff revenue.

[8] For an analysis with general equilibrium effects in the labor market, and orders of magnitude of its importance, see Cadot et al. (1997).

principals vying for influence over their common agent, the government, following the common-agency literature.

Consumers have identical tastes represented by a quasi-linear and additive utility function

$$u = c_0 + u(c_1) + u(c_2) + u(c_3)$$

where c_i stands for the consumption of final good i and the function u has the usual properties. It follows that, given that good 1 is consumed but also exported (hence not protected) while goods 2 and 3 are imported, in equilibrium $u'(c_1) = p_1^\star$, $u'(c_2) = p_2^\star(1+t_2)$ and $u'(c_3) = p_3^\star(1+t_3)$, where $p_i^\star$ is the world price of good i and t_1 and t_2 are ad-valorem tariffs.

2.1. Initial equilibrium

The political process is as follows. Organized into lobbies, competitive firms in sectors 1, 2 and 3, simultaneously offer contribution functions C_1, C_2 and C_3 to the government, all conditioned on a vector of trade-policy variables. The trade-policy variables are t_2, t_3, and a duty-drawback system whereby a fraction δ of the tariff paid on intermediate imports is rebated to exporters. Faced with these contribution functions, the government sets t_2, t_3, and δ so as to maximize a weighted average of social welfare and income from contributions, which we will call G.[9] That is, the government's problem is

$$\max_{t_2,t_3,\delta} G(t_2,t_3,\delta) = \sum_{i=1}^{3} C_i(t_2,t_3,\delta) + aW(t_2,t_3,\delta)$$

$$\text{s.t. } t_2 \geq 0,\ t_3 \geq 0,\ 1 \geq \delta \geq 0,$$

for some constant a. Let

$$\mathcal{L} = G(t_2,t_3,\delta) + \lambda(1-\delta)$$

where λ is a Lagrange multiplier. In a truthful equilibrium (see Bernheim and Whinston, 1986), the derivatives of contribution functions with respect to t_2,t_3, and δ are equal to the derivatives of the sectorial profit functions. Using this property, equilibrium conditions are

$$\frac{\partial \pi_i}{\partial t_3} = \frac{\partial C_i}{\partial t_3}, \quad i = 1,2,3 \tag{1}$$

$$\frac{\partial \pi_2}{\partial t_2} = \frac{\partial C_2}{\partial t_2}; \quad \frac{\partial \pi_2}{\partial \delta} = \frac{\partial C_2}{\partial \delta}; \quad \frac{\partial \pi_1}{\partial \delta} = \frac{\partial C_1}{\partial \delta} \tag{2}$$

[9] Export subsidies are not allowed here given that the WTO subsidy agreement bans its use. Note, however, that results are robust to the introduction of export subsidies as a trade policy instrument.

$$\frac{\partial \mathcal{L}}{\partial t_i} \leq 0, \quad t_i \geq 0, \quad t_i \frac{\partial \mathcal{L}}{\partial t_i} = 0, \; i = 2,3 \tag{3}$$

$$\frac{\partial \mathcal{L}}{\partial \delta} \leq 0, \quad \delta \geq 0, \quad \delta \frac{\partial \mathcal{L}}{\partial \delta} = 0, \tag{4}$$

$$1 - \delta \geq 0, \quad \lambda \geq 0, \quad \lambda(1 - \delta) = 0. \tag{5}$$

Eqs. (1)–(2) are truthfulness conditions, while (3)–(5) are Kuhn–Tucker conditions for the government. Given the technologies postulated, profit functions can be written as

$$\pi_1(t_3,\delta) = \{p_1^\star - \alpha_1 p_3^\star[(1 + (1 - \delta)t_3)]\}y_1 - w\ell_1,$$

$$\pi_2(t_2,t_3) = [p_2^\star(1 + t_2) - \alpha_2 p_3^\star(1 + t_3)]y_2 - w\ell_2,$$

$$\pi_3(t_3) = p_3^\star(1 + t_3)y_3 - w\ell_3.$$

Using the envelope theorem,

$$\frac{\partial \pi_1}{\partial t_3} = -(1 - \delta)p_3^\star \alpha_1 y_1 \leq 0, \quad \frac{\partial \pi_1}{\partial \delta} = t_3 p_3^\star \alpha_1 y_1 \geq 0,$$

$$\frac{\partial \pi_2}{\partial t_3} = -p_3^\star \alpha_2 y_2 < 0, \quad \frac{\partial \pi_2}{\partial t_2} = p_2^\star y_2 > 0, \tag{6}$$

$$\frac{\partial \pi_3}{\partial t_3} = p_3^\star y_3 > 0.$$

Note that with a full duty-drawback (i.e. when $\delta = 1$), producers of good 1 become indifferent to the level of the tariff on the intermediate good, i.e. $\partial \pi_1 / \partial t_3 = 0$. This does not apply, however, to producers of good 2, who serve the domestic market and are consequently not eligible for the duty-drawback.

As consumers have identical quasi-linear preferences, social welfare is the sum of income and consumer surplus, income being itself the sum of labor income, industry profits and tariff revenue. The tariff-revenue term is complicated by the presence of the duty-drawback scheme, which segments the intermediate-good market between sector-1 users, who are eligible for it, and sector-2 users, who are not. Given the availability of the scheme, sector-1 firms use only imported intermediate goods. In order to avoid a taxonomy of cases, we will assume that the domestic output of the intermediate good is not enough to cover the needs of sector 2 and final users, who accordingly use a mixture of home-produced and imported intermediates all priced at $p_3^\star(1 + t_3)$. Let $m_3 = c_3 + \alpha_1 y_1 + \alpha_2 y_2 - y_3$ stand for good 3's imports. Net tariff revenue on good-3 imports is, after deduction of duty-drawback repayments, $p_3^\star t_3(m_3 - \delta\alpha_1 y_1)$. Given this, welfare is:

$$W = w\ell + \pi_1(t_1,t_3,\delta) + \pi_2(t_2,t_3) + \pi_3(t_3) + p_2^\star t_2 m_2 + p_3^\star t_3(m_3 - \delta\alpha_1 y_1)$$
$$+ \sum_{i=1}^{3} u(c_i) - p_1^\star c_1 - p_2^\star(1+t_2)c_2 - p_3^\star(1+t_3)c_3,$$

where $\ell = \Sigma_{i=0}^{3} \ell_i$. Welfare terms are thus

$$\frac{\partial W}{\partial t_2} = p_2^\star y_2 + p_2^\star m_2 + p_2^\star t_2 m_2' + u'(c_2)c_2' p_2^\star - p_2^\star c_2 - p_2^\star(1+t_2)c_2' p_2^\star$$
$$= p_2^\star t_2 m_2' \leq 0 \tag{7}$$

for protection in sector 2, and

$$\frac{\partial W}{\partial t_3} = p_3^\star y_3 - p_3^\star(1-\delta)\alpha_1 y_1 - p_3^\star \alpha_2 y_2 + \frac{\partial}{\partial t_3}[p_3^\star t_3(m_3 - \delta\alpha_1 y_1)]$$
$$+ u'(c_3)c_3' p_3^\star - p_3^\star c_3 - p_3^\star(1+t_3)c_3' p_3^\star$$

for protection in sector 3. But note that $c_3 + \alpha_1 y_1 + \alpha_2 y_2 = y_3 + m_3$, and that[10]

$$\frac{\partial}{\partial t_3}[p_3^\star t_3(m_3 - \delta\alpha_1 y_1)] = p_3^\star\left[m_3 - \delta\alpha_1 y_1 + t_3\left(m_3' - \delta\alpha_1 \frac{\partial y_1}{\partial t_3}\right)\right]$$
$$= p_3^\star\left[m_3 - \delta\alpha_1 y_1 + t_3\left(m_3' - \delta\alpha_1 \frac{\partial^2 \pi_1}{\partial t_3 \partial t_1}\right)\right]$$
$$= p_3^\star\left[m_3 - \delta\alpha_1 y_1 + t_3\left\{m_3' - \delta\alpha_1 \frac{\partial}{\partial t_1}[-(1-\delta)\alpha_1 y_1]\right\}\right]$$
$$= p_3^\star[m_3 - \delta\alpha_1 y_1 + t_3[m_3' + \delta(1-\delta)\alpha_1^2 y_1']],$$

where y_1' is the own-price derivative of supply in sector 1. Combining these and rearranging slightly gives

$$\frac{\partial W}{\partial t_3} = p_3^\star t_3[m_3' + \delta(1-\delta)\alpha_1^2 y_1']. \tag{8}$$

Finally, the welfare effect of the duty-drawback at rate δ is

$$\frac{\partial W}{\partial \delta} = \frac{\partial \pi_1}{\partial \delta} + \frac{\partial}{\partial \delta}[p_3^\star t_3(m_3 - \delta\alpha_1 y_1)] = 0. \tag{9}$$

The absence of a welfare effect of the duty-drawback reflects the fact that it is a pure transfer entailing no welfare loss, since it affects neither the consumer price

[10] The last term in the second line below draws on the enveloped theorem, i.e., $y_1 = \partial\pi_1/\partial t_1$. In the third line, the last term draws on the fact that $\partial^2\pi_1/\partial t_3 \partial t_1 = \partial^2\pi_1/\partial t_1 \partial t_3$.

of good 1 nor its producer price, but only the price of an input in a Leontief production function.[11] Combining (6) with (7), (8), and (9) gives

$$\frac{\partial G}{\partial t_2} = p_2^{\star}(y_2 + at_2m_2'), \tag{10}$$

$$\frac{\partial G}{\partial t_3} = p_3^{\star}\{y_3 - (1-\delta)\alpha_1 y_1 - \alpha_2 y_2 + at_3[m_3' + \delta(1-\delta)\alpha_1^2 y_1']\}, \tag{11}$$

$$\frac{\partial G}{\partial \delta} = p_3^{\star} t_3 \alpha_1 y_1. \tag{12}$$

The function G is globally concave in t_2 and t_3, so the second-order condition holds for these instruments. We will assume in addition that interior solutions hold for both instruments since otherwise the whole problem of endogenous protection would become irrelevant. By contrast, (12) is clearly nonnegative no matter what, and strictly positive whenever $t_3 > 0$ (the duty-drawback is irrelevant if t_3 is zero). Therefore in equilibrium there is full drawback, i.e. $\delta^* = 1$. Using this condition to simplify (11), the first-order condition for t_3 reduces to

$$y_3 - \alpha_2 y_2 + at_3m_3' = 0,$$

or

$$t_3^* = \frac{y_3 - \alpha_2 y_2}{-am_3'}. \tag{13}$$

Finally, setting (10) equal to zero and solving for t_2 gives

$$t_2^* = \frac{y_2}{-am_2'}. \tag{14}$$

Together, t_2^*, t_3^* and $\delta^* = 1$ define the initial (pre-RTA) equilibrium.[12] Recall that sector 1 is the export sector and that sector 2 (along with sector 3) is an import competing sector. Hence sector 2 is not eligible for a duty-drawback.

Compared to a model with no intermediates, what is new here is the negative term involving the output of sector 2 in the numerator of (13). This term reflects counter-lobbying by producers in sector 2 against protection in sector 3, because protection raises the price of the intermediate good and consequently hurts their profits. However, sector 1, is not active in this counter-lobbying, because the full duty-drawback shelters it from the cost of intermediate-good protection. The

[11]Note that this implies that duty-drawbacks cannot be justified on welfare grounds under the assumptions in this paper. Panagariya (1992) provides a more general model where duty-drawbacks have ambiguous effects on welfare.

[12]Note that we would have obtained similar optimal tariffs had we assume that the government and the lobby engaged in Nash bargaining over contributions as in Maggi and Rodriguez-Clare (1998) instead of the common-agency game of Grossman and Helpman (1994).

absence of counter-lobbying by sector 1, because it benefits from full duty-drawback, tends *ceteris paribus*, to raise the equilibrium level of protection in sector 3 (and therefore to hurt sector 2 and consumers). Thus, duty-drawbacks have a protectionist bias.[13]

Note, incidentally, that the duty-drawback scheme creates intra-industry trade even under perfect competition. The reason is that producers of good 1 will always choose to export all their output if doing so makes them eligible for the duty-drawback (encouraging exports is indeed the scheme's objective) while domestic consumption of good 1 will be entirely covered by imports. A country having a duty-drawback scheme will then both export and import good 1.

3. Customs Union and duty-drawbacks

Suppose now that country *A* forms a Customs Union (CU) with the country absorbing sector 1's exports, country *B*, which then becomes its partner country. This situation will not be typical of most RTAs among, say sub-saharan African countries, since they trade small amounts of manufactures. But such a situation corresponds largely to the Mercosur case, at least between Argentina and Brazil, since they were both able to export substantial amount of manufactures to each other (see Yeats, 1998). It would also apply to countries in Asia that have duty-drawbacks and have the potential to export substantial amounts of manufactures to each other.[14]

Suppose then that the governments of *A* and *B* agree on an efficient solution for the CET, and then bargain over how they share the benefits of cooperation via monetary transfers ("shallow integration" in the terminology of Cadot et al., 1999).[15]

In this setup, let us first examine under which conditions duty-drawbacks would be eliminated for intra-regional exports, and if so what are the consequences for external tariffs.

[13]Note that the equilibrium tariffs reflect tariff escalation, in the sense that intermediate goods have higher levels of protection than consumer goods. The presence of duty-drawbacks, however reduces the extent of tariff escalation by increasing the tariffs on intermediate goods.

[14]Note that all the qualitative results in this section would also apply to the formation of a Free Trade Area. However, as shown by Cadot et al. (1999), external tariffs become a non-linear function of the pre-FTA tariffs and therefore would make our empirical work significantly more complicated.

[15]"Shallow integration" boils down to setting up the problem as if a common agency was maximizing the sum of member-country government's welfare functions, whereas under "deep integration", there is a single agency in charge of trade policy that takes into account union-wide lobbying, so that unlike shallow integration, country characteristics are aggregated.

3.1. Elimination of duty-drawbacks after CU formation

Article 12 of Mercosur declaration cmc/dec No. 10/94 stipulates that intra-regional exporters can no longer benefit from duty-drawbacks. To explain Mercosur's decision let us write the CU first order condition for the optimal level of duty-drawback for intra-regional trade.[16] In view of the application in Section 4, we use superscript M (for Mercosur) to denote the customs union. Recalling that country B absorbs all of country A exports of good 1 and using (12):

$$\frac{\partial G^M}{\partial \delta} = \frac{\partial G^A}{\partial \delta} + \frac{\partial G^B}{\partial \delta} = p_3^\star \tau_3 \alpha_1^A y_1^A - a^B p_1^\star \tau_1 \frac{\partial y_1^A}{\partial \delta} \tag{15}$$

where G^M is the CU's objective function (given by the sum of A's and B's objective function) and τ_i is the CET in sector i. The first term in (15) is as before the gain for the government of country A of imposing a duty-drawback. The second term is now the loss for country B in terms of tariff revenue of allowing exporters in A to benefit from duty-drawbacks. Indeed, the existence of a duty-drawbacks in intra-regional trade shifts outwards the export supply of exporters in A, which reduces tariff revenue for country B (as it diverts from rest-of-the world imports).

Using (6) and noting that $\partial y_1^A / \partial \delta = \partial^2 \pi_1^A / \partial \delta \partial \tau_1$, the right-hand side of (15) is always negative, and therefore at the optimum there are no duty-drawbacks ($\delta^M = 0$), if:

$$a^B > \frac{1 + \tau_1}{\tau_1 \epsilon_{S_1}^A} \tag{16}$$

where $\epsilon_{S_1}^A$ stands for the price-elasticity of supply of good 1 in country A. Thus, if the weight given to social welfare in country B's objective function is sufficiently high, then duty-drawbacks will be eliminated. The reason is that the gains in terms of contributions by producers of good 1 in A are not sufficient to compensate for the loss in terms of tariff revenue in B.

Taking as an example the average tariff in Mercosur which is around 14 percent, and assuming an average price-elasticity of supply around 1, (16) implies that a^B has to be larger than 8 for duty-drawbacks to be completely eliminated. Note that if import demand functions are non-concave, the second-order condition for the government's problem requires a^B to be larger than 1. Estimates of a for the United States in the 1980s yield values above 50 (see Goldberg and Maggi, 1999;

[16] It could be argued that allowing for duty-drawbacks within a CU makes little economic sense as this may create incentives for trade cross-hauling. The objective here is to show under which conditions it may also make little political-economy sense.

Gawande and Bandyopadhyay, 2000).[17] Given that Mercosur has eliminated duty-drawbacks for intra-regional trade, one can infer that the constraint in (16) was satisfied.[18] The implications for CET levels are studied in the next section.

3.2. CET after duty-drawback elimination

Several trade patterns can be envisaged when the CU is formed. Since we are interested in situations where lobbying takes place, we assume that exporters of good 1 in A sell in a protected market in B. This will be the case, if the following two assumptions are met.

First, let us assume that there is protection in sector 1, so that we can concentrate on the conditions when it will be profitable for A's producers to sell in B. Since duty-drawbacks are eliminated for intra-regional trade, this creates an incentive for exporters to re-direct their production from the region to the rest-of-the world. In such a situation the increase in counter-lobbying will not occur. In order to avoid this, we need to assume that producers always find it more profitable to sell within the regional market with protection and paying duties on intermediate purchases, than selling on the world market at the world market price, but not paying duties on intermediate purchases. Letting τ_1 be the CET on good 1, as before, this requires that:

$$p_1^{\star}[1+\tau_1-\alpha_1^A p_3^{\star}(1+\tau_3)] > p_1^{\star}(1-\alpha_1^A p_3^{\star})$$

which simplifies to:

Assumption 1. $\tau_1 > \alpha_1^A p_3^{\star}\tau_3$

Assumption 1, which is similar to the expression determining whether firms will sell in markets protected by rules of origin requirements (see e.g. Krueger, 1993), guarantees that selling in the market protected by the CET is more profitable than selling in the world market even if it involves forsaking the benefit of the duty-drawback.

Second, we suppose that A and B's combined output in sector 1 is not enough to serve the entire CU demand at the equilibrium price. Again, this situation is most representative of RTAs among developing countries, at least among countries that do not differ too much in size (like Argentina and Brazil). That is, letting $c_1^A + c_1^B$ be the CU consumption of good 1 at price $p_1^{\star}(1+\tau_1)$ and $y_1^A + y_1^B$ the CU output, we assume:

[17] Note that as shown by Grossman and Helpman (1994, p. 838), such high values for a imply that the government gives a similar weight to political contributions and aggregate welfare net of contribution in its objective function.

[18] Estimates of a in Argentina and Brazil are provided in Section 4.2.

Assumption 2. $c_1^A + c_1^B \geq y_1^A + y_1^B$

Thus, after the CU is formed, firms in sector 1 sell in a protected market (the partner country's), which was not the case before. This gives them a direct benefit. However, they are no longer eligible for the duty-drawback scheme so that they become sensitive to the rate of protection of the intermediate good. Through the truthfulness restriction, the degree of their sensitivity, given by the derivative of their profit function with respect to the CET in sector 3, i.e. τ_3, determines the intensity of their counter-lobbying.[19]

Turn now to the determination of the CET in sector 3. Recalling that duty-drawbacks are disallowed for intra-regional trade, i.e., that $\delta^M = 0$, the first order condition to the CET problem in the intermediate sector, is given by:

$$\frac{\partial G^M}{\partial \tau_3} = \frac{\partial G^A}{\partial \tau_3} + \frac{\partial G^B}{\partial \tau_3} \tag{17}$$

$$= p_3^{\star}(y_3^A - \alpha_1^A y_1^A - \alpha_2^A y_2^A + a^A \tau_3 m_3^{A'}) \tag{18}$$

$$+ p_3^{\star}(y_3^B - \alpha_1^B y_1^B - \alpha_2^B y_2^B + a^B \tau_3 m_3^{B'}) = 0 \tag{19}$$

Protection for sectors producing final goods would be given by an expression identical to (19), except that it would exclude the element that captures counter-lobbying on intermediate products.

Return to (19). To simplify, but also in view of empirical tractability for the application that follows, assume identical price effects on import demand for both countries in sector 3, i.e. that $m_3^{A'} = m_3^{B'} = \mu < 0$. Also, choose units so that $y_3^A + y_3^B = 1$. The assumption of identical price effects is motivated by lack of detailed information on import demand elasticities at a disaggregated level, whereas the normalization assumption is to avoid "size" effects in the estimation. Let t_3^A and t_3^B stand respectively for the levels of tariffs satisfying (13) for the home and partner countries respectively.

Then solving (19) for τ_3, and rearranging using (13) yields the expression that will be used in the estimation below:

$$\tau_3^{\star} = \frac{a^A}{a^A + a^B} t_3^A + \frac{a^B}{a^A + a^B} t_3^B + \frac{1}{\mu(a^A + a^B)}(\theta_3^A z_3^A + \theta_3^B z_3^B) \tag{20}$$

---

[19]Note that both assumptions would not be necessary, if we assumed that trade took place in differentiated products, which is probably a better approximation for trade in most manufactures, since then it would always pay to sell in both markets and it would always pay to obtain protection (a tariff would raise the price of the domestic substitute), though one would have to factor in terms-of-trade effects. In any event, a more general formulation would be considerably more cumbersome to develop.

where $\theta_j^A = (1 - \theta_j^B) = y_j^A/(y_j^A + y_j^B)$ is country A's share in the output of good j and

$$z_3^i = \frac{\alpha_1^i y_1^i}{y_3^i}$$

is the share of good 3's output in country i used as an intermediate in sector 1.

Expression (20) indicates that the CET is given by a weighted average of the existing optimal tariffs in both countries (these are the first two elements on the RHS of (20)) plus a third term that denotes the increase in counter-lobbying by the export sector against tariffs on the intermediate good due to the elimination of duty-drawbacks on intra-regional trade. The last term on the RHS of (20) is negative since $\mu < 0$, so its presence reduces the value of the CET. Note also that the increase in counter-lobbying would still be present in (20) if one did not impose a common import demand in each member country.[20]

Note that when substituting t_3^i, $i \in A,B$ in (20), we are implicitly assuming that, when lobbying the government, lobbies do not take into account the second-round effects of the adjustment in tariffs on their production levels. This assumption is not only probably closer to reality than the alternative which would take second-round effects into account, but also it is the only possible assumption in our empirical application on Mercosur.[21] Most importantly, to be able to substitute the existing tariffs will avoid excluding from the empirical analysis some important determinants of the tariff levels which cannot be directly measured.

To recapitulate, the simple political-economy model developed here shows that, if there is a possibility for exporters to obtain a duty-drawback, they will lobby to obtain the full drawback (which is what is usually observed), and that duty-drawbacks tend to raise the equilibrium rate of protection on intermediate goods. More importantly for our purposes, the model shows that under plausible conditions, a CU will alter lobbying incentives, leading to pressures to eliminate duty-drawbacks and to reduce the external protection on intermediate goods.

4. Application to Mercosur

We use Mercosur data to check whether the model's predictions are consistent with observed outcomes. Beyond data issues and the reasons stated in the

[20]One can show that if government's objective when setting tariffs is to maximize tariff revenue, then the CET would have been given by an expression similar to the one in (20), i.e., $\tau_3^* = 1/2(t_3^A + t_3^B) - 1/\mu(\theta_3^A z_3^A + \theta_3^B z_3^B)$. The difference is that the elimination of duty-drawbacks would have led to a higher CET rather than lower. Note that it would not be possible to endogenously explain the existence of duty-drawbacks in the pre-CU equilibrium if governments maximized tariff revenue.

[21]This is because to our knowledge there exists no disaggregated production data available for Mercosur members after 1994, and Mercosur's CET was implemented in 1995.

introduction, there are at least two practical reasons for our choice. First, steps towards putting in place a CET have gone much faster than in other recent RTAs; recall that the agreement was signed in 1991 and that the CET came into effect in 1995. Second, Mercosur is the only CU whose members previously had duty-drawbacks and which substantially eliminated barriers on internal trade. We discuss first data and econometric issues, then turn to results.

4.1. The empirical model

To estimate the effect of eliminating duty-drawbacks on the level of Mercosur's CET, we estimate a stochastic version of (20) on a cross-section of tariffs. To estimate the expression, we need to calculate the third term in that expression which requires information on input–output relations and on production at a fairly disaggregated level (ISIC 4 digit-level which includes 80 sectors). A table describing the characteristics of the 80 sectors used in the estimation is provided in the data appendix. The only Mercosur members for which industrial data was available at this level of disaggregation were Argentina and Brazil. Given that together they represent more than 85 percent of Mercosur production in any sector at the 3 digit ISIC classification level, the exclusion of Uruguay and Paraguay from the empirical analysis should not unduly affect our results.[22] Moreover, in their study of the determination of Mercosur's CET, Olarreaga and Soloaga (1998) concluded that Brazil's political lobbying variables performed as well in explaining variations in Mercosur's CET on their own as those of the four members together.

In Section 2, goods 1 and 2 were pure final goods whereas 3 only was usable both in final consumption and as an intermediate input. Now, let all goods be usable as final goods and as intermediates in the production of other goods. We need then to rewrite slightly the coefficient z_j^i. The total demand for good j as an intermediate in the production of all other goods k ($k = 1, \ldots, 80$), is $\Sigma_k \alpha_{jk} y_k$, where α_{jk} is its per unit requirement in the production of good k; thus,

$$z_j^i = \frac{\sum_k \alpha_{jk}^i y_k^i}{y_j^i}$$

and the share of good j's Mercosur output used as an intermediate in the production of other goods in the Mercosur is

$$z_j^M = \sum_{i=A,B} \theta_j^i z_j^i \tag{21}$$

where θ_j^i is i's share in the Mercosur's output of j. The higher is z_j^M, the stronger is

[22] See Olarreaga and Soloaga (1998).

the counter-lobbying against protection of j, and consequently, in accordance with (19) the lower is, ceteris paribus, the level of good j's equilibrium external tariff under the CET.

At the 4 digit ISIC classification level, Mercosur's CET is censored from above at its upper limit of 20 percent (four sectors reach this upper bound at this level of disaggregation). To allow for censoring, we estimate (20) using a Tobit model; i.e.

$$\tau_j = \begin{cases} \tau_j^\star & \text{if } \tau_j^\star < 20 \\ 20 & \text{if } \tau_j^\star \geq 20 \end{cases}$$

and

$$\tau_j^\star = \frac{a^A}{a^A + a^B} t_j^A + \frac{a^B}{a^A + a^B} t_j^B + \frac{1}{\mu(a^A + a^B)} z_j^M + \epsilon_j$$
$$= \beta_1 t_j^A + \beta_2 t_j^B + \beta_3 z_j^M + \epsilon_j \tag{22}$$

where subscript j stands for a sector, $j = 1, \ldots 80$, ϵ_j is the error term, and the expected signs are $\beta_1 > 0$, $\beta_2 > 0$ and $\beta_3 < 0$.

In estimating (22), no constraints are imposed on the values taken by β_1 and β_2, whereas the model suggests $\beta_1 = 1 - \beta_2$. The alternative then is to estimate this constrained version of (22) by taking t_j^A (for example) to the left-hand side of the equation. Thus, the equation to be estimated becomes:

$$\tau_j^\star - t_j^A = \beta_2 (t_j^B - t_j^A) + \beta_3 z_j^M + \epsilon_j \tag{23}$$

where the expected signs are as before. The advantage of (23) is that it is no longer censored and can therefore be estimated by OLS (or by weighted least squares to control for potential group data heteroscedasticity).

As discussed in Olarreaga et al. (1999), tariffs tend to be determined at the tariff line level and not at the industry level.[23] This implies that if the error is determined at the tariff line level and the number of tariff lines in each industry is not the same (as can be observed in the table in the data appendix the number of tariff lines varies from 1 in ISIC 3131 to 501 tariff lines in ISIC 3511), then the variance of the error term at the industry level will be negatively correlated with the number of lines in each industry, reducing the efficiency of our estimates. To correct for this potential heteroscedasticity, each observation at the industry level needs to be weighted by the number of tariff lines in each industry (i.e. multiplied by the square root of the number of tariff lines in each industry).

However, a problem with the above correction is that it assumes that the errors

[23] If not we would not observe variation in tariff levels within industries.

at the tariff line level are independently distributed. If observations within the same industry share a common unobserved determinant, then the above correction may reintroduce some heteroscedasticity. To test for this possibility, we follow Dickens (1990) and when necessary, we apply the correction he suggests which yields asymptotically efficient estimates.[24]

The data appendix describes data sources and provides a table with the data used in the estimations. The CET is the one negotiated in Ouro Preto in 1994 by Mercosur members. Tariffs or Argentina and Brazil are 1994 external official tariffs (corresponding to an FTA situation as by then more than 95 percent of their internal trade was free of tariffs). Trade data is the average of 1993, 1994 and 1995 whereas production data correspond to the industrial census of 1985 in Argentina and Brazil updated to 1994 using industrial production indices provided by UNIDO.

4.2. Did counter-lobbying increase in Mercosur?

Table 1 reports results of the estimation of (22) in the first column and of (23) in the second column. In both regressions, the coefficients have the expected sign and are statistically significant at the 99 percent level.[25] The regressors "account for" around 60 percent of the cross-sectorial variation in Mercosur's CET.

While it may be stretching the power of the model to interpret the values of β_1, β_2 in terms of welfare weights, it is nonetheless worthwhile to note the following. Unconstrained estimates suggest that Argentina and Brazil give relatively similar weights to social welfare in their objective function. However, the constrained estimates suggest that Argentina's trade policy authorities are significantly more concerned by social welfare than Brazil's trade policy authorities ($\hat{a}^A/\hat{a}^B = 1.27$). These estimates are consistent with the fact that, on average, Argentina's pre-CET average tariff is lower than Brazil's. Using estimates of β_3 and β_2 of Eq. (23) reported in Table 1, we can also provide estimates of a^A and a^B. Assume that $\mu = 1$, $\beta_3 = 1/(a^A + a^B)$. Noting that the units of τ are in percent and not in percentage points, one needs to divide the estimates of β_3 by 100. Thus $1/(a^A + a^B) = 0.05$. It is then straightforward to show that $a^A = 11.2$ and $a^B = 8.8$. This

[24] The test consists in verifying whether the error term of the weighted regression is correlated with the number of tariff lines in each industry. If this is the case, then one estimates consistently the variance of the common and individual error components by regressing the error of the weighted estimate on a constant and on $1/n_j$, where n_j is the number of tariff lines in industry j. To obtain asymptoticlly efficient estimates, one re-weighs the observations at the industry level using these variance estimates.

[25] Note that the negative coefficient on z^M also implies that government's objective is closer to the political-economy function used in this paper than one where government's maximise tariff revenue (see footnote 20).

Table 1
Estimating the increase in counter-lobbying[a]

	Tobit Eq. (22)	Constrained Eq. (23)
t^A	0.34	
	(0.09)★★	
t^B	0.42	
	(0.06)★★	
z^M	−4.51	−5.19
	(1.20)★★	(1.28)★★
$t^B - t^A$		0.44
		(0.07)★★
Constant	7.58	4.47
	(1.09)★★	(1.00)★★
R^2-adj.[b]	0.68	0.52
# obs.	80	80

[a] All estimations have used Dickens (1990) procedure correct for group data heteroscedasticity. Figures in parenthesis are standard errors. ★ stands for significance at the 95 percent level and ★★ at the 99 percent level.

[b] For the tobit regression the R^2 is calculated according to Veall and Zimmermann (1994) best predictor.

suggests that the inequality in (16) leading to the endogenous elimination of duty drawbacks is likely to be fulfilled in Argentina and Brazil.[26]

For our purposes, however, the most important result is that in both regressions, the sector's share of sales to other sectors enters with a negative sign, suggesting that, indeed, as predicted by a political-economy approach to the determination of the CET, intermediate goods producing sectors get less protection.

The results seem sufficiently promising to use our estimates to calculate the marginal effect of counter-lobbying on the CET from the coefficient estimates in Table 1. The results of this exercise are shown in Table 2. Let a $\bar{z}$ indicate the mean value of z^M in the sample, and $\hat{\beta}_z$ the estimated marginal effect of regressor z^M, whose value is given in Table 1. Then the change in the value of the mean value of the CET, $\Delta\bar{\tau}$ is given by: $\Delta\bar{\tau} = \hat{\beta}\bar{z}$. In our sample $\bar{z} = 0.68$.

A slight complication arises from the presence of censoring in our tobit estimate since the marginal effects should not include observations for tariffs on the upper bound, since these tariffs could not be higher in the absence of counter-lobbying given the structure of the tariff schedule. Therefore we need to weigh our estimated coefficients in the tobit regressions by the average probability of each observation being in the uncensored region. Given the low degree of censoring (5

[26] Note that these estimates suggest that the Argentinian government gives 9 percent more weight to political contributions than to aggregate welfare net of contributions in its objective function. A similar figure for the Brazilian government is 11 percent (see Grossman and Helpman, 1994 p. 838 for this derivation).

Table 2
Measuring the reduction in the CET due to counter-lobbying[a]

	z_{min} [b]	$\bar{z}$ [c]	z_{max} [d]
Tobit: Eq. (22)	−2.2	−3.0	−3.8
Const.: Eq. (23)	−2.7	−3.5	−4.4

[a] See text on how entries were computed. Values are expressed in percentage points.
[b] One standard deviation below $\hat{\beta}_3$.
[c] At $\hat{\beta}_3$.
[d] One standard deviation above $\hat{\beta}_3$.

percent) in our data, this probability is relatively high and equal to 0.98. Thus, for the tobit equation our estimated marginal effect is $\Delta\bar{\tau} = 0.98\hat{\beta}\bar{z}$.

Table 2 reports results of the importance of counter-lobbying in terms of percentage points reductions in the average CET for our different estimations using this procedure and one standard deviation below and above the estimated coefficient.[27] The total CET reduction associated with counter-lobbying varies from 2.2 to 4.4 percentage points (the average CET value in this sample is 13.9%). Hence, according to the model, in the absence of counter-lobbying, Mercosur's CET would have been between 16.1% and 18.3%. Taking the constrained estimates as reference, the average CET would have been 3.5 percentage points higher in the absence of increased counter-lobbying on intermediates' tariffs.

Table 3 indicates the top five and the bottom five industries where after the elimination of duty-drawbacks, counter-lobbying has led to the largest and smallest reductions in tariffs, respectively. The largest increase in counter-lobbying

Table 3
Top and Bottom 5 tariff reductions due to increased counter-lobbying[a]

	ISIC	CET (τ)	Fall in τ
Top 5	Non-metallic mineral prod. (3699)	9.4	−5.4
	Cement, lime and plaster (3692)	4.0	−5.3
	Pottery, earthenware (3610)	17.0	−5.2
	Glass and glass prod. (3620)	12.7	−5.2
	Structural Clay prod. (3691)	11.7	−5.2
Bottom 5	Wearing apparel (3220)	19.9	−0.1
	Leather finishing (3231)	9.5	−1.1
	Products of Leather (3233)	19.5	−1.1
	Footwear (3240)	20.0	−1.2
	Dairy prod. (3112)	14	−1.3

[a] Values of tariff reductions are expressed in percentage points and are computed using the constrained estimates.

[27] To give an example, the middle entry in row 1 of Table 2, −3.0 is obtained as follows: −3.0 = (0.98)(−4.51)(0.68).

on intermediate products tariffs occurred in industries 3699 (non-metallic mineral products), 3692 (cement, lime and platter), 3610 (pottery, china and earthware), 3620 (glass) and 3691 (structural clay). These tend to be sectors that are heavily used as intermediates in other sectors production and therefore which where more inclined to be subject to increase counter-lobbying on their tariffs. The smallest increase in counter-lobbying occurred in industries 3220 (wearing apparel), 3231 (tanneries and leather finishing), 3233 (leather products), 3240 (footwear) and 3112 (dairy products). These tend to be sectors which sell a little share of their output as input to other sectors. In non-metallic mineral products (3692), the tariff could have been 5.4 percentage points higher in the absence of increased counter-lobbying, which represents more than 50 percent of the actual CET. At the other end of the spectrum, for wearing apparel, the fall in tariff was a low 0.1 percentage points, which represents around 0.5 percent of the actual CET.

5. Concluding remarks

This paper used a political-economy framework to study the implications of duty-drawback schemes (promoted by the World Bank in many developing countries as a mechanism mitigating the anti-trade bias of existing tariffs) for the incentives of export industries to lobby against upstream tariffs on imported intermediates. In a model where duty-drawback schemes are jointly determined with tariffs as part of a political-economy equilibrium, we show that they reduce counter-lobbying incentives, leading, *ceteris paribus*, to higher tariff rates on imported intermediates used heavily in export industries.

Moreover, we showed that the formation of a CU will endogenously lead to the elimination of duty-drawbacks for intra-regional exports. This re-creates an incentive for counter-lobbying by users of intermediate goods, resulting in lower external tariffs on intermediate products, thereby formalizing a channel through which the "new" regionalism may, in the terminology of Bhagwati, be a stepping stone rather than a stumbling block in the move towards greater integration of the world economy.

The model's predictions were tested and confirmed in the case of Mercosur. Our estimates suggest that the CET would have been on average 3.5 percentage point higher (25 percent) in the absence of the increased counter-lobbying on intermediate products associated with the elimination of duty-drawbacks for intra-regional exports. Thus, the mechanism described above may partly explain the decline in external tariffs associated with the "new regionalism" defined by Ethier and Lawrence. Although our results could no doubt have been derived from alternative political-economy models, they also provide indirect vindication of the empirical implications of common-agency (and Nash-bargaining) models of trade protection.

Acknowledgements

We are grateful to Gustavo Bittencourt, Eric Bond, Caroline Freund, Kishore Gawande, Jaime Granados, Bernard Hoekman, Pravin Krishna, Phil Levy, John McLaren, Garry Pursell, Maurice Schiff, Isidro Soloaga, T.N. Srinivassan, David Tarr, Mark Thomas and participants at the "Leitner Conference on Political and Economic Aspects of Regional Integration", Yale University, and a Trade Seminar at the World Bank for very helpful comments and suggestions. We also thank Lili Tabada for excellent assistance. The views expressed here are those of the authors solely, and do not necessarily reflect those of the institutions to which they are affiliated.

References

Bhagwati, J., 1992. Regionalism and multilateralism: An overview. In: de Melo, J., Panagariya, A. (Eds.), New Dimensions of Regional Integration, pp. 21–51.

Cadot, O., de Melo, J., Olarreaga, M., 1997. Lobbying and the structure of protection, CEPR discussion paper # 1574, London.

Cadot, O., de Melo, J., Olarreaga, M., 1999. Regional Integration and lobbying for tariffs against non-members. International Economic Review 40, 635–658.

Cadot, O., de Melo, J., Olarreaga, M., 2001. Can regionalism ease the pain of multilateral trade liberalization? European Economic Review 45, 27–44.

Dickens, W., 1990. Error components in grouped data: is it ever worth weighting? Review of Economics and Statistics 72, 328–333.

Estevadeordal, A., Goto, J., Saez, R., 1999. The New Regionalism in the Americas: the case of Mercosur, mimeo, Inter-American Development Bank, Washington.

Ethier, W., 1998a. The new regionalism. The Economic Journal 108, 1149–1161.

Ethier, W., 1998b. Regionalism in a multilateral world. Journal of Political Economy 106, 1214–1245.

Freund, C., 2000. Multilateralism and the endogenous formation of preferential trade agreements. Journal of International Economics 52, 359–376.

Gawande, K., Bandyopadhyay, U., 2000. Is protection for sale? Evidence on the Grossman–Helpman theory of endogenous protection. Review of Economic and Statistcs 82, 139–152.

Goldberg, P., Maggi, G., 1999. Protection for sale: an empirical investigation. American Economic Review 89, 1135–1155.

Grossman, G., Helpman, E., 1994. Protection for sale. American Economic Review 84, 833–850.

Helpman, E., 1995. Politics and Trade Policy, CEPR discussion paper # 1269, London.

Inter-American Development Bank, 2000. Integration and Trade in the Americas, Periodic Note, December 2000.

Krishna, P., 1998. Regionalism and multilateralism: a political economy approach. Quarterly Journal of Economics 113, 227–2251.

Krueger, A., 1993. Free Trade Agreements as Protectionist Devices, NBER working paper 4352.

Krueger, A., Rajapatirana, S., 1999. The World Bank policies towards trade and trade policy reform, World Economy, 717–740.

Lawrence, R., 1999. Regionalism, multilateralism and deeper integration: changing paradigms for developing countries. In: Mendoza, M.R., Low, P., Kotschwar, B. (Eds.), Trade Rules in the Making: Challenges in Regional and Multilateral Negotiations. Brookings Institution Press.

Levy, P., 1997. A political-economic analysis of free-trade agreements. American Economic Review 87, 506–519.

Maggi, G., Rodriguez-Clare, A., 1998. The value of trade agreements in the presence of political pressures. Journal of Political Economy 106, 574–601.
Michalopoulos, C., 1999. Trade Policy and Market Access Issues for Developing Countries: Implications for the Millenium Round, Policy Research Working Paper 2214, The World Bank, Washington, DC.
Olarreaga, M., Soloaga, I., 1998. Endogenous tariff formation: the case of Mercosur. World Bank Economic Review 12, 297–320.
Olarreaga, M., Soloaga, I., Winters, L.A., 1999. What's Behind Mercosur's Common External Tariff, CEPR discussion paper 2310.
Panagariya, A., 1992. Input tariffs and duty drawbacks in the design of tariff reform. Journal of International Economics 32, 131–147.
Panagariya, A., 2000. Preferential trade liberalization: The traditional theory and new developments. Journal of Economic Literature 38, 287–331.
Veall, M., Zimmermann, K., 1994. Goodness of fit measures in the Tobit model. Oxford Bulletin of Economics and Statistics 56, 485–499.
Wu, C.-S., Chuang, S.-C., 1998. Duty-drawback mechanisms: the system in Taiwan (China) and recommendations for Costa Rica. In: Nash, J., Takacs, W. (Eds.), Trade Policy Reform: Lessons and Implications. World Bank Regional and Sectoral Studies, Washington, DC, p. 189–210.
Yeats, A., 1998. Does Mercosur's trade performance raise concerns about the effects of regional trade arrangements? World Bank Economic Review 12, 1–28.

Why OECD Countries Should Reform Rules of Origin

Olivier Cadot • Jaime de Melo

With preferential trade agreements on the rise worldwide rules of origin—which are necessary to prevent trade deflection—are attracting increasing attention. At the same time, preference erosion for Generalized System of Preferences (GSP) recipients is increasing resistance to further multilateral negotiations. Drawing on different approaches, this article shows that the current system of rules of origin that is used by the European Union and the United States in preferential trade agreements (including the GSP) and that is similar to systems used by other Organisation for Economic Co-operation and Development countries should be drastically simplified if developed economies really want to help developing economies integrate into the world trading system. In addition to diverting resources for administrative tasks, current rules of origin carry significant compliance costs. More fundamentally, it is becoming increasingly clear that they are often been designed to force developing economies to buy inefficient intermediate products from developed economies to "pay for" preferential access for the final product. The evidence also suggests that a significant share of the rents associated with market access (net of rules of origin compliance costs) is captured by developed economies. Finally, the restrictiveness of rules of origin is found to be beyond the levels that would be justified to prevent trade deflection, suggesting a capture by special interest groups. The article outlines some alternative paths to reforms. JEL codes: F13, F15

Rules of origin are an integral part of proliferating free trade agreements—countries belong to an average of six, according to a recent tally by the World Bank (2005, table 2.1)—and nonreciprocal preferential trade agreements such as the Generalized System of Preferences (GSP).[1] Given the lack of progress on harmonization at the World Trade Organization (WTO) and given that regionalism is here to stay, rules of origin are likely to be increasingly important in the world trading system.

doi;10.1093/wbro/lkm010 Advance Access publication October 4, 2007 23:77–105

The primary justification for rules of origin in preferential trade agreements is to prevent "trade deflection," or taking advantage of low external tariffs or weak customs-monitoring capacities to bring in imports destined for more protected markets in a trading bloc (possibly after superficial conditioning or assembly). In effect, rules of origin are needed to prevent trade deflection for all preferential trade agreements short of customs unions, where trade deflection is not an issue because members have a common external tariff. Beyond the largely unimportant issue of tariff revenue, what is at stake is the unwanted extension of preferences to out-of-bloc producers, which would erode the value of those preferences to eligible producers. In preferential trade agreements between developed and developing economies, rules of origin are also sometimes justified on "developmental" grounds because they can help foster integrated manufacturing activities in developing economy partners.

However, this article provides evidence that, by their complexity, rules of origin impose substantial compliance costs on preferred producers. For instance, in addition to regime-wide rules, the European Union has more than 500 product-specific rules of origin (Cadot, de Melo, and Pondard 2006). As a result, these rules are increasingly difficult to observe. In the least developed economies the rules divert scarce customs resources from other tasks such as trade facilitation.[2] In preferential trade agreements between developed and developing economies, forcing developing economy producers to source relatively inefficient intermediate goods locally or from developed economy partners rather than from the most price-competitive sources (as in, say, Asia) increases inefficiency and raises costs. The result is reduced value of preferences (compounding preference erosion in particular for least developed economies) and rent creation for developed country producers.

This potential for rules of origin to become a form of "export protection" was first observed by Krueger (1998) during negotiations for the North American Free Trade Agreement (NAFTA). It applies to all preferential trade agreements (including nonreciprocal preferential schemes) granted by Organisation for Economic Co-operation and Development (OECD) countries to developing economies. Moreover, there is an overwhelming evidence that this protectionist effect of rules of origin is not incidental but by design. Because rules of origin, unlike more traditional forms of trade protection such as voluntary export restraints or antidumping provisions, have so far largely escaped WTO disciplines; they are thus potentially a choice instrument for creeping protectionism.

New evidence reported in this article shows that the burden imposed by the rules of origin applied by the two main protagonists in preferential trade agreements, the European Union and the United States, is substantial whenever preferential margins are anything more than negligible. All told, the detailed evidence gathered here suggests that the current system of rules of origin applied by developed economies is out of hand and defeats both the spirit of reforms aimed at bringing greater transparency to the multilateral trading system and the development-friendly intent of preference schemes.

In a recent communication, the European Union decided to consider simplifying its rules of origin.[3] However, other OECD countries have so far refrained from reforming their rules and have opposed any discussion of reform of preferential rules of origin at the WTO. This article is a contribution to an overdue debate on how to design benign, transparent, and WTO-compatible rules of origin.

This article is organized as follows. The first section briefly recounts how product-specific rules of origin are defined in EU and U.S. preferential schemes and proposes an ordinal restrictiveness index summarizing their complexity. This index is shown to be correlated with EU and U.S. most favored nation tariffs (and thus, with the depth of trade preferences). The second section presents a simple framework for quantifying the costs associated with rules of origin: distortionary, administrative, and rent-transfer. The third section provides direct evidence of the effect of rules of origin on preference use and rent sharing using preference utilization rates and unit values. The fourth section qualifies the direct evidence by considering the Asian exception and the natural experiment provided by comparing the EU Everything But Arms initiative and the U.S. African Growth and Opportunity Act (AGOA), which have similar tariff-preference margins but different rules of origin. The fifth section provides further indirect evidence. The sixth section draws policy implications from the article's findings and makes recommendations for simplifying existing rules of origin.

Rules of Origin: Definition and Measurement

Rules of origin in preferential trade agreements have two components: a small set of regime-wide rules and a large set of product-specific rules, typically defined at the Harmonized System six-digit level of disaggregation (HS-6). Both rules together are to ensure sufficient transformation. Because the European Union and the United States are the main users of preferential trade schemes among OECD countries, this article follows the approach of Cadot, de Melo, and Portugal-Perez (2005), describing briefly the rules for NAFTA, which have been in place for a long time and correspond closely to those applied by the United States in other preferential trade agreements, and those for the European Union's "Pan-European system (PANEURO), "also called the "single-list" because it covers the common set of product-specific rules of origin that the European Union applies in all its preferential trade agreements (regime-wide rules differ across the European Union's preference schemes such as the GSP or Cotonou Agreement). The analysis starts with regime-wide rules then turns to product-specific rules of origin.

Regime-wide Rules

Regime-wide rules usually include five components (these and other terms are defined in the glossary at the end of the article):

- A *de minimis* (or tolerance) criterion that stipulates the maximum percentage of nonoriginating materials that can be used without affecting the origin of the final product.
- A cumulation rule.
- A provision on whether "roll-up" applies.
- The status of duty drawbacks.
- The applicable certification method.

Table 1 describes how these regime-wide rules differ between the European Union and the United States.

Table 1. EU and U.S. Examples of Regime-wide Rules of Origin

Preferential trade agreement	*De minimis* or tolerance rule	*Absorption (roll up)*	*Cumulation*	*Drawback allowed*	*Certification method*
NAFTA	7 percent (except agricultural and industrial products), 7 percent of weight for goods in chapters 50–63	Yes (except autos)	Bilateral	Not after 7 yrs	Self-certification
United States–Chile	10 percent (except agricultural and processed agricultural products)	Yes	Bilateral	Not mentioned	Self-certification
U. S.–GSP	10 percent, 10 percent of weight for goods in chapters 50–63	Not mentioned	Bilateral, limited diagonal	Not mentioned	Self-certification
Cotonou Agreement	15 percent	Yes	Full	Not mentioned	Two-step private and public and limited self-certification
EU GSP	10 percent (except goods in chapters 50–63)[a]	Yes	Bilateral, limited diagonal	Not mentioned	Two-step private and public and limited self-certification

Note: Classification is carried out at the six-digit Harmonized System tariff line level. Each cell is the percentage of tariff lines that have the rules of origin in the corresponding row and in the corresponding column.

[a] Goods in chapters 50–63 (textiles and apparel) do not benefit from a *de minimis* provision.

Source: Cadot, de Melo, and Portugal-Perez 2005, table 1.

Even for regime-wide rules, table 1 gives the impression of "made-to-measure" rules. It also shows that regime-wide rules differ across preferential trade agreements for the same developed economy partner, confirming the hub-and-spoke characteristic of preferential trade agreements between developed and developing economies. Certification methods also differ between EU and U.S. preferential trade agreements; certification is easier to carry out in U.S. agreements, at least in principle, than in EU ones.

Product-Specific Rules of Origin

Devising methods for determining sufficient processing (or substantial transformation) has turned out to be very complex in all existing preferential trade agreements because the Harmonized System was not designed to define the origin of goods. Three criteria are used by the European Union and the United States to determine whether sufficient transformation has taken place in activities requiring processing (that is, anything but crude products):

- A change of tariff classification (at various levels of the Harmonized System), meaning that the final product and its imported components should not belong to the same tariff classification (in other words, that the local processing should be substantial enough to induce a change of tariff classification).
- A critical threshold for value added (in short, a value content rule).
- A specific manufacturing process (a so-called "technical requirement").

For crude products the typical rule is "wholly obtained," which permits no foreign content whatsoever, although other rules apply in special cases, such as fish products.

Both NAFTA (whose rules are also used in other U.S. preferential trade agreements) and PANEURO have a long list of criteria—including such technical requirements as the "triple transformation" requirement in textiles and apparel, which requires apparel to be woven from originating fabric and yarn. Criteria also include exceptions (making them more stringent) and allowances (making them less stringent). NAFTA relies more heavily on changes of tariff classification, though often in combination with other criteria. PANEURO relies mostly on value content and wholly obtained criteria, with wholly obtained criteria prevalent for GSP and African, Caribbean, and Pacific (ACP) exports of primary products with little processing.

As Krishna (2006) points out, when analyzing rules of origin, the devil is in the details because the complexity of rules of origin is what provides an opportunity for special interests to influence their design and administration. While many facets of rules of origin have been explored, rigorous empirical study of their effects has been hampered by two difficulties, one relating to data on utilization rates, the other to measurement of the rules' restrictiveness.

First, data on preference utilization have been made freely available to the public only recently for the United States but not yet for the European Union (for example, Brenton and Manchin 2003 and the studies collected in Cadot, Estevadeordal *et al.* 2006).

Second, because rules of origin are a set of complex, heterogeneous legal rules, it has proved difficult to develop a reliable measure of their restrictiveness to serve as a synthetic indicator (much like effective rates of protection are a synthetic indicator of the restrictiveness of a country's trade regime). Estevadeordal (2000) has proposed an ordinal index of product-specific rules of origin restrictiveness (or *R*-index), taking values between one and seven, with higher values corresponding to more restrictive rules of origin. The index, constructed from a simple observation rule at the HS-6 level, where rules of origin are defined, is described below.

The observation rule is as follows (Cadot, de Melo, and Portugal-Perez 2005). Let *CC* stand for a change of chapter, *CH* for a change of heading, *CS* for a change of subheading, and *CI* for a change of item. A change of classification at the item level can be taken as less stringent than one at the subheading level, and so forth. So the criterion for classifying changes of tariff classification criteria is

$$CC > CH > CS > CI \tag{1}$$

But a change of tariff classification is often accompanied by one or two (in a few cases even three) additional requirements, such as value content rules, technical requirements, exceptions, or allowances. The observation rule assigns higher index values to changes of tariff classification when these requirements are added and lower ones in the case of allowances. For instance, a change of heading is given an index value of four, which rises to a five when accompanied by a technical requirement or exception but shrinks to three when accompanied by an allowance.

Though not amenable to quantification as effective rates of protection, the *R*-index plays the same analytical role; it is intended as an overall indicator of how trade-inhibiting the requirements that must be met by a product to obtain originating status. There is preliminary evidence that preferences have hidden compliance costs and that those compliance costs may be related to rules of origin. Table 2 shows evidence for the textile and apparel sector under NAFTA, the EU GSP, and the Cotonou Agreement (which grants tariff-free access for most ACP products to the EU market).[4] Although NAFTA's and Cotonou's preference margins are equal, at 10.4 percentage points, their utilization rates vary widely: 50 percent for Cotonou compared with 79.9 for NAFTA. Cotonou's low rate of uptake despite deep preferences suggests hidden barriers. ACP countries benefit from full rather than diagonal cumulation (that is, intermediate purchases from

Table 2. Preferences and Utilization Rates for Textiles and Apparel

Preferential trade agreement	*Number of observations*	*Utilization rate (percent)*	*Preference margin (percentage points)*
NAFTA (2001)	618	79.9	10.4
EU GSP (2004)	16,555 (HS-8) 12,920 (HS-6)	52.2	1.8
Cotonou Agreement (2004)	1,370 (HS-8) 1,175 (HS-6)	50.0	10.4

Note: Averages are unweighted. HS-6 is the six-digit Harmonized System level; HS-8 is the eight-digit Harmonized System level.

Source: Cadot, de Melo, and Portugal-Perez (forthcoming), table 3b.

Table 3. Preferences and Utilization Rates, All Goods

	Preference margin		
Preferential trade agreement	*$\tau \geq 4$ percent*[a]	*$\tau \geq 8$ percent*[a]	*$\tau \geq 12$ percent*[a]
North American Free Trade Agreement[b]	87 (1,239)	86.0 (558)	82.8 (287)
GSP[c]	50.2 (1,297)	52.5 (91)	66.2 (44)
Cotonou Agreement[c]	92.5 (1,627)	94.3 (892)	96.4 (566)

Note: Averages are unweighted. Numbers in parentheses are the number of tariff lines.

[a] $\tau_i = (t_i^{MFN} - t_i^{PREF})/(1 + t_i^{PREF})$ is the preference margin.

[b]Computed at the six-digit Harmonized System tariff-line level with 2001 data.

[c]Computed at the eight-digit Harmonized System tariff-line level with 2004 data for 92 countries (GSP) and 37 countries (Cotonou Agreement) qualifying for preferential market access.

Source: Cadot, de Melo, and Portugal-Perez. (forthcoming), table 2.

all partners qualify as originating) and a 15 percent tolerance rule compared with only 10 for the GSP, which also excludes the textile and apparel sector (chapters 50–63) from the 10 percent tolerance rule.

Table 3 shows that the evidence of hidden costs goes beyond the textile and apparel sector, where differences in uptake at similar margins may reflect composition effects. Define the preferential margin τ by the normalized difference between most favored nation and preferential tariffs

$$\tau_i = \frac{t_i^{\mathrm{MFN}} - t_i^{\mathrm{PREF}}}{1 + t_i^{\mathrm{MFN}}} \tag{2}$$

Table 3 shows that, contrary to expectations, when the preferential margin rises, utilization rates fall for NAFTA. This suggests that an omitted variable is positively

Table 4. Tariff Peaks and the *R*-index

	Restrictiveness-index value	
	North American Free Trade Agreement	*PANEURO*
Tariff peaks[a]	6.2 (257)	5.2 (780)
Low tariffs[b]	4.8 (1,432)	3.9 (3,241)
Total number of tariff lines	3,555	4,961

Note: Numbers in parentheses are numbers of tariff lines. Restrictiveness indexes are unweighted.
[a] Tariff lines whose tariffs exceed three times the GSP average.
[b] Tariffs lines whose tariffs are less than one-third of the GSP average.
Source: Cadot, de Melo, and Portugal-Perez 2005, table 3.

correlated with tariffs but negatively correlated with preference utilization. Rules of origin are an obvious culprit.

Table 4 shows that lines with tariff peaks (that is, with tariffs more than three times the average), where preferential margins are highest, do have higher *R*-index values than those with low tariffs. This relationship holds for both NAFTA and PANEURO.

Figure 1 confirms the patterns in tables 2–4; utilization rates do not really increase with tariff-preference margins. For NAFTA, they actually decrease due largely to the influence of the textile and apparel sector, where tariff preferences are deep and rules of origin stringent.

Quantifying the Effects of Rules of Origin

Although product-specific rules of origin, as already noted, take a variety of legal forms (changes of tariff classification, value content rules, technical requirement, and the like), they can all be represented conceptually as floors on domestic value added. Suppose that a producer in Madagascar wishes to sell a shirt under preferential access in the European Union, this shirt is made with both originating intermediate goods (that is, intermediate goods that are either local, EU-made, or imported from other qualifying countries, according to cumulation rules) and nonoriginating intermediate goods, say from Bangladesh, China, or India. Now assume that to satisfy origin requirements (whether change of tariff classification, value content rule, or technical requirement), the Malagasy producer uses a higher proportion of originating inputs than would be the case in the absence of rules of origin (which is precisely the rule's purpose).

Let superscript *R* denote a choice restricted by rules of origin. Unrestricted value added is va_i, and restricted value added is va_i^R, so rules of origin content

Figure 1. Average Utilization Rates for Different Preferential Margin Thresholds

GSP	NAFTA
43.7	86.1
50.2	87
56.8	86.4
52.5	86
71.4	84.8
66.2	82.8
46.8	81.9
45.4	77.8
55.9	78.5
54.7	76.6

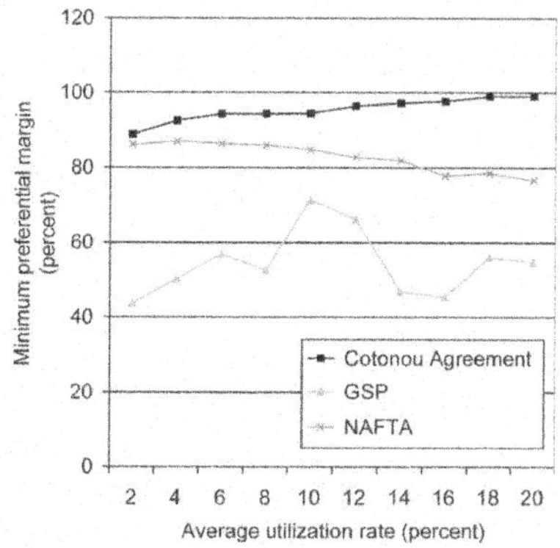

Note: Cotonou Agreement includes 37 countries, computed at the eight-digit Harmonized System level; GSP includes 92 countries, computed at the eight-digit Harmonized System level; and the NAFTA includes 3 countries, computed at the six-digit Harmonized System level. Data are unweighted averages computed at the most disaggregated tariff-line level (table 2). Averages are based on more than 100 observations except for GSP (minimum of 27 observations for preference margins, τ, equal to or greater than 20 percent.).
Source: Cadot, de Melo, and Pondard 2006.

reduces to $va_i^R > va_i$, whether or not it explicitly takes the form of a value content rule. Thus, conceptually a value content rule can be thought of as a generic rule that can play the role of all others by quantifying the objective common to all. This principle is important because it underlies an approach to rules of origin reform, discussed later, that substitutes a value content rule—possibly, although not necessarily, at differentiated rates across products—for the current array of instruments. It also highlights how information on rules of origin restrictiveness can be aggregated across instruments and subsumed into a single restrictiveness index, which itself can be then aggregated across product lines by averaging.

Five results emerge from the quantitative analysis of the relationship between rules of origin restrictiveness and preference uptake:

For a given preference margin a higher restrictiveness index translates into a lower utilization rate, all other things being equal.

For a given restrictiveness index a higher tariff-preference margin translates into a higher utilization rate, all other things being equal.

The compliance decisions of individual firms are binary; how the decisions aggregate into industry-wide utilization rates depends on the unobserved distribution of compliance costs.

A lower pass-through of tariff preferences for the least developed economies (due to low bargaining power) implies lower uptake of preferences, all other things being equal.

Improvements in the uptake of preferences can be obtained either from reductions in the restrictiveness of rules of origin or from cost-reducing administrative simplifications (such as transparent and uniform criterion).

The third result implies that the statistical relationship between *R*-index values, preference margins, and utilization rates can only be "noisy" (that is, affected by a large unexplained component) at the aggregate (product-line) level. But notwithstanding the noise introduced by unobserved firm characteristics (which could be investigated only with firm-level data that are not currently available), figure 1 suggests an unambiguous relationship between preference margins, rules of origin restrictiveness, compliance costs, and utilization rates. It also suggests that, without a proxy for rules of origin restrictiveness such as the *R*-index, attempting to evaluate the effect of tariff-preference margins on the uptake of those preferences may lead to omitted-variable bias.

Keeping in mind that this framework captures only some of the effects associated with rules of origin, several observations are in order.[5] First, administrative costs act as a technical barrier to trade; they result in resource waste, and in the welfare calculus of the effects of rules of origin they are more costly than the usual deadweight losses. Second, if costs are associated with certification, requests for preferential status would not be observed when preference margins are low. Third, compliance costs are particularly high for differentiated products, for which there can be quality as well as price differences between eligible (local) and noneligible intermediate goods. Because part of those costs is passed on to consumers in the countries that determine the rules of origin, high utilization rates does not necessarily imply that rules of origin have small effects.

Stiff rules of origin may inhibit or deflect trade altogether, not just the uptake of preferences. This was shown in the case of the Europe Agreements, free-trade agreements signed in 1991 between the European Union and the Central and Eastern European countries. Tumurchudur (2007a) showed that a large share of the exports from Central and Eastern Europe was deflected from EU markets by rules of origin, resulting in heavy losses. Evidence of trade-inhibiting effects is also apparent in the evolution of textile and apparel exports under AGOA and the Everything But Arms initiative, which is discussed in the exception and quasi-natural experiment section below.

Direct Evidence

In the absence of firm-level data Carrère and de Melo (2006) assume that the preference utilization rate for product line *i* (the percent of exports sent under the preferential regime rather than the most favored nation one), referred to as *Ui*, rises with the tariff-preference margin, τ_i (which may be just equal to the most favored nation tariff when preferential access means tariff-free access) and shrinks with rules of origin compliance costs c_i^R. That is, $U_i = f(\tau_i - c_i^R)$ where $f(\cdot)$ is an increasing function, and, $c_i^R = (RoO_i)$, where $g(\cdot)$ is an increasing function (true compliance costs are firm-specific and are thus unobserved; all that is observed is the presence of RoO_i). These assumptions lead to an estimable relation of the form

$$u_i = \lambda + \alpha\tilde{\tau}_i + \sum_k \theta_k RoO_{ik} + \varepsilon_i \tag{3}$$

where RoO_{ik} is a set of dummy variables indicating the presence of product-specific rules of origin (change of tariff classifications, exceptions, and so on). Results from estimating equation (3) on NAFTA data confirm that utilization rates rise with preferential margins and shrink in the presence of rules of origin (Cadot, de Melo, and Portugal-Perez 2005 for results using data for the European Union).

Carrère and de Melo (2006) combined their estimates with *R*-index values to compute an estimated ad valorem equivalent of total rules of origin compliance costs (administrative costs and costs due to higher input costs). Their estimates range from 3.5 percent for a change of chapter to more than 15 percent for combinations of rules of origin involving technical requirements. The strongly inhibiting effect of technical requirements appears to be an empirical regularity.

Even if the estimates are robust to a range of specifications, it is difficult to infer a sense of robustness from estimates derived from a relation like equation (3) because so much heterogeneity and so many "unobservables" influence preference uptake. Estimates have proved fairly sensitive to the inclusion of control variables, in particular when using EU GSP data.

An alternative is to restrict the analysis to products, for which the sole criterion used to determined origin is a value content. Drawing on the variation in EU value content criteria across product lines with value content the sole criterion, Cadot, Carrère, and Strauss-Kahn (2007) estimate an equation similar to equation (3), in which however the dummy variables for rules of origin are replaced with the continuous value content rule values.[6] Using dummy variables for Harmonized System sections to control for heterogeneity across sectors and restricting the sample to tariff lines with substantial tariff-preference margins (above 2 or 5 percent), they find that utilization rates rise, all other things being equal, with the maximum foreign content allowed by the value content rule.

Table 5. Estimated Effects on Preference Utilization and Rent Transfer of Relaxing a Value Content Requirement

	Preference margin			
	$\tau_i \geq 2\%$ *ACP + GSP*	$\tau_i \geq 5\%$ *ACP+ GSP*	$\tau_i \geq 2\%$ *GSP*	$\tau_i \geq 5\%$ *GSP*
Number of observations	19,261	5,958	13,448	4,305
Mean preferential margin ($\bar{\tau}$) (percent)	3.74	5.14	3.79	5.22
Mean utilization rate (percent)	0.12	0.17	0.17	0.22
Mean value content (percent of unit price)	58.8	58.2	58.9	58.6
Mean value of imports (euros)	1,475,182	2,376,301	986,979	159,694
Simulation: local content requirement reduced by 10 percentage points				
Change in preference utilization rate (percentage points)	2.0	5.2	2.5	1.7
Total rent transfer from increased utilization (millions of euros)[a]	21. 7	37. 4	25.3	11.6

[a]Evaluated at the mean value of imports.
Source: Authors' computations based on Cadot, de Melo, and Portugal-Perez (forthcoming), table 6.

Since a single value content criterion is a serious candidate for reform, at least in the case of the European Union (Stevens *et al.* 2006 and Cadot, de Melo, and Pondard 2006), table 5 reports two illustrative simulations based on these estimates. The mean local content requirement is 58 percent and preference margin 3–5 percent depending on the sample; mean utilization rates are rather low—between 12 and 22 percent. The bottom of the table shows the first-round effects (no supply response) of reducing the local-content requirement by 10 percentage points. Utilization rates rise by 2–5 percentage points (row 6), raising the rent transfer by €21–37 million, for a mean value of imports of €1.5–3.0 billion.

To fully grasp the welfare effects of rules of origin, the rent distribution between the exporting and importing country must be factored in. This implies estimating the pass-through effect of tariffs on consumer prices (that is, the extent to which preferences translate into a higher producer price for exporters). Estimates for AGOA preferences (Olarreaga and Özden 2005) and for the Caribbean Community (Özden and Sharma 2006) are that between one-third and one-half of tariff reductions are passed on to producers.

However, part of the border-price increase could reflect the compliance costs discussed above. Using a monopolistic-competition model with differentiated products in which Mexican exporters can export product j either to the rest of the world (under most favored nation status, at price p_j^M) or to the

Table 6. Exports, Unit Costs, and Prices under Preferential Market Access and a Binding Minimum Local Content Requirement

	Simulations				
	(1)	*(2)*	*(3)*[a]	*(4)*	*(5)*
Preference margin (percent)	10	10	10	10	10
Administrative unit costs (percent of unit price)	0	0	0	2.5	1.0
Unconstrained, minimum local content requirement (percent of unit price)	40	40	40	40	36
Constrained, minimum local content requirement (percent of unit price)		50	50	50	40
Preferential exports (percent change from scenario with no preferential access)	15.9	11.1	−0.15	7.1	10.7
Unit costs (percent change from scenario with no preferential access)	0	1.9	6.7	1.9	0.4
Unit net price (percent change from scenario with no preferential access)	2.9	3.0	3.4	2.2	2.1

Note: Unit net price set equal to 1, initial output to 100, and value-added to 20. All output is exported (40 percent to preference-receiving destination). For columns 1–4 nonoriginating inputs are set to 75 percent of intermediate good input purchases. This implies that initial (unconstrained) local content is $20 + 0.25\ (80) = 40$. Setting the minimum local content requirement at 50 percent implies reducing nonoriginating intermediate goods to 62.5 percent of intermediate good purchases. For column 5 nonoriginating inputs are set at 80 percent and reduced to 75 percent through the minimum local content rule.

[a]Same as column 2 but with low value for the elasticity of substitution between originating and nonoriginating materials (0.5 instead of 2).

Source: Authors' computations adapted from model in Cadot *et al.* 2005.

United States (under NAFTA, at price p_j^N), Cadot *et al.* (2005) estimate the following relationship

$$\text{NAFTA markup} = \alpha_0 + \alpha_1 \tau_j + \alpha_1 CC_j + \alpha_3 TECH_j + \varepsilon_j \tag{4}$$

where "NAFTA markup" is the percentage by which Mexico's NAFTA shipment prices are raised over comparable most favored nation shipment prices, CC_j is a dummy variable marking a change of tariff classification at the chapter level, and $TECH_j$ is a dummy variable marking a change of a technical requirement.

When estimated at the HS-8 level, equation (4) is the best tool to compare prices in different markets. With complete pass-through ($\mu = 1$ in equation (4) the estimated coefficient for α_1 would be close to one, but Cadot *et al.* (2005) find it substantially below one. They also obtain negative and significant estimates for (α_2, α_3) indicating that rules of origin costs are at least to some extent passed on to consumers. Once rules of origin are taken into account, the backward pass-through of preferences to producer prices falls from 80 percent of the margins to only 50 percent. They also show, using input–output links, that U.S. producers of intermediate goods are able to retain a substantial share of the rents generated by rules of origin downstream. That is, stiff rules of origin on, say, Mexican shirts exported to the United States significantly raise the price of fabric exported by the United States to Mexico for use in those shirts. This reflects the fact that rules of origin create a captive market for U.S. intermediate goods.

An Exception and a Quasi-Natural Experiment

The covariation of utilization rates and margins does not account for all the effects of rules of origin. Case studies such as those reported in Cadot, de Melo, and Pondard (2006) and Stevens *et al.* (2006) provide useful complementary evidence, although they conclude that each case is different, thereby explaining if not justifying the current maze. An exception and a quasi-natural experiment are drawn here, with both suggesting that rules of origin are, as they stand, unnecessarily restrictive.

Asian Exception

In a world where rules of origin are as cumbersome and complicated as they are (Estevadeordal and Suominen 2006 for a detailed description), Association of Southeast Asian Nations (ASEAN), Free Trade Area (AFTA) and the ASEAN-China Free Trade Area (ACFTA) stand out as exceptions. To obtain originating status (that is, to fulfill the criterion of sufficient processing), either the wholly obtained criterion (for a few agricultural products) or a single-value content rule requiring 40 percent local content (for most products) is used. This rule has been relaxed by allowing a choice between criteria for countries that found it too constraining. For instance, under ACFTA the importer can choose a change of tariff classification can be used as an alternative to the 40 percent local content for obtaining origin for leather goods, and some specific process criteria are also accepted for some textile products.[7]

So why are rules of origin under AFTA less stringent than elsewhere? First, until recently Asian regionalism was more about cooperation than about preferential trade. Under the aegis of the United States, Asia-Pacific Economic Cooperation was set up specifically to avoid preferential trade and the formation of an Asian trade bloc. Much of the region's integration in the world economy has been driven by unilateral tariff reductions. Second, regional trade has made possible the rise of the Asian manufacturing matrix in which labor-intensive stages of production initially carried out in Japan—and later in the Republic of

Korea—were outsourced to the region's lower wage countries. The resulting regional production networks have contributed to the price-competitiveness of Asia's exports, which has benefited the whole region. Stiff rules of origin would have jeopardized this successful model.

This "Asian exception" has been conducive to the successful development of Asian countries that have fully participated in "verticalizing" trade (the development of cross-border supply chains generating trade in intermediate products). In this unusual setup (relative to other global trading patterns), intraregional trade in politically sensitive final products where protection is highest was insignificant. Thus, the political-economy forces that would usually lead to the complex rules of origin observed elsewhere have not been at work so far. As a result, low-income countries such as Cambodia and Lao PDR have been able to participate in the fragmentation of production according to comparative advantage.[8] Arguably, Asia's simple and uniform rules of origin requirement is an example of the kind of rules of origin that would really be development-friendly.

AGOA and Everything but Arms: a Natural Experiment

In the textile and apparel sector, the choice area for obscure and trade-inhibiting rules of origin, the one notable exception is the U.S. preferences granted to 22 Sub-Saharan African least developed economies under AGOA. Thus, comparing African apparel exports to the European Union and the United States provides a quasi-experimental situation in which the effects of rules of origin on the uptake of trade preferences are analyzed. This quasi-experimental situation, first studied by Brenton and Özden (2005), comes from the combination of different rules of origin with very similar rates of preference margins (textiles and apparel receive approximately the same protection in the EU and U.S. markets. In 2001 the EU-15's most favored nation tariff was 10.1 percent compared with 11.7 percent for the United States, and duty-free access applied to both Everything But Arms eligible and the 34 AGOA-eligible African countries).

To qualify for preferential access to the U.S. market, an exporter must prove that the garments are produced, cut, and sewn in the area benefiting from preferential access (here, AGOA). Cotton products must be made from originating fabric, yarn, and thread, with diagonal cumulation somewhat relaxing the requirement, since fabric originating in other member countries qualifies. However, this rule, known as "the triple transformation" rule, was relaxed for 22 least developed economies under AGOA's "special regime," which permits the use of third-country fabric.[9] That is, the special regime reduces the transformation requirement to a single transformation (from fabric to garment).

Fifteen of AGOA's special regime beneficiaries are also eligible for the European Union's Everything But Arms initiative. But no such relaxation applies to exports to the European Union under either the Cotonou Agreement or Every But Arms preferences. EU rules of origin for apparel require production from originating yarn, which implies a "double transformation" from yarn to fabric and from fabric to clothing. The European Union's "double-transformation" rule obviously makes compliance difficult for countries that have no textile industry. Small or poor countries that cannot profitably produce fabric—weaving is a capital-intensive activity involving expensive machinery, particularly for woven products—should not, from an economic-efficiency viewpoint, set up the vertically integrated local value chains that would satisfy the double-transformation rule.

In apparel preference utilization rates are very high under both AGOA (97.36 percent in 2004) and Everything But Arms/Cotonou (94.9 percent). Cotonou has rules similar to those that Everything But Arms has for apparel. However, export volumes evolved quite differently for the 15 least developed economies that benefit from both schemes. Figure 2 shows a substantial increase in the value of apparel exports with AGOA's entry into force in 2000 (in particular for Lesotho and Madagascar). By contrast, the value of exports from this same group of countries did not rise following the adoption of Everything But Arms—in fact it fell slightly. Of course, the exports that remained flat for those countries should come as no surprise since they already benefited from Cotonou preferences, which give almost

Figure 2. Apparel Exports of 22 Countries Benefiting from the AGOA Special Regime, 2004

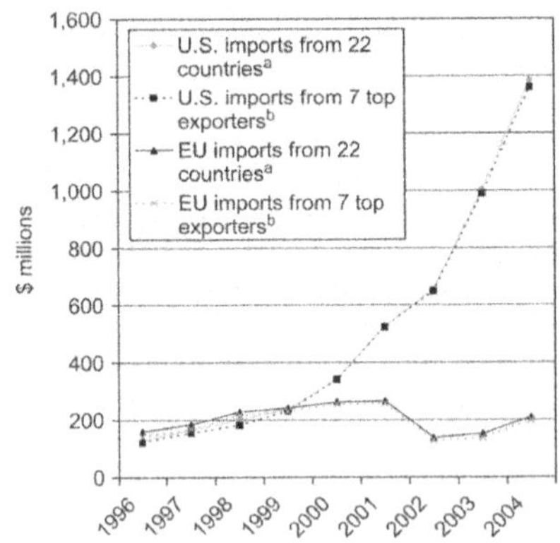

Note: [a]Benin, Botswana, Cameroon, Cape Verde, Ethiopia, Ghana, Kenya, Lesotho, Madagascar, Malawi, Mali, Mozambique, Namibia, Niger, Nigeria, Rwanda, Senegal, Sierra Leone, Swaziland, Tanzania, Uganda, and Zambia. [b]Botswana, Cameroon, Ghana, Kenya, Lesotho, Madagascar, Namibia, Nigeria, and Swaziland.
Source: Portugal-Perez (2007) based on the WTO Integrated Data Base[a]

as much access as Everything But Arms (with slightly more lenient rules on cumulation). In effect, nothing changed for them on this front, and along with other ACP countries they largely continued to request access under Cotonou, with which they were familiar, rather than Everything But Arms. But AGOA's special regime did not merely trigger a catch up of U.S.-bound exports toward already high levels of EU-bound exports; it dwarfed them. Thus, unlike AGOA's special regime neither Cotonou nor Everything But Arms appeared to have offered a preference mix (tariff preferences and rules of origin) conducive to export growth.

Because the data in figure 2 are computed at the HS-6 product level, it is safe to assume that heterogeneity in export composition is largely controlled for. This is confirmed by formal econometric evidence. In a model that controls for differences in preference margins and for demand shifters in the EU and U.S. markets, Portugal-Perez (2007) finds that relaxing rules of origin for apparel (captured by a dummy variable corresponding to the introduction of the AGOA's special regime) raised apparel exports significantly for beneficiary countries. Because the special regime was not introduced in the same year for all countries, its effects are well identified statistically, and Portugal-Perez' results strongly suggest that the difference in performance apparent in figure 2 is indeed attributable to differences in rules of origin regimes.

AGOA's special regime seems to have encouraged growth not only at the "intensive margin" (higher volumes) but also at the "extensive margin" (diversification by addition of new products). As new products were exported to both countries (an active extensive margin), the rate of increase in new products was several orders of magnitude higher for the U.S.-bound goods than for EU-bound ones, which is an important achievement. Product diversification is one measure of industrialization, particularly at early stages of the economic development process (Cadot, Carrère, and Strauss-Kahn 2007 and references therein). Controlling for other factors, countries that have a more diversified industrial base enjoy less volatile growth and are better poised to absorb shocks. Only three countries in Sub-Saharan Africa—Lesotho, Madagascar, and Senegal—export more than 50 products to either the European Union or the United States. Thus, if the development objective of rules of origin is to be taken seriously, encouraging export growth at the extensive margin is important, and in this regard Everything But Arms and Cotonou's performance are again disappointing compared with that of AGOA's special regime.

Taken together, the brief discussion here on the Asian exception and the comparison of AGOA with the Everything But Arms initiative suggests two results:

Limited differences between preferential regimes can have drastic effects on their performance; AGOA's relaxation of the triple transformation rule gave a significant boost to Sub-Saharan African apparel exports.

Utilization rates are an incomplete measure of the performance of preferential regimes, as the inhibiting effect of stiff rules of origin can be felt on trade volumes as well.

Indirect Evidence

Taking inspiration from the early work by Herin (1986) for EFTA, Cadot, de Melo, and Portugal-Perez (forthcoming) applied revealed-preference arguments to estimate upper and lower bounds of compliance costs. Arguably, this nonparametric approach could be more robust than the parametric evidence reported above. By revealed preference, for products with 100 percent utilization rates the net benefit of preferences is positive for all firms. Since everyone uses the preferences, the ad valorem equivalent of compliance costs cannot be larger than the tariff-preference margin. Conversely, for products with zero percent utilization rates, since no one uses the preferences, the compliance cost cannot be smaller than the preference margin.

For remaining sectors (those with utilization rates between 0 and 100 percent) the story is more complicated because of firm heterogeneity, so assumptions must be made. Cadot, de Melo, and Portugal-Perez (forthcoming) argue that, firm heterogeneity notwithstanding, the average exporter (in terms of compliance costs) is not too far from indifference between the preferential and the most favored nation regimes, which means that the compliance cost is about equal to the tariff-preference margin. Applying this reasoning gives trade-weighted ad valorem estimates of 4.7–8.2 percent depending on sectors for PANEURO and 1.8–1.9 percent for NAFTA—values in line with the econometric estimates of Carrère and de Melo (2006) reported earlier.

How then should requests for preferential status be interpreted when tariff preferences are nil? Beyond (likely) errors in data transcription, the logical possibility would be that administrative costs are negligible, but this contradicts the evidence (the nonparametric approach described in the previous paragraph gave estimates of pure administrative costs slightly above 3 percent in ad valorem form). Francois, Hoekman, and Manchin (2006) elegantly addressed this problem by modeling the determinants of utilization rates for EU trade with ACP countries in a switching-regression framework where the relationship between the variable of interest (utilization rates) and explanatory variables varies between two regimes: one for low-margin sectors and the other for high-margin ones. The dividing point between the two regimes is determined by the data using an algorithm developed by Hansen (2000).[10] They found that exporters start requesting preferences when preferential margins are in the 4.0–4.5 percent range, a result that is also broadly consistent with the nonparametric estimates of compliance costs reported above.

Other studies using aggregate bilateral trade data also suggest costs associated with the presence of rules of origin. Using a gravity model of bilateral trade, Anson *et al.* (2005) find that after controlling for the other determinants of the volume of bilateral trade, including the presence of free trade agreements, the intensity of bilateral trade is inversely related to the values taken by the *R*-index. Using a similar framework, Augier, Gasiorek, and Tang (2005) find that the volume of bilateral trade is lower when cumulation is on a bilateral rather than a full basis, leading them to suggest that rules of origin should be relaxed to allow for full cumulation.

The evidence reported so far in this article is overwhelming: rules of origin are burdensome and foster economic inefficiency. But this article also argues that they have a role in combating trade deflection, so calling them trade barriers is not enough. To make progress in designing "clean" rules of origin, a key part of the argument is to tell apart, in their current characteristics (and in particular their restrictiveness), how much is attributable to their antideflection role compared with how much is simply capture by special interests. Portugal-Perez (2006) tries to address this issue by decomposing variations in the *R*-index into a component attributable to trade deflection and one associated with lobbying or political-economy motives. He estimates this decomposition for Mexican textile and apparel exports to the United States under NAFTA using the following equation

$$RoO_i = \beta[TD_i] + \gamma[PE_i] + \varepsilon_i \qquad (5)$$

where (RoO_i) is *R*-index values at the HS-6 level. The regressors are the trade deflection vector, which includes a proxy for the extent of product differentiation (the more homogeneous the product, the more there is to gain from arbitraging even small differences in external tariffs), and differences in external tariffs (the larger these differences the more there is to arbitrage). Political-economy variables including the level of the United States' most favored nation tariff (a proxy for lobbying power) revealed comparative-advantage indexes and the value of Mexican exports to the rest of the world (a proxy for potential penetration of the U.S. market).

Portugal-Perez finds strong and quite robust correlations, suggesting that both sets of factors are at work in explaining cross-sectoral variations in rules of origin restrictiveness. Using estimated parameter values, he constructs a counterfactual distribution of *R*-index values across goods in the absence of political-economy correlates (that is, by setting $\gamma = 0$ in equation (5). The two distributions (actual and counterfactual) are reported in figure 3. They show that political-economy concerns (which shift the actual distribution to the right of the counterfactual) contribute to the overall restrictiveness of rules of origin. Drawing on the

Figure 3. Counterfactual Distribution for *R*-Index

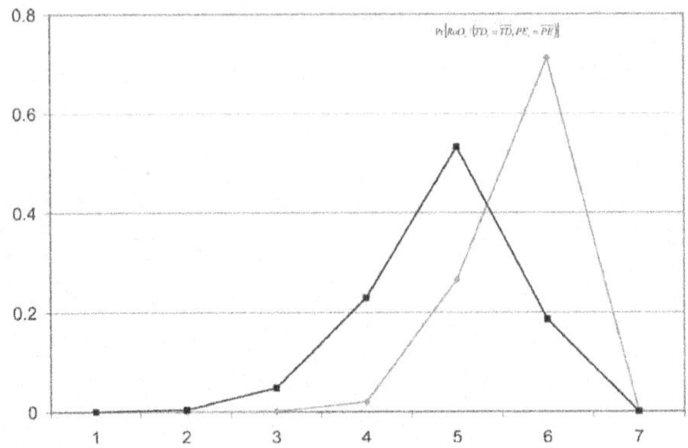

Source: Portugal-Perez 2006, figure 3.

estimates discussed earlier by Carrère and de Melo (2006), he concludes that capture by special interests may have raised the costs of rules of origin an average of 3.5–11 percent of good value, a very steep increase in the face of the shallow preferences that are generally granted.

Simulation methods provide another way of obtaining orders of magnitude of rules of origin effects on trade. Francois, Hoekman, and Manchin (2006) use their estimate of compliance costs to simulate the effects of trade liberalization by developed economies on low-income countries in a multiregional trade model. Despite preference erosion, low-income countries gain instead of losing from trade liberalization by the European Union because the "rectangle" deadweight losses associated with compliance costs are eliminated.

Table 6 provides alternative estimates from a partial-equilibrium perspective, taking as an example a GSP country benefiting from a 10 percent preferential margin in the EU (or U.S.) market (row 1) but forced to raise its minimum local content from the value in row 3 (40 percent, except in column 5) to the value in row 4 (50 percent, except in column 5). When present, administrative costs, also expressed as a percentage of the unit price, are given in row 2. The table's bottom three rows show the effect of rules of origin on equilibrium exports and prices.

Column 1 shows the benefits that accrue to the GSP producer from receiving a 10 percent preference margin with no constraint on the sourcing of inputs. For this constellation of elasticity (all are on the high side to reflect the likelihood that products from different origin are close substitutes, whether at the intermediate- or final-good level), the pass-through is 2.9 percent (row 7) out of a preference margin of 10 percent, in line with econometric estimates mentioned in the section on direct evidence. Exports increase by 16 percent, but costs do not increase because inputs are bought at constant world prices.

Column 2 shows what happens when the producer must reduce the use of nonoriginating materials to meet a value content rule of 50 percent (a 25 percent increase from column 1). For the example, where value added is 20 percent and unconstrained purchases of nonoriginating intermediate goods equal 75 percent of the value of total intermediate good purchases, raising the minimum local content from 40 to 50 percent implies that purchases of nonoriginating intermediate goods must be reduced to 62.5 percent. The result of forcing producers to shift away from preferred intermediate goods is a higher unit production cost resulting in lower export volume, with the 1.9 percent increase in unit cost passed on to EU and U.S. consumers. Matters get worse if substitution possibilities for materials from different origins are low (column 3), which might be the representative of industries with a lot of transformation and many production stages.[11]

Column 4 mirrors column 2 but adds administrative compliance costs of 2.5 percent. This further penalizes the GSP producer, even though part of this cost increase can again be passed on to consumers in the importing country. Of course, if GSP producers were competing with close substitutes, they would be unable to pass on the price increase. Finally, column 5 considers a simulation that might be fairly representative of an industry with enough originating intermediate good purchases that the shift to a 40 percent minimum local content would not affect producers much. In this case, the net price to producers might go up by about one-third of the preference margin, resulting in a modest supply response of about 10 percent.

Implications for Reform

If rules of origin are a legitimate way to prevent trade deflection by mandating that sufficient processing take place in the preferential zone, the accumulated evidence reported in this article indicates that they have gone vastly beyond that role, becoming akin to technical barriers to trade. Various estimates suggest that the compliance costs associated with meeting origin requirements in preferential trade agreements range between 3 and 5 percent of final product prices—a very stiff price tag for preference margins that are often thin, given that most favored nation tariffs are low in most sectors except textiles and apparel. Controlling for preferential margins, utilization rates are lower in product lines with more restrictive rules of origin and when producers are limited in the sourcing of their intermediate good purchases.

Because of their trade-inhibiting effects, rules of origin hinder the integration of preference-receiving least developed economies in the world economy and thus work at cross-purposes with the development-policy goals of EU and U.S. preferences. For Sub-Saharan African countries supplying apparel products to the European Union, even high utilization rates hide obstacles to export growth caused by the double-transformation requirement imposed on those products.

This article also shows that in the case of the European Union and the United States, the two largest users of preferential trade agreements, rules of origin are stricter for products with tariff peaks where preferences could be most valuable. The correlation between the presence of tariff peaks and that of highly restrictive rules of origin suggests capture by protectionist interests, a hypothesis largely confirmed by political-economy theory and evidence. Moreover, because rules of origin have so far escaped WTO disciplines—whereas other, more traditional trade-policy instruments are brought under increasingly stringent ones—they stand as a choice candidate for creeping protectionism.

Despite the prevalence of capture by special interests, two quasi-natural experiments point to broad directions for reform. First, the relaxation of the U.S. triple-transformation requirement in textile and apparel for Sub-Saharan African producers under AGOA has proved to strongly encourage export diversification and growth compared with exports destined to the European Union, which are subject to stricter rules under the Everything But Arms initiative (which otherwise features similar preference margins). Second, low-income Asian countries operating under simple and benign rules of origin have been able to rapidly integrate themselves into cross-border supply chains and have, as a result, tremendously benefited from the verticalization of world trade.

These observations suggest that a multilateral agenda for preferential rules of origin reform, a key step in bringing preferential trade agreements under WTO disciplines, would have to move along three dimensions: harmonization, simplification, and relaxation. Harmonization between trading blocs, although unlikely to be attained anytime soon, is desirable in view of the "spaghetti bowl" of preferential trade agreements and is a prerequisite for simple and mutually consistent cumulation rules. The European Union has set an example in this regard with the PANEURO system, designed precisely to facilitate cumulation across preferential zones.

For simplification arguments in favor of a single across-the-board rule are much like those in favor of uniform tariffs—that is, simplification fosters transparency and mitigates capture. Clearly, technical requirements should be targeted for elimination first because they are the most opaque, difficult to harmonize, and capture-prone instruments. Leaving aside agricultural products that could still operate under the wholly obtained criterion and keeping in mind that any uniform rule will affect industries and countries differently, two avenues could be considered; a simple change of tariff classification, say at the subheading (HS-6) level so that it is not too restrictive or a uniform value-content rule.

Some information can be gleaned in this regard from the European Union's recent review. The change of tariff classification has the advantage of simplicity, transparency, and low administrative costs. But the Harmonized System tariff nomenclature was designed to collect trade statistics, not to separate products and confer origin, so defining the change of tariff classification at a uniform level would produce erratic results across sectors. This would call for exceptions to uniformity, opening up a Pandora's Box of special deals. Moreover, a change of tariff classification that would not easily lend itself to differential treatment for least developed economies should be an objective (see below).

Notwithstanding conceptual clarity, a value content rule may be less than straightforward to apply in practice.[12] It may increase producer risk due to the sensitivity of costs to exchange-rate, wage, and commodity-price fluctuations and is also burdensome to apply for customs officials. However, it is simple to specify and transparent, and it allows for differential treatment of least developed economies. All told, if properly specified, it is the best candidate for an across-the-board criterion, ideally in combination, at the exporter's choice, with a change of tariff classification. In this spirit Tumurchudur (2007b) estimated for each good the maximum foreign content that would make a value content rule equivalent to the current array of NAFTA's rules of origin. Her method consisted of three steps.

First, she estimated the statistical relationship between utilization rates and rules of origin, including value content rules. Second, she inverted that relationship to find the rate of a value content rule that would give a utilization rate equal to the current one. Third, she calculated the trade-weighted average of that maximum content. This neutral average turns out to be a very low 21 percent of the good's value in maximum foreign content, confirming the diagnosis that NAFTA's rules of origin are very restrictive. More important, this rate provides a transparent and fully comparable benchmark which is to base discussions of reform and harmonization.

If the slow pace of harmonization talks at the WTO is any indication, the reform agenda described above may be overambitious by several orders of magnitude; even if the European Commission manages to complete the agenda, competition between systems may trigger similar rounds of simplification elsewhere, including in free trade agreements between developing economies in Africa and Latin America, whose rules of origin are often directly inspired by NAFTA and PANEURO. However, the outcome of the EU reform process is highly uncertain at this stage; moreover, even if the plan to adopt an across-the-board value content criterion survives, it is not clear that the rate of this value content rule would be uniform. Nor is it certain (perhaps even less) that it would relax the restrictiveness of the current system.

More immediate, win–win steps may be a better way to proceed. A simple first step would consist of eliminating rules of origin requirements for tariff lines with preferential margins below 3 or perhaps even 5 percent (the rate could be agreed upon in the context of multilateral negotiations at the WTO). This would be an all-around winning proposition since resources would be freed for other purposes, especially in developing economies, but also for consumers in developed economies, who would no longer bear part of the increased costs associated with compliance. A second step would be to allow for differential treatment not across sectors, but across beneficiaries, with low value content requirements for least developed economies reflecting the empirical observation that the "slices" of value added in least developed economies through cross-border production networks are generally thin. In this regard, the experience with the U.S. special regime granted in textile and apparel to African producers under AGOA is most encouraging.

Appendix. Glossary of terms

Harmonized System. A system of classification for traded goods in which all countries belonging to the World Customs Organization participate. It classifies traded goods into (by increasing order of disaggregation) 21 sections (one digit), 99 chapters (two digits), 1,417 items (four digits), and 4,998 subitems (six digits). Beyond that (eight- and ten-digit), classification systems are no longer harmonized across countries and are subject to frequent classification changes.

Preference Margin. The difference between most favored nation and preferential tariffs.

Preference Pass-Through. The percentage of a tariff-preference margin that is "appropriated" by exporters in the form of an increase in the export price. It is inversely related to the bargaining power of importers.

Preferential Status. Whether a good is eligible for the preferential tariff rate.

Technical Requirement. Rule of origin that imposes a certain type of production process or the use of certain specified technology or standard.

Trade Deflection. Use of the country with the lowest external tariff by importers in a free trade agreement (which reduces tariff revenue for others). This notion is distinct from Vinerian "trade diversion."

Utilization Rate. Share of exports shipped under the preferential (as opposed to most favored nation) regime.

Regime-wide Rules of Origin

Absorption or Roll-up. Principle that allows nonoriginating materials that have acquired origin by meeting specific processing requirements to maintain this origin when used as input in a subsequent transformation. In other words, the nonoriginating materials are no longer taken into account in calculating value added. The roll-up or absorption principle is used in most preferential trade agreements (in particular, the EU GSP and the Cotonou Agreement), although a few have exceptions for the automotive sector.

Cumulation. Principle that allows producers from one member country in a preferential trade agreement to import nonoriginating materials from another member country without affecting the final product's originating status. There are three types of cumulation rules: bilateral, diagonal, and full *Bilateral cumulation. It* is the most common type and applies to trade between two partners in a preferential trade agreement. It stipulates that producers in country A can use inputs from country B without affecting the final good's originating status as long as the inputs satisfy the area's rules of origin.

Diagonal Cumulation. Under *diagonal cumulation* (the basic principle of the EU's PANEURO system), countries in a preferential trade agreement can use materials that originate in any member country as if the materials originated in the country where the processing is undertaken. Under *full cumulation* all stages of processing or transformation of a product within countries in a preferential trade agreement can be counted as qualifying content regardless of whether the processing is sufficient to confer originating status to the materials themselves. Full cumulation allows for greater fragmentation of the production process than bilateral and diagonal cumulation.

Duty Drawbacks. Refunds to exporters of tariffs paid on imported intermediate good inputs. Many preferential trade agreements, especially in the Americas, mandate the elimination of duty-drawback schemes for exports to partner countries on the grounds that a duty drawback claimed by a producer in country A to export to country B would put that producer at a competitive advantage compared with domestic producers in country B given that the producer in country A already benefits from the elimination of intrabloc tariffs. Eliminating duty drawbacks as part of a preferential trade agreement can harm the profitability of final-good assembly for export to partner countries in the area, although tariff escalation, when present, already provides some protection for final-assembly operations (because it implies lower tariffs on intermediate goods than on final ones).

Product-Specific Rules of Origin

Allowance. An amendment to a mandated change of tariff classification that excludes some categories from noneligibility (that is, a final good belonging to, say, chapter 11 can embody imported inputs belonging to any other chapter or from chapter 11 itself but between headings *X* and *Y*).

Change of Tariff Classification. Rule of origin requiring that a final good made with imported inputs belong to a Harmonized System category that differs from that of its imported inputs (as proof of transformation). The mandated change of tariff classification can be specified at the chapter (two digits), heading (four digits), subheading (six digits), or item (eight digits) level.

Exception. An amendment to a mandated change of tariff classification that excludes some categories from eligibility (that is, a final good belonging to, say, chapter 11 can embody imported inputs belonging to any other chapter except headings X to Y).

Value Content. Rule of origin requiring a minimum percentage of local value (materials or value added) or a maximum percentage of foreign value.

Notes

Olivier Cadot is Professor of Economics at the University of Lausanne, associated scholar at Centre d'Etudes et de Recherches sur le Développement International (CERDI), and fellow at the Centre for Economic Policy Research (CEPR); his email address is olivier.cadot@unil.ch. Jaime de Melo (corresponding author) is Professor of Economics at the University of Geneva, associated scholar at CERDI, and fellow at CEPR; his email address is demelo@ecopo.unige.ch. The authors thank Paul Brenton and Marcelo Olarreaga for many useful suggestions and their colleagues and co-authors Céline Carrère, Antoni Estevadeordal, Alberto Portugal-Perez, Akiko Suwa-Eisenmann, and Bolormaa Tumurchudur for permission to draw on joint work. They also thank three referees for comments on a previous draft.

1. According to this same tally, 45 developing economies having signed bilateral trade agreements with a developed country, and 90 of the 109 preferential trade agreements between developed and developing economies have been created since 1990.

2. According to a survey administered by the World Customs Organization to customs officials in developing economies (as reported by Brenton and Imawaga 2004), 67 percent of respondents in

Sub-Saharan Africa agree that dealing with rules of origin under overlapping trade agreements causes problems, and a majority also agrees that rules of origin are more labor-intensive. Administering rules of origin detracts from other objectives of tax collection and trade facilitation.

3. Because meeting the requirements is difficult and appears unnecessarily complex, in view of the European Commission's objective to grant some preferential access to its market for GSP-eligible countries, on 16 March 2004 the commission adopted Communication COM (2005) on "The Rules of Origin in Preferential Trade Arrangements." The communication explores alternative rules of origin that would be simpler and more development friendly. A key proposal under consideration is to replace the current product-specific rules of origin with a single rule based on a minimum of originating value added.

4. By comparison, the average preferential margin (computed over tariff lines with positive tariffs) was 4.5 percent for NAFTA (almost all tariffs had been eliminated on NAFTA trade by 2001), 2.4 percent for GSP-eligible countries, and 4.6 for ACP countries (not eligible for Everything But Arms status). Data for the European Union are for 2004, when 62 percent of trade for GSP-eligible countries and over 80 percent of trade for ACP countries took place at zero tariffs (some ACP also benefited from Everything But Arms status at zero tariffs in the EU market).

5. Krishna (2006) discusses other effects that are more difficult to quantify: effects such as rules of origin-jumping investment and effects on intermediate prices. Thoenig and Verdier (2006) also consider the implications of rules of origin for multinationals confronted with outward-processing decisions.

6. The United States rarely uses a value content criterion as the sole requirement for origin, and when it does it tends to rely on a single 40 percent foreign content requirement. The European Union has value content criteria ranging from 50 to 15 percent of domestic value added.

7. Cumulation is, in principle, only diagonal (see the glossary in the appendix), but the domestic content can be calculated as an aggregate of value added in any ASEAN member state; so in effect AFTA provides for full cumulation, although, as noted by Brenton (2006), the rules stipulate that the final stage of manufacture must be carried out in the exporting member state (what constitutes "the final stage" is not defined). Because vertical links and outsourcing are very important in Asia, full cumulation considerably relaxes the requirements of satisfying origin.

8. To drive home the importance of trade in intermediate goods, consider the following example. On the basis of the input–output data in Baldwin (2006, table 1 for Indonesia, Malaysia, Philippines, and Thailand (middle-income Asian countries), an average of 35–40 percent of intermediate goods are sourced outside AFTA. For example, take an activity with 10 percent value-added and 40 percent nonoriginating intermediate goods—that is, 36 percent of the final unit product price is nonoriginating. Originating value for this activity would be 64 percent. Then take the plausible example of an activity with the same value added but with 60 percent of materials nonoriginating; originating value falls to 46 percent, barely above the 40 percent minimum currently stipulated in AFTA.

9. The special regime was recently extended until 2015. Figure 2 lists the 22 beneficiary countries.

10. The algorithm is in essence a grid search over cutoffs whose criterion is the minimization of the concentrated sum of squared errors of the ordinary least squares regressions in the two regimes.

11. The decline in exports to the preferential-giving destination suggests that producers would choose to export under most favored nation status. In the illustrative simulations reported here, with constant elasticity throughout and smooth substitution possibilities across the origin for intermediate good purchases and export destination sales, producers pass on cost increases to consumers.

12. The authors of this article are aware of concerns voiced by the private sector in the course of the EU review about the practical difficulty of a value content criterion for small firms and, if based on costs, its potential to force unwanted disclosure of strategic information to powerful EU buyers that would enhance their ability to squeeze rents from developing country producers.

References

Anson, J., O. Cadot, C. Carrère, A. Estevadeordal, J. de Melo, and B. Tumurchudur. 2005. "Rules of Origin in North-South Preferential Trading Arrangements with an Application to NAFTA." *Review of International Economics* 13(3):501–17.

Augier, P., M. Gasiorek, and C. Tang. 2005. "The Impact of Rules of Origin on Trade Flows." *Economic Policy* 20(43):567–24.

Baldwin, R. 2006. "Managing the Noodle Bowl: The Fragility of East Asian Regionalism." CEPR Discussion Paper 5561. Centre for Economic Policy Research, London.

Brenton, P. 2006. "Notes on Rules of Origin with Implications for Regional Integration in South East Asia." World Bank, Washington, D.C.

Brenton, P., and H. Imagawa. 2004. "Rules of Origin, Trade and Customs." In L. de Sokol, and J. Wulf eds., *Customs Modernization Handbook*. Washington, D.C.: World Bank.

Brenton, P., and M. Manchin. 2003. "Making EU Trade Agreements Work: the Role of Rules of Origin." *The World Economy* 26(5):755–69.

Brenton, P., and C. Özden. 2005. "Trade Preferences for Apparel and the Role of Rules of Origin: The Case of Africa." World Bank, Washington, D.C.

Cadot, O., C. Carrère, and V. Strauss-Kahn. 2007. "Export Diversification: What's Behind the Hump?" University of Lausanne, Switzerland.

Cadot, O., J. de Melo, and A. Portugal-Perez. 2005. "Market Access and Welfare under Free Trade Agreements: the Case of Textiles under NAFTA." *World Bank Economic Review* 19(3):379–405.

______. (forthcoming). "Rules of Origin for Preferential Trading Arrangements: Implications for the ASEAN FTA of EU and US Experience." *Journal of Economic Integration*.

Cadot, O., J. de Melo, and E. Pondard. 2006. "*Evaluating the Consequences of a Shift to a Value-added Method for Determining Origin in the European Union's GSP Preferential Scheme.*" Report prepared for the European Commission, Brussels.

Cadot, O., A. Estevadeordal, and A. Suwa-Eisenmann. 2006. "Rules of Origin as Export Subsidies." In O. Cadot eds., *The Origin of Goods: Rules of Origin in Regional Trade Agreements*. London: Oxford University Press.

Cadot, O., C. Carrère, J. de Melo, and B. Tumurchudur. 2006. "Product Specific Rules of Origin in EU and US Preferential Trading Arrangements: an Assessment." *World Trade Review* 5(2): 199–224.

Cadot, O., A. Estevadeordal, A. Suwa-Eisenmann, and T. Verdier eds. 2006. *The Origin of Goods: Rules of Origin in Regional Trade Agreements*. London: Oxford University Press.

Carrère, C., and J. de Melo. 2006. "Are Different Rules of Origin Equally Costly? Estimates from NAFTA." In O. Cadot eds., *The Origin of Goods: Rules of Origin in Regional Trade Agreements*. London: Oxford University Press.

Estevadeordal, A. 2000. "Negotiating Preferential Market Access: the Case of NAFTA." *Journal of World Trade* 34(1):141–66.

Estevadeordal, A., and K. Suominen. 2006. "Mapping Rules of Origin Around the World." In O. Cadot eds., *The Origin of Goods: Rules of Origin in Regional Trade Agreements*. London: Oxford University Press.

Francois, J., B. Hoekman, and M. Manchin. 2006. "Preference Erosion and Multilateral Trade Liberalization." *World Bank Economic Review* 20(2):197–216.

Hansen, B. 2000. "Sample Splitting and Threshold Estimation." *Econometrica* 68(3):575–603.

Herin, J. 1986. "Rules of Origin and Differences between Tariff Levels in EFTA and in the EC." EFTA Occasional Paper 13. Geneva: European Free Trade Agreement.

Krishna, K. 2006. "Understanding Rules of Origin." In O. Cadot eds., *The Origin of Goods: Rules of Origin in Regional Trade Agreements*. London: Oxford University Press.

Krueger, A.O. 1998. "Free Trade Areas versus Customs Unions." *Journal of Development Economics* 54(1):169–87.

Olarreaga, M., and C. Özden. 2005. "AGOA and Apparel: Who Captures the Tariff Rent in the Presence of Preferential Market Access?" *World Economy* 28(1):63–77.

Özden, C., and G. Sharma. 2006. "The Price Effects of Preferential Market Access: Caribbean Basin Initiative and the Apparel Sector." *World Bank Economic Review* 20(2):241–60.

Portugal-Perez, A. 2006. "Disentangling the Determinants of Rules of Origin in North-South Preferential Trade Agreements: Evidence for NAFTA." University of Geneva.

———. 2007. "The Costs of RoO in Apparel: African Apparel Exports to the US and EU." University of Geneva.

Stevens, C., M. Gasiorek, J. Chweijczak, and J. Kennan. 2006. "Creating Development Friendly Rules of Origin in the EU." Overseas Development Institute, International Economic Development Group, London. (www.odi.org.uk/iedg/publications/Rules_of_Origin_FinalReport.pdf).

Thoenig, M., and T. Verdier. 2006. "The Impact of RoO on Strategic Outsourcing: An IO Perspective." In O. Cadot eds., *The Origin of Goods: Rules of Origin in Regional Trade Agreements*. London: Oxford University Press.

Tumurchudur, B. 2007a. "Rules of Origin and Market Access in the Europe Agreements." University of Lausanne, Switzerland.

———. 2007b. "Reforming NAFTA's Rules of Origin." University of Lausanne, Switzerland.

World Bank. 2005. *Global Economic Prospects 2005: Trade, Regionalism and Development*. Washington, D.C.

WTO (World Trade Organization). 2002. "Rules of Origin in Regional Trade Agreements." WT/REG/W/45. Geneva, Switzerland.

Wulf, L. de, and J. Sokol eds. 2004. *Customs Modernization Handbook*. Washington, D.C.: World Bank.

3
The political economy of international migration in a Ricardo-Viner model

Jean-Marie Grether, Jaime de Melo and Tobias Müller

Introduction

Writing about the economic consequences of immigration in receiving countries from the standpoint of a labor economist, Borjas (1995) speaks of a resulting "immigration surplus" to underline that the benefits created by immigration usually outweigh any losses for natives in the receiving country. At the same time he notes that the condition for this gain to materialize is that the wages of natives diminish, which means that gainful immigration will generate distributional conflicts. Under most scenarios the efficiency gains are small relative to the redistribution of income caused by immigration. Yet, given the overall gains and the means at the disposals of the state to redistribute income, on economic grounds, at least, one might be inclined to expect a more positive attitude towards immigration than those expressed in recent surveys (see below). Bhagwati (1991), also writing from the point of view of receiving countries, but from the standpoint of a trade economist, notes that both politicians and economists in the European Union (EU) and the US support free trade while advocating restrictions on migrations, and argues that such attitudes can only be the consequence of being inconsistent in the application of utilitarian logic which would lead to the advocacy of the free immigration solution.

Indeed, any stylized description of the recent evolution of trade and migration policies would conclude that the barriers against the free movements of goods have been less intense than the restrictions countries have imposed on the international movement of labor (while policies with regard to the international movement of capital have also been generally more liberal than labor immigration policies). In other words, countries have been more open to the indirect inflow of factor services embodied in goods and to direct capital flows than to direct inflows of labor.

This chapter is concerned with the determinants of national policies towards immigration in receiving countries and recognizes that immigration policies are the result of the interaction of two factors: (i) standard economic analysis where benevolent policymakers are primarily concerned with efficiency; (ii) the preferences of the electorate which are driven by the impact of immigration on

Table 3.1 Foreigners and their characteristics

	1987	*1997*
Austria	4.3	9.1
Belgium	8.7	8.9
France	6.8	6.3
Germany	6.9	9.0
Italy	1.0	2.2
Switzerland	14.9	19.0
UK	3.2	3.6
US	6.2	9.3
Canada	15.4	17.4

Source: SOPEMI (1999).
Note: US and Canada: foreign-born population as a percentage of total population.

b: Education levels in EU countries (1995)

	Natives		*Immigrants*	
	Low	*High*	*Low*	*High*
UK	46.5	18.6	57.9	20.4
France	40.3	16.7	53.3	16.0
Germany	19.1	18.9	46.3	10.7
Austria	31.7	6.4	47.4	8.9
Spain	67.8	14.1	47.0	25.6
Italy	64.2	6.3	53.3	16.0
Denmark	25.4	22.1	31.6	29.0
Belgium	45.3	20.6	52.8	19.5
Sweden	27.2	23.3	30.3	24.9
Netherlands	24.0	18.6	40.2	16.0

Source: Razin, Sadka and Swagel (1998: Table 2).
Notes: Low education is less than first stage of secondary level; high education is completed third schooling level; medium (not shown) is the balance.

native factor-market returns. This discussion is largely carried out in terms of a small price-taking economy.

Table 3.1 gives characteristics of the labor force in a group of industrialized countries: the share of foreigners in the population (Table 3.1a) and comparative education levels (Table 3.1b). The figures in Table 3.1a show that foreigners' share in population has increased recently in most countries. The increase has been particularly strong in traditional "guest-worker" countries (Austria, Germany and Switzerland). Besides the temporary surge following the collapse of socialist regimes in Eastern Europe, the stylized pattern has been little permanent migration flows, with the flows being mostly for temporary migration and mostly concentrated in skilled labor.[1] The figures in Table 3.1b relate to European countries. They show that the share of low education individuals is generally smaller for natives than for immigrants, though the opposite is the case in Spain and Italy.

Going beyond the data in Table 3.1, recent migration trends raise a number of issues. First, why is it that legal immigrants coexist with illegal immigrants who are often all too visible? Second, why is it that the opposition towards what demographers call "primary migration" is remarkably strong,[2] even though some small economies like the Netherlands and Ireland have acute labor shortages, and in some larger economies like the UK and Germany steps are currently under way to bring in skilled workers?[3] Third, is there a link between the type of immigration and sector of activity? In the US it has been of a permanent kind rather than temporary and of a "meltingpot" type where the intersectoral distribution of immigrants and natives is similar, whereas in some EU countries it has been of a "guest-worker" type, where immigrants are seasonal and concentrated in a few sectors. And fourth, why are countries increasingly resorting to the use of eligibility criteria like capital and/or skill requirements?

The next section introduces the standard economic analysis primarily to identify when there is an immigration surplus. The following sections introduce political-economy elements into the analysis. We use a new specific-factor direct-democracy framework further developed in Grether et al. (2000) to analyze the determinants of attitudes towards immigration. First, we use the model to investigate the conditions under which natives will oppose (be in favor of) certain types of immigration, and how the level of immigration and exogenous changes such as globalization might alter attitudes. Next, we bring a slight modification to the model to show how one may observe simultaneously legal and illegal immigration. We then develop a dual labor market version to compare the "guest-worker" and "melting-pot" immigration systems. Concluding remarks follow in the final section.

Is there an immigration surplus?

In the introduction, our allusion to a "surplus" created by immigration referred to an aggregate model with only one good produced (as in the seminal paper by Berry and Soligo, 1969), thereby excluding trade, and more importantly minimizing the conflicts and controversies surrounding migration policy. In this section we review briefly the robustness to various modifications in an otherwise standard framework where policy choice is carried out by benevolent policymakers. The usefulness of looking into the robustness of the "immigration surplus" result is that if immigration leads to a welfare loss of natives on efficiency grounds, there is no need to extend the analysis along political economy dimensions to explain the resistance to immigration. First, we look for the robustness of the immigration surplus prediction in trade models and for the presence of distributional conflicts. We then consider extensions.

The impact of immigration in an open economy

In the closed-economy model presented by Borjas (1995), immigration alters factor returns so that benefits outweigh losses resulting from income redistribution effects. In fact, this outcome of redistributive conflict with efficiency gain also describes the effects of immigration in the short-run specific-factor model used later in the chapter. Thus, it is legitimate to check the robustness of this result in other international trade models.

Suppose then that the evaluation of the effects of immigration takes place over long periods. Then the long-run condition of zero profits replaces the rents earned by specific factors which are never equalized in the specific-factor model. Let us start with models where immigration takes place in a setting where free entry and exit imply zero long-run profits.

Take first the Heckscher-Ohlin (H-O) model where international trade has a strong disciplining effect on wages. We assume a two country world, where skilled labor, H, and unskilled labor, L, are the two factors entering identical constant returns to scale production functions describing the technology in each of two price-taking sectors. Since, in the absence of transport costs, goods prices will be equalized, unit costs must also be equal, which implies (in the plausible case of no factor intensity reversal) that wages are equalized (Factor Price Equalization or FPE), with wages entirely determined by world prices and technology parameters. The output mix consists of both products so that the economy is "diversified," and so long as it remains so, immigration will have no effect on factor rewards. Arbitrage via trade in goods will eliminate any incentive to migrate, but, in the absence of trade, as first shown by Mundell (1957), international factor mobility will also exhaust arbitrage gains, so that trade in goods and trade in factors are substitutes.[4] In this world where trade eliminates any incentive to migrate, if migration takes place in a small economy for exogenous reasons, it does not alter factor prices, and there is no "immigration surplus."[5]

The FPE proposition being obviously false, Trefler (1993, 1998) has shown that allowing for differences in productivity between sending and receiving countries leads to a modified FPE proposition where productivity-adjusted wages are the same, which rehabilitates empirically both the H-O and FPE theorems. To draw the welfare implications of this amendment, one must determine migrants' attributes. If productivity is an attribute of the worker (a migrant will have low productivity regardless of where he works), we are back in the previous setting and there are no welfare effects of migration. But if productivity is an attribute of the country (low productivity is then the result of poor policies), migration will raise productivity, and there will be a positive welfare effect from migration.

For large countries like the EU and US, sustained migration can, in addition, have income distribution effects. Migration of, say, skilled workers can be equivalent to increasing the relative supply of skilled-intensive goods, thereby lowering their relative price along with the wage of skilled workers. Also there is the possibility of a terms-of-trade effect as the relative price of skill-intensive goods is likely to fall.[6]

The terms-of-trade effect of migration is best captured in a Ricardian model (Findlay, 1982). Consider here a version in which an array of goods are produced with one unit of labor, with sending and receiving countries specialized in the production of different goods. To illustrate the effects of immigration take a three good model in which the destination country produces initially only good 1 so that $w/p_1=1/a_1$, and $w/p_i>1/a_i$, $i=2,3$. With immigration, the equilibrium condition in sector 1 is unaffected but the wage is driven down until $w/p_2=1/a_2$ while in the sending country the wage is bid up until $w^*/p_2=1/a^*_2$, which means, by the likewise equilibrium condition in sector 3, that p_3 has risen in the sending country. It is then clear that real wages per capita, *w/p,* of natives have fallen in terms of goods 2 and 3. As pointed by Trefler (1998), who develops this case further, what has happened is that by increasing the supply of good 1 and shifting the terms of trade against the host country, immigration serves to reduce the scarcity rents enjoyed by native workers. Thus general equilibrium adjustments result in a negative immigration "surplus."

What about increasing returns to scale? With external returns to scale, it is intuitive that the immigration surplus result will be restored if one thinks, for example, of opening up new land to cultivation like the prairie in nineteenth-century US: without immigrants production would have been insufficient to warrant investment in the railways. Trefler (1998) develops such a model and shows that immigration raises the productivity of domestic labor, though there is also a negative terms-of-trade effect so that it is possible that there is an optimal level of immigration beyond which further immigration reduces domestic welfare.[7]

In Europe, closer integration has increased factor mobility and diminished transport costs, although labour mobility is low, at least compared with the US where up to 20 percent of families move in any given year. Ludema and Wooton (1999) introduce imperfect labor mobility in an economic-geography model a la Krugman (1991). As a result, even though it is again impossible to identify an unequivocal immigration surplus, in this richer model the cumulative causation process triggered by a reduction in transport costs that is welfare-enhancing for the destination country and potentially immiserizing for the sending country may no longer occur. They show that for sufficiently mobile labor, progressive integration may initially lead to agglomeration, then again to diversification as trade costs are lowered further. Temporary dislocations in the face of increased market integration could then be avoided by a temporary restriction on factor movements, as for example in the Europe Agreements, where reduction in barriers to trade take place before migration of people is allowed.

Extensions

Wildasin first (1992, 1994) and subsequently Razin and Sadka (1995) pointed out that immigration will raise the costs of income redistribution if such a 'non-economic' objective is present. This is because factor mobility means that redistributive policies entail interjurisdictional externalities since it is no longer a local public good: redistributive policy from mobile towards fixed factors will be thwarted as mobile factors move (poor flock in and rich leave).

The implications of immigration for the functioning of a welfare system are examined in Razin and Sadka (1999a, 1999b) and Razin, Sadka and Swagel (1998) in an overlapping generations model where life spans two periods (young contribute to a pays-as-you-go pension scheme, while the old draw a pension). In this framework, even if immigrants are net receivers of the welfare system (in the US, according to calculations by Borjas (1994), foreign-born households are 10 percent of households receiving assistance but receive 13 percent of total assistance), so long as immigration (only the young immigrate) has no effect on wages, their arrival provides a positive externality on native population as they make a net contribution to public finances in the period in which they arrive. With immigrants reducing wages upon arrival, the welfare impact becomes ambiguous.

These, and other extensions (such as wage rigidity—see Razin and Sadka, 1995), modify and may reduce the efficiency gains of immigration, potentially pointing towards ambiguous effects of immigration on welfare in a standard optimizing framework. This conclusion is also reached when one introduces cultural preferences in the form of social capital into the analysis as in Schiff (1998, 1999). In this case, not considered here, immigration creates a negative externality that reduces welfare.

Determinants of individual preferences over immigration policy

To explore the political economy of immigration policy, we use the specific-factor or Ricardo-Viner model in a direct-democracy framework. The direct-democracy model is arguably the best-suited framework to represent how preferences over immigration are formed by the population at large. This is due to peoples' perception that absorbing immigrants will be partly via changes in one's wage.[8] Also, its links to the underlying economic model are more transparent than in other political economy approaches like the pressure group model where policy is the result of the maximization of a welfare function whose weights are often arbitrarily chosen.[9] As to the specific-factor model, its time-frame with short-term rents also probably corresponds to the time-frame envisaged by many voters when they form an opinion on immigration policy.[10]

Suppose then that every individual (or household) can vote on migration policy (i.e. whether he or she agrees to accept a given number of immigrants), and that no other issue is on the political agenda. Then preferences are single-peaked and the national stance towards immigration is determined by the median voter. We analyze this institutional setting in the context of a small price-taking open economy. Variations in income determine the attitude towards immigrants. Each native household is endowed with one unit of labor and a certain amount of capital. If immigration lowers a native's income, he or she will oppose it. Here we focus on legal immigration and on the effects of capital distribution among natives, and turn to illegal immigration later.

The economy produces two traded goods: X (import-competing) and Y (exporting), using three factors: unskilled labor (L) which is specific to sector X; skilled labor (H) which is specific to sector Y; and capital (K), which is the mobile factor.[11] Let k_X (k_Y) denote the capital to unskilled (skilled) labor ratio in X (Y). Denote the share of capital used in sector X by $\lambda_K \equiv K_X/\bar{K}$. Let ℓ be the share of unskilled individuals in total population $\ell \equiv \bar{L}/(\bar{L}+\bar{H})$. Define the index of between-group inequality in capital distribution, τ, as the ratio between capital per capita of unskilled households and the national capital per capita average. Letting K^L denote total ownership of capital of unskilled households, denote by $\theta_L \equiv K^L/\bar{K}$ the unskilled labor's ownership share of capital. Unskilled (skilled) migrants are denoted by M_L (M_H), and μ (γ) is the share of natives in the population of unskilled (skilled) households. Finally, it will prove useful for the graphical presentation to choose units so that native population equals the capital stock, with both set equal to unity. The following equations conveniently summarize the notation used in this section:

$$k_X \equiv K_X/\bar{L}; k_Y \equiv K_Y/\bar{H};$$

$$\ell \equiv \bar{L}/(\bar{L}+\bar{H});$$

$$\lambda_K \equiv K_X/\bar{K};$$

$$\theta_L \equiv K^L/\bar{K}; \tag{1}$$

$$\tau \equiv [K^L/\bar{L}]/[\bar{K}/(\bar{L}+\bar{H})] = \theta_L/\ell$$

$$\mu \equiv \bar{L}/(\bar{L}+M_L) \text{ or } \gamma \equiv \bar{H}/(\bar{H}+M_H);$$

$$\bar{L}+\bar{H}) \equiv \bar{K} \equiv 1$$

In this model, attitudes towards immigration will be determined by the interaction of three elements: (i) the number of migrants; (ii) the capital distribution among natives; (iii) the capital endowment of immigrants. We start from the simplest case where immigrants bring no capital with them, there are no immigrants initially ($\mu=\gamma=1$), and domestic capital is equally shared among national households ($\theta_L=\ell \Leftrightarrow \tau=1$). We then allow first for sustained immigration, and second for unequal distribution of capital ownership.

Infinitesimal immigration

To illustrate the current immigration policy debate in the majority of industrialized countries, we assume that immigrants are unskilled individuals, and that the export-competing sector is capital intensive (i.e. $k_X < k_Y$).

As the immigration surplus is a second-order efficiency gain, it cannot be reaped with marginal (or infinitesimal) immigration. This implies that global national income is unaffected (zero-sum property) and, as a consequence, if one type of household loses (opposes immigration), the other one necessarily wins (favors immigration). Thus, it is sufficient to analyze the attitude of one household category, say unskilled individuals.

The arrival of unskilled migrants will lead to an expansion of sector X that uses them intensively, through an improvement of the marginal productivity of capital ($V_x \rightarrow V_x'$ in Figure 3.1). The real return to both categories of domestic sector-specific labor factors will decrease, while capital remuneration goes up, so it is *a priori* unclear if unskilled households benefit from immigration. In Figure 3.1, A (D) is the loss of labor income of unskilled (skilled) households and A+B+C+D is the total increase in capital income. As aggregate national income does not change following an infinitesimal inflow of immigrants, the triangular areas B and C are negligible. This means that areas A and A+B are approximately identical, so that unskilled households will be exactly compensated from their labor income loss provided the amount of capital they own (K^L) is equal to the amount of capital which is used in sector X (K_X). In other words, if $K^L{}_C$ is the critical amount of capital owned by unskilled natives which leaves them indifferent to immigration, its value is given by$K^L{}_C = K_X$.

How does the actual capital ownership of unskilled natives compare with this critical amount? With capital evenly distributed among households, the share of capital owned by unskilled households is equal to their share in population (i.e. $\theta_L = \ell$). Indifference towards immigration (i.e. $K^L = K_X$) will arise if the share of capital owned by unskilled labor is equal to the share of capital used in sector X, i.e. if $\theta_L = \lambda_K$. This indifference condition is satisfied along the diagonal of the box represented in Figure 3.2. If $\theta_L = \ell < \lambda_K$, unskilled households own less than the critical amount, and the compensation effect from capital ownership is too weak to compensate for the loss of rents. In other words, unskilled households are, in a sense, "capital-poor": they suffer a net income loss and oppose immigration (this is represented by the dashed area in Figure 3.2). By the same reasoning, unskilled natives' attitudes are favorable towards immigration for points below the diagonal $(\theta_L = \ell > \lambda_K)$.

To determine whether unskilled natives will oppose or favor immigration, we need to know whether unskilled labor are "capital-rich" or "capital-poor." Think now of Figure 3.2 as an Edgeworth box which is possible by our choice of units. By the choice of units in equation (1), the share of unskilled labor in total population, ℓ and the share of capital in sector X, λ_K, are both equal to their respective stocks in the economy, i.e.$\ell = \overline{L}$ $\lambda_K = K_X$, and the choice of units also

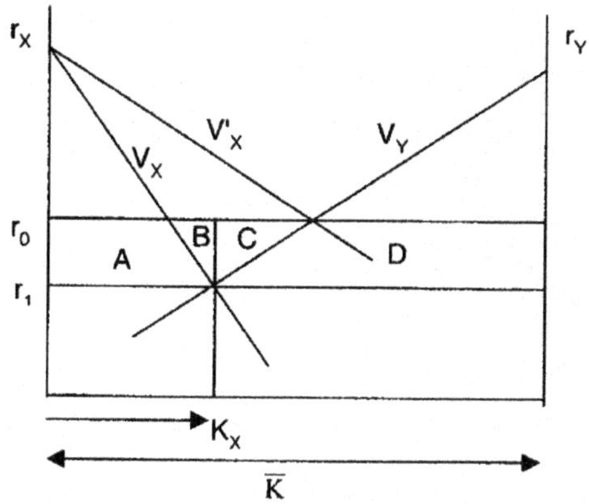

V_X: pre-migration marginal product of capital in sector X

V'_X: post-migration marginal product of capital in sector X

V_Y: marginal product of capital in sector Y

Figure 3.1 Infinitesimal immigration and factor rewards.

implies that $\bar{H}=1-\ell$ and $K_Y=1-\lambda_K$. This means that starting from, say, the SW corner of the box in Figure 3.2, one reads the allocation of unskilled labor to X going to the right along the horizontal axis while, if the NE corner represents the origin for industry Y, one reads the allocation of skilled labor to Y along the horizontal axis going from right to left. Thus any point in the box corresponds to a given allocation of skilled and unskilled labor and of the mobile capital between the two sectors.

Now, since we assumed that sector X is (unskilled) labor-intensive $(k_X<k_Y)$, whatever the allocation of capital, the permissible allocation of unskilled labor and of skilled labor will be below the diagonal. This means that, starting from a point like A (which would be on the dashed contract curve line if the economy were in long-run equilibrium), unskilled natives are necessarily capital-rich (since below the diagonal $k_X<k_Y$ or again $\theta_L=\ell>\lambda_K$) and they favor immigration.

What about national attitude? Given the zero-sum property of infinitesimal immigration, skilled natives adopt a position which is systematically opposed to that of unskilled natives (apart from the indifference case). This is represented in Figure 3.3a and b, with reversed dashed areas representing opposition to immigration. Combining both boxes one obtains Figure 3.3c, representing the national stance towards immigration according to which household group has the majority. For example, suppose that $\ell_0<0.5$, then (given that we have also assumed $k_X<k_Y$), the economy is in the shaded area (1) in figure 3.3(c). In that region, unskilled households are favorable to immigrants, but since they are the minority, the national attitude is one of opposition towards immigrants.[12]

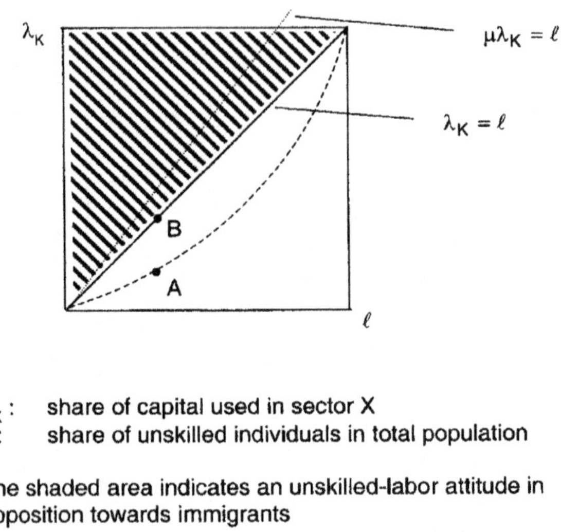

Figure 3.2 Attitude of unskilled natives towards immigration.

Note that all the previous analysis, which was based on an infinitesimal inflow of unskilled immigrants, remains valid if immigrants are skilled individuals. The reason is that both types of labor are analytically symmetric, and a reinterpretation of Figure 3.1 switching X and Y indices would lead exactly to the same results as far as critical capital ownership is concerned. In other words, Figure 3.3 represents the national attitude towards immigration, whatever the immigrants' skills.

In sum, as X is labor intensive and H is the majority group, it turns out that the nation as a whole unequivocally opposes immigration because it leads to a lower income of skilled natives, whose capital ownership is lower than the critical level that would make them indifferent. This result may seem surprising and rather inconsistent with actual immigration policies. In fact, it is highly dependent on the simplifying assumptions that underline the benchmark case which we adopted for expository purposes rather than for their realism. As will be shown below, relaxing these assumptions leads to a richer pattern of possible attitudes that will provide the basis for an interpretative discussion of results.

Sustained immigration

What happens if immigrants keep on flowing in? A quick, though incorrect, reaction would be to conclude that unskilled natives become progressively less prone to immigration because, as the share of capital used in industry X increases with the expansion of this sector, the critical capital ownership of

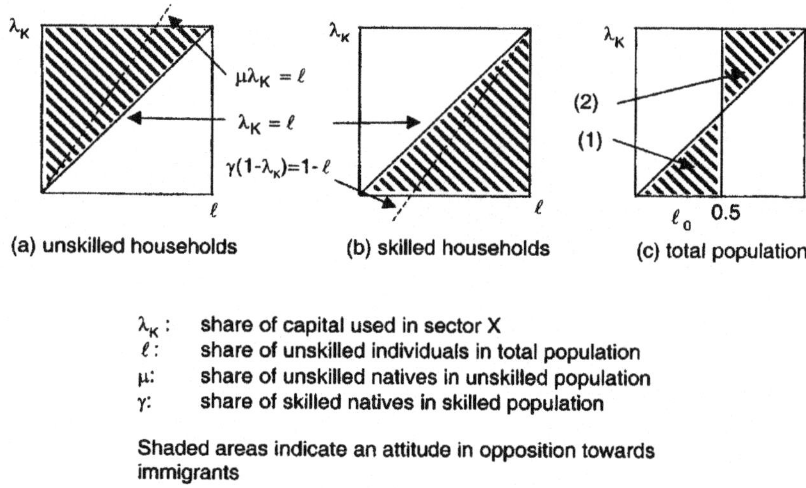

Figure 3.3 National attitude towards immigration.

unskilled natives, K_c^L becomes closer and closer to their effective capital ownership (an upward move from point A in Figure 3.2).

In fact the reverse is true: the critical capital ownership level of unskilled natives actually decreases, because since immigration is no longer infinitesimal, the zero-sum property no longer holds (one is in the "immigration surplus" situation discussed above). Hence, there is an increasing net gain from immigration that accrues to natives, making them more sympathetic towards immigrants. This "immigration surplus" situation is illustrated in Figure 3.4, where the sequential expansion of capital demand from sector X ($V_X^0 \rightarrow V_X^1 \rightarrow V_X^2$) leads to an ever increasing dashed area representing the net gain from immigration. Now, native unskilled households share their loss in rents with unskilled immigrant households.[13]

For skilled households, the critical capital level remains equal to the level of capital used in sector Y, so the analysis of Figure 3.3b remains unchanged. For unskilled households, because part of their income loss is now absorbed by the migrants already present, the compensatory requirement in terms of capital ownership is smaller. As illustrated in Figure 3.4, the critical amount of capital that leaves unskilled natives indifferent to immigration ($K_c^{L,2}=DE$)is equal to the amount of capital used in sector X ($K_X=DC$)times the share of natives in unskilled population, denoted by μ ($\mu \equiv \bar{L}/\bar{L}+M_L$) is the number of unskilled migrants, with $\mu=DE/DC$ at point C of Figure 3.4.

In terms of Figure 3.2, and provided ℓ is interpreted as the share of unskilled individuals in the voters' (not total) population, this leads to a rotation of the indifference line towards the left, whose expression is now given by $\mu\lambda_K=\ell$.

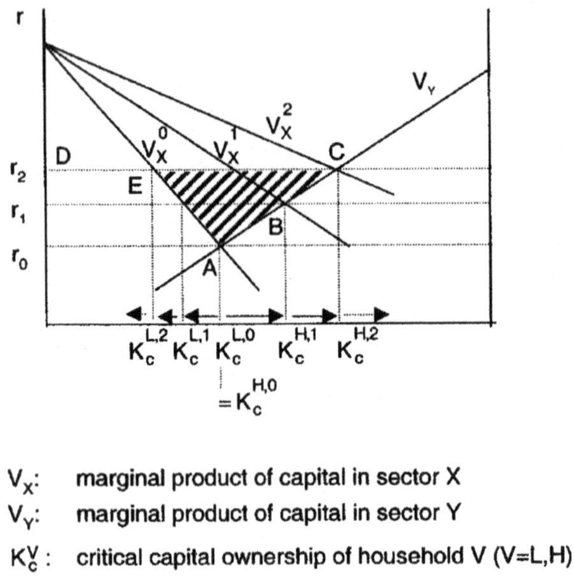

Figure 3.4 Sustained immigration.

Again, this is because the critical share of capital ownership for unskilled households is now smaller than the actual share of capital used in sector X, thereby decreasing the relative share of shaded areas in Figures 3.2 and 3.3a. Thus, an initial opposition may be softened and even reversed if a substantial immigration flow leads to sufficiently large net gains. However, recall that the attitude of skilled households (Figure 3.3b) remains unchanged. Thus, in terms of national attitude towards immigration (Figure 3.3c), it is only the shaded area (2) whose share would decrease, leaving area (1) unchanged.

As there is now an asymmetry between skilled and unskilled households, the skill level of immigrants matters. If immigrants are skilled individuals, the previous analysis is reversed: the indifference condition for unskilled households $(\lambda_K=\ell)$ remains unaltered, but skilled natives become more favorable to immigration. In Figure 3.3b, the indifference line for skilled households is now given by $\gamma(1-\lambda_K)=(1-\ell)$, where γ is the share of skilled natives in skilled population $(\gamma=\bar{H}/\bar{H}+M_H)$MH being the number of skilled migrants. In terms of national attitude (Figure 3.3c), area (2) is unchanged but area (1) is reduced.

Concurrently with the changes that have occurred in national attitudes towards immigration since the 1950s and 1960s when unskilled immigrants were welcomed, and the 1980s and 1990s when they were no longer welcome, the share of unskilled households has markedly declined. Suppose then that we apply our framework to a two-period analysis, and assume that $\ell_0>0.5>\ell$, so that native unskilled households started as a majority and became a minority (with a corresponding decrease in λ_K). In the presence of sustained migration, as the non-shaded areas in Figure 3.5a indicate, the median (native) voter changes from being in favor, to being against, unskilled immigration.[14] However, as depicted by Figure 3.5b, if immigrants are skilled and there is a substantial immigration surplus associated with their arrival, it may well be that the majority change leaves unaltered the favorable attitude towards skilled migrants.

Although this direct-democracy framework helps us to understand why attitudes towards skilled immigrants would be more favorable, it is still one in which unskilled natives (who are, according to our definition, "capital-rich") favor immigration, the reverse being true for skilled natives. This is particularly hard to reconcile with the survey-based results reported by Scheve and Slaughter (1999). Their econometric evidence using 1992 household survey data shows that, after controlling for gender, age, ideology, race, less-skilled (more-skilled) people prefer more-restrictionist (less-restrictionist) immigration policy. They also report that these results are robust to choice of the skill measure (occupational wage, years of schooling).

A straightforward extension to accommodate this result would be to assume that skilled (or unskilled) labor, rather than capital, is the mobile factor. In this case, every native would be opposed (favorable) to immigrants who (do not) share his or her skill level, irrespectively of capital ownership. An alternative is to introduce inequality in capital ownership among natives, as we do in the next section.

Unequal capital distribution across households

Relax now the assumption of equal capital ownership share among national households. We shall consider the case where capital is evenly distributed within each household group but capital per capita is different across groups (i.e there is "between" inequality).[15] Now the value of the index of between-group inequality, τ, defined in equation (1), is given by $\tau=\theta_L/\ell$ and $\tau<1$, under the plausible assumption that the per capita capital ownership of unskilled households is inferior to their share in total population. Recall that the definition of a "capital rich" ("capital poor") unskilled household is one for which $\theta_L>\lambda_K, (\theta_L<\lambda_K)$, so that the indifference line is now given by $\tau\ell=\lambda_K$.

Figure 3.6 draws the plausible case where $\tau<1$, so that the indifference line ($\lambda_K=\tau\ell$) has rotated clockwise with respect to Figure 3.3 ($\tau=1$). This leads to an increase of the area where unskilled (skilled) households are opposed (favorable) to immigrants, an intuitive result as between inequality has lowered the capital ownership of unskilled households. In the limiting case where unskilled natives do not own any capital ($\tau=0$), they become unambiguously opposed to immigration, while skilled natives systematically favor it, a result more consistent with the empirical evidence.

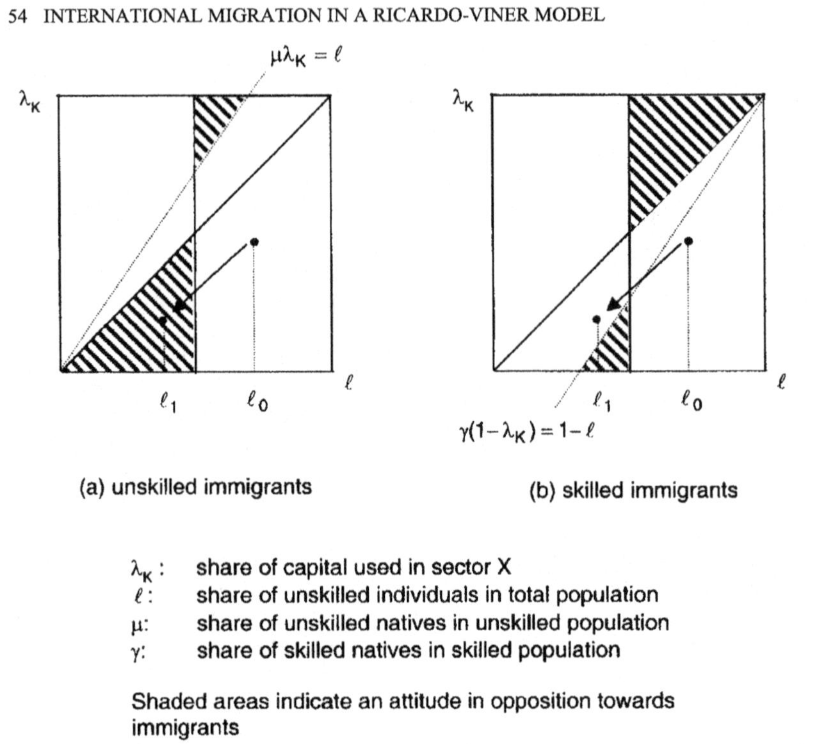

Figure 3.5 Population shares in the presence of sustained migration.

For the whole country, in Figure 3.6c, there is a net increase in the total shaded area (opposition to immigration). This suggests, in a probabilistic approach to reflect ignorance about the economy's parameter values, rising opposition towards immigration. Again, if one interprets these results in the light of the increased income inequality in the US (and to some extent in other receiving countries), the framework can help explain how the recent increase in income inequality is accompanied by a stiffening attitude towards unskilled immigration.

Another source of opposition towards immigration may come from globalization, reflected in an increase in the relative price of the exporting sector. Assume that the price of good Y increases or, alternatively, that a neutral technical progress in the same sector increases the marginal productivity of capital in the exporting sector. How would this affect the attitude towards immigrants? In itself, the shock would alter factor rewards (along the usual lines in the Ricardo-Viner model), but in fact the only thing that matters as far as households' attitudes are concerned is the impact on the critical capital ownership levels. And the answer is straight-forward: as the exporting sector expands, so does the share of capital used in sector Y. This means that skilled households face a higher critical capital level, the reverse being true for unskilled

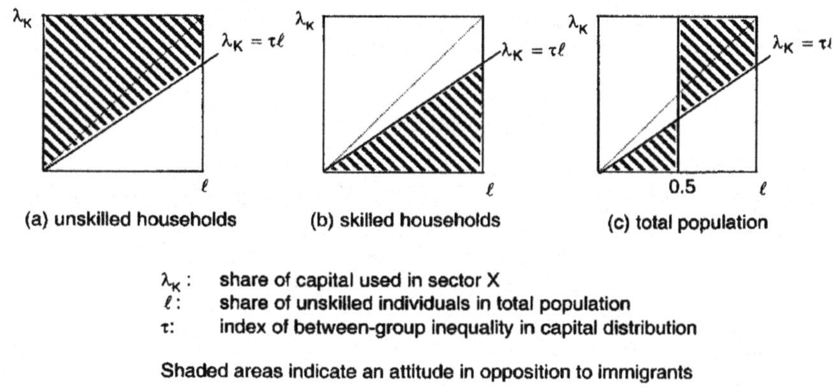

Figure 3.6 Inequality in capital distribution between households.

households. Thus, starting from an initial national indifference towards immigration (i.e. relaxing the assumption of differences in capital intensity between sectors for ease of exposition), like point B in Figure 3.2, we move downwards, making skilled households capital-poor and generating an opposition towards immigration since they are assumed to be the majority.

How are these results affected when immigrants also own capital? The basic difference from the previous analysis is that national factor rewards react both to the change in labor endowment and to the change in the capital stock. As both effects work in opposite directions, there is scope for a capital "compensation effect" on the immigrants' side, which might lead to a reversal of the net impact of immigration on factor rewards.

It can be shown that the critical capital ownership level of immigrants is exactly the same as that of the native unskilled in the benchmark case. If immigrants own more capital than this critical level, they become "capital-rich" and attitudes towards immigration are reversed. This may explain why capital requirements are a critical factor in the immigration policy of certain countries.

In sum, the Ricardo-Viner model provides a useful framework to analyze the changing pattern of attitudes towards legal immigration identified in industrialised countries. On the one hand, the loss of majority by unskilled natives is likely to have led to a reversal of national attitude from one of acceptance to one of opposition towards immigration. On the other hand, this stiffening of attitudes towards immigrants may have been exacerbated by globalization or by an increasing inequality of capital distribution among natives. At the same time, a relaxation of this anti-immigrants stance can be obtained by imposing capital requirements on immigrants, which, by the way, is being increasingly observed across receiving countries. Moreover, opposition towards skilled immigrants is less strong, particularly if the "immigration surplus" is large. In the next section, we show how a slight modification to the model makes it useful to examine the political economy of illegal immigration.

Why illegal migrants?

The Ricardo-Viner framework can be extended to the analysis of illegal immigration. Following Hillman and Weiss (1999a), we assume now that there is only one type of labor (L), which is the mobile factor, and two types of sector-specific capital (K_X, K_Y). There are two classes of households, "workers" each owning one unit of labor, and "capitalists" each owning one unit of either type of capital. Immigrants do not bring any capital with them. There are more workers than capitalists so the median voter is a worker.

Traded goods only

Start with the case where both goods are traded, and illegal immigrants are confined to one sector (illegal Mexicans in California employed in the garment and citrus fruit industries). Immigration, which brings down real wages, should never be observed, as it will be opposed by a majority of voters. However, illegal immigration may occur, and will be welcomed by capitalists. Suppose illegal immigration took place in the past, so that we start from an initial situation where there is already a substantial number of illegal immigrants in the country.[16] Moreover we assume that all illegal immigrants have been confined in sector X by an exogenous segregation process, which has displaced all native workers to sector Y.

This situation is depicted by Figure 3.7, where the number of illegal immigrants (M) is larger than the critical amount of immigrants that displaces the last native worker from sector X to sector Y ($M>M^*$). This means that native labor has become specific to sector Y and that the wage rate of natives (w_N) is higher than the wage rate of immigrants (w_I). In this case, as in a similar situation analyzed by Djajić (1997), native workers are "immunized" against additional illegal immigration. Indeed, any additional increase of the immigrant population (represented by the dotted lines in Figure 3.7) is Pareto improving for natives as it will depress the immigrants' wage while increasing the real return to K_Y and leaving unchanged both w_N and the real return to K_X.

What if immigration policy is now put up to a vote? If mass expulsion is not an option, the median voter will prefer to keep immigrants illegal rather than opt for an amnesty that would allow immigrants to enter sector Y and would bring down his or her wage to w^*. Moreover, a vote on additional illegal immigration would be positive as it would increase capital remuneration in sector Y while leaving indifferent native workers and sector X capitalists.

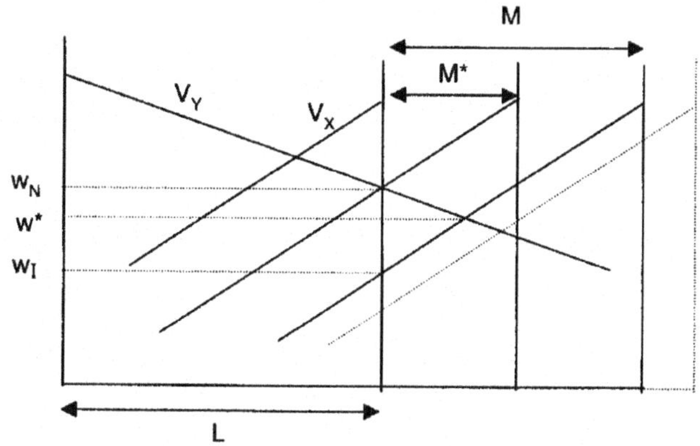

V_X: marginal product of labor in sector X
V_Y: marginal product of labor in sector Y
L: number of native workers
M: number of immigrants
M*: number of immigrants such that all natives are excluded from sector X.

Figure 3.7 Illegal immigration (labour is the mobile factor).

Non-traded sector

This illustrates the case where immigrants are confined to the lodging, restaurant and domestic help activities, as is the case in European countries with guest-worker systems. Provided that preferences are the same across household groups, the previous conclusion is reinforced if one of the two sectors produces non-traded goods. Suppose it is sector X, where illegal immigration is frequently observed, and start again from an initial situation where all natives are employed in sector Y (now the composite traded good). With respect to the analysis of Figure 3.7, the additional consequence of allowing more illegal immigration would be a decrease in the relative price of non-traded goods (there is an increase in the relative supply of non-traded goods while the relative demand is unchanged provided immigrants share a common consumption pattern with natives). This leaves every household better off than in the traded-goods case, generating a clear majority in favor of additional illegal immigration.[17]

The predictions here, according to which one would not vote to legalize illegal immigrants and where illegality permits the selective enforcement of restrictive immigration laws which confine immigrants to sectors where the median voter benefits from their presence, are supported by recent evidence. Hanson and Spilimbergo (1999a) show that illegal immigration between Mexico and the US responds to wage differences. In further work (Hanson and Spillimbergo, 1999b), they show that border enforcement efforts can be explained by the clashes in lobbying activities between sectors that use illegals intensively (apparel, fruits, lodging and restaurants) and hence lobby for lax enforcement, and labor unions that oppose lax enforcement. They also point out that an inefficient enforcement mix (at the border rather than the interior) is chosen for political economy reasons, though officially it is to avoid directly injuring the parties involved.

Dual labor markets and "guest-worker" migration

Segregation appears not only in the context of illegal immigration, but is observed in many countries even in the case of legal migration. The extent of segregation seems to depend on migration policy: it is more pronounced in countries with a "guest-worker" system than in countries favoring permanent immigration ("melting-pot").[18] Furthermore, Table 3.1 shows that among European countries, those with a "guest-worker" system (Germany, Austria, Switzerland) have experienced the greatest increases in the share of foreigners. From the viewpoint of political economy, one might therefore conjecture that the probability that immigration is accepted by natives depends on the type of immigration policy and thus on the extent of segregation it generates.

In the preceding section, we assumed complete sectoral segregation between natives and illegal immigrants. Here we investigate further the link between migration policy, (incomplete) sectoral segregation, and the political economy of immigration. To analyze this issue, we use an efficiency-wage model of a dual labor market with "good" and "bad" jobs. In this model, segregation and discrimination against immigrants are a consequence of the fact that migrants face different incentives and legal constraints than natives. On the one hand, migrants are likely to return to their home country (voluntarily or forced by limited work permits). On the other hand, preferential hiring regulations lead to discrimination against immigrants if good jobs are rationed.

We continue with the Ricardo-Viner small-country model with both goods traded, capital being the specific factor. Each native worker owns some quantity of capital, which is paid at the average return of the two sectors. The dual labor market is modelled in a standard efficiency-wage framework following Shapiro and Stiglitz (1984) and Bulow and Summers (1986). Work conditions in the primary and the secondary sectors are not identical. The primary sector, Y, offers good working conditions. By assumption, workers in this sector cannot be perfectly monitored. Thus firms prefer to pay wages above market-clearing levels in order to induce workers to supply effort. As a consequence, jobs are rationed in the primary sector and workers are queuing up for them. However, they can always find jobs in the secondary sector, X. These jobs are much less attractive and consist of repetitive tasks that can be easily monitored at negligible cost. The wage rate is set competitively in this sector. There is no unemployment.[19] First, we develop the model to show how the equilibrium is affected by an inflow of migrants, and second, we ask what type of system ("melting-pot" or "guest-worker") will be preferred by natives.

Segregation and discrimination in the efficiency wage model

Workers are assumed to be risk-neutral and to have identical instantaneous utility functions. Worker i holds a certain amount of capital k_i, and his indirect utility function is given by:

$$U = w + r_K k_i - e \tag{2}$$

where w is the wage, r_K is the average return to capital in the two sectors and e denotes effort. The variable e can take two values: 0 if the worker does not make any effort (i.e. if he "shirks"), and $e>0$ if he does not shirk. Workers are assumed to maximize expected utility over their infinite life horizon, using discount rate r.

Consider first the situation of natives. The problem of a worker in the primary sector who has to decide whether to shirk or not, can be analyzed by relating the utility levels that he can attain in the two cases. Let U_Y^s (U_Y^n) denote the expected present value of utility of a shirking (non-shirking) worker holding a primary-sector job. Let V_X denote the expected utility of a secondary-sector job. To relate these situations, the asset-equation approach introduced by Shapiro and Stiglitz (1984) is followed. A worker who shirks faces a probability d per unit time of being discovered and fired. Moreover, there is an exogenous probability q per unit time for each primary-sector job to end; in that case the worker takes up a job in the secondary sector. If a worker has a job in the primary sector, he receives wage w_Y. He earns the following return, according to whether he shirks or not:

$$rU_Y^n = w_Y + r_K k_i - e - q(U_Y^n - U_X) \tag{3}$$

$$rU_Y^s = w_Y + r_K k_i - (q+d)(U_Y^s - U_X) \tag{4}$$

A worker in the primary-sector does not shirk if $U_Y^n \geq U_Y^s$ At equilibrium, there is no shirking and this condition holds with equality since there is no reason for a primary-sector firm to pay a higher wage. Using equations (3) and (4), the no-shirking condition can be rewritten as follows:

$$d(U_Y^n - U_X) = e \tag{5}$$

The return to a job in the secondary sector is equal to:

$$rU_X = w_X + r_K k_i - e + \alpha(U_Y - U_X) \tag{6}$$

where α is the probability of moving from a secondary-sector job to a primary-sector job.

In a steady-state equilibrium, the flow out of the primary sector is qL_Y, where L_Y is native employment in the primary sector. The flow into the primary sector is $\alpha(L-L_Y)$, where L is total native employment. At equilibrium, these two must be equal. Thus, for natives α is given by $qL_Y/(L-L_Y)$. Using (3) and (6), the no-shirking condition (5) becomes:

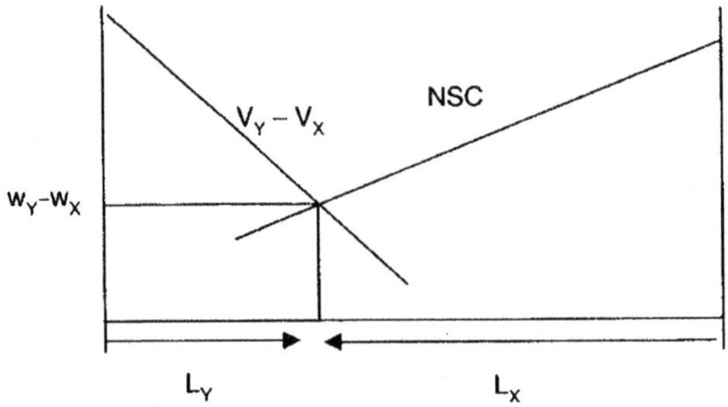

NSC: non-shirking constraint of natives
V_x: marginal product of labor in sector X (secondary sector)
V_Y: marginal product of labor in sector Y (primary sector)

Figure 3.8 Equilibrium in the dual labor market.

$$w_Y - w_x = \frac{e}{d}\left(r + \frac{qL}{L - L_Y}\right) \tag{7}$$

At equilibrium, the wage rate is equal to the marginal product of labor in each sector. Labor market equilibrium is depicted in Figure 3.8. The upward-sloping curve is the natives' no-shirking condition (7), and the downward-sloping curve represents the difference between marginal products of labor in the two sectors. The intersection determines the equilibrium wage differential and native employment in both sectors. Note that the employment of immigrants is considered exogenous in this figure, and that the equilibrium in the dual labor-market is inefficient. The distortion could be corrected by subsidising primary-sector (high-income) employment. Since such a measure would meet with strong political opposition, because of its anti-egalitarian implications, we assume that it is not realized.

The welfare outcome of immigration obviously depends on the migrants' incentives and on migration policy. Indeed, a distinctive characteristic of immigrants is their probability of return.[20] Therefore, even if migrants are identical to natives in all other respects, their incentive not to shirk is influenced by the probability of return to their home country. Moreover, the return probability is influenced by various aspects of migration policy, such as the existence of temporary work permits, or the government's attitude towards social and economic integration of immigrants. Other legal dimensions of migration policy are equally important. In most countries, migrants are granted equal rights in the host country's labor market only after a certain period of stay. Firms are compelled to prefer natives and "old" migrants over "new" migrants in their hiring decision.

All these factors contribute to segregation and thus discrimination against migrants. Since competition ensures that natives and migrants are paid the same wages, discrimination is of the type "equal pay for equal work, but not equal work." Hence migrants have smaller chances of finding "good" jobs than natives and suffer from sectoral segregation. The extent of segregation which results from these differences in incentives can be summarized by the following equation relating the migrants' chances of being employed in the primary sector to that of the natives:[21]

$$\frac{L^*_Y}{L^*} = (1-\zeta)\frac{L_Y}{L}; 0 < \zeta \leq 1 \tag{8}$$

where an asterisk on a variable denotes an immigrant and ζ measures the extent of segregation.

The choice of migration policy

Is it more likely that natives will vote in favor of immigration if the government applies a "guest-worker" system rather than a "melting-pot" policy? To analyze this issue, assume that capital is distributed unequally among native workers. Consider a worker (indexed by i) holding k_i units of capital. Immigration entails an identical change in his steady-state utility,

whether he works in the primary or the secondary sector. Indeed, differentiating equations (3) and (5) yields:

$$dU_Y = dU_X = (l/r)(dw_Y + k_i dr_K) \tag{9}$$

How does the critical level of capital, k_i^c(at which a native is indifferent towards immigration, i.e. $dU_X = dU_Y = 0$), depend on migration policy? Consider first, as a benchmark case, the standard Ricardo-Viner model without dual labor markets. Here the critical level of capital is given by the total per capita stock of capital, $(K_X+K_Y)/L$. By contrast, the "zero-sum" property of (infinitesimal) immigration is not preserved in the dual-labor-market model, as the equilibrium is inefficient. Immigration has a positive (negative) first-order effect on the natives' aggregate welfare if native employment in the primary-sector, L_Y, increases (decreases).[22] As a consequence, the critical level of capital is inferior (superior) to the per capita average capital stock, if native primary-sector employment increases (decreases) with immigration.

Thus the reaction of native primary-sector employment is crucial for the political economy of immigration. Immigration does not shift the natives' no-shirking constraint (NSC). Therefore the question whether L_Y increases with immigration reduces to whether the marginal-labor-product curve shifts upwards in Figure 3.8. In Müller (forthcoming), it is shown that this is more likely to happen if migration policy leads to a high degree of segregation, ζ.

It is instructive to consider the special case of a "guest-worker" system where segregation is maximized (ζ=1). As immigrants "push" natives towards the primary sector, the marginal-labor-product curve shifts to the right, and L_Y increases unambiguously with immigration. The critical level of capital is equal to:

$$k_i^c = \frac{K_X + K_Y}{L_Y + L_X[1 + \eta_Y / \varepsilon_Y]} \tag{10}$$

where η_Y is the absolute value of the inverse labor demand elasticity in the primary sector and ε_Y is the elasticity of the wage with respect to the primary-sector employment along the no-shirking constraint. Thus the "guest-worker" system implies a critical level of capital which is lower than the average capital per capita, since $k_i^c < (K_X + K_Y)/L$ If the distribution of capital is symmetric (or if the median capital level is not too far below the average), the median voter will therefore be in favor of immigration.

By contrast, with a non-discriminatory "melting-pot" policy (ζ=0), it is likely that the critical capital level exceeds the average per capita capital stock. In that case (and if the median capital level is not greater than the average), the majority of natives will vote against immigration.

Conclusions

This chapter has presented an overview of the determinants of migration policies in industrial countries. It has argued that overall, migration probably yields efficiency gains for natives (i.e. an immigration surplus), and an overall welfare gain, if compensation policies can be put in place. We have argued that it is a useful way to view immigration policies as largely determined by the electorate at large in representative democracies, as would be the case in a direct democracy, because of the strong positions taken by politicians and the electorate at large.

Using the direct-democracy framework in several variants of a specific-factors model, we have shown how it can help interpret several stylized facts about recent immigration policies: a stiffened stance towards immigration of the unskilled; coexistence of legals and illegals; lax enforcement towards illegals; a preference for 'guest-worker' programs; and a shift towards eligibility criteria included in immigration decisions.

While going beyond the framework of market-determined outcomes, and of policies determined by benevolent policymakers, the approach has remained grounded in the standard trade models. This has enabled us to relate trade and migration policies, as they are in policy and political debates. As a result, several aspects of migration policies, such as the determination of refugee policies towards asylum claims, have been left out. Neither have the links between foreign direct investment, trade policy and migration policy been examined.

Notes

1 See Zimmermann (1995) for a discussion of the phases of European migration and The Economist, May 6–12, 2000, for recent characteristics of immigration in the EU. For the US see Borjas (1994) and Trefler (1998).

2 A poll conducted on behalf of the European Commission shows that a significant majority of those interviewed believe that "immigrants are too many." This is particularly true in the four largest European countries, with 54 percent of Frenchmen, 57 percent of Germans, 51 percent of' Britons, and 64 percent of Italians believing the number of migrants to be excessive. And in the US, results of the US National Elections Survey of 1992, in which respondents were asked to reveal their preference over immigration policy on a scale of 1 (increase a lot), to 5 (decrease a lot) produced a mean of 3.6 and a standard deviation of 1.0 (Scheve and Slaughter, 1998).

3 The stiffening in attitude towards immigrants in the EU, especially towards low-skill ones, is all the more remarkable since according to the United Nations' Population Division projections based on current trends, the current flow of immigrants in the EU as a whole would have to reach 1.6 million a year to keep its working population stable, and 13.5 million a year to keep the ratio of pensioners to workers steady.

4 Wong (1995) explores systematically trade models in the presence of factor mobility. Venables (1999) explores the links between trade liberalization and factor mobility in a family of models. Faini and Grether (1997) and Grether et al. (1999) present models that accommodate the observed asymmetry between trade and migration policies.

5 Leamer and Levinsohn (1995) refer to this result as the Factor-Price-Insensitivity (FPI) theorem. However, with more tradable products than factors, we are in the multi-cone setting, so that with sufficiently large immigration shocks, the diversification cone will be altered and factor prices will change. Also, if both countries are in different cones, different goods are produced and trade will not eliminate incentives for factors to migrate.

6 Kenen (1971) analyzes the terms-of-trade effects of migration in an H-O model, but from the standpoint of the source country.

7 Though in a different context, this result is reminiscent of the discussion on the optimal population size where there are advantages (increasing returns to scale, sharing of public goods) and disadvantages (diminishing factor productivity, congestion effects). See Razin and Sadka (1997).

8 Scheve and Slaughter (1999) find that less-skilled workers are significantly more likely to prefer limiting immigrant inflows into the US, and that individuals form their opinions in accord with their interests as labor-force participants. This justifies the approach taken here. Their results also reject the "area analysis" framework used by labor economists according to which immigrants pressure the wages of similarly-skilled natives who reside in gateway communities where immigrants settle, but are in accordance with the "factor proportion analysis" where the pressure on wages is nationwide, as in the multi-cone H-O and Ricardo-Viner trade models.

64 INTERNATIONAL MIGRATION IN A RICARDO-VINER MODEL

9 For examples of the pressure-group approach, see Buckley (1996) and Mezza and Winden (1996).

10 Hillman and Weiss (1999b) suggest that voters probably find the H-O model appealing when formulating trade policy since it captures the indirect effect of labor (via embodiment in imports), and the Ricardo-Viner model when formulating immigration policy since immigrants compete directly with domestic labor. Bilal et al. (2000) provide an algebraic treatment of the long-run version of the model presented here with the same two goods and the assumption that the three factors, capital, unskilled labor and skilled labor, are mobile across sectors. Benhabib (1996) uses a similar approach in a one-sector economy.

11 An alternative would be to consider that skilled labor is the mobile factor; however, besides being less realistic in a two-sector context, this case is less interesting as the pattern of attitudes that emerge is independent of capital distribution (see Bilal et al., 2000).

12 Should the unskilled be the majority, then the economy is to the right of the "majority" line, and, since the economy is below the diagonal, the median voter would be favorable to unskilled immigration. And if Y were labor intensive, the economy would be above the diagonal, so that the results would, once again, be reversed.

13 This case also depicts the impact of an infinitesimal increase of unskilled migrants starting from an initial situation (like point B in Figure 3.4) where there are already immigrants in the country.

14 If migrants get progressively "assimilated" and vote, then the critical line in figure 3.5 rotates back to the diagonal, but the changes in attitudes would still be observed if the unskilled changed from majority to minority.

15 The case where capital is unevenly distributed within groups but the average capital per capita is identical between groups (within inequality) is treated in Grether et al. (2000) who also use a Beta distribution to examine numerically the case where capital ownership distribution is skewed to the left within each household group. The simulations reveal an "opposition cone" along the diagonal of Figure 3.3c, whose width depends on the skewness of the capital within each group.

16 This corresponds to the case analyzed by Hillman and Weiss, who also assume that undesired (from the point. of view of the median voter) illegal immigration has taken place. It is a shortcoming of the median voter framework that it is unsuitable to explain why illegal immigrants would have entered in the first place. A more appropriate framework is the pressure group model (see Hanson and Spilimbergo, 1991)), where industries that benefit from illegals make contributions in return for lower levels of enforcement while groups that oppose immigration, say unions (and perhaps other groups) make contributions for higher enforcement levels.

17 See Djajić (1997). This is all the more likely if one makes the assumption, as do Hillman and Weiss (1999a), that domestic (and legal immigrant) households have stronger preferences for non-traded goods than illegal immigrant. households.

18 Zimmermann (1994) shows that in "guest-worker" countries like Germany and Switzerland, immigrants are heavily represented in construction and manufacturing, as opposed to the United States, where the sectoral distributions of natives and immigrants are very similar.

19 For the effects of immigration in efficiency-wage models with unemployment, see Müller (2000) and Epstein and Hillman (2000), where the natives' willingness to exert effort increases with the number of immigrants.

20 In 1995, average return rates ranged from 1.5 percent for Netherlands to 7.8 percent for Germany, though much higher return rates are attained for particular groups (25.6 percent return rates for Polish immigrants in Germany) of for certain legal categories (10.3 percent for holders of annual work permits in Switzerland).

21 Equation (8) can be considered as a reduced form. The exact relation between segregation, discrimination and structural parameters (such as the return probability) is derived in Müller (forthcoming).

22 To see this, consider the variation of aggregate native welfare: $L_X\, dU_X + L_Y\, dU_Y = (l/r)\, L_X\, (dw_Y - dw_X) = [(1/r)\, (w_Y - w_X) - (e/d)]\, dL_Y$, where the expression between brackets is positive. Including the gain of secondary-sector workers, $(U_Y - U_X)\, dL_Y = (e/d)\, dL_Y$, does not change this qualitativc result.

References

Benhabib, J. (1996) "On the Political Economy of Immigration," *European Economic Review,* 40:1737–1743.

Berry, R.A. and R.Soligo (1969) "Some Welfare Aspects of International Migration," *Journal of Political Economy,* 77 (5): 778–794.

Bhagwati, J. (1991) "Free Traders and Free Immigrationists: Strangers or Friends," Working Paper 20, Russell Sage Foundation.

Bilal, S., J.M.Grether and J.de Melo (2000) "Attitudes Towards Immigration in a Direct Democracy: A Trade-Theoretic Approach," mimeo, University of Geneva.

Borjas, G. (1994) "Immigration and Welfare: 1970–90," Working Paper 4872, Cambridge, Mass.: National Bureau of Economic Research.

Borjas, G. (1995) "The Economic Benefits of Immigration," *Journal of Economic Perspectives,* 9 (2): 3–22.

Buckley, F.H. (1996) "The Political Economy of Immigration Policies," *International Review of Law and, Economics,* 16:81–99.

Bulow,J. and L.Summers (1986) "A Theory of Dual Labor Markets with Application to Industrial Policy, Discrimination, and Keynesian Unemployment," *Journal of Labor Economics,* 4 (3): 376–414.

Djajić, S. (1997) "Illegal Immigration and Resource Allocation," *International Economic Review,* 38 (1): 97–117.

Epstein, G. and A.Hillman (2000) "Social Harmony at the Boundaries of the Welfare State: Immigrants and Social Transfers", Working Paper 2414, London: Centre for Economic Policy Research.

Faini, R. and J.M.Grether (1997) "L'Ouverture au Commerce peut-elle réduire la Migration Nord-Sud," in J.de Melo and P.Guillaumont (eds), *Commerce Nord-Sud: Migration el Délocalisation,* Paris: Economica.

Findlay, R. (1982) "International Distributive Justice: A Trade Theoretic Approach," *Journal of International Economics,* 13:1–14.

Grether, J.M., J.de Melo and T.Müller, (1999) "Réflexions sur la non-équivalence entre politiques migratoires et politiques commerciales," in A.Bouët and J. le Cacheux (eds), *Globalisation et Politiques Economiques,* Paris: Economica.

Grether, J.M., J.de Melo and T.Müller (2000) "Why Have Attitudes Towards Immigration Changed?," in progress, University of Geneva.

Hanson, G. and A.Spilimbergo (1999a) "Illegal Immigration, Border Enforcement, and Relative Wages: Evidence from Apprehensions at the US-Mexico Border," *American Economic Review,* 89 (5): 1337–1357.

Hanson, G. and A.Spilimbergo (1999b) "Political Economy, Sectoral Shocks, and Border Enforcement," Working Paper 7315, Cambridge, Mass.: National Bureau of Economic Research.

Hillman, A. and A.Weiss (1999a) "A Theory of Permissible Immigration," *European Journal of Political Economy,* 15:585–604.

Hillman, A. and A.Weiss (1999b) "Beyond International Factor Movements: Cultural Preferences, Endogenous Preferences, Endogenous Policies and the Migration of' People: An Overview," in R.Faini, J.de Melo and K.Zimmermann (eds), *Migration: The Controversies and the Evidence,* Cambridge: Cambridge University Press, 76–90.

Kenen, P. (1971) "Migration, the Terms of Trade and Economic: Welfare in the Source Country," in J.N.Bhagwati et al. (eds), *Trade Balance of Payments and Growth: Essays in Honour of Charles Kindleberger,* Amsterdam: North-Holland.

Krugman, P. (1991) "Increasing Returns and Geography," *Journal of Political Economy,* 99:483–99.

Leamer, E.E. and J.Levinsohn (1995) "International Trade Theory: The Evidence," in G.Grossman and K.Rogoff (eds), *Handbook of International Economics, Vol. III,* Amsterdam: North-Holland.

Ludema, R. and I.Wooton (1999) "Regional Integration, Trade and Migration: Are Demand Linkages Relevant in Europe?," in R.Faini, J.de Melo and K. Zimmermann (eds), *Migration: The Controversies and the Evidence,* Cambridge: Cambridge University Press.

Mezza, I. and F.Winden (1996) "A Political Economic Analysis of Labor Migration and Income Redistribution," *Public Choice,* 88:333–63.

Müller, T. (2000) "Migration, Unemployment and Discrimination," Cahier du département d'économetrie No. 2000.03, University of Geneva.

Müller, T. (forthcoming) "Migration Policy in a Small Open Economy with a Dual Labor Market," *Review of International Economics.*

Mundell, R.M. (1957) "International Trade and Factor Mobility," *American Economic Review,* 47:321–335.

Razin, A. and E.Sadka (1995) "Resisting Migration: Wage Rigidity and Income Distribution," *American Economic Review,* Papers and Proceedings, 85 (2): 312–316.

Razin, A. and E.Sadka (1997) "International Migration and International Trade," in M.Rosenzweig and O.Stark (eds), *Handbook of Population and Family Economics,* Amsterdam: North-Holland.

Razin, A. and E.Sadka (1999a) "Migration and Pension with International Capital *Mobility" Journal of Public Economics,* 74 (2): 141–150.

Razin, A. and E.Sadka (1999b) "Unskilled Migration: A Burden or a Boon for the Welfare State," Working Paper 7013, Cambridge, Mass.: National Bureau of Economic Research.

Razin, A., E.Sadka and P.Swagel (1998) "Tax Burden and Migration: A Political Economy Theory and Evidence," Working Paper 6734, Cambridge, Mass.: National Bureau of Economic Research.

Scheve, K. and M.Slaughter (1998) "What Determines Individual Trade-Policy Preferences," Working Paper 6531, Cambridge, Mass.: National Bureau of Economic Research.

Scheve, K. and M.Slaughter (1999) "Labor-Market Competition, and Individual Preferences over Immigration Policy," Working Paper 6946, Cambridge, Mass.: National Bureau of' Economic Research.

Schiff, M.S. (1998) "Social Capital, Trade, and Optimal Migration Policy," Policy Research Working Paper 2044, World Bank.

Schiff, M.S. (1999) "Labor Market Integration in the Presence of Social Capital," Policy Research Working Paper 2222, World Bank.

Shapiro, C. and J.Stiglitz (1984) "Equilibrium Unemployment as a Worker-discipline Device," *American Economic Review,* 74:433–444.

SOPEMI (1999) *Trends in International Migration: Annual Report,* Paris: OECD.

Trefler, D. (1993) "International Factor Prices Differences: Leontief Was Right!," *Journal of Political Economy,* 101:961–987.

Trefler, D. (1998), "Immigrants and Natives in General Equilibrium Trade Models," in J.P.Smith (ed), *The Immigration Debate: Studies on the Economic, Demographic, and Fiscal Effects of Immigration,* Washington, D.C.: National Academy Press.

Venables, A. (1999) "Trade Liberalisation and Factor Mobility: an Overview," in R. Faini, J.de Melo and K.Zimmermann (eds), *Migration: The Controversies and the Evidence,* Cambridge: Cambridge University Press.

Wildasin, D. (1992) "Relaxation to Factor Mobility and Income Distribution," in P. Pestieau (ed.), *Public Finance in a World of Transition, Public Finance,* 47:216–32.

Wildasin, D. (1994) "Income Distribution and Migration," *Canadian Journal of Economics,* 27 (3): 637–656.

Wong, K. (1995) *International Trade in Goods and Factor Mobility,* Cambridge, Mass.: MIT Press.

Zimmermann, K. (1994) "European Migration: Push and Pull," Proceedings of the World Bank Annual Conference on Development Economics, The World Bank.

Zimmermann, K. (1995) "Tackling the European Migration Problem," *Journal of Economic Perspectives,* 9(2): 45–62.

Review of International Economics, 11(2), 253–267, 2003

Attitudes Towards Immigration: a Trade-Theoretic Approach

*Sanoussi Bilal, Jean-Marie Grether, and Jaime de Melo**

Abstract

The paper uses a three-factor (capital, low- and high-skill labor), two-household (low- and high-skill individuals), two-sector trade model to analyze the determinants of voter attitudes towards immigration under direct democracy, and to identify factors that would be coherent with both the observed increase in the skilled–unskilled wage differential and the stiffening attitudes towards low-skill capital-poor immigration. If the import-competing sector is intensive in the use of low-skill labor, and capital is the middle factor, an improvement in the terms of trade or neutral technical progress in the exporting sector leads nationals to oppose immigration of capital-poor low-skill households. An increase in income inequality is also likely to stiffen attitudes towards this type of capital-poor, low-skill immigration prevalent in Europe until recently.

1. Introduction

Incentives for international migration have largely been studied as responses to factor-reward differences with factors of production moving internationally to maximize income. The standard Heckscher–Ohlin model predicts that, on efficiency grounds, countries should be as open to the indirect inflow of factor services embodied in goods as to the direct flows of capital and labor. Yet, globalization of the world economy has revealed an asymmetry in policies as countries have become concurrently more open to flows of goods and capital and less open to direct flows of labor. Moreover, for countries receiving immigrants, restrictions have become more severe towards unskilled labor. At the same time there has been a widening disparity between the incomes of skilled and unskilled workers. This is in accordance with the Stolper–Samuelson predictions of increased globalization, suggesting that there is still some usefulness for the standard trade-theoretic framework when studying international factor migration, and that there may be causal links between changes in the external environment, the deterioration in the labor markets of many recipient countries, and the stiffening of attitudes towards immigration.

To be sure, to understand attitudes towards the movement of people, one must go beyond the standard economic framework where factors of production are apersonal entities. Broadening the framework to take into account the attributes of individuals as in models of locational choice (Hillman, 1994) or cultural preferences (Schiff, 1997) is indispensable to understand attitudes towards immigration. But it is hard to dismiss

*Bilal: International Economic Development Group, Overseas Development Institute, 111 Westminster Bridge Road, London SE1 7JD, UK. E-mail: s.bilal@odi.org.uk. Grether: University of Neuchâtel, Division Economique et Sociale, Pierre-à-Mazel 7, 2000 Neuchâtel, Switzerland. E-mail: jean-marie.grether@unine.ch. de Melo: University of Geneva, Département d'économie politique, 40 Boulevard du Pont-d'Arve, 1211 Genève 4, Switzerland. E-mail: jaime.demelo@ecopo.unige.ch. This is a revised version of a paper presented at the CEPR workshop "Globalization, Regional Integration and Development," Venice, 31 January/1 February 1998 and at a seminar at the University of Geneva. We thank Riccardo Faini, Ronald Jones, Tobias Müller, Arvind Panagariya, Maurice Schiff, an Associate Editor, a referee, and seminar participants for comments and the FNRS for financial support under grant 12-42011.94.

the view that, like others, immigration policies are usefully analyzed in a political-economy setting in which they are endogenously explained by economic and political self-interest and the institutional mechanisms of collective choice.[1] We study attitudes towards immigration in a model where attitudes are determined entirely by economic self-interest in a direct-democracy framework *à la* Mayer (1984), the simplest institutional mechanism of collective choice. We use a three-factor version of the two-good Heckscher–Ohlin model which allows us to consider two types of households (high-skill and low-skill) each owning varying degrees of capital.[2] We can thus study the effects of changes in the distribution of income on household attitudes towards immigration.

Section 2 presents the building blocks of the model: household factor ownership patterns and factor intensity conditions. Section 3 develops a simple graphical analysis that allows us to determine household attitudes towards immigration in terms of two parameters: a "similarity" index measuring differences in factor intensities and the household composition in the population. Section 4 carries out standard comparative statics exercises that establish how factor accumulation, terms-of-trade changes, and disembodied technical progress affect households' attitudes towards immigration. Section 5 interprets model-predicted results about changes in attitudes towards immigration in terms of broad stylized facts on the evolution of product and factor markets in receiving countries. For example, we introduce skewness in capital ownership within each household group and show how an increase in income inequality can lead to a stiffening in attitude towards capital-poor immigrants. Section 6 concludes.

2. The Model

As did the early users of the "3×2" model (Batra and Casas, 1976; Jones and Easton, 1983; Thompson, 1983), we assume a price-taking economy in international markets, and we take a long-run view by assuming that all factors are mobile across sectors. Two goods are produced, X_1 (imported) and X_2 (exported), with constant-returns-to-scale production functions using three factors, low-skill labor, high-skill labor, and capital (with endowments of L, H, and K, respectively). A one-household version of this model has been used by Davies and Wooton (1992) to study the effects of immigration on wages and the functional distribution of income. We discuss first assumptions about households, then turn to technology and determinants of factor prices.

Households

There are two types of households (v), each owning either one unit of low-skill labor ($v = l$) or one unit of high-skill labor ($v = h$) and a positive amount of capital (K_v). Households have identical and homothetic preferences. Household income depends on factor prices w_K, w_L, and w_H. Thus, the incomes of low- and high-skill households are $y_l = w_L + w_K K_l$ and $y_h = w_H + w_K K_h$, respectively. It is assumed that immigrants spend their income in the receiving country and only a fraction of them (initially set to one) are assimilated and vote.

Suppose a direct democracy in which people vote on immigration policy. In the absence of voting costs, a voter will favor entry of new immigrants, which we consider as permanent, if it increases her utility. Define the indirect utility of voter v as $U_v = U_v(p_1, p_2, y_v)$, where p_j is the domestic price of good j ($j = 1, 2$). Since goods' prices are fixed, even in the general case where immigrants dM ($dM = dL$ or dH) bring in capital

dK, we have $\partial p/\partial M = \partial p/\partial K = 0$. Thus, the condition for household v to favor immigration ($dU_v \geq 0$) reduces to

$$dy_v = \frac{\partial y_v}{\partial M}dM + \frac{\partial y_v}{\partial K}dK = dM\left[\left(\frac{\partial w_v}{\partial M} + \frac{\partial w_v}{\partial K}\frac{dK}{dM}\right) + \left(\frac{\partial w_K}{\partial M} + \frac{\partial w_K}{\partial K}\frac{dK}{dM}\right)K_v\right] \geq 0. \quad (1)$$

In expression (1), the first term in parentheses on the right-hand side gives the effect of immigration on labor income, the second the effect of immigration on capital income. It shows that a voter's attitude towards immigration depends on her skills ($v = h, l$), on her capital ownership (K_v), on which type of immigrants come in ($dM = dL, dH$), on how they are endowed in capital (dK/dM), and on how factor prices react to changes in factor endowments. We now turn to this latter determinant, leaving the systematic discussion of the former factors to section 3.

Factor Endowments and Factor Prices

To complete the model, we must specify factor-intensity assumptions. Presumably, countries that receive immigrants are net importers of low-skill-labor intensive products. Whether they are exporters of capital or rather of skilled-labor intensive products is more a matter of debate. To simplify presentation, we assume here that they export skilled-labor intensive products, which leaves capital as the "middle" factor.[3] If a_{ij} is the amount of factor i used in a unit of good j (with $i = L, H, K$ and $j = 1, 2$), this means that the following *factor extremity conditions* are satisfied:

$$a_{L1}/a_{L2} > a_{K1}/a_{K2} > a_{H1}/a_{H2}. \quad (2)$$

We know from Ruffin (1981) that in the 3 × 2 model the two extreme factors are "enemies" (i.e., an increase in the endowment of one of the extreme factors reduces the reward of the other, while increasing the reward of the middle factor), whereas the middle factor is everybody's "friend" (i.e., an increase in the endowment of the middle factor increases the wage of the extreme factors). Applied to our case, as both types of labor are enemies, this means that the middle factor, capital, whether it is owned by national households or brought in by immigrants, plays a (critical) compensatory role. This is straightforward from expression (1) on the voter's side: if immigrants bring in no capital ($dK/dM = 0$), the increase in capital reward ($dw_k/dM > 0$) mitigates and may overturn the decrease in wages ($dw_v/dM < 0$). But it is also true on the immigrants' side: as soon as they bring in capital, their impact on each source of households' income becomes ambiguous (as dw_i/dM and dw_i/dK have opposite signs $\forall i = K, L, H$).

To sort out these ambiguities, we need to extend Ruffin's analysis to allow for generalized endowment changes. Total differentiation of the usual zero-profit ($\Sigma_i a_{ij}w_i = p_j$) and full-employment ($\Sigma_j a_{ij}x_j = V_i$) conditions leads to a five-equation system with unknowns w_L, w_K, w_H, X_1, and X_2. As in Jones and Easton (1983, eq. 20), we solve implicitly for output changes from the extreme factor markets, which leads to the following reduced form for factor prices variations (using a circumflex to denote a relative change):

$$\theta_{L1}\hat{w}_L + \theta_{K1}\hat{w}_K + \theta_{H1}\hat{w}_H = \hat{p}_1, \quad (3)$$

$$\theta_{L2}\hat{w}_L + \theta_{K2}\hat{w}_K + \theta_{H2}\hat{w}_H = \hat{p}_2, \quad (4)$$

$$\xi_L\hat{w}_L + \xi_K\hat{w}_K + \xi_H\hat{w}_H = \hat{V}, \quad (5)$$

where θ_{ij} is the share of factor i in sector j's costs ($\theta_{ij} \equiv w_i a_{ij}/p_j$), ξ_i is the (general-equilibrium) economy-wide elasticity[4] of the use of the middle factor with respect to w_i, and $\hat{V}$ is given by the following expression:

$$\hat{V} = \hat{K} - (\alpha_L \hat{L} + \alpha_H \hat{H}), \tag{6}$$

where

$$\alpha_L \equiv (\lambda_K - \lambda_H)/(\lambda_L - \lambda_H), \quad \alpha_K \equiv (\lambda_L - \lambda_K)/(\lambda_L - \lambda_H) = 1 - \alpha_L, \tag{7}$$

and λ_i is the share of factor i used by sector 1. From (2), it is straightforward to show that $\lambda_L > \lambda_K > \lambda_H$, which means that α_L (or α_H) can be interpreted as the *index of similarity* between factor L (or H) and factor K.

The value taken by this similarity index depends on factor shares. To fix likely orders of magnitude, suppose that capital is used with the same intensity by both sectors ($\theta_{K1} = \theta_{K2}$). Then it can be shown[5] that the similarity index becomes

$$\alpha_L = \theta^L/(\theta^L + \theta^H), \quad \alpha_H = \theta^H/(\theta^L + \theta^H), \tag{7'}$$

where θ^i is the share of factor i in national income (e.g., $\theta^L \equiv w_L L/Y$, $Y \equiv w_L L + w_H H + w_k K$). Thus, in this special case (used in the comparative statics of section 4), the similarity index is equal to the share of the particular labor skill in total income accruing to labor.

The similarity index α_L (or α_H) also represents the sensitivity of the demand for the middle factor following a change in the supply of factor L (or H) when factor and product prices are kept constant and output changes are such that extreme factor markets are cleared. Thus, in (5), $\hat{V}$ can be interpreted as the difference between the growth in the capital stock and the increase in its demand induced by the growth of labor endowments (at constant prices and accommodating changes in output). If this difference is positive, factor growth will lead to an excess supply of capital, leading to a decrease in the middle factor's reward and an increase in the reward of extreme factors (this according to the friend–enemy relationship and to the left-hand side of equation (5), which represents the necessary adjustment of capital demand through factor rewards' changes). The reverse applies when $\hat{V} < 0$, while $\hat{V} = 0$ defines the set of factor growth rates that have no effect on factor prices.

Setting product prices constant, equations (3)–(5) lead to the following relationships between changes in factor prices and changes in factor endowments:

$$\hat{w}_K = -(1/\Delta)\hat{V}, \quad \hat{w}_L = \alpha_L (1/\Delta)(\theta^K/\theta^L)\hat{V}, \quad \hat{w}_H = \alpha_H (1/\Delta)(\theta^K/\theta^H)\hat{V}, \tag{8}$$

where Δ is a positive constant reflecting factor substitutability.[6]

Note that the change in each extreme factor reward (in the reward of the middle factor) is a positive (negative) function of $\hat{V}$, a result which is consistent with the interpretation of $\hat{V}$ as the change in the net supply of the middle factor.

3. Attitudes Towards Immigration

How do these changes in factor rewards translate into changes in attitudes towards immigration? As noted in the previous section, that attitude depends on the voter's skills, on capital endowment, and on the skills and capital endowment of immigrants. A useful property to start from is that, in this type of model, a marginal factor immigration leaves the income of residents unchanged.[7] With capital evenly distributed within each household category, an assumption we make until section 5, this implies that, as in Benhabib (1996), high-skill and low-skill households will always adopt an opposite attitude towards immigration.

In the following paragraphs we first show how the compensatory role of capital materializes in critical capital ownership levels for both residents and immigrants. Then we develop a graphical representation of how these capital-ownership levels and factor-intensity conditions interact to determine household attitudes following a marginal immigration.

Critical Capital Ownership Levels for Residents and Immigrants

Using (8), we can rewrite the change in each household income following immigration as[8]

$$dy_l = \left[-\frac{1}{\Delta}w_K\right][\hat{V}]\left[K_l - \alpha_L\frac{K}{L}\right], \quad dy_h = \left[-\frac{1}{\Delta}w_K\right][\hat{V}]\left[K_h - \alpha_H\frac{K}{H}\right], \tag{9}$$

which shows that income changes result from the multiplication of three terms, the first one being negative, while the signs of the other two are ambiguous, depending on capital ownership levels.

Consider first a Ruffin-type case, with an inflow of low-skill immigrants with no capital ownership. Then all wages will fall, as low-skill and high-skill labor are enemies. Does this imply that all households oppose immigration? Certainly not, because they own capital, and capital income increases. In fact we know, from the zero-sum property of aggregate income, that this overall increase in capital income will exactly match the decrease in labor income. However, apart from the very special case where capital is allocated over the two household categories in such a way as to keep their income unchanged, one group will lose, the other will gain. We call the former group "*capital-poor*" households, who will oppose immigrants, the latter "*capital-rich*" households, who will welcome them. As high-skill and low-skill labor are enemies, the same logic applies to the case of high-skill immigrants.

This is exactly what is conveyed by equation (9): as immigrants bring in no capital, $\hat{V}$ is negative, which makes the product of the first two terms positive. Whether the sign of the whole expression remains positive or not depends on the sign of the last term between brackets: it is positive if the household is capital-rich, which will be so provided her capital ownership, K_v, is larger than a critical level. It turns out that low-skill (high-skill) households are capital-rich if their capital ownership is larger than $\alpha_L(K/L)(\alpha_H(K/H))$. However, with capital equally distributed within each household group, as $K = K_L + K_H = LK_l + HK_h$, it is easy to show that one condition excludes the other. If, say, low-skill households are capital-poor, high-skill households are capital-rich, so they will never share the same attitude towards immigrants (except in the very special case where effective capital ownership is equal to the critical level in both groups so that every household is indifferent towards immigration).

Going beyond Ruffin-type immigration, what happens if immigrants also own capital? Again equation (9) tells us everything. As long as the capital brought by immigrants is below a critical level, $\hat{V}$ remains negative, leading to the same attitudes as those just described. In this case *immigrants* are "capital-poor." However, if the capital ownership of immigrants exceeds that critical level, they become "capital-rich" and the attitudes of residents are reversed because $\hat{V}$ changes sign (which implies, by (8), that the whole pattern of factor rewards' changes also reverses). It turns out that the critical capital ownership levels for immigrants are identical to those of the corresponding skill category of residents.

Table 1. Attitudes Towards Immigration and Critical Capital Ownership Levels

	Immigrants		
Low-skill households	*Capital-poor*[a]	*Capital-rich*[b]	*High-skill households*
capital-poor $K_l < \alpha_L K/L$	opposed *favorable*	favorable *opposed*	*capital-rich* $K_h > \alpha_H K/H$
capital-rich $K_l > \alpha_L K/L$	favorable *opposed*	opposed *favorable*	*capital-poor* $K_h < \alpha_H K/H$

K_v (K_v^M) is the effective capital ownership of household (immigrant) v.
[a] Either $K_l^M < \alpha_L K/L$ or $K_h^M < \alpha_H K/H$.
[b] Either $K_l^M > \alpha_L K/L$ or $K_h^M > \alpha_H K/H$.

The complete pattern of attitudes towards immigration, along with the different levels of critical capital ownership, are summarized in Table 1, with the position of high-skill residents in italics to distinguish them from low-skill ones. Note that attitudes are basically "capital-concerned": capital-poor households oppose capital-poor immigrants and vice versa, while the skill level of residents or immigrants only matters for the level of critical capital ownership. Moreover, inspection of critical capital ownership values reveals the following alternative interpretation of the similarity index:

PROPOSITION 1. *When capital ownership is evenly distributed within each group of households, α_L ($\alpha_H = 1 - \alpha_L$) is the share of total capital that must accrue to low-skill (high-skill) households to leave them just indifferent to immigration.*

This proposition underlines the graphical analysis of the next section.

A Graphical Representation of Attitudes Towards Immigration

It is now natural to compare the *critical* shares of capital ownership just identified above with the *effective* shares of capital owned by each category of households. Let us define these effective shares by $s_L \equiv K_L/K, s_H \equiv K_H/K$ and introduce two additional ratios:

$$\tau \equiv (K_L/L)/(K/L+H), \tag{10}$$

$$\ell \equiv L/(L+H). \tag{11}$$

In the above expressions, τ is an index of intergroup disparity of the distribution of capital ($\tau = 1$ when there is no interhousehold disparity in the distribution of capital and 0 when all capital ownership goes to the high-skill household group) while ℓ is the share of low-skill households in total population. Simple algebra shows that

$$s_L = \tau\ell, \quad s_H = 1 - \tau\ell. \tag{12}$$

Thus, attitudes towards immigration depend on the straightforward comparison between $\tau\ell$ and α_L: if $\tau\ell = s_L < \alpha_L$, low-skill households are capital-poor, but as $\alpha_L = 1 - \alpha_H$ and $s_L = 1 - s_H$, this implies that $s_H > \alpha_H$, so that high-skill households are capital-rich, which confirms again the opposite opinion held by the two household categories.

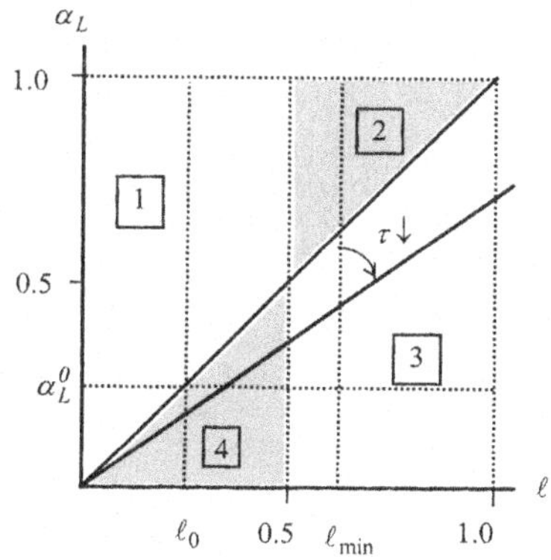

Figure 1. Determinants of National Attitude Towards Immigration

The national attitude towards immigration can now be depicted graphically as in Figure 1, on the basis of τ, ℓ, and α_L values. Indifference for all households is reached along the $\alpha_L = \tau\ell$ line, which coincides with the diagonal when $\tau = 1$. For all points above (below) this line, low-skill households are capital-poor (capital-rich), the reverse being true for high-skill households. Thus, if immigrants are capital-poor, all points above the indifference line correspond to cases where low-skill households oppose immigration, while positions are reversed below the indifference line. As national attitude will match the attitude of the majority group, in the clear areas 1 and 3 (the shaded areas 2 and 4), the economy favors (opposes) capital-poor immigration. If immigrants were capital-rich, all positions would be reversed. Finally, an increase in intergroup capital distribution disparity (a lower τ), which is represented by a clockwise rotation of the indifference line, would be associated with a widening of the range of (ℓ, α_L) values where low-skill households are capital-poor, leading to new shaded areas (not indicated in the figure).

In Figure 1, suppose that the share of low-skill labor is $\ell_0 < 0.5$ and that the similarity index takes the value $\alpha_L^0 = \ell_0$. Suppose also that there is no intergroup disparity in capital ownership ($\tau = 1$) and that immigrants are capital-poor in the sense defined above. In this case, poor households are a minority, but since both groups are indifferent to immigration, this is a borderline situation. Suppose now that $\alpha_L > \alpha_L^0$. Then, high-skill households will favor immigration (area 1), and since they are the majority, this implies that the political process, as modeled here, would be favorable to immigration of capital-poor immigrants. Conversely, if $\alpha_L < \alpha_L^0$, high-skill households (who are the majority) would oppose immigration and this would reflect the national attitude towards immigration. Finally, suppose that $\alpha_L = \alpha_L^0$, but that there is intergroup disparity in capital ownership ($\tau < 1$). Then, high-skill households that own more capital would be in favor of immigration (the intersection of the two dashed lines would now be in a clear area) and the economy would be favorable to immigration.

The assumption that all immigrants are assimilated and vote can easily be relaxed. Assume that only a proportion γ of resident low-skill households vote ($0 \le \gamma \le 1$). Then, remembering that $\ell \equiv L/(L + H)$, the condition for voting low-skill households to become the majority is $\ell > \ell_{min} = (\gamma + 1)^{-1}(0.5 \le \ell_{min} \le 1)$. In terms of Figure 1, this means that the vertical line beyond which there is a reversal of attitude towards immigration is shifted to the right to $\ell_{\min}$, leading to new shaded areas which are more akin to the attitude of high-skill households.

Finally, Figure 1 also illustrates how attitudes towards immigration would be handled in special cases. Suppose first that low-skill households own no capital ($\tau = 0$). Then, the attitude towards immigration will depend only on the share of low-skill households in the total population. Take next the 2 × 2 model. If high-skill (low-skill) labor and capital are used with the same intensities in both sectors, $\alpha_L = 0$ ($\alpha_L = 1$), then households are indifferent to immigration as marginal changes in endowments have no impact on factor rewards. Finally take the specific factor model, assuming that capital is the mobile factor. Then expressions (7) simplify ($\lambda_L = 1$, $\lambda_H = 0$) and the similarity index α_L (α_H) collapses to the share of the mobile factor used in sector 1 (2).

Results so far can be summarized as follows.[9]

PROPOSITION 2. *When capital ownership is evenly distributed within each group of households:*

(*a*) *low-skill and high-skill households always have opposite attitudes towards immigration;*

(*b*) *national attitude towards immigration is mainly "capital concerned," as households' attitudes are independent of the type of immigrants (but for the critical capital-ownership level of immigrants);*

(*c*) *when only a fraction of the low-skill households vote, immigration has an effect on aggregate voters' income and attitudes are more akin to those of high-skill households.*

4. Comparative Statics

How do changes in the economic environment affect attitudes towards immigration? We consider three exogenous changes. First there is growth through factor accumulation. In this case, critical-capital ownership levels for national households (see equation (9)) will be affected both directly, through factor endowment changes, and indirectly, through changes in the similarity index. This indirect effect is induced by variations in factor rewards (equation (8)), which derive from the comparative statics expressions (3) to (5).

Second, we take up changes in relative prices. It is widely perceived that a reduction in tariffs and other barriers to trade (such as the cost of doing business) have been important components of globalization that could have affected attitudes towards immigration. Here we proxy the effects of globalization by an exogenous rise in the relative price of the exporting sector (X_2).[10]

Third, there is the impact of technical progress. It is believed that technical progress has contributed, partially at least, to the increasing wage gap between workers of different skills. We deal with disembodied technical progress, either neutral or low-skill-labor saving.

The relevant comparative statics expressions are equations (3) to (5) with $\hat{p}_1 = 0$, $\hat{p}_2 > 0$, $\hat{V} = 0$ in the case of relative price changes and $\hat{p}_1 = -\nu_1$, $\hat{p}_2 = -\nu_2$, $\hat{V} = -\eta$ in the case of technical progress (where $\nu_j = \Sigma_i \theta_{ij} \hat{a}_{ij}^{ex}$, $\eta = \eta_k - (\alpha_L \eta_L + \alpha_H \eta_H)$, $\eta_i = \lambda_{i1} \hat{a}_{i1}^{ex} + \lambda_{i2} \hat{a}_{i2}^{ex}$ and $\hat{a}_{ij}^{ex}$ denotes the exogenous component of the rate of change of a_{ij}).

From the above, it is clear that neutral technical progress in sector 2 would be equivalent to an increase in the price of that sector. Hence, after dealing with the effects of a reduction of protection, we only treat across-the-board low-skill labor-saving technical progress in the following section. To save space, we only summarize the results; the derivations can be found in the appendix to Bilal et al. (1998).

Growth in Factor Endowments

To get qualitative results, we make two simplifying assumptions. First, we consider cases where only one factor's endowment changes at a time, namely a capital increase or an increase in the endowment of high-skill labor. Second, we neutralize for the direct effect of endowment changes. Thus, in the case of capital growth, we assume that it is spread evenly across households. In the case of labor growth, we assume that the initial capital endowment of the group is spread evenly across individuals. Then, at constant factor prices, the critical level of capital ownership would change proportionately to the individual ownership of capital, which neutralizes the direct effect of endowment changes. Variations in the attitude towards immigration are thus driven only by the indirect effect, through changes in the similarity index α_L.

It turns out that, in the general case, the sign of $\hat{\alpha}_L$ is ambiguous, depending on factor intensities and substitutability/complementarity between factors (reflected in the value taken by Δ in (8)). To resolve this ambiguity, we take the "symmetric" case mentioned above (i.e., $\theta_{K1} = \theta_{K2}$) and consider a one-level CES functional form for technology. Then, simple conditions can be derived under which an increase in factor endowment leads to changes in the similarity index and hence to changes in the attitudes towards immigration. These added restrictions also allow us to sign the effects of the other shocks on the value of the similarity index.

In the case of capital accumulation, α_L will fall if the elasticity of substitution is higher in sector 2, a plausible condition as this sector is the exporting one. As α_L falls, the critical-capital ownership level of high(low)-skill households increases (decreases), which means that this household category becomes more opposed (favorable) to immigration. To interpret this result, return to Figure 1 and suppose that initially $\tau = 1$, $\alpha = \alpha_L^0$, and $\ell = \ell_0$, which leads to indifference towards immigration, high-skill households being the majority. The increase in capital will shift the economy's point downwards, to shaded area 4, meaning opposition to (capital-poor) immigration, which reflects the new position of the majority group.

The impact of an increase in high-skill labor endowment is apparently more complex. On the one hand, it implies a decrease in ℓ which, starting from the same initial indifference point, would lead to a favorable national attitude towards (capital-poor) immigration. But on the other hand, it also leads to a change in α_L, which could run against the previous effect. However, it turns out that, in the "realistic" case where the elasticity of substitution is higher in the exporting sector, although α_L may eventually fall, it will never reverse the first effect. In sum, starting from indifference, an increase in high-skill labor endowment is likely to favor (capital-poor) immigration.

Increase in the Relative Price of the Exporting Sector

In the general case, an increase in the relative price of the exporting sector has an ambiguous impact on factor returns. However, if factors are substitutes, then as shown by Jones and Easton (1983), one obtains Stolper–Samuelson effects on the extreme factor returns, while the real return accruing to the middle factor depends on factor intensities and substitutability. In any case, to find out the effect on attitudes towards immigration, we need again to identify the effect of the shock on the value of the similarity index α_L.

With CES production functions, whatever the values of the elasticities of substitution, α_L unambiguously decreases following the increase in the relative price of the exporting sector (or a neutral technical progress in the same sector). Therefore, starting from the usual initial indifference point in Figure 1, this means that an increase in the relative price of the exporting sector (i.e., a reduction of protection) would generate an opposition to (capital-poor) immigration.

Low-Skill Labor-Saving Technical Progress

Finally, the effect of across-the-board labor-saving technical progress on factor prices is generally ambiguous. If factors are substitutes, although the change in the low-skill labor wage rate remains ambiguous, the wage rate of high-skill individuals falls while the return to capital increases. In the simple symmetric case of a CES production technology, if the elasticity of substitution is higher in the exporting sector, α_L increases unambiguously. Thus, starting from the usual indifference point in Figure 1, across-the-board low-skill labor-saving technical progress leads the economy to favor (capital-poor) immigration.

Results of the comparative statics can be summarized as follows.

PROPOSITION 3. *Suppose that: high-skill individuals are the majority; there is neither intergroup nor intragroup disparity in capital distribution; the capital factor share in total cost is the same in both sectors; technology is of the CES type with a higher elasticity of substitution in the exporting sector. Then, starting from an initial indifference, the national attitude towards (capital-poor) immigration will become:*

(*a*) *favorable in the case of an increase in high-skill labor or a low-skill labor-saving technical progress in both sectors;*
(*b*) *opposed in the case of an increase in the capital stock or an improvement in the terms of trade (which is equivalent to a neutral technical progress in the exporting sector).*

These results would be reversed if either low-skill individuals were the majority or immigrants were capital-rich.

5. Discussion

Consider the following often-cited stylized facts pertinent for the evolution of the labor market in recipient countries: (i) a decrease in the relative price of import-competing activities as a result of the globalization that has reduced protection; (ii) an increase in the skilled–unskilled wage gap; (iii) an increase in income (and capital) inequality; and (iv) technical progress, perhaps of the labor-saving variety.[11]

According to the results in section 4, via Stolper–Samuelson effects, globalization is consistent with the observed increase in the wage gap. So is neutral technical progress in the exporting sector. However, across-the-board low-skill labor-saving technical progress would lead to a reduction of the wage gap along the lines shown by Findlay and Grubert (1959) in the 2×2 case. In the symmetric case, endowment changes would leave the wage gap unchanged. In short, the dominant effect is the Stolper–Samuelson one. Now, if Stolper–Samuelson effects are dominant, as shown above, this would lead to a stiffening in attitudes towards capital-poor immigration. However, even in this simple symmetric case, once one allows for an increase in the share of high-skill households in the total population (which has no effect on the wage gap in this symmetric case), the attitude towards immigration is ambiguous since the effect of high-skill labor growth is favorable towards capital-poor immigration.

Assume now that capital ownership is not necessarily evenly distributed within households but follows a beta distribution. The probability density function for the capital ownership of household v is

$$f(K_v)=\frac{\Gamma(\beta_v+\gamma_v)}{\Gamma(\beta_v)\Gamma(\gamma_v)}\left(\frac{K_v}{c_v}\right)^{\beta_v-1}\left(1-\frac{K_v}{c_v}\right)^{\gamma_v-1}\left(\frac{1}{c_v}\right), \tag{13}$$

where K_v belongs to the interval $[0, c_v]$, $c_v > 0$, and Γ is the gamma function. For each household group, the upper-bound value c_v is obtained from the mean: $E(K_v) = c_v\beta_v/(\beta_v + \gamma_v) = K_v/V$, $V = H, L$. This distribution is symmetric (skewed to the left) if $\beta_v = \gamma_v(\beta_v < \gamma_v)$.

For simplicity, suppose that parameters describing the distribution of capital within each household group are the same for both groups (i.e., $\beta_l = \beta_h$, $\gamma_l = \gamma_h$).[12] Start with the case where the distribution is symmetric ($\beta = \gamma$) and there is no intergroup disparity in the distribution of capital ($\tau = 1$). In this case, we get exactly the same results as in the case of no intragroup disparity of capital ownership. This is because the number of people in each household group having the attitude of the other group's majority is the same (hence, Figure 2(a) is identical to Figure 1). Introduce now intergroup disparity in capital distribution ($\tau < 1$), maintaining the same symmetrical distribution for each household group (Figure 2(b)). Then, one is approximating the case where low-skill households have no capital and become systematically opposed to capital-poor immigrants.[13]

Introduce now skewness in the distribution of capital (with no intergroup disparity). Again suppose identical standard forms for each group (Figure 2(c)). Then, along the diagonal, although the mean voter would be indifferent to immigration, the median voter has lower capital in both groups, leading to a majority opposed to capital-poor immigration. As Figure 2(c) confirms, to reverse this unfavorable attitude towards immigration one must either alter the composition of the population or the value of the similarity index. Finally, Figure 2(d) combines intergroup disparity and within-group skewness by combining the parameters used in Figures 2(b) and 2(c).

Capital ownership distribution being highly skewed (see Wolff, 1996), Figures 2(c) or 2(d) are probably better guides of the roles of households composition and factor intensity differences in determining attitudes towards immigration. Also, taking a probabilistic approach to reflect ignorance about the economy's parameter values, note that, starting from Figure 2(a), where the shaded area is 1/4, an increase in intergroup and/or intragroup disparity increases the importance of the shaded area, which approximately could reach 5/8, reflecting a higher probability of opposition to capital-poor immigration.[14] After all, widening income disparities would appear to be coherent with the generalized move towards introducing capital requirements in immigration.

6. Conclusions

This paper has developed a model in which preferences towards immigration are determined by natives' perception of the impact of immigration on factor rewards. While noneconomic factors are likely to affect individual preferences (e.g., individual beliefs about civil rights and expectations regarding the cultural impact of immigrants), survey-based results indicate that individual preferences over immigration

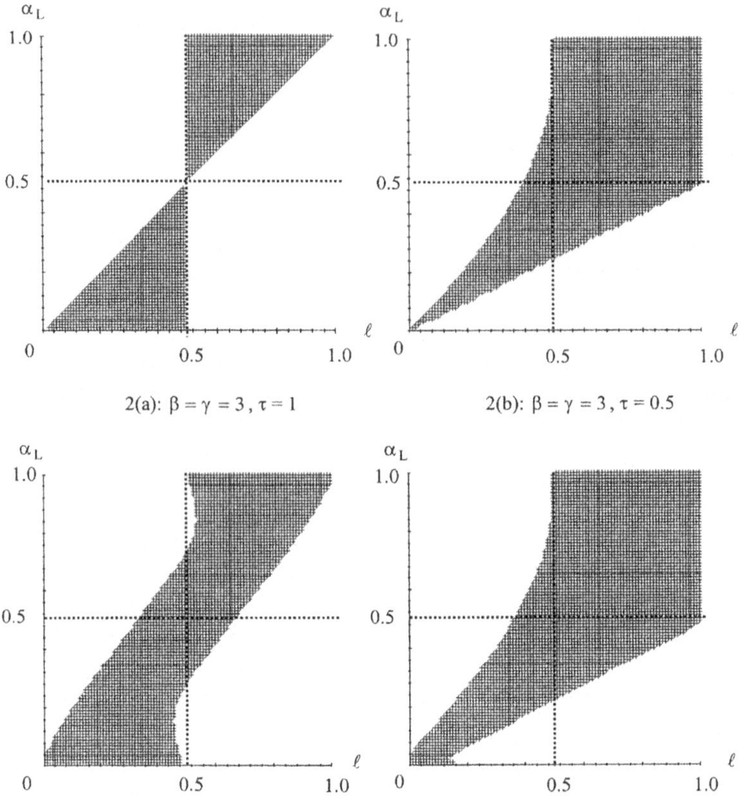

2(a): $\beta = \gamma = 3, \tau = 1$

2(b): $\beta = \gamma = 3, \tau = 0.5$

2(c): $\beta = 3, \gamma = 6, \tau = 1$

2(d): $\beta = 3, \gamma = 6, \tau = 0.5$

Figure 2. Capital Ownership Distribution and Attitudes Towards Immigration

policy in the United States are primarily determined by wage effects (see Scheve and Slaughter, 1999). These findings justify the approach taken here.

In spite of the complexity of the three-factor two-household model, we were able to show that so long as household capital-ownership disparities are intergroup, then attitudes towards immigration are determined by two parameters: an index of factor-use similarity (whose values can be approximated by readily available data on factor shares in export- and import-competing sectors) and the household composition of the population. At the same time, the model does not allow factor flows to have a net impact on the aggregate income of residents, as it fails in particular to take into account the possibility that immigration brings with it a number of externalities due to social and/or cultural differences. Also, an important dimension of globalization is the decline of the jobs "sheltered" from international competition. This is probably affecting attitudes towards immigration, an effect that could be captured in this framework only if it were extended to include a nontraded sheltered sector.

Nonetheless, the model provides a rich array of determinants of attitudes towards immigration. First, it highlights the importance of factor intensities in shaping attitudes towards immigration, in a model that introduces explicitly the role of capital-ownership and of the skill-level of potential immigrants, which have been at the center of the recent stiffening of attitudes towards low-skill (and/or capital-poor) immigrants. In this framework, we show that the model's predictions are coherent with the adverse impact on the attitudes towards immigration that might have occurred as a result of recent changes in OECD labor markets. For example, it shows that an increase in the capital stock and greater trade openness would both be consistent with a stiffening of attitudes towards capital-poor immigrants. Moreover, it suggests that the increasing income inequality (that may have been driven by the globalization process) could have reinforced the generalized move towards the introduction of capital requirements for immigrants.

References

Batra, R. and F. Casas, "A Synthesis of the Heckscher–Ohlin and the Neoclassical Models of International Trade," *Journal of International Economics* 6 (1976):21–38.

Benhabib, J., "On the Political Economy of Immigration," *European Economic Review* 40 (1996):1737–43.

Bilal, S., J.-M. Grether, and J. de Melo, "Determinant of Attitudes towards Immigration: a Trade-Theoretic Approach," discussion paper 1877, CEPR, London (1998).

Davies, J. and I. Wooton, "Income Inequality and International Migration," *Economic Journal* 102 (1992):789–802.

Ethier, W., "Bundled International Factor Mobility," in H. Kierzkowski (ed.), *Protection and Competition in International Trade: Essays in Honor of W. M. Corden*, Oxford: Blackwell (1987).

Findlay, R. and H. Grubert, "Factor Intensities, Technical Progress, and the Terms of Trade," *Oxford Economic Papers* 11 (1959):111–21.

Freeman, G.P., "Modes of Immigration Politics in Liberal Democratic States," *International Migration Review* 29 (1995):881–902.

Hillman, A., "The Political Economy of Migration Policy," in H. Siebert (ed.), *Migration: a Challenge for Europe: Symposium 1993*, Tübingen: Mohr (1994).

Hillman, A. and A. Weiss, "Beyond International Factor Movements: Cultural Preferences, Endogenous Policies and the Migration of People: an Overview," in R. Faini, J. de Melo, and K. Zimmermann (eds.), *Trade and Migration: the Issues and the Evidence,* Cambridge: Cambridge University Press (1999).

Jones, R. W. and S. T. Easton, "Factor Intensities and Factor Substitution in General Equilibrium," *Journal of International Economics* 15 (1983):65–99.

Jones, R. W. and J. A. Scheinkman, "The Relevance of the Two-Sector Production Model in Trade Theory," *Journal of Political Economy* 85 (1977):909–35.

Mayer, W., "Endogenous Tariff Formation," *American Economic Review* 74 (1984):970–85.

Müller, T., "Migration Policy in a Small Open Economy with a Dual Labour Market," *Review of International Economics* 11 (2003):130–43.

Schiff, M., "Migration et echanges: aspects positifs et normatifs," in J. de Melo and P. Guillaumont (eds.), *Commerce nord-sud, migration et délocalisation,* Economica, Paris (1997):33–54.

Ruffin, R. J., "Trade and Factor Movements with Three Factors and Two Goods," *Economics Letters* 7 (1981):177–82.

Scheve, K. F. and M. J. Slaughter, "Labor-Market Competition and Individual Preferences over Immigration Policy," NBER working paper6946 (1999).

Thompson, H., "Factor Migration and Income Distribution in International Trade," *Keio Economic Studies* 20 (1983):65–70.
Thompson, H. and D. Clark, "Factor Movements with Three Factors and Two Goods in the US Economy," *Economics Letters* 12 (1983):53–60.
Wellisch, D. and U. Walz, "Why do Rich Countries Prefer Free Trade Over Free Migration: the Role of the Modern Welfare State," *European Economic Review* 42 (1998):1595–612.
Wolff, E., "International Comparisons of Wealth Inequality," *Review of Income and Wealth* 42 (1996):433–51.
Wood, A., *North–South Trade, Employment and Inequality*, Oxford: Clarendon Press (1994).

Notes

1. Relying on the interest-group model, Freeman (1995) argues that benefits from immigration are concentrated among producers (who enjoy lower wages and face a higher demand) whereas the costs are diffused among the working population group (which earns lower wages). Hence, organized interests get more attention from political authorities than the general public does, and immigration policies appear more liberal than those that would be wished by the majority of the population. For a critical survey of the political-economy literature on immigration, see Hillman and Weiss (1999).
2. Benhabib (1996) also uses a direct-democracy model, but with one factor (and one sector). His model shares some of the properties of the model developed here, namely that an immigration policy that increases (lowers) the economy-wide average capital–labor ratio will be defeated if the median voter's capital–labor ratio is above (below) a critical capital ownership level. See Ethier (1987) for a treatment of bundled factor mobility in the $m \times n$ generalization of the Heckscher–Ohlin model.
3. This has the advantage of focusing on the most interesting case in terms of the variety of results. Davies and Wooton (1992) argue that the broad evidence suggests that the US belongs to this case, but Thompson and Clark (1983) suggest that low-skill labor may be the middle factor. The alternative case where high-skill labor is the middle factor is treated in Bilal et al. (1998).
4. It can be shown that $\xi_i = \sigma_k^i - (\alpha_L \sigma_L^i + \alpha_H \sigma_H^i)$, where σ_e^i is the economy-wide elasticity of the use of factor e ($e = K, L, H$) with respect to w_i ($i = K, L, H$), under the assumption that each industry's output is kept constant and α_L, α_H are defined in equation (7).
5. Multiplying the numerator and denominator of equation (7) by $Y/(p_1X_1)$ leads to $\alpha_L = (\theta^L/\theta^K)(\theta_{K1}\theta^H - \theta_{H1}\theta^K)/(\theta_{L1}\theta^H - \theta_{H1}\theta^L)$. This expression can be further simplified under the symmetry assumption, which implies that $\theta_{K1} = \theta_{K2} = \theta^K$ and that $\theta_{L1} + \theta_{H1} = \theta_{L2} + \theta_{H2} = \theta^L + \theta^H$.
6. $\Delta = (\alpha_L \xi_L/\theta^L + \alpha_H \xi_H/\theta^H - \xi_K/\theta^K)$; see Jones and Scheinkman (1977).
7. By the envelope theorem, the marginal impact of a unitary increase in any factor endowment on national income is equal to this factor reward, which means that total income of the incumbent factors remains unchanged. This zero-sum property of total income to marginal changes in immigration comes from the following assumptions: immigration is marginal, prices of goods are fixed, there is no redistribution policy (Wellisch and Walz, 1998), and the immigrants get paid the going wage, rather than some other wage as in, for example, the efficiency wage model with a dual labor market of Müller (2003).
8. From (9), remembering that $\alpha_L + \alpha_H = 1$ it is straightforward to check that $dY = \Sigma_l dy_l + \Sigma_h dy_h = 0$.
9. In the alternative case where high-skill labor is the middle factor, national attitude towards immigration becomes mainly "skill concerned": as in this case capital and low-skill labor are enemies, attitudes are independent on the capital ownership of households (although they do depend on the capital ownership of high-skill immigrants).
10. To be rigorous, one should take into account the redistributive effects of a reduction in trade barriers (e.g., who gets the resulting tariff revenue). This is ignored here.
11. Some have proposed (Wood, 1994) that globalization has induced "defensive" labor-saving technical progress in the labor-intensive import-competing sectors.

12. This implies identical standard forms for both groups (the standard form for the beta is obtained through the change of variable that restricts the domain to the interval [0, 1]).
13. For values of α_L approximating zero, the critical capital ownership level of high(low)-skill households is very high (low). But as high-skill households receive a higher proportion of total capital, a sufficient number of them go along with low-skill households to create a majority favorable to capital-poor immigration.
14. Of course different values would be obtained with other functional forms to represent the distribution of capital. We have used the beta since it makes it easy to reproduce the base case of no intragroup capital ownership disparity.

6 The Political Economy of Migration and EU Enlargement: Lessons from Switzerland

Jaime de Melo, Florence Miguet, and Tobias Müller

6.1 Introduction

The EU is about to take in ten European states as new members, raising its population by 28 percent to 480 million. Under current EU law, the new member states would benefit from the four basic freedoms of the Treaty of Rome. This means that people, capital, goods, and services would circulate freely between those states and all others in the union. Also, under current union law, welfare payments are attributable according to country of residence. As a result, despite the results from several studies suggesting that enlargement under current rules should have small positive aggregate effects on the welfare of EU15 citizens,[1] there is fear of adjustment difficulties with respect to the free movement of persons, especially in Austria and Germany. As the EU is worried that this issue threatens to affect public support for enlargement, a flexible system of transitional arrangements has been put forward in the negotiations with candidate countries.

The EU's position is based on opinion polls that suggest that EU citizens are reluctant to further immigration. In a 1997 Eurobarometer survey (European Commission 1997), in most European countries (except Finland, Spain, and Ireland) a majority of respondents indicated that they believed that further immigration would cause problems in their own countries. Moreover, only 12 percent of respondents in the EU thought that Eastern Europeans who wish to work in the west should be accepted without restrictions. These attitudes contrast with the rather modest labor market effects that can be expected from projected migration flows under EU enlargement.

Are attitudes toward EU enlargement linked to projected migration flows or stocks? According to a number of authors (Brücker et al. 2001; Dustmann and Preston 2000), attitudes toward immigration can be explained by three factors: labor market effects, welfare take-up, and racial or xenophobic prejudice. Most studies addressing the first factor have concentrated on estimating the change in stocks that would result from CEECs' accession to the EU.[2] Such an approach, however, gives an incomplete picture of the effects of EU enlargement, since enlargement will also involve a change in the legal status of workers in the labor market. For example, the bilateral guest worker and seasonal-worker arrangements that are currently in place between several EU members and the CEECs (see Boeri et al. 2001, table 4.4), which have good reasons to exist from a political-economy perspective, will have to be abolished once those CEECs are part of the EU. With few exceptions (Bauer, Lofstrom, and Zimmerman 2000; Brücker et al. 2001, chap. 2), these political-economy aspects of the migration consequences of enlargement have been largely ignored in the current debate (see section 6.2 for a theoretical exploration of this issue).

As to immigrants' potential for welfare dependence, Fertig and Schmidt (2001) show that natives' negative perception of immigrants in this regard is not in accordance with the moderate risk of immigrants' dependence on public assistance in Germany. Nonetheless, Sinn et al. (2001) consider the problem of immigrant welfare dependence serious enough to recommend delayed integration of immigrants into the social-welfare system in the receiving countries to avoid an erosion of the welfare state through competition between receiving countries. With regard to the role of non-economic factors in shaping attitudes toward immigration, it is difficult to gauge from the few studies available whether racial prejudices significantly influence attitudes toward EU enlargement.[3]

This chapter contributes to the debate on the political economy of migration policy. It recounts the Swiss experience with immigration policy, which is pertinent for the current debate along several dimensions. First, Switzerland has throughout its history absorbed a great number of immigrants, not only before 1974 (when European countries switched to a restrictive immigration policy), but also over the last twenty years (the share of foreigners in the Swiss population rose from 14 to 20 percent between 1980 and 2000). This increase is more important, in relative terms, than the projected rise in the immigrant stock in Germany following EU enlargement. At the same time, anti-immigration attitudes seem to be less widespread in Switzerland than in other European countries, according to a recent Eurobarometer survey (European Commission 2000, see section 6.4). It is therefore worthwhile to examine more closely the characteristics of Swiss migration policy.

Second, Switzerland has carried out reforms in immigration laws and policies that are close in spirit to several of the alternatives envisaged in the debate concerning enlargement, as discussed in European Commission 2001. Of particular interest, in the Swiss case, is the interaction of economic interests with the expression of these interests via the political system. Switzerland's system of direct democracy has forced the Swiss government to conduct its immigration policy so as to avoid the adoption of restrictive propositions by popular vote.

Third, the Swiss version of direct democracy is also interesting at the empirical level. Since 1970 the Swiss electorate has voted regularly on immigration policy, and individual surveys have been carried out after most votes. From the point of view of understanding attitudes toward immigration, the attitudes revealed by these post-election surveys are in sharp contrast to attitudes drawn from survey polls, which may suffer from "hypothetical bias."

The remainder of the chapter is structured as follows. Section 6.2 reviews the political-economy dimensions of immigration policy in a direct-democracy framework, which is relevant both for Switzerland and for interpreting the results from recent polls, taking into account that Swiss migration policy has been of the guest worker type and that labor markets in Switzerland are segmented. Section 6.3 then briefly recounts how the votes on referenda and popular initiatives have shaped Swiss immigration policy over the last thirty years. Section 6.4 examines a household survey conducted in connection with the 2000 vote in Switzerland on establishing a quota (slightly below the existing level) on the stock of immigrants. That poll allows us both to estimate the probability of voters' participation in terms of individual characteristics and to predict what the outcome would have been had all voters participated (the actual participation rate was 44 percent). Although it may not be valid to infer that such predictions correspond to what is captured in opinion polls (where there are no participation costs and all participate), it might provide a first handle on how EU citizens might in fact vote, if they really were brought to the booth. Conclusions follow in section 6.5.

6.2 The Political Economy of Immigration Policy

Attitudes toward immigrants, as expressed in opinion polls and at the voting booth, can be usefully decomposed into three components: cultural preferences or social capital, implications for the functioning of the welfare state, and economic effects (fear of unemployment and/

or lower wages). Cultural-preference aspects have been examined in Hillman and Weiss 1999a, Schiff 1998, and Schiff 1999 and have been summarized in Grether, de Melo, and Müller 2001. The welfare implications of EU enlargement have recently been covered in Sinn 2000, Brücker et al. 2001, and Boeri and Brücker 2001. Here we wish to emphasize the role of economic effects in the determination of migration policies in a direct-democracy framework.[4] We consider first the political economy of skill requirements, then explore whether low-skill immigration is likely to be accepted in a direct democracy if guest worker policies are pursued.

6.2.1 *Skilled or Unskilled Labor?*

Following in the footsteps of Canada and New Zealand, several countries have introduced a point system to determine the eligibility of applicant migrants; such point systems correspond to one of the transitional arrangements under consideration in the accession negotiations for the CEECs. As shown by Bauer, Lofstrom, and Zimmerman (2000), cross-country evidence seems to suggest better rates of immigrant assimilation for countries that have relied on such systems.

From a theoretical viewpoint, what policies regarding skill requirements for immigrants are likely to be adopted in a direct democracy? Benhabib (1996) considers this question in a median-voter framework in which capital is distributed unequally among natives. He assumes that there is a fixed pool of potential immigrants with different capital endowments (or skill levels). His main result is that if the median capital endowment of natives k_m is smaller than some critical level k_c, a minimum skill requirement for immigration approval will defeat any other policy under majority voting with pairwise alternatives.[5]

To gain some additional insight into this issue, consider a less general setting with only two alternatives up for vote: no immigration versus admission of a fixed number of immigrants. Differences in income determine the attitude toward immigrants. Each native household is endowed with one unit of labor and a certain amount of capital, which is unequally distributed among households. If immigration lowers the household's income, the household will oppose it. If no other issue is on the political agenda, preferences are single-peaked, and the national stance toward immigration is determined by the median voter. In this framework, when will the immigration option be accepted? Consider first the simple case of a constant-returns aggregate production function $F(K, L)$ and competitive labor markets. If the number of immigrants M is small relative to the number of natives N $(L = N + M)$, immigration produces the following change in income y of a resident endowed with k units of capital:[6]

$$\frac{dy/y}{dM/L} = \left(\frac{k_{\mathrm{I}} - \bar{k}}{\bar{k}}\right)\left(\frac{\bar{k} - k}{\bar{k}}\right)\left(\frac{s_{\mathrm{L}}(1 - s_{\mathrm{L}})}{\sigma(y/\bar{y})}\right), \tag{1}$$

where $\bar{k}$ is the country's aggregate capital-labor ratio, k_{I} the new immigrants' average capital-labor ratio, $\bar{y}$ per capita income, s_{L} the share of labor in national income, and σ the elasticity of substitution between labor and capital. Define the critical capital (or skill) level k_c as the level of capital k at which an individual is indifferent with respect to immigration. In this simple setup, the critical capital level k_c is equal to $\bar{k}$. If the distribution of capital, which should be interpreted as encompassing physical and human capital, is skewed to the right (as in figure 6.1), then the median skill level k_m is smaller than k_c, and the immigration option will be accepted if the immigrants' average skill level k_{I} is

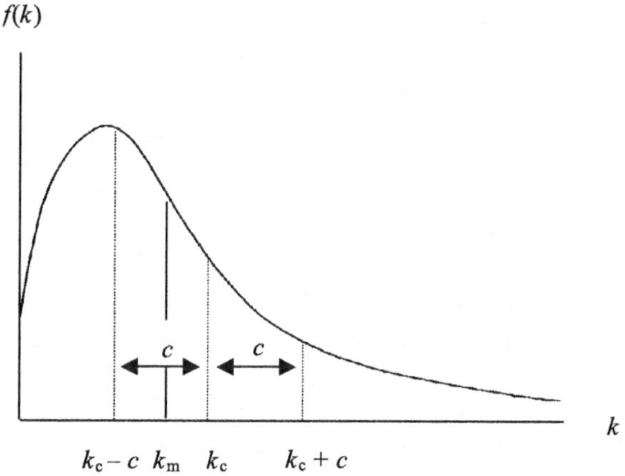

$f(k)$ density function of capital distribution
k_c critical capital level
k_m median of capital distribution
c voting costs

Figure 6.1
Skewed distribution of capital and attitudes toward immigration.

greater than the critical level k_c. By contrast, unskilled immigration ($k_I < k_c$) will be opposed.[7]

It is useful to relate this setting to the traditional analysis of immigration, which focuses on the efficiency gain ("immigration surplus") occurring with finite immigration. It should be noted, however, that the distributional changes produced by immigration are first-order effects, whereas the immigration surplus is only of the second order. As we emphasize distributional considerations in our politico-economic analysis, we neglect the efficiency gain by assuming that the immigration option that is up for vote involves only a small number of potential immigrants.

6.2.1.1 Voting Costs

The existence of voting costs might alter the above conclusion. Assume that, as in Mayer 1984, all individuals face identical voting costs, C. A voter will then take part in a vote about immigration only if the expected change in his income exceeds the voting costs, that is, if $|dy/dM| > C$. If the distribution of capital in the population is asymmetric, the outcome of the vote depends on voting costs. In particular, figure 6.1 makes it clear that if the distribution of capital is skewed to the right, it is possible that unskilled immigration ($k_I < k_c$) will be accepted by vote, even if this option is opposed by a majority of the population.[8] Indeed, among those who choose not to vote, in the example depicted in figure 6.1, a clear majority would be against unskilled immigration. The issue of participation will become prominent in the empirical analysis of section 6.4.

This first approach provides a good rationale for the recent implementation, in several European countries, of migration policies relying explicitly on skill criteria (e.g., the recent introduction of a "green card" in Germany; a similar scheme is underway in Switzerland). This simple framework is unable, however, to explain policies of temporary migration or of the guest worker type, which can be characterized as involving active recruitment of low-skill immigrants. Although these temporary migration policies were more prominent in the 1960s than they are today, they still play an important role in the current regulation of east-west migration. The remainder of this section will explore the channels through which these policies tend to decrease the critical capital level in a country, making it more likely for low-skill immigration to be accepted in a direct-democracy framework.[9]

6.2.2 *Guest Workers and Temporary Migration*

With the eastern enlargement of the EU, the current guest worker policies and temporary migration schemes that apply currently to CEEC workers will have to be abandoned for the *acquis communautaire*.[10] To understand how such a policy change would fare in a direct-democracy framework, it is crucial to examine why guest worker policies were adopted in the first place.

Most guest worker policies or temporary migration schemes aim at channeling immigrants into occupations or sectors in which they do not compete with native workers. The sectoral segregation between natives and migrants is either the direct result of legal regulations (e.g., work permits that limit the holders to working in certain sectors) or the indirect outcome of differing economic incentives. We discuss both cases in turn. To account for the structural effects of guest worker policies, the model is expanded to two sectors (Ricardo-Viner model).[11] The economy produces two traded goods: X (import-competing) and Y (export-competing), using three factors: labor (L), which is mobile between the two sectors, and two types of sector-specific capital (K_X, K_Y). We keep the assumption that capital is unequally distributed among natives; capital owners are paid at the average return of the two sectors. We assume furthermore that the median capital endowment (among voters) is smaller than the average capital-labor ratio and that immigrants are unskilled (i.e., they do not bring any capital with them when they migrate).

6.2.2.1 Traded Goods Only

Suppose first that both goods are traded, and guest workers are confined to one sector (guest workers are not only CEEC nationals, but also from other countries such as Turkey). In the absence of an immigration surplus, permanent immigration, which brings down real wages, should never be observed, as it will be opposed by a majority of voters. Guest worker immigration may occur, however, and will be welcomed by all individuals holding capital. Indeed, suppose we start from an initial situation in which there is already a substantial number of guest workers in the country. Moreover, assume that all guest workers have been confined to sector X by an exogenous segregation process that has displaced all native workers to sector Y. Such a segregation process can be implemented (as in the case of the CEEC workers in the EU countries) through a "rotation system" that grants

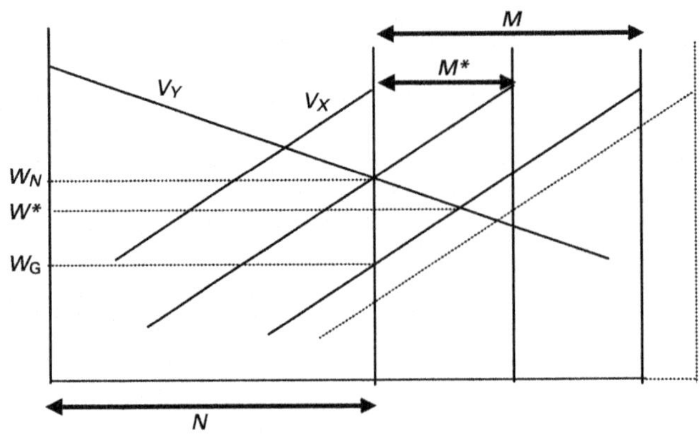

V_X marginal product of labor in sector X
V_Y marginal product of labor in sector Y
N number of native workers
M number of immigrants
M^* number of immigrants such that all natives are excluded from sector X

Figure 6.2
Guest workers in the Ricardo-Viner model.

only fixed-term labor contracts to immigrants and prevents them from making any change in occupation during their time of stay.

This situation is depicted in figure 6.2 where the number of guest workers (M) is larger than the critical amount of guest workers (M^*) that displaces the last native worker from sector X to sector Y ($M > M^*$). This means that native labor (N) has become specific to sector Y and that the wage rate of natives (w_N) is higher than the wage rate of guest workers (w_G). In this case, as shown by Djajic (1997), native workers are "immunized" against additional guest worker immigration. Indeed, any additional increase in the immigrant population (represented by the dotted lines in figure 6.2) is Pareto improving for natives, as it will depress the immigrants' wage while increasing the real return to K_Y and leaving unchanged both w_N and the real return to K_X.

What if immigration policy is now put up for vote in the host country? If mass expulsion of immigrants is not an option, the median voter will prefer keeping a guest worker system to introducing the free mobility of immigrants between sectors. Specifically in the case of the expanded EU, the latter option would allow CEEC immigrants to enter sector Y and would bring the natives' wage down to w^*. At the same time, the guest worker wage would increase from w_G to w^*, attracting more immigrants from the CEECs. Thus the free movement of persons between the CEECs and EU countries would be doubly opposed by voters in those countries. By contrast, a vote on additional guest worker immigration would be successful, as it would increase capital remuneration in sector Y while leaving indifferent native workers holding no capital.

This simple framework provides a rationale for the flexible system of transitional arrangements or the establishment of fixed-quota systems as envisaged in EU Commission 2001. These conclusions are reinforced if one modifies the setup to include a nontraded sector.

6.2.2.2 Nontraded Sector

Immigrants are often confined, in the countries that receive them, to working in the lodging, restaurant, and domestic-help sectors, both in the context of European countries with guest worker systems, and currently in the bilateral EU relations with the CEECs (see Boeri et al. 2001, section 5.2). Provided that preferences are the same across household groups, the previous conclusion is reinforced if one of the two sectors produces nontraded goods. Suppose that sector is sector X, in which guest worker immigration is frequently observed, and start again from an initial situation in which all natives are employed in sector Y (now the composite traded good). With respect to the analysis of figure 6.2, the additional consequence of allowing more guest worker immigration would be a decrease in the relative price of nontraded goods (the relative supply of nontraded goods increases, whereas the relative demand is unchanged, provided immigrants share a common consumption pattern with natives). This would leave every household better off than in the traded-goods case, generating a clear majority in favor of additional guest worker immigration.[12]

The predictions of the model that voters will not vote to abandon a guest worker system in favor of the free sectoral mobility of immigrants (and a fortiori, the free movement of persons) are supported by the history of Swiss migration policy.[13]

6.2.2.3 Segmented Labor Markets

It is probably unrealistic to assume that fixed-term labor contracts are the only source of segregation between natives and immigrants.

Segregation can also be observed in the case of immigrants who face no legal barriers to inter-sectoral mobility.[14] Also, the arguments developed above do not explain why the first M^* guest workers were accepted initially. A more realistic setup, analyzed in the same Ricardo-Viner framework by Müller (2003a, 2003b), is to assume that segregation takes place because immigrants and natives face different incentives in a segmented labor market. As immigrants are likely to return to their home country, their incentives differ from the incentives of natives. Discriminatory labor market regulations, such as the preferential hiring of natives, might reinforce this effect. In the context of a dual labor market, this difference in incentives leads to discrimination against immigrants if "good jobs" are rationed in an efficiency wage setup.

The dual labor market is modeled in a standard efficiency-wage framework following Shapiro and Stiglitz (1984) and Bulow and Summers (1986). We continue to use the Ricardo-Viner small-country model with both goods traded. Y is now the primary sector offering good working conditions, with firms paying above-market clearing wages to induce workers to supply effort, and X is the secondary residual sector, in which unattractive and repetitive jobs can be monitored at no cost. As a consequence, jobs are rationed in the primary sector, and workers are queuing up for them. They can always find jobs in the secondary sector, however, in which the wage rate is set competitively. There is no unemployment.[15]

At equilibrium, the wage rate is equal to the marginal product of labor in each sector. The labor market equilibrium with and without immigration is depicted in figure 6.3. The sectoral wage differential is determined by the no-shirking constraint. As the initial equilibrium in the dual labor market is inefficient, immigration produces not only the conventional "immigration surplus" (a second-order gain, represented in the figure by the two shaded triangles, that can be neglected if immigration is infinitesimal), but also a first-order change in efficiency (represented by the rectangle) due to the expansion of primary-sector employment (for simplicity, the wage differential is assumed constant in figure 6.3).

Whether the natives can reap a share of this first-order efficiency gain depends in particular on the immigrants' incentives and on migration policy. Indeed, a distinctive characteristic of immigrants in the existing EU countries is their probability of return to their countries of origin.[16] Therefore, even if migrants are identical to natives in all other

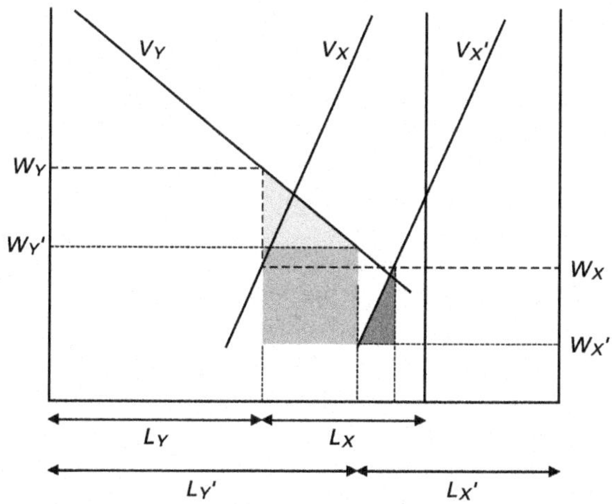

Figure 6.3
Immigration and the dual labor market.

respects, their incentive not to shirk is influenced by the probability that they will return to their home country, which depends indirectly on various aspects of the migration policy of the receiving country, such as the existence of temporary work permits and the government's attitude toward social and economic integration of immigrants. Also, firms in the receiving country are often forced by law to choose natives and "old" migrants over "new" migrants in their hiring decision.

All these factors contribute to segregation and thus to discrimination against migrants. Since competition ensures that natives and migrants are paid the same wages, discrimination is of the type "equal pay for equal work, but not equal work." Hence migrants have smaller chances of finding "good" jobs than natives and suffer from sectoral segregation. With segregation, immigration increases the natives' chances of finding a job in the primary sector and reaping a greater share of the efficiency gain represented by the shaded rectangle in figure 6.3.

These considerations suggest that the qualitative aspects of migration policy might influence political decisions concerning the desirability of further immigration. Indeed, it can be shown that a guest worker system makes a country more receptive to immigrants than a less discriminatory policy (de Melo, Miguet, and Müller 2002). In particular, an extreme guest worker policy (resulting in complete segregation) leads to a critical capital-labor ratio k_c that is smaller than the economy's average capital-labor ratio. If the distribution of capital in the economy is symmetric (or if the median capital level is not too far below the average), the median voter will therefore be in favor of immigration. Moreover, a less discriminatory policy regarding immigrant labor entails a critical capital level that is higher than in the extreme guest worker case.

Not only will the eastern enlargement of the EU create new immigration flows, but it will also improve the legal situation of CEEC nationals who are currently working in the EU under temporary migration or guest worker schemes. Such a policy change would improve the social and economic integration of immigrants and enhance their chances of finding "good" jobs in the economies of the countries that receive them. How would such a qualitative policy change fare in a popular vote? Grether, de Melo, and Müller (2001) show that if the median capital endowment among natives is below the average capital per capita, the improved integration of immigrants will be rejected by a majority of natives who fear the deterioration of their own economic situation. It should be emphasized that this is an inefficient outcome, since a policy of social integration would increase the number of good jobs at the expense of bad jobs and therefore improve the aggregate welfare of natives *and* immigrants (see Müller 2003a). Indeed, were immigrants allowed to vote, it is possible that a majority in favor of the policy change could be found.

In sum, our theoretical framework suggests three main conclusions. First, in the absence of segmented labor markets, voters will be in favor of a policy that imposes skill requirements on immigrants. Second, restricting the mobility of guest workers to nontraded sectors is likely to engender support for immigration. Third, with segmented labor markets a discriminatory migration policy, of the type used in the EU and Switzerland in the past, will obtain more support than an unrestricted migration policy, and natives are likely to oppose a shift from the former to the latter.

6.3 The Shaping of Switzerland's Immigration Policy

How does Switzerland's immigration experience compare to that of other developed countries? Table 6.1 depicts the evolution of the share of foreigners across European countries from 1950 to 1998, along with the share of EU foreigners among foreigners.[17] Switzerland stands out

Table 6.1
Foreign population in country of destination (as percentage of total population)

	1950	1960	1970	Share of EU foreigners, 1950–1970	1980	1985	1990	1998	Share of EU foreigners, 1998
North Europe									
Denmark	n.a.	n.a.	1.8[a]	n.a.	1.9	2.2	2.5	4.8	20.7
Sweden	1.8	2.5	5.0	95	5.0	4.6	4.7	5.6	40.0
Norway	0.5	0.7	2.0	n.a.	2.0	2.4	2.6	3.7	45.7
Finland	n.a.	n.a.	n.a.	n.a.	n.a.	0.0	0.4	1.6	18.4
Ireland	n.a.	n.a.	n.a.	n.a.	2.4	1.9	2.2	3.0	76.7
United Kingdom	3.4	4.5	5.7	60	3.0	3.1	3.2	3.8	40.0
Austria	11.0	n.a.	7.0	88	n.a.	4.0	4.1	9.1	13.0
Belgium	4.3	4.6	7.2	85	8.9	8.5	8.6	8.7	63.1
Netherlands	1.1	1.0	1.9	66	3.6	3.8	3.9	4.2	29.0
Switzerland[b]	6.1	10.8	17.2	96	14.1	14.6	14.7	19.0	62.0
Luxembourg	9.9	13.2	18.4	53	n.a.	26.5	26.3	35.6	87.0
France	4.2	4.6	5.3	61	6.8	n.a.	6.8	6.3	36.5
Germany	n.a.	1.2	4.5	77	5.6	5.6	7.4	8.9	25.3
South Europe									
Italy	0.1	0.1	0.2	39	0.1	0.1	1.2	2.1	13.7
Portugal	0.2	0.3	0.4	26	0.6	0.9	1.0	1.8	27.1
Spain	0.3	0.2	0.4	60	0.5	0.6	1.1	1.8	41.0
Total Europe	2.4	2.3	3.6	n.a.	3.7	3.9	4.4	5.3	n.a.

Source: Brücker et al. 2001a, table 1b.
Note: Data for 1950, 1960, and 1970 are derived from Census: They represent the share of foreign population in total population, except for the United Kingdom, where they represent the share of the foreign-born population. Data for 1980–1998 are derived from various national sources and represent foreign population share (in total population). n.a.: Not available.
[a] Percentage for 1975.
[b] Seasonal workers excluded.

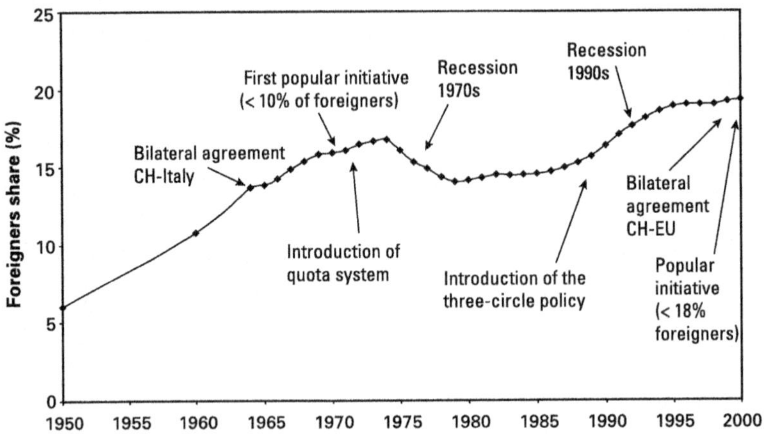

Figure 6.4
Foreign population share and migration policy in Switzerland.

from other European countries in two dimensions. First, compared with other European countries, with the exception of Austria (and Luxembourg), Switzerland had the highest initial share of foreigners in 1950 (6 percent), a lead it maintained until 1998, when the share had risen to 19 percent, whereas in Austria the share, which had started higher than Switzerland's (11 percent) actually fell over the same period. Second, although, as in all other countries, the share of EU nationals among foreigners in Switzerland has declined sharply over the last fifty years, the share of EU nationals among foreigners in Switzerland (62 percent in 1998) is still among the highest in Europe.

It is instructive to consider the history of Swiss migration policy in connection with the evolution of the foreign population share in Switzerland[18] (see figure 6.4). During the period of strong growth in the postwar period, labor shortages in Switzerland were met through immigration, with the foreigners' share in the population increasing from 5.8 to 9.1 percent between 1950 and 1960. But at the beginning of the 1960s, tensions started building, and the Swiss government issued two federal orders (in 1963 and 1964) aiming at limiting the inflow of immigrants into the country.[19]

In 1965, the first popular initiative attempting to limit the number of foreigners to 10 percent of the population (instead of the prevailing 15 percent) was launched. The initiative was later withdrawn. Confronted with this issue, in 1968, the government issued a new federal order aiming at stabilizing the stock of foreigners while at the same time making it easier for foreigners' children to become naturalized and giving leeway on exemptions to assuage economic interests. As the number of foreigners with renewable or long-term permits actually increased by close to 5 percent (instead of falling by 3 percent, as announced in the federal decree of 1968), a second initiative, also asking foreigners be limited to 10 percent of the population was launched in 1969; this time, the initiators gave up the possibility of withdrawing the initiative.

The 7 June 1970 vote on this initiative marks a watershed in Switzerland's policy toward immigrants (see table 6.2a). The initiative was the first in a series of popular initiatives taken to the polls over the next thirty years and the beginning of a policy based on a complex system of yearly quotas that is still in place today.[20] This vote also registered one of the highest participation rates (74 percent), and the proposal was rejected only narrowly, in spite of a last-ditch effort by the government to build consensus around its immigration policy by introducing further restrictions on immigration. But the system of popular initiatives (some aiming at controlling the flow of immigrants, others at improving the status of immigrants) has forced the Swiss government to compromise and to design, over the years, an effective, though not economically efficient, immigration policy.

During that period, the government was squeezed between economic interests seeking to avoid or reduce the impact of immigration quotas and the popular pressure to tighten them. Its response was to devise a complex system of quotas that gave it the flexibility to play both sides and to adjust rapidly to short-term objectives arising out of the combined pressures exerted by labor unions (pressing for binding quotas), firms (preferring loose quotas) and parts of the public (wishing to preserve cultural identity, as expressed in its xenophobic requests). For example, immigration to permit family reunification was not included in the quotas, nor was the conversion of seasonal to annual permits. These loopholes in the immigration laws led to the third popular initiative seeking to restrain immigration. The initiative's rejection, in a vote with a high participation rate, on 20 October 1974 by a two-thirds majority heralded the success of the government's give-and-take approach. One can conclude from the size of the majority that rejected the initiative that the conjunction of direct democracy and lobbying was shaping Switzerland's policy toward immigrants.

Table 6.2
Votes on immigration policy

Date	Contents	Result	Participation
a. Popular initatives[a]			
7 June 1970	Foreigners' share in population ≤ 10 percent (25 percent) in each canton (Geneva)	rejected 54%	74%
20 October 1974	Foreigners' share in population ≤ 12 percent (25 percent) in each canton (Geneva), with total in Switzerland ≤ 500,000 + Naturalizations ≤ 4,000 per year	rejected 65.8%	70%
13 March 1977	Foreigners' share in population ≤ 12.5 percent in Switzerland	rejected 70.5%	45%
13 March 1977	Naturalizations ≤ 4,000 per year	rejected 66.2%	45%
5 April 1981	Abolish seasonal-worker status + Indefinite renewal of working permits + Immigration flows to match emigration flows	rejected 83.8%	39%
4 December 1988	Immigration flows ≤ two-thirds of emigration flows (including asylum seekers) + Limit on seasonal workers and cross-border commuters	rejected 67.3%	52%
1 December 1996	Illegals cannot ask asylum seeker status + Restrictions on rights of appeal	rejected 53.7%	46%
24 September 2000	Foreigners' share in population ≤ 18 percent (including asylum seekers)	rejected 63.8%	45%
b. Referenda[b]			
6 June 1982	Counterproposal to the initiative of 5 April 1981: Indefinite renewal of working permits + Immigration flows to match emigration flows	rejected 50.4%	35%
4 December 1983	Tightening of naturalization criteria + Children of any Swiss citizen get Swiss nationality	accepted 60.8%	35%
4 December 1983	Loosening of naturalization requirements for foreigners' children, refugees, asylum seekers, and the nationless	rejected 55.2%	35%
5 April 1987	Distribution of asylum seekers across cantons + Faster admission process + Tightening of asylum law	accepted 67.3%	42%
5 April 1987	Amendment of the law regulating the stay and establishment of foreigners (e.g., imprisonment of dangerous asylum seekers or those who refuse to leave the country)	accepted 65.7%	42%

Table 6.2
(continued)

Date	Contents	Result	Participation
12 June 1994	Right of easier naturalization for young foreigners who grew up in Switzerland	rejected by cantons	46%
4 December 1994	Expanded search rights in asylum seekers' domiciles + Tightening of law on foreigners' rights	accepted 72.9%	43%
13 June 1999	Amendment of asylum law (i.e., less-restrictive provisory admission rights)	accepted 70.6%	45%
13 June 1999	Stricter criteria for asylum status + asylum seekers must be cooperative with authorities	accepted 70.8%	45%

[a] To be voted upon, an initiative must obtain 50,000 signatures (pre-1977) and 100,000 (starting in 1977). Acceptance of an initiative implies changes in the constitution.
[b] Laws or federal orders are put to vote if they obtain 50,000 signatures (1977 law).

The role of the democratic process was also evident in the 1981 vote on a popular initiative aimed at creating more equality between Swiss nationals and foreigners and eliminating the seasonal-worker status. This proposal was sharply opposed by the construction, catering, and agriculture sectors, which relied on labor from workers in this category. As these economic interests were opposed to the suppression of the seasonal-worker status but not to the equality principle, the government proposed a modification of the country's foreigners' law. As shown in table 6.2, both the popular initiative (in 1981) and the proposed law (in 1982) were rejected by the electorate. By that time, the foreign population was effectively stabilized, but as the proportion of annual permits had fallen from 70 percent in 1970 to 25 percent in 1980, flexibility in migratory policy was waning.

Only in the late 1980s, with the surge in asylum seekers and the prospects of a closer relationship with the EU, did immigration policy in Switzerland again begin to be questioned: On the one hand, distinguishing between economic and political motives for immigration was becoming difficult; on the other hand, the guest worker system appeared inappropriate if closer ties with the EU were to develop. Sensing that the European Economic Area (EEA) act would be rejected in a vote because it would call for an abolishment of the guest worker system, an immigration policy based on "cultural proximity" that was often referred to as the "three-circle policy" was adopted by the government.[21] In 1992, the referendum to join the EEA was nevertheless rejected by Swiss citizens.

The failure of the discriminatory cultural-proximity policy, Switzerland's participation in the international convention against racism in 1995, and the growing criticism of the quota system by the country's business sector led to the proposal in 1998 of a point system for immigration akin to the system in use in Canada and Australia. Although this proposal did not carry the day, the government did shift from a three-circle to a "two-circle" policy that would both accommodate the desire for closer ties with the EU (with 57 percent of the electorate accepting the proposed bilateral agreements with the EU in May 2000) and cater to anti-foreigner feelings in the population. Meanwhile, guest worker permits were cut in half to 88,000 per year during the 1990s.

What are the characteristics of the foreign population in Switzerland (now 20 percent of the total population, as noted in section 6.1) compared to that of other countries? With respect to the main categories of newly arriving immigrants, table 6.3 shows that, in 1998, Switzerland had an inflow composition similar to that of other countries: About 50 percent of immigrants were entering as workers, and 45 percent for family reunification purposes. In this table, Sweden stands out as having a large proportion of asylum seekers among its immigrant population, and France is distinguished from other countries of Europe in that the motivation for immigration to that country is less linked to work; the profile of its immigrants' reason for migrating resembles that of the United States.

Having noted that averages hide differences across nationalities, Brücker et al. (2001, 16) summarize as follows the socio-economic characteristics of immigrants in the EU. Immigrants to EU countries are concentrated in large cities and are younger than natives, with a higher proportion of males among migrants than among natives; migrants are also more than proportionally affected by unemployment. Most of these stylized characteristics apply to immigrants in Switzerland as well.[22] In the EU, immigrants generally have lower skill levels than natives, which is also the case in Switzerland if one considers immigrants from Southern Europe.[23] Brücker et al. also note that immigrants have an occupational status below that of natives with comparable skill levels. Foreigners in Switzerland have lower salaries and have lower chances of reaching upper-level positions in their firms' hierarchies than natives with comparable skill levels (Flückiger and Ramirez 2001).

Table 6.3
Immigration inflows by main categories

	Year	Workers[a]	Family reunification[a]	Asylum seekers and refugees[a]	Others[a]	Net inflow of foreigners[b]
Switzerland[c]	1998	50	45	5	0	1.1
Sweden	1997	2	55	21	22	0.4
France	1996	21	55	10	16	0.1
Italy[d]	1999	50	39	3	8	0.2
United Kingdom[e]	1998	45	50	5	0	0.4
United States[f]	1998	12	72	8	8	0.2
Canada[f]	1998	55	29	13	3	0.6
Australia[f]	1998	34	26	11	29	0.4

Sources: Brücker et al. 2001a, table 6, and OECD (2000a).
[a] As a percentage of total immigration to the country. With the exception of the United Kingdom and Switzerland, total inflows also include students, visitors, and so forth; thus the total does not sum to 100 percent.
[b] As percentage of total population in the country.
[c] Seasonal workers included.
[d] Inflow of foreigners: 1998.
[e] EU immigrants not included; inflow of foreigners: 1997.
[f] Inflows of permanent settlers.

6.4 Determinants of Attitudes and Voting Behavior

The analysis of surveys of individual voter attitudes in various countries points to the conclusion that attitudes toward immigration differ significantly among countries. Using cross-country data at the individual level from the International Social Survey Program (ISSP) for 1995, Bauer, Lofstrom, and Zimmerman (2000) find that most country dummy variables have a significant influence in their probit model, even if individual demographic and education variables are included. They conclude, rather tentatively, that sentiments toward immigrants are more favorable in countries using skill criteria in their immigration policies. By contrast, Brücker et al. (2001) work with country averages of a 1997 Eurobarometer poll to study attitudes toward immigration with respect to labor market effects, racism or xenophobia, and welfare take-up. Their strategy is to relate respondents' attitudes to country characteristics (previous growth rate, stock of foreigners, and rates of unemployment). In their sample of thirteen EU countries (Greece and Luxembourg are omitted), they find a significant positive relationship between fears that further immigration will cause problems domestically and the stock of foreign population in the country and a significant negative relationship between the unemployment rate in the country and apprehension about the negative effects of further immigration (Brücker et al. 2001, table 2.3).

How does Switzerland fit into this picture? Unfortunately, the 1995 ISSP and 1997 Eurobarometer surveys were not carried out for Switzerland. In figure 6.5, we report country averages, from a 2000 Eurobarometer survey that includes Switzerland, for the two questions in that survey that are closest to those analyzed by Brücker et al. (2001). It is striking in figure 6.5a that the inclusion of Switzerland upsets the pattern of consistently positive correlation between anti-immigration attitudes and the share of foreign population that exists in the other countries. In figure 6.5b, the negative correlation between anti-immigration attitudes and the unemployment rate reported by Brücker et al. (2001) is not reproduced for the thirteen EU member countries; it is even less well reflected if Switzerland is included. Switzerland can be considered an outlier among European countries in 2000: Having the highest foreign population share among those countries, it is the most open country toward foreigners. This result should, however, be interpreted with caution.[24]

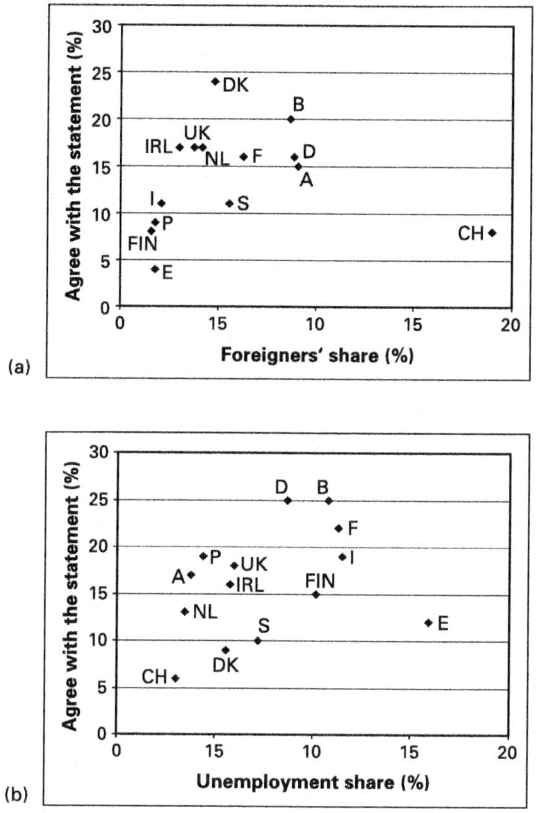

Countries:

A = Austria	E = Spain	NL = Netherlands
B = Belgium	F = France	P = Portugal
CH = Switzerland	FIN = Finland	S = Sweden
D = Germany	I = Italy	UK = United Kingdom
DK = Denmark	IRL = Ireland	

Figure 6.5
Attitudes toward immigrants: Eurobarometer survey, 2000: (a) "Other nationalities are disturbing"; (b) "Foreigners should be sent back."

Available responses were "agree with the statement," "disagree," or "don't know." The exact wording of the questions was as follows: (a) "Do you personally find the presence of people of another nationality disturbing in your daily life?" (b) "All immigrants, whether legal or illegal, from outside the EU and their children, even those who were born in your country, should be sent back to their country of origin." *Sources:* Eurobarometer survey 2000; OECD 2000 for 1998 foreigners' share; OECD 2001 for 1999 unemployment rate.

Because of its direct democracy, Switzerland provides a unique setting for analyzing the determinants of voters' attitudes toward immigration. After each national vote (since 1983), the GfS Institute carries out an individual-level survey (called *VOX*) asking Swiss citizens whether and how they voted. To elucidate the motivations behind voters' choices, the VOX polls also ask other questions concerning the issues at stake. Analysis of the data from this survey allows us to improve on existing studies of attitudes toward immigration (Scheve and Slaughter 1999, Citrin et al. 1997, Espenshade and Hempstead 1996, etc.) in two respects. First, the Swiss direct-democracy context enables us to address the issue of hypothetical bias, which hampers the analysis of conventional survey data.[25] Since Swiss voters are aware that if a popular initiative that is up for a vote is accepted, the proposed constitutional change reflected in the initiative will take place, there is no hypothetical bias. Second, the information on participation behavior provided by the survey data allows us to analyze how attitudes materialize in actual voting behavior. Indeed, the outcome of a vote is influenced by the decision to participate in the vote. Since it is likely that the decision to participate in a vote involving immigration policy and a voter's attitude toward immigration are not independent of one another, the outcome of a vote on immigration cannot accurately be inferred simply from survey questions on individuals' attitudes, as has been done in previous studies.

How can the decision to participate in a particular vote be explained if individuals are rational? If the result of the vote (yes/no) is the only politically relevant outcome of a referendum, then a citizen's motivation to vote is very weak, since his chances of changing the results of the vote are extremely small (the voting paradox). As is evident from the discussion of immigration policy in section 6.3, the voting paradox does not apply in the Swiss context: Even if a popular initiative is rejected, the outcome of the vote will be taken into account in later decisions by the government.[26] Thus the decision to participate in a popular vote can be interpreted more generally as a decision to influence the political process.

We turn now to the analysis of the Swiss vote in September 2000 on a popular initiative proposing that a limitation be imposed on the number of foreigners in the country. The initiative proposed that the Swiss constitution be changed to restrict the share of foreigners in the Swiss population to a maximum of 18 percent. Some categories of resident foreigners (e.g., academics, artists) would have been excluded from this count, but some non-residents (e.g., asylum seekers) would have been included. According to the definition of immigrant specified in the proposed constitutional change, the share of foreigners was 19.3 percent at the time of the vote. Therefore the initiative would have forced the government to limit immigration severely. The popular initiative was rejected by 63.7 percent of voters; the participation rate in the vote was 43.6 percent. The data that we are analyzing here come from an individual-level *VOX* survey that was carried out during the two weeks following the vote and includes 1,024 Swiss citizens over eighteen years old.

6.4.1 The Econometric Model

Our econometric framework is based on the direct-democracy model with voting costs discussed in section 6.2. To account for non-economic determinants of attitudes as well, we focus on immigration-induced changes in utility rather than income. The participation and voting decisions are modeled simultaneously by defining two dichotomous variables v (where $v = 1$ denotes a positive vote) and p (where $p = 1$ denotes participation) and two latent variables v^* and p^*:[27]

$$v^* = x'\beta + \varepsilon^*, \qquad v = 1 \quad \text{if } v^* > 0, \quad v = 0 \quad \text{otherwise,} \tag{2}$$

$$p^* = x'\alpha + z'\gamma + \xi^*, \qquad p = 1 \quad \text{if } p^* > 0, \quad p = 0 \quad \text{otherwise,} \tag{3}$$

where equations are normalized $(\text{Var}(\varepsilon^*) = \text{Var}(\xi^*) = 1)$. The interdependence between the decision to participate in the vote and a vote in favor of the popular initiative is captured by the fact that disturbances are assumed to be correlated: $\text{Corr}(\varepsilon^*\xi^*) = \rho$. Equations (2) and (3) can be interpreted as a simplified reduced form of a structural-voting model (see Krishnakumar and Müller 2003).

In this survey only individuals who participated in the vote were asked how they had voted. Therefore, equations (2) and (3) must be estimated using a bivariate probit model with censoring: For a given individual, v is not observed unless $p = 1$. The maximum-likelihood procedure that applies in this context was proposed by van de Ven and van Praag (1981).

In constructing the variables to estimate the model, we follow the literature (see, e.g., Citrin et al. 1997 and Scheve and Slaughter 1999) by distinguishing between economic and non-economic determinants of attitudes toward immigration. Economic determinants are related to

Table 6.4
Variables of the voting model

Variables	Mean	Standard deviation
Vote	0.283	0.451
Participation	0.579	0.494
Schooling (years)	12.650	2.113
Vocational education	0.636	0.481
Wage	5.045	2.981
Retired	0.205	0.404
Age	47.769	17.074
Unemployment share (canton)	1.845	0.837
Share of foreigners (agglomeration)	19.308	6.386
French speaking[a]	0.195	0.396
Italian speaking[a]	0.067	0.250
Female	0.485	0.500
Owner	0.481	0.500
Political orientation (0–10)	4.916	1.481

Note: There are 805 observations for all variables, except for the vote (466 observations).
[a] Reference group: German-speaking individuals.

the costs and benefits of immigration at the aggregate or individual level. At the individual level, economic determinants include in particular factor endowments such as the individual's skills and capital holdings. Non-economic determinants include individuals' political ideology, attitudes toward other cultures, and attitudes toward the civil rights of immigrants.[28]

From the viewpoint of an economist, the main question is whether skill or human capital is a significant determinant of attitudes toward immigration even if one controls for political ideology and other social and demographic variables. We explore carefully the role of economic determinants by using two different measures of skills. First, as a measure of educational attainment, we constructed an indicator of years of schooling according to the five education types reported in the survey (descriptive statistics of variables are given in table 6.4). The particularity of the dual education system in Switzerland is taken into account by defining a dummy variable that takes a value of one for individuals who received most of their secondary education as vocational training (apprenticeship, etc.).

Second, we used a wider measure of skills by including also on-the-job training. The two types of skills (schooling and on-the-job training) can be aggregated into a common indicator by appealing to Mincer's concept of "potential earnings." In Mincer's framework, observed wages and potential earnings are closely linked. To construct the aggregate skill measure ("earnings"), we applied a standard Mincer wage equation to data from the Swiss wage structure survey. The *earnings* indicator was constructed using the following equation:

$$\ln(\mathit{earnings}) = \text{constant} + 0.04(\mathit{experience}) - 0.5(\mathit{experience}^2/1000) + 0.09(\mathit{schooling}),$$

where *experience* is defined as $(\mathit{age} - \mathit{schooling} - 6)$.[29] The macroeconomic context is captured by the unemployment rate in the individual's canton of residence.[30] In addition, we use a variable measuring the share of foreigners in the population of the geographical area where the individual lives.

Among the non-economic determinants of attitudes toward immigration, we represent the political beliefs of citizens by a variable based on the individual's own judgment of his political position on a scale from 0 (left) to 10 (right). Cultural differences between the German-, French-, and Italian-speaking parts of Switzerland are captured by dummy variables for minorities. The participation equation furthermore includes dummy variables on gender and housing status (owner) and two continuous variables for age and age squared.

6.4.2 *Results*

We now report the results of four specifications of the voting and participation equations. Each specification includes one of the two skill measures and, in order to avoid problems of multicollinearity, either the cultural dummies or the other variables that are defined on a geographical basis (unemployed rate, share of foreigners). Indeed these variables are highly correlated since unemployment rates and the share of foreigners tend to be higher in the French and Italian speaking parts of Switzerland.

Before discussing the results in detail, it is useful to gauge the importance of the participation bias (sample selection bias) which can be done by estimating two versions of the model. First, the full model given by (2) and (3) is estimated using a bivariate probit model with censoring, as described above. Second, we ignore deliberately the selection mechanism and fit a standard probit model to equation (2),

Table 6.5
Estimation results of the voting model (specification 1)

	Probit	Probit with sample selection		
	Vote	Vote	Partici-pation	Marginal effect
Years of schooling	0.042 (1.17)	−0.068* (1.81)	0.113*** (4.72)	−0.027* (1.85)
Vocational education	0.565*** (3.60)	0.259 (1.61)	0.104 (1.01)	0.103 (1.59)
Age	−0.053** (2.22)	−0.072*** (3.92)	0.052*** (3.25)	−0.028*** (3.91)
Age squared/1,000	0.583** (2.56)	0.640*** (3.53)	−0.348** (2.17)	0.253*** (3.49)
Unemployment rate	−0.003 (0.03)	0.196** (2.16)	−0.323*** (4.39)	0.0776** (2.19)
Share of foreigners	−0.007 (0.54)	−0.017 (1.54)	0.029*** (2.94)	−0.007 (1.55)
Female			−0.159* (1.94)	
Owner			0.389*** (3.57)	
Political orientation	0.234*** (5.47)	0.151*** (3.71)	−0.440*** (4.28)	0.060*** (3.59)
Political orientation squared			48.168*** (4.38)	
Constant	−1.524* (1.90)	1.811** (2.03)	−2.028*** (3.73)	
Number of observations	466	805		
Number of uncensored observations		466		
Log-likelihood	−247.82	−720.25		
Rho		−0.92***		

Note: Absolute value of z-statistics in parentheses.
*significant at 10 percent. **significant at 5 percent. ***significant at 1 percent.

using only the part of the sample that includes observations on individuals who participated in the vote.

The results in table 6.5 demonstrate that the voting and participation decisions must be estimated simultaneously to explain (1) individuals' attitudes toward immigration and (2) the mechanism that links individual attitudes to actual voting behavior.[31] Indeed, the correlation ρ between the disturbances of the voting and participation equations is significantly different from zero, and its estimate is close to -1. As a consequence, the naive probit model yields biased results and would lead one to believe that schooling and the unemployment rate are not significant determinants of attitudes toward immigration.[32]

In the complete model with sample selection, the main parameters turn out to be significant and have the expected sign: A lower education level and right-wing convictions are associated with a higher probability of accepting the popular initiative.[33] The probability of voting "yes" decreases with age until it reaches a minimum around the age of fifty-six. This age-voting profile resembles (in the negative) an age-earnings profile. One might therefore be tempted to conclude that in this regression, *age* is a proxy for labor market experience (representing another measure of skill). That this is indeed the case can be seen in table 6.6, which reports the results of the three alternative specifications. When potential earnings (*wage*) are included in the equation (specifications 3 and 4), they contribute significantly to the explanation of voting and participation behavior, and in this case no independent influence of a voter's age can be identified.

It is interesting to note that a high foreign-population share in the voter's geographical area is not associated with an anti-immigration vote (specification 3 suggests rather the opposite). The effects of the remaining explanatory variables in the voting equation are rather robust with respect to the different specifications. Individuals living in cantons with high unemployment rates tend to be more hostile to immigration. Italian-speaking Swiss are significantly more opposed to immigration, which is certainly due to the specific situation of the labor market (with many low-wage workers along the Swiss-Italian border) and the strong influence of a local right-wing party (Lega).

The estimation of the participation equation yields interesting results in its own right. First, people from the political extremes are more likely to participate in the vote than those who hold centrist beliefs. Indeed, the probability of participation is related to the political scale in a U-shaped relationship, with the minimum (4.6) close to the sample

Table 6.6
Estimation results under different specifications

	Specification 2		Specification 3		Specification 4	
	Vote	Participation	Vote	Participation	Vote	Participation
Schooling	−0.073** (2.02)	0.115*** (4.84)				
Vocational education	0.259* (1.69)	0.064 (0.62)	0.230 (1.43)	0.108 (1.04)	0.223 (1.38)	0.066 (0.63)
Wage			−0.140** (2.03)	0.176*** (3.40)	−0.150** (2.16)	0.185*** (3.60)
Retired			−1.250** (2.30)	1.460*** (3.36)	−1.291** (2.36)	1.496*** (3.45)
Age	−0.071*** (4.00)	0.050*** (3.11)	−0.042 (1.51)	0.012 (0.53)	−0.037 (1.32)	0.006 (0.26)
Age squared/1,000	0.633*** (3.56)	−0.322** (2.03)	0.465* (1.70)	−0.093 (0.43)	0.413 (1.49)	−0.034 (0.16)
Unemployment rate			0.213** (2.40)	−0.330*** (4.49)		
Share of foreigners			−0.018* (1.68)	0.031*** (3.17)		
French speaking	0.133 (0.92)	−0.243** (2.02)			0.170 (1.17)	−0.243** (2.02)
Italian speaking	0.567** (2.37)	−0.818*** (4.27)			0.600*** (2.62)	−0.836*** (4.38)
Political orientation	0.149*** (3.83)	−0.442*** (4.36)	0.148*** (3.68)	−0.448*** (4.41)	0.144*** (3.72)	−0.450*** (4.57)

Political orientation squared		48.508***		48.764***		49.088***
		(4.47)		(4.48)		(4.67)
Female		−0.141*		−0.190**		−0.165**
		(1.76)		(2.33)		(2.07)
Owner		0.367***		0.396***		0.356***
		(3.38)		(3.31)		(2.72)
Constant	1.879**	−1.911***	0.986*	−0.504	0.983**	−0.307
	(2.25)	(3.58)	(1.83)	(1.09)	(2.02)	(0.70)
Number of observations	805		805		805	
Log-likelihood	−719.51		−725.16		−724.50	
Rho	−0.94***		−0.94***		−0.96***	

Note: Absolute value of z-statistics in parentheses.
*significant at 10 percent. **significant at 5 percent. ***significant at 1 percent.

Table 6.7
Probability of voting in favor of the popular initiative (sample averages, in percent, specification 1)

	Entire sample (805 observations)	Subsample of voters ($p = 1$) (466 observations)
Probit without sample selection		
$P\ (v = 1)$	27.4	28.3
Probit with sample selection		
$P\ (v = 1)$	54.6	51.8
$P\ (v = 1 \mid p = 1)$		28.3

mean (4.9). Second, participation is positively related to education, a result found in many other studies (see Mueller 1989, 365). Third, the participation of Swiss is greater in geographical areas in which there are many foreigners. Finally, the young, women, tenants, and minorities are less likely to go to the polls.

Turn now to the link between attitudes toward immigration and voting behavior. The estimates of marginal and conditional probabilities can inform us about this link (table 6.7 gives the average probabilities calculated both for the entire sample and the subsample including only people who participated). The conditional probability $P(v = 1 \mid p = 1)$ represents the model's fit for the outcome of the vote (the "yes" vote in the sample, 28.3 percent, is very well predicted). The marginal probability $P(v = 1)$ indicates how people voted or would have voted, whether they participated or not. For the entire sample, the average probability of accepting the initiative is 54.6 percent. This is a startling result. Had all Swiss citizens voted, the anti-immigration initiative would have been accepted!

The large divergence between the conditional and marginal probabilities can be explained by appealing to differences in observed and unobserved characteristics between those who voted and those who did not. It turns out that observed characteristics account for only a fairly small part of this difference. The participation and voting equations show, for example, that more-skilled individuals were more likely to participate and to reject the initiative. This effect, however, is quantitatively not very important, since the marginal probability of accepting the initiative is only slightly lower in the subsample of voters (51.8 percent) than in the entire sample (54.6 percent).[34]

The main difference between the marginal and conditional probabilities is due to the negative correlation between unobserved factors (disturbances) in the two equations. In other words, individuals who were more likely to participate than others *because of their unobserved characteristics* were generally more likely to reject the popular initiative. Indeed, this fact accounts for the large difference between the marginal probability (51.8 percent) and the conditional probability (28.3 percent) in the subsample of voters.[35]

To put these results into perspective, consider what would have happened if the Swiss government had followed opinion polls to define immigration policy, as some policymakers are tempted to do today in the context of EU enlargement. According to our econometric results, a general-opinion poll would have shown that more than half of Swiss voters were in favor of the popular initiative; interestingly, two "real" opinion polls came quite close to this conclusion.[36] Instead, the clear result of the vote was interpreted as a political signal of opposition to a restrictive immigration policy.

6.5 Conclusions

Perhaps the most controversial aspect of the ongoing negotiations about EU enlargement to the east is the free mobility of persons. Fears of a large inflow of immigrants have been apparent in recent EU-wide opinion polls. These fears are in sharp contrast with studies suggesting a net welfare gain from allowing the free mobility of persons to and from the CEECs, and with other studies predicting only moderate inflows of immigrants into the current EU member countries under free mobility.

This chapter informs the debate in two areas. First, we reviewed Switzerland's long-standing experience with immigration. We found that, compared with those of EU member countries as a whole, Swiss respondents in opinion polls are relatively more favorable to immigration in spite of Switzerland's having a higher stock of immigrants. The review of the debate and votes on initiatives and referenda over the last thirty years shows that the results at the election booth have influenced government policy on immigration, which has pursued a course accommodating the conflicting interests of unions, owners of businesses in sectors that are largely non-competitive internationally, and the public at large (as expressed in the results of the votes).

The resulting flexible system of annual quotas by worker categories combined with limited mobility and exemptions allowing the progressive transfer of immigrants from temporary to permanent status has successfully absorbed a large inflow of foreigners into Switzerland. Interestingly, many of the elements of this policy that have survived repeated challenges at the polls have been employed by EU members in their current immigration policies with the CEECs.

Second, and perhaps more interestingly, we have been able to show that the results from opinion polls are probably overly pessimistic, if interpreted as reflecting what people would actually vote if asked to. Indeed, drawing on a survey for the last immigration-related vote in Switzerland, which attempted to limit the stock of immigrants to its current level, we show that the government would have been tempted to put a limit on the number of immigrants if it had listened to opinion polls. In fact, the vote clearly rejected the proposal, confirming the notion that as in the contingent-valuation methods used to assess environmental damage, opinion polls are likely to suffer from hypothetical bias.

As to lessons for the current EU enlargement, it is interesting to contrast the Swiss experience with the debate on the EU's alleged "democratic deficit." Schematically, the Swiss political system derives its political legitimacy from direct-democratic procedures ("input legitimacy"), whereas the EU's legitimacy is based on the performance and efficient functioning of the decision-making process ("output legitimacy"). The EU's quasi-exclusive reliance on output legitimacy has prompted the criticism that the EU's political process suffers from a democratic deficit. But could the eastern enlargement have been carried through if voters in Western Europe had had the opportunity to oppose particularly sensitive issues, such as the free movement of persons? The Swiss experience suggests that large immigration flows can be absorbed in the context of a direct democracy, since the foreign population share of Switzerland has tripled over a forty-year period. But in the presence of populist right-wing movements, this absorption has been a long process. A flexible system of quotas and the gradual integration of immigrants turned out to be crucial in the case of Switzerland. Therefore, the Swiss experience suggests that the proper sequencing of policies toward immigrants during the transition period could turn out to be decisive for the political acceptance of EU enlargement.

Jaime de Melo, Florence Miguet, and Tobias Müller 161

Notes

This is a shortened version of de Melo, Miguet, and Müller 2002. The authors would like to thank Helge Berger, Fabrizio Carlevaro, Riccardo Faini, Thomas Moutos, Hans-Werner Sinn, Martin Werding, and participants at the CESifo workshops on EU enlargement in Munich (13–15 December 2001) and Delphi (13–14 September 2002) for useful suggestions and stimulating comments on previous drafts of the chapter. Financial support by the Swiss National Science Foundation (Grant 12-63953.00) is gratefully acknowledged.

1. See, e.g., Boeri and Brücker (2001), Brücker et al. 2001, and Sinn et al. 2001. The last study emphasizes, for Germany, potential problems during the transitional phase.

2. Evidence, mostly based on estimates of inflows from the ten aspiring countries, suggests that the stock of people (not only workers) would rise, after accession, to 4.0 million (up from the current 830,000), with their share in the EU population rising from 0.2 to 1.1 percent. The estimates suggest that the increase in immigrant population from enlargement will be largely concentrated in Germany, which is to absorb over two-thirds of the projected immigrant inflow, with an additional 10 percent to go to Austria. Sinn et al. (2001) forecast that between 3.4 and 4.3 percent of the population in acceding countries will flow to Germany, whereas Boeri and Brücker (2001) have a lower forecast (between 1.8 and 2.4 percent). According to Sinn et al. (2001), over the next fifteen years, the stock of immigrants in Germany would increase as a result of EU expansion to between 4 and 5 percent of the native population. Boeri and Brücker (2001) estimate that over the next thirty years, the share of immigrants from the CEEC10 in the German population would increase as a result of the expansion from 0.6 percent in 1998 to 3.5 percent in 2030 and in Austria from 1.3 to 5.5 percent. (As a reference, the stock of foreigners in Switzerland has more than tripled since the end of World War II to over 18 percent of the population.) Other estimates also suggest that past immigration has had little effect on unemployment, and that any negative impact on wages would be limited.

3. Dustmann and Preston (2000) find that racial prejudice is the most important component explaining negative inclination toward immigration from populations (e.g., West Indies, Asia) that are ethnically different from that of the receiving nation. By contrast, with regard to European immigrants, the estimated contributions of welfare and job concerns to negative feelings about immigration are as strong as those of racial prejudices.

4. The median-voter model employed in this chapter is well suited to representing how citizens' preferences over immigration translate into actual migration policies. Indeed, Scheve and Slaughter (1999) find that individuals form their opinions in accord with their interests as labor force participants. Moreover, the median-voter model gives a realistic description of the Swiss political system, in which people actually vote on immigration issues, and also of representative democracies in which governments monitor closely the public's mood on immigration. In the median-voter approach, the links to the underlying economic model are more transparent than in other political-economy approaches. Alternatively, one could rely on the pressure group model, in which policy is the result of the maximization of a welfare function whose weights are often arbitrarily chosen. For examples of this approach, see Buckley 1996 and Mezza and Winden 1996.

5. By symmetry, if $k_m > k_c$, a maximum skill requirement will defeat all other policy alternatives. Such a policy, however, might be difficult to enforce in the case of non-human capital, since immigrants might be able to conceal their capital holdings.

6. Equation (1) is obtained by differentiating $y = F_L + kF_K$, with $F_{KL} = -(L/K)F_{LL} = -(K/L)F_{KK}$ and $\sigma \equiv F_K F_K/(F_{KL}F)$.

7. See also Bilal, Grether, and de Melo 2003, which deals with the case of a beta distribution of capital in a direct-democracy model with three factors and two sectors.

8. Note that the voting costs c depicted in figure 6.1 are expressed in terms of capital per capita. They are linked to voting costs C through the following expression: $c = C\bar{k}^2\sigma L/((\bar{k} - k_{\mathrm{I}})s_{\mathrm{L}}s_{\mathrm{K}}\bar{y})$.

9. Consider the following simple example that lowers the critical capital level k_c (relative to the case considered above). Assume that, at the moment of the vote on migration policy, unskilled immigrants make up an important share of the initial population. If these immigrants do not have the right to vote, then k_c, equal to the average capital-labor ratio of the total population, is smaller than the average capital-labor ratio of the native population. Thus the capital endowment of the (native) median voter might well be greater than k_c. This case, however, which is reminiscent of the current Swiss situation, does not provide an explanation of why the (old) immigrants were accepted in the first place. The consequences of allowing for immigrants who do not have a right to vote in a Ricardo-Viner direct-democracy model are analyzed in Grether, de Melo, and Müller 2001.

10. Currently, in EU countries, immigration from the CEECs mostly takes the form of temporary migration, regulated either unilaterally by the host country or by bilateral agreements (see Boeri and Brücker 2001, table 4.4). Through these temporary migration programs, workers from the CEECs are channeled into occupations with low skill requirements. As a result, Boeri and Brücker (2001, 56) find that, although migrants from the CEECs are highly skilled, they work in the same sectors as other foreigners (i.e., labor-intensive sectors with a high share of unskilled workers).

11. The Ricardo-Viner model is a natural framework for examining the political-economy aspects of various migration policies in an open economy. Its time frame, with short-term rents, also probably corresponds to the time frame envisaged by many voters when they form an opinion on immigration policy. For example, Hillman and Weiss (1999b) suggest that voters probably find the Heckscher-Ohlin model appealing when formulating trade policy, since it captures the indirect effect on labor of trade in goods (via embodiment in imports), and the Ricardo-Viner model when formulating immigration policy, since immigrants compete directly with domestic labor.

12. See Djajic 1997. This is all the more likely if one makes the assumption, as do Hillman and Weiss (1999b) in the context of a similar analysis applied to illegal immigrants, that domestic (and permanent- or legal-immigrant) households have stronger preferences for nontraded goods than illegal-immigrant households.

13. In 1964, Italy pressured Switzerland to renegotiate the 1948 bilateral recruiting agreement between the two countries, leading to important improvements in the legal situation of Italian immigrants in Switzerland. The revised agreement aroused much opposition in Switzerland, triggering the creation of several anti-immigration movements. In 1981, the abolition of the seasonal-worker status was also opposed by a large majority of Swiss voters (see details in section 6.4).

14. The economic performance of ethnic Germans in the German labor market seems to be similar to (or even worse than) the performance of other immigrants, although ethnic Germans do not face any legal barriers to mobility and can be assumed to have better German language skills than other immigrants (Brücker et al. 2001, 58). This points to the conclusion that these immigrants suffer from an unequal access to the high-wage segment of the labor market.

15. For the effects of immigration in efficiency wage models with unemployment, see Müller 2003b and Epstein and Hillman 2000, in which the natives' willingness to exert effort increases with the number of immigrants.

16. In 1995, average return rates among the incumbent EU countries ranged from 1.5 percent for the Netherlands to 7.8 percent for Germany, though much higher return rates are observed for particular groups (e.g., 25.6 percent return rates for Polish immigrants in Germany) and for immigrant workers certain legal categories (e.g., 10.3 percent for holders of annual work permits in Switzerland).

17. Except for those for the United Kingdom, for which the figures are based on "foreign birth," the figures in table 6.1 are based on nationality. The statistics may misrepresent "immigrant pressure" for countries with high naturalization rates, like France and the United Kingdom. In the case of Switzerland, in 1990, 20.5 percent of residents were foreign born, and the foreign population share was 18.1 percent, indicating a lower rate of naturalization than in France and the United Kingdom. In 1999, foreigners accounted for 21.1 percent of the country's population. Excluding seasonal workers, asylum seekers, and short-stay foreigners, the share was 19.6 percent; excluding international workers and foreigners born in Switzerland, it was 16.3 percent.

18. A more detailed account of the recent history of Swiss migration policy can be found in Piguet and Mahnig 2000.

19. Even before the two orders were issued, foreign labor in Switzerland was grouped into three categories according to the type of work permit the workers held: seasonal (permit A), which prohibited the workers who held them from residing in the country more than nine months per year; annual renewable (permit B); and long-term (permit C), which allowed the establishment of residence. This reflected the view (expressed in the 1931 federal law on foreigners) that as long as they were not seeking residence, foreigners were welcome. This changed, under pressure from Italy, when the bilateral accord of 1964 allowed Italians residing in Switzerland for five years to change jobs and/or occupations, and relaxed time limits for family reunification and for obtaining long-term residence permits. This accord unleashed opposition in the media, to which the government replied by implementing its quota policy prior to ratifying the accord in March 1965.

20. Since 1970, yearly quotas for immigration have been established on the basis of data on return immigrants. To appease senescent sectors of the economy threatened with the loss of workers to expanding sectors, immigrants can change jobs only after one year, and they can change the canton in which they reside only after three years, with a consultative bargaining process at the canton level in cases of an excess number of demands for permits. The yearly quota policy averted a rise in unemployment during the economic crisis of the early 1970s, with the stock of foreigners diminishing by 86,000 between 1974 and 1976. As unemployment insurance was not compulsory at the time, many foreigners did not take it, which explains why the foreign population share fell by 2 percentage points during this crisis, but not in the subsequent crisis when unemployment insurance became compulsory in the early 1980s.

21. Under the three-circles policy, no restrictions were placed on immigration by citizens of EU and the European Free Trade Area (EFTA) countries (the first circle), whereas some restrictions were imposed on immigrants from a second circle of countries with close cultural ties to Switzerland (including Canadian, U.S. and CEEC citizens), with only exceptional admission of immigrants from the rest of the world, lumped together in a third circle.

22. The statistics for Switzerland (1999) are (nationals, foreigners): mean age (41, 33); male share (47.8 percent, 53.3 percent); urban dwellers (66.5 percent, 80.1 percent); unemployment rate (1.6 percent, 5.3 percent).

23. About two-thirds of foreigners living today in Switzerland come from Southern Europe (including Turkey and the former Yugoslavia). Note, however, that a substantial percentage of the immigrants from Northern Europe are highly skilled.

24. We are grateful to the editors for the following remarks. First, to the extent that some people move randomly in a regional context without paying attention to national borders, the fact that small countries have higher shares of foreign residents can be seen as a statistical artifact. Second, Eurobarometer data are known to be rather volatile over the years. Unfortunately, we are unable to carry out comparisons over time since there has been only one Eurobarometer survey (in 2000) with questions on immigration that included Switzerland.

25. Cummings, Harrison, and Rutström 1995 and Cummings et al. 1997 discuss the reasons why intentions may differ from actual behavior in the context of contingent methods for valuing environmental goods.

26. In certain circumstances, government decisions even anticipate the outcome of a popular vote. To prevent a popular initiative from being accepted by the voters, the government makes decisions that fulfill some of the initiative's demands. One example is the introduction of immigration quotas in the early 1970s, when a xenophobic popular initiative was up for vote (see section 6.3).

27. This model draws on Krishnakumar and Müller 2003.

28. The distinction between economic and non-economic determinants is, however, controversial and cannot be made easily in practice. For example, educational attainment is a measure of general human capital and is therefore an important determinant of an individual's wage. On the other hand, political values are certainly influenced by education as well. This double nature of education explains why Scheve and Slaughter (1999) classify education as an economic variable, whereas Citrin et al. (1997) interpret it as a demographic variable. A similar ambiguity arises for age, since it can be considered a proxy for work experience but also captures differences in political attitudes between generations.

29. The coefficients in this equation are based on a sample of Swiss men, bypassing problems associated with the measure of labor market experience (women) or schooling quality (foreign workers). To adapt the wage equation to the inactive citizens in our sample, we made some additional assumptions. For students, potential earnings are computed as if they were active citizens without experience. For the unemployed and people working in their home, potential earnings are computed as if they were active, but dummy variables are added to the regression to account for (unobserved) differences in work experience (as the coefficients of these dummies turn out not to be significant in the regression, they are not reported in the results). As the retired are no longer involved in the labor market, their attitude toward immigration is influenced by other considerations (such as the impact of immigration on social security). Therefore, their potential earnings are set to zero, and a dummy for the retired is included in the voting and participation equations.

30. In a dual labor market with unemployment, Müller (2003b) shows that the lower the unemployment rate, the greater are the chances that additional immigration is beneficial for natives.

31. As the four specifications do not differ significantly with respect to the problem of sample selection, we report results from only one of them.

32. To test the robustness of these results, we analyzed in addition two auxiliary questions. Those who participated in the vote were asked whether they agreed with the following statements: (1) "There are too many foreigners in Switzerland" and (2) "The current immigration policy is too lax; it should become tougher." Both estimations confirmed the crucial role of the variables *schooling* and *political ideology* (with p-values smaller than 0.005).

33. In contrast to the finding for participation, the square of the *political ideology* variable was found to have no significant influence on the vote; it was therefore dropped from the equation of the vote.

34. If there was no correlation between the disturbances of the two equations ($\rho = 0$), the conditional probability of voting "yes" would be equal to: $P(v = 1 \mid p = 1) = P(v = 1, p = 1)/P(p = 1) = P(v = 1)$. Therefore, the average of probabilities $P(v = 1)$ calculated on the subsample of voters represents the outcome of the vote as if omitted factors were not correlated across equations.

35. The ratio between the conditional and marginal probabilities is given by $P(v = 1 \mid p = 1)/P(v = 1) = P(v = 1, p = 1)/[P(p = 1) \cdot P(v = 1)]$. This ratio is equal to one if and only if $\rho = 0$.

36. According to a poll carried out in July 2000 and commissioned by Swiss television (DSR/TSR), 40 percent of respondents were in favor of the popular initiative, 42 percent were against, and 17 percent did not have an opinion. A similar poll, commissioned by the Swiss government in May 2000, concluded that the popular initiative would be accepted (see "Un Sondage sur l'Initiative des 18 percent secoue ses Opposants," *Le Temps*, 17 July 2000).

References

Bauer, T., M. Lofstrom, and K. F. Zimmerman. 2000. "Immigration Policy, Assimilation of Immigrants and Natives' Sentiments towards Immigrants: Evidence from 12 OECD Countries." Discussion paper no. 187, Institute for the Study of Labor (IZA), Bonn.

Benhabib, J. 1996. "On the Political Economy of Immigration." *European Economic Review* 40: 1737–1743.

Bilal, S., J.-M. Grether, and J. de Melo. 2003. "Determinants of Attitudes towards Immigration: A Trade-Theoric Approach." *Review of International Economics* 11, no. 2: 253–267.

Boeri, T., and H. Brücker. 2001. "The Impact of Eastern Enlargement on Employment and Labor Markets in EU Member States." Report for the European Commission, Berlin.

Brücker, H., G. Epstein, B. McCormick, G. St. Paul, A. Venturini, and K. Zimmerman. 2001. "Managing Migration in the European Welfare State." Mimeographed.

Bulow, J., and L. Summers. 1986. "A Theory of Dual Labor Markets with Application to Industrial Policy, Discrimination and Keynesian Unemployment." *Journal of Labor Economics* 23: 376–414.

Citrin, J., D. Green, C. Muste, and C. Wong. 1997. "Public Opinion toward Immigration Reform: The Role of Economic Motivation." *Journal of Politics* 59, no. 3: 858–881.

Cummings, R. G., S. Elliott, G. W. Harrison, and J. Murphy. 1997. "Are Hypothetical Referenda Incentive Compatible?" *Journal of Political Economy* 105, no. 3: 609–621.

Cummings, R. G., G. W. Harrison, and E. E. Rutström. 1995. "Homegrown Values and Hypothetical Surveys: Is the Dichotomous Choice Approach Incentive Compatible?" *American Economic Review* 85, no. 1: 260–266.

de Melo, J., F. Miguet, and T. Müller. 2002. "The Political Economy of Migration and EU Enlargement: Lessons from Switzerland." Discussion paper no. 3449, Centre for Economic Policy Research, London.

Djajic, S. 1997. "Illegal Immigration and Resource Allocation." *International Economic Review* 38, no. 1: 97–117.

Dustmann, C., and I. Preston. 2000. "Racial and Economic Factors in Attitudes to Immigration." Working paper no. 2542, Centre for Economic Policy Research, London.

Epstein, G., and A. Hillman. 2000. "Social Harmony at the Boundaries of the Welfare State: Immigrants and Social Transfers." Discussion paper no. 2414, Center for Economic Policy Research.

Espenshade, T., and K. Hempstead. 1996. "Contemporary American Attitudes toward U.S. Immigration." *International Migration Review* 30, no. 2: 535–570.

European Commission. 1997. "Racism and Xenophobia in Europe." Eurobarometer Opinion Poll no. 47.1, Brussels.

European Commission. 2000. "Eurobarometer: Public Opinion in the European Union." Report no. 53, Brussels.

European Commission. 2001. "The Free Movement of Workers in the Context of Enlargement." Information note. Brussels. Directorate General-V.

Faini, R., J. de Melo, and K. Zimmerman, eds. 1999. *Migration: The Controversies and the Evidence*. Cambridge, UK: Cambridge University Press.

Fertig, M., and C. Schmidt. 2001. First- and Second-Generation Migrants in Germany—What Do We Know and What People Think." Discussion paper no. 286, Institute for the Study of Labor, Bonn.

Flückiger, Y., and J. Ramirez. 2001. "Positions hiérarchiques et ségrégation par origine en Suisse." In *La migration et la Suisse: Résultats du programme national "Migrations et relations interculturelles,"* ed. H.-R. Wicker, R. Fibbi, and W. Haug, 275–301. Zurich: Seismo.

Grether, J.-M., J. de Melo, and T. Müller. 2001. "The Political Economy of International Migration in a Ricardo-Viner Model." In *International Migration: Trends, Policies and Economic Impact*, ed. S. Djajic, 42–68. London: Routledge.

Hillman, A., and A. Weiss. 1999a. "Beyond International Factor Movements: Cultural Preferences, Endogenous Policies and the Migration of People: An Overview." In *Migration: The Controversies and the Evidence*, ed. R. Faini, J. de Melo, and K. Zimmerman, 76–91. Cambridge, UK: Cambridge University Press.

Hillman, A., and A. Weiss. 1999b. "A Theory of Permissible Immigration." *European Journal of Political Economy* 15: 585–604.

Krishnakumar, J., and T. Müller. 2003. "Participation and Voting Behavior in a Direct Democracy: The Case of Migration Policy in Switzerland." Forthcoming.

Mayer, W. 1984. "Endogenous Tariff Formation." *American Economic Review* 74, no. 5: 970–985.

Mueller, D. C. 1989. *Public Choice II*. Cambridge: Cambridge University Press.

Müller, T. 2003a. "Migration Policy in a Small Open Economy with a Dual Labor Market." *Review of International Economics* 11, no. 1: 130–143.

Müller, T. 2003b. "Migration, Unemployment and Discrimination." *European Economic Review* 47, no. 3: 409–427.

OECD. 2000a. "Trends in International Migration." Système d'Observation Permanente des Migrations (SOPEMI) report, Paris.

OECD. 2000b. "Main Economic Indicators." Paris.

Piguet, E., and H. Mahnig. 2000. "Quotas d'immigration: L'expérience de la Suisse." Cahiers de migration internationale no. 37, International Labor Office Geneva.

Scheve, K., and M. Slaughter. 1999. "Labor-Market Competition and Individual Preferences over Immigration Policy." Working paper no. 6946, National Bureau of Economic Research, Cambridge, MA.

Schiff, M. 1998. "Trade, Migration, and Welfare: The Impact of Social Capital." Policy Research working paper no. 2044, World Bank, Washington, DC.

Schiff, M. 1999. "Labor Market Integration in the Presence of Social Capital." Policy Research working paper no. 2222, World Bank, Washington, DC.

SIDOS. 2000. "Eurobarometer for Switzerland." Swiss information and data archive service for the social sciences, Neuchâtel.

Shapiro, C., and J. Stiglitz. 1984. "Equilibrium Unemployment as a Worker-Discipline Device." *American Economic Review* 74: 433–444.

Sinn, H.-W. 2000. "EU Enlargement and the Welfare State." Working paper no. 307, CESifo, Munich.

Sinn, H.-W., G. Flaig, M. Werding, S. Munz, N. Düll, H. Hofmann, A. Hänlein, J. Kruse, H. J. Reinhard, and B. Schulte. 2001. "EU-Erweiterung und Arbeitskräftemigration: Wege zu einer schrittweisen Annäherung der Arbeitsmärkte." Ifo Beiträge zur Wirtschaftsforschung no. 2, München.

van de Ven, W. P. M. M., and B. M. S. van Praag. 1981. "The Demand for Deductibles in Private Health Insurance: A Probit Model with Sample Selection." *Journal of Econometrics* 17: 229–252.

Part IV

Challenges Ahead — An Inclusive Globalization and Environmental Policies

The Journal of International Trade & Economic Development
Vol. 17, No. 3, September 2008, 343–378

Openness, inequality and poverty: Endowments matter

Julien Gourdon[a], Nicolas Maystre[b] and Jaime de Melo[c]*

[a]*World Bank, Washington, USA, and CERDI, Clermont-Ferrand, France;* [b]*University of Geneva, Switzerland;* [c]*University of Geneva, Switzerland, CERDI, Clermont-Ferrand, France, and CEPR, London, UK*

(*Received August 2007; final version received December 2007*)

Using tariffs as a measure of openness, this paper finds consistent evidence that the conditional effects of trade liberalization on inequality are correlated with relative factor endowments. Trade liberalization, measured by changes in tariff revenues, is associated with increases in inequality in countries well-endowed with highly skilled workers and capital or with workers that have very low education levels. Similar, although less robust, results are also obtained when decile data are used instead of the usual Gini coefficients. Taken together, the results are strongly supportive of the factor-proportions theory of trade and suggest that trade liberalization in poor countries where the share of the labor force with little education is high raises inequality. Simulation results also suggest that relatively small changes in inequality as measured by aggregate measures of inequality, like the Gini coefficient, are magnified when estimates are carried out using decile data.

Keywords: international trade; income distribution; poverty

JEL Classification: F11, F16, D3

Introduction

The relation between openness, inequality and poverty within countries continues to be subject to considerable controversy in the debate about globalization and in the academic literature where the relative importance of the different transmission channels linking openness to inequality and poverty remains elusive. First, detailed case studies decomposing the sources of the evolution of income inequality within countries reveal very different patterns across countries. As for trade liberalization and openness – usually understood to mean the ease with which goods and services, factors of production (e.g. capital, labor and skills) move across countries as transaction costs fall – they are often used interchangeably and proxied by a trade-to-GDP ratio that captures many other features of a country's

*Corresponding author. Email: demelo@ecopo.unige.ch

ISSN 0963-8199 print/ISSN 1469-9559 online

DOI: 10.1080/09638190802136978
http://www.informaworld.com

exposure to trade beyond trade liberalization. Second, whether from specific trade liberalization episodes or from cross-country studies, the evidence on the relation between trade liberalization and inequality is conflicting (see for example, Bourguignon et al. 2005, Table 10.1). Third, in most cross-country studies, identification comes from cross-country variability in the inequality measure rather than within-country variability and no attempt is made to control for the source of the data on inequality.

If one were asked to point towards an emerging consensus, it would probably be that increasing openness has been reflected in a growing wage gap between skilled and unskilled wages. Moving to the association between openness and overall inequality (usually measured by the Gini coefficient) the evidence remains very mixed: many studies find no evidence of openness on inequality (Edwards 1997; Ravallion 2001; Dollar and Kraay 2002) or that openness increases (reduces) inequality at low (high) levels of development (Barro 2000; Milanovic 2005a). The literature is also characterized by a lack of robustness towards expectations from a trade liberalization on inequality derived from the standard factor-endowment-based trade model (Heckscher–Ohlin – HO for short). The literature has produced conflicting evidence that greater openness – usually measured by trade-to-GDP ratios – reduces (increases) inequality in developing (developed) countries. The literature also has produced muted support for the hypothesis that endowments matter along the expected lines, i.e. that countries relatively well-endowed with factors like natural resources that are unequally distributed, have greater income inequality. This lack of correlation between factor endowments and inequality should also come as a surprise to scholars working on the institutional foundations of development who generally find strong evidence that endowments matter in the evolution of a country's inequality (Hoff 2003). Finally, there is little support that trade liberalization reduces income inequality in countries that are relatively well-endowed in unskilled labor.[1]

In contrast to this agnosticism, following an exhaustive review of the evidence on trade liberalization and poverty, Winters et al. (2004) conclude that trade liberalization might be the easiest poverty-alleviating reform to accomplish, and the most powerful direct mechanism to alleviate poverty in a country. If so, knowing more about the links between trade policy and inequality is important since, from a political-economy perspective, knowledge about the links between openness and inequality will inform about the feasibility of policies that increase openness and are likely to reduce poverty.

We bring new evidence on this issue using two data sets covering a larger sample of developing countries than previous studies. First, we introduce fixed-effects in our panel estimation so that, even though the same functional form is imposed across countries, identification of the effects of changes in trade policy, and more indirectly of globalization, are confined to variations in that country's variables. We also broaden the range of control variables to address omitted variable bias. Second, unlike most previous studies, we find that endowments matter along the lines suggested by factor-endowment theory arguments reviewed in the following section. We find consistently that trade liberalization is associated with increases in inequality in countries that are relatively well-endowed with capital and with highly skilled workers, while it is associated with decreases in inequality in countries relatively well-endowed with primary educated (unskilled) workers and in arable land. On the other hand, as suggested by Wood (1994, 2002), we find that trade liberalization is associated with increases in inequality in countries relatively well-endowed with workers lacking basic education. We also show that it is important to control for the source of inequality data when investigating the correlates of inequality, and we provide suggestive simulations of the effects of trade liberalization on poverty.

The paper is organized as follows. The next section presents the framework and the data. Using data over the period 1980–2000, the second section establishes that the correlation between trade liberalization and inequality follows patterns predicted by factor-proportions theories. These results are largely confirmed with a data set based on deciles covering the period 1988–98 in the third section. The last section then concludes.

Framework and data

Framework

Take the standard factor-endowment model where a diversified price-taking economy operates under perfect competition. If the Heckscher–Ohlin–Vanek conditions are met (homothetic preferences, equal number of goods and factors of production), a change in trade policy under fixed factor supplies will raise the rewards of the relatively well-endowed factor.[2] To illustrate, in a two-factor-endowment world, with high-skilled (H) and low-skilled (L) workers (E_H,E_L; $w_H > w_L$; $INQ \equiv w_H/w_L$) and define the relative endowment of country i as $RE^i_j \equiv E^i_j/E^w_j$, where E^w_j is the world (sample) endowment of j. Then factor endowment theory suggests that a reduction in tariffs by country i will increase (decrease) inequality if it is relatively well endowed in E_H (E_L). Translated into an empirical setting where inequality is measured in terms of income, estimations inspired from factor endowment theory would suggest the following:

$$\Delta INQ_{it} = \alpha_0 \Delta Z_{it} + \alpha_1 \left(RE^{it}_H - RE^{it}_L\right) \Delta OPEN_{it} + \varepsilon_{it} \qquad (1)$$

where $OPEN_{it}$ is a measure of openness and Z_{it} a vector of control variables. In fact, most previous studies have estimated a relation in cross-section making it more difficult to isolate the effects of a change in openness on inequality.

To investigate the role of factors endowments on the effects of trade liberalization on inequality in a heterogeneous sample of countries, at least three issues must be tackled. First, the relation should be investigated within countries. Second, a plausible measure of changes in openness should be used. Finally, the list of factor endowments to be included should be informed by the characteristics of the sample.

As in earlier work, we use a panel data set, imposing the same functional form across countries, but include fixed effects for time and countries, which has typically not be done in most previous studies. For example, in their widely-cited study examined below, Spilimbergo et al. (1999) do not control for country-specific features that could account for differences in inequality such as labor market specificities emphasized by Rama (2002), productivity differences (see Easterly 2004) or institutions (Barro 2000). Nor do more recent studies (e.g. Milanovic 2005a) typically use such controls for heterogeneity.[3] Insofar as omitted factors do not change over time, the inclusion of fixed effects controls for such idiosyncratic factors. Since our data set covers a rather long period, and inevitably some of the relevant omitted variables will change over time, this needs to be kept in mind when interpreting results. Likewise, the validity of the results rests on the assumption that the data reflect a sufficiently stable relationship (this is why we exclude all transition economies from our samples) and that the same dynamics can be imposed on all countries, an assumption that is less likely to hold, but about which little can be done.

As discussed below, we use changes in tariffs as our measure of openness, a measure that captures directly the effects of trade policy and is reasonably well correlated with other proxies of openness.

Up to six endowment measures are included. Since the formulation measures endowment changes, unless these capture natural resources that can be considered in fixed supply, interpretation of the corresponding reduced form coefficients must recognize that it is unclear if the observed changes reflect a shift in supply or in demand, making it difficult to interpret the associated coefficient.

Wood (2002) provides a convenient summary of the different channels via which globalization might affect wage inequality. These channels help in the selection of factor endowments. Wood notes that as all forms of transaction costs fall with globalization, factor mobility (capital via FDI and Northern skilled K-workers in the terminology of Wood) is enhanced, leading to greater cooperation of Northern K-workers who travel to work with skilled workers in the South. In the South, workers with little or no-education (and hence low wages) would then be expected to be confined to non-traded activities.

In this set-up, trade liberalization would then not only lead to rising wages for skilled workers in the North and in the South, but under plausible assumptions, it would also lead to an increase in wage inequality in the South. In a two-sector model (tradables and non-tradables) with capital and two categories of workers (skilled and unskilled), in which the three household categories are not diversified in their factor-ownership holdings and the unskilled are confined to the non-tradable sector, Bensidoun et al. (2005) show formally that an increase in the wage of skilled labor (brought about by increased openness) will increase the value of the Gini index if the share of unskilled labor is large enough. Thus, we introduce three categories of labor, one of which has no-education. We provide evidence in support of this hypothesis.

To reflect the fact that many developing countries are well-endowed in natural resources and that, unlike human capital, these can be accumulated practically without limit by the few, in addition to capital which can also be accumulated by a minority, we include two natural resources: arable land, and mining and fuel. Trade liberalization would then increase the rents to owners of these resources. Insofar as these resources are distributed unequally, increasing openness in natural resource rich countries would increase income inequality (Bourguignon and Morrisson 1990; Fisher 2001; Leamer et al. 1999). Finally, we add endowment in physical capital. Since physical capital is also likely to be concentrated in the hands of few people because there is no natural upward limit to their accumulation, we expect that increasing openness in capital abundant countries would increase income inequality.

Sample and data

We use two data sets to measure inequality. Both data sets and how we constructed our measures of inequality and endowments are described in Appendix 2. Inequality is based on five-year average data spanning the 1980–2000 period. The measure of inequality is drawn from the extensively used Deininger and Squire (1996) data set (augmented to include the period 1995–2000 by the availability of the UNU-WIDER 2005 data). The second data set is a more recent 'high-quality' data set, World Income Distribution (WYD) available at approximately five-year intervals. It covers the period 1988–1998. Having two data sets is helpful for robustness checks. Furthermore, the WYD data set contains highly disaggregated data, which we use to quantify effects of trade liberalization on poverty.

The main weakness in the data set is the absence of a measure of financial openness. Miniane (2004) provides a summary of available indices of financial market integration. It turns out that even for the WYD data set, which only covers the 1988–98 period, about 2/3 of the countries in our data set would not have a measure of financial market integration. We have therefore decided not to tackle the issue of financial market integration (using FDI – as in, for example, Milanovic 2005 – would not be appropriate since it is largely an outcome variable).

Table 1 shows that our sample has a good representation across regions and that the developing countries are adequately represented. As a

Table 1. Countries in the sample.[a]

	Sample for the study in 1980–2000		Sample for the study in 1988–1998	
Regions	Number of countries	Number of obs.	Number of countries	Number of obs.
Developed	20	66	19	51
Africa and Middle East	14	42	10	23
Asia	10	36	11	29
Latin American	17	54	15	43
Total	61	198	55	146

Notes: List of countries is reported in Appendix 1.
[a]Transition and ex-USSR countries are excluded. Countries with less than two observations are also dropped from the sample.

reference, the often-cited study by Spilimbergo et al. (1999) had 17 developed and 17 developing countries in their sample.

Regarding the variable used to capture a country's outward-orientation, we use lagged tariffs i.e. $TAR_{i,t-5}$, (computed as the ratio of tariff revenues to imports) as a measure of trade openness. This is a more direct measure of openness than those often used previously (i.e. a trade output ratio, a 'trade adjusted ratio' obtained as a residual from an estimated relation of openness, or the Sachs and Warner 1995, index). As a consequence, our sample does not include the 1960–80 period covered in some of the earlier studies. Since most trade liberalization in developing countries started in the early 1980s, this may not be too damaging.

Figure 1 describes the main characteristics of the data at the regional level. The relative patterns of inequality remain unchanged across regional groupings, being the highest in Latin America and SSA throughout. Within regions, tariff dispersion fell and, except for the Middle East and North Africa (MENA) region, average tariffs declined during the sample period.

Table 2 gives regional averages for the two main variables of interest, the inequality measure and our measure of openness, tariffs computed from customs data (see Appendices 1 and 2). There is little variation in the average measure of inequality within regions and persistent differences across regions while the measure of protection indicates (on average) a downward trend in all regions except Africa. Since much of the trade reforms in the 1980s often consisted of replacing NTBs with tariffs, what appears as an increase in protection could in fact represent either a reduction, or no increase in protection. In selecting tariffs as our measure of openness, we take refuge in the often-made observation that the average tariff level is an adequate approximation of the restrictiveness of a country's trade regime, and arguably less controversial than other measures often used, which in any event, are not available (e.g. measures of NTBs).

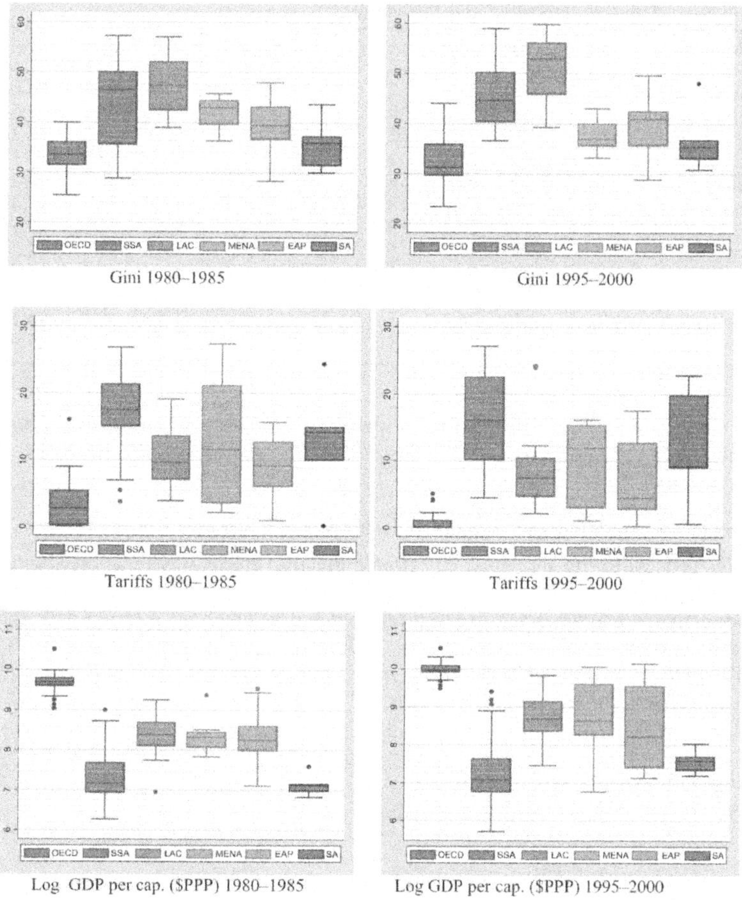

Figure 1. Box plots on Gini, tariffs and GDP per capita ($PPP) 1980–85 and 1995–2000.

However, as discussed in Appendix 2 and as shown in Tables A4a and A4b, the tariff measure is sufficiently correlated with other popular measures of trade restrictiveness that our results are only moderately sensitive to the choice of protection measure (see the discussion below on robustness in Section 3). As shown in Appendix 2, the correlation with the carefully constructed Wacziarg and Welch (2003) index is quite strong ($\rho = -0.56$). In the end, the strongest justification for using tariffs, besides the fact that it

Table 2. Data on inequality and openness.

Region	Year	Gini	Tariffs	Region	Year	Gini	Tariffs
Developed countries	1980	33.4	2.9	Latin America	1980	47.6	10.6
	1985	31.8	2.1		1985	48.1	13.6
	1990	33.1	1.7		1990	47.3	10.2
	1995	32.7	1		1995	49.8	7.1
East Asia	1980	40.9	6.7	Middle East	1980	42	19.8
	1985	40.7	8.1		1985	38.7	17.4
	1990	39.3	8.7		1990	38	19.1
	1995	39.2	6.4		1995	37.7	12.2
South Asia	1980	35.7	19.1	Africa	1980	44.6	16.7
	1985	35.9	27.1		1985	46.7	18.2
	1990	36.2	25.3		1990	50.5	18.1
	1995	37.8	15.2		1995	46.3	17.9

is a policy-based indicator, is their widespread availability and the likelihood that error measurements will be less than with other proposed measures.

Trade liberalization and inequality: endowments matter

We start exploring the basic HO prediction that trade liberalization should reduce inequality in low-income countries and increase it in high income countries. Next, we bring in factor endowments, which we interact with the tariff variable to isolate the effects of differing endowments on inequality. Throughout this section, the data cover the period 1980–2000 and the Gini coefficient is the inequality measure.

Openness, income and inequality

We start with the traditional specification:

$$INQ_{it} = D_i + YR_t + \alpha_1 \overline{Y}_{it} + \beta_1 TAR_{i,t-5} + \beta_2 (TAR_{i,t-5}{}^* \overline{Y}_{it}) + \sum_l \delta_l Z_{it} + \sum_{k=1,3} \gamma_k DS_{ikt} + e_{it}, \quad i = 1, \ldots, 76, t = 1, \ldots, 4 \quad (2)$$

In equation (2), the index of inequality is regressed on a set of country dummies (D_i) and year dummies (YR_t) to control for any common period shocks, on income per capita measured in PPP ($\bar{Y}_{it}$), on tariffs ($TAR_{i,t-5}$), lagged one-period to control for endogeneity and for the time it takes for tariffs to have an impact on inequality, on dummy variables (DS_{ikt}) to control for the source of inequality data (dummy variables for gross versus net income, income versus expenditure, and households versus individuals), and on a set of control variables (Z_{it}). Since our focus will be on endowments – which are all strongly correlated with income – in this first set of results we have not attempted to control for the endogeneity of income when estimating equation (2). All continuous variables are expressed in logarithms and all data are five year averages (this helps to control for autocorrelation and measurement error), giving us up to four observations across time.

The use of country fixed-effects reduces considerably the variance in inequality to be explained so that measurement errors are exacerbated even though taking five year averages should attenuate this problem (see Pritchett 2000). Having more data points within countries, as in for example Galiani and Porto (2006) who study the trade-liberalization wage-inequality relation in Argentina over 30 years, would clearly be a superior identification strategy, but such an option is not yet in the cards. Should an increase in openness (here lower values for TAR_{it-5}) raise inequality, it would be reflected in $\hat{\beta}_1 < 0$, while the relationship expected from a 'basic' factor-endowment (or HO) interpretation (with capital and labor as the sole endowments) would call for $\hat{\beta}_1 > 0, \hat{\beta}_2 < 0$ since lowering tariffs in high-income countries would be expected to increase inequality with a turning point at $\bar{Y} = -\frac{\beta_1}{\beta_2}$.

Estimates in Table 3 column 1, with no fixed effects, correspond to those usually found in the literature (e.g. Barro 2000; Ravallion 2001; Rama 2002). Under this specification, trade liberalization raises inequality in poor countries, but reduces it in rich countries (i.e. with income per capita higher than \$4722 PPP in column 1), in contradiction with HO expectations. The estimates also indicate less inequality in low inflation countries and in countries with a higher share of population between 40 and 59 years old (*Mature*), as in Higgins and Williamson (2002). The sign and coefficient estimates in column 1 are robust to the inclusion of year dummies (results not reported) which are included in the other estimates.

Adding dummy variables for the source of income inequality data in column 2 improves considerably the fit while increasing the significance of the coefficients discussed above. In particular, the results contrary to HO predictions continue to hold at a higher (now 5%) level of significance (the turning point is now \$3369). The coefficients of the dummies that control for the source of data on income inequality have the expected signs: Gini coefficients based on income or households are higher than those based on expenditure or individuals. Our first finding is that all studies should control for the source of income inequality data (a point already made by Ravallion 2001; Bensidoun et al. 2005). Since coefficient values on these dummies are always significant under our preferred estimation with FE (see below) and similar to those reported here in Tables 4 and 6, we do not comment further on this result.

Column 3 introduces fixed-effects (FE) into the estimation. Now, the sign of the coefficients for $(\hat{\beta}_1, \hat{\beta}_2)$ are reversed and are coherent with factor

Table 3. Inequality, income and openness.

Dependent variable	ln gini	ln gini	ln gini	ln gini
GDPpc	−0.05	−0.06c	0.04	0.02
	(1.10)	(1.86)	(0.46) – [0.60]	[0.40]
Tar_{t-5}	−4.23c	−3.98b	2.96	3.27c
	(1.91)	(2.05)	(1.25) – [1.47]	[1.69]
TAR_{t-5} × GDPpc	0.50c	0.49b	−0.34	−0.37
	(1.90)	(2.15)	(1.20) – [1.40]	[1.61]
Education	0.05	0.00	−0.05	
	(0.77)	(0.06)	(0.56) – [0.73]	
Mature	−0.45a	−0.44a	−0.09	
	(5.25)	(5.57)	(0.55) – [0.71]	
Ethnicity	0.02	0.02b		
	(1.43)	(2.07)		
Civil liberties	0.07	0.09b	0.02	
	(1.40)	(2.32)	(0.40) – [0.50]	
Inflation	0.06b	0.07a	0.02	0.02c
	(1.91)	(3.56)	(1.46) – [1.95]	[1.91]
Gross/net income		−0.01	−0.02	−0.02
		(0.37)	(0.85) – [1.15]	[1.23]
Income/expenditure		0.24a	0.15a	0.15a
		(6.44)	(3.20) – [4.91]	[4.89]
Households/individual		−0.00	0.06b	0.06a
		(0.02)	(2.36) – [3.46]	[3.43]
Constant	5.22a	5.03a	3.40a	3.36a
	(16.87)	(18.30)	(5.73) – [6.99]	[8.15]
Country fixed effects	No	No	Yes	Yes
Year effect	No	Yes	Yes	Yes
Observations	217	217	217	217
R-squared	0.44	0.60	0.91	0.90
No. of countries	66	66	66	66

Notes:
Absolute value of z statistics in parentheses (based on robust Huber–White standard errors) and in brackets (based on Beck and Katz (1995) Panel-corrected standard errors (PCSE)).
c: Significant at 10%; b: significant at 5%; a: significant at 1%.

endowments even though the coefficients are not significant at the 10% confidence interval with the standard heteroskedasticity-corrected (White) coefficients. Significance is slightly improved when we report Beck and Katz (1995) panel-corrected standard errors (PCSE), in brackets in column 3, and borderline significance is reached in column 4 when insignificant variables are excluded.[4] Our second conclusion is that results from studies that do not control for effects of omitted variables via FE are biased and that proxies for factor endowments effects behave according to expectations.

This reversal between OLS and OLS-within estimates can be understood from the data patterns in Figure 1. Since the richest countries (OECD) have the smallest tariffs and the lowest level of inequality through time, while SSA

Table 4. Inequality, factor endowments and openness.

Dependent variable	ln gini	ln gini	ln gini	ln gini	ln gini
GDP per capita	0.0345	0.0003	−0.0176	0.0464	0.0372
	(0.49)	(0.00)	(0.23)	(0.68)	(0.54)
MinFuel per Labor (MF/L)					0.1146b
					(2.20)
Arable Land per Labor (AT/L)	0.2590	0.1721	0.1796	−0.0295	−0.0802
	(1.56)	(1.01)	(1.06)	(0.22)	(0.59)
Capital per Labor (K/L)	−0.0318	−0.0328	−0.0621	−0.0320	−0.0235
	(0.49)	(0.50)	(0.92)	(0.49)	(0.36)
NoEd. per Labor (NO/L)	0.1239a				
	(3.28)				
BasEd. per Labor (BS/L)		0.0555			
		(1.04)			
SkillEd. per Labor (SK/L)			0.1190a		
			(3.94)		
SK/BS				0.0730b	0.0603c
				(2.12)	(1.73)
NO/(SK + BS)				0.1221a	0.1413a
				(3.47)	(3.80)
TAR_{t-5}	−0.2691	−0.2070	0.1491	−0.5080	−0.6347
	(0.57)	(0.43)	(0.35)	(1.22)	(1.55)
(MF/L) × (TAR_{t-5})					−0.0456
					(0.31)
(AT/L) × (TAR_{t-5})	0.0110	0.1088	−0.3616	0.2491	0.4535
	(0.02)	(0.21)	(0.81)	(0.55)	(0.94)
(K/L) × (TAR_{t-5})	−0.4953a	−0.2780	0.3229	−0.5188a	−0.5946a
	(2.74)	(1.57)	(1.52)	(2.63)	(2.99)

(continued)

Table 4. (*Continued*).

Dependent variable	ln gini	ln gini	ln gini	ln gini	ln gini
(NO/L) × (TAR_{t-5})	−1.4136a (2.83)				
(BS/L) × (TAR_{t-5})		0.1286 (0.31)			
(SK/L) × (TAR_{t-5})			−0.7412a (3.20)		
(SK/BS) × (TAR_{t-5})				−0.7341a (2.80)	−0.6630b (2.52)
(NO/(SK + BS)) × (TAR_{t-5})				−0.9660a (3.30)	−1.0853a (3.69)
Inflation	0.0349a (2.58)	0.0352b (2.56)	0.0291b (2.36)	0.0193 (1.44)	0.0187 (1.44)
Gross/net income	−0.0144 (0.79)	−0.0147 (0.81)	−0.0051 (0.28)	−0.0161 (0.90)	−0.0173 (1.00)
Income/expenditure	0.1507a (5.36)	0.1432a (5.16)	0.1362a (4.86)	0.1080a (3.78)	0.1098a (3.87)
Households/individual	0.0567a (2.96)	0.0630a (3.30)	0.0581a (3.08)	0.0663a (3.54)	0.0633a (3.44)
Country fixed effects	Yes	Yes	Yes	Yes	Yes
Year effect	Yes	Yes	Yes	Yes	Yes
Observations	210	210	210	202	202
# Countries	64	64	64	61	61

Notes:
Absolute value of z statistics in parentheses (based on Beck and Katz's PCSE).
c: Significant at 10%; b: significant at 5%; a: significant at 1%.

Table 5. Tariff reduction, inequality and factor endowments.

Variable	Percentile	5 percentage points tariff reduction*
(K/L)	0.25	0.4
	0.75	6.0
(SK/BS)	0.25	1.1
	0.75	4.7
(NO/(SK + BS))	0.25	−0.4
	0.75	5.4

*Percentage change in Gini coefficient.

countries have the lowest income par capita, the highest tariffs and the highest level of inequality, a level estimation will show that countries with low tariffs and high income per capita will have the lowest income inequality. However, such a relationship does not account for the impact of trade liberalization on inequality, which can only be captured in a within estimation.

Changes in inequality could be due to the effects of other ongoing reforms such as concurrent stabilization policies. For example, Wacziarg and Welch (2003) show that trade liberalization often occurs during periods of systemic reforms, including macro stabilization. Stabilization – here proxied by a reduction in inflation – is associated with a reduction in inequality (as in, for example, Dollar and Kraay 2002; Edwards 1997). However, including this control does not alter the relationship.

Trade liberalization, endowments and inequality

We now introduce relative endowments directly (rather than using income per capita as a proxy) interacting them with the openness measure as in previous studies (e.g. Bourguignon and Morrisson 1990; Spilimbergo et al. 1999; Fisher 2001). This allows us to test whether the conditional correlation of protection on inequality is sensitive to factor endowments. Results are reported in Table 4.

$$INQ_{it} = D_i + YR_t + \beta_1 TAR_{it-5} + \sum_{m=1,6} \phi_{1m} RE_{imt} + \sum_{m=1,6} \phi_{2m}(TAR_{it-5} * RE_{imt}) + \sum_{l} \delta_l Z_{it} + \sum_{k=1,3} \gamma_k DS_{ikt} + e_{it} \quad (3)$$

As suggested by factor-endowment-based theories, relative endowment ratios (RE_{imt}) are computed relative to the corresponding sample mean per worker endowment. The ratios are weighted by the trade share in GDP to account for the endowments of closed countries that do not compete in the world markets with other factors (to help comparisons, we use the formula in Spilimbergo et al. (1999) described in Appendix 2).

With the inclusion of fixed effects, control variables (Z_{it}) that vary little over time lost significance, so we start by including only inflation, GDP per capita (to keep results comparable with those in Table 3 and later on in Table 6) and the dummies for the source of inequality data. Because it is highly correlated with the endowment variables, per capita income is insignificant. However, the other controls keep the same signs and significance levels as in columns 4 and 5 of Table 3. Here, with factor endowments entering directly in the specification, we are particularly interested in the values of the interaction coefficients, ϕ_{2m}. A negative (positive) sign for these coefficients implies that a given trade liberalization increases (reduces) inequality more in countries relatively well-endowed in the corresponding factor.[5]

We include six endowments. Labor is broken down into three categories along the lines suggested by the discussion in the Framework and data section, and indicated in equation (3): non-educated labor, i.e. those who have never been to school or have not completed primary school (NO); primary-educated or labor with a basic education (BS); and those that have an education level beyond high-school (SK). Such a breakdown was carried out recently by Bensidoun et al. (2005) in a slightly different context.[6,7]

As to remaining endowments, Wood (2003) argues that arable land per worker (AT/L), as used by Spilimbergo et al. (1999), Fisher (2001) or Leamer et al. (1999) is not sufficient to encompass natural resources. He suggests the use of land per worker (T/L) since arable land per worker captures factor intensities in the production of food and raw materials but does not include mining and fuels, which are the less equally-distributed resources. This may explain why several studies find that a strong endowment in arable land is associated with decreases in inequality during trade liberalization (Spilimbergo et al. 1999). Thus, we use a direct measure of endowments in mining and fuels (MF/L), captured by production in minerals, fuels and coal, next to the measure of arable land. The capital per worker ratio (K/L) constitutes our sixth endowment.

Start with factor endowments. The coefficients on the factor endowment changes generally conform to a priori expectations. Along the lines suggested by the framework in Section 2.1, columns 1 and 3 show that inequality rises as the share of the non-educated (NO/L) and the share of skilled (SK/L) increases. As for the middle factor, labor with basic skills (BS/L), the coefficient in column 2 is insignificant. The capital-labor (K/L) coefficient is always insignificant. As for natural resources, an increase in mining and fuel (MF/L) is associated with an increase in inequality as predicted by theory and already observed in several previous studies (see column 5). The coefficient on arable land (AT/L) is insignificant.

Turning to the correlates of trade liberalization, the first three columns of Table 4 test the significance of endowments relative to labor. Column 1 confirms the expectation that trade liberalization in countries with relatively high endowments in K/L and NO/L is associated with a greater increase in inequality (negative coefficients for both interaction terms with lagged tariffs). Column 2 results also conform to factor endowment predictions since the coefficient on BS/L interacted with lagged tariffs is positive, but non-significant and the K/L interaction term loses significance. The same expected pattern also holds in column 3 with SK/L.[8] The result that trade liberalization is associated with greater increases in inequality in countries abundant in highly-educated labor is consonant with HO predictions.

To avoid perfect multicollinearity, column 4 controls for the skill composition of the labor force by including the three levels of education in two ratios: SK/BS and NO/(SK + BS). As expected, during a trade liberalization, countries with a relatively (to the sample average) strong endowment in SK/BS experience a greater increase in inequality and countries relatively well endowed in labor with no qualification (i.e. with high values of NO/(SK + BS) experience an increase in inequality during a trade liberalization. Finally, column 5 shows that the proxy for mineral resources is associated with increases in inequality (as is a relatively strong endowment in SK/BS and in NO/(SK + BS)).

We carried out several robustness checks. First, adding several macro-economic (inflation, investment, government expenditures, infrastructure stock, infrastructure quality and financial depth) and institutional variables (civil liberties) largely preserves those results (and the included macroeconomic variables often have the predicted signs, sometimes at statistically significant levels, as shown in Appendix 3, Table A5). For example, an improvement in infrastructure (column 4) or an increase in government expenditure (column 3) is associated with decreases in inequality whereas an increase in investment (column 1) is associated with increases in inequality. Second, similar results are obtained when we apply our preferred specification to quintile data from the UNU-WIDER (2005) database, even though the sample is smaller (45 countries instead of 61 because for some countries in the UNU-WIDER dataset estimates of quintile shares are not available, despite the availability of Gini coefficient estimates (Appendix 3, Table A6)). Third, in the absence of plausible instruments for tariffs that might be endogenous, we test for reverse causality by regressing inequality on future rather than past tariffs. The coefficients of interest become mostly insignificant, suggesting that reverse causality is not a problem. Fourth, the results are also robust to the exclusion of a small number of observations signaled as outliers by a test on residuals. The pattern of signs is also broadly similar when we exclude one region at a time (Appendix 3, Table A7). Finally, we replaced tariffs with alternative indices of trade liberalization (Appendix 3, Table A8). The signs (and often the significance) of our interaction terms are robust to the use of various trade ratios (see columns 2, 3 and 4). However, when we use the openness measures of Hiscox and Kastner (2002), Spilimbergo et al. (1999) and Pritchett (1996), respectively (see columns 5, 6 and 7), few coefficients of the interaction terms remain significant, although the signs remain the same (except in four cases). Overall, the results are moderately robust to alternative openness measures.

In sum, even though the results are sensitive to the choice of openness measure, overall they strongly suggest that endowments matter, both independently and interactively with tariffs justifying estimates of orders of magnitude of tariff changes on inequality.

Table 5 quantifies the effects of a five percentage point reduction in tariffs on Gini coefficient value for different quartiles of the distribution of endowments (the five percentage point reduction corresponds to the average observed reduction during the period for developing countries). Simulations are based on the last column of Table 4. As an example, this tariff reduction increases the value of the Gini coefficient by 0.4% for countries in the bottom quartile of the distribution of (K/L), while it increases inequality by 6.0% for those in the top quartile. A similar pattern holds for SK/BS, with the strongest effect for the ratio NO/(SK + BS). Since countries with a high share of non-educated population are also likely to be poorly endowed in capital, the two effects almost cancel each other.

Openness, inequality and poverty: further results

Arguably, in spite of controls for the type of survey, the data set used so far is of lesser quality than the more recent World Income Distribution (WYD)[9] data set that is drawn almost entirely from household surveys. As noted by Milanovic (2005b), surveys are appropriate to define welfare aggregates and to treat recipient units consistently across countries and time. The WYD data set, which also provides information on income levels by deciles, presents two advantages. First, it allows us to check for the robustness of our results in general, and also to avoid restricting our analysis to a specific inequality index, since we can work directly with decile data. Second, it is more appropriate to carry out estimates of the effects of trade liberalization on inequality and especially on poverty, both because the quality of the data is presumably higher, but also because the calculations can also be carried out directly from the household sample mean income per capita, $\bar{m}_{it}$, rather than from GDP per capita from national accounts.

Indeed, it has been argued that income measures from household survey data that is representative of the entire economy is a more reliable estimate of GDP than the corresponding measures from the national accounts. In particular, even though survey-based estimates of income have their own problems, Deaton (2005, 18) argues that: 'If we need to measure poverty in a way that will convince those who are skeptical of the idea that average growth reaches the poor, there is little choice but to use the surveys.' In our sample the correlation between annual income growth over 1988 and 1998 measured from the surveys, g_H, and its equivalent from national income, g_{PPP}, is surprisingly low ($\rho = 0.2917$). Moreover, regressing g_H on g_{PPP} gives (standard errors in parenthesis): $g_H = 0.029 + \underset{(0.357)}{0.706}\, g_{PPP}$; $R^2 = 0.0851$.

Following the approach and specification in equation (3), we regress the share of the *j*th decile in country *i* (multiplied by 10), θ_{ij} (which is defined as the ratio between the average income of the *j*th decile, y_{ijt}, and the sample mean income, $\bar{m}_{it}$) on $TAR_{i,t-5}$, the same set of relative endowments, RE_{it}, their interaction with $TAR_{i,t-5}$ and a set of controls, Z_{it}, including country and time dummies. As in Table 4, estimation is in double log form for all continuous variables and takes place for each decile:

$$\theta_{ij} \equiv \frac{y_{ijt}}{\bar{m}_{it}} = D_i + YR_t + \alpha_{1j}\bar{m}_{it} + \beta_{1j}TAR_{i,t-5} + \sum_{m=1,3} \phi_{1m}RE_{imt} + \sum_{m=1,3} \phi_{2m}(TAR_{i,t-5} * RE_{imt}) + \sum_{l} \delta_{jl}Z_{ilt} + DS_{it} + e_{ijt} \quad (4)$$

Table 6 reports the results for the bottom three and top three deciles (full results available in Appendix 3, Table A9).

Besides plausible estimates with the FE estimator (Milanovic 2005a, footnote 9, argues that because this panel is very short there is insufficient data variability to use such an estimator), the following patterns stand out. First, in spite of an insignificant correlation between GDP growth and sample mean income growth rates, the results obtained over this sample period by reconstructing the Gini index as a measure of inequality from decile data are in line with the results presented in Table 4, column 5.

Turning to the estimates obtained with data on income by deciles, the same patterns as those obtained in Table 4 continue to hold (remember however that when interpreting the results, opposite signs for the coefficients in columns 1 to 3 when compared with those in column 5 Table 4 correspond to similar results!). We still find that a reduction in protection decreases the share of the lower deciles and that this effect is more pronounced for countries that have a high K/L ratio while the opposite holds for countries with a high arable land AT/L ratio. However, when it comes to breaking down skills, the results lose significance suggesting a lack of robustness when a finer breakdown of skills is attempted. This should not be surprising because of the significant correlation across different endowment measures. Given the small time dimension and likely noise in the decile data, it is rather comforting that the signs are preserved and near significance is reached for the NO/(SK + BS) measure.

These results were submitted to several robustness checks.[10] We added government expenditure and/or an index of democracy and/or the

Table 6. Inequality, factor endowments and openness.

Dependent variable	ln θ_1	ln θ_2	ln θ_3	ln θ_8	ln θ_9	ln θ_{10}	ln gini
Tariffs_{t-5}	14.65a	6.08a	3.25a	−0.32	−0.7990a	−0.43	−1.14
	(3.88)	(4.12)	(3.23)	(0.93)	(2.66)	(0.49)	(1.47)
Mean income	−0.20	−0.13	−0.08	−0.05a	−0.0436b	0.13a	0.09b
	(1.48)	(1.62)	(1.23)	(2.76)	(2.51)	(2.99)	(2.06)
(K/L)	0.63b	0.19	0.11	0.06c	0.0341	−0.18a	−0.12c
	(2.27)	(1.35)	(0.97)	(1.92)	(0.89)	(2.61)	(1.65)
(AT/L)	0.76	0.03	0.07	0.43a	0.2673b	−0.69a	−0.27
	(0.83)	(0.08)	(0.27)	(4.57)	(2.08)	(3.01)	(1.30)
(MF/L)	−0.88b	−0.30c	−0.19c	−0.06b	−0.0314	0.19b	0.15b
	(2.24)	(1.90)	(1.91)	(2.00)	(1.08)	(2.50)	(2.22)
(SK/BS)	0.18	−0.02	−0.03	0.01	0.0489c	−0.00	0.01
	(1.00)	(0.22)	(0.49)	(0.42)	(1.86)	(0.12)	(0.29)
(NO/(SK + BS))	−0.06	−0.11	−0.09	−0.00	0.0406	0.06	0.07
	(0.29)	(1.20)	(1.09)	(0.07)	(1.44)	(1.33)	(1.09)
(K/L) × (Tariffs_{t-5})	3.80a	1.48a	0.86a	−0.33a	−0.4344a	0.10	−0.24
	(3.31)	(3.15)	(2.70)	(3.31)	(4.07)	(0.36)	(0.94)
(AT/L) × (Tariffs_{t-5})	−12.22a	−4.69a	−2.31a	0.05	0.3992	0.61	0.94
	(3.03)	(3.79)	(2.74)	(0.17)	(1.35)	(0.82)	(1.26)

(continued)

Table 6. (*Continued*).

Dependent variable	ln θ_1	ln θ_2	ln θ_3	ln θ_8	ln θ_9	ln θ_{10}	ln gini
(MF/L) × (Tariffs$_{t-5}$)	−0.58	−0.21	−0.17	0.05	−0.0082	0.01	0.05
	(1.07)	(0.93)	(1.04)	(0.74)	(0.13)	(0.07)	(0.40)
(SK/(BS)) × (Tariffs$_{t-5}$)	0.68	0.09	0.08	−0.00	0.1017	−0.55	−0.67c
	(0.56)	(0.14)	(0.18)	(0.02)	(0.61)	(1.54)	(1.91)
(NO/(SK + BS)) × (Tariffs$_{t-5}$)	2.00	0.94	0.59	0.13	0.1362	−0.70c	−0.55
	(1.42)	(1.60)	(1.18)	(1.05)	(0.93)	(1.92)	(1.37)
Inflation	−0.19b	−0.05	−0.02	0.00	0.0186	0.02	0.03c
	(2.38)	(1.52)	(0.71)	(0.47)	(0.92)	(0.94)	(1.88)
Income/expenditure	−0.20a	−0.09b	−0.08a	−0.00	0.0077	0.04	0.05b
	(2.80)	(2.56)	(2.63)	(0.20)	(0.62)	(1.60)	(2.15)
Country fixed effects	Yes	Yes	Yes	Yes	Yes	Yes	Yes
Year fixed effects	Yes	Yes	Yes	Yes	Yes	Yes	Yes
Observations	146	146	146	146	146	146	146
No. of countries	55	55	55	55	55	55	55

Notes: Absolute value of z statistics in parentheses (based on Beck and Katz's PCSE).
c: Significant at 10%; b: significant at 5%; a: significant at 1%.

investment in fixed capital, resulting in a large reduction in sample size. In general, the significant results in Table 6 carry on to this smaller sample (see Appendix 3, Table A10 for the version with the three macroeconomic variables at the same time).

Since the correlation between tariff reductions and inequality after controlling for endowments is still significant in this shorter time span, we used the coefficient estimates in Table 6 to simulate the average impact of a five-point decrease in tariff revenues (this corresponds to the average tariff reduction during that period) on the bottom and top three deciles for two aggregated developing 'regions': Latin America (15 countries) and East, South and South East Asia (11 countries excluding Japan and Singapore). Because the SSA region has only 10 observations spread over five countries, we do not report simulation results for that region.

In each case, after having checked for insensitivity to the exclusion of outliers, regional values are averaged over countries in the region and only statistically significant coefficients are used, which means that the simulations mostly capture the estimated effect of differences in K/L and AT/L ratios. Results of this simulation exercise are reported in Table 7.

Subject to the validity of imposing the same reaction to tariff liberalization across countries, in the absence of growth, trade liberalization reduces the income of the first three deciles (and mildly up to decile 7) with usually a small increase for the top three deciles (Table 7, row B). Wacziarg and Welch (2003) report in their sample an increase in average yearly growth (over a 7-year period) of 0.5 percentage points following trade liberalization. Row C suggests that this growth-induced effect of trade liberalization would not be sufficient to compensate for the adverse distributional implications for the poorest quintile.

Finally, the often-observed lack of sensitivity of aggregate measures of inequality to changes in the distribution of income is confirmed when inspecting the changes in the values of the Gini coefficients reported in Table 7 (in spite of the large changes in mean decile incomes, Gini coefficient values only change at the third decimal). Because of the many biases likely to remain in these estimates in spite of the inclusion of many control variables, it is difficult to comment with confidence on the additional information provided by the detailed results on the decile data.

As an alternative presentation of these orders of magnitude, Figure 2 reports country-level estimates of the simulated changes in the bottom and top quintiles of the distribution. The simulations are based on average values over the period. Because of the inclusion of fixed effects in our estimations, actual values of mean quintile shares are extremely close to those reported in Figure 2, obviating the need to comment on how the model fits the data. Gains and losses in the bottom quintile are mostly reflected in changes in the top quintile rather than the middle of the distribution.

Table 7. Simulated changes in decile income from a 5 percentage points reduction in tariffs.

		Decile 1	Decile 2	Decile 3	Decile 8	Decile 9	Decile 10
Latin America*	A	1.3% – 1.0%	2.5% – 2.3%	3.6% – 3.4%	11.6% – 11.5%	16.6% – 17.1%	38.0% – 38.1%
	B	348 – 280	704 – 636	1007 – 947	3306 – 3293	4763 – 4929	10994 – 11040
	C	2.1%	1.0%	0.6%	0.0%	−0.3%	0.0%
Asia*	A	3.0% – 2.2%	4.3% – 3.8%	5.2% – 4.9%	11.6% – 11.5%	15.1% – 15.3%	29.6% – 29.5%
	B	613 – 445	955 – 834	1184 – 1103	2704 – 2658	3486 – 3549	6692 – 6679
	C	3.1%	1.3%	0.7%	0.2%	−0.2%	0.0%

Notes:
Row A corresponds to the relative shift of the share due to a 5 points decrease of tariffs.
Row B corresponds to the shift of the absolute income of the share due to a 5 points decrease of tariffs.
Row C shows the corresponding annual real growth (over the 10 years) that would be necessary to keep each decile's income at its initial value.
Samples (number of observations per country in parenthesis next to the country).
Latin America [0.482, 0.483]*:
Argentina (3), Bolivia (3), Brazil (3), Colombia (3), Costa Rica (3), Dominican Republic (3), Ecuador (3), Jamaica (3), Mexico (3), Nicaragua (2), Panama (3), Paraguay (2), Peru (3), Uruguay (3) and Venezuela (3).
Asia [0.358, 0.357]*:
Bangladesh (2), China (2), India (3), Indonesia (2), Korea (3), Malaysia (3), Pakistan (3), Philippines (3), Singapore (3), Sri Lanka (3) and Thailand (3).
*Gini coefficients before and after simulated tariff reduction in brackets.

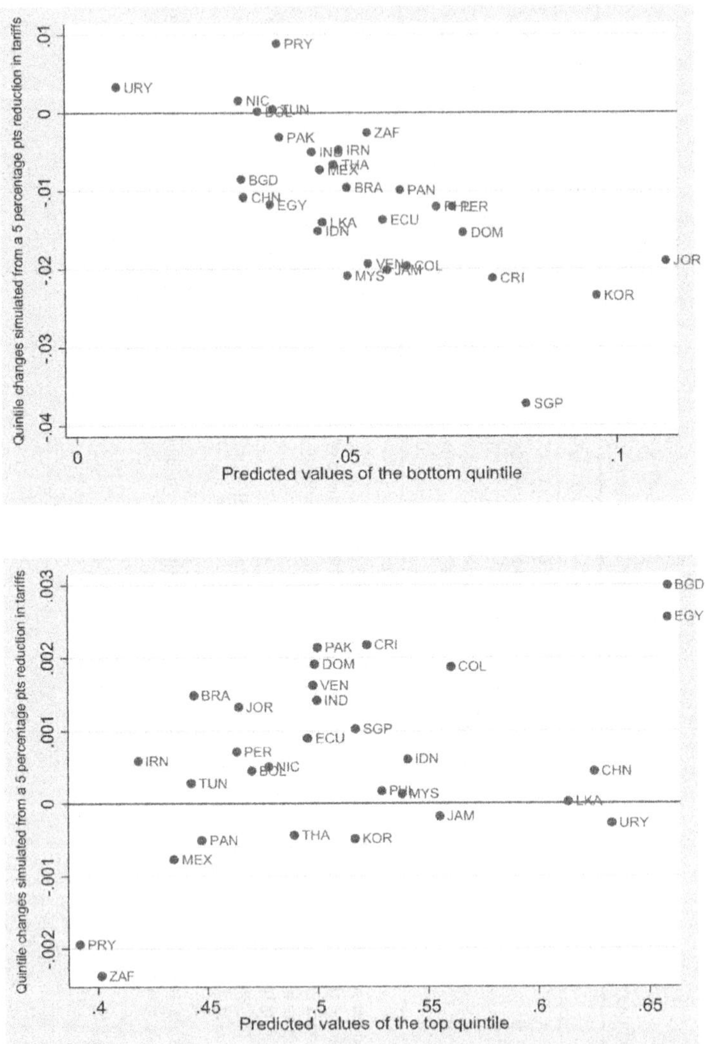

Figure 2. Simulated changes in quintile mean incomes of a 5 percentage points reduction in tariffs: (a) bottom quintile*, (b) top quintile*.
* Simulated quintile share before tariff reduction on the horizontal axis, and changes in quintile share following the tariff reduction (here, a 5 percentage points) on the vertical axis. For example, the average income share of the poorest 20% of Colombia (COL) is reduced from 6% of total income to 4% after the tariff reduction.

Conclusions

Much of previous research on the correlates of inequality has established that inequality is largely determined by factors that are quite different across countries and that change only slowly within countries. Notably, the effects of changes in trade policy, and of globalization more generally, have been difficult to detect. This paper has focused exclusively on within-country variations to trade policy changes while carefully disaggregating factor endowments. Overall, the results suggest that changes in inequality are correlated with changes in tariffs, which are quite robust to inclusion of various controls and to changes in sample periods.

Several patterns emerge from these conditional correlations that support the usefulness of resorting to factor-proportions theories of international trade when studying the effects of changes in trade policy on income distribution.

First, along with Stolper–Samuelson predictions, with income per capita serving as a proxy for factor endowments, trade liberalization is associated with an increase in inequality in high-income countries and a decrease in inequality in low-income countries, a result that has escaped most previous studies that have neglected to distinguish within-country from between-country effects.

Second, after accounting for several controls, when interacted with tariffs, factor endowments have the expected effects on inequality. Trade liberalization is associated with increases in inequality in capital-abundant and high-skill abundant countries. Increases in inequality are also positively correlated with trade liberalization in countries abundant in a non-educated labor force, although it decreases inequality in countries that are well-endowed with primary-educated labor. These results give support to the critics of globalization, who often point out that trade liberalization in poor countries leads to increases in inequality. We also demonstrate the need to control for the sources of income distribution when studying income inequality with several data sources for inequality. We also confirm the role of several indicators among the correlates associated with changes in inequality. For example, a reduction in macroeconomic instability (proxied by a reduction in inflation) consistently reduces within-country inequality.

While spurious correlation cannot be excluded, the results on the pattern of signs relating endowments to tariff changes are quite robust to the addition of several control variables. We find no evidence of reverse causality.

More tentative conclusions are reached when it comes to extending the analysis of distributional shifts by studying the whole income distribution rather than using aggregate distribution measures like the Gini or Theil coefficients. Over a shorter ten-year time-span, we obtain similar results with decile data, but the estimates often lack precision when we attempt to break down factor endowments beyond capital and labor to include skill and education levels. Nonetheless, even though measurement errors are probably exacerbated by the short temporal dimension, we would maintain that the relative robustness of the endowment effects to changes in specification justifies looking beyond averages and quantifying effects on the poor.

Acknowledgements

The authors thank Jean-Marie Baland, Olivier Cadot, Marco Fugazza, Sylviane Guillaumont, Sébastien Jean, Jaya Krishnakumar, Alessandro Nicita, Branko Milanovic, Marcelo Olarreaga, Mathias Thoenig, Jeffrey Williamson, Adrian Wood and seminar participants at UNCTAD (Geneva), T2M conference (Paris – PSE), the Universities of Milan and Namur for very helpful comments on an earlier draft. They also thank Branko Milanovic for providing them with his WYD data set and for answers to numerous queries. Annexes with detailed data sources and robustness checks are available from the authors upon request at http://www.unige.ch/ses/ecopo/demelo/Jaime.html

Notes

1. Perhaps this should not come as a surprise and not concern us too much if, via other channels, such as growth, increased openness reduces poverty. After all, HO theory should only be expected to inform us about the relation between endowments and factor rewards in response to a reform-induced change in relative factor demands rather than between endowments and overall income inequality, which is determined by many other factors. And, as pointed out by Baldwin (2004, 517) in his review of the trade liberalization and growth literature, since trade liberalization is rarely applied in isolation, it makes little sense to try to isolate its effects from those of associated policies. Anderson (2005) gives a survey of the conflicting evidence on openness and inequality, and Winters et al. (2004) survey the evidence between trade liberalization and poverty. Spilimbergo et al. (1999), Milanovic (2005a) and Bensidoun et al. (2005) are the studies most closely related to ours.
2. Let superscripts 1 and 0 stand for the change in factor prices associated with a change in trade policy. Then if technological choices are not affected by the change in trade policy: $(w^1 - w^0)\,(V^C - s^C\, V^W) \geq 0$ where s^C is country c's share in world (i.e. sample) income, and V^w is the sample average endowment. In the more general setting with no restrictions on the number of goods or factors, or on the rest-of-the-world, all that one can establish from profit maximization is a positive link between changes in prices and net exports and if technology choice is insensitive to price changes, then this correlation extends to factor price changes (see Ethier 1980 and Bensidoun et al. 2005).
3. Among the studies that control for heterogeneity, Edwards (1997) finds no evidence that openness or trade liberalization increases inequality. When including fixed effects, Barro (2000) finds no correlation between inequality and openness, echoing Ravallion's (2001) results.
4. To correct for heteroskedasticity, we used two estimators: the standard heteroskedasticity-consistent White (1980) estimator and the panel-corrected standard errors (PCSEs) estimator proposed by Beck and Katz (1995) which is shown to be as good or slightly superior to the robust estimator in Monte Carlo studies for small samples (see Beck and Katz 1996, Table 2). Hence we only report the PCSEs results in subsequent tables. Ethnicity is dropped from the FE estimates because it is time-invariant.
5. As a first exercise, not reported here, we replicated the same specification as Spilimbergo et al. (1999) confirming their results (i.e. a result in conformity with factor-endowment predictions for human capital but in contradiction with predictions for physical capital when using their openness variable ('adjusted'

trade ratio instead of tariffs). However, when using our preferred measure tariffs, increases in inequality are associated with relatively abundant endowments in capital following a reduction in tariffs (i.e. the coefficient on the interaction between relative endowment in capital per unit of labor, K/L, and the lagged tariff, is negative). To our knowledge, this plausible set of results has not been found in previous studies. However, with tariffs, the significance for the human capital endowment interactive term with tariffs disappears.

6. Bensidoun et al. (2005) argue that the Heckscher–Ohlin model is too restrictive, relying on factor-price-equalization (FPE) and hence identical production techniques in equilibrium. Using a more general approach that relaxes the FPE assumption (but still relies on other restrictive assumptions, like homothetic preferences and unchanged production techniques following trade liberalization), they show that factor price changes are correlated with the factor content of trade, leading them to test their model using constructed estimates of the labor-capital content of net exports instead of factor endowments on a similar D-S inequality data set for 53 countries. However, their results are not strictly comparable with ours (different sample with no SSA countries and a different definition of variables).
7. The index of human capital endowment (average years of schooling) is now replaced by these three different categories of skill levels. We take the NO, BS and SK variables from the Barro and Lee (2000) data set, which is available on a five-year basis that corresponds to the 5-year averages used for all our variables.
8. Owing to the high correlation between SK/L and K/L ($\rho = 0.84$), the coefficient on K/L changes sign and is almost significant statistically.
9. WYD can be downloaded from http://econ.worldbank.org/projects/inequality (accessed May 30, 2008).
10. We also ran the same regression without taking the logarithm of the LHS-variables, obtaining similar results. Regarding reverse causality, as previously, we ran the same regression using future trade rather than past values and the results become mostly insignificant, suggesting that reverse causality should not be a problem here (results are available upon request).

References

Anderson, E. 2005. Openness and inequality in developing countries: a review of theory and recent evidence. *World Development* 33, no. 7: 1045–63.

Baldwin, R.E. 2004. Openness and growth: what's the empirical relationship. In *Challenges to Globalization: Analyzing the Economics*, eds. R.E. Baldwin and A. Winters, 499–521. Chicago: The University of Chicago Press.

Barro, R. 2000. Inequality and growth in a panel of countries. *Journal of Economic Growth* 5: 5–32.

Barro, R.J., and J.-W. Lee. 2000. International data on educational attainment: updates and implications. CID Working Papers 42.

Beck, N., and J.N. Katz. 1995. What to do (and not to do) with time–series cross-section data. *The American Political Science Review* 89, no. 3: 634–47.

———. 1996. Nuisance vs. substance: specifying and estimating time-series cross-section models. *Political Analysis* 6: 1–36.

Bensidoun, I., S. Jean, and A. Sztulman. 2005. International trade and income distribution: reconsidering the evidence. CEPII Working Paper 17.

Bourguignon, F., F.H.G. Ferreira, and N. Lusting. 2005. A synthesis of the results. In *The Microeconomics of Income Distribution Dynamics: in East Asia and Latin America*, eds. F. Bourguignon, F.H.G. Ferreira, and N. Lusting, 357–406. Washington, DC: World Bank.

———. and C. Morrisson. 1990. Income distribution development and foreign trade. *European Economic Review* 34, no. 6: 1113–33.
Calderon, C., and L. Serven. 2004. *The Effects of Infrastructure Development on Growth and Income Distribution dataset*. World Bank. Available at: http://econ.worldbank.org/WBSITE/EXTERNAL/EXTDEC/EXTRESEARCH/0,,contentMDK:20699179~pagePK:64214825~piPK:64214943~theSitePK:469382,00.html (accessed on June 6, 2008).
Deaton, A. 2005. Measuring poverty in a growing world (or measuring growth in a poor world). *The Review of Economics and Statistics* 87, no. 1: 1–19.
Deininger, K., and L. Squire. 1996. A new data set measuring income inequality. *World Bank Economic Review* 10, no. 3: 565–92.
Dollar, D. 1992. Outward-oriented developing economies really do grow more rapidly: evidence from 95 LDCs, 1976–1985 from Global Development Finance & World Development Indicators. *Economic Development and Cultural Change* 40: 523–44.
———., and A. Kraay. 2002. Growth is good for the poor. *Journal of Economic Growth* 7: 195–225.
Edwards, S. 1997. Trade policy, growth and income distribution. *American Economic Review* 87, no. 2: 205–10.
Easterly, W.R. 2004. Globalization, inequality, and development: the big picture. *Monetary and Economic Studies* 22, no. S1: 57–87.
Easterly, W., and R. Levine. 1999. It's not factor accumulation: Stylized facts and growth models. *World Bank Economic Review* 15: 177–219.
Ethier, W. 1984. Higher dimensional issues in trade theory. In *Handbook of International Economics*, eds. R. Jones and P. Kenen, 1, 131–84. Amsterdam: North Holland.
Fisher, R. 2001. The evolution of inequality after trade liberalization. *Journal of Development Economics* 66, no. 2: 555–79.
Freedom House. 2005. Freedom in the World Reports. Washington, DC: Freedom House.
Galiani, S., and G. Porto. 2006. Trends in tariff reforms and trends in wage inequality. World Bank Policy Research Working Paper Series 3905.
Goldberg, P., and N. Pavcnik. 2004. Trade, inequality, and poverty: what do we know? Evidence from recent trade liberalization episodes in developing countries. NBER Working Paper 10593.
Heckscher, E. 1919. The effect of foreign trade on the distribution of income. *Economisk Tidskrift* 21, no. 1: 1–32.
Heston, A., R. Summers, and B. Aten. 2002. Penn World Table Version 6.1, Philadelphia, Center for International Comparisons at the University of Pennsylvania (CICUP).
Higgins, M., and J.G. Williamson. 2002. Explaining inequality the world round: cohort size, Kuznets curves, and openness. *Journal of Southeast Asian Studies* 40, no. 3: 268–302.
Hiscox, M.J., and S.L. Kastner. 2002. A general measure of trade policy orientations: gravity model-based estimates from 83 nations, 1960 to 1992. UCSD working paper.
Hoff, K. 2003. Paths of institutional development: a view from economic history. *World Bank Research Observer* 18, no. 2: 2205–26.
International Energy Annual. 2005. Energy Information Administration, available at http://www.eia.doe.gov/iea/ (accessed on December 14, 2007).
Kraay, A., N. Loayza, L. Serven, and J. Ventura. 2000. Country Portfolios, NBER Working Paper No. 7795.
La Porta, R., F. Lopez-de-Silanes, A. Schleifer, and R. Vishny. 1998. The Quality of Government, NBER Working Paper 6727.

Leamer, E. 1989. Measures of Openness. In *Trade Policy Issues and Empirical Analysis*, ed. R. Baldwin, 147–200. Chicago: University of Chicago Press.
———., H. Maul, S. Rodriguez, and P.K. Schott. 1999. Does natural resources abundance increase Latin American income inequality? *Journal of Development Economics* 59, no. 1: 3–42.
Mayer, T., and S. Zignago. 2005. Market Access in Global and Regional Trade, CEPII Working Paper No. 2005–02.
Marshall, M.G., and K. Jaggers. 2002. Polity IV Dataset. Available at: http://www.systemicpeace.org/polity/polity4.htm (accessed on December 14, 2007).
Milanovic, B. 2005a. Can we discern the effect of globalization on income distribution: evidence from household surveys? *World Bank Economic Review* 19, no. 1: 21–44.
———. 2005b. *Worlds Apart: Global and International Inequality 1950–2000*. Princeton: Princeton University Press.
Miniane, J. 2004. A new set of measures on capital account restrictions. *IMF Staff Papers* 51, no. 2: 276–308.
Ohlin, B. 1933. *Interregional and International Trade*. Cambridge, MA: Harvard University Press. Revised version published in 1968.
Pritchett, L. 1996. Measuring outward orientation in LDCs: can it be done? *Journal of Development Economics* 49, no. 2: 307–35.
———. 2000. Understanding patterns of economic growth: searching for hills among plateaus, mountains and plains. *World Bank Economic Review* 14, no. 2: 221–50.
Rama, M. 2002. Globalization, inequality and labor market policies. *Revue d'Economie du Développement* 1–2: 43–84.
Ravallion, M. 2001. Growth inequality and poverty: looking beyond averages. *World Development* 29, no. 11: 1803–15.
Rodrik, D. 2000. Comments on 'Trade, growth, and poverty', by D. Dollar and A. Kraay. Unpublished manuscript, Harvard University.
Sachs, J., and A. Warner. 1995. Economic reform and the process of global integration. *Brookings Papers on Economic Activity* 1: 1–118.
Spilimbergo, A., J.L. Londono, and M. Székely. 1999. Income distribution, factor endowments, and trade openness. *Journal of Development Economics* 59, no. 1: 77–101.
UNU–WIDER. 2005. *World Income Inequality Database, V 2.0a (June 2005), User Guide and Data Sources*. Helsinki, World Institute for Development Economics Research.
Vanek, J. 1968. The factor proportions theory: the N-factor case. *Kyklos* 21, no. 4: 749–56.
Wacziarg, R., and K.H. Welch. 2003. Trade liberalization and growth: new evidence. NBER Working Papers # 10152.
Winters, A., N. McCulloch, and A. McKay. 2004. Trade liberalization and poverty: the evidence so far. *Journal of Economic Literature* 42, no. 1: 72–115.
White, H. 1980. A heteroskedasticity-consistent covariance matrix and a direct test for heteroskedasticity. *Econometrica* 48, no. 4: 817–38.
Wood, A. 1994. *North–South Trade, Employment and Inequality: Changing Futures in a Skill-Driven World*. New York: Oxford University Press.
———. 2002. Globalization and wage inequalities: a synthesis of three theories. *Weltwirtchafliches Archiv* 138, no. 1: 54–82.
———. 2003. Could Africa be like America? In *Annual World Bank Conference on Development Economics: The New Reform Agenda*, eds. B. Pleskovic and N. Stern, 163–200. Washington, DC: World Bank.
World Bank. 2004. World Development Indicators on CD-ROM. Washington, DC: World Bank.

Appendices

Appendix 1: Data and data sources

Table A1. List of countries included in the sample 1980–2000 (Tables 2–5).

	Countries	Number of observations
Latin America	Argentina	3
	Barbados	1*
	Bolivia	2
	Brazil	3
	Chile	3
	Colombia	4
	Costa Rica	4
	Dominican Rep.	4
	Ecuador	3
	Guatemala	1*
	Guyana	1*
	Honduras	1*
	Jamaica	3
	Mexico	4
	Nicaragua	2
	Panama	4
	Paraguay	2
	Peru	4
	Trinidad & Tobago	2
	Uruguay	3
	Venezuela	4
Total	**17 (21*)**	**54 (58*)**
Developed Countries	Australia	4
	Austria	3
	Canada	4
	Cyprus	2
	Denmark	2
	Finland	3
	France	4
	Greece	4
	Ireland	3
	Italy	4
	Japan	4
	Netherlands	2
	New Zealand	2
	Norway	4
	Portugal	4
	Spain	4
	Sweden	4
	Switzerland	2
	United Kingdom	3
	United States	4
Total	**20**	**66**

(continued)

Table A1. (*Continued*).

	Countries	Number of observations
Africa and Middle East	Botswana	1*
	Burundi	1*
	Cameroon	2
	Egypt	2
	Ghana	3
	Iran	4
	Israel	3
	Jordan	4
	Kenya	3
	Lesotho	2
	Malawi	4
	Mali	1*
	Mauritius	3
	Rwanda	1*
	Sierra Leone	1*
	South Africa	4
	Tanzania	1*
	Tunisia	4
	Uganda	2
	Zambia	1*
	Zimbabwe	2
Total	**14 (21*)**	**42 (49*)**
Asia	Bangladesh	3
	China	1*
	India	4
	Indonesia	3
	Korea Rep.	4
	Malaysia	3
	Nepal	1*
	Pakistan	4
	Philippines	3
	Singapore	4
	Sri Lanka	4
	Thailand	4
Total	**10 (12*)**	**36 (38*)**

Note: * Indicates countries are excluded in our specifications with country fixed effects.

Table A2. List of countries included in the sample 1988–1998 (deciles from Milanovic 2005a).

	Countries	Number of observations
Africa and Middle East	Egypt	2
	Ghana	2
	Iran	3
	Jordan	3
	Kenya	2
	Lesotho	2
	South Africa	2
	Tunisia	3
	Uganda	2
	Zimbabwe	2
Total	**10**	**23**
Latin America	Argentina	3
	Bolivia	3
	Brazil	3
	Colombia	3
	Costa Rica	3
	Dominican Rep.	3
	Ecuador	3
	Jamaica	3
	Mexico	3
	Nicaragua	2
	Panama	3
	Paraguay	2
	Peru	3
	Uruguay	3
	Venezuela	3
Total	**15**	**43**
Asia	Bangladesh	2
	China	2
	India	3
	Indonesia	2
	Korea	3
	Malaysia	3
	Pakistan	3
	Philippines	3
	Singapore	2
	Sri Lanka	3
	Thailand	3
Total	**11**	**29**

(*continued*)

Table A2. (*Continued*).

	Countries	Number of observations
Developed Countries	Australia	2
	Austria	3
	Canada	3
	Cyprus	2
	Finland	2
	France	3
	Greece	3
	Ireland	3
	Israel	3
	Italy	3
	Japan	2
	Netherlands	3
	Norway	3
	Portugal	3
	Spain	2
	Sweden	3
	Switzerland	2
	United Kingdom	3
	United States	3
Total	**19**	**51**

Table A3. List of variables and sources.

Label	Content	Sources
Gini	Gini coefficients	UNI–WIDER (2005)
ShareX (X = 1, ..., 10)	Absolute income level of each decile normalized by the mean income. (X = 1 corresponds to the poorest 10% of the population and X = 10 to the richest 10%)	Milanovic (2005a)
Mean	It corresponds to the mean income derived from household surveys (in current $PPP)	Milanovic (2005a)
GDPpc	GDP per capita, PPP (constant 1995 international $)	Heston, Summers, and Aten (2002)
Capital	Capital per worker	Easterly and Levine (1999) and Kraay et al. (2000)
Land	Land per labor force and land arable per labor force	World Bank (2004)
Mining and fuel	Production of minerals, coal and oil	International Energy Annual (2005)
Education	Average years of schooling in the population over 15 years old	Barro and Lee (2000)
Non educated	Proportion of the population over 15 years non educated (or primary not completed)	Barro and Lee (2000)
Primary (based) educated	Proportion of the population over 15 years primary educated (completed) (or secondary not completed)	Barro and Lee (2000)
High (skilled) educated	Proportion of the population over 15 years high educated	Barro and Lee (2000)
Inflation	Annual growth rate of the GDP implicit deflator. The GDP implicit deflator is the ratio of GDP in current local currency to GDP in constant local currency	World Bank (2004)
Investment	Gross Fixed Capital Formation (in constant dollar)	World Bank (2004)
M2/Gdp	Money and quasi money comprise as % of Gdp	World Bank (2004)
Gov Expenditure	Total expenditure includes both current and capital expenditures as % of Gdp	World Bank (2004)
Mature	Share of the population between 40 and 59 years old	World Bank (2004)

(continued)

Table A3. (*Continued*).

Label	Content	Sources
Civil liberties	Measure the extent to which people are able to express their opinion openly without fears of reprisals and are protected in doing so by an independent judiciary	Freedom House (2005)
Democracy	Democracy is defined as 'general openness of political institutions'. The variable ranges from 0 (absence of democracy) to 10 (best)	Marshall and Jaggers (2002)
Ethnicity	Herfindhal index which measure the probability for two individuals to be in a different group each other	La Porta et al. (1998)
Infrastructure	Quantity (stock); Principal component analysis on road per km^2, telephone lines per workers, power Gigawatt per worker Quality: waiting times for phone com., energy losses, paved road	Calderon and Serven (2004)
Tariffs	Import duties comprise all levies collected on goods at the point of entry into the country. In % of imports	World Bank (2004)
Index Dollar	Index of price distortion	Dollar (1992)
Index Pritchett	Adjusted trade ratio: residual once we account for size and distance	Pritchett (1996)
Index Spilimbergo	Adjusted trade ratio: residual once we account for size, distance and difference in factor endowment	Spilimbergo, Londono, and Székely (1999)
Index Leamer	Adjusted net trade ratio: residual once we account for size, distance and difference in factor endowment	Leamer (1989)
Index Hiscox & Kastner	Fixed country years effect in a gravity model once we account for size, distance and difference in factor endowment	Hiscox and Kastner (2002)
Black market premium	Black market premium	World Bank (2004)
Index Wacziarg & Welch	Index taking value 0 or 1 depending on liberalization	Wacziarg and Welch (2003)
Tax Barro & Lee	Tax on capital and input	Barro and Lee (2000)
(X + M)/Gdp	Output trade ratio	World Bank (2004)

Appendix 2: Data construction

Inequality data sets

Results in Tables 3–5 use the Gini coefficients from the UNU–WIDER (2005), an update from the widely used Deininger and Squire [DS] (1996) database. The WIDER data base expands and provides more surveys than those used by DS. We use only the data that are labeled 'high quality' in WIDER as in DS. Regarding the mix of expenditure-based and income-based Gini coefficients, we take the data source into account by the use of dummies as we also use dummy variables to indicate if the recipient is a household or an individual. These different characteristics of the data also plague the DS data set. Those specificities are also controlled for by the use of dummy variables. Since we use 5-year average periods we use the same characteristics for a 5-year period. This does not create a problem since very few countries have different Gini characteristics on the period under cover (only 6 countries have Gini coefficients calculated both on income and expenditure).

The second dataset comes from Milanovic (2005a) is referred to as the WYD data set. It is used for the results reported in Tables 6 and 7 and is almost entirely based on micro (i.e. household-level) survey data. Data for about 2/3 of country-years are calculated directly from household surveys. As noted by Milanovic, this data presents two advantages relative to the other data bases. First, welfare aggregates as well as recipient units are defined consistently across countries and time. Second, information on income levels is provided by deciles (or, if necessary, even 'finer' partitions) rather than for only one or two synthetic inequality measures (e.g. Gini coefficient or Theil index). Since the data are sometimes based on Income and sometimes on expenditure data we also use dummies to control for data sources (this was not done in Milanovic 2005a).

How close are the inequality measures obtained from WIDER and from the DS–UNU–WIDER data? The first data set covers 61 countries (in the specification with fixed effects) and the second data set covers 55 of the 61 countries in the first data set. Whereas the first data set is obtained as a 5-year average for 4 periods (1980–85, 1985–90, 1990–95 and 1995–2000), the second gives data for three years 1988, 1993 and 1998. Using yearly from the first dataset, and calculating the Gini coefficient with the second dataset on a sample of 150 observations, yields a correlation coefficient of 0.94. This explains partly why the results in Table 6 are close to those obtained in Table 4.

Construction of the index of relative factor endowments

Let E_{ift} stand for per worker endowment of country i in factor f in year t and E^*_{ft} for the world per worker effective endowment of country i in factor f in year t, computed by weighting every country's endowment by the population and by the degree of openness. The world endowment is calculated on a dataset including 80 countries which have data on all the period under cover.

$$E^*_{ft} = \frac{\sum_i \left(E_{ift} \times pop_i \times \left(\frac{X+M}{GDP}\right)_i \right)}{\sum_i \left(pop_i \times \left(\frac{X+M}{GDP}\right)_i \right)}$$

The corresponding indicator of relative endowment is given by: $RE_{ift} = \ln \frac{(E_{ift})}{(E^*_{ft})}$

Robustness to alternative protection measures

Several authors (e.g. Goldberg and Pavcnik 2004; Rodrik 2000) reach the conclusion that tariffs capture relatively well the combined effects of trade policy changes. For example, Rodrik says that 'Tariff and non-tariff averages are reasonably accurate in ranking countries in terms of trade policy openness, and in showing changes in openness over time' (2000, 3). Andrew Rose provides on his web page a dataset including several measures of openness or protection which we use as robustness checks The correlation coefficients of the tariffs used in this study with several other measures of protection are given in Table A4a (level of significance in parenthesis).

However because tariffs do not take into account NTBs, we also compared several frequency indices of NTBs with our tariff measure at the HS-6 level using Jon Haveman's treatment of TRAINS data. We use the NTBs frequency index provided by the CEPII (in Mayer and Zignago 2005) to compare its average value for different range of tariff. As shown in Table A4b, the higher is the tariff the higher in the in the frequency index of NTBs whatever is the NTB (on quality or on quantity).

Taken together, the evidence in Tables A4a and A4b give support to tariffs as an adequate measure of protection for a large number of countries over an extended period of time.

Table A4a. Correlation Matrix of Protection Measures.

Correlation	(X + M)/ GDP	Index Leamer	Index Prichett	Index Spilimbergo	Waciarg & Welch	Dollar	Tax Barro & Lee	Index Hiscox Karstner	Black Market Premium
Observations	477	40	477	373	448	70	159	278	165
Tariffs	−0.15	−0.43	−0.08	−0.05	−0.56	−0.33	0.31	0.47	0.02
World Bank	(0.087)	(0.017)	(0.082)	(0.313)	(0.001)	(0.005)	(0.001)	(0.001)	(0.736)

Table A4b. Comparison of Tariffs with NTBs.

Tariffs	NTBs frequency index: All	NTBs frequency index: Quantity	NTBs frequency index: Quality
Tariff = 0%	0.09	0.01	0.06
Tariff > 5%	0.21	0.14	0.29
Tariff > 10%	0.24	0.16	0.32
Tariff > 15%	0.28	0.16	0.34
Tariff > 20%	0.30	0.19	0.36
Tariff > 30%	0.32	0.20	0.37

ANNALS OF ECONOMICS AND STATISTICS
NUMBER 97/98, JANUARY/JUNE 2010

FDI, the Brain Drain and Trade: Channels and Evidence

Artjoms IVLEVS
Bristol Business School, University of the West of England and GEP, University of Nottingham

Jaime DE MELO
Department of Political Economy, University of Geneva

This paper explores the links between the patterns of migration (high vs. low-skill), trade policy, and foreign direct investment (FDI) from the standpoint of sending countries. A skeleton general equilibrium model with a non-traded good and sector-specific labour is used to explore the effects of the skill-composition of exports on FDI. The model suggests that if exports are low-skill intensive, emigration of high-skill labour leads to positive FDI, suggesting that migration and FDI are complements. Cross-sectional analysis using FDI and emigration data for 102 migration-sending countries over the period 1990-2000 finds some support for this conjecture*.

I. Introduction

Globalization has become a major feature of the modern economic world. For many the integration of goods and factor markets is believed to bring substantial gains to the countries opening their borders to trade, foreign capital and migration, although labor markets are far from being integrated. For example, the annual earnings premium for a Mexican worker in the US is around $17,500 and multilateral negotiations on reducing barriers to labor mobility are not on the agenda. According to received wisdom, one would expect that the combination of sharp reduction in trade costs and policy-erected barriers to trade in goods would reduce migratory pressures as trade in goods would tend to close the wage gap across countries. In other words, one would expect that trade and migration are substitutes. Applying the same reasoning, one would expect that reductions in the barriers to investment, reflected in growing FDI, would also reduce migratory pressures; i.e. one would expect that FDI and migration are substitutes. Likewise, until recently trade and FDI were largely viewed as substitutes: high trade costs and policy-erected barriers to trade would be associated with an increase in what is now called horizontal or tariff-jumping FDI.

In spite of the joint determination of migration, investment (FDI) and trade, the large and growing theoretical and empirical literatures on the migration-investment-trade nexus have not been analyzed in an integrated framework. Diaspora and human capital effects have been emphasized

* JEL: F13, F22 / KEY WORDS: FDI, Brain Drain, Trade and Migration.

in the migration-FDI literature[1]; the nature of FDI (vertical or horizontal) has been emphasized in the FDI-trade literature[2]; and substitutability-complementarity relations have been emphasized in the trade-migration literature[3]. It should not be surprising then that in a recent survey of the literature, SCHIFF [2007] concludes that what he calls the MIT (for migration, investment and trade) linkages are complex, making it difficult to draw suggestive policy recommendations for source or sending countries.

Recent data on the skill-composition of emigration for 1990 and 2000 compiled by DOCQUIER and MARFOUK [2006] shows that it is especially South-North migration of skilled labor that has increased and that for all but the large developing countries, skilled emigration is a sizeable fraction of the labor force (DOCQUIER [2007], DOCQUIER, LOHEST and MARFOUK [2007], DEFOORT [2008]). Indeed, the availability of this data makes it possible to incorporate the skill-composition of emigration in the debate about the links between trade, migration and FDI and explore the channels through which emigration affects welfare in sending countries earlier identified in the "brain drain" literature[4].

This paper continues the exploration of the links between FDI, trade and the composition of migration, considering all three jointly. Section 2 sketches a Ricardo-Viner model of a price-taking economy with skilled and unskilled labor in which FDI flows respond to differences in rates of return and in which migration is considered exogenous reflecting barriers to immigration in receiving countries. This model provides a link between FDI, changes in trade costs, and changes in the skilled-unskilled migration pattern of the sending country. Owing to a lack of data to confront the

1. CHECCHI, DE SIMONE and FAINI [2007] question the virtuous circle between Human Capital (HC) and FDI proposed in the literature on the "brain gain" initiated by MOUNTFORD [1997]. Using data on skilled migration rates for 1990 and 2000, they find that tertiary enrolment is conditionally correlated positively with FDI (countries experiencing continuous FDI would then upgrade their skill content). However, at the same time the effect of this positive association on enrolments is eliminated by the negative correlation between tertiary school enrolment and emigration. Moreover, they obtain a negative conditional correlation between secondary enrolments and FDI.

2. Recent models of trade and FDI distinguish between vertical FDI (VFDI) that takes advantage of differences in factor costs and tariff-jumping or horizontal FDI (HFDI) that seeks to avoid trade costs. With high trade costs, horizontal FDI(HFDI) takes places, while with sufficiently different factor proportions between countries (and sufficiently low trade costs), vertical FDI (VFDI) will take place. In this framework developed by MARKUSEN [2002] and NAVARETTI and VENABLES [2005], HFDI substitutes for trade and VFDI creates trade. Using macro data, AMITI and WAKELIN [2003] find support for the predictions of these models. They find that investment liberalization among countries with similar factor endowments stimulates exports when trade costs are low, whereas investment liberalization reduces trade for countries with similar size and endowments when trade costs are high.

3. The literature on trade and migration has recently emphasized complementarities either because of credit constraints preventing the emigration of unskilled workers, or because of diaspora effects operating in the literature on ethnic networks in international trade. However, most of the evidence is for the US. Evidence supportive of complementarities in bilateral trade between host and sending countries has been found for the US (GOULD [1994], HEAD and RIES [1998], RAUCH and TRINIDADE [2002] and RAUCH and CASELLA [2003]). The role of diasporas has also been emphasized in several case studies on Information Technology between the US and India and between the US and Israel (ARORA and GAMBARDELLA [2005]). Again, relying on US data, KUGLER and RAPOPORT [2005, 2007] find that FDI in services are positively correlated with diaspora stocks indicating complementarities, whereas for manufactures unskilled diasporas and FDI are substitutes. DOCQUIER and LODIGIANI [2006] find evidence of positive externalities between skilled migration and FDI suggesting "brain gain" effects associated with skilled migration.

4. The "brain drain" literature has been challenged on several fronts. Three channels have been identified to transform a "brain drain" into a "brain gain" (i) skilled migrants remit relatively large amounts; (ii) selective immigration policies in host countries may raise the attractiveness of migration for high-skilled individuals, which in turn raises the private returns to education via a reduced supply inducing an additional investment in education in the host country; (iii) network effects may lead to technology transfer via FDI between host and sending countries

model's predictions directly with the data, section 3 estimates the relation between FDI and the skill-composition of emigration for a sample of 102 sending countries over the period 1990-2000. Results are encouraging, suggesting that the skill-composition of emigration highlighted by the model matters for the pattern of FDI inflows.

II. Migration, Trade and FDI: A Skeleton Model

In view of the importance of migration in many sending countries, we develop a model that captures some of the economy-wide effects associated with emigration and the skill-composition of emigrants. Emigration is considered exogenous (subject to emigration policies in receiving countries), and capital is internationally mobile, responding to differences in the return to capital. Take then an economy producing two goods, non-traded (N) and exported (E) and, to simplify, assume that all the production of the (E) sector is exported. Three fully-employed factors are available in fixed amounts in the economy: two types of industry-specific labor, L_N (employed in the non-traded sector) and L_E (employed in the export sector), and capital K; the supply structure is identical to the supply structure of the specific-factor (Ricardo-Viner) model. In addition, assume that labor is internationally mobile but sector-specific, while capital is intersectorally (within the economy) and internationally mobile with FDI responding to endogenously determined changes in the domestic return to capital[5].

Constant returns-to-scale neoclassical production functions with a constant elasticity of substitution between factors describe the technology. Let $a_{NN}(a_{EE})$ be the amount of specific factor $L_N(L_E)$ necessary to produce one unit of good of the non-traded (exported) good. The amount of capital (mobile factor) necessary to produce one unit of the non-traded (export) good is equal to $a_{KN}(a_{KE})$. Assume that all factors are fully employed.

Following JONES [1971], who was the first to formalise the link between factor prices, factor quantities and goods prices in a standard specific-factor (Ricardo-Viner) model, total differentiation of the system describing the zero profit and full employment conditions yields two expressions. The first expression (1.1) links the rewards to capital, the mobile factor, to prices and endowments and yields two familiar predictions from the standard specific factor model: first, emigration (i.e. a reduction in either type of sector specific labour) makes capital (the mobile factor) more abundant and decreases its rewards; second, any increase in a good price raises the rewards of capital, though by less than the price increase.

$$\hat{R} = \beta_N \hat{p}_N + \beta_E \hat{p}_E + \frac{1}{\Delta}\left(\lambda_{KN}\hat{L}_N + \lambda_{KE}\hat{L}_E - \hat{K}\right); \Delta > \qquad (1.1)$$

where a "^" over a variable denotes the percentage change in that variable; R is the reward to the mobile factor; p_N and p_E are goods' prices; For $j = N,E$, we have

$$\beta_j = \frac{\lambda_{Kj}}{\Delta}\frac{\sigma_j}{\theta_{jj}} > 0$$

5. There is support for this hypothesis. For example, FRIEDBERG [2001] finds a significant positive relationship between source and destination country sector employment for Russian immigrants to Israel in the nineties.

where θ_{ij} is factor i's ($i = L_N, L_E, K$) share in total income generated in sector j; λ_{Kj} is the fraction of capital factor absorbed by the sector j; σ_j is the elasticity of substitution between factors in sector j:

$$\sigma_j = \frac{\hat{\alpha}_{Kj} - \hat{\alpha}_{jj}}{\hat{R}_j - \hat{R}_K}$$

and

$$\Delta = \sum_{j=N,E} \lambda_{Kj} \frac{\sigma_j}{\theta_{jj}} > 0$$

The second expression (1.2) links changes in outputs to changes in factor endowments, and to changes in prices, with the limiting case of no output responsiveness to price changes (a rectangular PPF) when the elasticities of factor substitution tend to zero $(\Omega \to 0 \; if \; \sigma_E \to 0 \; and \; \sigma_N \to 0)$.

$$\begin{aligned}(\hat{N} - \hat{E}) &= \Omega(\hat{p}_N - \hat{p}_E) + (\hat{L}_N - \hat{L}_E) \\ &+ \frac{1}{\Delta}\left(\frac{\theta_{KN}\sigma_N}{\theta_{NN}} - \frac{\theta_{KE}\sigma_E}{\theta_{EE}}\right)\left(\hat{K} - \lambda_{KN}\hat{L}_N - \lambda_{KE}\hat{L}_E\right)\end{aligned} \tag{1.2}$$

where $\Omega = \theta_{KN} \frac{\sigma_N}{\theta_{NN}} \beta_E + \theta_{KE} \frac{\sigma_E}{\theta_{EE}} \beta_N$.

Suppose momentarily that both goods are traded and the economy is small with fixed goods prices $(\hat{p}_E = \hat{p}_D = 0)$. Then emigration of either type of labor will cause a decrease in the capital reward and a capital outflow or "negative" FDI. Thus, if both goods produced were perfectly tradable as in most trade models, capital "follows" labor: migration and FDI (or capital movements) are substitutes as in MUNDELL [1957].

To keep the model tractable we minimize the number of parameters by taking a representative consumer with a homothetic utility function consuming an imported good, M, along with the non-traded good. We postulate a CES utility function to model the aggregate demand for a home and imports good:

$$Q(M,N,\sigma) = \left[\chi \, M^{(\sigma-1)/\sigma} + (1-\chi) \, N^{(\sigma-1)/\sigma}\right]^{\sigma/(\sigma-1)} \tag{1.3}$$

where Q(.) is utility over the domestic non-traded and imported goods, χ is a parameter that weights the import good relative to the domestic good, and σ is the constant elasticity of substitution between domestic and imported good.

Utility maximization yields:

$$\frac{M}{N} = k\left(\frac{p_N}{p_M}\right)^{\sigma} \tag{1.4}$$

where

$$k = \left(\frac{\chi}{1-\chi}\right)^{\sigma}$$

is a constant capturing expenditure shares and p_N and p_M are unit prices.

In this simple model, the revenue-equal-expenditure constraint implies balanced trade, i.e.:

$$\bar{\pi}_M M = \bar{\pi}_E E \tag{1.5}$$

with the bar on the foreign-currency prices of traded goods (π_M, π_E) reflecting the small-country assumption for traded goods. Letting world prices equal to one by choice of units, in the absence of trade taxes, consumers and producers face world prices, i.e. $p_M = e\bar{\pi}_M$ and $p_E = e\bar{\pi}_E$ where e converts foreign currency units to domestic currency units. In the more general case, when there are barriers to trade (e.g. tariffs), the relative price guiding domestic decisions will be given by

$$\frac{p_M}{p_E} = \frac{\mu\bar{\pi}_M}{\bar{\pi}_E}\,;\, \mu > 1$$

and where $d\mu<0$ captures the effects reduction in importing costs; and equation (1.5) can be rewritten as:

$$\frac{E}{M} = \frac{\mu\bar{\pi}_M}{\bar{\pi}_E} \tag{1.6}$$

The model is closed by choosing a numéraire, say the exchange rate. Then, the relative price of the non-traded good, or the real exchange rate, $e^R = 1/p_D$, is the equilibrating variable.

II.*1* *The Link Between Migration and Capital Flows*

Consider now the links between migration (assumed to be exogenous) and induced capital flows. To find the effect of migration on the reward to capital and consequently on FDI flows, consider first the change in the price of the non-traded good induced by labor flows and in a second step the effect on the reward to capital. Solve then the system consisting of (1.2) and the log differentials of (1.4) and (1.5) assuming that only labor endowments change and export and import prices are exogenous. This gives the system:

$$\begin{aligned}
&(\hat{N}-\hat{E}) = \Omega\,\hat{p}_N + \left(\hat{L}_N - \hat{L}_E\right) + \frac{1}{\Delta}\left(\frac{\theta_{KN}\sigma_N}{\theta_{NN}} - \frac{\theta_{KE}\sigma_E}{\theta_{EE}}\right)\left(-\lambda_{KN}\hat{L}_N - \lambda_{KE}\hat{L}_E\right) \\
&\hat{M}-\hat{N} = \sigma\,\hat{p}_N \\
&\hat{M}-\hat{E} = 0
\end{aligned} \tag{1.7}$$

Solving (1.7) provides the expression linking the equilibrium domestic price to factor endowments.

$$\hat{p}_N = -\frac{1}{(\sigma+\Omega)}\left(\alpha_N\hat{L}_N + \alpha_E\hat{L}_E\right) \tag{1.8}$$

where

$$\alpha_N = 1 - \lambda_{KN}\frac{1}{\Delta}\left(\frac{\theta_{KN}\sigma_N}{\theta_{NN}} - \frac{\theta_{KE}\sigma_E}{\theta_{EE}}\right) > 0$$

$$\alpha_E = -1 - \lambda_{KE}\frac{1}{\Delta}\left(\frac{\theta_{KN}\sigma_N}{\theta_{NN}} - \frac{\theta_{KE}\sigma_E}{\theta_{EE}}\right) < 0$$

The impact of factor endowment changes on the domestic price is straightforward. From (1.8), emigration of labor specific to the non-traded sector raises the relative price of the non-traded good while emigration of labor specific to the export-sector lowers the relative price of the non-traded good. The adjustment mechanism is as follows: a decrease [increase] in the relative supply of non-traded labor L_N increases [decreases] its relative marginal product putting upward [downward] pressure on the relative price of the non-traded good. In the limit, if the two consumption goods become perfectly substitutable, the effect of labor emigration on the non-traded good price vanishes.

Substituting (1.8) into (1.1) shows that labor emigration affects the reward to capital through a familiar direct effect and indirectly via the induced change in the relative price of the non-traded good according to the following expression:

$$\hat{R} = +\frac{1}{\Delta}\left(\lambda_{KN}\hat{L}_N + \lambda_{KE}\hat{L}_E\right) - \frac{1}{(\sigma+\Omega)}\beta_N\left(\alpha_N\hat{L}_N + \alpha_E\hat{L}_E\right)$$

with the indirect effect vanishing when goods are perfect substitutes in consumption $(\sigma \to \infty)$ or the marginal rate of transformation in production is infinite $(\Omega \to \infty)$. Rearranging the above expression yields:

$$\begin{aligned}\hat{R} &= \frac{\lambda_{KN}}{\Delta}\frac{(\sigma-\sigma_N)}{(\sigma+\Omega)}\hat{L}_N + \frac{\left(\frac{\sigma_N}{\theta_{NN}}\left(\frac{\lambda_{KN}}{\lambda_{KE}} + \theta_{KN}\right) + \sigma\right)}{(\sigma+\Omega)}\hat{L}_E \\ &= \gamma_N\hat{L}_N + \gamma_E\hat{L}_E\end{aligned} \tag{1.9}$$

Emigration of labour which is specific to the export sector leads to a reduction in the rewards to capital, i.e. to FDI outflow ($\gamma_E > 0$). Emigration of labor which is specific to the non-traded sector is ambiguous $(\gamma_N > 0 \Leftrightarrow \sigma > \sigma_N\ ;\ \gamma_N < 0 \Leftrightarrow \sigma < \sigma_N)$ – in particular, factor substitutability in production of non-traded good (σ_N) combined with low substitutability in consumption (σ) leads to an increase in the reward to capital, and hence to FDI inflow.

II.*2 The Link Between Trade Costs and Capital Flows*

Add now the effects of a change in importing costs. Solving the system consisting of (1.2) and the log differentials of (1.4) and (1.6) yields the expression for the change in the home good price:

$$\hat{p}_N = \frac{\hat{\mu}(\sigma-1)}{(\sigma+\Omega)} - \frac{1}{(\sigma+\Omega)}\left(\alpha_N\hat{L}_N + \alpha_E\hat{L}_E\right) \tag{1.10}$$

If imports and non-traded goods are sufficiently good substitutes in consumption ($\sigma > 1$), then a reduction in tariffs ($d\mu$<0) which lowers the relative price of imports will lead to a decrease in the price of the home good, p_N. If the elasticity of substitution between the imported and non-traded goods is less than 1, the price of the non-traded good will increase when tariffs go down.

The effect of changes in importing costs on the reward to capital is given by (substitute (1.10) into (1.1)):

$$\hat{R} = \left(\frac{\beta_N (\sigma - 1)}{\sigma + \Omega} \right) \hat{\mu} + \gamma_N \hat{L}_N + \gamma_E \hat{L}_E \tag{1.11}$$

If the elasticity of substitution between imported and domestic goods is less than 1, the reduction in importing costs (lower μ) will result in a higher price of capital and positive FDI. Importantly, the effect of a reduction in importing costs on FDI works independently of the effects of the composition of emigration.

II.3 *Summarizing Model Predictions and Identifying Testable Hypotheses*

To sum up, the skeleton model is useful to investigate Migration-FDI and Trade-FDI links. Starting with Migration-FDI links, it indicates that emigration of different types of labour may have may have different impacts on FDI: emigration of labour which is specific to the export sector will always have a negative effect on FDI; emigration of labor specific to the non-traded sector will lead to positive FDI if the degree of production factor substitution in the non-traded sector is higher than the degree of substitution of non-traded and imported goods in consumption ($\sigma < \sigma_N$).

To test these predictions empirically, we concentrate on developing and transition economies – which are also the most likely to be emigration-sending countries. Short of data on emigration by sector of employment (in our case, exports and non-traded), we use the data on emigrant stocks by education level in 1990 and 2000 from DOCQUIER and MARFOUK [2006]. To "connect" these data to our model, we make a restricting assumption that in a typical migration sending country export activities are less skill-intensive than the production of non-traded goods. While the low skill intensity of exports is plausible and easy to justify (e.g. agriculture or unskilled-labor intensive exports like clothing and footwear), it is less clear that, on average, the non-traded sector is high-skilled intensive. However, for many migrant-sending countries, the high-skilled manufacturing sector is negligible and most high-skilled labor is employed in skill-intensive non-traded sectors – e.g. education, medical services and government administration. Along these lines, BHARGAVA and DOCQUIER [2008] provide an example of high-skilled non-traded-sector specific migration, i.e. the very high rates of medical brain drain for a number of small developing countries.

If in addition imports and non-traded goods are poor substitutes in consumption, the first prediction from the model is:

(i) High-skill emigration in developing countries will be positively correlated with higher levels of FDI

As to the Trade-FDI links, an increase in tariffs will lead to negative FDI, if imports and domestic goods are weak substitutes in consumption ($\sigma < 1$). Assuming again that in developing countries consumers cannot easily substitute imports for domestically produced non-traded goods and services, the second prediction is:

(ii) In developing countries higher tariffs will be associated with lower FDI.

ARTJOMS IVLEVS AND JAIME DE MELO

III. Empirical Specification and Data

III.1 Specification

We estimate the following model:

$$FDI_i = \beta_0 + \beta_1 Migration\ Skill\ Gap_i + \beta_2 Trade\ Restrictiveness_i + \gamma Control\ Variables_i + \delta Regional\ Dummies + \varepsilon_i \quad (1.12)$$

where

(i) FDI_i represents the flow of foreign direct investment to country *i* between 1990 and 2000. Our preferred measure is the average annual net FDI (inflows minus outflows) as a percentage of GDP between 1990 and 2000[6]. As a check on the sensitivity of our results we also use, as a second measure, the difference in net FDI stocks (as a percentage of GDP) between 1990 and 2000.

(ii) *Migration Skill Gap*$_i$ captures the change in high-skilled labour supply relative to the change in low-skilled labour supply due to migration in country *i* between 1990 and 2000. Precisely, we define *Migration Skill Gap* as

$$\frac{\Delta Stock\ of\ Emigrants_{High\ skilled,2000-1990}}{Labour_{High\ skilled,1990}} - \frac{\Delta Stock\ of\ Emigrants_{Low\ skilled,2000-1990}}{Labour_{Low\ skilled,1990}}$$

and express it in percentage points. For example, if between 1990 and 2000 in country *i* the supply of high-skilled labour decreased, due to migration, by 10%, and the supply of low-skilled labour decreased by 5%, our measure of the migration skill gap will be equal to 5 percentage points.

(iii) *Trade Restrictiveness* represents the importing costs (see section 3.2 for more detail);

(iv) *Control Variables* is a vector which controls the following (see section 3.2 for more detail): export skill intensity; GDP, population and the share of workers with tertiary education at the beginning of the period (1990); the changes in GDP, population and the share of workers with tertiary education over 1990-2000; the index of political stability; the index of linguistic fractionalization; and a measure of remoteness.

(v) and ε_i is the error term.

III.2 Sample and Data Sources

The sample of migration sending countries is chosen by excluding 26 "traditional" immigration-receiving countries[7], developed Asian countries (Korea, Malaysia , Singapore, Taiwan and Hong Kong), and Gulf countries (Bahrain, Kuwait, Qatar, Saudi Arabia and the United Arab Emirates)[8] from the whole sample of countries covered by DOCQUIER and MARFOUK [2006]. Given the availability of data for the other variables, this gives us a sample of 102 countries (see TABLE A.IV for the list).

6. By taking averages, we are also able to cope with the problem of missing data for countries which became independent in the early 1990s (e.g. countries in Central and Eastern Europe).

7. Australia, Austria, Belgium, Canada, Cyprus, Denmark, Finland, France, Germany, Greece, Iceland, Ireland, Israel, Italy, Japan, Luxembourg, Malta, the Netherlands, New Zealand, Norway, Portugal, Spain, Sweden, Switzerland, the United Kingdom, and the United States.

8. These countries are excluded because of high skill intensity of exports making them less comparable to other MSC and/or being potentially immigration receiving countries.

The appendix describes data sources in detail. The dependent variable (net inflows of FDI as percentage of GDP) is constructed using the UNCTAD inward and outward foreign direct investment data[9]. Migration data come from DOCQUIER and MARFOUK [2006] and BEINE et al. [2007][10]. The database contains information on emigration stocks by educational attainment (low, medium, high) in 1990 and 2000[11].

Among the key variables included in the model, we had difficulty obtaining an indicator of the change in a country's trade policy for our large sample with many small countries, including islands. We refrained from constructing an index residually from a regression estimating trade volumes and opted for the average tariffs in 1996-2000 from the World Bank Trade Data Base[12].

As for control variables, the skill-intensity of exports is approximated by the share of machinery and transport equipment (Section 7 of Standard International Trade Classification (SITC)) in total exports, a category listed among the most skill-intensive industries by e.g. ROMALIS [2004] (see his TABLE I). Two variables are included to proxy for the risk premium and socio-political environment: the index of political stability (increasing values corresponding to more stability) from the World Bank Aggregate Governance Indicators, and an index of linguistic fractionalization (higher values corresponding to higher diversity)[13] from ALESINA et al. [2003].

Remoteness is measured by the inverse of the distance-weighted GDP and comes from Andrew Rose's database. For each country i and year t, remoteness is defined as

$$R_{it} = 1/\left(\sum_j \frac{GDP_{jt}}{D_{ij}}\right)$$

where j represents all other countries (except i) and D_{ij} is the distance in km between the capitals of countries i and j.

Finally, in view of the stylized differences in regional patterns of emigration (see DOCQUIER and MARFOUK [2006]), we also include as controls regional dummy variables for small developing islands (defined as in DOCQUIER and MARFOUK [2006]), transition economies (Central and Eastern European countries, including former Yugoslavian and Soviet Union Republics, and Albania), Middle East and North African (MENA) countries, Africa, Asia and Latin America.

9. For six countries in our sample – Cameroon, Central Africa, Gabon, Iran, Panama and South Africa – FDI outflows are higher than inflows (negative values for the dependent variable).

10. Using data from BEINE et al [2007] we control for the age of entry of high-skilled immigrants (at least 22 years of age). This allows us to exclude emigrants who obtained their education in the country of destination and never participated in the labour force of their country of origin.

11. Restricting the change in labour force to changes in the composition of emigration neglects factors other than emigration that affect education levels, such as education policies and linkages between human capital and emigration. Short of modelling the supply of skills directly as in e.g. CHECCHI et al. [2007], we include among the controls some of the factors affecting the supply of skills (income per capita and its growth rate). Controls also include factors affecting the investment climate like measures of political stability. This said, the results in CHECCHI et al. suggest the potential for reverse causality since educational decisions are linked to past FDI and past migration.

12. This period is chosen because of close to complete data availability for the sample because for the period 1990-1995 tariff data is missing for many countries. We also experimented with interpolation to fill missing data to measure trade liberalization as (tariff (2000)-tariff (1990)/1+ tariff (1990)). We also computed 10 years tariff average. Neither was significant.

13. If population shares of n linguistic groups in a country are $p_1, p_2, \ldots, p_n$, the index of linguistic fractionalization is given by $F = 1 - \sum_{i=1}^{n} p_i^2$.

III.2 Endogeneity of Migration

A major challenge concerning the estimation of our results is reverse causality since the relationship between FDI and migration is likely to go both ways[14]. One the one hand, migration influences FDI through the change in the return to capital (as our model suggests) or via other channels such as migrant networks (not included in the model but controlled for in TABLE III). On the other hand, FDI is also likely to influence migration, and in particular that of skilled labour. Higher levels of FDI may increase the demand for skilled labour or increase overall income, thereby reducing migration. Or, if financial constraint to migration is binding, higher income generated by FDI may lead to higher outflows of workers.

To correct for potential endogeneity, we estimate our results with instrumental variables. As an instrument for our migration skill gap variable, we use the stocks of migrants in 1980 in the USA and Canada as percentage of sending-country population (these are the only two countries with sufficient data for our sample)[15] . The justification for this choice is that the prior stock of emigrants is likely to meet the exclusion restriction, i.e. to be potentially correlated with migration but not directly with FDI. Arguably, more migrants from developing countries in 1980 in the USA and Canada would make the subsequent migration easier via migrant networks. At the same time, migrants who arrived in the USA and Canada before 1980 would be less likely to influence FDI in 1990-2000, since they are less informed about recent investment opportunities in their home countries. Indeed, it is likely that the longer the migrant has lived abroad, the less likely he would be to have information about current investment opportunities in the source country and convey this information to potential investors. In other words, recent migrants are the most knowledgeable about where and how to invest in their home countries. This is especially true for developing countries where political regimes and administrative procedures/laws etc. often change.

As to the data source for our instrument – the sum of stocks of migrants in the USA and Canada from developing countries in 1980 relative to the home country populations – it comes from the official USA and Canada 2000 Population Census statistics. In particular, the 2000 Population Censuses of these countries contain (the publically and electronically available) information on whether the foreign-born residents (from practically all countries of the world) arrived before 1980, between 1980 and 1990, or between 1990 and 2000[16].

14. Education levels influence both FDI and migration decisions, and past migration has been found to influence current FDI through network effects, CHECCHI et al. [2007]). FDI is also sensitive to the political and economic environment of the host country.

15. We have tried several other variables to instrument our migration differential variable (among others: infant mortality rate, healthy life expectancy, adolescent fertility rate, government health expenditure, the spread of HIV, measles, malaria, pneumonia, the number of people affected in natural disasters, number of people affected by floods etc), but have encountered the common problem of weak instruments (in particular, the Cragg-Donald statistic did not exceed 4).

16. Migrants who arrived to the USA or Canada before 1980, but died between 1980 and 2000 cannot be accounted for, since we can use only 2000 Census data. Census data for 1980 and 1990 are either unavailable or extremely limited and in all cases not sufficiently disaggregated by country of origin. In our sample, stocks of migrants in the USA and Canada are highly correlated ($\rho = 0.69$) so that results are unaffected if we use as instrument the stock in either country rather than the sum of stocks.

IV. Results

TABLE I reports the results with robustness and sensitivity checks reported in TABLES II and III. Consider first OLS results. Regardless of the definition of skills, TABLE I shows that, after taking into account the controls, FDI and a change in the pattern of emigration towards skilled labour are positively correlated. Thus, a reduction in the relative supply of skilled labour (more emigrants) attracts FDI, i.e. the pattern of observed emigration and FDI are complement. Using alternative definitions for the measurement of the skill composition of emigration in columns [1] – [3], and after taking into account the separate influence exerted by the controls, a 1 percentage point decrease in the relative supply of skilled labour between 1990 and 2000 was associated with an increase in annual FDI (as a percentage of GDP) of about 0.02 percentage points. Thus, an increase in skilled- labour emigration (net of low-skilled emigration) of e.g. 10 percentage points between 1990 and 2000 was associated with an increase in FDI inflows by 0.2 percentage points annually (as a share of GDP). The OLS result is significant at 1%.

Turning to the IV results (columns [4] – [6] of TABLE I), we find that the instrument is significant at the 1% level in the first stage regression and (depending on the definition of the skill composition), explains 20-31% of the variation of the migration variable. The Cragg-Donald F-statistic is sufficiently high (ranging from 21 to 38), confirming that the coefficient of the instrument in the first stage regression is different from 0. As to the IV results, in all specifications, the migration coefficient values increase to 0.026-0.038 and remain highly significant.

Comfortingly, most of the controls have the expected signs and several are significant. The negative partial correlation between GDP (controlling for population) and FDI inflows conforms to predictions. Note, however, that this correlation would also be consistent with another interpretation if income per capita is a proxy for differences in factor endowments. Then, low income-per-capita countries would, as suggested by the neoclassical growth model, attract VFDI. At the same time, the impact of the relative change in the share of the high-skilled workers affects FDI flows negatively and significantly so. This result can be explained as follows. *Higher relative change* in the variable could be an indication of *lower initial levels* of the variable. The negative and significant coefficient of the change in the share of the high-skilled is then not surprising, assuming that the investors prefer countries with higher skilled labour force[17].

We also find that average 1996-2000 tariffs are negatively correlated with net FDI inflows, as predicted by our theoretical framework. However, given that the average tariffs do not measure the changes in trade policy over the period, it is difficult to put much significance on this result.

The sign of the coefficient associated with the linguistic variable is interesting. Linguistic fractionalisation is negatively associated with FDI inflows. This result is in line with previous evidence indicating an adverse impact of linguistic and ethnic heterogeneity on various social

17. One reviewer suggested that the negative coefficient of the relative change in the share of the highly skilled could be seen as supportive of the main prediction of our model. However, in our setting, the emigration of the highly skilled and the increase in the share of the highly skilled in the domestic labour force would have different effects on the price of the mobile factor (capital) and, subsequently, FDI. If the government policy is to increase the quantity and the quality of education, it would probably be matched with the increases or improvements of the productive capacity (capital). On the contrary, in the case of emigration of the highly skilled, especially if it is triggered by the sudden policy shock of the immigration-receiving country, the capital stock will adjust more slowly, giving rise to the differential between the domestic and world price of capital and FDI. Therefore, the coefficient of the migration differential variable should be regarded as the price (general equilibrium) effect. The relative change in the share of the highly skilled affects FDI through different channels (e.g. as a signal of the general skill level of the domestic labour force) and is used in the regressions to control for the changes in educational policies.

and economic variables, e.g. the provision of public goods, the literacy rate, the extent of corruption and political freedom, the incidence of civil wars, and growth (see e.g. EASTERLY and LEVINE [1997], LA PORTA et al. [1999], ALESINA et al. [2003], MONTALVO and REYNAL-QUEROL [2005a, 2005b]).

TABLE I. — Correlates of FDI in Migration-sending Countries

Dependent variable: Average annual FDI (as % of GDP) between 1990 and 2000						
	(1) OLS	(2) OLS	(3) OLS	(4) IV	(5) IV	(6) IV
$\Delta L_H/L_{H(1990)} - \Delta L_L/L_{L(1990)}$, in %(.)	0.020***			0.031***		
	(0.004)			(0.007)		
$\Delta L_H/L_{H(1990)} + \Delta L_M/L_{M(1990)} - \Delta L_L/L_{L(1990)}$, in %(.)		0.018***			0.026***	
		(0.003)			(0.006)	
$\Delta L_H/L_{H(1990)} - \Delta L_M/L_{M(1990)} - \Delta L_L/L_{L(1990)}$, in %(.)			0.021***			0.038***
			(0.004)			(0.009)
Remoteness	7.238	8.335	5.727	12.586*	12.680*	12.448*
	(6.784)	(6.810)	(6.784)	(7.088)	(6.918)	(7.489)
Average tariffs, 1996-2000, in %	–0.077**	–0.075**	–0.080**	–0.063*	–0.064*	–0.062*
	(0.034)	(0.034)	(0.034)	(0.034)	(0.033)	(0.036)
Skill intensive exports, in %	0.033*	0.033*	0.033*	0.037**	0.036**	0.038*
	(0.020)	(0.019)	(0.020)	(0.019)	(0.018)	(0.020)
Ln (GDP), 1990	–0.761**	–0.738**	–0.788**	–0.709**	–0.692**	–0.735**
	(0.299)	(0.298)	(0.302)	(0.287)	(0.280)	(0.303)
GDP growth, 1990-2000, in %	0.000	–0.000	0.000	–0.001	–0.001	–0.002
	(0.008)	(0.008)	(0.008)	(0.008)	(0.007)	(0.008)
Share of high-skilled, 1990, in %	–0.054	–0.045	–0.063	–0.077	–0.058	–0.104
	(0.070)	(0.070)	(0.071)	(0.068)	(0.065)	(0.074)
Change in the share of high-skilled, 1990, in %	–0.019***	–0.018***	–0.020***	–0.026***	–0.023***	–0.030***
	(0.005)	(0.005)	(0.005)	(0.006)	(0.006)	(0.007)
Ln (Population), 1990	0.309	0.322	0.297	0.243	0.280	0.190
	(0.339)	(0.338)	(0.342)	(0.326)	(0.316)	(0.346)
Population growth, 1990-2000, in %	–0.056*	–0.053*	–0.060**	–0.051*	–0.048*	–0.056*
	(0.028)	(0.028)	(0.028)	(0.027)	(0.026)	(0.029)
Political stability, 1996	–0.626	–0.579	–0.674*	–0.723*	–0.632*	–0.857**
	(0.385)	(0.383)	(0.389)	(0.371)	(0.359)	(0.399)
Linguistic fractionalisation, 2001	–2.135**	–2.204**	–2.054**	–2.191**	–2.272**	–2.073**
	(0.955)	(0.952)	(0.964)	(0.912)	(0.890)	(0.965)
MENA	0.071	0.043	0.105	0.007	–0.014	0.038
	(1.099)	(1.096)	(1.109)	(1.050)	(1.023)	(1.111)
Africa	–1.717	–1.669	–1.736	–2.446**	–2.182**	–2.834**
	(1.072)	(1.065)	(1.083)	(1.096)	(1.046)	(1.201)
Small Islands	0.189	0.063	0.420	–1.590	–1.287	–2.036
	(1.539)	(1.540)	(1.542)	(1.754)	(1.669)	(1.926)
Transition Economics	–0.131	–0.055	–0.233	0.158	0.187	0.116
	(1.349)	(1.345)	(1.359)	(1.296)	(1.265)	(1.371)
Latin America	–0.889	–1.140	–0.588	–1.229	–1.488	–0.847
	(1.042)	(1.044)	(1.047)	(1.011)	(0.999)	(1.056)
Constant	17.533***	16.413***	18.848***	16.680***	15.343***	18.648***
	(4.515)	(4.516)	(4.546)	(4.333)	(4.269)	(4.554)
Instrument[a]: *coeff. 1st stage, standard error*				17.736***	21.116***	14.356***
				(3.263)	*(3.424)*	*(3.138)*
Partial R^2 of excl. instrument				0.26	0.31	0.20
Cragg-Donald F-stat (p-value)				29.55	38.04	20.93
				(0.000)	(0.000)	(0.000)
Number of observations R^2	102	102	102	102	102	102
	0.577	0.580	0.570	0.533	0.556	0.476

Standard errors in parentheses

[a]Stock of migrants in the USA and Canada in 1980 as % of sending country population.

*$p < 0.10$, **$p < 0.05$, ***$p < 0.01$

$\Delta L_i/L_i$, i = *high, medium, low*, is the change in emigration slock of labor with skill level i between 1990 and 2000 (positive, if emigration stock increased) with respect to total labor force with skill level i in 1990, expressed in %.

Political stability index ranges from -2.5 to 2.5. Higher values correspond to better governance outcomes.

Linguistic fractionalization index ranges from 0 to 1. Higher values correspond to higher linguistic and religious diversity.

Asia is the reference group for regions.

The OLS result is robust to a different measure of FDI when we use the difference in stocks of net FDI (as % of GDP) between 2000 and 1990 as dependent variable (col. [1] and [2] in TABLE II). Again, we find that a more than proportional outflow of high-skill labour between 1990 and 2000 is associated with a positive change in FDI stock. Specifically, a 10 percentage point increase in relatively high skilled emigration in 1990-2000 is associated with 1.2 (OLS) – 2.3 (IV) percentage point increase of FDI stock (as % of GDP).

TABLE II. — Correlates of FDI: Robustness and Sensitivity Checks

Dependent variable	Stock of FDI (% of GDP) in 2000 - stock of FDI (% of GDP) in 1990		Average annual FDI (as % of GDP) between 1990 and 2000: Without transition economies		Without Small island economies	
	(1)	(2)	(3)	(4)	(5)	(6)
	OLS	IV	OLS	IV	OLS	IV
$\Delta L_H/L_{H(1990)} - \Delta L_L/L_{L(1990)}$, in %(.)	0.120***	0.229***	0.019***	0.028***	0.010**	0.039
	(0.031)	(0.059)	(0.004)	(0.007)	(0.004)	(0.071)
Remoteness	-19.924	33.415	2.194	7.148	14.188**	15.009*
	(57.946)	(61.587)	(7.268)	(7.499)	(6.679)	(7.843)
Average tariffs, 1996-2000, in %	-0.512*	-0.374	-0.063*	-0.053	-0.034	-0.047
	(0.292)	(0.291)	(0.037)	(0.035)	(0.033)	(0.048)
Skill intensive exports, in %	0.104	0.140	0.035	0.037*	0.041**	0.035
	(0.167)	(0.163)	(0.024)	(0.022)	(0.018)	(0.024)
Ln (GDP), 1990	-7.484***	-6.973***	-0.620*	-0.581*	-0.988***	-0.862*
	(2.556)	(2.493)	(0.331)	(0.308)	(0.290)	(0.453)
GDP growth, 1990-2000, in %	-0.041	-0.055	0.003	0.001	-0.004	-0.004
	(0.067)	(0.065)	(0.008)	(0.008)	(0.007)	(0.008)
Share of high-skilled, 1990, in %	0.392	0.167	-0.058	-0.069	-0.055	-0.073
	(0.598)	(0.590)	(0.091)	(0.084)	(0.059)	(0.081)
Change in the share of high-skilled, 1990, in %	-0.122***	-0.189***	-0.017***	-0.024***	-0.011**	-0.029
	(0.045)	(0.054)	(0.006)	(0.007)	(0.005)	(0.046)
Ln (Population), 1990	4.971*	4.320	0.254	0.214	0.585*	0.494
	(2.897)	(2.829)	(0.370)	(0.344)	(0.305)	(0.413)
Population growth, 1990-2000, in %	-0.709***	-0.662***	-0.066*	-0.060*	-0.014	-0.058
	(0.241)	(0.235)	(0.034)	(0.032)	(0.027)	(0.113)
Political stability, 1996	-3.806	-4.772	-0.552	-0.655*	-0.170	-0.530
	(3.284)	(3.220)	(0.414)	(0.390)	(0.347)	(0.979)
Linguistic fractionalisation, 2001	-7.630	-8.191	-2.174**	-2.191**	-1.611*	-2.443
	(8.161)	(7.927)	(1.056)	(0.978)	(0.847)	(2.281)
MENA	2.420	1.789	0.023	-0.036	0.301	0.263
	(9.391)	(9.121)	(1.151)	(1.067)	(0.950)	(1.081)
Africa	-3.986	-11.255	-1.009	-1.652	-2.288**	-2.625*
	(9.154)	(9.521)	(1.142)	(1.142)	(0.956)	(1.372)
Small Islands	4.087	-13.653	0.638	-0.764	-	-
	(13.145)	(15.244)	(1.635)	(1.780)		
Transition Economies	-14.907	-12.017	-	-	1.949	0.201
	(11.519)	(11.264)			(1.296)	(4.592)
Latin America	2.871	-0.512	-0.533	-0.876	-0.207	-1.088
	(8.904)	(8.788)	(1.102)	(1.046)	(0.890)	(2.414)
Constant	137.7***	129.2***	15.678***	14.718***	14.941***	15.861***
	(38.567)	(37.652)	(5.295)	(4.945)	(4.136)	(5.218)
Instrument[a] : *coeff. 1st stage standard error*		17.736***		17.731***		2.718
		(3.263)		(3.811)		(4.548)
Partial R^2 of excl. instrument		0.26		0.26		0.005
Cragg-Donald F-stat (p-value)		29.55		21.65		0.36
		(0.000)		(0.000)		(0.552)
Number of observations	102	102	80	80	91	91
R^2	0.450	0.370	0.605	0.570	0.435	0.107

Standard errors in parentheses

[a] Stock of migrants in the USA and Canada in 1980 as % of sending country population.

* $p < 0.10$, ** $p < 0.05$, *** $p < 0.01$

See notes of TABLE I.

Results are also robust to a change in sample when transition economies (col. [3] and [4] of TABLE II) and small developing island economies (col. [5] and [6]) are excluded. Using OLS, we still obtain a significant and positive coefficient of relatively high-skilled emigration. However, excluding small island economies reduces by half the value of the coefficient. Using 1980 migrant stock in the USA and Canada as an instrument, there is no change in results when transition economies are excluded, but we notice that these instruments are no longer valid if small islands are excluded from our sample[18].

IV.*1* *Controlling for Networks*

In spite of the included controls and the above robustness checks, this apparently robust correlation might be spurious, as it might reflect some omitted variable affecting both FDI and emigration. Among the more important possibilities, changes in immigration policies in host countries might have fostered diasporas which in turn could have contributed to changes in the perception about the attractiveness of FDI, or to changes in FDI policies in migration-sending countries. To see if this diaspora channel might be important, we purge from the data an estimate of FDI-related networks.

To control for the importance of networks (see DOCQUIER and LODIGIANI [2007]), we use data by DOCQUIER, LOWELL and MARFOUK [2007] to build migration data by country of destination. In a first step we find the three main migrant destinations for all sending countries, which for most countries in our sample account for close to 90% of migrants. In a second step, we calculate for each sending country the percentage of the stock of FDI that comes from the three main destinations of migrants (we find the major origins of FDI in the UNCTAD country profiles, although sometimes only flow data for certain years (e.g. 2000) are available). We then subtract the share of FDI coming from the migrant destination countries from the aggregate FDI value to isolate "networks-related FDI" from total FDI inflows. As a result of this construction of bilateral migration and FDI, we lose 40% of observations.

The results from this new set of estimates are reported in TABLE III and are still broadly supportive of the complementarity results reported in TABLES I and II. Not surprisingly, with this smaller sample, estimates are less precise. If the dependent variable is the average annual FDI (col. [1]), the migration (high-skilled less low-skilled) variable is positive, but insignificant. However, if the dependent variable is the difference in the stock of FDI (col. [3]), the migration variable is positive and significant at the 5% level. With IV estimates (see cols. (2) and (4)), the value of the migration coefficient increases, and the coefficient is significant at 10%[19].

18. Clearly other instruments would be desirable for a restricted sample of developing countries that would exclude small islands, though there is no a priori reason to exclude small islands, especially in an otherwise small cross-section sample.

19. We have also tried the 1990 stock of skilled migrants as an alternative measure for networks. However, the use of both the stock of migrants and the migration differential variable in one regression results in multicollinearity (both variables are highly correlated). The estimated coefficient of the stock is then significant, while the migration differential variable becomes insignificant.

TABLE III. — Estimates Excluding Diaspora-Related FDI

Dependent variable	Average annual FDI (% of GDP) between 1990 and 2000, excluding FDI from three major migrant destinations		Stock of FDI (% of GDP) in 2000- stock of FDI (% of GDP) in 1990, excluding FDI from three major migrant destinations	
	OLS	*IV*	*OLS*	*IV*
	(1)	(2)	(3)	(4)
$\Delta L_H/L_{H(1990)} - \Delta L_L/L_{L(1990)}$ in %(.)	0.009 (0.005)	0.015* (0.008)	0.093** (0.035)	0.094* (0.052)
Remoteness	9.513 (8.218)	10.574 (7.093)	62.326 (53.265)	62.433 (45.284)
Average tariffs, 1996-2000, in %	–0.066 (0.051)	–0.062 (0.044)	–0.353 (0.333)	–0.353 (0.281)
Skill intensive exports, in %	0.016 (0.024)	0.019 (0.021)	0.160 (0.159)	0.160 (0.135)
Ln (GDP), 1990	–0.704** (0.342)	–0.633** (0.301)	-7.081*** (2.217)	-7.074*** (1.921)
GDP growth, 1990-2000, in %	–0.004 (0.010)	–0.006 (0.008)	–0.113* (0.062)	–0.113** (0.054)
Share of high-skilled, 1990, in %	–0.069 (0.088)	–0.054 (0.077)	–0.174 (0.573)	–0.173 (0.491)
Change in the share of high-skilled, 1990, in %	–0.003 (0.010)	–0.006 (0.009)	–0.015 (0.065)	–0.015 (0.059)
Ln (Population), 1990	0.368 (0.371)	0.318 (0.320)	5.386** (2.403)	5.380*** (2.046)
Population growth, 1990-2000, in %	–0.030 (0.049)	–0.012 (0.046)	–0.247 (0.321)	–0.245 (0.296)
Political stability, 1996	–0.217 (0.538)	–0.173 (0.461)	–1.077 (3.489)	–1.073 (2.945)
Linguistic fractionalisation, 2001	–1.320 (1.255)	–1.207 (1.076)	1.700 (8.135)	1.712 (6.872)
MENA	1.335 (2.759)	0.825 (2.412)	0.464 (17.881)	0.412 (15.397)
Africa	–0.683 (3.065)	–1.571 (2.774)	–10.387 (19.865)	–10.477 (17.710)
Small Islands	2.498 (3.029)	0.874 (3.095)	3.085 (19.635)	2.920 (19.758)
Transition Economics	2.321 (2.724)	1.746 (2.398)	7.550 (17.653)	7.492 (15.313)
Latin America	0.689 (2.906)	–0.163 (2.634)	5.526 (18.839)	5.439 (16.817)
Constant	11.901** (5.496)	11.156** (4.749)	87.086** (35.622)	87.010*** (30.323)
Instrument[a]: *coeff. 1st stage standard error*		14.064*** (3.033)		14.064*** (3.033)
Partial R^2 of excl. instrument		0.33		0.33
Cragg-Donald F-stat (p-value)		21.51 (0.000)		21.51 (0.000)
Number of observations	61	61	61	61
R^2	0.568	0.555	0.590	0.590

Standard errors in parentheses

[a]Stock of migrants in the USA and Canada in 1980 as % of sending country population.

$*p < 0.10$, $**p < 0.05$, $***p < 0.01$

See notes of TABLE I.

V. Conclusions

This paper investigated the channels linking FDI, migration and trade for migration-sending countries in a unified framework suitable for empirical investigation with macro data. Assuming that FDI responds to changes in the reward to capital, we investigate the effects of changes in the skill composition of the labour force through migration (emigration is assumed exogenous and determined by immigration policies in host countries) on FDI. If exports in migration sending countries are relatively less skill intensive than non-traded goods, a skewed pattern of emigration towards skilled labour which raises the price of the non-traded good will also raise the net capital reward, thereby leading to positive FDI. In this set-up, emigration of skilled labour is complementary with FDI, i.e. the outflow of higher skilled labour leads to capital inflows.

Correlations on a sample of 102 developing countries using emigration rates by skill for 1990 and 2000 support this conjecture. Over 1990-2000, the conditional correlation between FDI flows and the pattern of emigration suggests that, after controlling for countries' GDP per capita, education level and other factors, an increase in the emigration rate of high-skilled workers (net of low-skilled emigration) by 10 percentage points is associated with an increase in annual FDI (as a share of GDP) of about 0.2 percentage points.

The complementarity between skilled emigration and FDI is generally robust notably to different measures of FDI and to different samples. The correlation suggesting complementarity is also fairly robust to an alternative estimation on a smaller sample in which diaspora-related FDI has been purged. Taken together, the results are supportive of studying the migration-trade-FDI nexus in a general equilibrium setting taking into account the skill composition of emigrants.

The results also extend the channels through which linguistic fractionalization diversity affect developing-country performance. Whereas previous channels emphasized growth and corruption, we find here that linguistic fractionalization is negatively correlated with FDI inflows.

ACKNOWLEDGEMENTS

We thank Mario Piacentini for many helpful conversations and suggestions, and Giovanni Facchini, Céline Carrère, Frédéric Docquier, Hubert Jayet, Marcelo Olarreaga, Maurice Schiff and Mathias Thoenig and participants at the Lille, Riga and Warsaw conferences for comments. All remaining errors are our own.

Correspondence: Artjoms Ivlevs – Bristol Business School, UWE, Frenchay Campus, Coldharbour Lane, Bristol, BS16 1QY, United Kingdom.
Email: a.ivlevs@uwe.ac.uk.

Appendix

TABLE A.I — Data Sources and Definitions

Name of Variable	Definition	Source
FDI: $\left(\Delta K_{it}^{*} / Y_{it}\right)$	Net FDI as % of GDP	UNCTAD data base
GDP	GDP in 1990	WDI indicators
Population	Population in 1990	WDI indicators
Share of high-skilled, 1990	Share of high skill in the labor force	Docquier and Marfouk (2006)
Remoteness	Inverse of distance-weighted GDP	A. Rose database
Average tariffs	Average tariffs in 1996-2000	Ng database
Skill intensive exports	Machinery and transport /total exports	SITC, section 7
Political stability, 1996	Political stability -2.5 (less stable)$<PS_i+2.5$ (more stable)	World Bank Aggregate Governance Indicators
Linguistic fractionalisation, 2001	Linguistic fractionalization [0 (low diversity) … 1 (high diversity)]	Alesina et al. (2003)

TABLE A.II — Summary Statistics

Variable	Observ.	Mean	Std. Dev.	Min	Max
average annual FDI (as % of GDP), 1990-2000	102	2.47	2.86	-5.25	14.72
stock of FDI (% of GDP) in 2000 – stock of FDI (% of GDP) in 1990	102	16.06	21.42	-48.34	124.85
$\Delta L_H/L_{H(1990)} - \Delta L_L/L_{L(1990)}$	102	34.66	82.66	-6.75	504.77
$\Delta L_H/L_{H(1990)} + \Delta L_M/L_{M(1990)} - \Delta L_L/L_{L(1990)}$	102	21.90	69.06	-27.86	473.35
$\Delta L_H/L_{H(1990)} - \Delta L_M/L_{M(1990)} - \Delta L_L/L_{L(1990)}$	102	28.28	75.34	-5.23	489.06
Remoteness	102	0.18	0.06	0.07	0.33
Average tariffs, 1996-2000, in %	102	15.67	8.09	0.24	38.13
Skill intensive exports, in %	102	10.16	14.64	0.04	76.13
Ln (GDP), 1990	102	22.83	1.83	17.47	26.86
GDP growth, 1990-2000, in %	102	31.37	40.24	-64.39	180.15
Share of high-skilled, 1990, in %	102	6.93	6.16	0.10	20.10
Change in the share of high-skilled, 1990, in %	102	44.92	52.16	-10.00	300.00
Ln (Population), 1990	102	15.88	1.74	11.60	20.85
Population growth, 1990-2000, in %	102	18.47	14.52	-13.55	53.22
Political stability, 1996	102	-0.27	0.82	-2.92	0.98
Linguistic fractionalisation, 2001	102	0.41	0.30	0.01	0.92
MENA	102	0.10	0.30	0	1
Africa	102	0.29	0.46	0	1
Small Islands	102	0.11	0.31	0	1
Transition Economies	102	0.22	0.41	0	1
Latin America	102	0.17	0.37	0	1
Stock of migrants in the USA and Canada in 1980 as % of sending country pop.	102	0.92	2.40	0.00	12.34
Average annual FDI (% of GDP) between 1990 and 2000, excluding FDI from three major migrant destinations	61	1.97	2.22	-2.65	10.15
Stock of FDI (% of GDP) in 2000- stock of FDI (% of GDP) in 1990, excluding FDI from three major migrant destinations	61	12.76	14.75	-15.20	66.28

TABLE A.III — Correlation Matrix Between Independent Variables

	Migration	Remoteness	Average tariffs	Skilled Exports	Ln(GDP)	GDP growth
Migration $\Delta L_H/L_{H(1990)} - \Delta L_L/L_{L(1990)}$	1.00					
Remoteness	0.10	1.00				
Average tariffs	0.08	0.21	1.00			
Skill intensive exports	-0.13	-0.38	-0.28	1.00		
Ln (GDP), 1990	-0.38	-0.21	-0.15	0.43	1.00	
GDP growth	0.09	0.29	0.23	-0.01	-0.01	1.00
Share of high-skilled	-0.27	-0.46	-0.50	0.36	0.35	-0.47
Change in the share of high-skilled	0.41	0.22	0.17	-0.20	-0.19	0.19
Ln (Population)	-0.35	-0.03	0.04	0.18	0.80	0.13
Population Growth	0.04	0.49	0.29	-0.33	-0.27	0.55
Political Stability	0.15	-0.07	-0.19	0.25	-0.30	0.01
Linguistic Fractionalisation	0.00	0.25	0.09	-0.19	-0.13	0.00
Latin America	-0.12	0.19	-0.21	0.01	0.21	0.16
MENA	-0.09	-0.19	0.27	-0.08	0.13	0.20
Africa	0.07	0.48	0.14	-0.30	-0.35	0.11
Small Islands	0.47	0.22	0.29	-0.11	-0.41	0.03
Transition	-0.17	-0.66	-0.45	0.32	0.20	-0.64

TABLE A.III — Correlation Matrix Between Independent Variables (continued)

	High-skilled: share	High-skilled: change	Ln (pop)	Population growth	Political stability	Ling. fract.
Share of high-skilled	1.00					
Change in the share of high-skilled	-0.46	1.00				
Ln (Population)	0.01	0.00	1.00			
Population growth	-0.56	0.24	0.02	1.00		
Political stability	0.18	-0.26	-0.55	-0.27	1.00	
Linguistic fractionalisation	-0.29	0.15	0.16	0.31	-0.24	1.00
Latin America	0.24	-0.12	0.03	0.10	-0.05	-0.31
MENA	0.00	0.09	0.07	0.22	-0.15	-0.19
Africa	-0.55	0.21	-0.01	0.50	-0.18	0.61
Small Islands	-0.24	0.06	-0.54	-0.11	0.35	-0.22
Transition	0.67	-0.32	-0.02	-0.77	0.21	-0.16

Note: see TABLE A.I for definition of variables

TABLE A.IV — List of Countries by Region

Middle East and North Africa (MENA)	Algeria, Egypt, Iran, Jordan, Lebanon, Morocco, Oman, Syria, Tunisia and Yemen
Small Islands	the Bahamas, Comoros, Fiji, Guyana, Jamaica, Mauritius, Papua New Guinea, Saint Lucia, Saint Vincent and the Grenadines, Sao Tome and Principe, Trinidad and Tobago.
Transition Economies	Albania, Armenia, Azerbaijan, Belarus, Bulgaria, Croatia, Czech Republic, Estonia, Georgia, Hungary, Kazakhstan, Latvia, Lithuania, Macedonia, Moldova, Poland, Romania, Russia, Slovakia, Slovenia, Turkmenistan and Ukraine.
Latin America	Argentina, Belize, Bolivia, Brazil, Chile, Colombia, Costa Rica, Ecuador, Guatemala, Honduras, Mexico, Nicaragua, Panama, Paraguay, Peru, Uruguay, Venezuela
Africa	Benin, Botswana, Burkina Faso, Burundi, Cameroon, Central African Republic, Cote d'Ivoire, Ethiopia, Gabon, the Gambia, Ghana, Guinea, Kenya, Lesotho, Madagascar, Malawi, Mali, Mozambique, Namibia, Niger, Nigeria, Senegal, South Africa, Sudan, Swaziland, Tanzania, Togo, Uganda, Zambia, Zimbabwe.
Asia	Bangladesh, Cambodia, China, India, Indonesia, Mongolia, Nepal, Pakistan, Philippines, Thailand, Turkey, Vietnam

References

ALESINA, A., A. DEVLEESCHAUWER, W. EASTERLY, S. KURLAT and R. WACZIARG (2003): "Fractionalization", *Journal of Economic Growth*, Vol 8, No. 2, pp. 155-194. [111,114,118]

AMITI, M. and K. WAKELIN (2003): "Investment Liberalization and International Trade," *Journal of International Economics*, Vol. 61, pp.101-126. [104]

ARORA, A. and A. GAMBARDELLA, eds., (2005): *From Underdogs to Tigers: The Rise and Growth of the Software Industry in Brazil, China, India, Ireland and Israel*, Oxford University Press. [104]

BHARGAVA, A., and F. DOCQUIER (2008): "HIV Pandemic, Medical Brain Drain, and Economic Development in Sub-Saharan Africa," *World Bank Economic Review*, Vol. 22, pp. 345-367. [109]

BEINE, M., F. DOCQUIER and H. RAPOPORT (2007): "Measuring International Skilled Migration: New Estimates Controlling for Age of Entry," *World Bank Economic Review*, Vol. 21, No. 2, pp. 249-254. [111]

CHECCHI, D., G. De SIMONE and R. FAINI (2007): "Skilled Migration, FDI and Human Capital," *Centro Luca d'Agliano WP*, No. 235. [104,111,112]

DEFOORT, C. (2008): "Tendances de long terme en migrations internationales: analyse à partir de 6 pays receveurs," *Population-E* 63, pp. 285-318. [104]

DOCQUIER, F. (2007): "Brain Drain and Inequality Across Nations," forthcoming *Revue d'Economie du Développement.* [104]

DOCQUIER, F., O. LOHEST and A. MARFOUK (2007): "Brain Drain in Developing Countries," *World Bank Economic Review*, Vol. 21, No. 2, pp. 193-218. [104]

DOCQUIER, F. and E. LODIGIANI (2007): "Skilled Migration and Business Networks," Open Economies Review, online DOI 10.1007/s11079-008-9102-8. [116]

DOCQUIER, F., and A. MARFOUK (2006): "International Migration by Educational Attainment (1990-2000) – Release 1.1," in C. Ozden and M. Schiff, eds., International Migration, Remittances and Development, Palgrave Macmillan: New York. [104,109,110,111,118]

DOCQUIER, F., B.L. LOWELL and A. MARFOUK (2007): "A Gendered Assessment of Highly Skilled Immigration," *Population and Development Review*, Vol. 35, No. 2, pp. 297-322. [116]

EASTERLY, W. and R. LEVINE (1997): "Africa's Growth Tragedy: Policies and Ethnic Divisions," *Quarterly Journal of Economics*, Vol. 112, No. 4, pp. 1203- 1250. [114]

FRIEDBERG, R.M. (2001): "The Impact of Mass Migration on the Israel Labor Market," *Quarterly Journal of Economics,* Vol. 116, pp. 1373-1408. [105]

GOULD, D.M. (1994): "Immigrant Links to the Home Country: Empirical Implications for U.S. Bilateral Trade Flows", *The Review of Economic and Statistics*, Vol. 76, No. 2, pp. 302-316. [104]

HEAD, K. and J. RIES (1998): "Immigration and Trade Creation: Econometric Evidence from Canada", *Canadian Journal of Economics,* Vol. 31, No. 1, pp. 47-62. [104]

JONES, R. (1971): "A Three-Factor Model in Theory, Trade and History," in: Bhagwati J. et al., eds., *Trade, Balance of Payments and Growth*, North-Holland. [105]

KUGLER, M. and H. RAPOPORT (2005): "Skilled Emigration, Business Networks and Foreign Direct Investment," *CESIFO WP* No. 1455. [104]

KUGLER, M. and H. RAPOPORT (2007): "International Labor and Capital Flows: Complements or Substitutes?" *Economic Letters*, Vol. 1, No. 2, pp. 155-162. [104]

LA PORTA, R., F.A. LOPEZ-DE-SILANES, SHLEIFER and R. VISHNY, (1999): "The Quality of Government," *Journal of Law, Economics and Organization*, Vol. 15, pp. 222-279. [114]

MARKUSEN, J. R. (2002): *Multinational Firms and the Theory of International Trade*, Cambridge, MIT Press. [104]

MONTALVO, J.G. and M. REYNAL-QUEROL (2005a): "Ethnic Polarization, Potential Conflict, and Civil Wars," *American Economic Review*, Vol. 95, No. 3, pp. 796-816. [114]

MONTALVO, J.G. and M. REYNAL-QUEROL (2005b): "Ethnic Diversity and Economic Development," *Journal of Development Economics*, Vol. 76, pp. 293-323. [114]

MOUNTFORD A. (1997): "Can a Brain Drain Be Good For Growth in the Source Economy?," *Journal of Development Economics,* Vol. 53, pp. 287-303. [104]

MUNDELL, R. (1957): "International Trade and Factor Mobility", *American Economic Review, Vol.* 47, No. 2, pp. 321-335. [106]

NAVARETTI, G.B. and A. VENABLES (2004): *Multinational Firms in the World Economy*, Princeton, Princeton University Press. [104]

RAUCH, J.E. and A. CASELLA (2003): "Overcoming Informational Barriers to International Resource Allocation: Prices and Group Ties," *Economic Journal*, Vol. 113, pp. 21-42. [104]

RAUCH, J.E. and V. TRINDADE (2002): "Ethnic Chinese Networks in International Trade", *Review of Economics and Statistics*, Vol. 48, No. 1, pp. 7-35. [104]

ROMALIS, J. (2004): "Factor Proportions and the Structure of Commodity Trade," *American Economic Review*, Vol. 94, No. 1, pp. 67-97. [111]

SCHIFF, M. (2007): "Migration, Investissement et Commerce: relation et implications politiques: Commentaires," *Revue d'Economie du Développement*, Vol. 23, No. 2-3, pp. 1-35. [104]

Trade in a 'Green Growth' Development Strategy

*Issues and Challenges**

Jaime de Melo†

This paper discusses the state of knowledge about the trade-related environmental consequences of a country's development strategy along three channels: (i) direct trade-environment linkages (overexploitation of natural resources and trade-related transport costs);(ii) 'virtual trade' in emissions resulting from production activities; (iii) the product mix attributes of a 'green-growth' strategy (environmentally preferable products and goods for environmental management). Main conclusions are the following. Trade exacerbates over-exploitation of natural resources in weak institutional environments, but there is little evidence that differences in environmental policies across countries has led to significant 'pollution havens'. Trade policies to 'level the playing field' would be ineffective and result in destructive conflicts in the WTO. Lack of progress at the Doha round suggests the need to modify the current system of global policy making.

Key words: Environmental goods, natural resources, green growth, trade, climate.
JEL Classification: F18, Q56.

1 PRELIMINARIES

A sustainable growth is a development strategy that meets the need of the current generation without hindering the ability of future generations to meet their own needs implying sufficient economic forces to offset the exhaustibility of finite resources (Bruntland report (UN, 1987)). A sustainable growth strategy

* This is a revised and shortened version of de Melo (2012). I am grateful to the World Bank and to the FERDI for financial support, to Mike Toman for helpful conversations and to Jean-Marie Grether, Nicole Mathys, Gisèle Schmid, Ronald Steenblink and conference participants for comments on an earlier draft.

† University of Geneva and FERDI. E-mail: Jaime.demelo@unige.ch

must also recognize nature's limited ability to act as a sink for human activities, implying that the environment is itself a limited resource. Sustainable growth thus requires dealing with the by-products of human activity (solid pollutants, toxic pollutants, CO_2 emissions) as well as exhaustibility (fossil fuels and minerals, temperature increase) and renewability (fish, forests) in an economically meaningful time frame. A well-developed growth literature leading to the Hartwick (1977) rule has established that growth is sustainable in the face of declining natural capital when natural capital is not an essential input (i.e. it can be substituted by physical and human capital). Then, the rents from the exploitation of the resource have to be invested in building the substitutes (human and physical capital stock) needed to generate the continuous technological change that shifts the depletion point of the natural resource indefinitely.

Where then does trade enter into a 'green growth' strategy? From the perspective of a trade economist it begins with the 'Columbian exchange' when, starting in the 15th century, global trade transformed the planet into a single ecological system that has had a profound influence on ecological diversity and indirectly on the exhaustibility of natural resources. This transformation would not have occurred in the absence of international trade. Here I take a shorter-term and narrower perspective, asking how current and future trade and trade policies enter a green-growth development strategy. My focus is on reviewing evidence on how trade affects the quality of the environment defined to include local and trans-border pollution and the sustainable use of natural resources. A few preliminaries serve to set the contours of the debate.

In the case of pollution-intensive tradable manufacturing activities (e.g. the energy-intensive industries that are also heavy emitters of GHGs), the problem is the possibility of "outsourcing" the pollution. If the pollution damage is mostly local, such as SO_2 emissions, then internalizing the damage through the application of a corrective tax or a technological standard will, in principle, solve the problem except for the possibility that these polluting activities may migrate to "pollution havens" since trade-leakage allows firms to escape the reach of their governments' environmental policies. If the pollution is global (as in GHG emissions), while the corrective instruments are the same, the solution requires collective action.

In the case of natural resources, the effects of trade depend on the property rights regime. When these can be secured, trade will be welfare-increasing. When property-rights are ill-defined, or when there is open-access, international trade is likely to lead to over-exploitation or disappearance of the resource. Then a restriction on trade or a ban on trade in endangered species would be the appropriate policy in an environment where resources are open-access.

To be effective, the policy requires cooperation from trading partners, as for instance, in the ban of trade in ivory. By contrast, an environmental policy to regulate local pollution does not require cooperation to the extent that "virtual trade in pollution" is limited.

A few environmental problems like climate change are truly global. In this case, collective action is necessary and, so far, little role has been attributed to international trade in solving them, notably the climate change problem. In effect, trade is of limited help in designing a global climate regime. First, it cannot resolve the property rights issue of who has the right to do what. Second, by implication, it is of limited help in determining how to implement the Common but Differentiated Responsibility (CBDR) principle enshrined in the 1994 United Nations Framework Convention on Climate Change (UNFCCC) in anticipation of the, yet to be taken, actions to internalize the global externality caused by climate change. Being a trans-border externality, courts have no jurisdiction to award rights. Power and political process determine implicit property-right outcomes.

Yet, trade can be a facilitator in designing policies for global public goods by widening the range of potentially beneficial outcomes in the negotiations and an open World Trading System will help technological diffusion of 'green growth' technologies. Trade can also play a strategic role in the exercise of transnational power via threatened or actual trade measures if the necessary cooperation is not forthcoming. Along more traditional lines, trade policies can be used to compensate for the competitiveness effects of differences in environmental policies across countries. Barrett (2003) reviews the literature on International Environmental Agreements and Ederington (2010) reviews the implications of linking trade and environmental agreements.

As emphasized by Whalley (2011), in a linked climate-trade-finance regime that goes beyond the current global policy coordination regime envisioned at Bretton Woods in 1944, climate now offers the prospect of potentially stronger trade disciplines beyond those negotiated at the WTO. Recognizing that the link between trade and environmental policies is more direct than when the Bretton Woods regime was set up raises the question of the appropriateness of negotiating trade and environmental policies separately and of how trade and environmental policies fit in the current global policy coordination architecture and whether this architecture is appropriate. Apart from some concluding remarks, in spite of its emphasis on global issues, this survey does not deal with the architecture of the current global policy regime or the desirability of linking trade and environmental policies. Nor does it cover the role of an open World Trade System in facilitating technological transfer and adoption.

The paper emphasizes the evidence brought to the debate and is organized as follows. Section 2 presents three channels through which trade and trade policy have an impact on the sustainability of a growth strategy. Examples of how trade and trade policy operate across these channels are discussed in the following three sections. Section 3 discusses direct trade-related pressures on the environment: over-exploitation of natural resources in weak institutional environments and environmental damage caused by transport activities. Section 4 reviews evidence on the twin effects of leakage and border-tax adjustments for local and global pollutants arguing that these might be less than what has been supposed. Section 5 addresses the problems associated with the likely capture by powerful groups of GHG emitters that will result in inefficient policies that will be passed on to consumers who, in turn, will resist these policies.

Section 6 concludes with remarks on the adequacy of the current system of global policy-making in which environmental and trade policies are odd bedfellows.

2 NATURAL RESOURCES, THE ENVIRONMENT, AND TRADE: CHANNELS OF INTERACTION

Figure 1 isolates three channels of interaction between a development strategy and its environmental implications and where trade enters into these links. The first is in the pattern of production: does the development strategy manage adequately the environment, and does it produce goods and services that are 'environmentally-friendly' (in the sense of being 'green' since just about all human activities are harmful to the environment)? The second channel works through the by-product externalities that inevitably accompany human activities, externalities that are becoming increasingly global. The third channel covers the direct effects of trade on the environment.

The pattern of production (a). Whether a country is pursuing a 'green-growth' development strategy depends first on its product mix and on the production processes it uses (energy from fossil fuel or from renewables). Production activities (relation (a)) distinguish between tradable environment-related products and other products. For the tradable environment-related products and services, their impact on the environment depends on whether their production helps manage the environment better (Goods for Environmental Management – GEMs such as pumps for air pollution control) or if they are environmentally preferable products (EPPs such as solar panels). For both GEMs and EPPs, reducing barriers to trade for these goods (or subsidizing the production of clean energy) is good for the environment.[1] This could take place in the context of multilateral trade negotiations (as under the Doha Round) or at a less ambitious plurilateral level (as in the case of several plurilateral agreements, e.g. the Information Technology Agreement signed under the Uruguay Round). However, these goods are difficult to identify and little progress has occurred under the current multilateral negotiations.

Figure 1: *Natural Resources, the Environment, and Trade*

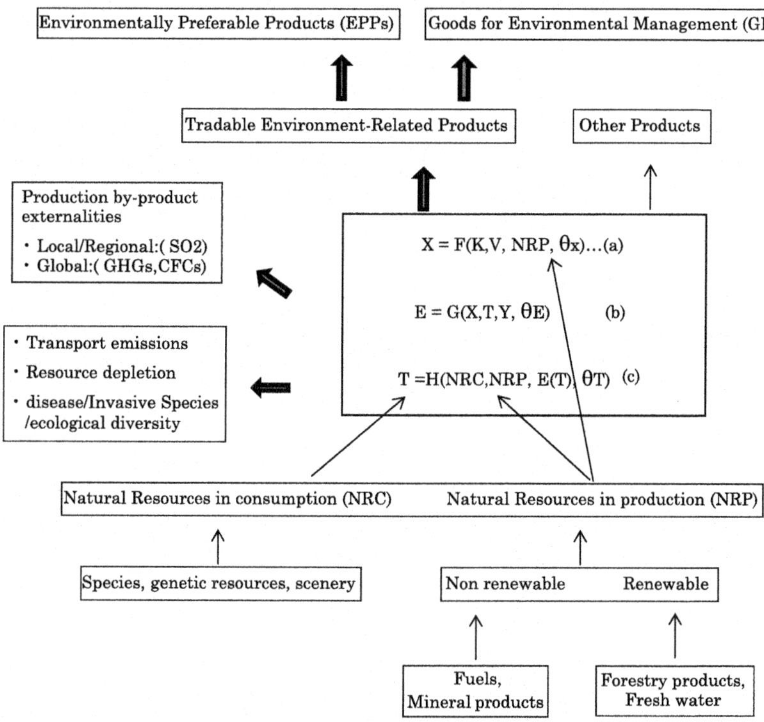

(a) X= Output; K= physical and human capital; V=Intermediate inputs, NRP= Natural resources in production; θ_X=Output-related policies (e.g. taxes or subsidies on fossil fuels)
(b) E= output-related emissions; Y=per capita income; θ_E= caps/taxes on emissions
(c) T= environment-related Trade; NRC=natural resources in consumption; E(T)=Emission related to transport; θ_T=border taxes
GHG= Green-house gases; CFC=chlorofluorocarbons; SO= Sulfuric oxides;

[1] Policy levers are captured by θ_X in relation (a) and θ_T in relation (c). Examples of policies would be taxes/subsidies on fossil fuels, subsidies on renewable energies or on biofuels, trade taxes or trade bans on endangered species.

Natural resources can be categorized as non-renewable (fuels, mineral products), or renewable (forestry products, fresh water). Goods are produced with natural resources in production (NRP). These are the raw materials that enter production (relation (a)). Natural resources also enter directly as natural resources in consumption (NRC such as fish, biodiversity and genetic resources). Both NRC and NRP goods may be characterized by poorly-defined property-rights which may be exacerbated because they are traded (relation (c)). In both cases, the appropriate policy consists of correcting the externality at source (e.g. establishing property rights or applying production/consumption taxes) and if the entire production is traded (e.g. ivory) a trade tax or trade ban is also the first-best policy. Difficulties in implementing the appropriate policy can be due to property rights or open-access (often the case for NRC, i.e. endangered species) or for strong vested interests reflected in lobbying activities (often the case for NRP, i.e. fossil fuels).

Strong geographic concentration is a key characteristic of many natural resources. Close to 90% of world proven oil reserves are concentrated in 15 countries, and the same pattern holds for non-ferrous metals and other mineral products. All the wortld's largest industrial economies are net importers of these goods typically concentrated in the 'South'. The resulting 'North-South' trade gives rise to the traditional gains from trade between countries with different factor endowments: countries rich in natural resources will export the services of these factors in exchange for the services of human and physical capital. However because of their exhaustibility or slow rate of renewal, the traditional gains from trade can be overshadowed by the depletion of these resources in the exporting country due to trade-related over-exploitation resulting in tensions between countries. [2]

'Virtual' trade in fresh water is an example of gains from trade in natural resources. It is a renewable resource that is essentially non-traded and very

[2] Because natural resources are indispensable inputs for production and are also necessary for maintaining a high quality of human life, their unequal distribution across countries is also a source of friction. Contrary to most industrial and agricultural products, where importing countries seek protection from imports, countries abundant in natural resources seek to restrict their exports. It is estimated that export taxes are twice as likely in natural-resource sectors than in other sectors and export taxes from natural resources are a third higher than their share in total trade (WTO (2010, section D)). The reasons for restraining exports of natural resources include fiscal needs, rent-shifting, the desire for diversification through processing of raw materials by keeping prices low for downstream activities and protecting the environment.

concentrated geographically. Water enters into the production of agricultural products, especially crops and, like electricity, is traded indirectly. In spite of the distortions created by the implicit subsidy to water usage around the world – as water is rarely priced at opportunity cost – it is estimated that the gains from trade in water-intensive agricultural commodities saves around 20% of total water use, i.e. is equivalent to a 20% yearly increase in the world's supply of water.[3]

By-product externalities (b). The second channel through which trade affects the environment is indirect. Since close to half of world production is traded the (usually negative) externalities related to the production activities (described above) add on to the negative impacts of production itself. The determinants of these externalities are summarized in relation (b). They include the scale of activity, income per capita, Y, which is taken here as a proxy for environmental policies, composition effects related to the pattern of specialization, and technique effects. Insofar as trade 'causes' growth, there is a scale effect leading to a deterioration of the quality of the environment. Trade can also accelerate the adoption of 'clean' techniques of production, as a more open trade regime increases the adoption of clean technologies.[4] Antweiler, Copeland and Taylor (2001) and others have proposed and implemented decompositions of the pollution content of trade trying to establish whether or not trade is 'good for the environment'. Section 4 discusses the empirical evidence based on this approach.

Application of second-best theory again recommends that these externalities be corrected at source, i.e. that corrective taxes, θ_E, be applied on industries that pollute. For local pollutants, such as SO2, corrective measures like the cap-and-trade systems have been successful (e.g. the US Clean Air Act

[3] For reference, water subsidies are estimated at $55 billion, almost all in non-OECD countries while non-nuclear energy subsidies are estimated at $300 billion with 2/3 in non-OECD countries. With 80% of fresh water entering agricultural production, pricing water at opportunity cost would drastically change the pattern of comparative advantage in agricultural products across countries and would lead to less water-intensive consumption patterns. Taxing the water content of exported agricultural products would be second-best even though exporters would likely improve their terms-of-trade. In any case, it would be strongly opposed by farmers.

[4] Most evidence on the two-way causality between trade and growth points to a causality from a more open trade regime to higher growth (see e.g. Frankel and Romer (1999) and Wacziarg and Welch (2008)). A large empirical literature exploring the trade-productivity reviewed in Keller (2010) suggests that in addition to R&D expenditures and spillovers, technical progress comes through imports.

of 1990).[5] So the remaining issue and the question for the role of trade in environmental policy is the extent to which these industries are footloose. The review of empirical evidence in section 4 suggests that fears of 'pollution havens' have been exaggerated in the case of local pollutants. As to global pollutants like GHG emissions, few national economic policy measures have been applied, so there is little evidence.

Direct Trade-Environment Linkages (c). Besides the production pattern and the related production externalities, direct effects of trade on the environment constitute a third channel. Three effects are singled out in relation (c). First, trade requires international transport which itself pollutes the environment. Ideally, life cycle analysis taking into account trade-related emissions would determine if trade, as opposed to local production, is friendlier towards the environment. Second, trade alters the profitability of harvesting natural resources. In the absence of corrective measures, often made difficult by poorly-defined property rights, these resources can be depleted more rapidly than would be optimal in the case of non-renewable resources, and overexploited in the case of renewable resources (e.g. fishing). Applying second-best theory would call for the corrective measure being applied in production, but since these natural resources are often entirely exported, export taxes, θ_T, are equivalent to a domestic measure. Third, trade affects a country's ecology as invasive species and the spreading of diseases are directly related to international trade. These aspects will not be discussed here.[6] Nor will I cover other trade activities like the prospects of 'green tourism', which can provide strong impetus to improve the management of natural resources and the environment.

Under each channel, accompanying policies can improve the quality of the environment (policies that correct externalities) or worsen it (policies that create distortions). In each case, because of the magnitude of the externalities or distortions, substantial rents are created that impede the implementation of the efficient policies (e.g. carbon taxes, removal of subsidies on fishing) through lobbying activities. These direct linkages are now discussed.

---

[5] Chan and al. (2012) argue that the cap-and-trade system has been quite efficient and, above all successful politically, because the 'grandfathering' of emissions permits won political support. See Tirole (2009) about the economic effects of a cap-and-trade in reducing the global warming.

[6] How invasive species brought about (often involuntarily) by trade have led to our 'single' ecological system is described in Mann (2011). Fischer (2010) discusses how the characteristics of species (sedentary or migratory, pests or not, a local or global resource stock) will affect resource management, and hence the choice of trade policy.

3 DIRECT TRADE-ENVIRONMENT LINKAGES

Many natural resources are renewable over time according to biological processes (influenced by trade but not covered here). Their depletion by harvesting activities has been largely driven by international trade made possible by the huge fall in transport costs for natural resources.[7] The multilateral trade system poses a double threat for the management of natural resources. First, by erasing borders, trade liberalization and other reductions in international transaction costs (including facilitating the transfer of technologies that raise the productivity of harvesting) contribute directly to the increasingly untenable pressure on resource stocks. Second, as discussed in section 5, obligations attached to WTO membership can hamstring governments in their attempts to manage their resources by disallowing trade-restrictive measures, or, more simply, countries may be unable to reach an agreement on the necessary actions to be taken.

3.1 Trade-related Pressures on Natural Resources

When opening a natural resource (e.g. timber or buffalo hides) to trade, the resource price becomes determined on international markets and is no longer self-regulating. If the resource stock is not managed optimally, opening to trade is likely to exacerbate a pre-existing open-access problem (Bulte and Barbier (2005), Copeland and Taylor (2009)). If all rents from resource extraction are dissipated by over-exploitation, then the country will be made worse off by trade. There are also secondary effects. Shifting production towards resource-intensive sectors may have general equilibrium 'resource curse' effects, as employment in manufacturing–where there may be economies of scale or spillover benefits for growth–falls.[8]

---

7 According to WTO, over the period 1870 to 1990, transport costs of natural resources have fallen by 90% (WTO (2010, section D)).

8 By affecting the relative price of agricultural land, international trade in natural resources also affects biodiversity which may rise, fall or change in composition across partners. Species with a lower replenishing rate are likely to succumb to pressures from trade. The management of migratory wildlife also creates problems for the preservation of habitat across jurisdictions. Some natural resources are pests while others have complementary impacts on biodiversity. These ecological effects of trade in natural resources are not covered here. Bulte and Barbier (2005) develop several models that show the ambiguous role of opening up to trade in the typical second-best situation characterizing natural resources. Also see Fischer (2010) and WTO (2010, section C)).

Following Chichilnisky (1994), a large theoretical literature has explored the possibility that weak governance in the South can confer an "apparent" comparative advantage in trade in a natural resource. If, in addition, the North cannot manage resources optimally either, unless recovery rates are sufficient, stocks in the North could also be driven to collapse. Example are the 19th Century slaughter of buffalo in the US to sustain the European demand for hides (Taylor (2011)) and currently fisheries, a global common pool resource that has seen all-round overexploitation (Moltke (2011)). Remarkably, as discussed in section 6, in spite of accumulated evidence for over forty years, the international community has been unable to take the needed measures to improve the management of fisheries.

Asymmetry of resource-management regimes across countries means that global resources with "enclosed" property rights will be better sustained by trade while putting pressure on the remaining «unenclosed» resources. Copeland and Taylor (2009) identify three factors that will contribute to determining whether higher resource prices brought about by trade will lead to better management of the resource rather than raising the return to evading enforcement. The first factor is the ability of the resource to generate competitive returns (representing the opportunity cost of labor in other activities) without resource exhaustion. The second is the level of regulatory power to manage the natural resource. This power is likely to be low in many resource-abundant countries. Finally, the third factor is the size of the labor supply. It should not be too large so as to avoid increased returns to cheating as the probability of being caught falls. If natural resources were not geographically concentrated, an opening to trade could then lead to an all-around increase in welfare as comparative advantage would lie in the North (i.e. in the country with a better property rights regime) and the fall in the resource price in the South would lead to an improvement in the property rights regime in the South as the returns to cheating would fall (Copeland and Taylor (2009)).

However, this welfare-increasing outcome from opening to trade or from trade liberalization is unlikely because of the great geographical concentration of natural resources in low-income countries reflecting the pattern that high-income countries are overwhelmingly net importers of natural resources (WTO (2o10, p.49). In addition, in low-incomes countries, the ability to enforce property rights is likely to be weakened by the lobbying and corruption made possible by the rents associated with the extraction of natural resources. In sum, it is difficult to dispel the possibility that trade in natural resources exported by poor countries, –especially for resources with low replenishment rates–will do more harm than good. Trade would then lead to a loss of natural capital and to negative 'genuine savings', possibly resulting in an unsustainable development path. In this case, cooperation from importing countries (presumably with better institutions) would help alleviate the resource curse problem.

A large (and still-growing) empirical literature tries to identify the presence of a robust 'natural resource curse'. This, however, need not be the case (see the summaries in Lederman and Maloney (2007) and Van der Ploeg (2011)). When explored comprehensively across channels and across countries, the findings are varied, with the outcome dependent on the institutional set-up and other determinants unrelated to trade (e.g. geography or fractionalization of the population).[9] Perhaps less emphasized is the finding that environments rich in natural resources engender institutional weaknesses as groups attempt to capture rents (Mehlum, H., K. Moene and R. Torvik (2006)). This curse-via-politics is largely endogenous to the political environment and not subject to improvements by governments in power who have a vested interest in blocking institutional change. Recipients of the rents can also block the trade reforms that would reduce distortions and improve the management of natural resources. For example, drawing on the Doing Business data, in a large sample of 133 countries, Amin and Djankov (2008) find that the proclivity to undertake micro-reforms that reduce trade distorting regulation is much lower in countries whose exports are more concentrated in abundant natural resources.[10]

3.2 Transport-Related Emissions

The elasticity of trade to world income has increased from around 2.0 in the 1960s to 3.7 in the 2000s (Freund (2009)). For environmentalists, this is evidence that international trade is a direct contributor to deterioration of the environment. Transport costs (national and international) account for approximately 13% of global CO2 emissions with about two-thirds of the

[9] The early literature mistakenly used resource dependence as a measure of resource abundance. When this distinction is made the 'resource curse' effects found in the early literature are dampened (Brunnschweiler and Bulte (2008)). Evidence shows that resource dependence and institutional quality are negatively correlated (Isham et al. (2005)). The outcome of natural resource abundance and performance also depends on the institutional setting (Bhattacharya and Hodler (2008)).

[10] Collier and Hoeffler (2004) were the first to give evidence that conflicts are more likely to be driven by greed to get hold of the rents than by grievances due to ethnic or religious conflicts. Bulte and Brunschweiler (2009) contest this result suggesting that conflict increases dependence on resource extraction (captured by the share of primary exports) while resource abundance (measured by resource stocks) is associated with a reduced probability of civil war.

emissions related to manufacturing activity. With the relocation of manufacturing activity to Asia, shipping volume has increased by 50% over the past 20 years. Shipping now accounts for about 90 percent of the volume of global trade and about 3 percent of global CO2 emissions. Also, oceangoing ships use bunker fuel and so emit about 15 percent of global nitrogen oxides and between 5 and 8 percent of global sulfur oxide emissions, all contributing to respiratory illnesses, cardiopulmonary disorders and lung cancers, particularly among people who live near heavy ship traffic (70% of emissions are within 400 km of land).[11]

Two studies give orders of magnitude of transport-related GHG emissions related to international trade. Using detailed emissions for 7 sectors and 62 countries covering the period 1990 to 2000, Grether et al. (2010) compute an order of magnitude of the contribution of trade to SO2 emissions. Having defined a no-trade equilibrium, adding up emissions coming from trade-related composition effects and trade-related transport activities, they estimate that global worldwide SO2 manufacturing emissions were increased through trade by 16 percent in 1990 and 13 percent in 2000.[12]

Cristea et al. (2011) produce a more systematic 'bottom-up' estimate of trade-related emissions (emissions from producing what is traded, i.e. traded goods in manufacturing activities, plus transport-related emissions from international transport disaggregated according to mode of transport). They show that, world-wide, one third of trade-related emissions come from international transportation with a great variation in contribution across countries. For example, their world share estimates for (output) [exports, imports] are:

[11] The US EPA estimates that applying a 400 km buffer zone along Canadian and US coastlines would save up to 8300 lives a year by 2020 (International Herald Tribune, April 26, 2010 "Controlling Pollution from Ships") As expected, there was a strong opposition from Asian exporters to the proposal of a tax on fuel for shipping by the EU even though the proposal stated that the proceeds would be rebated to developing countries. There was also a strong opposition from the US when the EU announced it would impose a carbon tax on all flights in and out of the EU because US exports mostly use air transport.

[12] Their estimate is in two steps. First, they define an anti-monde in which countries are forced to produce what they consume in the trade equilibrium. International trade then increases emissions by 10% in 1990 and by 3.5% in 2000, the fall is largely a reflection of the all-around decline in emission-intensity. Second, they consider emissions caused by international transport. Using a rough decomposition by mode of transport, they estimate that international-trade related emissions accounted for about 5-9% of total SO2 manufacturing emissions. Adding trade and transport-cost related emissions, their estimates suggest that SO2 transport-related emissions have gone from accounting for roughly one third to three quarters of total trade-related emissions over the 1990-2000 period.

China (20.8%) [3.5%, 6.7%]; India (4.9%) [0.6%,1.5%]; U.S. (12.0%) [32.5%, 10.7%]. These estimates reveal the great reliance of the US on air cargo which is the most emission-intensive mode of transport.[13] Thus, when one takes into account emissions from international transport, the US emission per dollar traded is higher than for India or China, but lower for regions that are distant from their trade partners (e.g. South America).

Interestingly, the growth of Regional Trade Agreements has led to a change in modal transport as deep integration across partners has led to greater trade with adjacent partners with a shift to rail and road modes of transport. Currently, the average tariff for land-adjacent partners is 1% and 5.5% for non-adjacent partners. Multilateral trade liberalization would then result in a shift in transport mode towards aviation and maritime transport. Thus, when Cristea et al. (2011) simulate the effect of free trade, they find that aviation and maritime transport grow relative to land transport as trade shifts towards more distant partners, CO2 emissions related to output grow by 0.4% and transport-related emissions grow by 8%.

Among others, a green-growth development strategy would benefit from a change in technology in maritime transport. Drawing on the successful MARPOL treaty on discharging waste at sea, which successfully imposed a new double-hull technology on tankers, Barrett (2008) suggests that the network characteristic of transport technology, which has the characteristic of a 'tipping-point' treaty, could be exploited to design a sectoral treaty to reduce GHG emissions. Because of the network characteristic of transport technology, a threshold in participation would lead to full participation. However, because of the differences in the intensity of transport modes across partners, reaching an agreement would be difficult.

4 POLLUTION HAVENS, TRADE LEAKAGES AND BORDER TAX ADJUSTMENTS

Environmentalists fear that, by reducing transport costs and trade barriers, globalization would shift "dirty" goods (products that cause mostly local

[13] Estimates draw on GTAP data so they include only CO2 emissions from fossil-fuel combustion, cement production and gas flaring. Differences in emissions across transport modes are substantial. Taking an estimate of their emission averages per tonnes-km (t-km) of transport services gives the following estimates across transport modes (CO2 grams per t-km in parenthesis): maritime (≈10g/t-km); land (≈70g/t-km); air (≈700g/t-km).

pollution) from the 'North' to the 'South' leading to an increase in the pollution content of imports (PCI) of the North according to the "Pollution haven hypothesis" (PHH) and to a worldwide increase in the production of dirty products since these are now produced in the South with more pollution-intensive techniques. For local pollutants, environmental measures and reductions to trade barriers have however not lead to significant shifts in production towards countries with lax environmental policies. For global pollutants causing climate change, such as the accumulation of greenhouse gases in the atmosphere, little effort at curbing emissions has been undertaken so that we mostly rely on ex-ante simulations. I review both types of pollutants, starting with the local one.

4.1 Pollution Havens?

The existence of pollution havens rests on the assumption that the polluting industries can migrate. Yet, this is unlikely to be important in practice since the more tradable energy-intensive and heavily polluting industries are also largely weight-reducing industries. Smelting non-ferrous metals (and the processing of paper from wood) usually takes place close to extraction sites to avoid transport costs (Ederington et al 2005). Grether and de Melo (2004) estimate a bilateral-trade gravity model for each one of the 'dirty' industries and an aggregate of 'clean' industries.[14] They find a consistently higher coefficient for the distance coefficient for dirty industries. This, and the fact that extraction in natural-resource-based industries cannot migrate, suggests that transport costs would deter relocation of much processing to countries with lower regulation standards, making energy-intensive polluting industries unlikely to be footloose. [15]

---

[14] SO2 and CO2 emission patterns across industries are very similar as the same six industries are the main emitters for both gases: petroleum products, pulp and paper, non-ferrous metals, iron and steel, chemicals, building material – cement. These are energy-intensive industries and hence heavy emitters of CO2. The coefficient of correlation between CO2 and SO2 emissions is higher than 0.9 for UK industries for the average over 1990-2000.

[15] Using data on SO2 emission intensities Grether et al. (2009) estimate that over the period 1990-2000 SO2 emissions fell by 9.8% with a technique effect contributing to a fall by 14% while the scale effect contributed to an increase in emissions of 9.5%. Between-country shifts contributed to a reduction of 2.4% and between-sector shifts within countries to another reduction of 3%. Dean and Lovely (2010) also decompose changes in the pollution intensity (air and water) of Chinese exports and imports during 1995-2004 and find a small composition effect and a larger effect from the shift towards cleaner production processes.

Suppose, however, that pollution-intensive industries can migrate. To fix the terms of the debate about the pollution haven hypothesis (PHH), consider the following simple hypothetical example. Two countries, North (N) and South (S), produce two goods, a 'dirty' and a (completely) 'clean' good under perfect competition in a Heckscher-Ohlin framework, with pollution per unit of output of the dirty good being initially identical in N and S so that both countries are the same in all respects except that N has a higher income per capita than S. Let environmental quality be a normal good. Stricter environmental standards in N will lower emissions per unit of output and abatement costs will raise the unit price of the dirty good in N. N will then import the dirty good and hence its trade will be «embodied» with emissions (i.e. $PCI_{NS} > 0$),. Conversely, S will import the clean good from its partner and in this setting with no intra-industry trade $PCI_{SN} = 0$. The literature refers to this environmental-policy induced effect as the pollution haven (PH) effect and to the emissions embodied in trade as "virtual trade in emissions" or as the "balance of emissions embodied in trade" (BEET). In this particular example, $BEET_N > 0$ and $BEET_S = 0$. A reduction in trade barriers, will lead S to specialize in the production of dirty products as S has a comparative advantage in dirty products due to the environmental policy in N. Globalization thus increases PCI_{NS} in conformity with the PHH (some of the previously dirty production in N is now carried out in S probably under less-stringent environmental standards). If the dirty industry is capital intensive and N is relatively well-endowed in capital, then if N and S had the same environmental policies, we would only observe a Factor endowment (FE) effect as N would have a comparative advantage in dirty products. Taking the two effects together, under the plausible assumption that the FE effect reduces the PCI and the PH effect increases it, globalization will obey the PHH if PH is positive and dominates the FE effect.

Grether et al. (2011) provide a first global test of the PHH hypothesis with data for a large sample of countries and industries. They estimate the contribution of the PH and FE effects to the total PCI for 10 major pollutants and find that almost always the PH effect is positive and the FE effect is negative. For four out of 10 pollutants the PHH is vindicated, but that the net contribution of these effects is always small, between 5% and 10% of the total effect confirming in a large sample of countries that factors other than environmental policy are important in determining competiveness. Their large sample also reveals the importance of composition effects across groups of countries. Thus even though the FE and PH effects are important in North-South (NS) and SN trade, much trade is accounted for by intra-regional NN trade among Northern countries. However, with an increase in SS trade in recent years, the contribution of the PHH to the PCI would be expected to increase.

In a Heckscher-Ohlin world, increasing Foreign Direct Investment (FDI) would lead to an increase in PCI_{NS}. World trade, however, is increasingly fragmented, in great part as a result of globalization that has reduced transaction costs. Taking into account outsourcing, the presence of FDI could however, lead to a decline in PCI_{NS}. Consider a model with a continuum of intermediates as in Feenstra and Hanson (1997) where intermediates are ranked by decreasing pollution-intensity and the location of production between N and S depends on relative production costs (inclusive of pollution taxes). As shown by Dean and Lovely (2010), FDI to the South (often directed towards 'special economic zones' producing goods for export) will lower the cost of capital and shift comparative advantage along the continuum of goods towards less pollution-intensive activities. Hence, in this setting, contrary to the standard PHH debate, FDI lowers PCI_{NS}. They find support that the pollution intensity of trade falls and is lower for processing trade. In their sample, the pollution intensity of exports is lower the larger the share of processing exports and the larger the share of FDI in total investment. They conclude that their results could suggest evidence that, over the period, foreign investors brought greener technologies than their local counterparts.

4.2 Climate Change Mitigation, Leakages and Border tax Adjustments

Comparative-advantage-based shifts in CO2 emissions. Throughout the Kyoto Protocol (KP) negotiation period (1995-2005)), CO2 emission transfers from developing to developed countries through trade were 1.2 Gt, an estimate that exceeded the target of KP1 emission reductions (Peters et al. 2011) indicating that, as feared by environmentalists, virtual trade in carbon has adverse unintended consequences for climate policy. Other estimates also conclude that the pattern of trade between developed and developing countries has been shifting with a rising import-export ratio of energy-intensive products in high-income OECD countries (especially the US) and the opposite in low and middle-income countries (especially China).[16] The upshot is that, contrary to what is reported in the production-based UNFCCC statistics, Annex B countries have continued to contribute to the growth in emissions.

These estimates suggest three remarks. First, the territorial-based caps under the KP have thus far allowed Annex B countries to meet their target because of their positive BEET, so that any cap on emissions should be on consumption (as under the Montreal Protocol)and not on production (as under the KP).

[16] See World Bank (2008, figures 2.2,2.3,2.4).

Second, developing countries whose exports are carbon-intensive can be expected to continue opposing joining a successor to KP. Third, the importance of carbon-intensive exports by developing countries to developed countries suggests that countries like China might be willing to undertake more substantial climate-mitigation commitments in exchange for firmer trade disciplines that would guarantee them access to carbon-intensive markets in the OECD.[17]

Policy-induced leakage estimates. The above estimates can be considered passive or comparative-advantage based (as opposed to policy-induced and subject to leakage). Turning to policy –induced leakage estimates, Kee et al. (2010) use a gravity model to estimate the effects on exports of OECD countries of carbon taxes and energy-efficiency standards, both captured by dummy variables using 3-digit ISIC data for manufacturing exports over the period 1988-2005. They find no evidence of a loss of competitiveness from a carbon tax for energy-intensive industries when exporting countries impose a carbon tax, but a significant reduction in bilateral trade the year that efficiency standards are applied, whether the efficiency standard is applied by the exporting or by the importing country. They conclude that this evidence suggests that subsidies and exemptions to the energy-intensive industries must have compensated for the disadvantages imposed by the carbon tax, a plausible interpretation in view of the powerful lobbying activities by these industries. Another study on carbon imports estimates that the volume of trade "caused" by KP is small and that close to half of carbon savings due to the KP signature have been offset by increases in non-signatories.[18]

[17] Using a Leontief-type multi-region input-output model, similar to the method used by Peters et al. (2011) in their calculations, Atkinson et al. (2010), compute first-order effects from applying a 50$/ton tax on the carbon content of imports across all countries. They estimate that this tax would amount to an export tax rate of around 10% for China's exports across destinations. In comparison, EU exports would face an average export tax rate of 1.2% and the US of 3.1%. This just confirms that taxing CO2 is a tax on developing countries. It also explains why, some countries, like China are already starting to tax their exports of CO2 intensive goods since it is better to collect the tax oneself than to hand over the revenue to foreigners.

[18] Drawing on data for 38 countries (26 of which have ratified Kyoto), and 12 sectors over the period 1995-2005, Aichele and Felbermayr (2010) examine the impact of different GHG policies on trade flows and emissions. They estimate that carbon imports are on average 12% higher if the importer has ratified Kyoto and his trading partner not. Confirming previous work, the effect is most important in energy intensive industries, where robust evidence for carbon leakage was found for seven sectors. Their findings suggest that, even though the volume of trade "caused" by Kyoto is rather small, on average about 40% of carbon savings due to the ratification of the Kyoto protocol has been offset by increasing emissions in non-committing countries.

The limits of trade policy to mitigate GHG emissions. In OECD countries, around 70% of national income is produced in services and only 15-25% in manufactures, limiting any effect of trade policies on reduction in emissions on the production side. Besides, emission intensities often vary more across countries within an industry than across industries, implying that using trade policy to correct for differences in carbon policies would call for country-directed rather than industry-level measures (Dong and Whalley (2010)). Such measures would be in violation of the MFN treatment at the WTO unless they were part of a Regional Trade Agreement (RTA).[19]

Global multi-regional general-equilibrium trade (MR-GE) models have been used extensively to answer several questions on climate mitigation policies: (i) damage estimates necessary to elicit participation in cooperative agreements and required compensation to bring about participation; (ii) emission reductions from carbon taxes and leakage rates from sub-global carbon taxes, and; (iii) the incidence of Border Tax Adjustments (BTAs) to compensate for differences in carbon taxes.

In principle, international trade expands the bargaining set for reaching a cooperative climate agreement, but small countries will not participate unless they receive compensation because of the sharing of benefits with non-participants. Cai et al. (2009) analyze the participation decision in a skeleton MR-GE model in which temperature change caused by CO2 emissions related to consumption enter negatively in the consumer's utility function. In this set-up, lower consumption has two effects on welfare. It increases welfare directly through a lower rise in global temperature, and indirectly through reduced demand for imports, which improves the country's terms-of-trade. Calibrating the utility function parameters on the Stern (2005) damage estimates, they show that a 10% damage (i.e reduction in GDP) from a 1% reduction in consumption would be necessary for the US or China to participate in a treaty if they are linked through trade. In the absence of trade, the damage would have to be close to 50% and a 50% reduction in CO2 emissions would reduce GDP by 2-3%. In a follow-up, Tan and Whalley (2010), estimate that transfers of 150$ billion per year would compensate the BRICS for their participation in an across-the-board reduction in emissions of 30% over a fifty-year period.

[19] Dong and Whalley (2010) examine reasons for carbon-motivated RTAs and requirements for WTO compatibility of such agreements (no selective actions against high-emitting countries and the possibility of invoking article XX to avoid covering all trade). Then, these RTAs could include extension of preferences to low-emission products, but also BTAs to offset anti-competitive effects. As under the Montreal Protocol , the RTAs could also include penalties against those who do not join the agreement.

Carbon taxes to reduce emissions will lead to a shift from tradables towards non-tradables as the latter are less energy-intensive. For example, Pigott et al. (1992) estimate that an 80% reduction in CO2 emissions compared to their 1990 level across regions would reduce world trade by 50%, suggesting an elasticity of trade to CO2 of two-thirds. Factoring in the greater substitution possibilities across energy sources in the longer term, a guess-estimate would be that a 10% reduction in CO2 emissions could result in a 3% reduction in world trade. In practice, not all countries will apply carbon pricing. A typical model estimate is that, in the absence of a border tax adjustment (BTA), estimated leakage rates are in the 10%-20% range. For example, if the EU (or the US) were to cut emissions individually by 20%, the leakage rate would be around 35% but it is only 20% when both cut emissions together (Boehringer et al. 2010).

MR-GE models have also been used to provide estimates of the effects of border tax adjustments (BTAs) to prevent carbon leakage. The estimates suggest that a BTA reduces leakage by half. The reason for the relative inefficiency of a BTA is that a tax on the CO2 content of imports has a strong terms-of-trade effect in favor of the country that imposes the BTA, leading to a change in comparative advantage.

The models also give estimates of the different BTAs that have been proposed in the political debate. A first proposal circulated in the US would be to adjust the price of imports by applying the CO2 tax in the US to the total (direct and indirect) carbon content of imports, perhaps along with a relief from paying the tax for exporters. A second proposal would be to tax imports on the basis of the carbon content of imports (US legislation would oblige importers to buy emission allowances equivalent to the carbon content of imports). Mattoo et al. (2009), estimate that if industrial countries were to reduce emissions by 17% without applying a BTA, manufacturing exports by developing countries would remain unchanged but would fall by about 2% under the first proposal, and by 15% under the second proposal. Should developed countries try to impose across-the-board taxation on imports based on their carbon content, there would be a collision between developed and developing countries at the WTO.

5 IMPLEMENTATION DIFFICULTIES: POLITICAL ECONOMY CONSIDERATIONS

It is estimated that a tax of $100 per ton of CO2 would be necessary to keep any global temperature rise to around 2^0 C generating annual rents close to a trillion dollars and that the annual fossil fuel subsidies that should be eliminated are worth over $400 billion. Acting on both measures continues to face strong opposition and any serious action to mitigate climate change will have to face up to contestable rents far beyond those that have ever been at stake in the world trading system. The failed negotiations to deal with fishery subsidies and climate change mitigation show the inadequacy of the current subsidy rules and the resistance to take the measures necessary for developing a green-growth development strategy. These inadequacies are compounded by Special and Differential Treatment (S&DT) and the Common but Differentiated Responsibility (CBDR) principles at the climate change negotiations.

5.1 Natural Resources: Fisheries

Market imperfections and institutional failures, both of which impede the full internalization of the true social value of the environment, have often been aggravated by government interventions. This phenomenon has been amply documented by the so-called 'perverse subsidies' including energy subsidies, water subsidies, almost all fishing subsidies, and most recently subsidies for bio-fuels. Credit and fiscal incentives for activities such as livestock and land conversion in forest areas contribute to a loss of biological diversity that can be exacerbated by trade. As with all market imperfections, second-best theory would call for the removal of subsidies accorded to the oil industries and the costing of fossil-fuel extraction (fracking, deterioration of physical infrastructure, contamination of acquifers) that would go a long way towards raising the profitability of other, more efficient, renewable energies.[20] But most of these subsidies which have global implications for a green-growth development strategy regrettably continue to be "non-actionable" under the GATT.

Particularly interesting is the case of fisheries, a natural resource that shares some of the same characteristics as climate, but that has the advantage of being "observable" since fish stocks have been known to be declining since the early seventies. Resolving the overexploitation of fisheries requires: (i) improvement in the management of fisheries by giving/selling secure and enforceable rights to fishermen to solve the open-access problem; (ii) reform

[20] Worldwide, according to the International Energy Agency (2011), subsidies to renewable energies are estimated at 67$ billion and the corresponding figure for consumption subsidies for fossil fuels (including for biofuels) at 400$ billion. Across the EU where taxation is decided at the national level, the gap in the price of electricity is still around 4 to 1 (Nordstrom (2009)).

the subsidy system which boils down to eliminating virtually all subsidies to the industry.[21]

After the failed Seattle negotiations where fishery subsidies were prominent on the agenda, they reappeared in article 28 of the Doha ministerial "...participants shall also aim to clarify and improve WTO disciplines on fishery subsidies, taking into account the importance of this sector for developing countries". Three years into the negotiations, major fishing countries who had developed a dominant position in the industry acquiesced that most subsidies were indeed harmful as the Hong Kong ministerial recognized explicitly that governments should strengthen disciplines on subsidies including through "the prohibition of certain fisheries subsidies that contribute to overcapacity and over-fishing", subject to S&DT for developing countries (Von Moltke, 2011, p. 154). But progress on defining *de minimis* rules for S&DT to exclude the large fishing nations (China, Peru and others) met with fierce resistance and no agreement could be reached. In the end, agreeing on compensation in fisheries has proved as elusive as the application of the CBDR principle under Kyoto.

5.2 Border Tax Adjustments to Mitigate Climate change

Just as in the case of fisheries, dealing with rent transfers nationally and internationally will dominate efficiency considerations both because the bulk of the electorate is opposed to a carbon tax and because high GHG emitters are powerful groups in the energy, construction, transportation and manufacturing sectors.[22]. Moore (2010) takes the steel industry, a heavy CO2 emitter for which it is difficult to detect the carbon footprint, as a case to illustrate the political-economy difficulties of implementing a carbon border tax. He shows that none among the possible border adjustment schemes would meet the necessary economic, political, environmental, legal, and administrative constraints needed to gain the necessary support for implementation. These constraints are: (i) domestic firm buy-in; (ii) foreign firm buy-in;

[21] Worldwide, fisheries account for 170 million jobs and generate revenues of around $85 billion per year with subsidies in the 25-35$ billion range, all of which (except those for management) contribute directly or indirectly to overexploitation. About 37% of fish catch is traded internationally. Details in Von Moltke (2011, chaps. 1 and 2).

[22] Messerlin (2011) draws the parallel between climate and water policies, arguing that both communities face the same foes (protectionist pressures from strong lobby groups, e.g. steel producers and farmers) and friends (exporters of environmentally-friendly products) in their quest to pursue the efficient policies (remove water subsidies and tax carbon).

(iii) administrative capability; (iv) adherence to WTO rules (articles I on non-discrimination and III on national treatment; and (v) incentives for CO2 reduction by foreign firms. Since several technologies are available to produce steel, it would be necessary for the country wishing to impose a border adjustment to firms in foreign countries to distinguish among foreign firm types. The complicated administrative procedures implied by any choice of border adjustment raises the spectre of adopting a system of rules of origin that would attempt, through bureaucratic means, to identify the true source of products whose origin is unclear from their physical characteristics. Such a system would in all likelihood be captured by lobbies as has been the case for rules of origin in the context of preferential market access (see Cadot and de Melo, 2007) or more recently by industry lobbies in the submission lists of environmental goods that would be up for negotiated reductions in protection at the Doha negotiations (Balineau and de Melo (2013)).

Mathys and de Melo (2011) discuss the exceptional sensitivity of these rent transfers in the political debate in the EU and the US and take the promotion of biofuels as an example of rent capture in action and of a perverse incentive. [23] Getting support for mitigation policies under a cap may then prove to be very costly. Mathys and de Melo conclude that, just as anti-dumping was the price to pay for countries to sign up to the Single Undertaking as part of the Uruguay round grand package, free allowances (or very limited auctioning) may be the political price to pay in the application of mitigation policies. As in the case of biofuels, such support would result in large transfers from consumers to producers. In a study of the ETS cap, Demailly and Quirion (2008) estimate that a 15 per cent reduction in CO2 emissions under free allowances would raise the net profit margin of industries under the cap by seven percentage points, an increase coming from a 10 per cent fall in consumer surplus. And of course, aluminium, which is highly tradable (i.e. very substitutable across suppliers), is not covered in the emission cap since, even with free allowances, the possibility to raise prices and pass on the costs to consumers would be very limited. As to total leakage estimates, at 8%, these are estimated to be small.

[23] Even though estimates suggest that at most half a dozen sectors might be subject to significant carbon leakage, 164 sectors (sub-sectors) have been considered by the EU Commission as exposed to "significant risk of carbon leakage" meaning that they would be up to get 100 percent free allocations. Messerlin (2010) notes that these are the sectors that have succeeded in obtaining contingent-protection measures at the WTO.

6 CONCLUDING REMARKS: TRADE POLICIES FOR A GREEN GROWTH STRATEGY[24]

The current architecture for global policy making rests on the Bretton Woods institutions: the IMF, the World Bank, and the WTO. These institutions were designed to manage interactions between countries that did not involve the physical linkages that have been growing since the early 1960s. The failure to make progress in the negotiations on EGS and on reforms of fishery subsidies in the current Doha Round leads one to question whether we have the right global architecture to handle trade and environment polices for a green-growth strategy. Besides participation by all parties involved, are there any lessons from the evolution of the World Trading System for the design of green-growth trade policies? Here are a few for consideration.

A regional approach with leeway. Looking back at the early days of the GATT, participation was among a small group of countries where negotiation was easier than under the now unwieldy WTO where unanimity is required for all major decisions. The GATT thus made progress towards free trade with agreements that bound nations in ways that did not impinge on their national sovereignty. It is indeed the straightjacket imposed by the Single Undertaking and the Dispute Settlement Mechanism under the WTO that has been largely the cause of the stalemate in the Doha round. It is now widely believed that the live-and-let-live approach under the GATT was the key to its success in delivering the global public good provided by the current World Trading System (Baldwin (2010)). Applying this insight to environment and trade policies, it is likely that the shift to a bottom-up approach has greater chances of success than the previous top-down approach under the KP. Many environmental issues are likely to be better dealt with at the regional level. An example is the many environmental directives under Maastricht Treaty which allows the European Commission to make legally binding decisions for member states. States can still renegotiate, or even withdraw from the Union, so that while their sovereignty has been diluted, their essential rights remain intact. Through a succession of decisions, the incentive for member states to exercise rights has been reduced. Given the large discrepancies in emission intensities across countries within a given sector, it is likely that a regional approach where emission intensities are more similar would be implemented more easily.

Guiding policy principles. If possible, carbon taxes should be levied on domestic CO_2 emissions with the objective of converging towards a unique

[24] Cf Mathys and de Melo (2012).

carbon tax. This approach by price incentives should continue to be strongly encouraged because of its transparency, its efficiency and its alleviation of the requirement of compensatory transfers. Likewise, if a Carbon Credit Trading System (CCTS) is adopted, although not required, auctioning of permits should be encouraged, trade-related GHG measures should be limited, like-products should be defined at a broad enough level of aggregation (4-digit HS for Hufbauer et al., 2009) and the modalities for border adjustments and the management of the CCTS should be flexible. Countries that would subscribe to such a "green code" would benefit from a "peace clause" so as to avoid being subject to WTO disputes. This sensible approach may, however, be difficult to implement as all activities would want to qualify for "green space status" and the request for flexibility could easily lead to a made-to-measure rather than to a transparent code, although implementation at a regional level would have greater chances of success.

As to the principles for guiding trade policies, first the MFN and NT (national treatment) principle would seem to offer the best joint disciplines on the two threats discussed here: carbon tariffs and carbon border taxes. Since carbon tariffs are calculated on a country basis rather than on a product basis, goods with different CO2 intensity would get charged the same tariff. Emerging countries would want the MFN to be preserved. Developed countries would want to keep the option of imposing carbon border taxes (exports do not pay the carbon tax, but the tax is paid at the rate of the carbon tax in the importing country much like the VAT is administered across countries with different domestic taxes). Thus developed countries would like to preserve the NT principle. So the non-discrimination principle of the WTO enshrined in the MFN + NT principle would be the best compromise even though there is clear room for abuse. Non-discrimination would be the best compromise because, as argued by Messerlin (2011), border taxes have lower discriminatory capacity than contingent instruments available at the WTO (anti-dumping, antisubsidy and antisafeguards). Also, with the growing importance of outsourcing in world trade, any border tax should be calculated on an ad-valorem basis and on the basis of the CO2 content in value-added (and not on the gross value of the trade flow), though this complicates considerably its application.

Other elements of the WTO rules, especially those on subsidies would need to be modified. Currently, the huge subsidies on oil as well as the farm subsidies, including on fisheries, water, and biofuels are either 'non actionable' or have not been challenged at the WTO. These subsidies should be eliminated while subsidies appropriately targeted to meet climate objectives (e.g. for R&D in clean energy) should be allowed. This will not be an easy task, but it needs to be tackled. Likewise, export taxes which are distortionary and are allowed under the current WTO rules should be banned (an export tax on CO2 intensive products is a subsidy to the domestic consumption of these same goods).

Under this approach, with these 'simple' rules, much progress would be more likely to take place in a small group of countries, which would be an easier route than a Multilateral Treaty. As mentioned above, unilateral reduction in tariffs was the way most progress was made in the early rounds of trade negotiations. Of course, unilateral action is certainly easier to envisage in the case of tariff reductions where most gains are internalized than under GHG emissions where all gains are equally shared so that the need for collective action is much greater. Under this simpler architecture, in the initial steps forward, the UN process, which still requires unanimity, would be by-passed.

RÉFÉRENCES

AICHELE, R. and G. FELBERMAYR (2010) "Kyoto and the Carbon Content of Trade", FZID DP # 10-2010.

AMIN, M. and S. DJANKOV (2009), "Natural Resources and Reforms", PRWP #4882, The World Bank.

ANTWEILER, W., B. COPELAND and S. TAYLOR (2001),"Is Free Trade Good for the Environment? " *American Economic Review*, Vol. 91(4), pp.877-908.

ATKINSON G., K. HAMILTON, G. RUTA and D. VAN DER MENSBRUGGHE (2010), "Trade in 'Virtual' Carbon", World Bank Policy Research Working Paper 5194.

BALDWIN, R. (2010), "Understanding the GATT's Wins and the WTO's Woes", CEPR Policy Insight #49.

BALINEAU, G. and J. de MELO (2013), "Removing Barriers to Trade on Environmental Goods: An Appraisal", *World Trade Review*, forthcoming.

BARRETT, S. (2003) *Environment and Statecraft: The Strategy of Environmental Treaty-Making*, Oxford University Press.

BARRETT, S. (2008), "A Portfolio System of Climate Treaties", Discussion Paper 08-13, Harvard Kennedy School.

BHATTACHARYA, S. and R. HODLER, (2008). "Natural Resources, Democracy and Corruption", *European Economic Review*, 54(4), 608-21.

BOEHRINGER, C., C. FISCHER and K. ROSENDAHL (2010), "The Global Effects of Subglobal Climate Policies", *BE Journal of Economic Analysis and Policy*, BE Press vol. 10(2), p. 13.

BRUNNSCHWEILER, C. and E. H. BULTE (2008), "The Resource Curse Revisited: A Tale of Paradoxes and Red-Herrings", *Journal of Environmental Economics and Management*, 55(3), 248-64.

BRUNNSCHWEILER, C. and E. H. BULTE (2009), "Natural Resources and Violent Conflict: Resource Abundance, Dependence and the Onset of Civil Wars", Oxford Economic Papers, 61(4), 651-74.

BULTE, E. and E.B. BARBIER (2005) "Trade and Renewable Resources in a Second-best World: An Overview", *Environmental and Resource Economics*, 30(4), 423-63.

CADOT, O. and J. DE MELO (2007), "Why OECD Countries Should Reform their Rules of Origin", *World Bank Research Observer*.

CAI, Y., R. RIEZMAN, and J. WHALLERY (2009) International Trade and the Negotiability of Global Change Agreements", NBER #14711.

CHAN, G., R. STAVINS, R. STOWE, R. SWEENEY (2012), "The SO2 allowance-trading system and the Clean Air Act Amendments of 1990: Reflections on 20 years of policy Innovation", *National Tax Journal*, 65, 419-52.

CHICHILNISKY, G. (1994), "North-South Trade and the Global Environment", *American Economic Review*, 84(4), 851-74.

COLLIER, P. and A. HOEFFLER (2004), "Greed and Grievance in Civil War", *Oxford Economic Papers*, 56(4), 563-95.

COPELAND, B.R. and S. TAYLOR (2009) "Trade,Tragedy, and the Commons", *American Economic Review*, 99 (2009), 725-49.

CRISTEA, A., D. HUMMELS, L. PUZZELO, and M. AVETISYAN (2011) "Trade and the Greenhouse Gas Emission from International Freight Transport", NBER #17117.

DEAN, J. and M. LOVELY (2010) "Trade Growth, Production Fragmentation, and China's Environment" in R. Feenstra and S. Wei eds. *China's Growing Role in World Trade*, University of Chicago Press and NBER, 429-69.

DEMAILLY, D. and P. QUIRION (2008), "European Emission Trading Scheme and Competitiveness: A Case Study of the Iron and Steel Industry", *Energy Economics*, 30(4), 2009-27.

DONG, Y. and J. WHALLEY (2010) "Carbon, Trade Policy, and Carbon Free Trade Areas", *The World Economy,* Vol. 33(9), pp. 1073-1094.

EDERINGTON J. (2010) "Should Trade Agreements Include Environmental Policy?", *Review of Environmental Economics and Policy*, 4(1), 103-21

EDERINGTON J., LEVINSON A. and J. MINIER (2005),"Footloose and Pollution-Free", *Review of Economics and Statistics*, Vol. 87 (1), pp. 92-99.

FEENSTRA, R. and G. HANSON (1997), "Foreign Direct Investment and Relative Wages: Evidence from Maquiladoras", *Journal of International Economics*, 42(3-4), 371-93.

FISCHER, C. (2010) "Does Trade Help or Hinder the Conservation of Natural Resources", *Review of Environmental Economics and Policy*, 4(1), 103-21.

FRANKEL, J. and D. ROMER (1999) "Does Trade Cause Growth?", *American Economic Review*, 89(3), 379-99.

FREUND, C. (2009), "The Trade Response to Global Downturns: Historical Evidence", PRWP#5015.

GRETHER, J.M, N. MATHYS and J. DE MELO (2009), "Scale, Technique, and Composition Effects in SO2 Manufacturing Emissions", *Environmental and Resource Economics*, vol. 43(2), 257-74.

GRETHER, J.M, N. MATHYS and J. DE MELO (2010), "Is Trade Bad for the Environment? Decomposing world-wide SO2 Emissions", *Review of World Economics,* vol. 145(4), 713-29.

GRETHER J.-M., N.A. MATHYS and J. DE MELO (2011), "Unravelling the world-wide pollution haven effect", *Journal of International Trade and Economic Development,* ifirst July (2010).

GRETHER, J.-M. and J. DE MELO, (2004), "Globalization and dirty industries: Do pollution havens matter?" in R.E. Baldwin and A. Winters eds., *Challenges to Globalization: Analyzing the Economics*, University of Chicago Press, pp. 167-208.

HARTWICK, J.M. (1977), "Intergenerational Equity and the Investing of Rents from Exhaustible Resources", *American Economic Review,* 66, 972-74.

HUFBAUER, G., S. CHARNOVITZ, and J. KIM (2009), „*Global Warming and the World Trading System"*. Washington, DC: Peterson Institute for International Economics.

ISHAM, J., M. WOOLCOCK, L. PRITCHETT and G. BUSBY (2005), "The Varieties of Resource Experience: Natural Resource Exports and the Political Economy of Growth", *World Bank Economic Review*, 19(2), 141-74.

KEE, H.L., H. MA, and M. MANI (2010) " The Effects of Domestic Climate Change Measures on International Competitiveness", *The World Economy*, 33(6), 820 9.

KELLER, W. (2010) "International Trade, Foreign Direct Investment and Technology Spillovers" in *Handbook of the Economics of Innovation*, edited by B. Hall and N. Rosenberg, Elsevier North-Holland.

LEDERMAN, D. and W. MALONEY, eds. (2007)) *Natural Resources, Neither Curse nor Destiny*, Stanford University Press.

MANN, C. W. (2011) *1493: Uncovering the New World Columbus Created,* A. Knopf, New York.

MATHYS, N., and MELO, J. de (2011), "Political Economy Aspects of Climate Change Mitigation Efforts", *The World Economy*, 34(11), 1938-54.

MATHYS, N., and MELO, J. de (2012), " Concilier les Politiques Commerciales et les Politiques Climatiques", *Revue d'Economie du Développement,* n° 2, 57-83.

MATTOO A. and A. SUBRAMANIAN (2010), "Equity in Climate Change", Policy Research Working Paper 5383, World Bank.

MATTOO, A., SUBRAMANIAN A., D. VAN DER MENSBRUGGHE and JIANWU He (2009) "Reconciling Climate Change and Trade Policy", World Bank Policy research discussion paper 5123.

MEHLUM, H., K. MOENE, R. TORVIK (2006), «Institutions and the Resource Curse», *Economic Journal*, 116 (50), 1-20.

MELO, J. de and N. MATHYS (2011), "Trade and Climate Change Policies after the Crisis" chp. 23 in M. Haddad and Ben Sheperd eds. *Managing Openness: Trade and Outward-Oriented Growth after the Crisis,* The World Bank.

MESSERLIN, P. (2010), "Climate Change and Trade Policy: from Mutual Destruction to Mutual Support", PRWP#5378.

MESSERLIN P. (2011), "Climate, Trade, and Water: A Grand Coalition?" *The World Economy*, 34(11), 1883-1910.

MOLTKE, A. Von (2o11) ed., *Fisheries Subsidies, Sustainable Development and the WTO* ,UNEP, Earthscan.

MOORE, M. (2010) "Implementing Carbon Tariffs: A Fool's Errand?", World Bank Working paper #5359.

NORDSTROM, H (2009), "The Microcosm of Climate Change Negotiations : What Can we Learn from the European Union?", ICTSD, Geneva.

PETERS G. P, J. MINX, C. WEBER, and O EDENHOFER (2011), "CO2 embodied in international trade with implications for global climate policy", *Proceedings of the National Academy of Sciences*, http://www.pnas.org/content/early/2011/04/19/1006388108

PIGOTT, R. J. WHALLEY and R. WIGLE (1992), " International Lionkages and Carbon Reduction Initiatives" ch. 6 in K. Anderson and R. Blackhurst eds., *The Greening of World Trade Issues*, Harvester and Wheatsheaf.

PLOEG, R. van der (2011), "Natural Resources: Curse or Blessing?", *Journal of Economic Literature*, 49(2), 366-420.

STERN, R. (2005), *The Economics of Climate Change: The Stern Review*, Cambridge University Press.

TAYLOR, M.S. (2011), "Buffalo Hunt: International Trade and the Virtual Extinction of the North American Bison", *American Economic Review*, 101(7), 3162-95.

TAN, H., and J. WHALLEY (2010), "The Potential Global and Developing Country Impacts of Alternative Emission Cuts and Accompanying Mechanisms for the Post Copenhagen Process", NBER #16090.

TIROLE, J. (2009), "Politique Climatique: Une Nouvelle Architecture Internationale" Rapport au Conseil d'Analyse Economique.

WACZIARG, R. and WELCH (2008), "Trade Liberalization and Growth; New Evidence", *World Bank Economic Review,* 22(2), 187-231.

WHALLEY, J. (2011), "What Role for Trade in a Post 2012 Global Climate Policy Regime?", *The World Economy*, 34(11), 1844-1862.

WORLD BANK (2008), *International Trade and Climate Change: Economic, Legal, and Institutional Experiences*, The World Bank, 144p.

WTO Report (2010), *Report on 2010 World Trade.*

The Journal of International Trade & Economic Development
Vol. 21, No. 1, February 2012, 131–162

Routledge
Taylor & Francis Group

Unravelling the worldwide pollution haven effect

Jean-Marie Grether[a]*, Nicole Andréa Mathys[b] and Jaime de Melo[c]

[a]*University of Neuchâtel, Neuchâtel, Switzerland;* [b]*University of Neuchâtel and Swiss Federal Office of Energy, Neuchâtel and Bern, Switzerland;* [c]*University of Geneva and CEPR, Geneva, Switzerland*

(*Received 10 May 2009; final version received 10 December 2009*)

This paper tackles the 'pollution haven' argument by estimating the pollution content of imports (PCI). The PCI is then decomposed into three components: (i) a 'deep' component (i.e. traditional variables unrelated to the environmental debate); (ii) a factor endowment component and (iii) a 'pollution haven' component reflecting the impact of differences in environmental policies. The estimation is carried out for 1987 for an extensive data set covering 10 pollutants, 48 countries and 79 ISIC four-digit sectors. Decompositions based on cross-section econometric estimates suggest a significant pollution haven effect, which increases the PCI of the North because of stricter environmental regulations in the North. At the same time, the factor endowment effect lowers the PCI of the North, as the North is relatively well-endowed in capital and pollution-intensive activities are capital intensive. On a global scale, because the bulk of trade is intra-regional with a high North-North share, these effects are small relative to the 'deep' determinants of the worldwide PCI. Robustness checks performed on a more recent dataset, but limited to sulphur dioxide, confirm these results. In sum, differences in factor endowments and environmental policies only marginally affected the PCI of world trade at the end of the 1980s.

Keywords: trade and the environment; pollution haven effect; factor endowment effect

1. Introduction

For the environmentally minded, globalization reflected in rising trade shares in world GDP is worrisome – directly, because the activity of trading itself generates pollution, and indirectly because lower environmental standards generate a comparative advantage in 'dirty' industries for developing countries. In this context, globalization, which reduces transport costs and/or trade barriers, would shift investment and production of 'dirty' goods to the South. As a result, globalization would lead to an increase in

*Corresponding author. Email: jean-marie.grether@unine.ch

ISSN 0963-8199 print/ISSN 1469-9559 online

http://dx.doi.org/10.1080/09638190903552040
http://www.tandfonline.com

the pollution content of imports (PCI) by the North in conformity with what has been called the 'pollution haven (PH) hypothesis' (henceforth PHH), and to a worldwide increase in the production of dirty products. Likewise, the literature has emphasized that a tightening of environmental standards in the North would lead industries to relocate to the South according to what is referred to as the 'pollution haven (PH) effect'. Overall, it is fair to say that empirical support for the PHH is weak, while the PH effect, which is often taken for granted has, apart from recent empirical support for the US, also been elusive.[1]

In his review of the state of knowledge on the PHH, Taylor (2005) points out that the literature lacks a compelling multi-country test of the PHH, noting that the challenge for empiricists is to develop 'clever methods that eliminate the need for some of the data'. This paper is a first step in this direction. We argue (with some supporting evidence) that one can assume constancy in emissions per unit of labour. This allows us then to carry out a systematic global estimation of the pollution content of trade across all industrial sectors, in which we disentangle the role of factor endowments and environmental policies from the more fundamental (or 'deep') determinants of bilateral trade. However, because this assumption is strong, we also check that results still hold in the case of SO_2, the only pollutant for which emission data are available across countries and sectors.

To our knowledge, this global exercise is novel. As an example of what transpires from our estimates, consider the usual version of the PH effect identified in the literature. Because of a shift in comparative advantage, a tightening of Northern environmental standards will increase the pollution content of imports by the North. But what about the South? In reality, developing countries are also importing dirty products, and they may even be larger importers of those goods if one takes into account the fact that highly polluting activities are often capital-intensive (referred to as the factor-endowment (FE) effect in the literature). So a tightening of Northern environmental standards will also decrease the pollution content of imports by the South, leading to an ambiguous change of the global pollution content of North–South trade. But composition effects do not stop here since trade includes intra-regional (i.e. North–North and South–South) trade. The framework proposed in this paper weighs the importance of the PH and FE effects, taking into account composition effects that have been ignored so far in the literature.

Although we carry out robustness checks, data limitations force us to make assumptions about emission intensities so that it should be seen as first-time estimates of orders of magnitude of the PHH for a large set of countries in the late 1980s, taking into account the following issues discussed in the debate. First, both PH and FE effects are quantified in a setting with a large set of developed (North) and developing (South) countries. Second, 79 four-digit manufacturing sectors are covered (not only the five dirtiest usually aggregated into one sector) and the analysis is carried out for ten categories of pollutants. Third, to identify the PH effect, we use the lead content of gasoline (and other indicators) as a proxy for environmental stringency used in lieu of income per capita. Finally, a flexible gravity-type framework provides a good control for non-environment-related determinants of the pollution content of trade.

Section 2 discusses briefly the PH and FE effects, arguing that they can be usefully captured by the pollution content of trade (in our case, the pollution content of imports (PCI)). Section 3 constructs estimates of the PCI for ten pollutants for a large cross-section of countries and industries accounting for roughly 60% of world trade. Section 4 estimates a model of bilateral trade in emissions (one for each pollutant) in which factor endowments, environmental policies, and 'deep' determinants (i.e. all remaining determinants) are separately identified. These estimates then serve to decompose the relative importance of the PH and FE effects in the debate on the PHH. In addition to standard robustness checks on the main dataset, Section 5 drops the assumption of constancy of emissions per worker and introduces alternative proxies for environmental regulation. Section 6 concludes.

2. The pollution content of trade: a framework

A simple example serves to introduce the notion of the pollution content of trade, measured here by the pollution content of imports (PCI). The example illustrates how the PCI serves to analyse the trade and the environment relationship by identifying a PH effect and a FE effect. We then present a framework of bilateral commodity trade that is useful to link the PCI to underlying determinants.

2.1. The pollution haven effect: an illustrative identification

To fix the terms of the debate about the PH effect, and to motivate the choice of the pollution content of imports (PCI), consider the following simple hypothetical example in a Heckscher–Ohlin framework.[2] Two countries, North (N) and South (S), produce two goods, a 'dirty' and a (completely) 'clean' good, with pollution per unit of output of the dirty good being initially identical in N and S so that both countries are the same in all respects except that N has a higher income per capita than S. Assume then that environmental quality is a normal good. Stricter environmental standards in N will lower emissions per unit of output and abatement costs will raise the unit price of the dirty good. N will then import the dirty good and hence its trade will be 'embodied' with emissions (i.e. $PCI_{NS} > 0$). Conversely, S will import the clean good from its partner and so the PCI of S will be zero as there is no intra-industry trade in a Heckscher–Ohlin setting (i.e. $PCI_{SN} = 0$). Therefore, in this two-commodity world, the PCI of N from S is positive ($PCI_{NS} > 0$) and the PCI of S from N is zero ($PCI_{SN} = 0$) since S imports the clean good. Differences in environmental standards alone lead to trade and to an increase in world pollution since the opportunity to trade has led to a shift in the production of the dirty good to S.

Next, consider two experiments involving the gains from trade specialization. First, consider globalization via a reduction in transport costs, or a reduction in trade barriers. This will lead S to specialize in the production of dirty products. Globalization thus increases PCI_{NS} in conformity with what has been called the PH hypothesis (some of the previously dirty production in N is now carried out in S under less-stringent environmental standards). As a second experiment, consider a tightening of environmental regulations in N. This is also expected to lead to a relocation of dirty industries from N to S, increasing PCI_{NS} further through what is referred to as the PH effect in the literature.

Bring in now factor endowment differences, supposing that dirty industries are capital intensive (as assumed in Copeland and Taylor 2003) and that N is relatively well-endowed in capital. If the PH effect was small (as suggested by recent US-based evidence mentioned above), then the FE effect on comparative advantage could well dominate. Assume this to be the case. Then, S will be importing the dirty good although it has lower environmental standards, a configuration referred to as reflecting the FE hypothesis according to Copeland and Taylor (2004).

Starting from this new configuration, consider again the two experiments above. A reduction in transport costs and/or trade liberalization, might then lead dirty activities to move to N, resulting in an increase in dirty imports of S from N. Conversely, a tightening of environmental policy in N will have the reverse effect, with dirty activities moving to S and increasing PCI_{NS}.

Clearly, in a multi-commodity world, PCI_{NS}, $PCI_{SN} \neq 0$, and if the relative strength of the PH effect dominates, one would expect to observe $PCI_{NS} > PCI_{SN}$. Thus, the relative strength of the PH versus the FE effect is a determinant shaping the worldwide allocation of the PCI between groups of countries. It also plays a crucial role regarding the impact of globalization or environmental policy changes on the pollution content of trade.

To get a full picture of the factors underlying the evolution of the worldwide pollution content of trade, scale (N and S have different economic weight and both may grow) and technique (abatement activities are different in N and S and vary across time) effects should also be factored in, as well as differences in emission intensities across commodities. And since the debate on trade and the environment is usually couched in terms of the contribution of rich and poor countries, compositional effects across regions should also be taken into account. The framework below shows how this can be done.

2.2. *Framework*

Any suitable framework for a positive analysis of the PHH needs to make a distinction between clean and dirty sectors in terms of their damage to the environment and to link environmental damage directly to production activities. This is best done by embedding emission intensities per unit of activity in a multi-sector bilateral trade framework at the industry level. This allows the exploitation of the variance in the data on commodity trade and on emission intensities.

A recasting of Romalis (2004) provides this framework. He considers a two-region (North and South) setting in which countries are identical in each country grouping and in which preferences are represented by a single consumer sharing identical homothetic preferences across all countries. In each country, a continuum of industries are ranked by factor intensity (in his case, skilled and unskilled labour and in ours capital and labour) with production taking place under monopolistic competition with increasing returns to scale. Firms can costlessly differentiate their products. Transport costs lead to a departure from factor price equalization, which pins down the trade structure, while monopolistic competition gives rise to N-S intra-industry trade. Romalis (2004) produces evidence in support of his model, showing that a typical Northern's country market share of skilled intensive products rises with the skill-intensity of the industry. Translating his results to our setting, a typical Northern country's market share of capital-intensive pollution-intensive products rises with the capital intensity of the industry.

For our purposes, the combination of transport costs and monopolistic competition in Romalis' model results in predictions about the location of production and bilateral trade in each industry. Trade shares depend on the interaction of factor intensities and relative factor costs, which in turn depend on relative factor abundance and policies. To translate these predictions into our bilateral setting, let M_{ijs} denote imports of sector s by country i from country j, Δkl_{ijs} the differences in capital-labour intensities for industry s, and $\Delta\theta_{ij}$ the difference in the stringency of the environmental policies between i and j (assumed to have the same impact on emissions across sectors). Let Ω_{ij} capture other exogenous (or 'fundamental') determinants of bilateral trade at the national level, which in our gravity-type approach include distance and other country-specific determinants of bilateral trade. Then the model can be expressed as:

$$M_{ijs} = f(\Omega_{ij}, \Delta kl_{ijs}, \Delta\theta_{ij}) \quad (1)$$

To establish the desired link between trade volumes and the pollution content of trade measured by the PCI, we disaggregate across pollutants and sectors. The disaggregation across sectors to recognize that the usual two-sector 'dirty/clean' distinction is insufficient.[3] As usual, there is a trade-off between the variance in the data by proceeding at a disaggregate level and introducing measurement errors that lead to less precise and less robust results.

Let then emissions per US dollar of production in country j, sector s and pollutant k be given by g_{js}^k and define two PCI measures: (i) total import-embodied emissions across sectors, Z_{ij}^k, (expressed in terms of physical units of pollution) and average emission intensities, G_{ij}^k, (expressed as physical units of pollution per one US dollar of imports). The two PCI measures of country i from country j for pollutant k, are then given by:[4]

$$Z_{ij}^k = \sum_s g_{js}^k M_{ijs}; \quad G_{ij}^k \equiv \frac{Z_{ij}^k}{M_{ij}} = \sum_s g_{js}^k \mu_{ijs} \tag{2}$$

where $M_{ij} = \Sigma_s M_{ijs}$ and μ_{ijs} is the share of sector s in country i imports from country j. For each pollutant, the total PCI indicator (similar indicators have been previously used by Antweiler 1996 and Ederington et al. 2004) and the average PCI are used in the econometric estimates. In our view, investigating changes in the volume of pollution embodied in worldwide trade (i.e. in PCI) is the simplest, most direct step to do in the analysis of the PH effect.

3. Measuring the PCI

The PCI measures in Section 2 are now constructed for a sample of 48 countries (29 developing and 19 developed countries) using sectoral data on emissions for the US for 1987, which is the only source of comprehensive data on emissions for a large number of pollutants.[5] These emissions coefficients are available from the US IPPS for 14 pollutants (here aggregated into ten pollutants – see Table A3 in the Appendix). They are computed for 79 four-digit ISIC industries (see Hettige et al. 1995).[6]

It is clear that having emissions coefficients for only one year is a major drawback and that applying US coefficients to a large sample of countries that includes developed and developing countries is problematic. How we deal with this problem will be explained shortly. While estimations and decompositions are carried out for ten pollutants, to save space we discuss results for three pollutants widely used in other studies: sulphur dioxide in the air (SO_2), total toxic pollution (TPTT) and biological oxygen demand in water (BOWT) and report the decompositions for all pollutants later. All three pollutants generate relatively small trans-border externalities beyond those embodied in trade.[7]

Emission intensities in the IPPS database are only reported for the US, but we have to apply them to all countries in the sample. For the reasons discussed below, we assume constancy of emission intensities per worker across countries. Consider first the following supporting evidence on SO_2. Olivier and Berdowski (2001) have constructed country-specific SO_2 emission coefficients for a large sample of countries on the basis of data collected for a small number of manufacturing sectors. Using several methods, Grether, Mathys and de Melo (2009) disaggregate this data into seven sectors and 62 countries and show that, for SO_2 at least, emissions per unit of labour are similar across Northern and Southern countries, while there is a large difference in emissions per unit of output between North and South (see Figure 1).

Second, using these same SO_2 data, we searched for a systematic relation between emissions per capita and development characteristics. Sector-specific White-robust regressions using PPP GDP per capita[8] as the explanatory variable confirm the pattern in Figure 1, i.e. that intensities per USD are significantly lower in richer countries. However, when intensities per worker are used instead of emissions per dollar of output as the explained variable, the coefficient is non-significant. Results (reported in Appendix Table A4) suggest that emissions per worker are roughly constant across countries, indicating that higher emissions per capita in the South are compensated for by lower labour productivity in the South (since $e_X \equiv E/X$, $a_L \equiv L/X$, $e_L \equiv E/L$, then $e_X \equiv e_L a_L$).[9]

Third, and again on the basis of the same SO_2 data, Section 5.2 shows that the orders of magnitude suggested by the present paper do not depend on whether emissions per worker are kept fixed or allowed to vary across countries.

Figure 1. SO_2 emission intensities for north and south.
Note: North: United States, Canada, High income Asia and Europe. South: Latin America, Africa and Low income Asia.

Fourth, the constancy of emissions intensities by worker is in accordance with the evidence in Hettige et al. (2000) who found that emissions per employee are roughly constant across countries for one of our pollutants – biochemical oxygen demand in water (BOWT).

On the basis of this evidence, we adjust the US per employee IPPS coefficients, $e^k_{L,US,s}$, by each country's industry labour–output ratio $a^S_{L,J} \equiv L_{js}/X_{js}$, i.e. $g^k_{js} = e^k_{L,US,s}(a^S_{LJ})$ which amounts to assuming a constancy of emissions per unit of labour (Section 5 uses the country-specific SO_2 emission intensities to check the robustness of our results to this assumption).

Table 1 summarizes, for the two country groupings (North and South), the main factors at stake: the constructed indices of PCI on the assumption of the constancy of e_L, the proxy for the stringency of environmental policy, and factor endowments (specific variables that are used are explained and justified in Section 4).

Three patterns stand out in the data. First, as expected, the proxy indicator for environmental policy – the lead content of gasoline – indicates a much

Table 1. Environmental stringency index, factor endowments, imports and pollution-haven ratios by country grouping.

Variable (units)	Statistics	North** (19 countries)	South** (29 countries)
Lead Content (Grams/Gallon)	Mean (C.V.)	0.24 (0.76)	0.58 (0.43)
Capital/Labor (1987 Thousand US Dollars per employee)	Mean (C.V.)	88.94 (0.38)	9.67 (0.89)
Imports* (Million Current US Dollars)	Mean (C.V.)	930 (815)[a] (1.34)	99 (92)[b] (1.30)
PCI-BOWT* (Million Pounds)	Mean (C.V.)	1.19 (1.29)	0.17 (1.00)
	PH-Ratio[c]	0.89	
PCI-SO_2* (Million Pounds)	Mean (C.V.)	7.24 (1.31)	1.27 (1.32)
	PH-Ratio[c]	0.67	
PCI-TPTT* (Million Pounds)	Mean (C.V.)	5.39 (1.18)	0.86 (1.11)
	PH-Ratio[c]	0.63	

Notes: Data are averages over 1986–1988. PH-Ratios for the remaining pollutants are reported in appendix table A3.

*Bilateral data averaged by importer.

**The split by income group used 11,000$ as break point which corresponds to the trough in the bimodal distribution. See table A1 for the list of countries.

[a]N-N; [b]S-S trade in parenthesis; [c]see equation (3) for the definition.

C.V.: Coefficient of variation, PCI: Pollution content of imports, BOWT: Biological oxygen demand in water, SO_2: Sulfur dioxide in the air, TPTT: Total Toxic Pollution.

more stringent environmental policy in the North, and even if this is an imperfect proxy, the difference in average values is large, suggesting room for strong PH effect in the data. Second, as would be suggested if FE effects were important, there is a great difference in the average capital–labour endowment ratios between the two groups of countries. Third, again not surprisingly, the volume of trade is much larger for the North, suggesting that composition effects might be important depending on the pattern of trade of the North. This is further confirmed by the share of intra-regional trade figures in parenthesis in total imports for both the North and the South. For both groups of countries, inter-regional trade is only about 10% of total trade.

Finally, the bottom of the table reports the 'pollution haven ratio' for each one of the three pollutants defined for pollutant k as the ratio of the average PCI for high-income (denoted by subscript 'N') to low-income (denoted by subscript 'S') countries (for the PH-ratios of the remaining pollutants, see Appendix Table A3):

$$PH^k = \frac{G_N^k}{G_S^k} \tag{3}$$

According to the reasoning in Section 2.1, should the PHH find support in the raw (but constructed) data, and should most trade be inter- rather than intra-regional, one would expect to find $PH^k > 1 \forall k$,. The presumption here is that the PH effect dominates the FE effect. In fact, as shown in the bottom of the table, the opposite is the case for all three pollutants reported in the table (but also for the other pollutants). To go further and elucidate why the average PCI is systematically lower in the North (i.e. $PH^k > 1 \forall k$), one needs to disentangle and take out the impact of the fundamental determinants of trade that are embodied in the constructed PCI. It could well be that the PCI is mainly determined by these more fundamental determinants of trade patterns than those identified in the PHH debate.

4. Unravelling the pollution haven effect

To disentangle the correlates of the PCI, we estimate the relation suggested by equation (1). Assuming that determinants enter multiplicatively and omitting pollutant superscript k, the PCI of country i's imports from country j, Z_{ij}, can be decomposed into a 'deep' determinant component, Ω_{ij} (i.e. the import-embodied pollution that would occur for reasons unrelated to environmental policy and endowments), an FE effect, κ_{ij}, and a PH effect, ℓ_{ij}:

$$Z_{ij} = \Omega_{ij} \kappa_{ij} \ell_{ij} \tag{4}$$

This multiplicative form between the three components is easy to handle, particularly in a gravity-like framework and it is also convenient to carry out the decomposition that is proposed in the next section. We proceed in two steps. First, we regress for each pollutant k, the bilateral PCI, Z_{ij}, on a set of explanatory variables capturing the effects identified in equation (4). In a second step, we use the estimated coefficients to decompose the total predicted PCI for each pollutant into the three components, namely 'deep', 'FE', and 'PH' effects.

Estimation uses 1987 data and is based on a gravity-type equation (5) which is convenient to include the 'fundamental' determinants of bilateral trade. The PH effect is captured by differences in the lead content of gasoline presented in Table 1.[10]

The capital–labour ratio serves as proxy for endowment differences, i.e. captures the FE effect. To avoid erroneously attributing variations in bilateral PCIs to the two effects of interest, it is important to have as complete as possible set of control variables in the vector of 'deep' determinants. Thus, the sets of α and β coefficients control for these 'deep' determinants of bilateral trade, the former set relating to gravity-type controls, and the latter including other controls. The gravity-type controls include log distance ($DIST_{ij}$), the extent of the potential market ($MKT_{ij} = \ln(GDP_i{*}\ GDP_j)$), proxied by the product of GDPs (since these cannot be entered individually in the presence of fixed effects), common religion (CR_{ij}), common language (CL_{ij}) and landlockedness (LL_{ij}). Importer (DM_j) and exporter (DE_i) dummy variables control for country-specific omitted determinants.

$$
\begin{aligned}
lnZ_{ij}^{k} = {} & \alpha_o + \alpha_1 DIST_{ij} + \alpha_2 MKT_{ij} + \alpha_3 CR_{ij} + \alpha_4 CL_{ij} + \alpha_5 LL_{ij} \\
& + \beta_{1i} DE_i + \beta_j DM_j + \beta_3 \Delta SK_{ij} + \beta_4 \Delta HK_{ij} + \beta_5 \Delta COAL_{ij} \\
& + \beta_6 \Delta OIL_{ij} + \gamma_1 \Delta LEAD_{ij} + \gamma_2 \Delta KL_{ij} + \varepsilon_{ij} \qquad (5)
\end{aligned}
$$

As further control variables, we include proxies for differences in natural resource endowments across countries, oil production $\left(\Delta OIL_{ij} = \ln(\frac{OIL_i}{OIL_j})\right)$ and coal production $\left(\Delta COAL_{ij} = \ln\left(\frac{COAL_i}{COAL_j}\right)\right)$ since it is known that many pollution-generating activities are linked to the weight-reducing activities associated with the processing of primary products that are natural-resource based and hence less sensitive to differences in environmental policies. We also include two measures of skills since it has sometimes been claimed that pollution intensive activities are also skill-intensive (see Cole and Elliott 2005). The two variables are differences in the skill ratio (i.e. (skilled + base skills)/unskilled labour) $\left(\Delta SK_{ij} = \ln\left(\frac{SK_i}{SK_j}\right)\right)$, and differences in the ratio of high skilled labour (skilled/base skills), $\left(\Delta HK_{ij} = \ln\left(\frac{HK_i}{HK_j}\right)\right)$. To sum up, one may expect these control variables to be related to the bilateral PCI, although their influence is ultimately an empirical matter.[11]

To these variables we add the PH and FE variables mentioned above, namely the difference in the maximum lead content of gasoline $\left(\Delta LEAD_{ij} = \ln\left(\frac{LEAD_i}{LEAD_j}\right)\right)$, and the difference in capital-labour ratios $\left(\Delta KL_{ij} = \ln\left(\frac{KL_i}{KL_j}\right)\right)$.

Equation (5) is estimated for each one of the ten pollutants for average values over the 1986–88 period and observations with aggregate bilateral trade below a threshold of \$10,000 are dropped (leading to a loss of 3% of observations). Results for the three selected pollutants are discussed below (results for the remaining seven pollutants are summarized in Figure 2, see section 4.2).

Three objections come to mind when estimating equation (5) by OLS.[12] First, the results could be entirely driven by the volume of trade rather than the composition of trade. To address this potential shortcoming, we regress the average (G_{ij}^k) instead of the total PCI (Z_{ij}^k), thereby focusing only on the composition effect. As the trade volume dimension is absent, the traditional gravity-type control variables should in principle all disappear. However, we maintain distance as a regressor to control for the fact that dirty industries are predominantly weight-reducing activities (see supporting evidence in, for example, Grether and de Melo 2004) and hence might be particularly sensitive to transport costs. The alternative specification then becomes:

$$\begin{aligned}\ln G_{ij}^k = \tilde{\alpha}_o + \tilde{\alpha}_1 DIST_{ij} + \tilde{\beta}_1 DE_i + \tilde{\beta}_2 DM_j \\ + \tilde{\beta}_3 \Delta SK_{ij} + \tilde{\beta}_4 \Delta HK_{ij} + \tilde{\beta}_5 \Delta COAL_{ij} \\ + \tilde{\beta}_6 \Delta OIL_{ij} + \tilde{\gamma}_1 \Delta LEAD_{ij} + \tilde{\gamma}_2 \Delta KL_{ij} + \tilde{\varepsilon}_{ij}\end{aligned} \quad (6)$$

Second, one could object to the inclusion of intra-regional trade in the context of an estimation of the PH effect which is supposed to operate between, rather than within, regions so that all intra-regional bilateral trade (i.e. N-N and S-S) should be deleted. Thus, as a robustness check, we also report estimates of equation (5) over a sample that excludes intra-regional trade. However, as intra-regional trade should also respond to the same determinants as N-S and S-N trade, and since we are interested in capturing the PH and FE effects at the worldwide level, we consider that the relevant coefficient estimates for the decomposition exercise are those derived from the whole sample.

Finally, one could object that *LEAD* may be endogenous (as suggested by Ederington and Minier 2003, who found evidence that environmental policy has partly served as a substitute for protection using aggregate data). To deal with this potential problem, we also instrument *LEAD* by the UN's measure of Human development (the HDI). To be an appropriate instrument, the HDI has to be correlated with environmental regulation and orthogonal to the error term of the PCI regression. We expect that the HDI, takes into account different development dimensions of countries, and will be directly correlated with environmental regulation (which it is). Our maintained hypothesis is that the PCI is not directly affected by the HDI since environmental policies would be the main channels through which institutional and policy choices are likely to influence the PCI. So, in the absence of a better instrument, we stick to the

HDI as an instrument for the potential endogeneity of the environmental policy proxy, checking robustness to the choice of environmental proxy in Section 5.1, and arguing that environmental policy may not be a substitute for protection at the aggregate bilateral level.

4.1. Correlates of the PCI

Table 2 reports results for the two specifications (5 and 6), the two samples (world or NS only), and for the three selected pollutants: SO_2, BOWT, and TPTT. Overall, results are encouraging. Consider estimates of equation (5): first, the signs of the variables of interest are as expected in all specifications, and significant most of the time. The same comment applies to the gravity-related controls. For example, the coefficient on distance is negative and slightly higher than the 'average' estimate of –1.0 from meta studies, which is what one might expect since weight-reducing dirty industries are more sensitive to transport costs than clean industries (see, for example, the estimates in Grether and de Melo 2004). Likewise, common language and common religion enhances trade. Finally, landlockdness (0 if neither country in the dyad is landlocked, 1 if one is and 2 if both are) has a negative correlation with trade volume presumably via higher transport costs. As to the other controls for which we have no a priori expectations, they are only significant in some specifications.

Second, as to the comparison between OLS and 2SLS estimates for equation (5), coefficients do not change sign and, except for BOWT, are very similar in terms of significance for all variables apart from LEAD, which becomes significant through the instrumentation.[13]

In the first stage regression, the coefficient of LEAD is –1.45 and significant at the 1% level. The F-statistics take a value of 56.4, signifying the absence of a weak instrument problem. In the absence of other suitable instruments, we cannot test for the exogeneity of LEAD and we rely on the 2SLS estimates for the simulations reported below.

When we abstract from volume effects, and hence focus on detecting PH and FE effects in the composition of bilateral trade (equation (6)), we still find the same signs for both variables of interest. Finally, estimates are sufficiently close when the sample is restricted to North-South bilateral trade flows, indicating that the results of decompositions reported below would not be overly sensitive to the choice of sample. However, in two out of three cases the contribution of the FE effect would be larger if we were to carry out decompositions based on this restricted sample.

In sum, we retain from the estimates in Table 2 that the data support the presence of PH and FE effects, although the OLS estimates for LEAD are not significant in two cases. The average values of endowments and policies reported in Table 1 allow one to deduce the sign of these effects on PCI_{NS} and PCI_{SN}. Thus, starting from the 'deep' determinants of bilateral trade, the PCI_{NS} will be reduced through the 'FE' effect because the North has a

Table 2. Pollution content of imports regressions, 1987.

	Biochemical Oxygen Demand Water (BOWT)				SO_2 in the air (SO_2)				Total Toxic Pollution Intensity (TPTT)			
	Total PCI		Av. PCI	NS PCI	Total PCI		Av. PCI	NS PCI	Total PCI		Av. PCI	NS PCI
	OLS	2SLS	2SLS	2SLS	OLS	2SLS	2SLS	2SLS	OLS	2SLS	2SLS	2SLS
Δlead	−0.16***	−0.32***	−0.39***	−0.39***	−0.02	−0.21***	−0.19***	−0.20***	−0.01	−0.21***	−0.20***	−0.21***
	[5.31]	[5.22]	[10.28]	[5.37]	[0.60]	[3.86]	[6.53]	[3.05]	[0.52]	[4.26]	[7.71]	[3.36]
Δ Capital/Labor	−0.11	−0.29***	−0.42***	−0.2	−0.18**	−0.16**	−0.36***	−0.44***	−0.19**	−0.12*	−0.41***	−0.32***
	[1.22]	[3.29]	[6.22]	[1.54]	[2.44]	[2.05]	[7.01]	[3.76]	[2.18]	[1.77]	[9.04]	[2.95]
Δ Skill Ratio[a)]	0.09	0.33**	−0.23*	−0.05	0.50***	0.47***	−0.14	0.18	0.38***	0.30**	−0.50***	−0.04
	[0.81]	[1.97]	[1.93]	[0.33]	[5.24]	[3.14]	[1.48]	[1.29]	[4.22]	[2.20]	[6.18]	[0.33]
Δ High Skill Ratio[b)]	−0.18	−1.89***	0.17	−1.20***	−0.62***	−2.08***	0.21	−0.97***	−0.43*	−1.78***	0.92***	−0.55**
	[0.75]	[7.64]	[0.91]	[4.59]	[3.17]	[9.44]	[1.46]	[4.08]	[1.91]	[9.01]	[7.30]	[2.45]
Δcoal	−0.02	0.01	−0.10***	0.14***	0.03**	0.04**	−0.09***	0.18***	0	0.01	−0.16***	0.14***
	[0.79]	[0.43]	[5.88]	[3.80]	[2.03]	[2.19]	[6.52]	[5.38]	[0.02]	[0.36]	[13.50]	[4.51]
Δoil	0.03	0	0.01	0.28***	0.05***	0.02	0.02	0.27***	0.04*	0	−0.01	0.22***
	[1.04]	[0.07]	[0.74]	[5.82]	[2.93]	[0.66]	[1.21]	[6.09]	[1.98	[0.18]	[0.51]	[5.12]
Distance	−1.34***	−1.34***	−0.24***	−1.55***	−1.32***	−1.32***	−0.20***	−1.51***	−1.25***	−1.25***	−0.11***	−1.39***
	[15.35]	[21.23]	[5.91]	[13.12]	[15.96]	[23.58]	[6.39]	[14.05]	[15.87]	[24.95]	[3.92]	[13.59]
GDP_i*GDP_j	0.94***	0.55***		0.61***	0.96***	0.59***		0.63***	0.93***	0.57***		0.61***
	[22.00]	[43.30]		[28.91]	[24.74]	[51.77]		[32.56]	[22.33]	[56.43]		[33.73]
Common Language	1.14***	1.14***		0.50***	1.00***	1.00***		0.70***	0.92***	0.92***		0.49***
	[7.52]	[8.24]		[2.93]	[6.74]	[8.15]		[4.53]	[6.79]	[8.34]		[3.37]
Common Religion	0.72***	0.72***		0.34	0.74***	0.74***		0.37*	0.67***	0.67***		0.35*
	[5.18]	[4.52]		[1.63]	[5.34]	[5.25]		[1.94]	[6.42]	[5.29]		[1.92]
Landlocked	−0.67**	−2.08***		−0.44	−0.46*	−1.57***		0.11	−0.54**	−1.54***		−0.43
	[2.49]	[7.67]		[1.33]	[1.99]	[6.52]		[0.35]	[2.11]	[7.13]		[1.50]
Observations	2107	2107	2107	1109	2107	2107	2107	1109	2107	2107	2107	1109
R-squared	0.73	0.73	0.34	0.78	0.74	0.74	0.47	0.8	0.78	0.78	0.49	0.81

Notes: Dependent variable (in log): Total PCI: Total bilateral PCI, Av. PCI: Average bilateral PCI, NS PCI: Total bilateral PCI between North and South. Absolute value of t statistics in brackets, in 2SLS regressions lead is instrumented with the human development index, first stage F statistics are 48.50 for the average PCI regressions and 56.43 for the others, fixed effects are not reported.

*Significant at 10%; **significant at 5%; ***significant at 1%, [a)](skilled + base skills)/unskilled, [b)]skilled/base skills.

comparative advantage in dirty products. Likewise, because of more stringent environmental standards, the PCI_{NS} will be increased through the 'PH' effect. The opposite patterns will hold for PCI_{SN}. However, to go further, we need to take into account the fact that there is horizontal trade that will be reflected in PCI_{NN} and PCI_{SS} values with the worldwide effect being a weighted average of vertical and horizontal trade flows. We now carry out a decomposition of the PCI into its constituent parts.

4.2. Decomposing the PCI into the PH and the FE effects

For each region, normalize the deep determinants of the PCI to unity. Then, for each pollutant k, the total percentage increase in the PCI due to the FE and the PH effects will be given by:

$$1 + TOT = (1 + FE)(1 + PH) \tag{7}$$

where FE and PH are the respective percentage increases in the PCI due to each effect.

Decomposition results are reported in Table 3 for the three pollutants with overall decomposition results for the ten pollutants reported in Figure 2. Take, for example, biochemical oxygen demand in water (BOWT). Starting from the base (or 'fundamental') PCI, adding differences in factor endowments reduces the PCI by 4% while adding differences in environmental regulations increases the PCI by 11% so that, taken together, the two effects increase the world PCI by 7%, which is also shown in Figure 2. Next focus on the PH effect. The worldwide result (11% increase) is in fact a weighted average of the PH effect on intra-regional flows (13%) and the PH effect on inter-regional flows (1%), with corresponding weights of 88% and 12%. Similarly, the aggregate PH effect on inter-regional flows is decomposed into a Northern (173%) and a Southern (−70%) component, with import shares being respectively 29% and 71%.

Several patterns stand out in Table 3. Start with row 1. As emphasized by participants in the PH debate, whatever the pollutant, Northern imports from the South display a significant PH effect, resulting in a strong increase in the PCI. Likewise the FE effect is also estimated to have a significant impact on the PCI in the opposite direction. Move to row 2, which gives the corresponding decomposition for Southern imports from the North. A reverse pattern of similar magnitude is evident. As shown along row 3, these countervailing forces naturally tend to cancel out, so that FE and PH effects on overall trade are several orders of magnitude smaller than on isolated (either Northern or Southern) inter-regional trade. As could be expected, the net impact is driven by the Northern pattern, but the mitigating impact of the Southern PCI (at least more than a quarter of vertical PCI) should not be underestimated. Composition effects are also evident when comparing

Table 3. Decomposition of the PCI into the FE and the PH-Effect (%).

Row	Import flows [a)]	Number of observations	Biochemical Oxygen Demand Water (BOWT)			SO_2 in the air (SO_2)			Total Toxic Pollution Intensity (TPTT)		
			FE-effect	PH-effect	TOT-effect	FE-effect	PH-effect	TOT-effect	FE-effect	PH-effect	TOT-effect
1	NS	544	−68	173	−14	−44	114	20	−38	106	27
2	SN	565	127	−70	−33	61	−65	−44	42	−64	−49
3	NS + SN	1109	−19	1	−19	−13	15	1	−8	8	−1
4	NN	342	−1	13	12	−1	9	9	0	−3	−3
5	SS	656	−22	−16	−34	−1	−6	−7	−5	−9	−13
6	NN + SS	998	−2	13	11	−1	9	8	0	−3	−4
7	World	2107	−4	11	7	−3	10	6	−2	−1	−3
			Ω	Ω k	Ω k ℓ	Ω	Ω k	Ω k ℓ	Ω	Ω k	Ω k ℓ
8	Share of NS in NS + SN		75	29	79	70	45	83	63	42	81
9	Share of NN in NN + SS		97	98	98	95	96	96	95	95	95
10	Share of NS + SN in World		14	12	11	22	20	21	24	22	24

Notes:
[a)]NS: North imports from the South, SN: South imports from the North, NN: North imports from the North, SS: South imports from the South.
Along rows: TOT = (1 + FE)*(1 + PH) −1. For example for row 7: (1−0.04)*(1 + 0.11)− 1 ≈ 0.07. Due to rounding, the decomposition only holds approximate l.
Along columns: $AGG_v = \theta^*CMP_1 + (1\text{-}\theta)^*CMP_2$ where AGG_v is the aggregate effect (v = NS + SN, NN + SS, World) CMP_1 and CMP_2 are the two corresponding components and θ is the share of CMP_1 in the relevant PCI (Ω for the FE and the TOT effects, Ω k for the PH effect, Ω k ℓ is only reported for the sake of completeness).

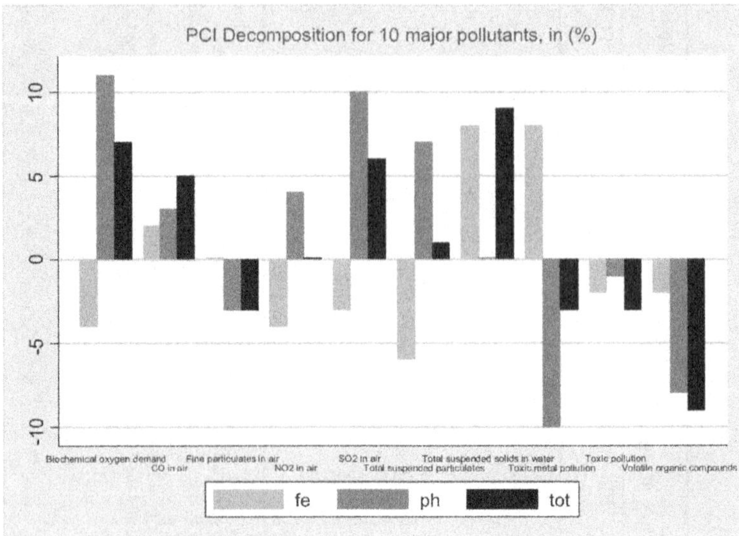

Figure 2. The pollution-haven hypothesis for ten major pollutants, 1987.
Notes: (TOT) is the sum of the factor-endowment (FE) and the pollution-haven (PH) effects according to the decomposition given by equation (7).

relative magnitudes in rows 4 and 5. First, intra-regional FE and PH effects are much smaller than corresponding inter-regional effects. Second, since 75% of the world PCI is accounted for by intra-regional trade, the overall effects are much smaller than those that one would obtain if considering only North–South trade, as is done in typical case studies carried out for industrialized countries. These two results corroborate results by Ederington et al. (2005) who find stronger PH effects for inter-regional than intra-regional trade and conclude that because of the dominance of N-N trade in global trade, PH effects are likely to be small.

Finally, note that the relative strength of PH and FE effects is not invariant across pollutants, a result that is confirmed by the differences in estimates across pollutants in Figure 2. For two out of the three pollutants of Table 3, the PH effect dominates the FE effect whatever the type of imports considered, while for the third pollutant (biochemical oxygen demand), the PH effect is only dominated in the case of Northern imports from the South.

Figure 2 compares, side by side, the results of the decomposition for the ten pollutants. Recall that the PHH is said to hold if the PH effect is positive and dominates the FE effect. No clear-cut verdict emerges as to the strength of the PHH since it holds for four (biological oxygen demand, SO_2, total suspended particulates and NO_2) out of the ten pollutants. For one pollutant, toxic metal pollution, both the FE and the PH effect go in the opposite direction of what would be expected. 'Iron and steel' and 'non-ferrous metals' are the two main polluting industries in this case and hence a possible explanation for this counter-intuitive result could be the fact that these are weight-reducing and hardly mobile industries (as also suggested in Grether and de Melo 2004). For the remaining pollutants, effects are either small or support either the PH or the FE effect, but not both.

These decompositions also provide an estimate of the possible reduction in the worldwide PCI if there were a complete harmonization of environmental policies, meaning that the worldwide PH effect on the PCI could be suppressed, by equalizing environmental regulation between countries. The harmonization effect can be approximately read off the relevant PH columns in Table 3 by changing the sign (the exact estimate would be given by $(-x/(1 + x/100))$ where x is the percentage change reported in Table 3). For the three pollutants in Table 3, harmonization of environmental policies would reduce the PCI by roughly 10% for biochemical oxygen demand and SO_2 and increase it by 3% in the case of total toxic pollution. For CO, NO_2 and total suspended particulates, a harmonization would also lead to decreased pollution of the world PCI, while for fine particulates, toxic metal pollution and volatile organic compounds, an equalization of environmental regulations would lead to increased PCI (for total suspended solids in water and toxic pollution, the effects would be small). This reasoning could give a hint on which pollutants international harmonization efforts should be concentrated. Note that in this exercise the relative level of regulation does not matter, because only differences between countries would influence trade flows, while in a real-world policy scenario regulation levels would be of major importance.

5. Robustness checks

Two exercises are carried out. Section 5.1 computes confidence intervals and checks sensitivity to the selection of the GDP threshold used for the construction of income groups. Section 5.2 tackles the sensitivity of results for SO_2 emissions to dropping the assumption of the constancy of e_L and to the selection of two alternative proxies for environmental regulation.

5.1. Robustness check on the main dataset

As to the estimates in Tables 2 and 3, three sensitivity tests suggest overall robustness. First, we computed confidence intervals for the predicted values of the different PCI levels. Results are reported in Appendix Table A5. The sign of the individual effects does not change most of the time, but there are several changes in the total effects. Aggregate worldwide effects remain small, and one can conclude that we obtain the same orders of magnitude. Second, we checked for changes in the selection of per capita GDP threshold. Two alternative thresholds were considered to add or take away five countries to the original group of 19 Northern countries versus 29 Southern countries. Results reported in Appendix Table A6, show that the overall patterns are quite insensitive to this change of definition. Third, arguing that environmental stringency is endogenous to bilateral trade flows at the sector level is questionable. Indeed, one might argue that environmental stringency is less likely to be endogenous when bilateral trade data are used along with national environmental regulation. In fact, endogeneity would apply if environmental regulation were a substitute for protection. This would be most likely if either environmental regulation was sector specific and/or trade flows were only country, and not country-pair, specific. We therefore also report results based on the simple OLS regression (see Table A7 in Appendix). Results are very similar.

5.2. *Robustness to data availability: results for SO_2 emissions*[14]

Tables 4 and 5 report results of two explorations with SO_2 emission data for 2000 (based on the data prepared in Grether et al. 2009). First, we introduce two alternative proxies for environmental stringency, namely, the environmental regulatory regime index (Esty and Porter 2005) and the air pollution regulation index from the WEF's Global competitiveness report. These proxies are only available for recent years, and not for all countries, hence our sample is reduced to 39 (38 for the regulatory regime index) countries.[15] Second, we relax the assumption of the constancy of emission per worker (on the same set of reduced countries).

Regression results are reported in Table 4. Columns 2–5 report results when US emission coefficients are applied to all countries, while columns 6–9 report corresponding results when country-specific emission coefficients are used. For each case, OLS and 2SLS results are reported. The variables of interest always have the expected sign (note that a sign reversal is expected for the first line in Table 2, as a higher lead content means a lower environmental stringency) and are most of the time highly significant. Results are also very similar across the different specifications. Table 5 shows the corresponding decomposition results and confirms previous findings. Although composition effects lead to a variety of patterns at the aggregate level, results for the first two rows, which relate to North–South trade, are perfectly in line with those of Table 3.

Table 4. Pollution content of imports regressions for SO_2, 2000.

	US emission coefficients				Country-specific emission coefficients			
	Air Pollution Regulation		Regulatory Regime Index		Air Pollution Regulation		Regulatory Regime Index	
	OLS	2SLS	OLS	2SLS	OLS	2SLS	OLS	2SLS
Δ Environmental stringency	1.96***	1.60***	1.44***	2.57***	2.68***	3.23***	1.13***	2.39***
	[5.04]	[4.11]	[5.89]	[10.06]	[6.94]	[7.56]	[4.78]	[8.56]
Δ Capital/labour	−1.35***	−1.24***	−0.78***	−0.97***	−0.65***	−0.96***	−0.17	−0.39***
	[8.62]	[8.22]	[6.13]	[7.71]	[3.93]	[5.79]	[1.30]	[2.82]
Δ Skill ratio	−0.28***	−0.33***	0.07	0.31***	−0.15*	−0.08	−0.33***	−0.07
	[3.54]	[4.02]	[1.01]	[3.44]	[1.77]	[0.90]	[4.55]	[0.66]
Δ High skill ratio	0.19***	−0.11	0.22	0.78***	0.02	0.18**	−0.04	0.60***
	[2.87]	[1.52]	[1.58]	[9.25]	[0.22]	[2.31]	[0.30]	[6.40]
Δ Coal	−0.08***	−0.27***	−0.08**	−0.13***	−0.13***	−0.27***	−0.21***	−0.26***
	[2.96]	[9.94]	[2.10]	[4.13]	[4.42]	[8.92]	[6.35]	[7.63]
Δ Oil	0.09***	−0.01	0.22***	0.27***	0.12***	−0.04	0.19***	0.25***
	[3.33]	[0.26]	[4.79]	[7.36]	[3.61]	[1.00]	[4.34]	[6.25]
Distance	−1.44***	−1.44***	−1.40***	−1.40***	−1.41***	−1.41***	−1.39***	−1.37***
	[20.84]	[22.76]	[18.91]	[20.31]	[18.85]	[20.37]	[17.40]	[18.39]
GDP*i**GDP*j*	1.25***	0.45***	1.03***	0.48***	1.10***	0.48***	1.10***	0.49***
	[26.08]	[40.75]	[8.11]	[42.53]	[22.84]	[39.73]	[8.54]	[38.98]

(*continued*)

Table 4. (*Continued*).

	US emission coefficients				Country-specific emission coefficients			
	Air Pollution Regulation		Regulatory Regime Index		Air Pollution Regulation		Regulatory Regime Index	
	OLS	2SLS	OLS	2SLS	OLS	2SLS	OLS	2SLS
Common language	0.84***	0.84***	0.86***	0.86***	0.87***	0.87***	0.90***	0.90***
	[6.19]	[5.43]	[6.29]	[5.39]	[5.77]	[5.16]	[5.94]	[5.18]
Common religion	−0.01	−0.12	0.09	0.10	−0.02	−0.02	−0.01	−0.01
	[0.20]	[0.19]	[0.74]	[0.78]	[0.39]	[0.34]	[0.09]	[0.09]
Landlocked	0.07	−0.36*	−0.45**	−1.47***	−1.10***	−1.90***	−1.10***	−2.24***
	[0.40]	[1.94]	[2.07]	[8.96]	[6.29]	[9.53]	[4.80]	[9.66]
Observations	650	650	600	600	650	650	600	600
R-squared	0.86	0.86	0.86	0.86	0.85	0.85	0.85	0.85

Notes:

See text for sample size. Dependent variable (in log): Total bilateral PCI.

Absolute value of t statistics in brackets, in 2SLS regressions the environmental index is instrumented with the human development index, first stage F statistic is 115 with the air pollution regulation index and 72 with the regulatory regime index. A higher value of the index implies a more stringent policy. Fixed effects are not reported.

*Significant at 10%; **significant at 5%; ***significant at 1%, [a](skilled + base skills)/unskilled, [b]skilled/base skills.

Table 5. Decomposition of the PCI into the FE and the PH-effect (%): Results for SO_2 with two alternative measures of environmental regulation.

Row	Import flows[a)]	Obs.		US emission coefficients						Country-specific emission coefficients					
				Air Pollution Regulation			Regulatory Regime Index			Air Pollution Regulation			Regulatory Regime Index		
		Air Reg.	Reg. Index	FE-effect	PH-effect	TOT-effect	FE-effect	PH-effect	TOT-effect	FE-effect	PH-effect	TOT-effect	FE-effect	PH-effect	TOT-effect
1	NS	165	154	−86	118	−70	−77	321	−1	−80	472	12	−49	285	97
2	SN	165	154	163	−56	15	145	−81	−53	237	−84	−45	68	−81	−68
3	NS + SN	330	308	−41	−23	−54	63	−60	−34	−33	53	3	−8	53	40
4	NN	110	110	−3	4	1	−3	−6	−9	−2	12	10	−1	−5	−6
5	SS	210	182	−76	−11	−79	−62	−18	−67	−56	−3	−58	−28	−23	−45
6	NN + SS	320	292	−19	3	−16	−12	−7	−18	−28	7	−23	−11	−11	−21
7	World	650	600	−24	−1	−25	2	−22	−21	−29	17	−17	−11	1	−10

Notes: Decompositions using coefficient estimates reported in Table 4. See Table 3 for definitions and evaluation of the decomposition.

6. Conclusions

This paper contributes to the debate on trade and the environment by extending the usual case studies (one country or a few products) to a systematic analysis of the content of individual pollutants in global trade at the most disaggregated level for which one can hope to get available emission data. While the results share the limitations of other studies due to the absence of more systematic emission data, the paper goes beyond previous contributions that focus on a handful of 'dirty' industries or a case study of a specific pollutant or a specific country. In our unravelling of the PH effect, we have controlled for the transport cost component of the PCI as well as other 'deep' determinants of the bilateral pollution content of trade. This has allowed us to better isolate the role of differences in factor endowments and environmental policies. We do find evidence of traditional PH and FE effects that have often been elusive in the literature, although these effects cannot be said to be systematic nor quantitatively important or as robust as one would wish across all pollutants.

This said, the results suggest diversity in magnitudes across pollutants and a rather small contribution of the PHH factors in the overall PCI of world trade, notably because of composition factors usually not considered in the debate. Thus, for several pollutants, the PCI of the North is lower because, on average, its endowments are favourable to activities with high emissions and, likewise its PCI is higher for other pollutants because of the probable delocalization of dirty industries to the South associated with stricter environment policies in the North. Yet, for each one of the ten pollutants we find that these effects contribute to less than 10% of the overall determinants of import-embodied emissions. Taken together, at least for 1986–88, it would appear that differences in factor endowments and environmental policies have only marginally affected the pollution content of world trade, although the impact has been stronger on vertical (North–South) trade flows. These results carry over for one pollutant, SO_2, for which country-specific emissions and alternative environmental proxies are available for the year 2000. Much as in an earlier debate around the Leontief paradox regarding the factor content of US trade, better data will be required to get a firmer grasp of the quantitative importance of the effects involved.

Acknowledgements

We thank Werner Antweiler, Andrea Baranzini, Marius Brülhart, Olivier Cadot, Matthew Cole, Céline Carrère, Robert Elliott, Gene Grossman, Jaya Krishnakumar, Bernard Sinclair-Desgagné, Scott Taylor, David Wheeler, two referees and participants at the ETSG meeting in Dublin (2005) and a seminar at the PSE in 2007 for comments on an earlier draft. This is an extensively revised version of Grether et al. (2006). Financial support from the Swiss National Fund under research grant No 100012-109926 is gratefully acknowledged. The usual disclaimers apply. Appendices referred to in the text are available from the authors upon request.

Notes

1. Although the PH effect is obviously a worldwide issue involving rich and poor countries, faced with lack of data, researchers have conducted their investigations by carrying out 'partial' studies. Effects contributing to the location of economic activity (see the illustrative example in Section 2) have often been analyzed in the context of firm case studies (e.g. Eskeland and Harrison 2002) or case studies of a particular pollutant (e.g. Antweiler et al. 2001 for SO_2 emissions). Several studies on the US, controlling for unobserved heterogeneity and the endogeneity of environmental policy, have detected a significant PH effect (Cole et al. 2005; Ederington et al. 2004, 2005; Levinson and Taylor 2008, using a panel data set of US industries). When covering more countries, the analysis is often limited to specific sectors (e.g. Cole and Elliott 2003a) with less clear-cut results.
2. We could have carried out the analysis by measuring the pollution content of exports. Since the econometric analysis is carried out on bilateral trade, both approaches are in effect equivalent. Because export data are less reliable, we use imports to minimize measurement errors.
3. The traditional approach relies on the less accurate comparison between 'clean' and 'dirty' sectors. It is true that, at the three-digit ISIC level, the group of 'dirty' sectors (reported in Table A2 in Appendix 2) does not seem to change much across pollution criteria (e.g. actual emissions versus abatement costs, see Mani and Wheeler 1997). However, the definition of 'clean' sectors is more ambiguous, and the intermediate sectors that are dropped from the usual analysis of clean versus dirty industries often represent a substantial part of the PCI (up to 50% for some pollutants according to our estimates, see Table A3 in Appendix 2). Moreover, at the four-digit ISIC level, the classification of dirty sectors is not robust across pollutants. Two examples taken from the IPPS coefficients of the World Bank establish the superiority of our approach. Take first the manufacture of leather products (ISIC 3233) which is one of the cleanest activities in terms of SO_2 released in the air, but also one of the most polluting in terms of metal toxic pollution. Take next sugar factories and refineries (ISIC 3118): this has the opposite pattern, releasing much SO_2 in the air, but negligible toxic pollution. Overall, more than a quarter of ISIC four-digit categories exhibit a similar pattern, ranking in the top ten most polluting sectors according to one pollution criteria and among the ten cleanest according to another.
4. The *average* pollution content can also be called average pollution *intensity*.
5. See Appendix Table A1 for a list of the countries.
6. Variables are described in Appendix 1 and Appendix Table A6.
7. SO_2 is mainly emitted by fossil fuel combustion. It may cause respiratory diseases and damage trees and crops. It is also a prime source of acid rain, which damages forests and buildings and contributes to the acidification of lakes and streams. Toxic pollution is measured as toxic chemicals in air, land and water (the rank correlation between the total measure and the media-specific measure is 0.93 for air, 0.87 for land and 0.46 for water). It causes damage to internal organs, neurological functions and can result in decreased hutching success, reproductive problems and cancers. Biological oxygen demand in water measures how much oxygen is being used by aerobic micro-organisms to decompose organic matter (e.g. dead plants, leaves, manure, sewage, food waste). If these bacteria use too much of the dissolved oxygen, then not enough will be left for other organisms.
8. GDP per capita square terms turn out not to be significant.
9. In the absence of factor price equalization through trade, if within-sector differences in technology are Hicks neutral, a labour-abundant poor country

will use a more labour intensive technique of production. Thus, constant emissions per unit of labour would be consistent with higher emission intensities per unit of output in low-income countries.

10. This index is a market-share weighted sum of the maximum lead content of different gasolines (see Grether and Mathys 2002, and Appendix 1 for further details). It has been used by Hilton and Levinson (1998), Damania et al. (2003), Fredriksson et al (2005) and Cole et al. (2006) as a proxy for environmental policy.
11. For reference, Antweiler, Copeland and Taylor (2001) estimate the correlates of per capita concentration intensities in 103 cities as: $(z/N)_{kt} = \alpha_0(K/L)_{kt} + \alpha_1 Y_{kt}$ $\alpha_2((X + M)/Y)_{kt} + \ldots$ where Y is GDP k is an index for 43 countries and $t = 1, \ldots, 16$ years and $+ \ldots$ indicates the inclusion of country fixed effects, interaction terms for the three RHS variables plus squared values of the three RHS variables. In this specification, α_0 and interaction terms capture composition effects, while α_1 captures the combined scale and technique effects and α_2 captures the trade-induced effect. Cole and Elliott (2003b) estimate a fairly similar relationship, but with emission intensities per capita as the LHS variable.
12. We checked for heteroskedacity by using the Poisson estimator suggested in Santos Silva and Tenreyro (2006) obtaining similar results.
13. There are two reasons why the estimate on the LEAD coefficient might be biased towards zero. First if the lead content of gasoline is relatively important with respect to total PCI and countries import refined gasoline with lead content meeting national requirements, then there could be a positive correlation between total PCI and lead content. Second if lead content is a proxy for environmental awareness, consumers will have a relatively clean consumption structure leading to a positive correlation between lead content and the PCI. However, given the level of disaggregation, it is unlikely that such substitution effects will be captured by the data.
14. We thank two anonymous referees for having suggested this additional robustness check.
15. For the detailed country list, see Table A1 in the Appendix.

References

Antweiler, W. 1996. The pollution terms of trade. *Economic Systems Research* 8, no. 4: 361–5.

Antweiler, W., B. Copeland, and S. Taylor. 2001. Is free trade good for the environment? *American Economic Review* 91, no. 4: 877–908.

Barro, R.J., and J.-W. Lee. 2000. International data on educational attainment: Updates and implications. CID Working Paper No. 42.

CIA's World Factbook. http://www.cia.gov/cia/publications/factbook/docs/profileguide.html.

Cole, M.A., and R.J.R. Elliott. 2003a. Do environmental regulations influence trade patterns? Testing old and new trade theories. *The World Economy* 26, no. 8: 1163–86.

Cole, M.A., and R.J.R. Elliott. 2003b. Determining the trade-environment composition effect: The role of capital, labor and environmental regulations. *Journal of Environmental Economics and Management* 46, no. 3: 363–83.

Cole, M.A., and R.J.R. Elliott. 2005. FDI and the capital intensity of dirty sectors: A missing piece of the pollution haven puzzle. *Review of Development Economics* 9, no. 4: 530–48.

Cole, M.A., R.J.R. Elliott, and K. Shimamoto. 2005. Why the grass is not always greener: The competing effects of environmental regulations and factor intensities on US specialization. *Ecological Economics* 54, no. 1: 95–109.

Cole, M.A., R.J.R. Elliott, and P. Fredriksson. 2006. Endogenous pollution havens: Does FDI influence environmental regulations? *Scandinavian Journal of Economics* 108, no. 1: 157–78.

Copeland, B.R., and M.S. Taylor. 2003. *Trade and the environment: Theory and evidence*. Princeton, NJ: Princeton University Press.

Copeland, B.R., and M.S. Taylor. 2004. Trade, growth and the environment. *Journal of Economic Literature* 42: 7–71.

Damania, R., P.G. Fredriksson, and J.A. List. 2003. Trade liberalization, corruption and environmental policy formation: Theory and evidence. *Journal of Environmental Economics and Management* 46, no. 3: 490–512.

Ederington, J., and J. Minier. 2003. Is environmental policy a secondary trade barrier? An empirical analysis. *Canadian Journal of Economics* 36, no. 1: 137–54.

Ederington, J., A. Levinson, and J. Minier. 2004. Trade liberalization and pollution havens. *Advances in Economic Analysis & Policy* 4, no. 2. Article 6.

Ederington, J., A. Levinson, and J. Minier. 2005. Footloose and pollution-free. *The Review of Economics and Statistics* 87, no. 1: 92–9.

Eskeland, G., and A. Harrison. 2002. Moving to greener pastures? Multinationals and the pollution haven hypothesis. *Journal of Development Economics* 63, no. 1: 1–23.

Esty, D.C., and M.E. Porter. 2005. National environmental performance: An empirical analysis of policy results and determinants. *Environment and Development Economics* 10, no. 4: 391–434.

Fredriksson, P.G., E. Neumayer, R. Damania, and S. Gates. 2005. Environmentalism, democracy and pollution control. *Journal of Environmental Economics and Management* 45: 343–65.

Gourdon, J., N. Maystre, and J. de Melo. 2008. Openness, inequality and poverty: Endowments matter. *Journal of International Trade & Economic Development* 17, no. 3: 343–78.

Grether, J.-M., and N.A. Mathys. 2002. *Lead content of gasoline 1983–1995*. Switzerland: University of Neuchâtel.

Grether, J.-M., and J. de Melo. 2004. Globalization and dirty industries: Do pollution havens matter? In *Challenges to globalization: Analyzing the economics*, ed. R.E. Baldwin, and A. Winters, 167–208. Chicago, IL: University of Chicago Press.

Grether, J.-M., N. Mathys, and J. de Melo. 2009. Trade, technique and composition effects in SO_2 manufacturing emissions, 1990–2000. *Environmental and Resource Economics* 43, no. 2: 257–74.

Hettige, H.P., M. Mani, and D. Wheeler. 2000. Industrial pollution in economic development: the environmental Kuznets curve revisited. *Journal of Development Economics* 62, no. 2: 445–76.

Hettige, H.P., P. Martin, M. Singh, and D. Wheeler. 1995. *The industrial pollution projection system*. WPS 1431. Washington, DC: The World Bank.

Hilton, F.G.H., and A. Levinson. 1998. Factoring the environmental Kuznets curve: Evidence from automotive lead emissions. *Journal of Environmental Economics and Management* 35, no. 2: 126–41.

Levinson, A., and S. Taylor. 2008. Unmasking the pollution haven effect. *International Economic Review* 49, no. 1: 223–54.

Mahajan, S. 2001. Estimates of capital stock. Mimeo, PRMEP, World Bank.

Mani, M., and D. Wheeler. 1997. In search of pollution havens? Dirty industry in the world economy, 1960–95. In *Trade, global policy, and the environment*, ed. P. Fredriksson, WBDP 402. Washington, DC: World Bank.

Nicita, A., and M. Olarreaga. 2007. Trade, production and protection, 1976–04. *World Bank Economic Review* 21, no. 1: 265–71.

Olivier, J.G.J., and J.M. Berdowski. 2001. Global emissions sources and sinks. In *The climate system*, ed. J. Berdowski, R. Guicherit, and B.J. Heij, 33–78. Lisse, The Netherlands: A.A. Balkema Publishers/Swets & Zeitlinger Publishers.
Romalis, J. 2004. Factor proportions and the structure of commodity trade. *American Economic Review* 94, no. 1: 67–97.
Santos Silva, J.M.C., and S. Tenreyro. 2006. The log of gravity. *The Review of Economics and Statistics* 88, no. 4: 641–58.
Taylor, M.S. 2005. Unbundling the pollution haven hypothesis. *B.E. Journals in Economic Analysis & Policy* 4, no. 2. article 8.
World Bank. 2004. World Bank development indicators. CD-ROM, Washington, DC.
World Economic Forum. *Global Competitiveness Report 2001–2002*.
World Energy Council. 2004. *Survey of energy sources*. Amsterdam: Elsevier.

Appendix 1. Data description

Bilateral trade flows are taken from the 'Trade and Production Database' by Nicita and Olarreaga (2007). Imports (imports are known to be more reliable than exports) for 48 developing and developed countries are available at the 4-digit ISIC level (see Appendix A1 for a country-list). To transform real bilateral trade flows into the pollution content of imports we used the World Bank's 'Industrial Pollution Pojection System' (IPPS). See Hettige et al. (1995) for a detailed description. These IPPS coefficients allow us to estimate the amount of pollution (in pounds or kilograms) emitted per employee by four-digit ISIC. In total, ten different pollutants (see Table A3 in Appendix 2 for a detailed list of these pollutants) are proposed. Concerning the exact measure, we use the lower bound estimation of pollution per employee. Note that these IPP coefficients are, strictly speaking, only available for 1987 for the US industries. Hettige, Mani and Wheeler (2000) show that pollution/labour ratios seem to be roughly constant across countries. Hence using employment/output ratios by three-digit industry (four-digit data are not available) and country from the 'Trade and Production Database' allows us to compute a pollution per dollar of import coefficient specific to each country.

The distance and the common language variables are taken from the CEPII database. The common religion variable has been constructed on the basis of the *CIA's World Factbook* and GDP values are extracted from the World Bank's (2004) WDI Indicators. Capital and labour endowment data are from Sandeep Mahajan (2001). Skill ratios and coal and oil production have been taken from Gourdon, Maystre and de Melo (2008). The human development index for 1987 has been extracted from the UN website.

The data source for the maximum lead content in gasoline has been elaborated by Grether and Mathys (2002) on the basis of Octel's Worldwide Gasoline Survey. More precisely the average has been worked out by using different types of gasoline and weighting them by their market share. Therefore, the proxy constructed takes into account the importance of the different types of gasoline in the overall market. If one admits that it is generally more costly to produce gasoline with low lead contents, the selected variable represents not only the maximum lead content observed, but also, and this is the important feature, in some sense the enforced legal limit of lead content in gasoline. Since it is impossible for the moment to obtain an index of environmental stringency for the 1980s for a large set of countries, the average maximum lead content represents at least one of the most important environmental indicators. Note also that Damania et al. (2003) showed that this indicator is closely correlated with other proxies for environmental stringency.

Table A1. Countries in the sample.

Argentina	Jordan
Australia*	Japan*
Austria*	Kenya
Bolivia	Korea, Rep.
Canada*	Sri Lanka
Chile	Mexico
China	Malawi
Cameroon	Malaysia
Colombia	Netherlands*
Costa Rica	Norway*
Denmark*	New Zealand*
Ecuador	Pakistan
Egypt, Arab Rep.	Panama
Spain*	Peru
Finland*	Philippines
France*	Portugal*
United Kingdom*	Singapore*
Greece*	Sweden*
Guatemala	Thailand
Honduras	Trinidad and Tobago
Indonesia	Turkey
India	Uruguay
Ireland*	United States*
Italy*	Venezuela, RB

Note: *Stands for developed economies, i.e. economies where the average GDP per capita over the sample period in 1995 PPP dollars is higher than $11,000.
The following countries are not covered in the robustness section on SO_2 emissions: Cameroon, Guatemala, Sri Lanka, Malawi, New Zealand, Pakistan, Portugal, Thailand, Trinidad and Tobago. When using the regulatory regime index: Turkey is also absent from the sample.

Table A2. Dirty and clean sectors.

Dirty		Clean	
ISIC 3-digit	Description	ISIC 3-digit	Description
341	Paper and products	321	Textiles
351	Industrial chemicals	382*	Machinery except electrical
369	Other non-metallic mineral products	383*	Machinery electrical
371	Iron and steel	384	Transport equipment
372	Non-ferrous metals	385	Professional and scientific equipment

Note: *These sectors have been classified as overall clean. When only looking at pollution intensity in heavy metals however they are on ranks 8 and 9 respectively. Source: Copeland and Taylor (2003).

Table A3. Pollutants.

IPPS-Pollutants - per employee, lower bound		Pollution share of dirty sectors (in %)*	PH-Ratio
TPTT	Toxic pollution intensity – TOTAL	73	0.63
MPTT	Toxic metal pollution intensity – TOTAL	85	0.70
S2AI	SO2 – AIR	65	0.67
N2AI	NO2 – AIR	61	0.69
COAI	CO – AIR	59	0.79
VOAI	Volatile organic compounds – AIR	59	0.52
FPAI	Fine particulates – AIR	64	0.75
TSAI	Total suspended particulates – AIR	48	0.56
BOWT	Biochemical oxygen demand – WATER	79	0.89
TSWT	Total suspended solids – WATER	91	0.53

Note: *Dirty sectors account for 18% of total imports.

Table A4. Regressions of SO_2 emission per worker (per dollar) on constant and GDP per capita PPP in constant 2000 international dollars.

	Emission per worker		Emission per dollar	
Sectors	GDP per capita	F-stat	GDP per capita	F-stat
Refineries, coke and gas	1.59 (1.31)	1.49	−5.91*** (1.96)	9.05
Iron and steel	0.134 (1.28)	0.01	−6.03*** (1.64)	13.57
Non-ferrous metals	4.03* (2.33)	3.00	−4.83** (2.21)	4.78
Chemicals	1.65 (1.67)	0.97	−5.85*** (1.67)	12.19
Building materials (cement)	−0.55 (1.32)	0.18	−9.31*** (1.18)	61.94
Pulp and paper	1.69 (1.44)	1.39	−6.57*** (1.46)	20.14

Note:
F-stat: F-statistic of the whole regression (including the constant).
$S0_2$ Emission data are from Grether et al (2009).
*Significant at 10%; **significant at 5%; ***significant at 1%.

Table A5. Confidence intervals for the decomposition estimates (%).

Import flows[a)]	Number of observations	Biochemical Oxygen Demand Water (BOWT) FE-effect		BOWT PH-effect		BOWT TOT effect		SO_2 in the air (SO_2) FE-effect		SO_2 PH-effect		SO_2 TOT effect		Total Toxic Pollution Intensity (TPTT) FE-effect		TPTT PH-effect		TPTT TOT effect	
NS	544	−75	−60	167	180	−34	12	−53	−34	107	122	−3	47	−48	−27	101	111	4	55
SN	565	118	138	−77	−63	−50	−11	56	66	−73	−55	−58	−26	38	47	−72	−56	−61	−35
NS + SN	1109	−26	−11	−17	20	−38	6	−18	−5	−3	33	−20	26	−15	−1	−8	23	−21	23
NN	342	−1	−1	9	17	8	16	−1	0	5	13	4	13	0	0	−7	0	−7	1
SS	656	−26	−18	−16	−15	−38	−31	−4	1	−6	−5	−10	−4	−7	−3	−9	−8	−16	−11
NN + SS	998	−2	−1	9	16	7	15	−1	0	5	12	4	12	0	0	−7	0	−7	0
World	2107	−6	−2	5	17	−1	14	−5	−1	3	16	−2	15	−4	0	−7	5	−11	5

Notes: 95% Confidence intervals on the predicted values are reported.
[a)]See notes Table 3.

Table A6. Decomposition of the PCI into the FE and the PH-Effect (in %) with changing income group definition.

			Biochemical Oxygen Demand Water (BOWT)			SO_2 in the air (SO_2)			Total Toxic Pollution Intensity (TPTT)		
Import flows[a]	Income group definition[b]	Number of observations	FE-effect	PH-effect	TOT-effect	FE-effect	PH-effect	TOT-effect	FE-effect	PH-effect	TOT-effect
NS	Initial	544	−86	173	−14	−44	114	20	−38	106	27
	Higher	473	−54	111	−3	−40	112	27	−33	97	31
	Lower	549	−69	166	−20	−46	16	11	−40	99	19
SN	Initial	565	127	−70	−33	61	−65	−44	42	−64	−49
	Higher	489	78	−60	−28	46	−58	−38	32	−56	−42
	Lower	575	164	−63	−3	76	−52	−16	52	−53	−29
NS + SN	Initial	1109	−19	1	−19	−13	15	1	−8	8	−1
	Higher	962	−8	−3	−12	−8	12	3	−5	4	−1
	Lower	1124	−31	20	−17	−19	30	5	−15	25	6
NN	Initial	342	−1	13	12	−1	9	9	0	−3	−3
	Higher	182	−1	16	14	−1	11	10	0	−3	−3
	Lower	550	0	11	11	1	7	8	1	−6	−4
SS	Initial	656	−22	−16	−34	−1	−6	−7	−5	−9	−13
	Higher	963	−33	−12	−41	−12	−3	−15	−11	−7	−17
	Lower	433	−29	−21	−45	−10	−11	−19	−11	−14	−23
NN + SS	Initial	998	−2	13	11	−1	9	8	0	−3	−4
	Higher	1145	−3	15	11	−2	9	8	−1	−3	−4
	Lower	983	0	11	10	−0	6	7	1	−6	−5

Notes:
[a] See notes for Table 3.
[b] Higher: Threshold at US $15,000; Greece, Ireland, Portugal, Singapore and Spain become Southern countries.
[c] Lower: Threshold at US $6500; Argentina, Korea, Mexico, Trinidad Tobago and Uruguay become Northern countries.

Table A7. Decomposition of the PCI into the FE and the PH-Effect (%). Results from OLS regression, previous 2SLS results in parenthesis.

Row	Import flows[a)]	Number of observations	Biochemical Oxygen Demand Water (BOWT)			SO_2 in the air (SO_2)			Total Toxic Pollution Intensity (TPTT)		
			FE-effect	PH-effect	TOT-effect	FE-effect	PH-effect	TOT-effect	FE-effect	PH-effect	TOT-effect
1	NS	544	−36 (−86)	90 (173)	21 (−14)	−50 (−44)	8 (114)	−46 (20)	−52 (−38)	7 (106)	−49 (27)
2	SN	565	39 (127)	−40 (−70)	−17 (−33)	67 (61)	−7 (−65)	55 (−44)	66 (42)	−6 (−64)	57 (−49)
3	NS + SN	1109	−16 (−19)	31 (1)	11 (−19)	−42 (−13)	5 (15)	−39 (1)	−45 (−8)	4 (8)	−42 (−1)
4	NN	342	−1 (−1)	11 (13)	10 (12)	−2 (−1)	1 (9)	0 (9)	−1 (0)	0 (−3)	0 (−3)
5	SS	656	−6 (−22)	−8 (−16)	−14 (−34)	0 (−1)	0 (−6)	0 (−7)	−7 (−5)	−1 (−9)	−8 (−13)
6	NN + SS	998	−2 (−2)	11 (13)	10 (11)	−2 (−1)	1 (9)	0 (8)	−1 (0)	0 (−3)	−1 (−4)
7	World	2107	−2 (−4)	13 (11)	10 (7)	−14 (−3)	2 (10)	−12 (6)	−17 (−2)	1 (−1)	−16 (−3)

Notes:

[a)]NS: North imports from the South, SN: South imports from the North, NN: North imports from the North, SS: South imports from the South.

Along rows: TOT = (1 + FE)*(1 + PH) −1,

Along columns: $AGG_v = \theta * CMP_1 + (1-\theta) * CMP_2$ where AGG_v is the aggregate effect (v = NS + SN, NN + SS, World) CMP_1 and CMP_2 are the two corresponding components and θ is the share of CMP_1 in the relevant PCI (Ω for the FE and the TOT effects, Ω k for the PH effect, Ω k ℓ is only reported for the sake of completeness).

Table A8. Variable description.

Variable	Description	Source
E/L	Pollution per employee	IPPS, World Bank (for SO2: Grether et al. 2009)
L/X	Inverse labour productivity	Trade and Production Database, 1976–2000
M	Bilateral import flows	Trade and Production Database, 1976–2000
DIST	Geodesic Distance between the most important cities	http://www.cepii.fr
MKT	Product of GDPs	World Bank Development Indicator 2004
CR	Common Religion	Correlation Coefficient, based on CIA's World Factbook
CL	Dummy for common language	http://www.cepii.fr
LL	Dummy for landlockedness	http://www.cepii.fr
SK	Proportion of population over 15 years with completed primary education with respect to population with less than 4 years of schooling in 1987.	Barro and Lee (2000)
HK	Proportion of population over 15 years with completed high education with respect to population with less than 4 years of schooling in 1987.	Barro and Lee (2000)
COAL	Production of coal	World Energy Council (2004)
OIL	Production of oil	World Energy Council (2004)
LEAD	Average maximum lead content in gasoline	Octels world wide gasoline survey, prepared base available on http://www2.unine.ch/Jahia/site/irene/op/edit/pid/12149?matrix=101
	Alternative measures of environmental regulation:	World Economic Forum report
	Air pollution regulation	Esty and Porter (2005)
	Regulatory Regime Index	
K/L	Capital to labour ratio	Sandeep Mahajan (PRMEP), World Bank (2001)
HDI	Human development indicator for 1987	United Nations Database